D0826398

Head First
Android Development

Wouldn't it be dreamy if there were a book on developing Android apps that was easier to understand than the space shuttle flight manual? I guess it's just a fantasy...

Dawn Griffiths
David Griffiths

CARLSBAD CITY LIBRARY
CARLSBAD, CA 92011

O'REILLY®

Beijing · Cambridge · Köln · Sebastopol · Tokyo

Head First Android Development

by Dawn Griffiths and David Griffiths

Copyright © 2015 David Griffiths and Dawn Griffiths. All rights reserved.

Printed in the United States of America.

Published by O'Reilly Media, Inc., 1005 Gravenstein Highway North, Sebastopol, CA 95472.

O'Reilly Media books may be purchased for educational, business, or sales promotional use. Online editions are also available for most titles (*http://safaribooksonline.com*). For more information, contact our corporate/institutional sales department: (800) 998-9938 or *corporate@oreilly.com*.

Series Creators:	Kathy Sierra, Bert Bates
Editor:	Meghan Blanchette
Cover Designer:	Karen Montgomery
Production Editor:	Melanie Yarbrough
Production Services:	Jasmine Kwityn
Indexer:	Bob Pfahler
Page Viewers:	Mum and Dad, Carl

Printing History:

June 2015: First Edition.

Mum and Dad →

← Rob and Lorraine

The O'Reilly logo is a registered trademark of O'Reilly Media, Inc. The *Head First* series designations, *Head First Android Development*, and related trade dress are trademarks of O'Reilly Media, Inc.

Many of the designations used by manufacturers and sellers to distinguish their products are claimed as trademarks. Where those designations appear in this book, and O'Reilly Media, Inc., was aware of a trademark claim, the designations have been printed in caps or initial caps.

While every precaution has been taken in the preparation of this book, the publisher and the authors assume no responsibility for errors or omissions, or for damages resulting from the use of the information contained herein.

No kittens were harmed in the making of this book, but several pizzas were eaten.

ISBN: 978-1-449-36218-8

[M]

AUG 2 8 2015

[2015-06-09]

To our friends and family. Thank you so
much for all your love and support.

Authors of Head First Android Development

Dawn Griffiths

David Griffiths

Dawn Griffiths started life as a mathematician at a top UK university, where she was awarded a first-class honors degree in mathematics. She went on to pursue a career in software development and has 20 years experience working in the IT industry.

Before writing Head First Android Development, Dawn wrote three other Head First books (*Head First Statistics*, *Head First 2D Geometry* and *Head First C*) and has also worked on a host of other books in the series.

When Dawn's not working on Head First books, you'll find her honing her Tai Chi skills, reading, running, making bobbin lace, or cooking. She particularly enjoys spending time with her wonderful husband, David.

David Griffiths began programming at age 12, when he saw a documentary on the work of Seymour Papert. At age 15, he wrote an implementation of Papert's computer language LOGO. After studying pure mathematics at university, he began writing code for computers and magazine articles for humans. He's worked as an agile coach, a developer, and a garage attendant, but not in that order. He can write code in over 10 languages and prose in just one, and when not writing, coding, or coaching, he spends much of his spare time traveling with his lovely wife—and coauthor—Dawn.

Before writing *Head First Android Development*, David wrote three other Head First books: *Head First Rails*, *Head First Programming* and *Head First C*.

You can follow us on Twitter at *https://twitter.com/HeadFirstDroid*.

Table of Contents (Summary)

Table of Contents (the real thing)

Intro

Your brain on Android. Here *you* are trying to *learn* something, while here your *brain* is, doing you a favor by making sure the learning doesn't *stick*. Your brain's thinking, "Better leave room for more important things, like which wild animals to avoid and whether naked snowboarding is a bad idea." So how *do* you trick your brain into thinking that your life depends on knowing how to develop Android apps?

getting started

Diving In

Android has been taking the world by storm.

Everybody wants a smart phone or tablet, and Android devices are hugely popular. In this book we'll teach you how to **develop your own apps**, and we'll start by getting you to build a basic app and run it on an Android Virtual Device. Along the way you'll meet some of the basic components of all Android apps such as *activities* and *layouts*.

All you need is a little Java know-how...

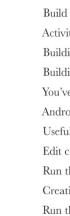

Device   Activity   Layout

building interactive apps

Apps That Do Something

2

Most apps need to respond to the user in some way.

In this chapter you'll see how you can make your apps *a bit more interactive*. You'll see
how you can get your app to *do* something in response to the user, and **how to get
your activity and layout talking to each other** like best buddies. Along the way we'll
take you a bit **deeper** into *how Android actually works* by introducing you to **R**, the
hidden gem that glues everything together.

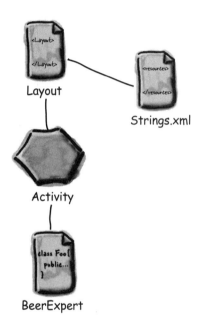

Layout

Strings.xml

Activity

BeerExpert

multiple activities and intents

State Your Intent

Most apps need more than one activity.

So far we've just looked at single-activity apps, which is fine for simple apps. But when things get more complicated, just having the one activity won't cut it. We're going to show you **how to build apps with multiple activities**, and how you can get your apps talking to each other using *intents*. We'll also look at how you can use intents to **go beyond the boundaries of your app** and **make activities in other apps on your device perform *actions***. Things just got a whole lot more powerful...

3

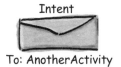

Intent

To: AnotherActivity

Hey, user. Which activity do you want to use this time?

CreateMessageActivity

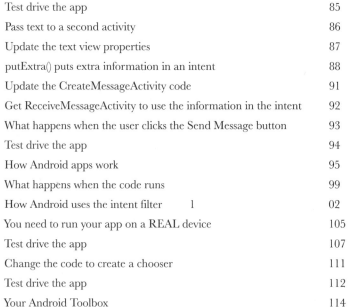

Android

User

4

the activity lifecycle

Do one thing and do it well

Activities form the foundation of every Android app.

So far you've seen how to create activities, and made one activity start another using an intent. But *what's really going on beneath the hood?* In this chapter we're going to dig a little deeper into **the activity lifecycle**. What happens when an activity is *created* and *destroyed*? Which methods get called when an activity is *made visible and appears in the foreground*, and which get called when the activity *loses the focus and is hidden*? And **how do you save and restore your activity's state**?

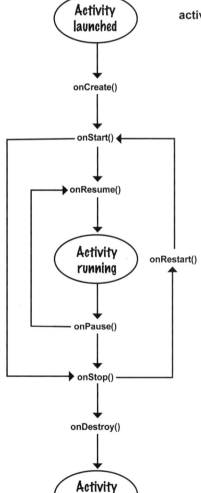

the user interface

Enjoy the View

Let's face it, you need to know how to create great layouts.

5

If you're building apps you want people to *use*, you need to make sure they **look just the way you want**. So far we've only scratched the surface when it comes to creating layouts, so it's time to *look a little deeper*. We'll introduce you to more **types of layout** you can use, and we'll also take you on a tour of the **main GUI components** and *how you use them*. By the end of the chapter you'll see that even though they all look a little different, all layouts and GUI components have *more in common than you might think*.

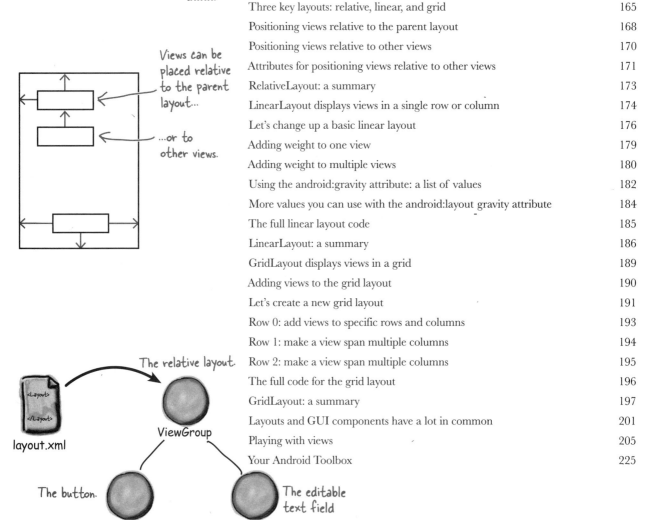

Views can be placed relative to the parent layout...

...or to other views.

The relative layout.

layout.xml

ViewGroup

The button.

View

View

The editable text field

6

list views and adapters

Getting Organized

Want to know how best to structure your Android app?

You've learned about some of the basic building blocks that are used to build apps, and now *it's time to get organized*. In this chapter we'll show you how you can take a bunch of ideas and **structure them into an awesome app**. We'll show you how **lists of data** can form the core part of your app design, and how **linking them together** can create a *powerful and easy-to-use app*. Along the way, you'll get your first glimpse of using **event listeners** and **adapters** to make your app more dynamic.

Display a start screen with a list of options.

Display a list of the drinks we sell.

Show details of each drink.

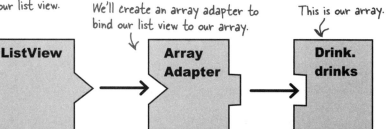

This is our list view.

We'll create an array adapter to bind our list view to our array.

This is our array.

ListView → **Array Adapter** → **Drink. drinks**

fragments

Make it Modular

You've seen how to create apps that work in the same way irrespective of the device they're running on.

But what if you want your app to *look and behave differently* depending on whether it's running on a *phone* or a *tablet*? In this chapter we'll show you how to make your app choose the **most appropriate layout for the device screen size**. We'll also introduce you to **fragments**, a way of creating *modular code components* that can be *reused by different activities*.

So the fragment will contain just a single list. I wonder... When we wanted to use an activity that contained a single list, we used a ListActivity. Is there something similar for fragments?

nested fragments

Dealing with Children

You've seen how using fragments in activities allow you to reuse code and make your apps more flexible.

In this chapter we're going to show you *how to nest one fragment inside another.* You'll see how to use the **child fragment manager** to tame unruly fragment transactions. Along the way you'll see why *knowing the differences between activities and fragments* is so important.

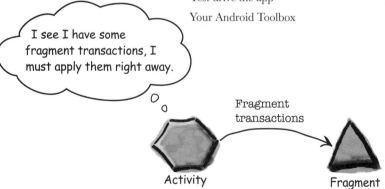

I see I have some fragment transactions, I must apply them right away.

Fragment transactions

Activity

Fragment

action bars

Taking Shortcuts

9

Everybody likes a shortcut.

And in this chapter you'll see how to add shortcuts to your apps using **action bars**. We'll show you how to start other activities by **adding action items** to your action bar, how to share content with other apps using the **share action provider**, and how to navigate up your app's hierarchy by implementing **the action bar's Up button**. Along the way you'll see how to give your app a consistant look and feel using **themes**, and introduce you to the Android support library package.

This is what the share action looks like on the action bar. When you click on it, it gives you a list of apps to share content using.

API 21? A perfect match.

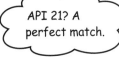

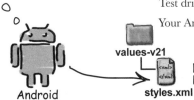

values-v21

styles.xml

Name: AppTheme
Parent: Theme.Material.Light

Android

10

navigation drawers

Going Places

Apps are so much better when they're easy to navigate.

In this chapter we're going to introduce you to the **navigation drawer**, a slide-out panel that appears when you swipe the screen with your finger or click an icon on the action bar. We'll show you how to use it to display a *list of links* that take you to **all the major hubs of your app**. You'll also see how *switching fragments* makes those hubs **easy to get to** and **fast to display**.

The content goes in a FrameLayout. You want the content to fill the screen. At the moment it's partially hidden by the drawer.

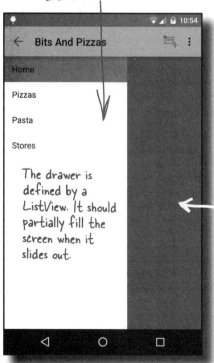

The drawer is defined by a ListView. It should partially fill the screen when it slides out.

SQLite databases

Fire up the Database

If you're recording high scores or saving tweets, your app will need to store data. And on Android you usually keep your data safe inside a **SQLite database**. In this chapter, we'll show you how to *create a database*, *add tables* to it, and *prepopulate it with data*, all with the help of the friendly **SQLite helper**. You'll then see how you can cleanly roll out *upgrades* to your database structure, and how to *downgrade* it if you need to pull any changes.

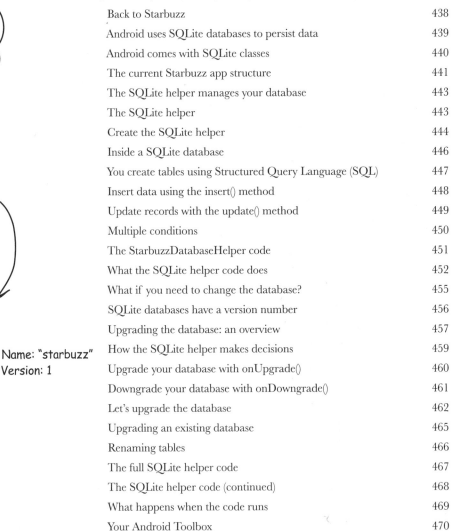

Your database, sir. Will that be all?

onCreate()

SQLite helper

DRINK

Name: "starbuzz"
Version: 1

SQLite database

cursors and asynctasks

Connecting to Databases

12

So how do you connect your app to a SQLite database?

So far you've seen how to create a SQLite database using a SQLite helper. The next step is to get your activities to access it. In this chapter you'll find out how to use **cursors** to *get data from the database*, how to *navigate* cursors and how to *get data from them*. You'll then find out how to use **cursor adapters** to connect them to list views. Finally, you'll see how writing efficient *multi-threaded code* with **AsyncTask**s will keep your app speedy.

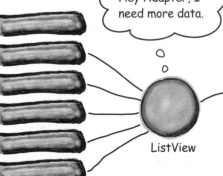

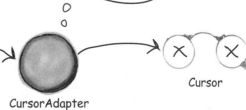

services

At Your Service

There are some operations you want to keep on running, irrespective of which app has the focus.

As an example, If you start playing a music file in a music app, you'd probably expect it to keep on playing when you switch to another app. In this chapter you'll see how to use **services** to deal with situations just like this. Along the way you'll see how use some of **Android's built-in services**. You'll see how to to keep your users informed with the *notification service*, and how the *location service* can tell you where you're located.

activity_main.xml

Android
Location
Service

getMiles()

MainActivity.java

1.11

OdometerService.java

The number of miles traveled.

material design

Living in a Material World

14

With API level 21, Google introduced Material Design.

In this chapter we'll look at **what Material Design is**, and how to make your apps fit in with it. We'll start by introducing you to **card views** you can reuse across your app for a *consistent look and feel*. Then we'll introduce you to the **recycler view**, the list view's flexible friend. Along the way you'll see how to **create your own adapters**, and how to completely change the look of a recycler view with just *two lines of code*.

art

The Android Runtime

Android apps need to run on devices with low powered processors and very little memory.

Java apps can take up a lot of memory and because they run inside their own Java Virtual Machine (JVM), Java apps can take a long time to start when they're running on low-powered machines. Android deals with this by not using the JVM for its apps. Instead it uses a very different virtual machine called the Android Runtime (ART). In this appendix we'll look at how ART gets your Java apps to run well on a small, low-powered device.

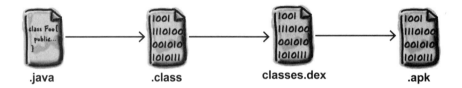

.java   .class   classes.dex   .apk

adb

The Android Debug Bridge

In this book we've focused on using an IDE for all your Android needs. But there are times when using a command line tool can be plain useful, like those times when Android Studio can't see your Android device but you just *know* it's there. In this chapter we'll introduce you to the Android Debug Bridge (or adb), a command line tool you can use to communicate with the emulator or Android devices.

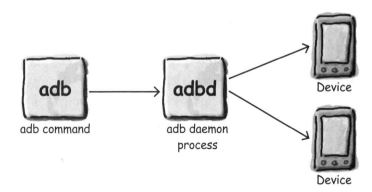

adb command   adb daemon process

The Android Emulator

Ever felt like you were spending all your time waiting for the emulator?

There's no doubt that using the Android emulator is useful. It allows you to see how your app will run on devices other than the physical ones you have access to. But at times it can feel a little... sluggish. In this appendix we're going to explain why the emulator can seem slow, Even better, we'll give you a few tips we've learned for **speeding it up**.

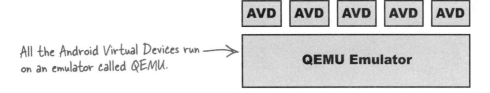

All the Android Virtual Devices run on an emulator called QEMU. →

The Top Ten Things (we didn't cover)

Even after all that, there's still a little more.

There are just a few more things we think you need to know. We wouldn't feel right about ignoring them, and we really wanted to give you a book you'd be able to lift without extensive training at the local gym. Before you put down the book, **read through these tidbits**.

The battery's running low, in case anyone's interested.

Android

how to use this book

Intro

In this section, we answer the burning question:
"So why DID they put that in a book on Android?"

Who is this book for?

If you can answer "yes" to all of these:

1 Do you already know how to program in Java?

2 Do you want to master Android app development, create the next big thing in software, make a small fortune, and retire to your own private island? ←

OK, maybe that one's a little far-fetched. But, you gotta start somewhere, right?

3 Do you prefer actually doing things and applying the stuff you learn over listening to someone in a lecture rattle on for hours on end?

this book is for you.

Who should probably back away from this book?

If you can answer "yes" to any of these:

1 Are you looking for a quick introduction or reference book to developing Android apps?

2 Would you rather have your toenails pulled out by 15 screaming monkeys than learn something new? Do you believe an Android book should cover *everything*, especially all the obscure stuff you'll never use, and if it bores the reader to tears in the process, then so much the better?

this book is ***not*** for you.

[Note from Marketing: this book is for anyone with a credit card... we'll accept PayPal, too.]

We know what you're thinking

"How can *this* be a serious book on developing Android apps?"

"What's with all the graphics?"

"Can I actually *learn* it this way?"

We know what your *brain* is thinking

Your brain craves novelty. It's always searching, scanning, *waiting* for something unusual. It was built that way, and it helps you stay alive.

So what does your brain do with all the routine, ordinary, normal things you encounter? Everything it *can* to stop them from interfering with the brain's *real* job—recording things that *matter*. It doesn't bother saving the boring things; they never make it past the "this is obviously not important" filter.

How does your brain *know* what's important? Suppose you're out for a day hike and a tiger jumps in front of you—what happens inside your head and body?

Neurons fire. Emotions crank up. *Chemicals surge.*

And that's how your brain knows…

This must be important! Don't forget it!

But imagine you're at home or in a library. It's a safe, warm, tiger-free zone. You're studying. Getting ready for an exam. Or trying to learn some tough technical topic your boss thinks will take a week, ten days at the most.

Just one problem. Your brain's trying to do you a big favor. It's trying to make sure that this *obviously* unimportant content doesn't clutter up scarce resources. Resources that are better spent storing the really *big* things. Like tigers. Like the danger of fire. Like how you should never have posted those party photos on your Facebook page. And there's no simple way to tell your brain, "Hey brain, thank you very much, but no matter how dull this book is, and how little I'm registering on the emotional Richter scale right now, I really *do* want you to keep this stuff around."

Your brain thinks THIS is important.

Great. Only 600 more dull, dry, boring pages.

Your brain thinks THIS isn't worth saving.

We think of a "Head First" reader as a <u>learner</u>.

So what does it take to *learn* something? First, you have to *get* it, then make sure you don't *forget* it. It's not about pushing facts into your head. Based on the latest research in cognitive science, neurobiology, and educational psychology, *learning* takes a lot more than text on a page. We know what turns your brain on.

Some of the Head First learning principles:

Make it visual. Images are far more memorable than words alone, and make learning much more effective (up to 89% improvement in recall and transfer studies). It also makes things more understandable. **Put the words within or near the graphics** they relate to, rather than on the bottom or on another page, and learners will be up to *twice* as likely to solve problems related to the content.

Use a conversational and personalized style. In recent studies, students performed up to 40% better on post-learning tests if the content spoke directly to the reader, using a first-person, conversational style rather than taking a formal tone. Tell stories instead of lecturing. Use casual language. Don't take yourself too seriously. Which would *you* pay more attention to: a stimulating dinner-party companion, or a lecture?

Get the learner to think more deeply. In other words, unless you actively flex your neurons, nothing much happens in your head. A reader has to be motivated, engaged, curious, and inspired to solve problems, draw conclusions, and generate new knowledge. And for that, you need challenges, exercises, and thought-provoking questions, and activities that involve both sides of the brain and multiple senses.

Get—and keep—the reader's attention. We've all had the "I really want to learn this, but I can't stay awake past page one" experience. Your brain pays attention to things that are out of the ordinary, interesting, strange, eye-catching, unexpected. Learning a new, tough, technical topic doesn't have to be boring. Your brain will learn much more quickly if it's not.

Touch their emotions. We now know that your ability to remember something is largely dependent on its emotional content. You remember what you care about. You remember when you *feel* something. No, we're not talking heart-wrenching stories about a boy and his dog. We're talking emotions like surprise, curiosity, fun, "what the…?", and the feeling of "I rule!" that comes when you solve a puzzle, learn something everybody else thinks is hard, or realize you know something that "I'm more technical than thou" Bob from Engineering *doesn't*.

Metacognition: thinking about thinking

If you really want to learn, and you want to learn more quickly and more deeply, pay attention to how you pay attention. Think about how you think. Learn how you learn.

Most of us did not take courses on metacognition or learning theory when we were growing up. We were *expected* to learn, but rarely *taught* to learn.

But we assume that if you're holding this book, you really want to learn how to develop Android apps. And you probably don't want to spend a lot of time. If you want to use what you read in this book, you need to *remember* what you read. And for that, you've got to *understand* it. To get the most from this book, or *any* book or learning experience, take responsibility for your brain. Your brain on *this* content.

The trick is to get your brain to see the new material you're learning as Really Important. Crucial to your well-being. As important as a tiger. Otherwise, you're in for a constant battle, with your brain doing its best to keep the new content from sticking.

So just how *DO* you get your brain to treat programming like it was a hungry tiger?

There's the slow, tedious way, or the faster, more effective way. The slow way is about sheer repetition. You obviously know that you *are* able to learn and remember even the dullest of topics if you keep pounding the same thing into your brain. With enough repetition, your brain says, "This doesn't *feel* important to him, but he keeps looking at the same thing *over* and *over* and *over*, so I suppose it must be."

The faster way is to do **anything that increases brain activity,** especially different *types* of brain activity. The things on the previous page are a big part of the solution, and they're all things that have been proven to help your brain work in your favor. For example, studies show that putting words *within* the pictures they describe (as opposed to somewhere else in the page, like a caption or in the body text) causes your brain to try to makes sense of how the words and picture relate, and this causes more neurons to fire. More neurons firing = more chances for your brain to *get* that this is something worth paying attention to, and possibly recording.

A conversational style helps because people tend to pay more attention when they perceive that they're in a conversation, since they're expected to follow along and hold up their end. The amazing thing is, your brain doesn't necessarily *care* that the "conversation" is between you and a book! On the other hand, if the writing style is formal and dry, your brain perceives it the same way you experience being lectured to while sitting in a roomful of passive attendees. No need to stay awake.

But pictures and conversational style are just the beginning…

Here's what WE did:

We used **pictures**, because your brain is tuned for visuals, not text. As far as your brain's concerned, a picture really *is* worth a thousand words. And when text and pictures work together, we embedded the text *in* the pictures because your brain works more effectively when the text is *within* the thing it refers to, as opposed to in a caption or buried in the body text somewhere.

We used **redundancy**, saying the same thing in *different* ways and with different media types, and *multiple senses*, to increase the chance that the content gets coded into more than one area of your brain.

We used concepts and pictures in **unexpected** ways because your brain is tuned for novelty, and we used pictures and ideas with at least *some **emotional*** content, because your brain is tuned to pay attention to the biochemistry of emotions. That which causes you to *feel* something is more likely to be remembered, even if that feeling is nothing more than a little **humor**, **surprise**, or **interest.**

We used a personalized, **conversational style**, because your brain is tuned to pay more attention when it believes you're in a conversation than if it thinks you're passively listening to a presentation. Your brain does this even when you're *reading*.

We included **activities**, because your brain is tuned to learn and remember more when you **do** things than when you *read* about things. And we made the exercises challenging-yet-doable, because that's what most people prefer.

We used **multiple learning styles**, because *you* might prefer step-by-step procedures, while someone else wants to understand the big picture first, and someone else just wants to see an example. But regardless of your own learning preference, *everyone* benefits from seeing the same content represented in multiple ways.

We include content for **both sides of your brain**, because the more of your brain you engage, the more likely you are to learn and remember, and the longer you can stay focused. Since working one side of the brain often means giving the other side a chance to rest, you can be more productive at learning for a longer period of time.

And we included **stories** and exercises that present **more than one point of view,** because your brain is tuned to learn more deeply when it's forced to make evaluations and judgments.

We included **challenges**, with exercises, and by asking **questions** that don't always have a straight answer, because your brain is tuned to learn and remember when it has to *work* at something. Think about it—you can't get your *body* in shape just by *watching* people at the gym. But we did our best to make sure that when you're working hard, it's on the *right* things. That **you're not spending one extra dendrite** processing a hard-to-understand example, or parsing difficult, jargon-laden, or overly terse text.

We used **people**. In stories, examples, pictures, etc., because, well, *you're* a person. And your brain pays more attention to *people* than it does to *things*.

Here's what YOU can do to bend your brain into submission

So, we did our part. The rest is up to you. These tips are a starting point; listen to your brain and figure out what works for you and what doesn't. Try new things.

Cut this out and stick it on your refrigerator.

- -

① Slow down. The more you understand, the less you have to memorize.

Don't just *read*. Stop and think. When the book asks you a question, don't just skip to the answer. Imagine that someone really *is* asking the question. The more deeply you force your brain to think, the better chance you have of learning and remembering.

② Do the exercises. Write your own notes.

We put them in, but if we did them for you, that would be like having someone else do your workouts for you. And don't just *look* at the exercises. **Use a pencil.** There's plenty of evidence that physical activity *while* learning can increase the learning.

③ Read "There Are No Dumb Questions."

That means all of them. They're not optional sidebars, ***they're part of the core content!*** Don't skip them.

④ Make this the last thing you read before bed. Or at least the last challenging thing.

Part of the learning (especially the transfer to long-term memory) happens *after* you put the book down. Your brain needs time on its own, to do more processing. If you put in something new during that processing time, some of what you just learned will be lost.

⑤ Talk about it. Out loud.

Speaking activates a different part of the brain. If you're trying to understand something, or increase your chance of remembering it later, say it out loud. Better still, try to explain it out loud to someone else. You'll learn more quickly, and you might uncover ideas you hadn't known were there when you were reading about it.

⑥ Drink water. Lots of it.

Your brain works best in a nice bath of fluid. Dehydration (which can happen before you ever feel thirsty) decreases cognitive function.

⑦ Listen to your brain.

Pay attention to whether your brain is getting overloaded. If you find yourself starting to skim the surface or forget what you just read, it's time for a break. Once you go past a certain point, you won't learn faster by trying to shove more in, and you might even hurt the process.

⑧ Feel something.

Your brain needs to know that this *matters*. Get involved with the stories. Make up your own captions for the photos. Groaning over a bad joke is *still* better than feeling nothing at all.

⑨ Write a lot of code!

There's only one way to learn to develop Android apps: **write a lot of code**. And that's what you're going to do throughout this book. Coding is a skill, and the only way to get good at it is to practice. We're going to give you a lot of practice: every chapter has exercises that pose a problem for you to solve. Don't just skip over them—a lot of the learning happens when you solve the exercises. We included a solution to each exercise—don't be afraid to **peek at the solution** if you get stuck! (It's easy to get snagged on something small.) But try to solve the problem before you look at the solution. And definitely get it working before you move on to the next part of the book.

Read me

This is a learning experience, not a reference book. We deliberately stripped out everything that might get in the way of learning whatever it is we're working on at that point in the book. And the first time through, you need to begin at the beginning, because the book makes assumptions about what you've already seen and learned.

We assume you're new to Android, but not to Java.

We're going to be building Android apps using a combination of Java and XML. We assume that you're familiar with the Java prorgamming language. If you've never done any Java programming *at all*, then you might want to read *Head First Java* before you start on this one.

We start off by building an app in the very first chapter.

Believe it or not, even if you've never developed for Android before, you can jump right in and start building apps. You'll also learn your way around Android Studio, the official IDE for Android development.

The examples are designed for learning.

As you work through the book, you'll build a number of different apps. Some of these are very small so you can focus on a specific part of Android. Other apps are larger so you can see how different components fit togeher. We won't complete every part of every app, but feel free to experiment finish them off yourself. It's all part of the learning experience. The source code for all the apps here: *https://tinyurl.com/HeadFirstAndroid*.

The activities are NOT optional.

The exercises and activities are not add-ons; they're part of the core content of the book. Some of them are to help with memory, some are for understanding, and some will help you apply what you've learned. ***Don't skip the exercises.***

The redundancy is intentional and important.

One distinct difference in a Head First book is that we want you to *really* get it. And we want you to finish the book remembering what you've learned. Most reference books don't have retention and recall as a goal, but this book is about *learning*, so you'll see some of the same concepts come up more than once.

The Brain Power exercises don't have answers.

For some of them, there is no right answer, and for others, part of the learning experience of the Brain Power activities is for you to decide if and when your answers are right. In some of the Brain Power exercises, you will find hints to point you in the right direction.

The technical review team

Edward

Technical reviewers:

Edward Yue Shung Wong has been hooked on coding since he wrote his first line of Haskell in 2006. Currently he works on event driven trade processing in the heart of the City of London. He enjoys sharing his passion for development with the London Java Community and Software Craftsmanship Community. Away from the keyboard, find Edward in his element on a football pitch or gaming on YouTube (@arkangelofkaos).

Tony Williams is a Java and Android developer.

Acknowledgments

Our editor:

Many thanks to our editor **Meghan Blanchette** for picking up the Head First reins. Her feedback and insight has been invaluable. We've appreciated all the times she told us our words had all the right letters, but not necessarily in the right order.

Thanks also to **Bert Bates** for teaching us to throw away the old rulebook and for letting us into his brain. This book has been so much better because of Bert's reactions and feedback.

Meghan Blanchette

The O'Reilly team:

A big thank you goes to **Mike Hendrickson** for having confidence in us and asking us to write the book in the first place; **Courtney Nash** for all her help in the early stages of the book; and the **early release team** for making early versions of the book available for download. Finally, thanks go to **Melanie Yarbrough**, **Jasmine Kwityn** and the rest of the production team for expertly steering the book through the production process and for working so hard behind the scenes.

Family, friends, and colleagues:

Writing a Head First book is a rollercoaster of a ride, and this one's been no exception. This book might not have seen the light of day if it hadn't been for the kindness and support of our family and friends. Special thanks go to **Andy P**, **Steve**, **Colin**, **Jacqui**, **Angela**, **Paul B**, **Mum**, **Dad**, **Carl**, **Rob** and **Lorraine**.

The without-whom list:

Our technical review team did a great job of keeping us straight and making sure what we covered was spot on. We're also grateful to all the people who gave us feedback on early releases of the book. We think the book's much, much better as a result.

Finally, our thanks to **Kathy Sierra** and **Bert Bates** for creating this extraordinary series of books.

Safari® Books Online

 Safari Books Online (*www.safaribooksonline.com*) is an on-demand digital library that delivers expert content in both book and video form from the world's leading authors in technology and business. Technology professionals, software developers, web designers, and business and creative professionals use Safari Books Online as their primary resource for research, problem solving, learning, and certification training.

Safari Books Online offers a range of product mixes and pricing programs for organizations, government agencies, and individuals. Subscribers have access to thousands of books, training videos, and prepublication manuscripts in one fully searchable database from publishers like O'Reilly Media, Prentice Hall Professional, Addison-Wesley Professional, Microsoft Press, Sams, Que, Peachpit Press, Focal Press, Cisco Press, John Wiley & Sons, Syngress, Morgan Kaufmann, IBM Redbooks, Packt, Adobe Press, FT Press, Apress, Manning, New Riders, McGraw-Hill, Jones & Bartlett, Course Technology, and dozens more. For more information about Safari Books Online, please visit us online.

1 getting started

 Diving In

Android has taken the world by storm.

Everybody wants a smartphone or tablet, and Android devices are hugely popular. In this book, we'll teach you how to **develop your own apps**, and we'll start by getting you to build a basic app and run it on an Android Virtual Device. Along the way, you'll meet some of the basic components of all Android apps, such as **activities** and **layouts**. **All you need is a little Java know-how...**

Welcome to Androidville

Android is the world's most popular mobile platform. At the last count, there were over *one billion* active Android devices worldwide, and that number is growing rapidly.

Android is a comprehensive open source platform based on Linux and championed by Google. It's a powerful development framework that includes everything you need to build great apps using a mix of Java and XML. What's more, it enables you to deploy those apps to a wide variety of devices—phones, tablets and more.

So what makes up a typical Android app?

Layouts define what each screen looks like

A typical Android app is comprised of one or more screens. You define what each screen looks like using a **layout** to define its appearance. Layouts are usually defined using XML, and can include GUI components such as buttons, text fields, and labels.

Java code defines what the app should do

Layouts only define the *appearance* of the app. You define what the app *does* by writing Java code. A special Java class called an **activity** decides which layout to use and tells the app how to respond to the user. As an example, if a layout includes a button, you need to write Java code in the activity to define what the button should do when you press it.

Sometimes extra resources are needed too

In addition to Java code and layouts, Android apps often need extra resources such as image files and application data. You can add any extra files you need to the app.

Android apps are really just a bunch of files in particular directories. When you build your app, all of these files get bundled together, giving you an app you can run on your device.

We're going to build our Android apps using a mixture of Java and XML. We'll explain things along the way, but you'll need to have a fair understanding of Java to get the most out of this book.

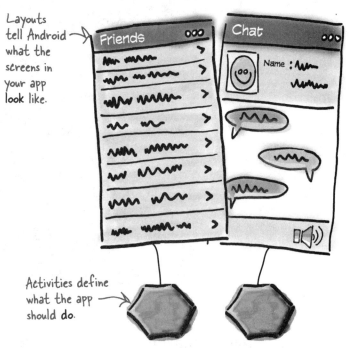

Layouts tell Android what the screens in your app look like.

Activities define what the app should **do**.

Resources can include → sound and image files.

The Android platform dissected

The Android platform is made up of a number of different components. It includes core applications such as Contacts, a set of APIs to help you control what your app looks and how it behaves, and a whole load of supporting files and libraries. Here's a quick look at how they all fit together:

Don't worry if this seems like a lot to take in.

At this stage, we're just giving you an overview of what's included in the Android platform. We'll explain the different components in more detail as and when we need to.

Android comes with a set of core applications such as Contacts, Calendar, Maps, and a browser.

When you build your apps, you have access to the same APIs used by the core applications. You use these APIs to control what your app looks like and how it behaves.

Underneath the application framework lies a set of C and C++ libraries. These libraries get exposed to you through the framework APIs.

Underneath everything else lies the Linux kernel. Android relies on the kernel for drivers, and also core services such as security and memory management.

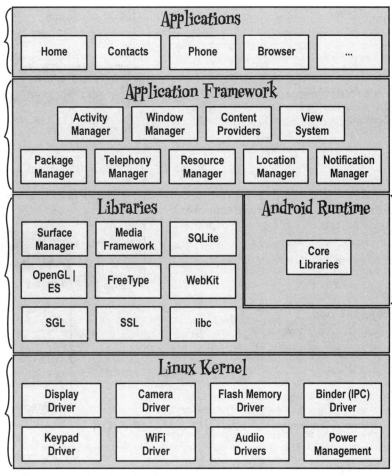

The Android runtime comes with a set of core libraries that implement most of the Java programming language. Each Android app runs in its own process.

The great news is that all of the powerful Android libraries are exposed through the APIs in the application framework, and it's these APIs that you use to create great Android apps. All you need to begin is some Java knowledge and a great idea for an app.

Here's what we're going to do

So let's dive in and create a basic Android app. There are just a few things we need to do:

① **Set up a development environment.**
We need to install Android Studio, which includes all the tools you need to develop your Android apps.

② **Build a basic app.**
We'll build a simple app using Android Studio that will display some sample text on the screen.

③ **Run the app in the Android emulator.**
We'll use the built-in emulator to see the app up and running.

④ **Change the app.**
Finally, we'll make a few tweaks to the app we created in step 2, and run it again.

there are no Dumb Questions

Q: Are all Android apps developed in Java?

A: You can develop Android apps in other languages too, but the truth is most developers use Java.

Q: How much Java do I need to know for Android app development?

A: You really need experience of Java SE. If you're feeling rusty, we suggest getting a copy of *Head First Java* by Kathy Sierra and Bert Bates.

Q: Do I need to know about Swing and AWT?

A: Android doesn't use Swing or AWT, so don't worry if you don't have Java desktop GUI experience.

You are here.

getting **started**

Set up environment
Build app
Run app
Change app

Your development environment

Java is the most popular language used to develop Android applications. Android devices don't run *.class* and *.jar* files. Instead, to improve speed and battery performance, Android devices use their own optimized formats for compiled code. That means that you can't use an ordinary Java development environment—you also need special tools to convert your compiled code into an Android format, to deploy them to an Android device and to let you debug the app once it's running.

All of these come as part of the **Android SDK**. Let's take a look at what's included.

The Android SDK

The Android Software Development Kit contains the libraries and tools you need to develop Android apps:

SDK Platform
There's one of these for each version of Android.

SDK Tools
Tools for debugging and testing, plus other useful utilities. It also features a set of platform dependent tools.

Sample apps
If you want practical code examples to help you understand how to use some of the APIs, the sample apps might help you.

ANDROID SDK

These are just some of the main points.

Documentation
So you can get to the latest API documentation offline.

Android support
Extra APIs that aren't available in the standard platform.

Google Play Billing
Allows you in integrate billing services in your app.

Android Studio is a special version of IntelliJ IDEA

IntelliJ IDEA is one of the most popular IDEs for Java development. Android Studio is a version of IDEA that includes a version of the Android SDK and extra GUI tools to help you with your app development.

In addition to providing you with an editor and access to the tools and libraries in the Android SDK, Android Studio gives you templates you can use to help you create new apps and classes, and it makes it easy to do things such as package your apps and run them.

Install Java

Set up environment
Build app
Run app
Change app

Android Studio is a Java development environment, so you need to make sure the right version of Java is installed on your machine.

First, check the Android Studio system requirements to see which versions of the Java Development Kit (JDK) and Java Runtime Edition (JRE) you need. You can see the system requirements here:

Oracle and Google sometimes change their URLs. If these URLs don't work, do a search.

> *http://developer.android.com/sdk/index.html#Requirements*

When you know which versions of the JDK and JRE you need, you can get them from here and install them:

> *http://www.oracle.com/technetwork/java/javase/downloads/index.html*

Then install Android Studio

If this URL has changed, search for Android Studio in developer.android.com.

Once you have Java up and running, you can download Android Studio from here:

> *https://developer.android.com/sdk/installing/index.html?pkg=studio*

This page also includes installation instructions. Follow the instructions to install Android Studio on your computer. Once you've installed Android Studio, open it and follow the instructions to add the latest SDK tools and support libraries.

We're not including installation instructions in this book as they can get out of date pretty quickly. Follow the online instructions and you'll be fine.

When you're done, you should see the Android Studio welcome screen. You're ready to build your first Android app.

This is the Android Studio welcome screen. It includes a set of options for things you can do.

there are no
Dumb Questions

Q: You say we're going to use Android Studio to build the Android apps. Do I have to?

A: Strictly speaking, you don't have to use Android Studio to build Android apps. All you need is a tool that will let you write and compile Java code, plus a few other specialist tools to convert the compiled code into a form that Android devices can run.

Q: So I can use my own IDE?

A: Android Studio is the official Android IDE, but Eclipse is also popular. You can see further details here: *https://developer. android.com/tools/sdk/eclipse-adt.html*.

Q: Can I write Android apps without using an IDE?

A: It's possible, but it's more work. Most Android apps are now created using a build tool called *gradle*. Gradle projects can be created and built using a text editor and a command line.

Q: A build tool? So is gradle like ANT?

A: Similar, but gradle is much more powerful than ANT. Gradle can compile and deploy code, just like ANT, but it also uses Maven to download any third-party libraries your code needs. Gradle also uses Groovy as a scripting language, which means you can easily create quite complex builds with gradle.

Q: Most apps are built using gradle? I thought you said a lot of developers use Android Studio?

A: Android Studio provides a graphical interface to gradle, and also to other tools for creating layouts, reading logs and debugging.

Build a basic app

Now that you've set up your development environment, you're ready to create your first Android app. Here's what the app will look like:

This is the name of the application.

This is a very simple app, but that's all you need for your very first Android app.

There'll be a small piece of sample text right here that Android Studio will put in for us.

Let's build the basic app

Whenever you create a new app, you need to create a new project for it. Make sure you have Android Studio open, and follow along with us.

1. Create a new project

The Android Studio welcome screen gives you a number of options for what you want to do. We want to create a new project, so click on the option for "Start a new Android Studio project".

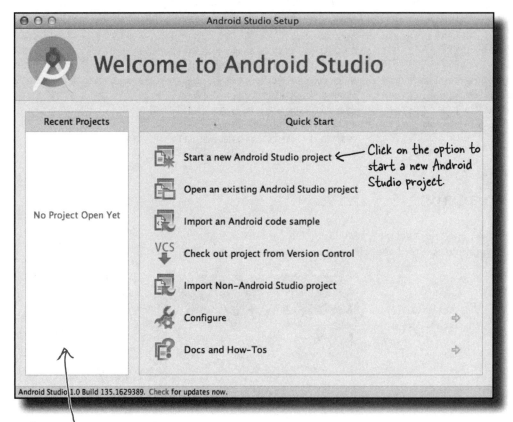

Click on the option to start a new Android Studio project.

Any projects you create will appear here. This is our first project, so this area is currently empty.

Building a basic app (continued)

2. Configure the project

You now need to configure the app by saying what you want to call it, what company domain to use, and where you would like to store the files.

Android Studio uses the company domain and application name to form the name of the package that will be used for your app. As an example, if you give your app a name of "My First App" and use a company domain of "hfad.com", Android Studio will derive a package name of `com.hfad.myfirstapp`. The package name is really important in Android, as it's used by Android devices to *uniquely identify your app*.

Enter an application name of "My First App", a company name of "hfad.com", and accept the default project location. Then click on the Next button.

Watch it!

The package name must stay the same for the lifetime of your app.

It's a unique identifier for your app and used to manage multiple versions of the same app.

The application name is shown in the Google Play Store and various other places, too.

The wizard forms the package name by combining the application name and the company domain.

All of the files for your project will be stored here.

Building a basic app (continued)

☑ Set up environment
→ ☐ **Build app**
☐ Run app
☐ Change app

3. Specify the API level

You now need to indicate which API level of Android your app will use. API levels increase with every new version of Android. Unless you only want your app to run on the very newest devices, you probably want to specify one of the older APIs.

Here, we're choosing API level 15, which means it will be able to run on most devices. Also, we're only going to create a version of our app to run on phones and tablets, so we'll leave the other options unchecked.

← You'll see more about the different API levels on the next page.

When you've done this, click on the Next button.

The minimum required SDK is the lowest version your app will support. Your app will run on devices with this level API or higher. It won't run on devices with a lower API.

○ ○ ○   Create New Project

New Project
Android Studio

Select the form factors your app will run on

Different platforms require separate SDKs

☑ Phone and Tablet

→ Minimum SDK   [API 15: Android 4.0.3 (IceCreamSandwich)] ⬍

Lower API levels target more devices, but have fewer features available. By targeting API 15 and later, your app will run on approximately **87.9%** of the devices that are active on the Google Play Store. Help me choose.

☐ TV

Minimum SDK   [API 21: Android 5.0 (Lollipop)] ⬍

☐ Wear

Minimum SDK   [API 21: Android 5.0 (Lollipop)] ⬍

☐ Glass

Minimum SDK   [Glass Development Kit Preview (Google Inc.) (API 19)] ⬍

[Cancel]   [Previous]   [Next]   [Finish]

Android Versions Up Close

You've probably heard a lot of things about Android that sound tasty. Things like Ice Cream Sandwich, Jelly Bean, KitKat, and Lollipop. So what's with all the confectionary?

Android versions have a version number and a codename. The version number gives the precise version of Android (e.g., 5.0), while the codename is a slightly more generic "friendly" name that may cover several versions of Android (e.g., Lollipop). The API level refers to the version of the APIs used by applications. As an example, the equivalent API level for Android version 5.0 is 21.

Version	Codename	API level
1.0		1
1.1		2
1.5	Cupcake	3
1.6	Donut	4
2.0	Eclair	5
2.01	Eclair	6
2.1	Eclair	7
2.2.x	Froyo	8
2.3 - 2.3.2	Gingerbread	9
2.3.2 - 2.3.7	Gingerbread	10
3.0	Honeycomb	11
3.1	Honeycomb	12
3.2	Honeycomb	13
4.0 - 4.0.2	Ice Cream Sandwich	14
4.0.3-4.0.4	Ice Cream Sandwich	15
4.1	Jelly Bean	16
4.2	Jelly Bean	17
4.3	Jelly Bean	18
4.4	KitKat	19
4.4	KitKat (with wearable extensions)	20
5.0	Lollipop	21

Hardly anyone uses these versions.

Most devices use one of these APIs.

When you develop Android apps, you really need to consider which versions of Android you want your app to be compatible with. If you specify that your app is only compatible with the very latest version of the SDK, you might find that it can't be run on many devices in the first instance. You can find out the percentage of devices running particular versions here: *https://developer.android.com/about/dashboards/index.html.*

✓ Set up environment
Build app
Run app
Change app

Activities and layouts from 50,000 feet

The next thing you'll be prompted to do is add an activity to your project. Every Android app is a collection of screens, and each screen is comprised of an activity and a layout.

An **activity** is **a single, defined thing that your user can do**. You might have an activity to compose an email, take a photo, or find a contact. Activities are usually associated with one screen, and they're written in Java.

A **layout** describes **the appearance of the screen.** Layouts are written as XML files and they tell Android how the different screen elements are arranged.

Let's look in more detail at how activities and layouts work together to create a user interface:

Layouts define how the user interface is presented.

Activities define actions.

① The device launches your app and creates an activity object.

② The activity object specifies a layout.

③ The activity tells Android to display the layout on screen.

④ The user interacts with the layout that's displayed on the device.

⑤ The activity responds to these interactions by running application code.

⑥ The activity updates the display...

⑦ ...which the user sees on the device.

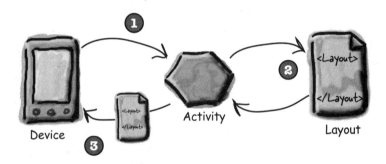

Now that you know a bit more about what activities and layouts are, let's go through the last couple of steps in the wizard and get it to create a basic activity and layout.

Building a basic app (continued)

4. Create an activity

The next screen gives you a series of templates you can use to
create an activity and layout. You need to choose one. We're
going to create an app with a basic activity and layout, so
choose the Blank Activity option and click the Next button.

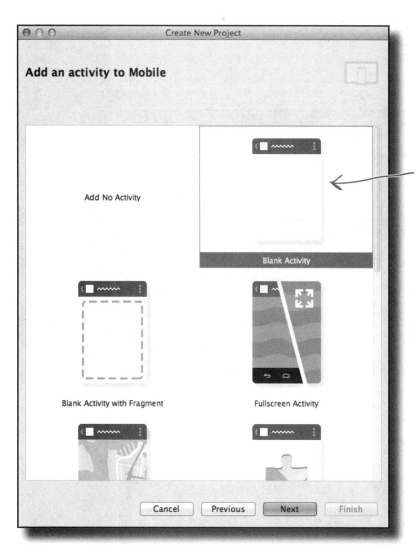

There are other types of
activity you can choose
from, but make sure you
select the Blank Activity
option.

Building a basic app (continued)

Set up environment
Build app
Run app
Change app

5. Configure the activity

You will now be asked what you want to call the screen's activity and layout. You will also need to say what the title of the screen will be, and specify a menu resource name. Enter an activity name of "MainActivity", and a layout name of "activity_main". The activity is a Java class, and the layout is an XML file, so the names we've given here will create a Java class file called *MainActivity.java* and an XML file called *activity_main.xml*.

When you click on the Finish button, Android Studio will build your app.

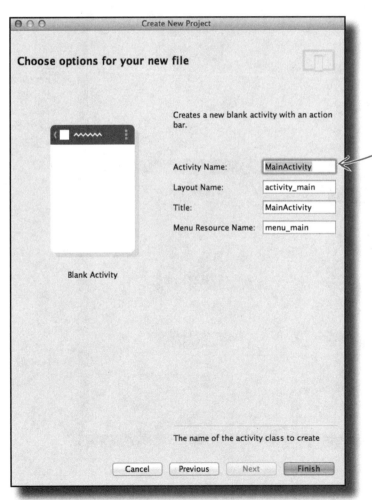

Give the activity a name of "MainActivity" and the layout a name of "activity_main". Accept the defaults for the other options.

You've just created your first Android app

So what just happened?

⭐ **The Android Studio wizard created a project for your app, configured to your specifications.**
You defined which versions of Android the app should be compatible with, and the wizard created all of the files and folders needed for a basic valid app.

⭐ **It created a basic activity and layout with template code.**
The template code includes layout XML and activity Java code, with sample "Hello world!" text in the layout. You can change this code.

When you finish creating your project by going through the wizard, Android Studio automatically displays the project for you.

Here's what our project looks like (don't worry if it looks complicated right now, we'll break it down over the next few pages):

This is the project in Android Studio.

Android Studio creates a complete folder structure for you

An Android app is really just a bunch of valid files in a particular folder structure, and Android Studio sets all of this up for you when you create a new app. The easiest way of looking at this folder structure is with the explorer in the leftmost column of Android Studio.

The explorer contains all of the projects that you currently have open. To expand or collapse folders, just click on the arrows to the left of the folder icons.

Choose the project option here to see the files and folders that make up your project.

This is the name of the project.

Click on these arrows to expand or collapse the folders.

These files and folders are all included in your project.

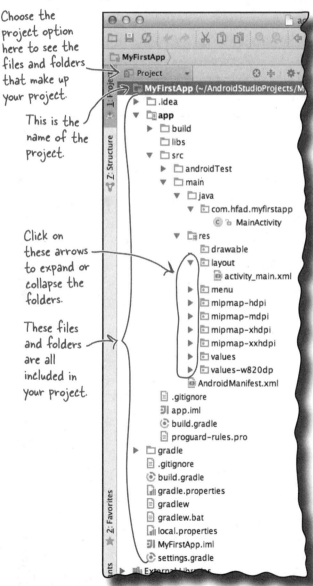

The folder structure includes different types of files

If you browse through the folder structure, you'll see that the wizard has created various types of files and folders for you:

⭐ **Java and XML source files**
These are the activity and layout files the wizard created for you.

⭐ **Android-generated Java files**
There are some extra Java files you don't need to touch which Android Studio generates for you automatically.

⭐ **Resource files**
These include default image files for icons, styles your app might use, and any common String values your app might want to look up.

⭐ **Android libraries**
In the wizard, you specified the minimum SDK version you want your app to be compatible with. Android Studio makes sure it includes the relevant Android libraries for this version.

⭐ **Configuration files**
The configuration files tell Android what's actually in the app and how it should run.

Let's take a closer look at some of the key files and folders in Androidville.

Useful files in your project

Android Studio projects use the gradle build system to compile and deploy your apps. Gradle projects have a standard layout. Here are some of the key files and folders you'll be working with:

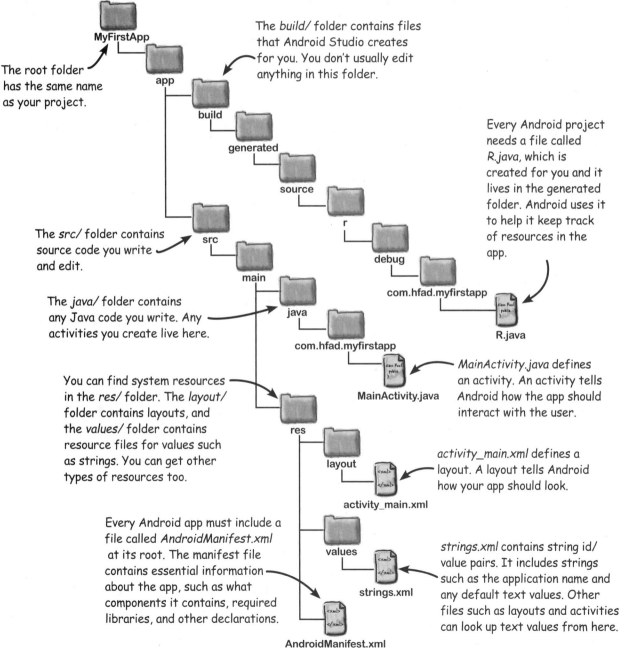

The root folder has the same name as your project.

The *build/* folder contains files that Android Studio creates for you. You don't usually edit anything in this folder.

The *src/* folder contains source code you write and edit.

Every Android project needs a file called *R.java*, which is created for you and it lives in the generated folder. Android uses it to help it keep track of resources in the app.

The *java/* folder contains any Java code you write. Any activities you create live here.

You can find system resources in the *res/* folder. The *layout/* folder contains layouts, and the *values/* folder contains resource files for values such as strings. You can get other types of resources too.

MainActivity.java defines an activity. An activity tells Android how the app should interact with the user.

activity_main.xml defines a layout. A layout tells Android how your app should look.

Every Android app must include a file called *AndroidManifest.xml* at its root. The manifest file contains essential information about the app, such as what components it contains, required libraries, and other declarations.

strings.xml contains string id/ value pairs. It includes strings such as the application name and any default text values. Other files such as layouts and activities can look up text values from here.

Edit code with the Android Studio editors

Set up environment
Build app
Run app
Change app

You view and edit files using the Android Studio editors. Double-click on the file you want to work with, and the file contents will appear in the middle of the Android Studio window.

The code editor

Most files get displayed in the code editor. The code editor is just like a text editor, but with extra features such as color coding and code checking.

Double-click on the file in the explorer...

...and the file contents appear in the editor panel.

The design editor

If you're editing a layout, you have an extra option. Rather than edit the XML, you can use the design editor. The design editor allows you to drag GUI components onto your layout, and arrange them how you want. The code editor and design editor give different views of the same file, so you can switch back and forth between the two.

You dictate which editor you're using with these tabs.

These are different views of the same file. The first view shows the code, and the second view shows the design.

WHAT'S MY PURPOSE?

Here's the code from a layout file Android Studio generated for us. We know you've not seen layout code before, but just see if you can match each of the descriptions at the bottom of the page to the correct lines of code. We've done one to get you started.

activity_main.xml

```xml
<RelativeLayout xmlns:android="http://schemas.android.com/apk/res/android"
xmlns:tools="http://schemas.android.com/tools"
android:layout_width="match_parent"
android:layout_height="match_parent"
android:paddingLeft="16dp"
android:paddingRight="16dp"
android:paddingTop="16dp"
android:paddingBottom="16dp"
tools:context=".MainActivity">

<TextView
    android:text="@string/hello_world"
    android:layout_width="wrap_content"
    android:layout_height="wrap_content" />

</RelativeLayout>
```

Add padding to the screen margins.

Include a `TextView` GUI component for displaying text.

Make the text wrap horizontally and vertically.

Display the value of a string resource called `hello_world`.

Make the layout the same width and height as the screen size on the device.

WHAT'S MY PURPOSE? SOLUTION

Here's the code from a layout file Android Studio generated for us. We know you've not seen layout code before, but just see if you can match each of the descriptions at the bottom of the page to the correct lines of code. We've done one to get you started.

activity_main.xml

```xml
<RelativeLayout xmlns:android="http://schemas.android.com/apk/res/android"
xmlns:tools="http://schemas.android.com/tools"
android:layout_width="match_parent"
android:layout_height="match_parent"
android:paddingLeft="16dp"
android:paddingRight="16dp"
android:paddingTop="16dp"
android:paddingBottom="16dp"
tools:context=".MainActivity">

<TextView
    android:text="@string/hello_world"
    android:layout_width="wrap_content"
    android:layout_height="wrap_content" />

</RelativeLayout>
```

Add padding to the screen margins.

Include a TextView GUI component for displaying text.

Make the text wrap horizontally and vertically.

Display the text value of a string resource called hello_world.

Make the layout the same width and height as the screen size on the device.

Now let's see if you can do the same thing for some activity code. **This is example code, and not the code that Android Studio will have generated for you.** Match the descriptions below to the correct lines of code.

MainActivity.java

```
package com.hfad.myfirstapp;

import android.os.Bundle;
import android.app.Activity;

public class MainActivity extends Activity {

    @Override
    protected void onCreate(Bundle savedInstanceState) {
        super.onCreate(savedInstanceState);
        setContentView(R.layout.activity_main);
    }
}
```

This is the package name.

These are Android classes used in **MainActivity**.

Specifies which layout to use.

Implement the **onCreate()** method from the **Activity** class. This method is called when the activity is first created.

MainActivity extends the Android class **android.app.Activity**.

WHAT'S MY PURPOSE? SOLUTION

Now let's see if you can do the same thing for some activity code. **This is example code, and not the code that Android Studio will have generated for you.** Match the descriptions below to the correct lines of code.

MainActivity.java

```java
package com.hfad.myfirstapp;

import android.os.Bundle;
import android.app.Activity;

public class MainActivity extends Activity {

    @Override
    protected void onCreate(Bundle savedInstanceState) {
        super.onCreate(savedInstanceState);
        setContentView(R.layout.activity_main);
    }
)
```

This is the package name.

These are Android classes used in **MainActivity**.

Specifies which layout to use.

Implement the **onCreate()** method from the **Activity** class. This method is called when the activity is first created.

MainActivity extends the Android class **android.app.Activity**.

Run the app in the Android emulator

So far you've seen what your Android app looks like in Android Studio and got a feel for how it hangs together. But what you *really* want to do is see it running, right?

You have a couple of options when it comes to running your apps. The first option is to run them on a physical device. But what if you don't have one to hand, or you want to see how it looks on a type of device you don't have?

An alternative option is to use the **Android emulator** that's built into the Android SDK. The emulator enables you to set up one or more **Android virtual devices** (AVDs) and then run your app in the emulator *as though it's running on a physical device*.

So what does the emulator look like?

Here's an AVD running in the Android emulator. It looks just like a phone running on your computer.

The emulator is an application that re-creates the exact hardware environment of an Android device: from its CPU and memory, through to the sound chips and the video display. The emulator is built on an existing emulator called QEMU, which is similar to other virtual machine applications you may have used, like VirtualBox or VMWare.

The exact appearance and behavior of the AVD depends on how you've set up the AVD in the first place. The AVD here is set up to mimic a Nexus 4, so it will look and behave just like a Nexus 4 on your computer.

Let's set up an AVD so that you can see your app running in the emulator.

The Android emulator allows you to run your app on an Android virtual device (AVD). The AVD behaves just like a physical Android device. You can set up numerous AVDs, each emulating a different type of device.

Once you've set up an AVD, you can see your app running on it. Android Studio launches the emulator for you.

Just like a physical phone, you need to unlock it before you start using it. Simply click on the lock icon and drag it upward.

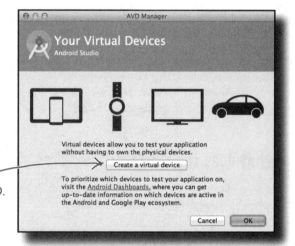

Set up environment
Build app
Run app
Change app

Creating an Android Virtual Device

There are a few steps you need to go through in order to set up an AVD within Android Studio. We'll set up a Nexus 4 AVD running API level 21 so that you can see how your app looks and behaves running on this type of device. The steps are pretty much identical no matter what type of device you want to set up.

Open the Android Virtual Device Manager

The AVD Manager allows you to set up new AVDs, and view and edit ones you've already created. Open it by selecting Android on the Tools menu and choosing AVD Manager.

If you have no AVDs set up already, you'll be presented with a screen prompting you to create one. Click on the "Create a virtual device" button.

Click on the "Create a virtual device" button to create an AVD.

Select the hardware

On the next screen, you'll be prompted to choose a device definition. This is the type of device your AVD will emulate. You can choose a variety of phone, tablet, wear, or TV devices.

We're going to see what our app looks like running on a Nexus 4 phone. Choose Phone from the Category menu and Nexus 4 from the list. Then click the Next button.

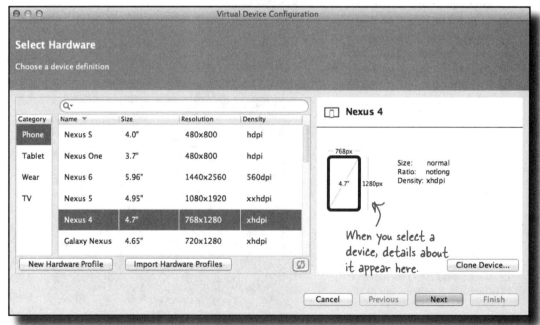

When you select a device, details about it appear here.

Creating an AVD (continued)

Select a system image

Next, you need to select a system image. The system image gives you an installed version of the Android operating system. You can choose the version of Android you want to be on your AVD, and what type of CPU (ARM or x86).

You need to choose a system image for an API level that's compatible with the app you're building. As an example, if you want your app to work on a minimum of API level 15, choose a system image for *at least* API level 15. We're going to use a system image for API level 21. Choose the option for Lollipop 21 armeabi-v7a with a target of Android 5.0.1. Then click on the Next button.

If you don't have this system image installed, you'll be given the option to download it.

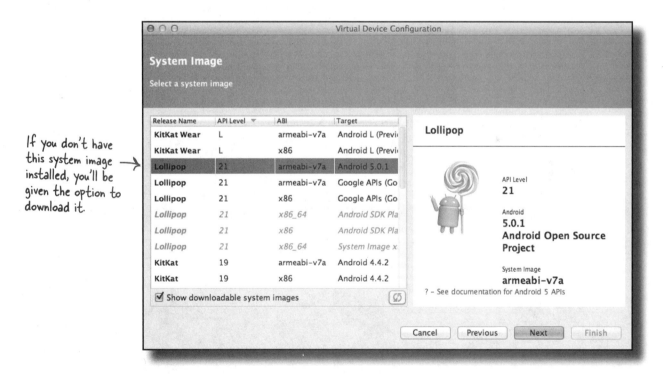

We'll continue setting up the AVD on the next page.

Creating an AVD (continued)

Verify the AVD configuration

On the next screen, you'll be asked to verify the AVD configuration. This screen summarizes the options you chose over the last few screens, and gives you the option of changing them. Accept the options, and click on the Finish button.

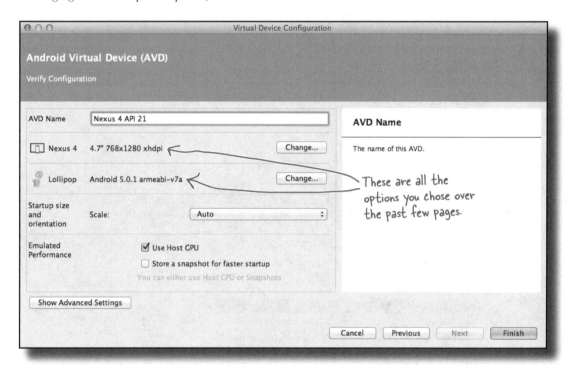

The AVD Manager will create the AVD for you, and when it's done, display it in the AVD Manager list of devices. You may now close the AVD Manager.

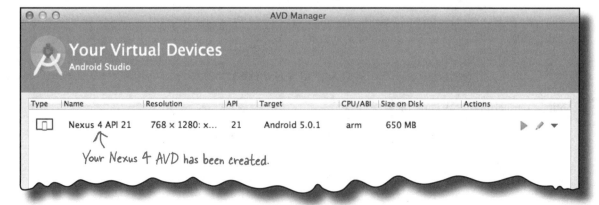

Run the app in the emulator

Set up environment

Build app

→ **Run app**

Change app

Now that you've set up your AVD, let's run the app on it. To do this, choose the "Run 'app'" command from the Run menu. When you're asked to choose a device, make sure the "Launch emulator" option is selected, along with the Nexus 4 AVD you just created. Then click on the OK button.

While we wait patiently for the AVD to appear, let's take a look at what happens when you choose Run.

Compile, package, deploy and run

Choosing the Run option doesn't just run your app. It also deals with all the preliminary tasks that are needed for the app to run:

This is the AVD we just created.

Libraries   Resources

Java file   Bytecode   APK file

▶ Run

Emulator

Emulator

> ## An APK file is an Android application package. It's basically a JAR or ZIP file for Android applications.

① The Java source files get compiled to bytecode.

② **An Android application package, or APK file, gets created.**
The APK file includes the compiled Java files, along with any libraries and resources needed by your app.

③ **Assuming there's not one already running, the emulator gets launched with the AVD.**

④ Once the emulator has been launched and the AVD is active, the APK file is uploaded to the AVD and installed.

⑤ **The AVD starts the main activity associated with the app.**
Your app gets displayed on the AVD screen, and it's all ready for you to test out.

be patient

Set up environment ☑
Build app ☑
Run app ➡
Change app

You can watch progress in the console

It can sometimes take quite a while for the emulator to launch with your AVD—often *several minutes*. The great news is that you can see what's happening using the Android Studio console. The console gives you a blow-by-blow account of what the gradle build system is doing, and if it encounters any errors, you'll see them highlighted in the text.

We suggest finding something else to do while waiting for the emulator to start. Like quilting, or cooking a small meal.

You can find the console at the bottom of the Android Studio screen:

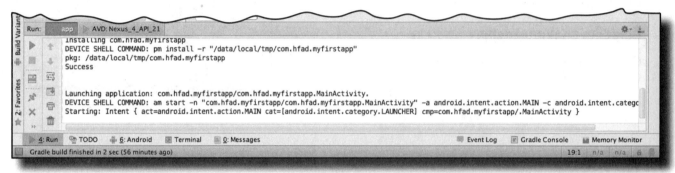

Here's the output from our console window when we ran our app:

Android Studio launches the emulator with AVD Nexus4, the AVD we just set up.

```
Waiting for device.
/Applications/adt-bundle-mac/sdk/tools/emulator -avd Nexus_4_API_21 -netspeed full -netdelay none
Device connected: emulator-5554
Device Nexus_4_API_21 [emulator-5554] is online, waiting for processes to start up..
Device is ready: Nexus_4_API_21 [emulator-5554]          The AVD is up
Target device: Nexus_4_API_21 [emulator-5554]            and running.
Uploading file
        local path: /Users/dawng/AndroidStudioProjects/MyFirstApp/app/build/outputs/apk/app-debug.apk
        remote path: /data/local/tmp/com.hfad.myfirstapp
Installing com.hfad.myfirstapp
DEVICE SHELL COMMAND: pm install -r "/data/local/tmp/com.hfad.myfirstapp"
pkg: /data/local/tmp/com.hfad.myfirstapp          Upload and install the APK file.
Success
Launching application: com.hfad.myfirstapp/com.hfad.myfirstapp.MainActivity.
DEVICE SHELL COMMAND: am start -n "com.hfad.myfirstapp/com.hfad.myfirstapp.MainActivity" -a
android.intent.action.MAIN -c android.intent.category.LAUNCHER
Starting: Intent { act=android.intent.action.MAIN cat=[android.intent.category.LAUNCHER]
cmp=com.hfad.myfirstapp/.MainActivity }
```

Finally, our app is launched by starting the main activity for it. This is the activity the wizard created for us.

Test drive

So let's look at what actually happens on screen when you run your app.

First, the emulator fires up in a separate window. The emulator takes a while to load the AVD, but then after a bit you see the locked screen of the AVD.

The emulator launches...

... and here's the locked AVD. It looks and behaves just like a real Nexus 4 device.

When you unlock the AVD screen by swiping the padlock icon upward, you see the app you just created. The application name appears at the top of the screen, and the default sample text "Hello world!" is displayed in the screen.

This is the title of the application.

Here's the sample text the wizard created for us.

Hello world!

Android Studio created the sample text "Hello world!" for us without us having to tell it.

Here's the app running on the AVD.

What just happened?

Let's break down what happens when you run the app:

1 Android Studio launches the emulator, loads the AVD, and installs the app.

2 When the app gets launched, an activity object is created from MainActivity.java.

3 The activity specifies that it uses the layout activity_main.xml.

4 The activity tells Android to display the layout on the screen. The text "Hello world!" gets displayed.

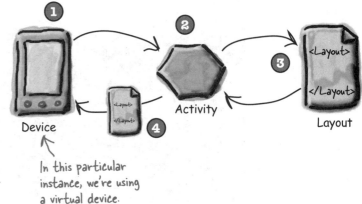

Device

In this particular instance, we're using a virtual device.

Activity

Layout

---

there are no Dumb Questions

Q: You mentioned that when you create an APK file, the Java source code gets compiled into bytecode and added to the APK. Presumably you mean it gets compiled into Java bytecode, right?

A: It does, but that's not the end of the story. Things work a little differently on Android.

The big difference with Android is that your code doesn't actually run inside an ordinary Java VM. It runs on the Android runtime (ART) instead, and on older devices it runs in a predecessor to ART called Dalvik. This means that you write your Java source code, compile it into *.class* files using the Java compiler, and then the *.class* files get stitched into a single file in DEX format, which is smaller, more efficient bytecode. ART then runs the DEX code. You can see more details about this in Appendix A.

Q: That sounds complicated. Why not just use the normal Java VM?

A: ART can convert the DEX bytecode into native code that can run directly on the CPU of the Android device. This makes the app run a lot faster, and use a lot less battery power.

Q: Is a Java virtual machine really that much overhead?

A: Yes. Because on Android, each app runs inside its own process. If it used ordinary JVMs, it would need a lot more memory.

Q: Do I need to create a new AVD every time I create a new app?

A: No, once you've created the AVD you can use it for any of your apps. You may find it useful to create multiple AVDs in order to test your apps in different situations. As an example, you might want to create a tablet AVD so you can see how your app looks and behaves on larger devices.

Refining the app

Over the past few pages, you've built a basic Android app and seen it running in the emulator. Next, we're going to refine the app you've built.

At the moment, the app displays the sample text "Hello world!" that the wizard put in for us as a placeholder. You're going to change that text to say something else instead. So what do we need to change in order to achieve that? To answer that, let's take a step back and look at how the app is currently built.

My First App

Sup doge

You're going to change the text here to say something other than "Hello word!".

The app has one activity and one layout

When we built the app, we told Android Studio how to configure it, and the wizard did the rest. The wizard created a basic activity for us, and also a default layout.

The activity controls what the app does

Android Studio created an activity for us called *MainActivity.java*. The activity specifies what the app **does** and how it should respond to the user.

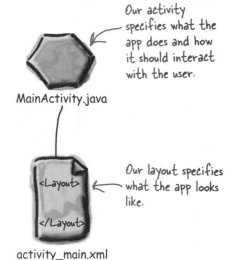

Our activity specifies what the app does and how it should interact with the user.

MainActivity.java

The layout controls the app appearance

MainActivity.java specifies that it uses the layout Android Studio created for us called *activity_main.xml*. The layout specifies what the app **looks like**.

Our layout specifies what the app looks like.

activity_main.xml

We want to change the appearance of the app by changing the text that's displayed. This means that we need to deal with the Android component that controls what the app looks like. We need to take a closer look at the *layout*.

☑ Set up environment
☑ Build app
☑ Run app
→ □ **Change app**

What's in the layout?

We need to change the sample "Hello world!" text that Android Studio created for us, so let's start with the layout file *activity_main.xml*. If it isn't already open in an editor, open it now by finding the file in the *app/src/main/res/layout* folder in the explorer and double-clicking on it.

The design editor

There are two ways of viewing and editing layout files in Android Studio: through the **design editor** and through the **code editor**.

When you choose the design option, you can see that the sample text "Hello world!" appears in the layout as you might expect. But what's in the underlying XML?

Let's see by switching to the code editor.

The design editor.

Hello world!

Here's the sample text.

You can see the design editor by choosing "Design" here.

The code editor

When you choose the code editor option, the content of *activity_main.xml* is displayed. Let's take a closer look at.

The code editor.

To see the code editor, click on "Text" in the bottom tab.

☑ Set up environment
☑ Build app
☑ Run app
→ ☐ **Change app**

activity_main.xml has two elements

Here's the code from *activity_main.xml* that Android Studio generated for us.

```
<RelativeLayout xmlns:android="http://schemas.android.com/apk/res/android"
    xmlns:tools="http://schemas.android.com/tools"
    android:layout_width="match_parent"
    android:layout_height="match_parent"
    ...
    tools:context=".MainActivity" >

    <TextView
        android:text="@string/hello_world"
        android:layout_width="wrap_content"
        android:layout_height="wrap_content" />

</RelativeLayout>
```

This is the <RelativeLayout> element.

Android Studio gave us more XML here, but you don't need to think about that just yet.

This is the <TextView> element nested within the <RelativeLayout> element.

This is the full path of activity_main.xml.

MyFirstApp

app/src/main

res

layout

activity_main.xml

The code contains two elements.

The first element is the `<RelativeLayout>` element. This element tells Android to display items on the layout in relative positions. You can use `<RelativeLayout>`, for instance, to center items in the middle of the layout, align them to the bottom of the screen on your Android device, or position them relative to other items.

The second element is the `<TextView>` element. This element is used to display text to the user. It's nested within the `<RelativeLayout>`, and in our case it's being used to display the sample text "Hello world!".

The key part of the code within the `<TextView>` element is the first line. What do you notice?

Watch it!

Android Studio sometimes displays the values of references in place of actual code.

As an example, it may display `"Hello world!"` *instead of the real code* `"@string/hello_world"`. *Any such substitutions should be highlighted in the code editor, and clicking on them or hovering over them with your mouse will reveal the true code.*

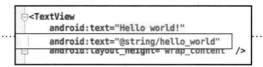

```
<TextView
    android:text="Hello world!"
    android:text="@string/hello_world"
    android:layout_height="wrap_content" />
```

```
<TextView
    android:text="@string/hello_world"
    android:layout_width="wrap_content"
    android:layout_height="wrap_content" />
```

The TextView element describes the text in the layout.

What do you notice about this line?

The layout file contains a reference to a string, not the string itself

The key part of the `<TextView>` element is the first line:

```
android:text="@string/hello_world" />
```

`android:text` means that this is the `text` property of the `<TextView>` element, so it specifies which text should be displayed in the layout. But why does it say "`@string/hello world`" rather than "Hello world!"? What does this actually mean?

Let's start with the first part, `@string`. This is just a way of telling Android to look up a text value from a string resource file. In our case, Android Studio created a string resource file for us called *strings.xml*, located in the *app/src/main/res/values* folder.

The second part, `hello world`, tells Android to **look up the value of a resource with the name `hello_world`**. So `@string/hello_world` means "look up the string resource with the name `hello_world`, and use the associated text value."

> **Put string values in strings.xml rather than hardcoding them. strings. xml is a resource file used to hold name/value pairs of strings. Layouts and activities can look up string values using their name.**

...for string resource hello_world.

Display the text...
```
android:text="@string/hello_world" />
```

> That seems complicated. Why doesn't activity_main.xml just include the text? Surely that's simpler?

There's one key reason: localization

Say you've created an app and it's a big hit on your local Google Play Store. But you don't want to limit yourself to just one country or language—you want to make it available internationally and for different languages.

Separating out text values into *strings.xml* makes dealing with issues like this much easier. Rather than having to change hardcoded text values in a whole host of different activity and layout files, you can simply replace the *strings.xml* file with an internationalized version.

Using *strings.xml* as a central resource for text values also makes it easier to make global changes to text across your whole application. If your boss needs you to change the wording in an app because the company's changed its name, only *strings.xml* needs to be changed.

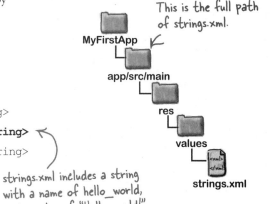

Let's look in the strings.xml file

Android Studio created a string resource file for us called *strings.xml*, so let's see if it contains a `hello_world` resource. Use the explorer to find it in the *app/src/main/res/values* folder, and open it by double-clicking on it.

Here's what our code in the *strings.xml* file looks like:

```xml
<?xml version="1.0" encoding="utf-8"?>
<resources>
    <string name="app_name">My First App</string>
    <string name="hello_world">Hello world!</string>
    <string name="action_settings">Settings</string>
</resources>
```

strings.xml includes a string with a name of hello_world, and a value of "Hello world!".

As you can see, there's a line of code that looks just like what we are looking for. It describes a string resource with a name of `hello_world`, and a value of "Hello world!":

```xml
<string name="hello_world">Hello world!</string>
```

Update strings.xml to change the text

So let's change the sample text in the app. If you've not already done so, find the file *strings.xml* in the Android Studio explorer, and double-click on it to open it.

Here's the code from the file. You need to look for the string with the name "hello_world", and change its corresponding text value from "Hello world!" to "Sup doge":

```xml
<?xml version="1.0" encoding="utf-8"?>
<resources>
    <string name="app_name">My First App</string>
    <string name="hello_world">Hello world! Sup doge</string>
    <string name="action_settings">Settings</string>
</resources>
```

Change the value here from "Hello world!" to "Sup doge".

Once you've updated the file, go to the File menu and choose the Save All option to save your change.

String Resource Files Up Close

strings.xml is the default resource file used to hold name/value pairs of strings so that they can be referenced throughout your app. It has the following format:

> The <string> element identifies the name/value pairs as strings.

> The <resources> element identifies the contents of the file as resources.

```xml
<?xml version="1.0" encoding="utf-8"?>
<resources>
    <string name="app_name">My First App</string>
    <string name="hello_world">Hello world!</string>
    <string name="action_settings">Settings</string>
</resources>
```

There are two things that allow Android to recognize *strings.xml* as being a string resource file:

★ **The file is held in the folder app/src/main/res/values.**
XML files held in this folder contain simple values, such as strings and colors.

★ **The file has a ‹resources› element, which contains one or more ‹string› elements.**
The format of the file itself indicates that it's a resource file containing Strings. The `<resources>` element tells Android that the file contains resources, and the `<string>` element identifies each String resource.

This means that you don't need to call your String resource file *strings.xml*; if you want, you can call it something else, or split your Strings into multiple files.

Each name/value pair takes the form

> `<string name="`**string_name**`">`**string_value**`</string>`

where `string_name` is the identifier of the string, and `string_value` is the String value itself.

A layout can retrieve the value of the String using

> `"@string/string_name"` ← This is the name of the string whose value we want to return.

> "string" tells Android to look for a string resource of this name.

getting **started**
- [x] **Set up environment**
- [x] **Build app**
- [x] **Run app**
→ [x] **Change app**

Take the app for a test drive

Once you've edited the file, try running your app in the emulator again by choosing the "Run 'app'" command from the Run menu. You should see that your app now says "Sup doge" instead of "Hello world!".

Here's the updated version of our app running in the emulator.

The sample text now says "Sup doge" instead of "Hello world!".

---

there are no Dumb Questions

Q: Do I absolutely have to put my text values in a string resource file such as *strings.xml*?

A: It's not mandatory, but Android gives you warning messages if you hardcode text values. It might seem like a lot of effort at first, but it makes things like localization much easier. It's also easier to use String resources to start off with, rather than patching them in afterward.

Q: How does separating out the String values help with localization?

A: Suppose you want your application to be in English by default, but in French if the device language is set to French. Rather than hardcode different languages into your app, you can have one String resource file for English text, and another resource file for French text.

Q: How does the app know which to use?

A: Put your default English strings resource file in the *app/src/main/res/values* folder as normal, and your French resource file in a new folder called *app/src/main/res/values-fr*. If the device is set to French, it will use the strings in the *app/src/main/res/values-fr* folder. If the device is set to any other language, it will use the strings in *app/src/main/res/values*.

Q: The layout code Android Studio generated for me looks a little different than the book's examples. Should I be concerned?

A: Android Studio may give you slightly different XML depending on which version you're using. You don't need to worry about this, because from now on you'll be learning how to roll your own layout code anyway, so you'll replace a lot of what Android Studio gives you.

Your Android Toolbox

**You've got Chapter 1 under
your belt and now you've
added Android basic concepts
to your toolbox.**

You can download
the full code for
the chapter from
https://tinyurl.com/
HeadFirstAndroid.

BULLET POINTS

- Versions of Android have a version number, API level, and code name.

- Android Studio is a special version of IntelliJ IDEA that interfaces with the Android Software Development Kit (SDK) and the gradle build system.

- A typical Android app is comprised of activities, layouts, and resource files.

- Layouts describe what your app looks like. They're held in the *app/src/main/res/layout* folder.

- Activities describe what you app does, and how it interacts with the user. The activities you write are held in the *app/src/main/java* folder.

- *strings.xml* contains string name/value pairs. It's used to separate out text values from the layouts and activities, and supports localization.

- *AndroidManifest.xml* contains information about the app itself. It lives in the *app/src/main* folder.

- An AVD is an Android Virtual Device. It runs in the Android emulator and mimics a physical Android device.

- An APK is an Android application package. It's like a JAR file for Android apps, and contains your app bytecode, libraries, and resources. You install an app on a device by installing the APK.

- Android apps run in separate processes using the Android runtime (ART).

- `RelativeLayout` is used to place GUI components in relative positions in a layout.

- The `TextView` element is used for displaying text.

2 building interactive apps

Apps That Do Something

I wonder what happens if I press the button marked "ejector seat"?

Most apps need to respond to the user in some way.

In this chapter, you'll see how you can make your apps **a bit more interactive**. You'll see how you can get your app to *do* something in response to the user, and **how to get your activity and layout talking to each other** like best buddies. Along the way, we'll take you a bit **deeper into how Android actually works** by introducing you to **R**, the hidden gem that glues everything together.

You're going to build a Beer Adviser app

In the Chapter 1, you saw how to create a basic app using the Android Studio New Project wizard, and how to change the text displayed in the layout. But when you create an Android app, you're usually going to want the app to *do* something.

In this chapter, we're going to show you how to create an app that the user can interact with: we'll be creating a Beer Adviser app. In the app, users can select the types of beer they enjoy, click a button, and get back a list of tasty beers to try out.

Here's how the app will be structured:

1   **The layout specifies what the app will look like.**
It includes three GUI components:

- A drop-down list of values called a spinner, which allows the user to choose which type of beer they want.
- A button that when pressed will return a selection of beer types.
- A text field that displays the types of beer.

2   **The file strings.xml includes any string resources needed by the layout—for example, the label of the button specified in the layout.**

3   **The activity specifies how the app should interact with the user.**
It takes the type of beer the user chooses, and uses this to display a list of beers the user might be interested in. It achieves this with the help of a custom Java class.

3   **The custom Java class contains the application logic for the app.**
It includes a method that takes a type of beer as a parameter, and returns a list of beers of this type. The activity calls the method, passes it the type of beer, and uses the response.

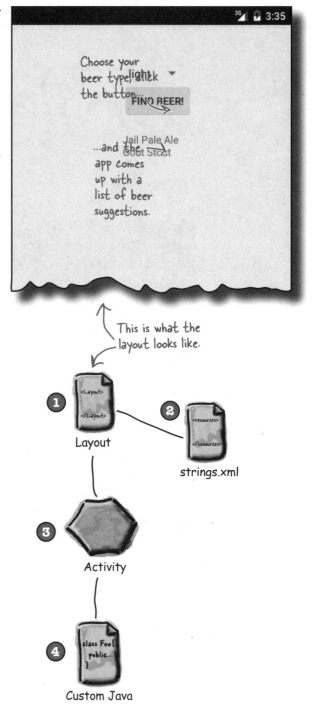

Here's what you need to do

So let's get to work and build the Beer Adviser app. There are a few steps you need to go through (we'll tackle these throughout the rest of the chapter):

① **Create a project.**
You're creating a brand-new app, so you'll need to create a new project. Just like before, you'll need to create a basic layout and activity.

② **Update the layout.**
Once you have a basic app set up, you need to amend the layout so that it includes all the GUI components your app needs.

③ **Wire the layout to the activity.**
The layout only creates the visuals. To add smarts to your app, you need to wire the layout to the Java code in your activity.

④ **Write the application logic.**
You'll add a Java custom class to the app, and use it to make sure users get the right beer based on their selection.

Create the project

→ ☐ **Create project**
☐ **Update layout**
☐ **Connect activity**
☐ **Write logic**

Let's begin by creating the new app (the steps are similar to those we used in the previous chapter):

★ Open Android Studio and choose "Start a new Android Studio project" from the welcome screen. This starts the wizard you saw in Chapter 1.

★ When prompted, enter an application name of "Beer Adviser", making your package name `com.hfad.beeradviser`.

★ We want the app to work on most phones and tablets, so choose a minimum SDK of API 15, and make sure the option for "Phone and Tablet" is ticked. This means that any phone or tablet that runs the app must have API 15 installed on it as a minimum. Most Android devices meet this criteria.

★ Choose a blank activity for your default activity. Call the activity "FindBeerActivity" and the accompanying layout "activity_find_beer". Accept the default values for Title and Menu Resource Name, as we won't be using these.

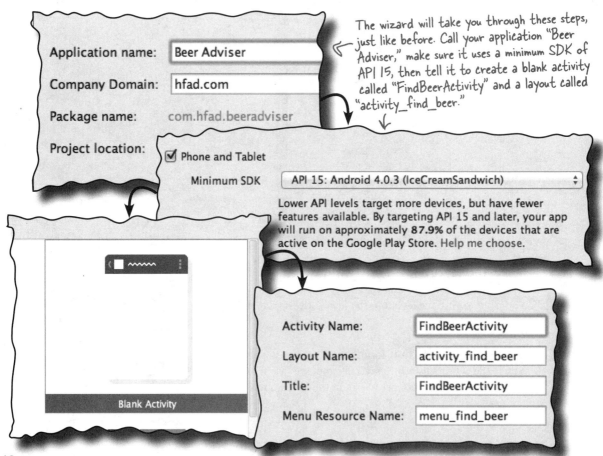

The wizard will take you through these steps, just like before. Call your application "Beer Adviser," make sure it uses a minimum SDK of API 15, then tell it to create a blank activity called "FindBeerActivity" and a layout called "activity_find_beer."

Application name:	Beer Adviser
Company Domain:	hfad.com
Package name:	com.hfad.beeradviser
Project location:	

☑ Phone and Tablet

Minimum SDK — API 15: Android 4.0.3 (IceCreamSandwich)

Lower API levels target more devices, but have fewer features available. By targeting API 15 and later, your app will run on approximately **87.9%** of the devices that are active on the Google Play Store. Help me choose.

Blank Activity

Activity Name:	FindBeerActivity
Layout Name:	activity_find_beer
Title:	FindBeerActivity
Menu Resource Name:	menu_find_beer

We've created a default activity and layout

When you click on the Finish button, Android Studio creates a new project containing an activity called *FindBeerActivity.java* and a layout called *activity_find_beer.xml*. Let's start by changing the layout file. To do this, go to the *app/src/main/res/layout* folder, and open the file *activity_find_beer.xml*.

Just like before, the wizard has created a default layout for us with a "Hello world!" <TextView> element on the page like this:

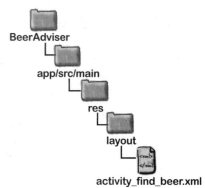

BeerAdviser

app/src/main

res

layout

activity_find_beer.xml

The layout XML

```
<RelativeLayout xmlns:android="http://schemas.android.com/apk/res/android"
    xmlns:tools="http://schemas.android.com/tools"
    android:layout_width="match_parent"
    android:layout_height="match_parent"
    android:paddingLeft="16dp"
    android:paddingRight="16dp"
    android:paddingTop="16dp"
    android:paddingBottom="16dp"
    tools:context=".FindBeerActivity">

    <TextView
        android:text="@string/hello_world"
        android:layout_width="wrap_content"
        android:layout_height="wrap_content" />

</RelativeLayout>
```

These elements relate to the layout as a whole. They determine the layout width and height, along with any padding in the layout margins.

The design editor

The <TextView> in the XML is reflected in the design editor.

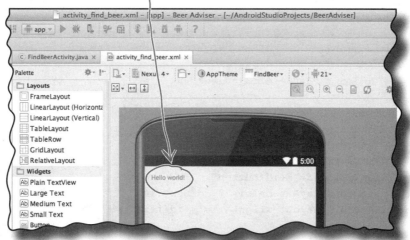

Adding components with the design editor

There are two ways of adding GUI components to the layout: via XML or using the design editor. Let's start by adding a button via the design editor.

To the left of the design editor, there's a palette that contains GUI components you can drag to your layout. If you look in the Widgets area, you'll see that there's a Button component. Click on it, and drag it into the design editor.

Here's the palette.

Here's the Button. Drag it over to the layout.

We placed ours under the "Hello world!" text.

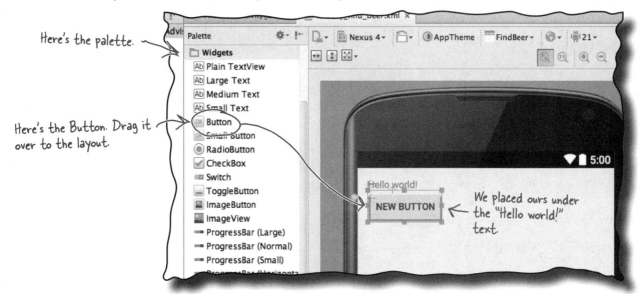

Changes in the design editor are reflected in the XML

Dragging GUI components to the layout like this is a convenient way of updating it. If you switch to the code editor, you'll see that adding the button via the design editor has added some lines of code to the file:

The code the design editor adds depends on where you place the button. It's likely that your layout XML will look different to ours, but don't worry, we're changing it soon.

```
...
<TextView
    android:text="@string/hello_world"
    android:layout_width="wrap_content"
    android:layout_height="wrap_content"
    android:id="@+id/textView" />

<Button
    android:layout_width="wrap_content"
    android:layout_height="wrap_content"
    android:text="New Button"
    android:id="@+id/button"
    android:layout_below="@+id/textView"
    android:layout_alignLeft="@+id/textView" />
...
```

The TextView element we had before has been given an ID.

There's a new Button element that describes the new button you've dragged to the layout. We'll look at this in more detail over the next few pages.

activity_find_beer.xml has a new button

The editor added a new <Button> element to *activity_find_beer.xml*:

```
<Button
        android:layout_width="wrap_content"
        android:layout_height="wrap_content"
        android:text="New Button"
        android:id="@+id/button"
        android:layout_below="@+id/textView"
        android:layout_alignLeft="@+id/textView" />
```

A button in Androidville is a push-button that the user can press to trigger an action. It includes properties controlling its position, size, appearance, %and what methods it should call in the activity. These properties aren't unique to buttons—other GUI components including text views have them too.

Buttons and text views are subclasses of the same Android View class

There's a very good reason why buttons and text views have properties in common—they both inherit from the same Android **View** class. You'll find out more about this later in the book, but for now, here are some of the more common properties.

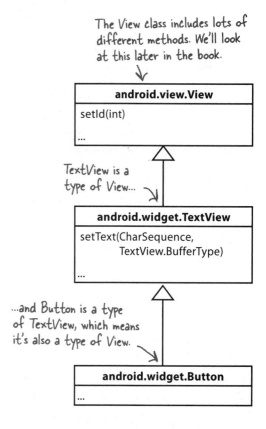

The View class includes lots of different methods. We'll look at this later in the book.

android:id

This gives the component an identifying name. The ID property enables you to control what components do via activity code, and also allows you to control where components are placed in the layout:

```
android:id="@+id/button"
```

android:text

This tells Android what text the component should display. In the case of <Button>, it's the text that appears on the button:

```
android:text="New Button"
```

android:layout_width, android:layout_height

These properties specify the basic width and height of the component. "wrap_content" means it should be just big enough for the content:

```
android:layout_width="wrap_content"
android:layout_height="wrap_content"
```

- [x] Create project
- [ ] **Update layout** ←
- [ ] Connect activity
- [ ] Write logic

A closer look at the layout code

Let's take a closer look at the layout code, and break it down so that you can see what it's actually doing (don't worry if your code looks a little different, just follow along with us):

The RelativeLayout element.

```
<RelativeLayout xmlns:android="http://schemas.android.com/apk/res/android"
    xmlns:tools="http://schemas.android.com/tools"
    android:layout_width="match_parent"
    android:layout_height="match_parent"
    android:paddingLeft="16dp"
    android:paddingRight="16dp"
    android:paddingTop="16dp"
    android:paddingBottom="16dp"
    tools:context=".FindBeerActivity">
```

This is the text view

```
    <TextView
        android:text="@string/hello_world"
        android:layout_width="wrap_content"
        android:layout_height="wrap_content"
        android:id="@+id/textView" />
```

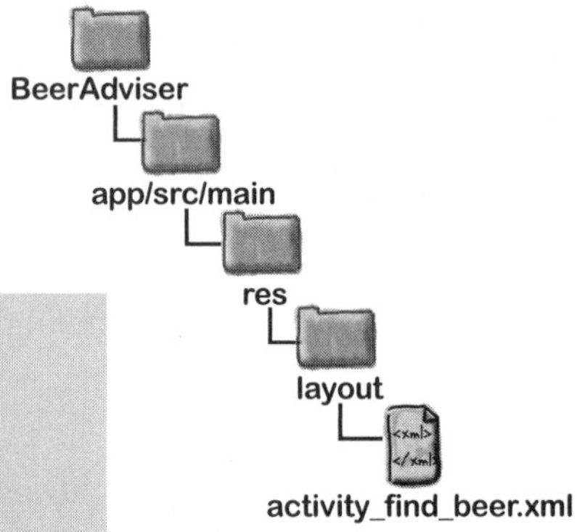

BeerAdviser
app/src/main
res
layout
activity_find_beer.xml

This is the button.

```
    <Button
        android:layout_width="wrap_content"
        android:layout_height="wrap_content"
        android:text="New Button"
        android:id="@+id/button"
        android:layout_below="@+id/textView"
        android:layout_alignLeft="@+id/textView" />
```

```
</RelativeLayout>
```

← This closes the RelativeLayout element.

The RelativeLayout element

The first element in the layout code is `<RelativeLayout>`. The `<RelativeLayout>` element tells Android that the different GUI components in the layout should be displayed *relative* to each other. As an example, you can use it to say that you want one component to appear to the left of another one, or that you want them to be aligned or lined up in some way.

← There are other ways of laying out your GUI components too. You'll find out more about these later on.

In this example, the button appears directly underneath the text view, so the button is displayed relative to the text view.

The TextView element

The first element inside the `<RelativeLayout>` is the `<TextView>`:

```
...
    <TextView
        android:text="@string/hello_world"
        android:layout_width="wrap_content"
        android:layout_height="wrap_content"
        android:id="@+id/textView" />
...
```

No properties have been set to specify where the text view should appear in the layout, so by default Android displays it in the upper-left corner of the screen. Notice that the text view has been given an ID of `textView`. You'll see why this is needed when we look at the next element.

The Button element

The final element inside the `<RelativeLayout>` is the `<Button>`:

```
...
    <Button
        android:layout_width="wrap_content"
        android:layout_height="wrap_content"
        android:text="New Button"
        android:id="@+id/button"
        android:layout_below="@+id/textView"
        android:layout_alignLeft="@+id/textView" />
...
```

When we added our button to the layout, we positioned the button so that it was underneath the text view, and so that the left edge of the button lined up with the left edge of the text view. We positioned the button *relative* to the text view, and this is reflected in the XML:

```
android:layout_below="@+id/textView"
android:layout_alignLeft="@+id/textView"
```

There are different ways of writing the layout XML in order to produce the same visual effect. As an example, the XML above specifies that *the button is positioned below the text view*. An equivalent statement would be to say that *the text view is positioned above the button*.

Using a relative layout means that GUI components will be positioned relative to each other.

The text view is displayed in the upper-left corner by default.

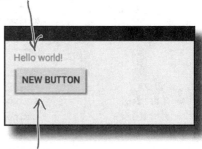

The button is set to appear below the text view, and with its left edge vertically aligned to the left edge of the text view.

Changes to the XML...

You've seen how changes you make in the design editor are reflected in the layout XML. The opposite applies too—any changes you make to the layout XML are applied to the design.

Try this now. Replace your *activity_find_beer.xml* code with the following:

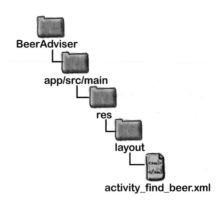

BeerAdviser

app/src/main

res

layout

activity_find_beer.xml

```xml
<RelativeLayout xmlns:android="http://schemas.android.com/apk/res/android"
    xmlns:tools="http://schemas.android.com/tools"
    android:layout_width="match_parent"
    android:layout_height="match_parent"
    android:paddingBottom="16dp"
    android:paddingLeft="16dp"
    android:paddingRight="16dp"
    android:paddingTop="16dp"
    tools:context=".FindBeerActivity" >
```

A spinner is the Android name for a drop-down list of values. It allows you to choose a single value from a selection.

```xml
<Spinner
    android:id="@+id/color"
    android:layout_width="wrap_content"
    android:layout_height="wrap_content"
    android:layout_alignParentTop="true"
    android:layout_centerHorizontal="true"
    android:layout_marginTop="37dp" />
```

This element displays a spinner in the layout. A spinner is a drop-down list of values.

Place a button below the spinner and left-align it to the spinner.

```xml
<Button
    android:id="@+id/find_beer"
    android:layout_width="wrap_content"
    android:layout_height="wrap_content"
    android:layout_alignLeft="@+id/color"
    android:layout_below="@+id/color"
    android:text="Button" />
```

Place a text view below the button and left-align it to the button.

```xml
<TextView
    android:id="@+id/brands"
    android:layout_width="wrap_content"
    android:layout_height="wrap_content"
    android:layout_alignLeft="@+id/find_beer"
    android:layout_below="@+id/find_beer"
    android:layout_marginTop="18dp"
    android:text="TextView" />
```

Do this!

Replace the contents of *activity_find_beer.xml* with the XML shown here.

```xml
</RelativeLayout>
```

...are reflected in the design editor

Once you've changed the layout XML, switch to the design editor. Instead of a layout containing a text view with a button underneath it, you should now see a text view displayed below a button.

Above the button we have a **spinner**. A spinner is the Android term for a drop-down list of values. When you touch it, it expands to show you the list so that you can pick a single value.

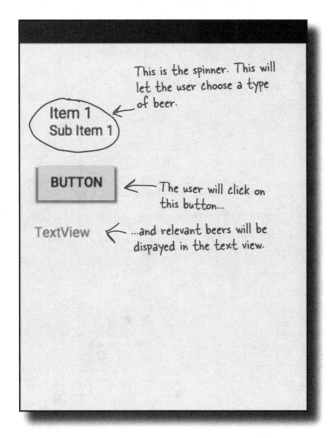

This is the spinner. This will let the user choose a type of beer.

Item 1
Sub Item 1

BUTTON

The user will click on this button...

TextView

...and relevant beers will be dispayed in the text view.

A spinner provides a drop-down list of values. It allows you to choose a single value from a set of values.

GUI components such as buttons, spinners, and text views have very similar attributes, as they are all types of View. Behind the scenes, they all inherit from the same Android View class.

We've shown you how to add GUI components to the layout with the aid of the design editor, and also by adding them through XML. In general, you're more likely to hack the XML to get the results you want without using the design editor. This is because editing the XML directly gives you more direct control over the layout, and means that you're not dependent on the IDE.

Create project
Update layout
Connect activity
Write logic

Use string resources rather than hardcoding the text

There's one more thing we need to change before we try running the app. At the moment, the button and text view both use hardcoded string values for their text properties. As we mentioned in Chapter 1, it's a good idea to change these to use the strings resource file *strings.xml* instead. While this isn't strictly necessary, it's a good habit to get into. Using the strings resource file for static text makes it easier to create international versions of your app, and if you need to tweak the wording in your app, you'll be able to do it one central place.

Open up the *app/src/main/res/values/strings.xml* file. When you switch to the XML view, it should look something like this:

```xml
<?xml version="1.0" encoding="utf-8"?>
<resources>

    <string name="app_name">Beer Adviser</string>
    <string name="hello_world">Hello world!</string>
    <string name="action_settings">Settings</string>

</resources>
```

These are strings that Android Studio created for us.

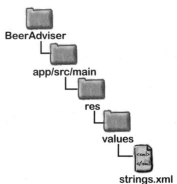

First, delete the "hello_world" resource, as we're no longer using it. Then, add a new resource called "find_beer" with a value of "Find Beer!". After you've done that, add a new resource named "brands" but don't enter anything for the value.

Your new code should look like this:

```xml
...
    <string name="app_name">Beer Adviser</string>
    <string name="hello_world">Hello world!</string>
    <string name="action_settings">Settings</string>
    <string name="find_beer">Find Beer!</string>
    <string name="brands"></string>
...
```

You need to remove the hello_world string resource, and add in two new ones called find_beer and brands.

Change the layout to use the string resources

Next, let's change the button and text view elements in the layout XML to use the two string resources we've just added.

Open up the *activity_find_beer.xml* file, and make the following changes:

⭐ Change the line `android:text="Button"` to `android:text="@string/find_beer"`.

⭐ Change the line `android:text="TextView"` to `android:text="@string/brands"`.

```
...
    <Spinner
        android:id="@+id/color"
        android:layout_width="wrap_content"
        android:layout_height="wrap_content"
        android:layout_alignParentTop="true"
        android:layout_centerHorizontal="true"
        android:layout_marginTop="37dp" />

    <Button
        android:id="@+id/find_beer"
        android:layout_width="wrap_content"
        android:layout_height="wrap_content"
        android:layout_alignLeft="@+id/color"
        android:layout_below="@+id/color"
        android:text="@string/find_beer" />
```
← *This will display the value of the find_beer string resource on the button.*

```
    <TextView
        android:id="@+id/brands"
        android:layout_width="wrap_content"
        android:layout_height="wrap_content"
        android:layout_alignLeft="@+id/find_beer"
        android:layout_below="@+id/find_beer"
        android:layout_marginTop="18dp"
        android:text="@string/brands" />
...
```
← *This will display the value of the brands string resource in the TextView. While this is currently blank, this ensures any future changes to the string value will get picked up.*

BeerAdviser
app/src/main
res
layout
activity_find_beer.xml

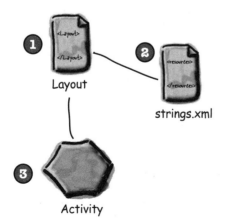

Let's take the app for a test drive

☑ Create project
☐ Update layout
☐ Connect activity
☐ Write logic

We still have more work to do on the app, but let's see how it's looking so far. Save the changes you've made, then choose the "Run 'app'" command from the Run menu. When prompted, select the option to launch the emulator.

Wait patiently for the app to load, and eventually it should appear.

Try touching the spinner. It's not immediately obvious, but when you touch the spinner, it presents you with a drop-down list of values—it's just at this point we haven't added any values to it.

Beer Adviser

This is the spinner, but it has no values in it.

FIND BEER!

The button is underneath the spinner, and also left-aligned to it.

Here's what we've done so far

Here's a quick recap of what we've done so far:

1 **We've created a layout that specifies what the app will look like.**
It includes a spinner, a button, and a text view.

2 **The file strings.xml includes the string resources we need.**
We've added a label for the button, and an empty string for the brands.

3 **The activity specifies how the app should interact with the user.**
Android Studio has created a basic activity for us, but we haven't done anything with it yet.

Layout

strings.xml

Activity

there are no Dumb Questions

Q: The layout looks slightly different when you run it compared with how it looks in the design editor. Why's that?

A: The design editor does its best to show you how the layout will look, but it has a few limitations. Our layout XML specfies that the spinner should be centered horizontally, for instance, but this may not be obvious from the design editor.

In practice, you're always best off working directly with the XML. This gives you a more accurate picture of what's going on, and gives you a finer degree of control too.

Q: I thought there was a text view too?

A: There is, it's just that at the moment it doesn't contain any text so you can't see it. You'll see it later on in the chapter when we get the text view to display some text.

Add values to the spinner

At the moment, the layout includes a spinner, but it doesn't have anything in it. Whenever you use a spinner, you need to get it to display a list of values so that the user can choose the value they want.

We can give the spinner a list of values in pretty much the same way that we set the text on the button and the text view: by using a **resource**. So far, we've used *strings.xml* to specify single String values. All we need to do is specify an *array* of String values, and get the spinner to reference it.

> **Resources are noncode assets, such as images or strings, used by your app.**

Adding an array resource is similar to adding a string

As you already know, you can add a string resource to *strings.xml* using

```
<string name="string_name">string_value</string>
```

where `string_name` is the identifier of the String, and `string_value` is the String value itself.

To add an array of Strings, you use the following syntax:

```
<string-array name="string_array_name">
    <item>string_value1</item>
    <item>string_value2</item>
    <item>string_value3</item>
    . . .
</string-array>
```

← This is the name of the array.

} These are the values in the array. You can add as many as you need.

where `string_array_name` is the name of the array, and `string_value1`, `string_value2`, `string_value3` are the individual String values that make up the array.

Let's add a `string-array` resource to our app. Open up *strings.xml*, and add the array like this:

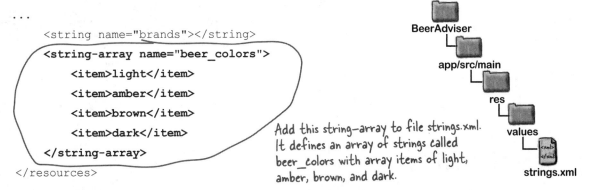

```
    . . .
    <string name="brands"></string>
    <string-array name="beer_colors">
        <item>light</item>
        <item>amber</item>
        <item>brown</item>
        <item>dark</item>
    </string-array>
</resources>
```

Add this string-array to file strings.xml. It defines an array of strings called beer_colors with array items of light, amber, brown, and dark.

BeerAdviser
app/src/main
res
values
strings.xml

Get the spinner to reference a string-array

A layout can reference a string-array using similar syntax to how it would retrieve the value of a string. Rather than use

    "@string/string_name"

you use the syntax

    "@array/array_name"

Use @string to reference a string, and @array to reference an array.

where `array_name` is the name of the array.

Let's use this in the layout. Go to the layout file *activity_find_beer.xml* and add an `entries` attribute to the spinner like this:

```
...
    <Spinner
        ...
        android:layout_marginTop="37dp"
        android:entries="@array/beer_colors" />
...
```

This means "the entries for the spinner come from array beer_colors"

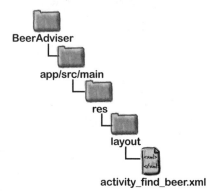

BeerAdviser
app/src/main
res
layout
activity_find_beer.xml

Test drive the spinner

So let's see what impact these changes have had on our app. Save your changes, then run the app. You should get something like this:

Create project
Update layout
Connect activity
Write logic

By default the top item in the spinner is selected.

Click on the spinner to see its entries.

When you click on a value, it gets selected.

We need to make the button do something

So far, we've added new GUI components to the layout, and populated a spinner with an array of values. What we need to do next is make the app react to the value we select in the spinner when the button is clicked. We want our app to behave something like this:

① **The user chooses a type of beer from the spinner.**
The user clicks on the button to find matching beers.

② **The layout specifies which method to call in the activity when the button is clicked.**

③ **The method in the activity retrieves the value of the selected beer in the spinner and passes it to the getBrands() method in a Java custom class called BeerExpert.**

④ **BeerExpert's getBrands() method finds matching brands for the type of beer and returns them to the activity as an ArrayList of Strings.**

⑤ **The activity gets a reference to the layout text view and sets its text value to the list of matching beers.**
This is displayed on the device.

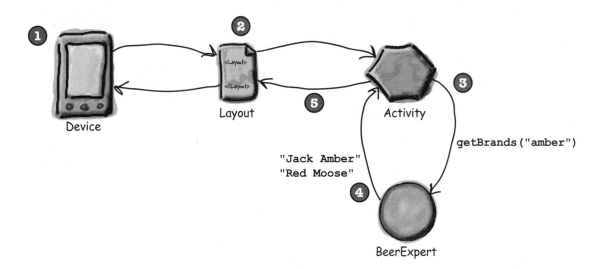

Let's start by getting the button to call a method.

Make the button call a method

☑ Create project
☑ Update layout
Connect activity
Write logic

Whenever you add a button to a layout, it's likely you'll want it to do something when the user clicks on it. To do this, you need to get the button to call a method in your activity.

To get a button to call a method in the activity when it's clicked, we need to make changes to two files:

⭐ **We need to change the layout file activity_find_beer.xml.**
We'll specify which method in the activity will get called when the button is clicked.

⭐ **We need to change the activity file FindBeerActivity.java.**
We need to write the method that gets called.

Let's start with the layout.

Use onClick to say which method the button calls

It only takes one line of XML to tell Android which method a button should call when it's clicked. All you need to do is add an `android:onClick` attribute to the `<button>` element, and give it the name of the method you want to call:

android:onClick="method_name" ← *This means "when the compenent is clicked, call the method in the activity called method_name".*

Let's try this now. Go to the layout file *activity_find_beer.xml*, and add a new line of XML to the `<button>` element to say that method `onClickFindBeer()` should be called when the button is clicked:

```
    ...

        <Button
            android:id="@+id/find_beer"
            android:layout_width="wrap_content"
            android:layout_height="wrap_content"
            android:layout_alignLeft="@+id/color"
            android:layout_below="@+id/color"
            android:text="@string/find_beer"
            android:onClick="onClickFindBeer" />

    ...
```

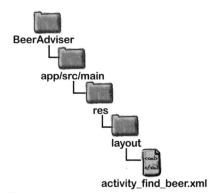

When the button is clicked, call method onClickFindBeer() in the activity. We'll create the method in the activity over the next few pages.

Once you've made these changes, save the file.

Now that the layout knows which method to call in the activity, we need to go and write the method. Let's take a look at the activity.

What activity code looks like

When we first created a project for our app, we asked the wizard to create a basic activity for us called `FindBeerActivity`. The code for this activity is held in a file called *FindBeerActivity.java*. Open this file by going to the *app/src/main/java* folder and double-clicking on it.

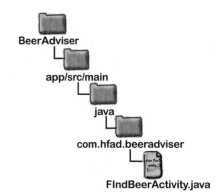

BeerAdviser

app/src/main

java

com.hfad.beeradviser

FindBeerActivity.java

When you open the file, you'll see that Android Studio has generated a lot of Java code for you. Rather than taking you through all the code that Android Studio has created for you, we want you to replace it with the code below. This is because a lot of the activity code that Android Studio has generated is unnecessary, and we want you to focus on the fundamentals of Android itself rather than the quirks of a single IDE. So delete the code that's currently in *FindBeerActivity.java*, and replace it with the code shown here:

```java
package com.hfad.beeradviser;

import android.os.Bundle;
import android.app.Activity;

public class FindBeerActivity extends Activity {

    @Override
    protected void onCreate(Bundle savedInstanceState) {
        super.onCreate(savedInstanceState);
        setContentView(R.layout.activity_find_beer);
    }
}
```

The class extends the Android Activity class.

This is the onCreate() method. It's called when the activity is first created.

setContentView tells Android which layout the activity uses. In this case, it's activity_find_beer.

The above code is all you need to create a basic activity. As you can see, it's a class that extends the `android.app.Activity` class, and implements an `onCreate()` method.

All activities have to extend the `Activity` class. The `Activity` class contains a bunch of methods that turn your Java class from a plain old Java class into a full-fledged, card-carrying Android activity.

All activities also need to implement the `onCreate()` method. The `onCreate()` method gets called when the activity object gets created, and it's used to perform basic setup such as what layout the activity is associated with. This is done using the `setContentView()` method. In the example above, `setContentView(R.layout.activity_find_beer)` tells Android that this activity uses `activity_find_beer` as its layout.

On the previous page, we added an `onClick` attribute to the button in our layout and gave it a value of `onClickFindBeer`. We need to add this method to our activity so it will be called when the button gets clicked. This will enable the activity to respond when the user touches a button in the user interface.

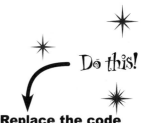

Do this!

Replace the code in your version of *FindBeerActivity.java* with the code shown on this page.

Add an **onClickFindBeer()** method to the activity

Create project
Update layout
Connect activity
Write logic

The onClickFindBeer() method needs to have a particular signature, otherwise it won't get called when the button specified in the layout gets clicked. The method needs to take the following form:

```
public void onClickFindBeer(View view) {

}
```

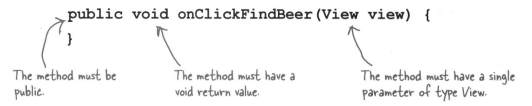

The method must be public.

The method must have a void return value.

The method must have a single parameter of type View.

If the method doesn't take this form, the method won't respond when the user touches the button. This is because behind the scenes, Android looks for a public method with a void return value, with a method name that matches the method specified in the layout XML.

The View parameter in the method may seem unusual at first glance, but there's a good reason for it being there. The parameter refers to the GUI component that triggers the method (in this case, the button). As we mentioned earlier, GUI components such as buttons and text views are all types of View.

So let's update our activity code. Add the onClickFindBeer() method below to your activity code:

> **If you want a method to respond to a button click, it must be public, have a void return type, and take a single View parameter.**

We're using this class, so we need to import it.

```
...
import android.view.View;

public class FindBeerActivity extends Activity {
...
    //Call when the user clicks the button
    public void onClickFindBeer(View view){
    }
}
```

Add the onClickFindBeer() method to FindBeerActivity.java.

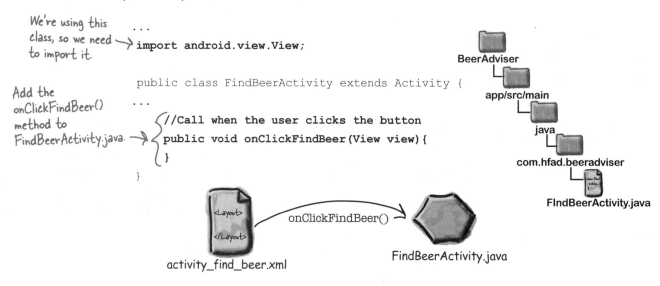

activity_find_beer.xml

onClickFindBeer()

FindBeerActivity.java

BeerAdviser
app/src/main
java
com.hfad.beeradviser
FindBeerActivity.java

onClickFindBeer() needs to do something

Now that we've created the `onClickFindBeer()` method in our activity, the next thing we need to do is get the method to do something when it runs. We need to get our app to display a selection of different beers that match the beer type the user has selected.

In order to achieve this, we first need to get a reference to both the spinner and text view GUI components in the layout. This will allow us to retrieve the value of the chosen beer type from the spinner, and display text in the text view.

Use findViewById() to get a reference to a view

We can get a handle for our two GUI components using a method called `findViewById()`. The `findViewById()` method takes the ID of the GUI component as a parameter, and returns a `View` object. You then cast the return value to the correct type of GUI component (for example, a `TextView` or a `Button`).

Here's how you'd use `findViewById()` to get a reference to the text view with an ID of brands:

We want the view with an ID of brands.

```
TextView brands = (TextView) findViewById(R.id.brands);
```

brands is a TextView, so we have to cast it as one.

Take a closer look at how we specified the ID of the text view. Rather than pass in the name of the text view, we passed in an ID of the form `R.id.brands`. So what does this mean? What's R?

R.java is a special Java file that gets generated by the Android tools whenever you create or build your app. It lives within the *app/build/generated/source/r/debug* folder in your project in a package with the same name as the package of your app. Android uses R to keep track of the resources used within the app, and among other things it enables you to get references to GUI components from within your activity code.

If you open up *R.java*, you'll see that it contains a series of inner classes, one for each type of resource. Each resource of that type is referenced within the inner class. As an example, R includes an inner class called `id`, and the inner class includes a `static final brands` value. The line of code

```
(TextView) findViewById(R.id.brands);
```

uses this value to get a reference to the `brands` text view.

R is a special Java class that enables you to retrieve references to resources in your app.

***R.java* gets generated for you.**

You don't change any of the code within R, but it's useful to know it's there.

Once you have a View, you can access its methods

☑ Create project
☑ Update layout
☑ Connect activity
→ ☐ **Write logic**

The findViewById() method provides you with a Java version of your GUI component. This means that you can get and set properties in the GUI component using the methods exposed by the Java class. Let's take a closer look.

Setting the text in a TextView

As you've seen, you can get a reference to a text view in Java using

```
TextView brands = (TextView) findViewById(R.id.brands);
```

When this line of code gets called, it creates a TextView object called brands. You are then able to call methods on this TextView object.

Let's say you wanted to set the text displayed in the brands text view to "Gottle of geer". The TextView class includes a method called setText() that you can use to change the text property. You use it like this:

```
brands.setText("Gottle of geer");
```
← Set the text on the brands TextView to "Gottle of geer"

Retrieving the selected value in a spinner

You can get a reference to a spinner in a similar way to how you get a reference to a text view. You use the findViewById() method as before, only this time you cast the result as a Spinner:

```
Spinner color = (Spinner) findViewById(R.id.color);
```

This gives you a Spinner object whose methods you can now access. As an example, here's how you retrieve the currently selected item in the spinner, and convert it to a String:

```
String.valueOf(color.getSelectedItem())
```
← This gets the selected item in a spinner and converts it to a String.

The code

```
color.getSelectedItem()
```

actually returns a generic Java object. This is because spinner values can be something other than Strings, such as images. In our case, we know the values are Strings, so we can use String.valueOf() to convert the selected item from an Object to a String.

Update the activity code

You now know enough to write some code in the onClickFindBeer()
method. Rather than write all the code we need in one go, let's start by
reading the selected value from the spinner, and displaying it in the text view.

Activity Magnets

Somebody wrote a new **onClickFindBeer()** method using fridge magnets
for us to slot into our activity. Unfortunately, a freak kitchen whirlwind has
dislodged the magnets. Can you piece the code back together again?

The code needs to retrieve the type of beer selected in the spinner, and then
display the type of beer in the text view.

```
//Call when the button gets clicked
public void onClickFindBeer(................... view) {

    //Get a reference to the TextView
    ....................... brands = ..................... ........................ ( ..................... );

    //Get a reference to the Spinner
    Spinner ................ = ..................... ........................ ( ................. );

    //Get the selected item in the Spinner
    String ..................... = String.valueOf(color. ................................. );

    //Display the selected item
    brands. ................ (beerType);
}
```

TextView   color   findViewById   setText   R.id.color

(TextView)   findView   R.view.brands   R.id.brands

Button   findView   View   R.view.color   findViewById

getSelectedItem()   beerType   (Spinner)

You won't
need to use
all of the
magnets.

Activity Magnets Solution

Somebody wrote a new **onClickFindBeer()** method using fridge magnets for us to slot into our activity. Unfortunately, a freak kitchen whirlwind has dislodged the magnets. Can you piece the code back together again?

The code needs to retrieve the type of beer selected in the spinner, and then display the type of beer in the text view.

```
//Call when the button gets clicked
public void onClickFindBeer( View view) {

    //Get a reference to the TextView
    TextView brands = (TextView) findViewById( R.id.brands );

    //Get a reference to the Spinner
    Spinner color = (Spinner) findViewById ( R.id.color );

    //Get the selected item in the Spinner
    String beerType = String.valueOf(color. getSelectedItem() );

    //Display the selected item
    brands. setText (beerType);
}
```

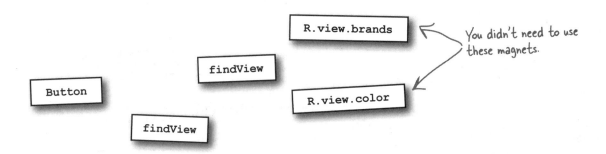

R.view.brands

findView

Button

findView

R.view.color

You didn't need to use these magnets.

The first version of the activity

Our cunning plan is to build the activity in stages, and test it as we go along. In the end, the activity will take the selected value from the spinner, call a method in a custom Java class, and then display matching types of beer. For this first version, our goal is just to make sure that we correctly retrieve the selected item from the spinner.

Here is our activity code, including the method you pieced together on the previous page. Apply these changes to *FindBeerActivity.java*, then save them:

```
package com.hfad.beeradviser;

import android.os.Bundle;
import android.app.Activity;
import android.view.View;
import android.widget.Spinner;
import android.widget.TextView;
```

We're using these extra classes.

BeerAdviser
app/src/main
java
com.hfad.beeradviser
FindBeerActivity.java

```
public class FindBeerActivity extends Activity {

    @Override
    protected void onCreate(Bundle savedInstanceState) {
        super.onCreate(savedInstanceState);
        setContentView(R.layout.activity_find_beer);
    }
```

← *We've not changed this method.*

```
    //Call when the button gets clicked
    public void onClickFindBeer(View view) {
        //Get a reference to the TextView
        TextView brands = (TextView) findViewById(R.id.brands);
        //Get a reference to the Spinner
        Spinner color = (Spinner) findViewById(R.id.color);
        //Get the selected item in the Spinner
        String beerType = String.valueOf(color.getSelectedItem());
        //Display the selected item
        brands.setText(beerType);
    }
}
```

findViewById returns a View. You need to cast it to the right type of View.

getSelectedItem returns an Object. You need to turn it into a String.

What the code does

Before we take the app for a test drive, let's look at what the code actually does.

① **The user chooses a type of beer from the spinner and clicks on the Find Beer button. This calls the public void onClickFindBeer(View) method in the activity.**

The layout specifies which method in the activity should be called when the button is clicked via the `android:onClick` property of the button.

Layout   FindBeerActivity

② **The activity gets references to the TextView and Spinner GUI components using calls to the findViewById() method.**

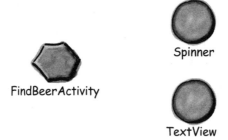

Spinner

FindBeerActivity

TextView

③ **The activity retrieves the currently selected value of the spinner, and converts it to a String.**

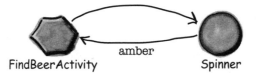

FindBeerActivity   amber   Spinner

④ **The activity then sets the text property of the TextView to reflect the currently selected item in the spinner.**

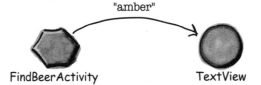

"amber"

FindBeerActivity   TextView

Test drive the changes

Make the changes to the activity file, save it, and then run your app. This time when we click on the Find Beer button, it displays the value of the selected item in the spinner.

The type of beer selected is displayed in the text view.

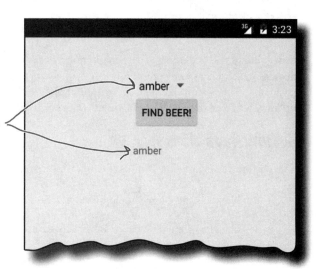

there are no
Dumb Questions

Q: I added a string to my *strings.xml* file but I can't see it in *R.java*. Why isn't it there?

A: Android Studio, generates *R.java* when you save any changes you've made. If you've added a resource but can't see it in *R.java*, check that your changes have been saved.

R.java also gets updated when the app gets built. The app builds when you run the app, so running the app will also update *R.java*.

Q: The values in the spinner look like they're static as they're set to the values in the `string-array`. Can I change these values programmatically?

A: You can, but it's more complicated than just using static values. We'll show you later in the book how you can have complete control over the values displayed in components such as spinners.

Q: What type of object is returned by `getSelectedItem()`?

A: It's declared as type `Object`. Because we used a `string-array` for the values, the actual value returned in this case is a `String`.

Q: In this case? Isn't it always?

A: You can do more complicated things with spinners than just display text. As an example, the spinner might display an icon next to each value. As `getSelectedItem()` returns an `Object`, it gives you a bit more flexibility.

Q: Does the name of `onClickFindBeer` matter?

A: All that matters is that the name of the method in the activity code matches the name used in the button's `onClick` attribute in the layout.

Q: Why did we replace the activity code that Android Studio created for us?

A: IDEs such as Android Studio include lots of time-saving functions and utilities that can save you a lot of time. They generate a lot of code for you, and sometimes this can be useful. When you're learning a new language or development area such as Android, we think it's best to learn about the fundamentals of the language rather than what the IDE generates for you. This way you'll develop a greater understanding of it, which you'll then be able to use no matter which IDE you use.

Building the custom Java class

As we said at the beginning of the chapter, the Beer Adviser app decides which beers to recommend with the help of a custom Java class. The custom Java class is written in plain old Java, with no knowledge of the fact it's being used by an Android app.

Custom Java class spec

The custom Java class should meet the following requirements:

⭐   The package name should be `com.hfad.beeradviser`.

⭐   The class should be called `BeerExpert`.

⭐   It should expose one method, `getBrands()`, that takes a preferred beer color (as a String), and return a `List<String>` of recommended beers.

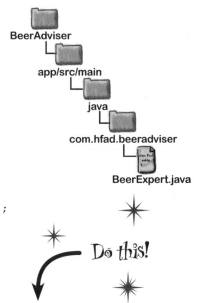

Layout

strings.xml

Activity

We need to create a Java class that the activity can use to find out which beer brands to suggest.

BeerExpert

Build and test the Java class

Java classes can be extremely complicated and involve calls to complex application logic. You can either build and test your own version of the class, or use our sophisticated version of the class shown here:

```java
package com.hfad.beeradviser;
import java.util.ArrayList;
import java.util.List;

public class BeerExpert {
    List<String> getBrands(String color) {
        List<String> brands = new ArrayList<String>();
        if (color.equals("amber")) {
            brands.add("Jack Amber");
            brands.add("Red Moose");
        } else {
            brands.add("Jail Pale Ale");
            brands.add("Gout Stout");
        }
        return brands;
    }
}
```

This is pure Java code, nothing Androidy about it.

BeerAdviser

app/src/main

java

com.hfad.beeradviser

BeerExpert.java

Do this!

Add the BeerExpert class to your project. Highlight the *com.hfad.beeradviser* package in the *app/src/main/java* folder, and go to File→New...→Java Class. A new class will be created in the package.

Enhance the activity to call the custom Java class so that we can get REAL advice

In version two of the activity we need to enhance the onClickFindBeer() method to call the BeerExpert class for beer recommendations. The code changes needed are plain old Java. You can try to write the code and run the app on your own, or you can turn the page and follow along.

Sharpen your pencil

Enhance the activity so that it calls the BeerExpert getBrands() method and displays the results in the text view.

```java
package com.hfad.beeradviser;

import android.os.Bundle;
import android.app.Activity;
import android.view.Menu;
import android.view.View;
import android.widget.Spinner;
import android.widget.TextView;
import java.util.List;          ← We added this line for you.

public class FindBeerActivity extends Activity {
    private BeerExpert expert = new BeerExpert();
...
    //Call when the button gets clicked
    public void onClickFindBeer(View view) {
        //Get a reference to the TextView
        TextView brands = (TextView) findViewById(R.id.brands);
        //Get a reference to the Spinner
        Spinner color = (Spinner) findViewById(R.id.color);
        //Get the selected item in the Spinner
        String beerType = String.valueOf(color.getSelectedItem());




    }
}
```

You'll need to use the BeerExpert class to get the beer recommendations, so we added this line for you too.

↑ You need to update the onClickFindBeer() method.

Sharpen your pencil
Solution

Enhance the activity so that it calls the BeerExpert getBrands() method and displays the results in the text view.

```
package com.hfad.beeradviser;

import android.os.Bundle;
import android.app.Activity;
import android.view.Menu;
import android.view.View;
import android.widget.Spinner;
import android.widget.TextView;
import java.util.List;

public class FindBeerActivity extends Activity {
    private BeerExpert expert = new BeerExpert();
...
    //Call when the button gets clicked
    public void onClickFindBeer(View view) {
        //Get a reference to the TextView
        TextView brands = (TextView) findViewById(R.id.brands);
        //Get a reference to the Spinner
        Spinner color = (Spinner) findViewById(R.id.color);
        //Get the selected item in the Spinner
        String beerType = String.valueOf(color.getSelectedItem());
```

```
//Get recommendations from the BeerExpert class

List<String> brandsList = expert.getBrands(beerType);  ← Get a List of brands.

StringBuilder brandsFormatted = new StringBuilder();  ← Build a String using
                                                         the values in the List.
for (String brand : brandsList) {

    brandsFormatted.append(brand).append('\n');  ← Display each brand
                                                    on a new line.
}

//Display the beers

brands.setText(brandsFormatted);  ← Display the results in
                                     the text view.
```

```
    }
}
```

↖

Using the BeerExpert requires pure Java code, so don't worry if your code looks a little different than ours.

Activity code version 2

Here's our full version of the activity code. Apply the changes to your version of *FindBeerActivity.java*, make sure you've added the BeerExpert class to your project, and save your changes:

```java
package com.hfad.beeradviser;

import android.os.Bundle;
import android.app.Activity;
import android.view.Menu;
import android.view.View;
import android.widget.Spinner;
import android.widget.TextView;
import java.util.List;
```
← We're using this extra class.

BeerAdviser
app/src/main
java
com.hfad.beeradviser
FindBeerActivity.java

```java
public class FindBeerActivity extends Activity {
    private BeerExpert expert = new BeerExpert();
```
↖ Add an instance of BeerExpert as a private variable.

```java
    @Override
    protected void onCreate(Bundle savedInstanceState) {
        super.onCreate(savedInstanceState);
        setContentView(R.layout.activity_find_beer);
    }


    //Call when the button gets clicked
    public void onClickFindBeer(View view) {
        //Get a reference to the TextView
        TextView brands = (TextView) findViewById(R.id.brands);
        //Get a reference to the Spinner
        Spinner color = (Spinner) findViewById(R.id.color);
        //Get the selected item in the Spinner
        String beerType = String.valueOf(color.getSelectedItem());
        //Get recommendations from the BeerExpert class
        List<String> brandsList = expert.getBrands(beerType);
        StringBuilder brandsFormatted = new StringBuilder();
        for (String brand : brandsList) {
            brandsFormatted.append(brand).append('\n');
        }
        //Display the beers
        brands.setText(brandsFormatted);
    }
}
```
← Use the BeerExpert class to get a List of brands.

← Build a String, displaying each brand on a new line

← Display the String in the TextView.

What happens when you run the code

1 **When the user clicks on the Find Beer button, the onClickFindBeer() method in the activity gets called.**
The method creates a reference to the spinner and text view, and gets the currently selected value from the spinner.

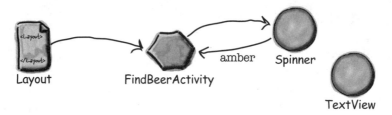

2 **The onClickFindBeer() calls the getBrands() method in the BeerExpert class, passing in the type of beer selected in the spinner.**
The getBrands() method returns a list of brands.

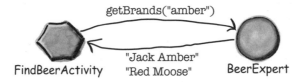

3 **The onClickFindBeer() method formats the list of brands and uses it to set the text property in the text view.**

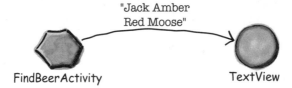

Test drive your app

Once you've made the changes to your app, go ahead and run it. Try selecting different types of beer and clicking on the Find Beer button.

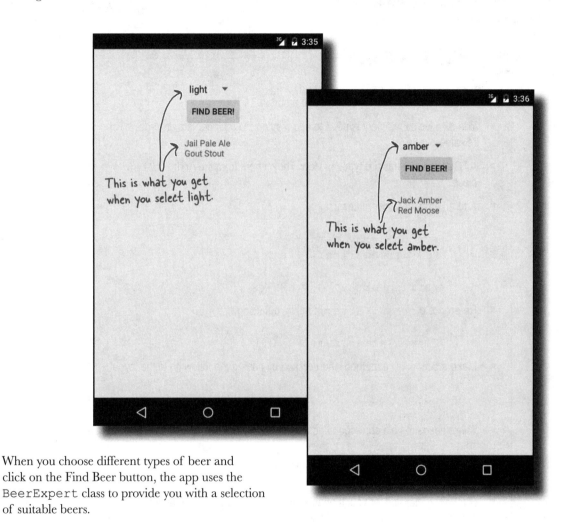

This is what you get when you select light.

This is what you get when you select amber.

When you choose different types of beer and click on the Find Beer button, the app uses the `BeerExpert` class to provide you with a selection of suitable beers.

Your Android Toolbox

You've got Chapter 2 under your belt and now you've added building interactive Android apps to your toolbox.

You can download the full code for the chapter from https://tinyurl.com/HeadFirstAndroid.

BULLET POINTS

- The `Button` element is used to add a button.

- The `Spinner` element is used to add a spinner. A spinner is a drop-down list of values.

- All GUI components are types of view. They inherit from the Android `View` class.

- Add an array of string values using:

```
<string-array name="array">
    <item>string1</item>
    ...
</string-array>
```

- Reference a `string-array` in the layout using:

```
"@array/array_name"
```

- Make a button call a method when clicked by adding the following to the layout:

```
android:onClick="clickMethod"
```

There needs to be a corresponding method in the activity:

```
public void clickMethod(View view) {
}
```

- *R.java* is generated for you. It enables you to get references for layouts, GUI components, Strings, and other resources in your Java code.

- Use `findViewById()` to get a reference to a view.

- Use `setText()` to set the text in a view.

- Use `getSelectedItem()` to get the selected item in a spinner.

- Add a custom class to an Android project by going to File menu→New...→Java Class.

3 multiple activities and intents

State Your Intent

I sent an intent asking who could handle my ACTION_CALL, and was offered all **sorts** of activities to choose from.

Most apps need more than one activity.

So far we've just looked at single-activity apps, which is fine for simple apps. But when things get more complicated, just having the one activity won't cut it. We're going to show you **how to build apps with multiple activities**, and how you can get your apps talking to each other using *intents*. We'll also look at how you can use intents to **go beyond the boundaries of your app** and **make activities in other apps on your device perform actions**. Things just got a whole lot more powerful...

Apps can contain more than one activity

Earlier in the book, we said that an activity is a single, defined thing that your user can do, such as displaying a list of recipes. If your app is simple, this may be all that's needed.

A lot of the time, you'll want users to do *more* than just one thing—for example, adding recipes as well as displaying a list of them. If this is the case, you'll need to use multiple activities: one for displaying the list of recipes and another for adding a single recipe.

The best way of seeing how this works is to see it in action. You're going to build an app containing two activities. The first activity will allow you to type a message. When you click on a button in the first activity, it will launch the second activity and pass it the message. The second activity will then display the message.

> An activity is a single focused thing your user can do. If you chain multiple activities together to do something more complex, it's called a task.

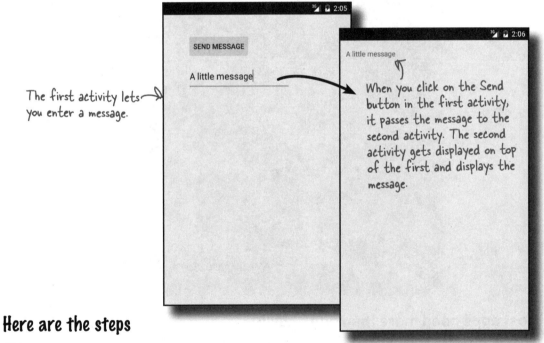

The first activity lets you enter a message.

When you click on the Send button in the first activity, it passes the message to the second activity. The second activity gets displayed on top of the first and displays the message.

Here are the steps

1 Create a basic app with a single activity and layout.

2 Add a second activity and layout.

3 Get the first activity to call the second activity.

4 Get the first activity to pass data to the second activity.

Here's the app structure

The app contains two activities and two layouts.

1 **When the app gets launched, it starts activity CreateMessageActivity.**
This activity uses the layout *activity_create_message.xml*.

2 **The user clicks on a button in CreateMessageActivity.**
This launches activity `ReceiveMessageActivity`, which uses layout *activity_receive_message.xml*.

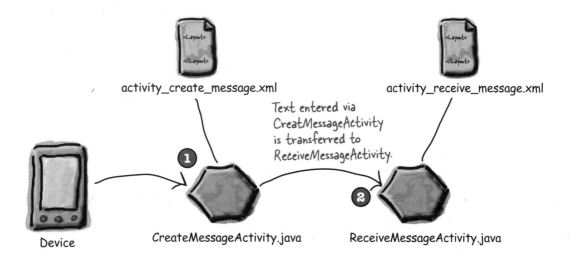

activity_create_message.xml

Text entered via CreatMessageActivity is transferred to ReceiveMessageActivity.

activity_receive_message.xml

Device

CreateMessageActivity.java

ReceiveMessageActivity.java

Create the project

You create a project for the app in exactly the same way you did in previous chapters. Create a new Android Studio project for an application named "Messenger" with a package name of com.hfad.messenger. The minimum SDK should be API 15 so that it will work on most devices. You'll need a blank activity called "CreateMessageActivity" with a layout called "activity_create_message" so that your code matches ours.

On the next page, we'll update the activity's layout.

Create 1st activity
Create 2nd activity
Call 2nd activity
Pass data

Update the layout

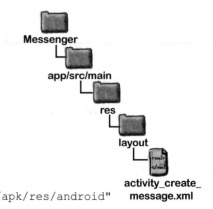

Here's the XML for the *activity_create_message.xml* file. We removed the
<TextView> that Android Studio created for us, and replaced it with
<Button> and <EditText> elements. The <EditText> element gives
you an editable text field you can use to enter data.

Change your *activity_create_message.xml* file to match the XML here:

```xml
<RelativeLayout xmlns:android="http://schemas.android.com/apk/res/android"
    xmlns:tools="http://schemas.android.com/tools"
    android:layout_width="match_parent"
    android:layout_height="match_parent"
    android:paddingBottom="16dp"
    android:paddingLeft="16dp"
    android:paddingRight="16dp"
    android:paddingTop="16dp"
    tools:context=".CreateMessageActivity" >

    <Button
        android:id="@+id/send"
        android:layout_width="wrap_content"
        android:layout_height="wrap_content"
        android:layout_alignParentLeft="true"
        android:layout_alignParentTop="true"
        android:layout_marginLeft="36dp"
        android:layout_marginTop="21dp"
        android:onClick="onSendMessage"
        android:text="@string/send" />

    <EditText
        android:id="@+id/message"
        android:layout_width="wrap_content"
        android:layout_height="wrap_content"
        android:layout_alignLeft="@+id/send"
        android:layout_below="@+id/send"
        android:layout_marginTop="18dp"
        android:ems="10" />

</RelativeLayout>
```

Replace the <TextView> Android Studio gives you with the <Button> and <EditText>.

Clicking on the button runs the onSendMessage() method in the activity.

This is a String resource.

This describes how wide the <EditText> should be. It should be wide enough to accommodate 10 letter M's.

**The <EditText> element
defines an editable text
field for entering text. It
inherits from the same
Android View class as the
other GUI components
we've seen so far.**

Update strings.xml...

The button we added has a text value of @string/send. This means we need to add a string called "send" to *strings.xml* and give it a value. This value is the text we want to appear on the button. Do this now:

```
...
    <string name="send">Send Message</string>
...
```

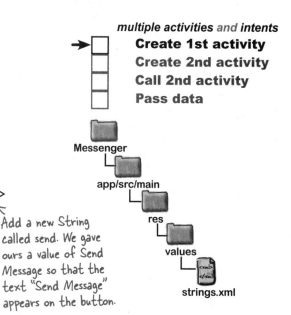

multiple activities and intents
Create 1st activity
Create 2nd activity
Call 2nd activity
Pass data

Messenger

app/src/main

res

values

strings.xml

Add a new String called send. We gave ours a value of Send Message so that the text "Send Message" appears on the button.

...and add the method to the activity

The line in the `<Button>` element

```
android:onClick="onSendMessage"
```

means that the `onSendMessage()` method in the activity will fire when the button is clicked. Let's add this method to the activity now.

Open up the *CreateMessageActivity.java* file and replace the code Android Studio created for you with the following:

```
package com.hfad.messenger;

import android.app.Activity;
import android.os.Bundle;
import android.view.View;


public class CreateMessageActivity extends Activity {

    @Override
    protected void onCreate(Bundle savedInstanceState) {
        super.onCreate(savedInstanceState);
        setContentView(R.layout.activity_create_message);
    }


    //Call onSendMessage() when the button is clicked
    public void onSendMessage(View view) {
    }
}
```

We're replacing the code that Android Studio created for us, as most of the code it creates isn't required.

The onCreate() method gets called when the activity is created.

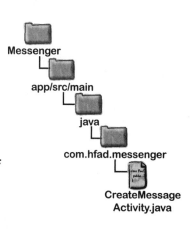

Messenger

app/src/main

java

com.hfad.messenger

CreateMessage Activity.java

This method will get called when the button's clicked. We'll complete the method body as we work our way through the rest of the chapter.

Now that you've created the first activity, let's move on to the second.

Create the second activity and layout

Create 1st activity
Create 2nd activity
Call 2nd activity
Pass data

Android Studio has a wizard that lets you add extra activities and layouts to your apps. It's like a cut-down version of the wizard you use to create an app, and you use it whenever you want to create a new activity.

To create the new activity, choose File → New → Activity, and choose the option for Blank Activity. You will be presented with a new screen where you can choose options for your new activity.

Every time you create a new activity and layout, you need to name them. Give the new activity a name of "ReceiveMessageActivity" and the layout a name of "activity_receive_message". Check that the package name is "com. hfad.messenger". Accept the rest of the defaults, and when you're done, click on the Finish button.

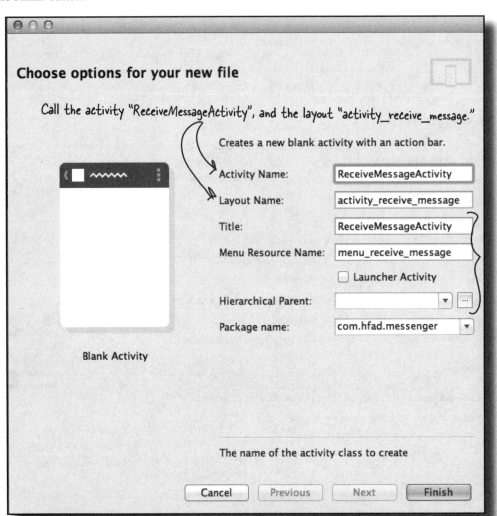

Choose options for your new file

Call the activity "ReceiveMessageActivity", and the layout "activity_receive_message."

Creates a new blank activity with an action bar.

Activity Name:	ReceiveMessageActivity
Layout Name:	activity_receive_message
Title:	ReceiveMessageActivity
Menu Resource Name:	menu_receive_message
☐ Launcher Activity	
Hierarchical Parent:	▼ ...
Package name:	com.hfad.messenger ▼

Blank Activity

Accept the rest of the defaults, as all we're interested in is creating a new activity and layout. We'll replace most of the code Android Studio gives us.

The name of the activity class to create

Cancel   Previous   Next   **Finish**

What just happened?

When you clicked on the Finish button, Android Studio created a shiny new activity file for you, along with a new layout. If you look in the explorer, you should see that a new file called *ReceiveMessageActivity.java* has appeared in the *app/ src/main/java* folder, and a file called *activity_receive_message. xml* has appeared under *app/src/main/res/layout*.

> Here's the new activity and layout we just created. There are now two activities and layouts in the app.

Each activity uses a different layout. `CreateMessageActivity` uses the layout *activity_ create_message.xml*, and `ReceiveMessageActivity` uses the layout *activity_receive_message.xml*.

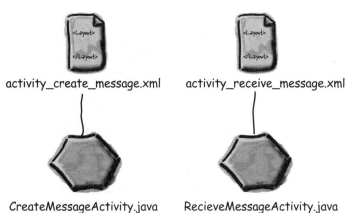

activity_create_message.xml   activity_receive_message.xml

CreateMessageActivity.java   RecieveMessageActivity.java

Behind the scenes, Android Studio also made a configuration change to the app in a file called *AndroidManifest.xml*. Let's take a closer look.

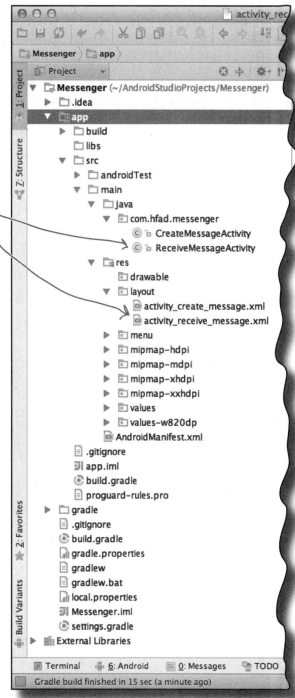

Welcome to the Android manifest file

Create 1st activity
Create 2nd activity
Call 2nd activity
Pass data

Every Android app must include a file called *AndroidManifest.xml*. You can find it in the *app/src/main* folder of your project. The *AndroidManifest.xml* file contains essential information about your app, such as what activities it contains, required libraries, and other declarations. Android creates the file for you when you create the app. If you think back to the settings you chose when you created the project, some of the file contents should look familiar.

Here's what our copy of *AndroidManifest.xml* looks like:

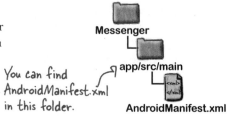

Messenger

app/src/main

You can find
AndroidManifest.xml
in this folder.

AndroidManifest.xml

```xml
<?xml version="1.0" encoding="utf-8"?>
<manifest xmlns:android="http://schemas.android.com/apk/res/android"
    package="com.hfad.messenger" >

    <application
        android:allowBackup="true"
        android:icon="@mipmap/ic_launcher"
        android:label="@string/app_name"
        android:theme="@style/AppTheme" >

        <activity
            android:name=".CreateMessageActivity"
            android:label="@string/app_name" >
            <intent-filter>
                <action android:name="android.intent.action.MAIN" />
                <category android:name="android.intent.category.LAUNCHER" />
            </intent-filter>
        </activity>

        <activity
            android:name=".ReceiveMessageActivity"
            android:label="@string/title_activity_receive_message" >
        </activity>

    </application>
</manifest>
```

← This is the package name we specified.

Android Studio gave our app a default icon. We'll look at this later in the book.

The theme affects the appearance of the app. We'll look at this later.

If you develop Android apps without an IDE, you'll need to create this file manually.

This is the first activity, Create Message Activity.

This bit specifies that it's the main activity of the app.

This says the activity can be used to launch the app.

This is the second activity, Receive Message Activity.

Android Studio added these lines for us when we added the second activity.

Every activity needs to be declared

All activities need to be declared in *AndroidManifest.xml*. If an activity isn't declared in the file, the system won't know it exists. And if the system doesn't know it exists, the activity will never run.

You declare an activity in the manifest by including an `<activity>` element inside the `<application>` element. In fact, *every* activity in your app needs a corresponding `<activity>` element. Here's the general format:

> If I'm not included in AndroidManifest.xml, then as far as the system's concerned, I don't exist and will never run.

Activity

```
<application
    ...          ← Each activity needs to be declared
    ...>           inside the <application> element.

    <activity          ← This line is mandatory.
        android:name="activity_class_name"
        android:label="@string/activity_label"   ← This line is optional,
                                                    but Android Studio
        ...                                          completes it for us.
        ...>  ← The activity may have other properties too.
    ...

    </activity>
    ...

</application>
```

The following line is mandatory and is used to specify the class name of the activity::

```
android:name="activity_class_name"
```

`activity_class_name` is the name of the class, prefixed with a ".". In this case, it's `.ReceiveMessageActivity`. The class name is prefixed with a "." because Android combines the class name with the name of the package to derive the *fully qualified* class name.

This line is optional and is used to specify a user-friendly label for the activity:

```
android:label="@string/activity_label"
```

It's displayed at the top of the screen when the activity runs. If you leave this out, Android will use the name of the application instead.

The activity declaration may include other properties too, such as security permissions, and whether it can be used by activities in other apps.

Watch it!

The second activity was automatically declared because we added it using the Android Studio wizard.

If you add extra activities manually, you'll need to edit AndroidManifest.xml yourself. If you use another IDE, it may not be added for you.

An intent is a type of message

So far we've created an app with two activities in it, and each activity has its own layout. When the app is launched, our first activity, `CreateMessageActivity`, will run. What we need to do next is get `CreateMessageActivity` to call `ReceiveMessageActivity` when the user clicks the Send Message button.

Whenever you want an activity to start a second activity, you use an **intent**. You can think of an intent as an "intent to do something". It's a type of message that allows you to bind separate objects (such as activities) together at runtime. If one activity wants to start a second activity, it does it by sending an intent to Android. Android will start the second activity and pass it the intent.

You can create and send an intent using just a couple of lines of code. You start by creating the intent like this:

```
Intent intent = new Intent(this, Target.class);
```

The first parameter tells Android which object the intent is from, and you can use the word `this` to refer to the current activity. The second parameter is the class name of the activity that needs to receive the intent.

Once you've created the intent, you pass it to Android like this:

```
startActivity(intent);
```

This tells Android to start the activity specified by the intent.

Once Android receives the intent, it checks everything's OK and tells the activity to start. If it can't find the activity, it throws an **`ActivityNotFoundException`**.

You start an activity by creating an intent and using it in the startActivity() method.

The intent specifies the activity you want to receive it. It's like putting an address on an envelope.

↓ Intent

To: AnotherActivity

startActivity() starts the activity specified in the intent.

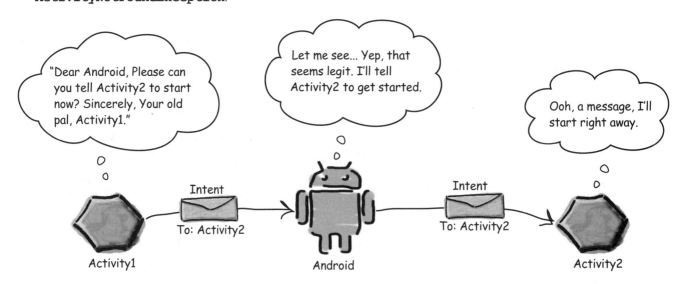

"Dear Android, Please can you tell Activity2 to start now? Sincerely, Your old pal, Activity1."

Let me see... Yep, that seems legit. I'll tell Activity2 to get started.

Ooh, a message, I'll start right away.

Intent — To: Activity2

Intent — To: Activity2

Activity1　　　Android　　　Activity2

Use an intent to start the second activity

Let's put this into practice and use an intent to call
ReceiveMessageActivity. We want to launch the activity
when the user clicks on the Send Message button, so we'll add the
two lines of code to our onSendMessage() method.

Make the changes highlighted below:

```
package com.hfad.messenger;

import android.app.Activity;
import android.content.Intent;
import android.os.Bundle;
import android.view.View;


public class CreateMessageActivity extends Activity {

    @Override
    protected void onCreate(Bundle savedInstanceState) {
        super.onCreate(savedInstanceState);
        setContentView(R.layout.activity_create_message);
    }


    //Call onSendMessage() when the button is clicked
    public void onSendMessage(View view) {
        Intent intent = new Intent(this, ReceiveMessageActivity.class);
        startActivity(intent);
    }


}
```

We need to import the Intent class android.content.Intent as we're using it in onSendMessage().

We've not changed this method.

Messenger
app/src/main
java
com.hfad.messenger
CreateMessage Activity.java

Start activity ReceiveMessageActivity.

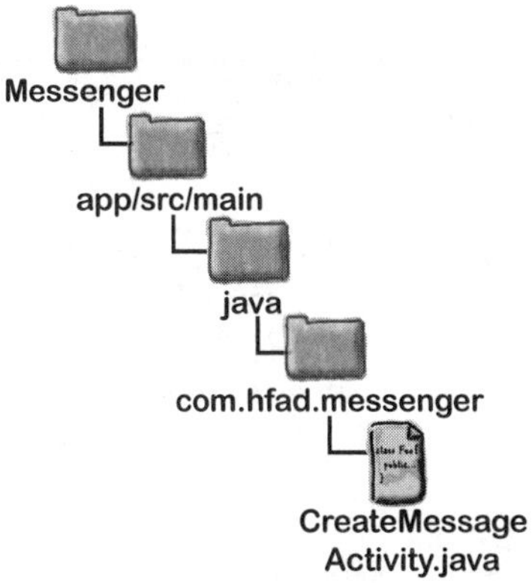

So what happens now when we run the app?

Create 1st activity ✓

Create 2nd activity ✓

Call 2nd activity →

Pass data

What happens when you run the app

Before we take the app out for a test drive, let's go over how the app we've developed so far will function:

1 **When the app gets launched, the main activity, CreateMessageActivity starts.**
When it starts, the activity specifies that it uses layout *activity_create_ message.xml*. This gets displayed in a new window.

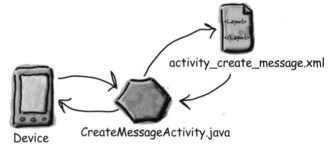

2 **The user clicks on a button.**
The onSendMessage() method in CreateMessageActivity responds to the click.

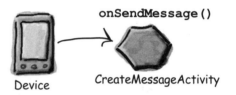

3 **The onSendMessage() method tells Android to start activity ReceiveMessageActivity using an intent.**
Android checks that the intent is OK, and then it tells ReceiveMessageActivity to start.

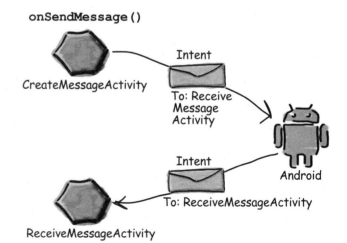

The story continues...

4 When ReceiveMessageActivity starts, it specifies that it uses layout *activity_receive_message.xml* and this gets displayed in a new window.

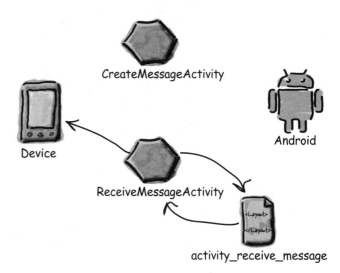

CreateMessageActivity

Android

Device

ReceiveMessageActivity

activity_receive_message

Test drive the app

Save your changes, and then run the app. `CreateMessageActivity` starts, and when you click on the Send Message button, it launches `ReceiveMessageActivity`.

☑ **Create 1st activity**
☑ **Create 2nd activity**
→ ☑ **Call 2nd activity**
☐ **Pass data**

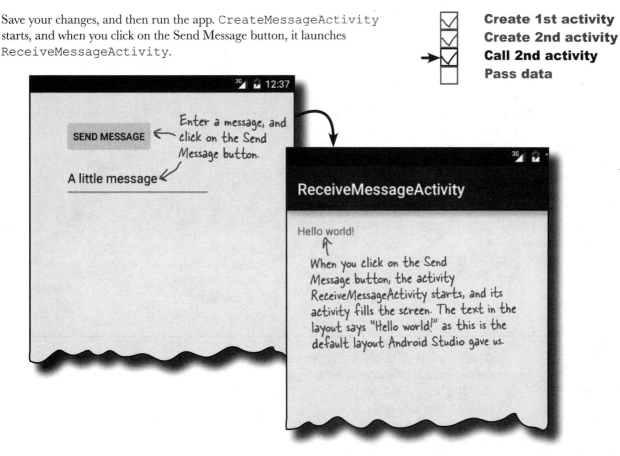

3G 📶 🔋 12:37

SEND MESSAGE ← Enter a message, and click on the Send Message button.

A little message ←

ReceiveMessageActivity

Hello world!

When you click on the Send Message button, the activity ReceiveMessageActivity starts, and its activity fills the screen. The text in the layout says "Hello world!" as this is the default layout Android Studio gave us.

Create 1st activity

Create 2nd activity

Call 2nd activity

Pass data

Pass text to a second activity

So far we've coded `CreateMessageActivity` to start
`ReceiveMessageActivity` when the Send Message button is
pressed. Next, we'll get `CreateMessageActivity` to pass text to
`ReceiveMessageActivity` so that `ReceiveMessageActivity`
can display it. In order to accomplish this, we'll do three things:

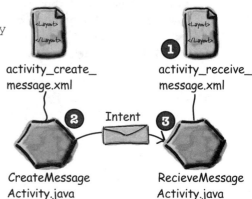

activity_create_
message.xml

activity_receive_
message.xml

CreateMessage
Activity.java

Intent

RecieveMessage
Activity.java

1 Tweak the layout *activity_receive_message.xml* so that we
can display the text. At the moment it's the default
layout the wizard gave us.

2 Update *CreateMessageActivity.xml* so that it gets the text
the user inputs. It then needs to add the text to the
intent before it sends it.

3 Update *ReceiveMessageActivity.java* so that it displays the
text sent in the intent.

Let's start with the layout

Here's the *activity_receive_message.xml* layout that Android Studio
created for us:

```
<RelativeLayout xmlns:android="http://schemas.android.com/apk/res/android"
    xmlns:tools="http://schemas.android.com/tools"
    android:layout_width="match_parent"
    android:layout_height="match_parent"
    android:paddingLeft="16dp"
    android:paddingRight="16dp"
    android:paddingTop="16dp"
    android:paddingBottom="16dp"
    tools:context="com.hfad.messenger.ReceiveMessageActivity">

    <TextView
        android:text="@string/hello_world"
        android:layout_width="wrap_content"
        android:layout_height="wrap_content" />
</RelativeLayout>
```

*Here's the
text view that
currently appears
in the layout.*

Messenger

app/src/main

res

layout

activity_receive_
message.xml

Exercise

We need to make a couple of changes to the layout. We need to give the `<TextView>`
element an ID of "message" so that we can reference it in our activity code, and we need to stop
the String "Hello world!" from appearing. How should we change the layout? Have a go before
looking at the next page.

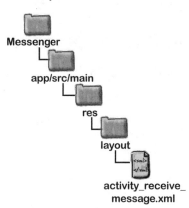

Update the text view properties

We need to update a couple of things in the layout.

First, we need to give the `<TextView>` element an ID. You have to add an ID to any GUI components you need to reference in your activity code, as this gives you a way of referencing it in your Java code. We also need to stop the text "Hello world!" from appearing.

You can do both these things by updating the layout like this:

```
<RelativeLayout xmlns:android="http://schemas.android.com/apk/res/android"
    xmlns:tools="http://schemas.android.com/tools"
    android:layout_width="match_parent"
    android:layout_height="match_parent"
    android:paddingLeft="16dp"
    android:paddingRight="16dp"
    android:paddingTop="16dp"
    android:paddingBottom="16dp"
    tools:context="com.hfad.messenger.ReceiveMessageActivity">

    <TextView
        android:id="@+id/message"
        android:text="@string/hello_world"
        android:layout_width="wrap_content"
        android:layout_height="wrap_content" />

</RelativeLayout>
```

← This line gives the `<TextView>` an ID of message.

Remove the line that sets the text to @string/hello_world.

Rather than delete the code that says

```
android:text="@string/hello_world"
```

we could have updated *strings.xml* to give the String resource `hello_world` an empty value. We decided not to here as the only text we'll ever want to display in the text view is the message passed to it by `CreateMessageActivity`.

Now that we've updated the layout, we can get to work on the activities.

there are no Dumb Questions

Q: Do I have to use intents? Can't I just construct an instance of the second activity in the code for my first activity?

A: That's a good question, but no, that's not the "Android way" of doing things. One of the reasons is that by passing intents to Android, Android knows the sequence in which activities are started. This means that when you click on the Back button on your device, Android knows exactly where to take you back to.

putExtra() puts extra information in an intent

Create 1st activity
Create 2nd activity
Call 2nd activity
Pass data

You've seen how you can create a new intent using

```
Intent intent = new Intent(this, Target.class);
```

You can add extra information to this intent that can be picked up by the activity you're targeting so it can react in some way. To do this, you use the `putExtra()` method

> **`intent.putExtra("message", value);`**

putExtra() lets you put extra information in the message you're sending.

Intent

To: ReceiveMessageActivity
message: "Hello!"

where `message` is a String name for the value you're passing in, and `value` is the value. The `putExtra()` method is overloaded so `value` has many possible types. As an example, it can be a primitive such as a `boolean` or `int`, an array of primitives, or a `String`. You can use `putExtra()` repeatedly to add numerous extra data to the intent. If you do this, make sure you give each one a unique name.

There are many different options for the type of value. You can see them all in the Google Android documentation. Android Studio will give you a list as you type code in too.

How to retrieve extra information from an intent

The story doesn't end there. When Android tells `ReceiveMessageActivity` to start, `ReceiveMessageActivity` needs some way of retrieving the extra information that `CreateMessageActivity` sent to Android in the intent.

There are a couple of useful methods that can help with this. The first of these is

> **`getIntent();`**

`getIntent()` returns the intent that started the activity, and you can use this to retrieve any extra information that was sent along with it. How you do this depends on the type of information that was sent. As an example, if you know the intent includes a String value with a name of "message", you would use the following:

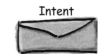

Intent

To: ReceiveMessageActivity
message: "Hello!"

```
Intent intent = getIntent();
String string = intent.getStringExtra("message");
```

← Get the intent.

← Get the string passed along with the intent that has a name of "message".

You're not just limited to retrieving String values. As an example, you can use

> **`int intNum = intent.getIntExtra("name", default_value);`**

to retrieve an `int` with a name of `name`. `default_value` specifies what `int` value you should use as a default.

```
package com.hfad.messenger;

import android.os.Bundle;
import android.app.Activity;
import android.content.Intent;
import android.view.View;

..............................................................................................................

public class CreateMessageActivity extends Activity {

    @Override
    protected void onCreate(Bundle savedInstanceState) {
        super.onCreate(savedInstanceState);
        setContentView(R.layout.activity_create_message);
    }

    //Call onSendMessage() when the button is clicked
    public void onSendMessage(View view) {

        ..................................................................................................

        ..................................................................................................

        Intent intent = new Intent(this, ReceiveMessageActivity.class);

        ..................................................................................................

        startActivity(intent);
    }
}
```

Pŏŏl Puzzle

Your **job** is to take code segments from the pool and place them into the blank lines in *CreateMessageActivity. java*. You may **not** use the same code segment more than once, and you won't need to use all the code snippets. Your **goal** is to make the activity retrieve text from the message <EditText> and add it to the intent.

These code snippets were not needed here.

Pool snippets:

EditText
EditText
import
putExtra
String
messageView
putExtraString
"message"
=
;
R.id.message
messageView
getText()
findViewById
=
;
.
android.widget.EditText
messageText
messageText
intent
(
)
;
)
,
toString()
.

```
package com.hfad.messenger;

import android.os.Bundle;
import android.app.Activity;
import android.content.Intent;
import android.view.View;
import android.widget.EditText;
```
You need to import the EditText class.

```
public class CreateMessageActivity extends Activity {

    @Override
    protected void onCreate(Bundle savedInstanceState) {
        super.onCreate(savedInstanceState);
        setContentView(R.layout.activity_create_message);
    }

    //Call onSendMessage() when the button is clicked
    public void onSendMessage(View view) {
        EditText messageView = (EditText) findViewById(R.id.message);
        String messageText = messageView.getText().toString();
        Intent intent = new Intent(this, ReceiveMessageActivity.class);
        intent.putExtra("message", messageText);
        startActivity(intent);
    }
}
```

Pool Puzzle Solution

Your **job** is to take code segments from the pool and place them into the blank lines in *CreateMessageActivity.java*. You may **not** use the same code segment more than once, and you won't need to use all the code snippets. Your **goal** is to make the activity retrieve text from the message <EditText> and add it to the intent.

Get the text from the editable text field with an ID of message.

Add the text to the intent, giving it a name of "message".

These code snippets were not needed here.

putExtraString

Update the CreateMessageActivity code

We updated our code for *CreateMessageActivity.java* so that it takes the text the user enters on the screen and adds it to the intent. Here's the full code (make sure you update your code to include these changes, shown in bold):

```java
package com.hfad.messenger;

import android.os.Bundle;
import android.app.Activity;
import android.content.Intent;
import android.view.View;
import android.widget.EditText;

public class CreateMessageActivity extends Activity {

    @Override
    protected void onCreate(Bundle savedInstanceState) {
        super.onCreate(savedInstanceState);
        setContentView(R.layout.activity_create_message);
    }

    //Call onSendMessage() when the button is clicked
    public void onSendMessage(View view) {
        EditText messageView = (EditText)findViewById(R.id.message);
        String messageText = messageView.getText().toString();
        Intent intent = new Intent(this, ReceiveMessageActivity.class);
        intent.putExtra(ReceiveMessageActivity.EXTRA_MESSAGE, messageText);
        startActivity(intent);
    }
}
```

You need to import the EditText class android.widget.EditText as you're using it in your activity code.

Get the text that's in the EditText.

Start ReceiveMessageActivity with the intent.

Create an intent, then add the text to the intent. We're using a constant for the name of the extra information so that we know CreateMessageActivity and ReceiveMessageActivity are using the same String. We'll add this to ReceiveMessageActivity on the next page.

Messenger
└ app/src/main
  └ java
    └ com.hfad.messenger
      └ CreateMessage Activity.java

Now that `CreateMessageActivity` has added extra information to the intent, we need to retrieve the information and use it.

Get ReceiveMessageActivity to use the information in the intent

Create 1st activity
Create 2nd activity
Call 2nd activity
Pass data

Now that we've changed `CreateMessageActivity` to add text to the intent, we'll update `ReceiveMessageActivity` so that it uses the text.

We're going to get `ReceiveMessageActivity` to display the message in its text view when the activity gets created. As the activity's `onCreate()` method gets called as soon as the activity is created, we'll add the code to this method.

To get the message from the intent, we'll first get the intent using the `getIntent()` method, then get the value of the message using `getStringExtra()`.

Here's the full code for *ReceiveMessageActivity.java* (replace the code that Android Studio generated for you with this code, and then save all your changes):

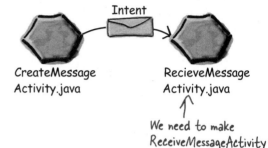

Intent

CreateMessage
Activity.java

RecieveMessage
Activity.java

We need to make
ReceiveMessageActivity
deal with the intent it
receives.

```java
package com.hfad.messenger;

import android.os.Bundle;
import android.app.Activity;
import android.content.Intent;
import android.widget.TextView;

public class ReceiveMessageActivity extends Activity {

    public static final String EXTRA_MESSAGE = "message";

    @Override
    protected void onCreate(Bundle savedInstanceState) {
        super.onCreate(savedInstanceState);
        setContentView(R.layout.activity_receive_message);
        Intent intent = getIntent();
        String messageText = intent.getStringExtra(EXTRA_MESSAGE);
        TextView messageView = (TextView)findViewById(R.id.message);
        messageView.setText(messageText);
    }
}
```

We need to import
the Intent and
TextView classes.

This is the name of the extra value we're passing in the intent.

Get the intent, and get
the message from it using
getStringExtra().

Add the text to the message text view.

Messenger

app/src/main

java

com.hfad.messenger

ReceiveMessage
Activity.java

Before we take the app for a test drive, let's run through what the code does.

What happens when the user clicks the Send Message button

1 **When the user clicks on the button, the onSendMessage() method is called.**
Code within the onSendMessage() method creates an intent to start activity ReceiveMessageActivity, adds a message to the intent, and passes it to Android with an instruction to start the activity.

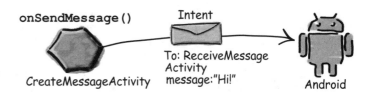

onSendMessage()

Intent

CreateMessageActivity

To: ReceiveMessage Activity
message:"Hi!"

Android

---

2 **Android checks that the intent is OK, and then tells ReceiveMessageActivity to start.**

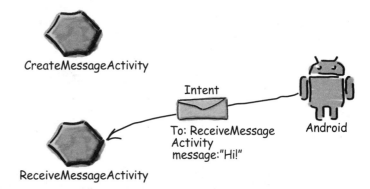

CreateMessageActivity

Intent

To: ReceiveMessage Activity
message:"Hi!"

Android

ReceiveMessageActivity

---

3 **When ReceiveMessageActivity starts, it specifies that it uses layout *activity_receive_message.xml*, and this gets displayed on the device.**
The activity updates the layout so that it displays the extra text included in the intent.

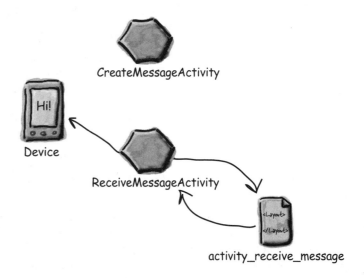

CreateMessageActivity

Hi!

Device

ReceiveMessageActivity

activity_receive_message

Test drive the app

Make sure you've updated the two activities, save your changes, and then run the app. `CreateMessageActivity` starts, and when you enter some text and click on the Send Message button, it launches `ReceiveMessageActivity`. The text you entered is displayed in the text view.

Here's the text we entered, successfully passed via the intent to the second activity.

These are both full-screen, but we've snipped away some of the blank space.

We can change the app to send messages to other people

Now that we have an app that sends a message to another activity, we can change it so that it can send messages to other people. We can do this by integrating with the message sending apps already on the device. Depending on what apps the user has, we can get our app to send messages via Messaging, Gmail, Google+, Facebook, Twitter...

Hey, hold it right there! That sounds like a freaky amount of work to get the app working with all those apps. And how the heck do I know what apps people have on their devices anyway? Get real.

It's not as hard as it sounds due to the way Android is designed to work.

Remember right at the beginning of the chapter when we said that tasks are multiple activities chained together? Well, **you're not just limited to using the activities within your app**. You can go beyond the boundaries of your app to use activities within *other* apps as well.

How Android apps work

As you've seen, all Android apps are composed of one or more activities, along with other components such as layouts. Each activity is a single defined focused thing the user can do. As an example, apps such as Gmail, Google+, Messaging, Facebook, and Twitter all have activities that enable you to send messages, even though they may achieve this in different ways.

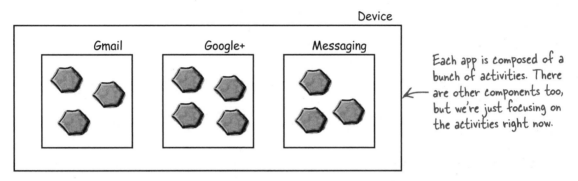

Each app is composed of a bunch of activities. There are other components too, but we're just focusing on the activities right now.

Intents can start activities in other apps

You've already seen how you can use an intent to start a second activity within the same app. The first activity passes an intent to Android, Android checks it, and then Android tells the second activity to start.

The same principle applies to activities in other apps. You get an activity in your app to pass an intent to Android, Android checks it, and then Android tells the second activity to start *even though it's in another app*. As an example, we can use an intent to start the activity in Gmail that sends messages, and pass it the text we want to send. Instead of writing our own activities to send emails, we can use the existing Gmail app.

You can create an intent to start another activity even if the activity is within another app.

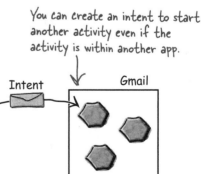

This is the app you've been working on throughout the chapter.

This means that you can build apps that perform far more powerful tasks by chaining together activities across the device.

But we don't know what apps are on the device

There are three questions we need answers to before we can call activities in other apps:

⭐ How do we know activities are available on the user's device?

⭐ How do we know which of these activities are appropriate for what we want to do?

⭐ How do we know how to use these activities?

The great news is that we can solve all of these problems using **actions**. Actions are a way of telling Android what standard operations activities can perfom. As an example, Android knows that all activities registered for a send action are capable of sending messages.

What you're going to do next is learn how to create intents that use actions to return a set of activities that you can use in a standard way—for example, to send messages.

Here's what you're going to do

1 **Create an intent that specifies an action.**
The intent will tell Android you want to use an activity that can send a message. The intent will include the text of the message.

2 **Allow the user to choose which app to use.**
The chances are there'll be more than one on the device capable of sending messages, so the user will need to pick one. We want the user to be able to choose one every time they click on the Send Message button.

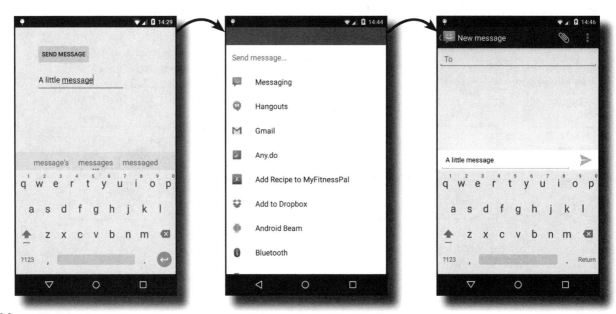

Create an intent that specifies an action

So far you've seen how to create an intent that launches a specific activity using

```
Intent intent = new Intent(this, ReceiveMessageActivity.class);
```

The intent is an **explicit intent**; you explicitly tell Android which class you want it to run.

> We've told the intent which class it's intended for, but what if we don't know?

If there's an action you want done but you don't mind which activity does it, you create an **implicit intent**. You tell Android what sort of action you want it to perform, and you leave the details of which activity performs it to Android.

How to create the intent

You create an intent that specifies an action using the following syntax:

```
Intent intent = new Intent(action);
```

where action is the type of activity action you want to perform. Android provides you with a number of standard actions you can use. As an example, you can use Intent.ACTION_DIAL to dial a number, Intent.ACTION_WEB_SEARCH to perform a web search, and Intent.ACTION_SEND to send a message. So if you want to create an intent that specifies you want to send a message, you use

```
Intent intent = new Intent(Intent.ACTION_SEND);
```

Adding extra information

Once you've specified the action you want to use, you can add extra information to it. We want to pass some text with the intent that will form the body of the message we're sending. To do this, you use the following lines of code:

```
intent.setType("text/plain");
intent.putExtra(Intent.EXTRA_TEXT, messageText);
```

> These attributes relate to Intent.ACTION_SEND. They're not relevant for all actions.

where messageText is the text you want to send. This tells Android that you want the activity to be able to handle data with a MIME data-type of "text/plain", and also tells it what the text is.

You can make extra calls to the putExtra() method if there's additional information you want to add. As an example, if you want to specify the subject of the message, you can also use

```
intent.putExtra(Intent.EXTRA_SUBJECT, subject);
```

> If subject isn't relevant to a particular app, it will just ignore this information. Any apps that know how to use it will do so.

where subject is the message subject.

> You can find out more about the sorts of activity actions you can use and the extra information they support in the Android developer reference material: http://tinyurl.com/n57qb5.

Change the intent to use an action

We'll update *CreateMessageActivity.java* so that we create an implicit
intent that uses a send action. Make the changes highlighted below,
and save your work:

```
package com.hfad.messenger;

import android.os.Bundle;
import android.app.Activity;
import android.content.Intent;
import android.view.View;
import android.widget.EditText;

public class CreateMessageActivity extends Activity {

    @Override
    protected void onCreate(Bundle savedInstanceState) {
        super.onCreate(savedInstanceState);
        setContentView(R.layout.activity_create_message);
    }


    //Call onSendMessage() when the button is clicked
    public void onSendMessage(View view) {
        EditText messageView = (EditText)findViewById(R.id.message);
        String messageText = messageView.getText().toString();
        Intent intent = new Intent(this, ReceiveMessageActivity.class);
        intent.putExtra(ReceiveMessageActivity.EXTRA_MESSAGE, messageText);
        Intent intent = new Intent(Intent.ACTION_SEND);
        intent.setType("text/plain");
        intent.putExtra(Intent.EXTRA_TEXT, messageText);
        startActivity(intent);
    }
}
```

Messenger
└ app/src/main
  └ java
    └ com.hfad.messenger
      └ CreateMessage
        Activity.java

Remove these two lines. ➞

Instead of creating an intent that's
explicitly for ReceiveMessageActivity, we're
creating an intent that uses a send action.

Let's break down what happens when the user clicks
on the Send Message button.

What happens when the code runs

① **When the onSendMessage() method is called, an intent gets created. The startActivity() method passes the intent to Android.**

The intent specifies an action of ACTION_SEND, and a MIME type of text/plain.

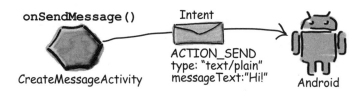

② **Android sees that the intent can only be passed to activities able to handle ACTION_SEND and text/plain data. Android checks all the activities, looking for ones that are able to receive the intent.**

If no actions are able to handle the intent, an ActivityNotFoundException is thrown.

Aha, an implicit intent. I need to find all the activities that can handle ACTION_SEND, data of type text/plain, and have a category of DEFAULT.

③ **If just one activity is able to receive the intent, Android tells the activity to start and passes it the intent.**

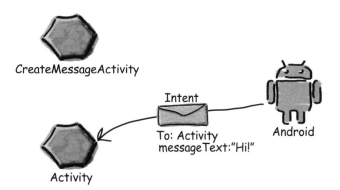

The story continues...

4 If more than one activity is able to receive the intent, Android displays an activity chooser dialog and asks the user which one to use.

CreateMessageActivity

Hey, user. All of these activities can send a message for you. Which one do you want?

Android

User

---

5 When the user chooses the activity she wants to use, Android tells the activity to start and passes it the intent. The activity displays the extra text contained in the intent in the body of a new message.

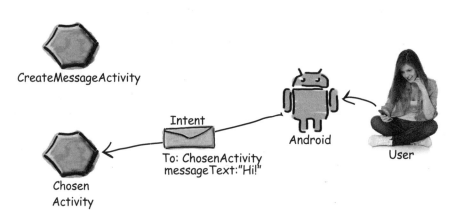

CreateMessageActivity

Intent

To: ChosenActivity
messageText:"Hi!"

Chosen
Activity

Android

User

In order to create the activity chooser dialog, Android must know which activities are capable of receiving the intent. On the next couple of pages we'll look at how it does this.

The intent filter tells Android which activities can handle which actions

When Android is given an intent, it has to figure out which activity, or activities, are able to handle it. This process is known as **intent resolution**.

When you use an *explicit* intent, intent resolution is straightforward. The intent explicitly says which component the intent is directed at, so Android has clear instructions about what to do. As an example, the following code explicitly tells Android to start `ReceiveMessageActivity`:

```
Intent intent = new Intent(this, ReceiveMessageActivity.class);
startActivity(intent);
```

When you use an *implicit* intent, Android uses the information in the intent to figure out which components are able to receive it. It does this by checking the intent filters in every app's copy of *AndroidManifest.xml*.

An **intent filter** specifies what types of intent each component can receive. As an example, here's the entry for an activity that can handle an action of `ACTION_SEND`. The activity is able to accept data with MIME types of text/plain or image:

```
<activity android:name="ShareActivity">
    <intent-filter>
        <action android:name="android.intent.action.SEND"/>
        <category android:name="android.intent.category.DEFAULT"/>
        <data android:mimeType="text/plain"/>
        <data android:mimeType="image/*"/>
    </intent-filter>
</activity>
```

This tells Android the activity can handle ACTION_SEND.

The intent filter must include a category of DEFAULT or it won't be able to receive implicit intents.

These are the types of data the activity can handle.

The intent filter also specifies a **category**. The category supplies extra information about the activity such as whether it can be started by a web browser, or if it's the main entry point of the app. An intent filter ***must*** include a category of `android.intent.category.DEFAULT` if it's to receive implicit intents. If an activity has no intent filter, or it doesn't include a category name of `android.intent.category.DEFAULT`, it means that the activity can't be started with an implicit intent. It can only be started with an *explicit* intent using the fully qualified component name.

How Android uses the intent filter

When you use an implicit intent, Android compares the information given in the intent with the information given in the intent filters specified in every app's *AndroidManifest.xml* file.

Android first considers intent filters that include a category of `android.intent.category.DEFAULT`:

```
<intent-filter>
    <category android:name="android.intent.category.DEFAULT"/>
    ...
</intent-filter>
```

Intent filters without this category will be omitted as they can't receive implicit intents.

Android then matches intents to intent filters by comparing the action and MIME type contained in the intent with those of the intent filters. As an ← example, if an intent specifies an action of `Intent.ACTION_SEND` using:

It will also look at the category of the intent filter if one is supplied by the intent. This isn't used very often, so we're not covering how to add categories to intents.

```
Intent intent = new Intent(Intent.ACTION_SEND);
```

Android will only consider activities that specify an intent filter with an action of `android.intent.action.SEND` like this:

```
<intent-filter>
    <action android:name="android.intent.action.SEND"/>
    ...
</intent-filter>
```

Similarly, if the intent MIME type is set to "text/plain" using

```
intent.setType("text/plain");
```

Android will only consider activities that can accommodate this type of data:

```
<intent-filter>
    <data android:mimeType="text/plain"/>
    ...
</intent-filter>
```

If the MIME type is left out of the intent, Android tries to infer the type based on the data the intent contains.

Once Android has finished comparing the intent to the component intent filters, it sees how many matches it finds. If Android finds a single match, Android starts the component (in our case, the activity) and passes it the intent. If it finds multiple matches, it asks the user to pick one.

BE the Intent

Your job is to play like you're the intent on the right and say which of the activities described below are compatible with your action and data. Say why, or why not, for each one.

Here's the intent.

```java
Intent intent = new Intent(Intent.ACTION_SEND);
intent.setType("text/plain");
intent.putExtra(Intent.EXTRA_TEXT, "Hello");
```

```xml
<activity android:name="SendActivity">
    <intent-filter>
        <action android:name="android.intent.action.SEND"/>
        <category android:name="android.intent.category.DEFAULT"/>
        <data android:mimeType="*/*"/>
    </intent-filter>
</activity>
```

```xml
<activity android:name="SendActivity">
    <intent-filter>
        <action android:name="android.intent.action.SEND"/>
        <category android:name="android.intent.category.MAIN"/>
        <data android:mimeType="text/plain"/>
    </intent-filter>
</activity>
```

```xml
<activity android:name="SendActivity">
    <intent-filter>
        <action android:name="android.intent.action.SENDTO"/>
        <category android:name="android.intent.category.MAIN"/>
        <category android:name="android.intent.category.DEFAULT"/>
        <data android:mimeType="text/plain"/>
    </intent-filter>
</activity>
```

BE the Intent Solution

Your job is to play like you're the intent on the right and say which of the activities described below are compatible with your action and data. Say why, or why not, for each one.

```
Intent intent = new Intent(Intent.ACTION_SEND);
intent.setType("text/plain");
intent.putExtra(Intent.EXTRA_TEXT, "Hello");
```

✓ This activity accepts ACTION_SEND and can handle data of any MIME type so it can respond to the intent.

```
<activity android:name="SendActivity">
    <intent-filter>
        <action android:name="android.intent.action.SEND"/>
        <category android:name="android.intent.category.DEFAULT"/>
        <data android:mimeType="*/*"/>
    </intent-filter>
</activity>
```

✗ This activity doesn't have a category of DEFAULT so can't receive the intent.

```
<activity android:name="SendActivity">
    <intent-filter>
        <action android:name="android.intent.action.SEND"/>
        <category android:name="android.intent.category.MAIN"/>
        <data android:mimeType="text/plain"/>
    </intent-filter>
</activity>
```

✗ This activity can't accept ACTION_SEND intents, only ACTION_SENDTO. ACTION_SENDTO allows you to send a message to someone specified in the intent's data.

```
<activity android:name="SendActivity">
    <intent-filter>
        <action android:name="android.intent.action.SENDTO"/>
        <category android:name="android.intent.category.MAIN"/>
        <category android:name="android.intent.category.DEFAULT"/>
        <data android:mimeType="text/plain"/>
    </intent-filter>
</activity>
```

You need to run your app on a REAL device

So far we've been running our apps using the emulator. The emulator only includes a small number of apps, and there may well be just one app that can handle ACTION_SEND. In order to test our app properly, we need to run it on a physical device where we know there'll be more than one app that can support our action—for example, an app that can send emails and an app that can send messages.

Here's how you go about getting your app to run on a physical device.

1. Enable USB debugging on your device

On your device, open "Developer options" (in Android 4.0 onward, this is hidden by default). To enable it, go to Settings → About Phone and tap the build number seven times. When you return to the previous screen, you should be able to see "Developer options."

Yep, seriously.→

Within "Developer options," tick the box to enable USB debugging

You need to enable USB debugging.

2. Set up your system to detect your device

If you're using a Mac, you can skip this step.

If you're using Windows, you need to install a USB driver. You can find the latest instructions here:

http://developer.android.com/tools/extras/oem-usb.html

If you're using Ubuntu Linux, you need to create a udev rules file. You can find the latest instructions on how to do this here:

http://developer.android.com/tools/device.html#setting-up

3. Plug your device into your computer with a USB cable

Your device may ask you if you want to accept an RSA key that allows USB debugging with your computer. If it does, you can tick the "Always allow from this computer" option and choose OK to enable this.

You'll get this message if your device is running Android 4.2.2 or higher.

Specify action
Create chooser

Running your app on a real device (continued)

4. Run your app in Android Studio as normal

Android Studio will install the app on your device and launch it. You may be asked to choose which device you want to run your app on. If so, select your device from the list available and click OK.

The first device listed is our emulator.

Here's our physical device.

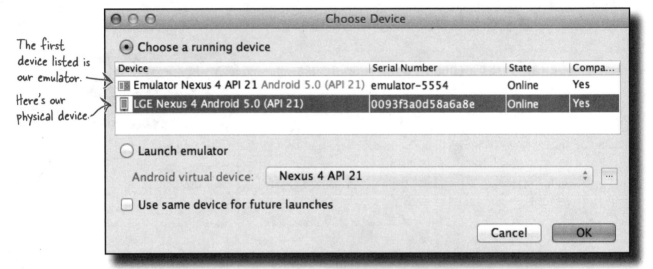

And here's the app running on the physical device

You should find that your app looks about the same as when you ran it through the emulator. You'll probably also find that your app installs and runs quicker too.

Now that you know how to run the apps you create on your own device, you're all set to test the latest changes to your app.

Test drive the app

Try running the app using the emulator, and then using your own device. The results you get will depend on how many activities you have on each that support using the Send action with text data.

If you have one activity

Clicking on the Send Message button will take you straight to that app.

> We only have one activity available on the emulator that can send messages with text data, so when we click on the Send Message button, Android starts the activity.

If you have more than one activity

Android displays a chooser and asks you to pick which one you want to use. It also asks you whether you want to use this action just once or always. If you choose always, the next time you click on the Send Message button it uses the same activity by default.

> We have lots of suitable activities available on our physical device. We decided to use the Messaging app. We selected the "always" option—great if we always want to use Messaging, not so great if we want to use a different one each time.

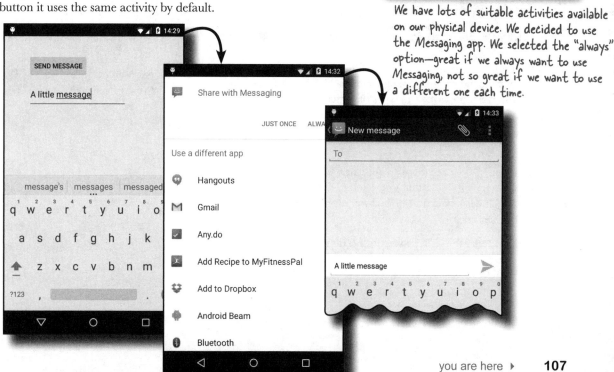

> Here's the message.

What if you ALWAYS want your users to choose an activity?

You've just seen that if there's more than one activity on your device that's capable of receiving your intent, Android automatically asks you to choose which activity you want to use. It even asks you whether you want to use this activity all the time or just on this occasion.

There's just one problem with this default behavior: what if you want to *guarantee* that users can choose an activity every time they click on the Send Message button? If they've chosen the option to always use Gmail, for instance, they won't be asked if they want to use Twitter next time.

Fortunately, there's a way around this. You can create a chooser that asks you to pick an activity without asking if you always want to use it.

> createChooser() allows you to specify a title for the chooser dialog, and doesn't give the user the option of selecting an activity to use by default. It also lets the user know if there are no matching activities by displaying a message.

Intent.createChooser() displays a chooser dialog

You can achieve this using the `Intent.createChooser()` method. This method takes the intent you've already created, and wraps it in a chooser dialog. The big difference in using this method is that you're not given the option of choosing a default activity—you get asked to choose one every time.

You call the `createChooser()` method like this:

This is the intent you created earlier.

```
Intent chosenIntent = Intent.createChooser(intent, "Send message...");
```

You can pass in a title for the chooser that gets displayed at the top of the screen.

The method takes two parameters: an intent and an optional `String` title for the chooser dialog window. The `Intent` parameter needs to describe the types of activity you want the chooser to display. You can use the same intent we created earlier, as this specifies that we want to use `ACTION_SEND` with textual data.

The `createChooser()` method returns a brand-new `Intent`. This is a new explicit intent that's targeted at the activity chosen by the user. It includes any extra information supplied by the original intent, including any text.

To start the activity the user chose, you need to call

```
startActivity(chosenIntent);
```

We'll take a closer look over the next couple of pages at what happens when you call the `createChooser()` method.

What happens when you call createChooser()

This is what happens when you run the following two lines of code:

```
Intent chosenIntent = Intent.createChooser(intent, "Send message...");
startActivity(chosenIntent);
```

① **The createChooser() method gets called.**

The method includes an intent that specifies the action and MIME type that's required.

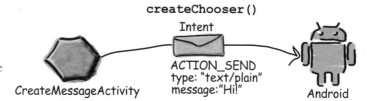

createChooser()

Intent

CreateMessageActivity

ACTION_SEND
type: "text/plain"
message:"Hi!"

Android

---

② **Android checks which activities are able to receive the intent by looking at their intent filters.**

It matches on the actions, type of data, and categories they can support.

I see, I need to create a chooser for activities that support the SEND action and text/plain data.

CreateMessageActivity

Android

---

③ **If more than one activity is able to receive the intent, Android displays an activity chooser dialog and asks the user which one to use.**

This time it doesn't give the user the option of always using a particular activity, and it displays "Send message..." in the title.

If no activities are found, Android still displays the chooser but shows a message to the user telling her there are no apps that can perform the action.

CreateMessageActivity

Hey, user. Which activity do you want to use this time?

Android

User

The story continues...

Specify action
→ **Create chooser**

④ **When the user chooses which activity she wants to use, Android returns a new explicit intent describing the chosen activity.**
The new intent includes any extra information that was included in the original intent, such as any extra text.

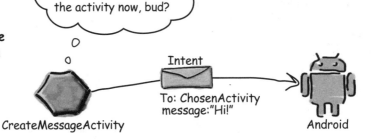

She wants to use Activity2. Here's the intent.

Intent

CreateMessageActivity   ChosenActivity message:"Hi!"   Android   User

⑤ **The activity asks Android to start the activity specified in the intent.**

Thanks for the intent, Android. Can you start the activity now, bud?

Intent

CreateMessageActivity   To: ChosenActivity message:"Hi!"   Android

⑥ **Android asks the activity specified by the intent to start, and then passes it the intent.**

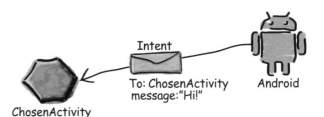

CreateMessageActivity

Intent

ChosenActivity   To: ChosenActivity message:"Hi!"   Android

Change the code to create a chooser

We'll change the code so that the user gets asked which activity they want to use to send a message every time they click on the Send Message button. We'll update the `onSendMessage()` method in *CreateMessageActivity.java* so that it calls the `createChooser()` method, and we'll add a string resource to *strings.xml* for the chooser dialog title.

Update strings.xml...

We want the chooser dialog to have a title of "Send message...". Add a string called "chooser" to *strings.xml*, and give it the value "Send message..." (make sure to save your changes):

```
...
<string name="chooser">Send message...</string>
...
```

...and update the onSendMessage() method

We need to change the `onSendMessage()` method so that it retrieves the value of the chooser string resource in *strings.xml*, calls the `createChooser()` method, and then starts the activity the user chooses. Update your code as follows:

```
...
    //Call onSendMessage() when the button is clicked
    public void onSendMessage(View view) {
        EditText messageView = (EditText)findViewById(R.id.message);
        String messageText = messageView.getText().toString();
        Intent intent = new Intent(Intent.ACTION_SEND);
        intent.setType("text/plain");
        intent.putExtra(Intent.EXTRA_TEXT, messageText);
        String chooserTitle = getString(R.string.chooser);          ← Get the chooser title.
        Intent chosenIntent = Intent.createChooser(intent, chooserTitle);
        startActivity(Intent);                                       ↑
        startActivity(chosenIntent);   ← Start the activity          Display the chooser dialog.
    }                                    that the user selected.
...
```

The `getString()` method is used to get the value of a string resource. It takes one parameter, the ID of the resource (in our case, this is `R.string.chooser`):

```
getString(R.string.chooser);    ←  If you look in R.java, you'll find chooser
                                    in the inner class called string.
```

Now that we've updated the app, let's run the app to see our chooser in action.

Test drive the app

Save your changes, then try running the app again.

If you have one activity

Clicking on the Send Message button will take you straight to that app just like before.

> There's no change here— Android continues to take you straight to the activity.

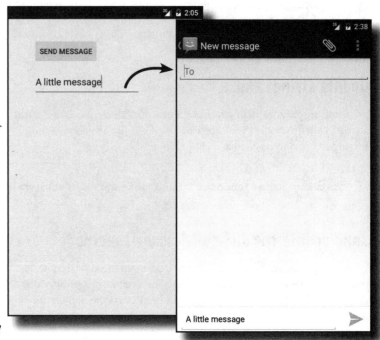

If you have more than one activity

Android displays a chooser but this time it doesn't ask us if we always want to use the same activity. It also displays the value of the chooser string resource in the title.

> Here's the chooser we created with createChooser(). It no longer gives us the option of using a particular activity every time.

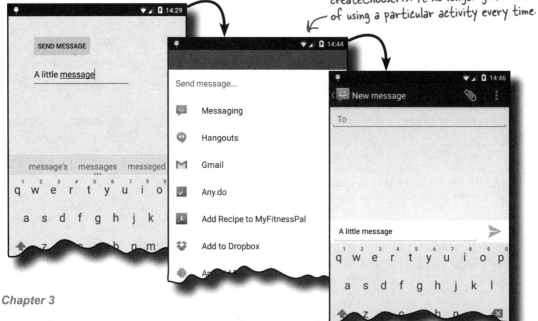

If you have NO matching activities

If you have no activities on your device that are capable of sending messages, the `createChooser()` method lets you know by displaying a message.

This behavior is another benefit to using the `createChooser()` method. The `createChooser()` method is able to deal with situations where no activities can perform a particular action.

If you want to replicate this for yourself, try running the app in the emulator, and disable the Messaging app that's on there.

there are no
Dumb Questions

Q: So I can run my apps in the emulator or on a physical device. Which is best?

A: Each one has its pros and cons.

If you run apps on your physical device, they tend to load a lot quicker than using the emulator. It's also useful if you're writing code that interacts with the device hardware.

The emulator allows you to run apps against many different versions of Android, screen resolutions, and device specifications. It saves you from buying lots of different devices.

The key thing is that you make sure you test your apps thoroughly using a mixture of the emulator and physical devices before releasing them to a wider audience.

Q: Should I use implicit or explicit intents?

A: It comes down to whether you need Android to use a specific activity to perform your action, or whether you just want the action done. As an example, suppose you wanted to send an email. If you don't mind which email app the user uses to send it, just as long as the email gets sent, you'd use an implicit intent. On the other hand, if you needed to pass an intent to a particular activity in your app, you'd need to use an explicit intent. You need to explicity say which activity needs to receive the intent.

Q: You mentioned that an activity's intent filter can specify a category as well as an action. What's the difference between the two?

A: An action specifies what an activity can do, and the category gives extra detail. We've not gone into details about the category because you don't often need to specify a category when you create an intent.

Q: You say that the `createChooser()` method displays a message in the chooser if there are no activities that can handle the intent. What if I'd just used the default Android chooser and passed an implicit intent to `startActivity()`?

A: If the `startActivity()` method is given an intent where there are no matching activities, an `ActivityNotFoundException` is thrown. If you don't catch this using a `try/catch` block, it may cause your app to crash.

Your Android Toolbox

You've got Chapter 3 under your belt and now you've added multiple activity apps and intents to your toolbox.

> You can download the full code for the chapter from https://tinyurl.com/HeadFirstAndroid.

BULLET POINTS

- A task is two or more activities chained together.

- The `<EditText>` element defines an editable text field for entering text. It inherits from the Android `View` class.

- You can add a new activity in Android Studio by choosing File → New... → Activity.

- Each activity you create must have an entry in *AndroidManifest.xml*.

- An **intent** is a type of message that Android components use to communicate with one another.

- An explicit intent explicitly specifies the component the intent is targeted at. You create an explicit intent using
  `Intent intent = new Intent(this, Target.class);`

- To start an activity, call `startActivity(intent)`. If no activities are found, it throws an `ActivityNotFoundException`.

- Use the `putExtra()` method to add extra information to an intent.

- Use the `getIntent()` method to retrieve the intent that started the activity.

- Use the `get*Extra()` methods to retrieve extra information associated with the intent. `getStringExtra()` retrieves a String, `getIntExtra()` retrieves an int, and so on.

- An activity action describes a standard operational action an activity can perform. To send a message, use `Intent.ACTION_SEND`.

- To create an implicit intent that specifies an action, use
  `Intent intent = new Intent(action);`

- To describe the type of data in the intent, use the `setType()` method.

- Android resolves intents based on the named component, action, type of data, and categories specified in the intent. It compares the contents of the intent with the intent filters in each app's *AndroidManifest.xml*. An activity must have a category of `DEFAULT` if it is to receive an implicit intent.

- The `createChooser()` method allows you to override the default Android activity chooser dialog. It allows you to specify a title for the dialog, and doesn't give the user the option of setting a default activity. If no activities can receive the intent it is passed, it displays a message. The `createChooser()` method returns an `Intent`.

- You retrieve the value of a string resource using `getString(R.string.stringname);`

4 the activity lifecycle

Being an Activity

...so I told him that if he didn't onStop() soon, I'd onDestroy() him with a cattle prod.

Activities form the foundation of every Android app.

So far you've seen how to create activities, and made one activity start another using an intent. But *what's really going on beneath the hood?* In this chapter, we're going to dig a little deeper into **the activity lifecycle**. What happens when an activity is **created** and **destroyed**? Which methods get called when an activity is **made visible and appears in the foreground**, and which get called when the activity **loses the focus and is hidden**? And **how do you save and restore your activity's state**?

How do activities really work?

So far you've seen how to create apps that interact with the user, and apps that use multiple activities to perform tasks. Now that you have these core skills under your belt, it's time to take a deeper look at how activities *actually work*. Here's a recap of what you know so far, with a few extra details thrown in.

 An app is a collection of activities, layouts, and other resources.
One of these activities is the main activity for the app.

Each app has a main activity, as specified in the file AndroidManifest.xml.

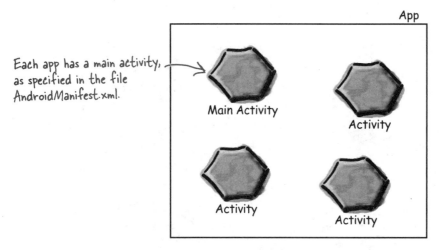

 By default, each app runs within its own process.
This helps keep your apps safe and secure. You can read more about this in Appendix i (which covers the Android runtime, or ART) at the back of this book.

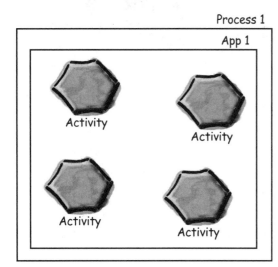

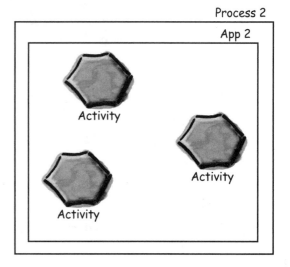

⭐ **You can start an activity in another application by passing an intent with startActivity().**

The Android system knows about all the installed apps and their activities, and uses the intent to start the correct activity.

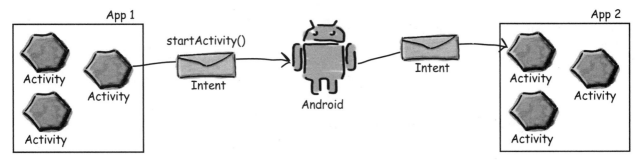

⭐ **When an activity needs to start, Android checks if there's already a process for that app.**

If one exists, Android runs the activity in that process. If one doesn't exist, Android creates one.

⭐ **When Android starts an activity, it calls its onCreate() method.**

onCreate() is always run whenever an activity gets created.

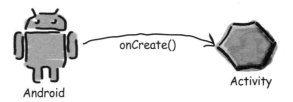

But there are still lots of things we don't yet know about how activities function. How long does the activity live for? What happens when your activity disappears from the screen? Is it still running? Is it still in memory? And what happens if your app gets interrupted by an incoming phone call? We want to be able to control the behavior of our activities in a *whole range of different circumstances*, but how?

The Stopwatch app

In this chapter, we're going to take a closer look at how activities work under the hood, common ways in which your apps can break, and how you can fix them using the activity lifecycle methods. We're going to explore the lifecycle methods using a simple Stopwatch app as an example.

The Stopwatch app consists of a single activity and a single layout. The layout includes a text view showing you how much time has passed, a Start button that starts the stopwatch, a Stop button that stops it, and a Reset button that resets the timer value to zero.

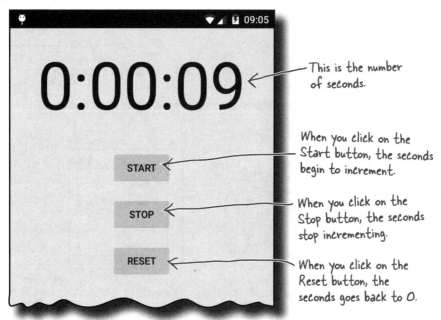

This is the number of seconds.

When you click on the Start button, the seconds begin to increment.

When you click on the Stop button, the seconds stop incrementing.

When you click on the Reset button, the seconds goes back to 0.

Build the app

You have enough experience under your belt to build the app without much guidance from us. We're going to give you just enough code to be able to build the app yourself, and then you can see what happens when you try to run it.

Start off by creating a new Android project for an application named "Stopwatch" with a package name of com.hfad. stopwatch. The minimum SDK should be API 15 so it can run on most devices. You'll need an activity called "StopwatchActivity" and a layout called "activity_stopwatch".

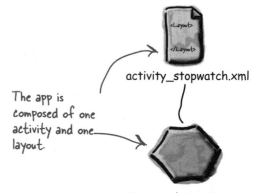

activity_stopwatch.xml

The app is composed of one activity and one layout.

StopwatchActivity.java

The stopwatch layout code

Here's the XML for the layout. It describes a single text view that's used to display the timer, and three buttons to control the stopwatch. Replace the XML currently in *activity_stopwatch.xml* with the XML shown here:

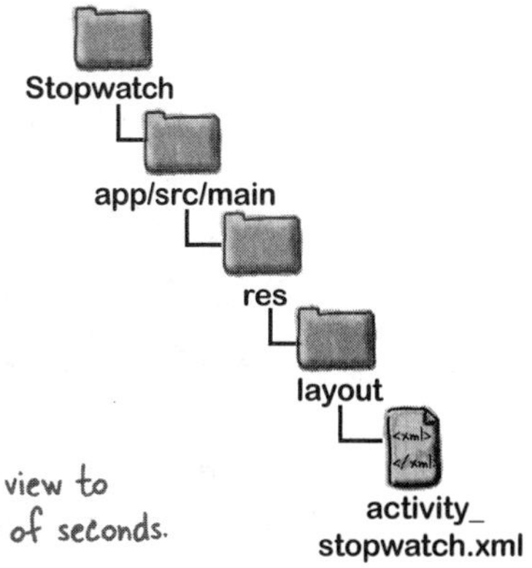

```xml
<RelativeLayout xmlns:android="http://schemas.android.com/apk/res/android"
    xmlns:tools="http://schemas.android.com/tools"
    android:layout_width="match_parent"
    android:layout_height="match_parent"
    android:paddingBottom="16dp"
    android:paddingLeft="16dp"
    android:paddingRight="16dp"
    android:paddingTop="16dp"
    tools:context=".StopwatchActivity" >

    <TextView
        android:id="@+id/time_view"
        android:layout_width="wrap_content"
        android:layout_height="wrap_content"
        android:layout_alignParentTop="true"
        android:layout_centerHorizontal="true"
        android:layout_marginTop="0dp"
        android:text=""
        android:textAppearance="?android:attr/textAppearanceLarge"
        android:textSize="92sp" />

    <Button
        android:id="@+id/start_button"
        android:layout_width="wrap_content"
        android:layout_height="wrap_content"
        android:layout_below="@+id/time_view"
        android:layout_centerHorizontal="true"
        android:layout_marginTop="20dp"
        android:onClick="onClickStart"
        android:text="@string/start" />
```

Stopwatch
app/src/main
res
layout
activity_stopwatch.xml

We'll use this text view to display the number of seconds.

These attributes make the stopwatch timer nice and big.

This is for the Start button. It calls a method called onClickStart() when it gets clicked.

The layout code continues over the page.

The layout code (continued)

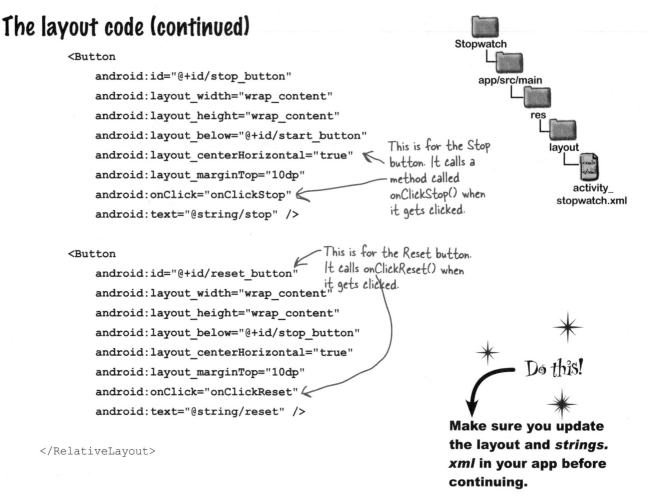

```
<Button
    android:id="@+id/stop_button"
    android:layout_width="wrap_content"
    android:layout_height="wrap_content"
    android:layout_below="@+id/start_button"
    android:layout_centerHorizontal="true"
    android:layout_marginTop="10dp"
    android:onClick="onClickStop"
    android:text="@string/stop" />
```

This is for the Stop button. It calls a method called onClickStop() when it gets clicked.

```
<Button
    android:id="@+id/reset_button"
    android:layout_width="wrap_content"
    android:layout_height="wrap_content"
    android:layout_below="@+id/stop_button"
    android:layout_centerHorizontal="true"
    android:layout_marginTop="10dp"
    android:onClick="onClickReset"
    android:text="@string/reset" />
```

This is for the Reset button. It calls onClickReset() when it gets clicked.

```
</RelativeLayout>
```

Do this!

Make sure you update the layout and *strings. xml* in your app before continuing.

The stopwatch strings.xml file

The layout uses three extra String values, one for the text value of each button. These values are String resources, so need to be added to *strings. xml*. Add the string values below to *strings.xml*:

```
...
    <string name="start">Start</string>
    <string name="stop">Stop</string>
    <string name="reset">Reset</string>
...
```

These are the button labels.

The layout is done! Next, let's move on to the activity.

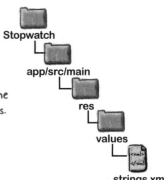

How the activity code will work

The layout defines three buttons that we'll use to control the stopwatch. Each button uses its onClick attribute to specify which method in the activity should run when the button is clicked. When the Start button is clicked, the onClickStart() method gets called, when the Stop button is clicked the onClickStop() method gets called, and when the Reset button is clicked the onClickReset() method gets called. We'll use these method to start, stop, and reset the stopwatch.

When you click on the Start button, the onClickStart() method is called.

When you click on the Stop button, the onClickStop() method is called.

When you click on the Reset button, the onClickReset() method is called.

We'll update the stopwatch using a method we'll create called runTimer(). The runTimer() method will run code every second to check whether the stopwatch is running, increment the number of seconds and display the number of seconds in the text view.

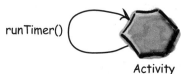

runTimer()

Activity

To help us with this, we'll use two private variables to record the state of the stopwatch. We'll use an int called seconds to track how many seconds have passed since the stopwatch started running, and a boolean called running to record whether the stopwatch is currently running.

We'll start by writing the code for the buttons, and then we'll look at the runTimer() method.

Add code for the buttons

When the user clicks on the Start button, we'll set the `running` variable to `true` so that the stopwatch will start. When the user clicks on the Stop button, we'll set `running` to `false` so that the stopwatch stops running. If the user clicks on the Reset button, we'll set `running` to `false` and `seconds` to 0 so that the stopwatch is reset and stops running.

Replace the contents of *StopwatchActivity.java* with the code below:

START → running=true

STOP → running=false

RESET → running=false seconds=0

```java
package com.hfad.stopwatch;

import android.os.Bundle;
import android.app.Activity;
import android.view.View;

public class StopwatchActivity extends Activity {

    private int seconds = 0;
    private boolean running;
```
Use seconds and running to record the number of seconds passed and whether the stopwatch is running.

```java
    @Override
    protected void onCreate(Bundle savedInstanceState) {
        super.onCreate(savedInstanceState);
        setContentView(R.layout.activity_stopwatch);
    }

    //Start the stopwatch running when the Start button is clicked.
    public void onClickStart(View view) {
        running = true;
    }
```
This gets called when the Start button is clicked.

Start the stopwatch running.

```java
    //Stop the stopwatch running when the Stop button is clicked.
    public void onClickStop(View view) {
        running = false;
    }
```
This gets called when the Stop button is clicked.

Stop the stopwatch running.

```java
    //Reset the stopwatch when the Reset button is clicked.
    public void onClickReset(View view) {
        running = false;
        seconds = 0;
    }
}
```
This gets called when the Reset button is clicked.

Stop the stopwatch running and set the seconds to 0.

Stopwatch

app/src/main

java

com.hfad.stopwatch

Stopwatch Activity.java

The runTimer() method

The next thing we need to do is create the `runTimer()` method. The `runTimer()` method will get a reference to the text view in the layout, format the contents of the `seconds` variable into hours, minutes, and seconds, and then display the results in the text view. If the `running` variable is set to `true`, it will increment the `seconds` variable. Here's the code:

```java
private void runTimer() {
    final TextView timeView = (TextView)findViewById(R.id.time_view);
    ...
    int hours = seconds/3600;
    int minutes = (seconds%3600)/60;
    int secs = seconds%60;
    String time = String.format("%d:%02d:%02d",
            hours, minutes, secs);
    timeView.setText(time);
    if (running) {
        seconds++;
    }
    ...
}
```

Get the text view.

Format the seconds into hours, minutes, and seconds. This is plain Java code.

Set the text view text.

If running is true, increment the seconds variable.

We've left out a bit of code here. We'll look at that on the next page.

We need this code to keep looping so that it increments the `seconds` variable and updates the text view every second. We need to do this in such a way that we don't block the main Android thread.

In non-Android Java programs, you can perform tasks like this using a background thread. In Androidville, this is a problem—only the main Android thread can update the user interface, and if any other thread tries to do so, you get a `CalledFromWrongThreadException`.

The solution is to use a `Handler`. We'll look at this on the next page.

Handlers allow you to schedule code

A `Handler` is an Android class you can use to schedule code that should be run at some point in the future. You can also use it to post code that needs to run on a different thread. In our case, we're going to use a `Handler` to schedule the stopwatch code to run every second.

To use the `Handler`, you wrap the code you wish to schedule in a `Runnable` object, and then use the `Handler` `post()` and `postDelayed()` methods to specify when you want the code to run. Let's take a closer look at these mehods.

The post() method

The `post()` method posts code that needs to be run as soon as possible (which is usually almost immediately). The `post()` method takes one parameter, an object of type `Runnable`. A `Runnable` object in Androidville is just like a `Runnable` in plain old Java, a job you want to run. You put the code you want to run in the `Runnable`'s `run()` method, and the `Handler` will make sure the code is run as soon as possible. Here's what the method looks like:

```
final Handler handler = new Handler();
handler.post(Runnable);
```
← You put the code you want to run in the Handler's run() method.

The postDelayed() method

The `postDelayed()` method works in a similar way to the `post()` method except that you use it post code that should be run in the future. The `postDelayed()` method takes two parameters: a `Runnable` and a `long`. The `Runnable` contains the code you want to run in its `run()` method, and the `long` specifies the number of milliseconds you wish to delay the code by. The code will run as soon as possible after the delay. Here's what the method looks like:

```
final Handler handler = new Handler();
handler.postDelayed(Runnable, long);
```
← Use this method to delay running code by a specified number of milliseconds.

On the next page, we'll use these methods to update the stopwatch every second.

The full runTimer() code

To update the stopwatch, we're going to repeatedly schedule code using the Handler with a delay of 1,000 milliseconds each time. Each time the code runs, we'll increment the seconds variable and update the text view.

Here's the full code for the runTimer() method:

```
private void runTimer() {
    final TextView timeView = (TextView) findViewById(R.id.time_view);
    final Handler handler = new Handler();    ← Create a new Handler.
    handler.post(new Runnable() {    ← Call the post() method, passing in a new Runnable. The post()
        @Override                       method processes codes without a delay, so the code in the
        public void run() {             Runnable will run almost immediately.
            int hours = seconds/3600;
            int minutes = (seconds%3600)/60;
            int secs = seconds%60;                        The Runnable run() method
            String time = String.format("%d:%02d:%02d",   ← contains the code you want to
                    hours, minutes, secs);                be run—in our case, the code
            timeView.setText(time);                       to update the text view.
            if (running) {
                seconds++;
            }
            handler.postDelayed(this, 1000);    ← Post the code in the Runnable to be run again
        }                                          after a delay of 1,000 milliseconds, or 1 second.
    });                                            As this line of code is included in the Runnable
}                                                  run() method, this will keep getting called.
```

Using the post() and postDelayed() methods in this way means that the code will run as soon as possible after the required delay, which in practice means almost immediately. While this means the code will lag slightly over time, it's accurate enough for the purposes of exploring the lifecycle methods in this chapter.

We want the runTimer() method to start running when StopwatchActivity gets created, so we'll call it in the activity onCreate() method:

```
protected void onCreate(Bundle savedInstanceState) {
    ...
    runTimer();
}
```

We'll show you the full code for the activity on the next page.

The full StopwatchActivity code

Here's the full code for *StopwatchActivity.java*. Update your code with our changes below.

```
package com.hfad.stopwatch;

import android.os.Bundle;
import android.os.Handler;
import android.app.Activity;
import android.view.View;
import android.widget.TextView;

public class StopwatchActivity extends Activity {
    //Number of seconds displayed on the stopwatch.
    private int seconds = 0;
    //Is the stopwatch running?
    private boolean running;


    @Override
    protected void onCreate(Bundle savedInstanceState) {
        super.onCreate(savedInstanceState);
        setContentView(R.layout.activity_stopwatch);
        runTimer();
    }

    //Start the stopwatch running when the Start button is clicked.
    public void onClickStart(View view) {
        running = true;
    }

    //Stop the stopwatch running when the Stop button is clicked.
    public void onClickStop(View view) {
        running = false;
    }
```

Use seconds and running to record the number of seconds passed and whether the stopwatch is running.

We're using a separate method to update the stopwatch. We're starting it when the activity is created.

This gets called when the Start button is clicked.

Start the stopwatch running.

This gets called when the Stop button is clicked.

Stop the stopwatch running.

Stopwatch
app/src/main
java
com.hfad.stopwatch
Stopwatch
Activity.java

The activity code (continued)

```
//Reset the stopwatch when the Reset button is clicked.
public void onClickReset(View view) {
    running = false;
    seconds = 0;
}
```

Stop the stopwatch running and set the seconds to 0.

This gets called when the Reset button is clicked.

Stopwatch

app/src/main

java

com.hfad.stopwatch

StopwatchActivity.java

```
//Sets the number of seconds on the timer.
private void runTimer() {
    final TextView timeView = (TextView)findViewById(R.id.time_view);
    final Handler handler = new Handler();
    handler.post(new Runnable() {
        @Override
        public void run() {
            int hours = seconds/3600;
            int minutes = (seconds%3600)/60;
            int secs = seconds%60;
            String time = String.format("%d:%02d:%02d",
                    hours, minutes, secs);
            timeView.setText(time);
            if (running) {
                seconds++;
            }
            handler.postDelayed(this, 1000);
        }
    });
}
```

Get the text view.

Use a Handler to post code.

Format the seconds into hours, minutes, and seconds.

Set the text view text.

If running is true, increment the seconds variable.

Post the code again with a delay of 1 second.

Let's look at what happens when the code runs.

Do this!

Make sure you update your activity code with our changes.

What happens when you run the app

1 **The user decides she wants to run the app.**
She clicks on the icon for the app on her device.

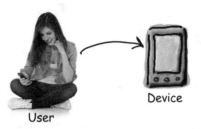

Device

User

2 **The AndroidManifest.xml file for the app specifies which activity to use as the launch activity.**
An intent is constructed to start this activity using `startActivity(intent)`.

AndroidManifest.xml   Android

3 **Android checks if there's already a process running for the app, and if not, creates a new process.**
It then creates a new activity object—in this case, for `StopwatchActivity`.

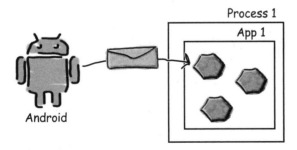

Process 1

App 1

Android

The story continues

④ **The onCreate() method in the activity gets called.**
The method includes a call to setContentView(), specifying a layout, and then
starts the stopwatch with runTimer().

⑤ **When the onCreate() method finishes, the layout gets displayed on the device.**
The runTimer() method uses the seconds variable to determine what text to display
in the text view, and uses the running variable to determine whether to increment
the number of seconds. As running is initially false, the number of seconds isn't
incremented.

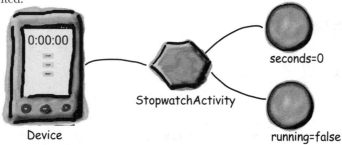

---

there are no
Dumb Questions

Q: Why does Android run an app inside a separate process?

A: For security and stability. It prevents one app accessing the data of another. It also means if one app crashes, it won't take others down with it.

Q: Why have an onCreate() method? Why not just put that code inside a constructor?

A: Android needs to set up the environment for the activity after it's constructed. Once the environment is ready, Android calls onCreate(). That's why code to set up the screen goes inside onCreate() instead of a constructor.

Q: Couldn't I just write a loop in onCreate() to keep updating the timer?

A: No, onCreate() needs to finish before the screen will appear. An endless loop would prevent that happening.

Q: runTimer() looks really complicated. Do I really need to do all this?

A: It's a little complex, but whenever you need to schedule code like this, the code will look similar to runTimer().

Test drive the app

When we run the app in the emulator, the app works great. We can start, stop, and reset the stopwatch without any problems at all—the app works just as you'd expect.

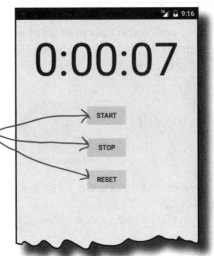

These buttons work as you'd expect. The Start button starts the stopwatch, the Stop button stops it, and the Reset button sets the stopwatch back to 0.

But there's just one problem...

When we ran the app on a physical device, the app worked OK up until someone rotated the device. When the device was rotated, the stopwatch set itself back to 0.

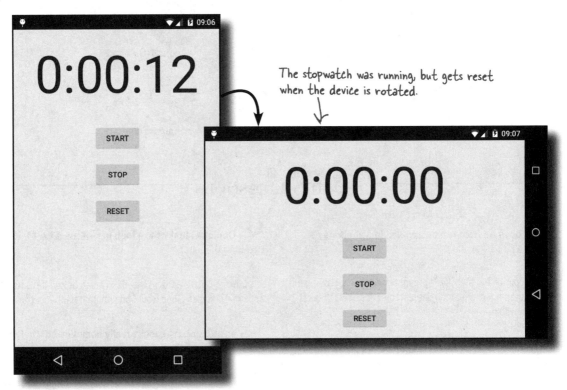

The stopwatch was running, but gets reset when the device is rotated.

In Androidville, it's surprisingly common for apps to break when you rotate the device. Before we fix the problem, let's take a closer look at what caused it.

What just happened?

So why did the app break when the user rotated the screen?
Let's take a closer look at what really happened.

1 **The user starts the app, and clicks on the start button to set the stopwatch going.**

The runTimer() method starts incrementing the number of seconds displayed in the time_view text view using the seconds and running variables.

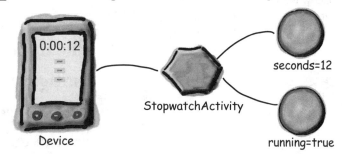

2 **The user rotates the device.**

Android sees that the screen orientation and screen size has changed, and it destroys the activity, including any variables used by the runTimer() method.

3 **StopwatchActivity is then re-created.**

The onCreate() method runs again, and the runTimer() method gets called. As the activity has been re-created, the seconds and running variables are set to their default values.

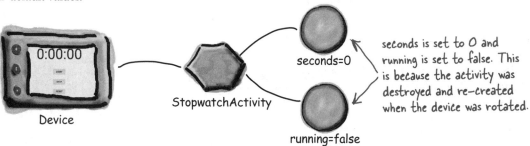

seconds is set to 0 and running is set to false. This is because the activity was destroyed and re-created when the device was rotated.

Rotating the screen changes the device configuration

When Android runs your app and starts an activity, it takes into account the **device configuration**. By this we mean the configuration of the physical device (such as the screen size, screen orientation, and whether there's a keyboard attached) and also configuration options specified by the user (such as the locale).

Android needs to know what the device configuration is when it starts an activity because it can impact what resources are needed for the application. A different layout might need to be used if the device screen is landscape rather than portrait, for instance, and a different set of string values might need to be used if the locale is French.

The device configuration includes options specified by the user (such as the locale), and options relating to the physical device (such as the orientation and screen size). A change to any of these options results in the activity being destroyed and re-created.

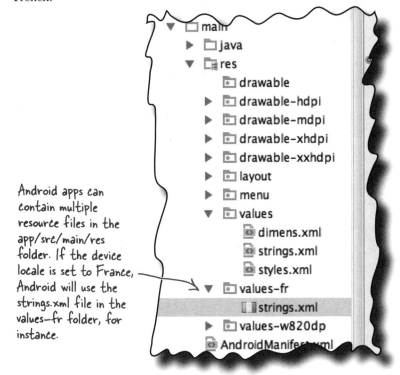

Android apps can contain multiple resource files in the app/src/main/res folder. If the device locale is set to France, Android will use the strings.xml file in the values-fr folder, for instance.

When the device configuration changes, anything that displays a user interface needs to be updated to match the new configuration. If you rotate your device, Android spots that the screen orientation and screen size has changed, and classes this as a change to the device configuration. It destroys the current activity, and then re-creates it again so that resources appropriate to the new configuration get picked up.

From birth to death: the states of an activity

When Android creates and destroys an activity, the activity moves from being launched, to running, to being destroyed.

The main state of an activity is when it's **running** or **active**. An activity is running when it's in the foreground of the screen, has the focus, and the user can interact with it. The activity spends most of its life in this state. An activity starts running after it has been launched, and at the end of its life, the activity is **destroyed**.

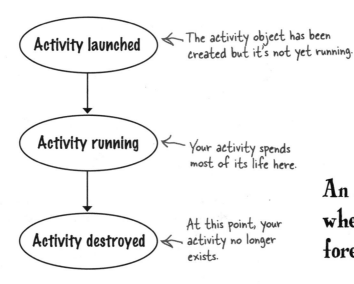

The activity object has been created but it's not yet running.

Your activity spends most of its life here.

At this point, your activity no longer exists.

> An activity is running when it's in the foreground of the screen.

When an activity moves from being launched to being destroyed, it triggers key activity lifecycle methods: the onCreate() and onDestroy() methods. These are lifecycle methods that your activity inherits, and which you can override if necessary.

The onCreate() method gets called immediately after your activity is launched. This method is where you do all your normal activity setup such as calling setContentView(). You should always override this method. If you *don't* override it, you won't be able to tell Android what layout your activity should use.

> onCreate() gets called when the activity is first created, and it's where you do your normal activity setup.

The onDestroy() method is the final call you get before the activity is destroyed. There are a number of situations in which an activity can get destroyed—for example, if it's been told to finish, if the activity's being re-created due to a change in device configuration, or if Android has decided to destroy the activity in order to save space.

> onDestroy() gets called just before your activity gets destroyed.

We'll take a closer look at how these methods fit into the activity states on the next page.

The activity lifecycle: from create to destroy

Here's an overview of the activity lifecycle from birth to death. As you'll see later in the chapter, we've left out some of the details, but at this point we're just focusing on the onCreate() and onDestroy() methods.

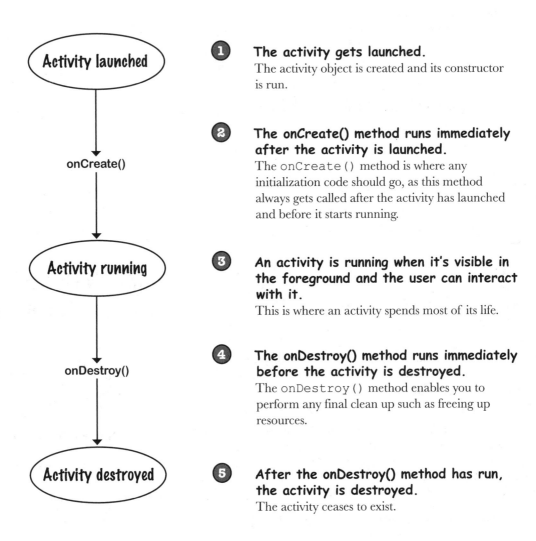

1 **The activity gets launched.**
The activity object is created and its constructor is run.

2 **The onCreate() method runs immediately after the activity is launched.**
The onCreate() method is where any initialization code should go, as this method always gets called after the activity has launched and before it starts running.

3 **An activity is running when it's visible in the foreground and the user can interact with it.**
This is where an activity spends most of its life.

4 **The onDestroy() method runs immediately before the activity is destroyed.**
The onDestroy() method enables you to perform any final clean up such as freeing up resources.

5 **After the onDestroy() method has run, the activity is destroyed.**
The activity ceases to exist.

Your activity inherits the lifecycle methods

As you saw earlier in the book, your activity extends the `android.app.Activity` class. It's this class that gives your activity access to the Android lifecycle methods:

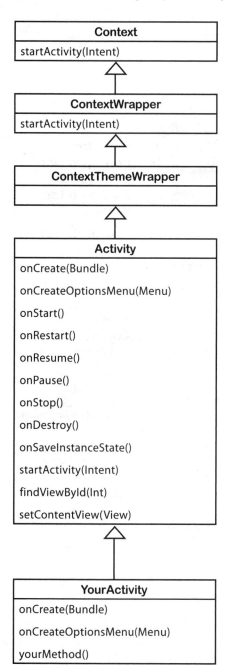

Context abstract class
(android.content.Context)

An interface to global information about the application environment. Allows access to application resources, classes, and application-level operations.

ContextWrapper class
(android.content.ContextWrapper)

A proxy implementation for the Context.

ContextThemeWrapper class
(android.view.ContextThemeWrapper)

The ContextThemeWrapper allows you to modify the theme from what's in the ContextWrapper.

Activity class
(android.app.Activity)

The Activity class implements default versions of the lifecycle methods. It also defines methods such as findViewById(Int) and setContentView(View).

YourActivity class
(com.hfad.foo)

Most of the behavior of your activity is handled by superclass methods. All you do is override the methods you need.

How do we deal with configuration changes?

As you saw, our app went wrong when the user rotated the screen. The activity was destroyed and re-created, which meant that local variables used by the activity were lost. So how do we get around this issue? How do we deal with device configuration changes such as a change to the screen orientation?

There are two options: we can either tell Android to bypass restarting the activity, or we can save its current state so that the activity can re-create itself in the same state. Let's look at these two options in more detail.

Bypass re-creating the activity

The first option is to tell Android not to restart the activity if there's been a configuration change. While we're going to show you how to do this, bear in mind that it's usually not the best option. This is because when Android re-creates the activity, it makes sure it uses the right resources for the new configuration. If you bypass this, you may have to write a bunch of extra code to deal with the new configuration yourself.

You can tell Android not to re-create an activity due to a configuration change by adding a line to the activity element of the *AndroidManifest.xml* file like this:

```
android:configChanges="configuration_change"
```

where `configuration_change` is the type of configuration change.

In our case, we'd want to get Android to bypass a change to the screen orientation and screen size, so we'd need to add the following code to the *AndroidManifest.xml* file:

```
<activity
    android:name="com.hfad.stopwatch.StopwatchActivity"
    android:label="@string/app_name"
    android:configChanges="orientation|screenSize" >
```

Watch it!

Only deal with configuration changes this way as a last resort.

You'll bypass built-in Android behavior that could cause problems.

Stopwatch

app/src/main

AndroidManifest.xml

The | means we need to bypass both configuration changes. This is because most devices have a rectangular screen, so rotating the device changes both the orientation and the screen size.

If Android encounters this type of configuration change, it makes a call to the `onConfigurationChanged(Configuration)` method instead of re-creating the activity:

```
public void onConfigurationChanged(Configuration config) {

}
```

You can implement this method to react to the configuration change if you need to.

Or save the current state...

The better way of dealing with configuration changes which you'll use most often is to save the current state of the activity, and then reinstate it in the onCreate() method of the activity.

To save the current state of the activity, you need to implement the onSaveInstanceState() method. The onSaveInstanceState() method gets called before the activity gets destroyed, which means you get an opportunity to save any values you want to retain before they get lost.

The onSaveInstanceState() method takes one parameter, a Bundle. A Bundle allows you to gather together different types of data into a single object:

```java
public void onSaveInstanceState(Bundle savedInstanceState) {
}
```

The onCreate() method gets passed the Bundle as a parameter. This means that if you add the values of the running and seconds variables to the Bundle, the onCreate() method will be able to pick them up when the activity gets re-created. To do this, you use Bundle methods to add name/value pairs to the Bundle. These methods take the form:

```java
bundle.put*("name", value)
```

where bundle is the name of the Bundle, * is the type of value you want to save, and name and value are the name and value of the data. As an example, to add the seconds int value to the Bundle, you'd use:

```java
bundle.putInt("seconds", seconds);
```

You can save multiple name/value pairs of data to the Bundle.

Here's our onSaveInstanceState() method in full:

```java
@Override
public void onSaveInstanceState(Bundle savedInstanceState) {
    savedInstanceState.putInt("seconds", seconds);
    savedInstanceState.putBoolean("running", running);
}
```

Save the values of the seconds and running variables to the Bundle.

Now that we've saved our variable values to the Bundle, we can use them in our onCreate() method.

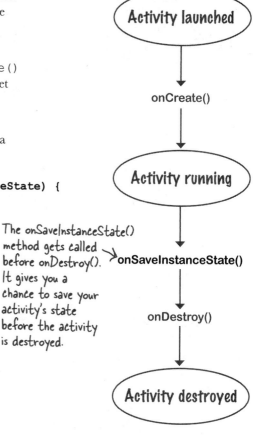

The onSaveInstanceState() method gets called before onDestroy(). It gives you a chance to save your activity's state before the activity is destroyed.

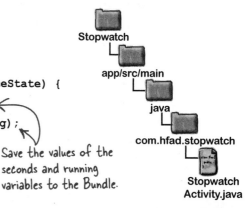

...then restore the state in onCreate()

As we said earlier, the `onCreate()` method takes one parameter, a `Bundle`. If the activity's being created from scratch, this parameter will be null. If, however, the activity's being re-created and there's been a prior call to `onSaveInstanceState()`, the `Bundle` object used by `onSaveInstanceState()` will get passed to the activity:

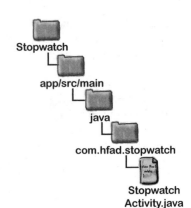

Stopwatch

app/src/main

java

com.hfad.stopwatch

Stopwatch
Activity.java

```
protected void onCreate(Bundle savedInstanceState) {
    ...
}
```

You can get values from `Bundle` by using methods of the form

bundle.get*("name");

where `bundle` is the name of the `Bundle`, * is the type of value you want to get, and name is the name of the name/value pair you specified on the previous page. As an example, to get the `seconds` `int` value from the `Bundle`, you'd use:

int seconds = bundle.getInt("seconds");

Putting all of this together, here's what our `onCreate()` method now looks like:

```
protected void onCreate(Bundle savedInstanceState) {
    super.onCreate(savedInstanceState);
    setContentView(R.layout.activity_stopwatch);
    if (savedInstanceState != null) {
        seconds = savedInstanceState.getInt("seconds");
        running = savedInstanceState.getBoolean("running");
    }
    runTimer();
}
```

Retrieve the values of the seconds and running variables from the Bundle.

So how does this work in practice?

Do this!

Make sure you update your onCreate() method and add the onSaveInstanceState() method.

What happens when you run the app

① **The user starts the app, and clicks on the start button to set the stopwatch going.**

The `runTimer()` method starts incrementing the number of seconds displayed in the `time_view` text view.

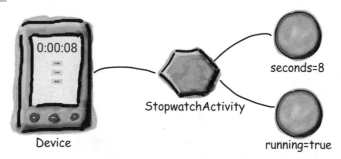

② **The user rotates the device.**

Android views this as a configuration change, and gets ready to destroy the activity. Before the activity is destroyed, `onSaveInstanceState()` gets called. The `onSaveInstanceState()` method saves the seconds and running values to a `Bundle`.

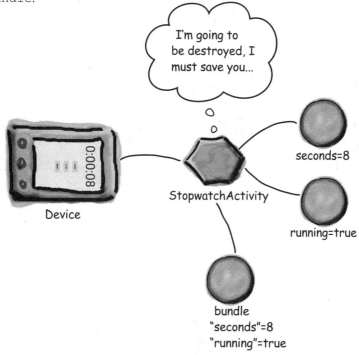

The story continues

4 **Android destroys the activity, and then re-creates it.**

The onCreate() method gets called, and the Bundle gets passed to it.

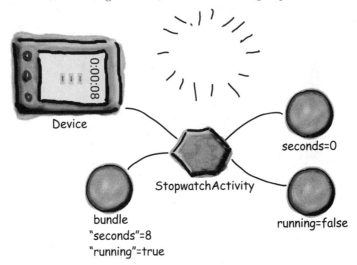

5 **The Bundle contains the values of the seconds and running variables as they were before the activity was destroyed.**

Code in the onCreate() method set the current variables to the values in the Bundle.

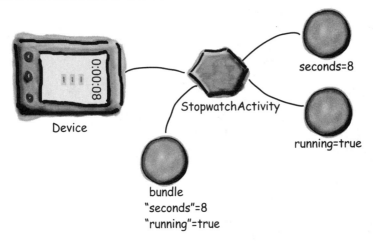

6 **The runTimer() method gets called, and the timer picks up where it left off.**

The stopwatch gets displayed on the device.

Test drive the app

Make the changes to your activity code, then run the app. When
you click on the Start button, the timer starts, and it continues
when you rotate the device.

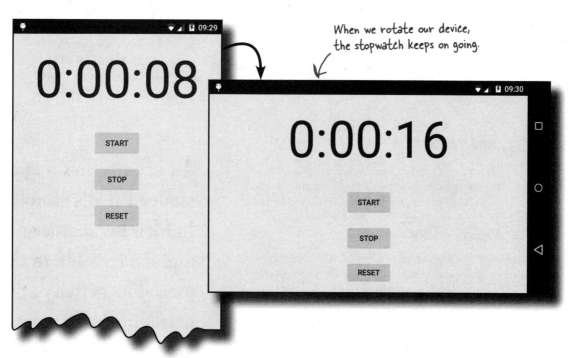

*When we rotate our device,
the stopwatch keeps on going.*

---

there are no
Dumb Questions

Q: Why does Android want to
re-create an activity just because I
rotated the screen?

A: The onCreate() method is
normally used to set up the screen. If your
code in onCreate() depended upon
the screen configuration (for example, if
you had different layouts for landscape
and portrait) then you would want
onCreate() to be called every time
the configuration changed. Also, if the user
changed the locale, you might want to re-
create the UI in the local language.

Q: Why doesn't Android
automatically store every instance
variable automatically? Why do I have
to write all of that code myself?

A: You might not want every instance
variable stored. For example, you might
have a variable that stores the current
screen width. You would want that
variable to be recalculated the next time
onCreate() is called.

Q: Is a Bundle some sort of Java
map?

A: No, but it's designed to work like a
java.util.Map. Bundles have
additional abilities to maps, for example,
Bundles have the ability to be sent
between processes. That's really useful,
because it allows the Android OS to stay in
touch with the state of an activity.

There's more to an activity's life than create and destroy

So far we've looked at the create and destroy parts of the activity lifecycle,and you've seen how to deal with configuration changes such as a change in the screen orientation. But there are other events in an activity's life that you might want to deal with to get the app to behave in the way you want.

As an example, suppose the stopwatch is running and you get a phone call. Even though the stopwatch isn't visible, it will continue running. But what if you want the stopwatch to stop while it's hidden, and resume once the app is visible again?

← Even if you don't really want your stopwatch to behave like this, it's a great excuse to look at more lifecycle methods.

Start, stop, and restart

Fortunately, it's easy to handle actions that relate to an activity's visibility if you use the right lifecycle methods. In addition to the onCreate() and onDestroy() methods, which deal with the overall lifecycle of the activity, there are other lifecycle methods that deal with an activity's visibility.

There are three key lifecycle methods that deal with when an activity becomes visible or invisible to the user. These methods are onStart(), onStop(), and onRestart(). Just as with onCreate() and onDestroy(), your activity inherits them from the Android Activity class.

onStart() gets called when your activity becomes visible to the user.

onStop() gets called when your activity has stopped being visible to the user. This might be because it's completely hidden by another activity that's appeared on top of it, or because the activity is going to be destroyed. If onStop() is called because the activity's going to be destroyed, onSaveInstanceState() gets called before onStop().

onRestart() gets called after your activity has been made invisible, before it gets made visible again.

We'll take a closer look at how these fit in with the onCreate() and onDestroy() methods on the next page.

An activity has a state of stopped if it's completely hidden by another activity and isn't visible to the user. The activity still exists in the background and maintains all state information.

The activity lifecycle: the visible lifetime

Let's build on the lifecycle diagram you saw earlier in the chapter, this time including the onStart(), onStop(), and onRestart() methods (the bits you need to focus on are in bold):

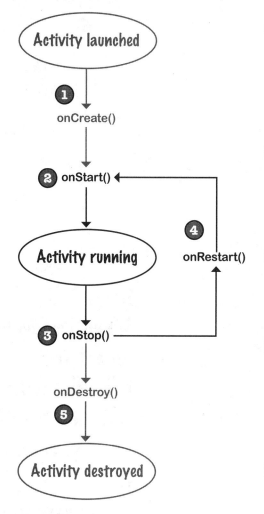

1 **The activity gets launched, and the onCreate() method runs.**
Any activity initialization code in the onCreate() method runs. At this point, the activity isn't yet visible, as no call to onStart() has been made.

2 **The onStart() method runs after the onCreate() method. It gets called when the activity is about to become visible.**
After the onStart() method has run, the user can see the activity on the screen.

3 **The onStop() method runs when the activity stops being visible to the user.**
After the onStop() method has run, the activity is no longer visible.

4 **If the activity becomes visible to the user again, the onRestart() method gets called followed by onStart().**
The activity may go through this cycle many times if the activity repeatedly becomes invisible and visible again.

5 **Finally, the activity is destroyed.**
The onStop() method will usually get called before onDestroy(), but it may get bypassed if the device is extremely low on memory.

Watch it!

If your device is extremely low on memory, onStop() might not get called before the activity is destroyed.

We need to implement two more lifecycle methods

There are two things we need to do to update our Stopwatch app. First, we need to implement the activity's `onStop()` method so that the stopwatch stops running when the app isn't visible. Once we've done that, we need to implement the `onStart()` method so that the stopwatch starts again when the app is visible. Let's start with the `onStop()` method.

Implement onStop() to stop the timer

You override the `onStop()` method in the Android `Activity` class by adding the following method to your activity:

```
@Override
protected void onStop() {
        super.onStop();
}
```

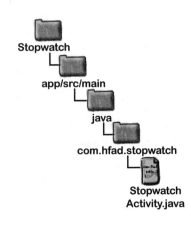

Stopwatch

app/src/main

java

com.hfad.stopwatch

Stopwatch
Activity.java

Whenever you override one of the Android lifecycle methods, it's important that you first call up the `onStop()` method in the superclass using:

```
super.onStop();
```

There are a couple of reasons for this. First, you need to make sure that the activity gets to perform all of the actions in the superclass lifecycle method. Second, Android will never forgive you if you bypass this step—it will generate an exception.

We need to get the stopwatch to stop when the `onStop()` method is called. To do this, we need to set the value of the `running` boolean to false. Here's the complete method:

```
@Override
protected void onStop() {
    super.onStop();
    running = false;
}
```

When you override an activity lifecycle method, you need to call the superclass method. If you don't, you'll get an exception.

So now the stopwatch stops when the activity is no longer visible. The next thing we need to do is get the stopwatch to start again when the activity becomes visible.

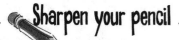

Sharpen your pencil

Now it's your turn. Change the activity code so that if the stopwatch was running before **onStop()** was called, it starts running again when the activity regains the focus.

```java
public class StopwatchActivity extends Activity {
    private int seconds = 0;
    private boolean running;

    @Override
    protected void onCreate(Bundle savedInstanceState) {
        super.onCreate(savedInstanceState);
        setContentView(R.layout.activity_stopwatch);
        if (savedInstanceState != null) {
            seconds = savedInstanceState.getInt("seconds");
            running = savedInstanceState.getBoolean("running");
        }
        runTimer();
    }

    @Override
    public void onSaveInstanceState(Bundle savedInstanceState) {
        savedInstanceState.putInt("seconds", seconds);
        savedInstanceState.putBoolean("running", running);
        savedInstanceState.putBoolean("wasRunning", wasRunning);
    }

    @Override
    protected void onStop() {
        super.onStop();
        running = false;
    }
```

Here's the first part of the activity code. You'll need to implement the onStart() method and change other methods slightly too.

Sharpen your pencil
Solution

Now it's your turn. Change the activity code so that if the stopwatch was running before **onStop()** was called, it starts running again when the activity regains the focus.

```java
public class StopwatchActivity extends Activity {
    private int seconds = 0;
    private boolean running;
    private boolean wasRunning;
```

We added a new variable, wasRunning, to record whether the stopwatch was running before the onStop() method was called so that we know whether to set it running again when the activity becomes visible again.

```java
    @Override
    protected void onCreate(Bundle savedInstanceState) {
        super.onCreate(savedInstanceState);
        setContentView(R.layout.activity_stopwatch);
        if (savedInstanceState != null) {
            seconds = savedInstanceState.getInt("seconds");
            running = savedInstanceState.getBoolean("running");
            wasRunning = savedInstanceState.getBoolean("wasRunning");
        }
        runTimer();
    }
```

We'll restore the state of the wasRunning variable if the activity is re-created.

```java
    @Override
    public void onSaveInstanceState(Bundle savedInstanceState) {
        savedInstanceState.putInt("seconds", seconds);
        savedInstanceState.putBoolean("running", running);
        savedInstanceState.putBoolean("wasRunning", wasRunning);
    }
```

Save the state of the wasRunning variable.

```java
    @Override
    protected void onStop() {
        super.onStop();
        wasRunning = running;
        running = false;
    }
```

Record whether the stopwatch was running when the onStop() method was called.

```java
    @Override
    protected void onStart() {
        super.onStart();
        if (wasRunning) {
            running = true;
        }
    }
}
```

Implement the onStart() method. If the stopwatch was running, set it running again.

The updated StopwathActivity code

We updated our activity code so that if the stopwatch was running before it lost the focus, it starts running again when it gets the focus back. Make the changes to your code:

```java
public class StopwatchActivity extends Activity {
    private int seconds = 0;
    private boolean running;
    private boolean wasRunning;

    @Override
    protected void onCreate(Bundle savedInstanceState) {
        super.onCreate(savedInstanceState);
        setContentView(R.layout.activity_stopwatch);
        if (savedInstanceState != null) {
            seconds = savedInstanceState.getInt("seconds");
            running = savedInstanceState.getBoolean("running");
            wasRunning = savedInstanceState.getBoolean("wasRunning");
        }
        runTimer();
    }

    @Override
    public void onSaveInstanceState(Bundle savedInstanceState) {
        savedInstanceState.putInt("seconds", seconds);
        savedInstanceState.putBoolean("running", running);
        savedInstanceState.putBoolean("wasRunning", wasRunning);
    }

    @Override
    protected void onStop() {
        super.onStop();
        wasRunning = running;
        running = false;
    }

    @Override
    protected void onStart() {
        super.onStart();
        if (wasRunning) {
            running = true;
        }
    }
    ...
```

A new variable, wasRunning, records whether the stopwatch was running before the onStop() method was called so that we know whether to set it running again when the activity becomes visible again.

Restore the state of the wasRunning variable if the activity is re-created.

Save the state of the wasRunning variable.

Record whether the stopwatch was running when the onStop() method was called.

Implement the onStart() method. If the stopwatch was running, set it running again.

Stopwatch

app/src/main

java

com.hfad.stopwatch

Stopwatch Activity.java

What happens when you run the app

1 **The user starts the app, and clicks the Start button to set the stopwatch going.**
The runTimer() method starts incrementing the number of seconds displayed in the time_view text view.

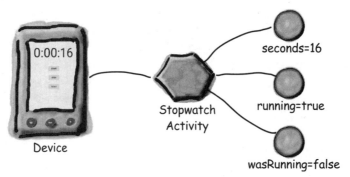

Device

Stopwatch
Activity

seconds=16

running=true

wasRunning=false

2 **The user navigates to the device home screen so the Stopwatch app is no longer visible.**
The onStop() method gets called, wasRunning is set to true, running is set to false, and the number of seconds stops incrementing.

The activity still exists even though it's not visible.

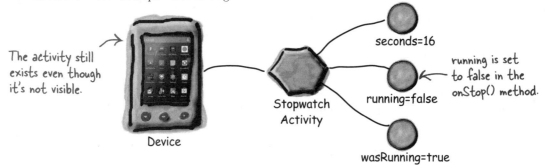

Device

Stopwatch
Activity

seconds=16

running=false

running is set to false in the onStop() method.

wasRunning=true

3 **The user navigates back to the Stopwatch app.**
The onStart() method gets called, running is set to true, and the number of seconds starts incrementing again.

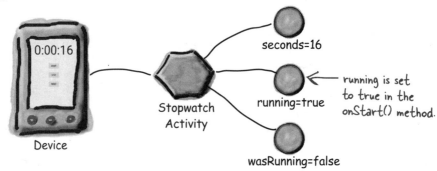

Device

Stopwatch
Activity

seconds=16

running=true

running is set to true in the onStart() method.

wasRunning=false

Test drive the app

Save the changes to your activity code, then run the app. When you click on the Start button the timer starts, it stops when the app is no longer visible, and it starts again when the app becomes visible again.

We set our stopwatch going, then switched to the device home screen.

The stopwatch had paused while the app wasn't visible.

The stopwatch started again when we went back to it.

---

there are no Dumb Questions

Q: Could we have used the onRestart() method instead?

A: onRestart() is used when you only want code to run when an app becomes visible after having previously been invisible. It doesn't run when the activity becomes visible for the first time. In our case, we wanted the app to still work when we rotated the device.

Q: Why should that make a difference?

A: When you rotate the device, the activity is destroyed and a new one is created in its place. If we'd put code in the onRestart() method instead, it wouldn't have run when the activity was re-created. The onStart() method gets called in both situations.

But what if an app is only partially visible?

So far you've seen what happens when an activity gets created and destroyed, and you've also seen what happens when an activity becomes visible, and when it becomes invisible. But there's one more situation we need to consider: when an activity's visible but doesn't have the focus.

When an activity is visible but doesn't have the focus, the activity is paused. This can happen if another activity appears on top of your activity that isn't full-size or that's transparent. The activity on top has the focus, but the one underneath is still visible and is therefore paused.

The stopwatch activity is still visible, but it's partially obscured and no longer has the focus.

This is an activity from another app that's appeared on top of the stopwatch.

An activity has a state of paused if it's lost the focus but is still visible to the user. The activity is still alive and maintains all its state information.

There are two lifecycle methods that deal with when the activity is paused and when it becomes active again: `onPause()` and `onResume()`. `onPause()` gets called when your activity is visible but another activity has the focus. `onResume()` is called immediately before your activity is about to start interacting with the user. If you need your app to react in some way when your activity is paused, you need to implement these methods.

You'll see on the next page how these methods fit in with the rest of the lifecycle methods you've seen so far.

The activity lifecycle: the foreground lifetime

Let's build on the lifecycle diagram you saw earlier in the chapter, this time including the onResume() and onPause() methods (the new bits are in bold):

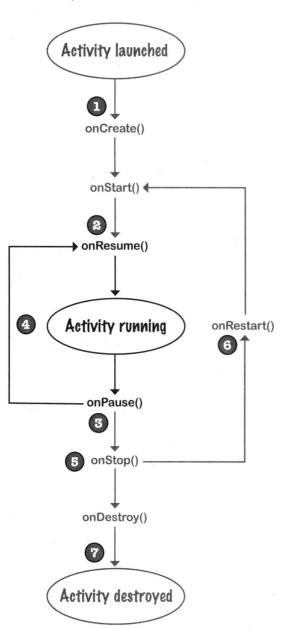

1 **The activity gets launched, and the onCreate() and onStart() methods run.**
At this point, the activity is visible, but it doesn't have the focus.

2 **The onResume() method runs after the onStart() method. It gets called when the activity is about to move into the foreground.**
After the onResume() method has run, the activity has the focus and the user can interact with it.

3 **The onPause() method runs when the activity stops being in the foreground.**
After the onPause() method has run, the activity is still visible but doesn't have the focus.

4 **If the activity moves into the foreground again, the onResume() method gets called.**
The activity may go through this cycle many times if the activity repeatedly loses and regains the focus.

5 **If the activity stops being visible to the user, the onStop() method gets called.**
After the onStop() method has run, the activity is no longer visible.

6 **If the activity becomes visible to the user again, the onRestart() method gets called, followed by onStart() and onResume().**
The activity may go through this cycle many times.

7 **Finally, the activity is destroyed.**
As the activity moves from running to destroyed, the onPause() method gets called before the activity is destroyed. The onStop() method usually gets called too.

Earlier on you talked about how the activity is destroyed and a new one is created when the user rotates the device. What happens if the activity is paused when the device is rotated? Does the activity go through the same lifecycle methods?

That's a great question, so let's look at this in more detail before getting back to the Stopwatch app.

The original activity goes through all its lifecycle methods, from `onCreate()` to `onDestroy()`. A new activity is created when the original is destroyed. As this new activity isn't in the foreground, only the `onCreate()` and `onStart()` lifecycle methods get called:

Original Activity

```
Activity launched
      |
  onCreate()
      |
❶ onStart()
      |
  onResume()
      |
Activity running
      |
❷ onPause()
      |
  onStop()
      |
  onDestroy()
      |
Activity destroyed
      ❸
```

Replacement Activity

```
Activity launched
      |
  onCreate()
      |
  onStart() ❹
```

❶ **The user launches the activity.**
The activity lifecycle methods `onCreate()`, `onStart()`, and `onResume()` get called.

❷ **Another activity appears in front of it.**
The activity `onPause()` method gets called.

❸ **The user rotates the device.**
Android sees this as a configuration change. The `onStop()` and `onDestroy()` methods get called, and Android destroys the activity. A new activity is created in its place.

❹ **The activity is visible but not in the foreground.**
The `onCreate()` and `onStart()` methods get called. As the activity is only visible and doesn't have the focus, `onResume()` isn't called.

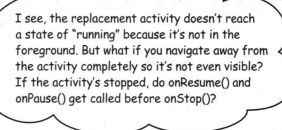

I see, the replacement activity doesn't reach a state of "running" because it's not in the foreground. But what if you navigate away from the activity completely so it's not even visible? If the activity's stopped, do onResume() and onPause() get called before onStop()?

Activities can go straight from onStart() to onStop() and bypass onPause() and onResume().

If you have an activity that's visible, but never in the foreground and never has the focus, the onPause() and onResume() methods *never get called*.

The onResume() method gets called when the activity appears in the foreground and has the focus. If the activity is only visible behind other activities, the onResume() method doesn't get called.

Similarly, the onPause() method gets called when the activity is no longer in the foreground. If the activity is never in the foreground, this method won't get called.

If an activity stops or gets detroyed before it appears in the foreground, the onStart() method is followed by the onStop() method. onResume() and onPause() are bypassed.

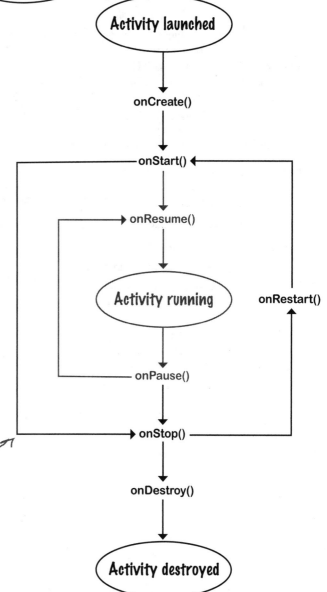

Stop the stopwatch if the activity's paused

Let's get back to the Stopwatch app.

So far we've made the stopwatch stop if the Stopwatch app isn't visible, and made it start again when the app becomes visible again. In addition to this, let's get the stopwatch to stop if the activity is paused, and start again when the activity is resumed. So which lifecycle methods do we need to implement?

The easy answer is that we need to use the onPause() and onResume() methods, but we can take this one step further. **We'll use these methods to replace the calls to onStop() and onStart() that we've already implemented**. If you look again at the lifecycle diagram, calls are made to onPause() and onResume() *in addition to* onStop() and onStart() whenever an activity is stopped and started. We'll use the same methods for both situations as we want the app to behave in the same way.

Here's our version of the onPause() method:

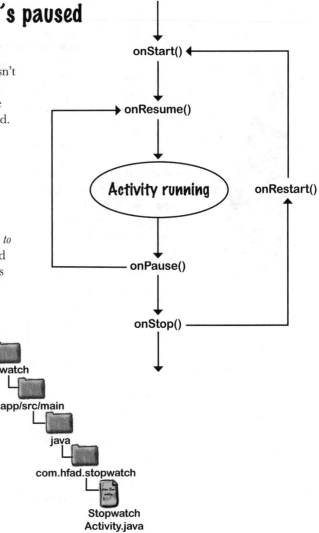

```java
@Override
protected void onPause() {
    super.onPause();
    wasRunning = running;
    running = false;
}
```

And here's the onResume() method:

```java
@Override
protected void onResume() {
    super.onResume();
    if (wasRunning) {
        running = true;
    }
}
```

So let's see what happens when we run the app.

Do this!

Replace the onStop() and onStart() methods in your code with the onPause() and onResume() methods shown here.

What happens when you run the app

1 **The user starts the app, and clicks on the start button to set the stopwatch going.**
The runTimer() method starts incrementing the number of seconds displayed in the time_view text view.

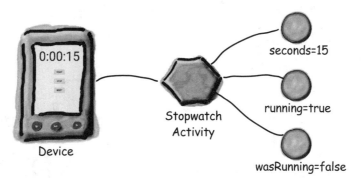

2 **Another activity appears in the foreground, leaving StopwatchActivity partially visible.**
The onPause() method gets called, wasRunning is set to true, running is set to false, and the number of seconds stops incrementing.

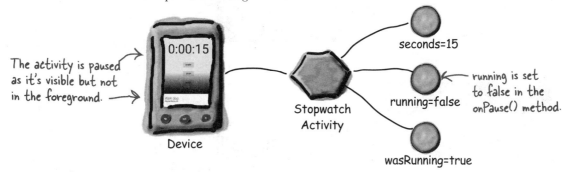

The activity is paused as it's visible but not in the foreground.

running is set to false in the onPause() method.

3 **When StopwatchActivity returns to the foreground, the onResume() method gets called, running is set to true, and the number of seconds starts incrementing again.**

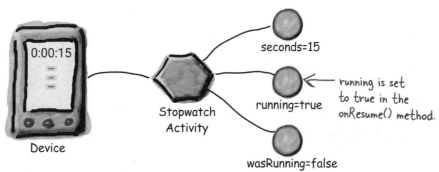

running is set to true in the onResume() method.

Test drive the app

Save the changes to your activity code, then run the app. When you click on the Start button, the timer starts; it stops when the app is partially obscured by another activity, and it starts again when the app is back in the foreground.

We started our stopwatch. It paused when the activity was partially obscured.

The stopwatch started again when the activity came back into the foreground.

---

there are no Dumb Questions

Q: As some of the lifecycle methods aren't always called, it sounds like this can lead to some flaky apps. Is that right?

A: In certain circumstances, Android may choose not to call methods like `onStop()` and `onPause()`. These methods usually contain code to clean up the app.

`onCreate()` and `onStart()` will *always* be called at the correct time, and this means that your app can also make sure it begins in the right shape. That's far more important.

The key thing is that you really get which lifecycle methods get called under what circumstances.

The complete activity code

Here's the full *StopwatchActivity.java* code for the finished app:

```
package com.hfad.stopwatch;

import android.os.Bundle;
import android.os.Handler;
import android.app.Activity;
import android.view.View;
import android.widget.TextView;

public class StopwatchActivity extends Activity {
    //Number of seconds displayed on the stopwatch.
    private int seconds = 0;
    //Is the stopwatch running?
    private boolean running;
    private boolean wasRunning;

    @Override
    protected void onCreate(Bundle savedInstanceState) {
        super.onCreate(savedInstanceState);
        setContentView(R.layout.activity_stopwatch);
        if (savedInstanceState != null) {
            seconds = savedInstanceState.getInt("seconds");
            running = savedInstanceState.getBoolean("running");
            wasRunning = savedInstanceState.getBoolean("wasRunning");
        }
        runTimer();
    }

    @Override
    protected void onPause() {
        super.onPause();
        wasRunning = running;
        running = false;
    }

    @Override
    protected void onResume() {
        super.onResume();
        if (wasRunning) {
            running = true;
        }
    }
}
```

Use seconds, running, and wasRunning to record the number of seconds passed, whether the stopwatch is running, and whether the stopwatch was running before the activity was paused.

Stopwatch
app/src/main
java
com.hfad.stopwatch
Stopwatch
Activity.java

Get the previous state of the stopwatch if the activity's been destroyed and re-created.

← If the activity's paused, stop the stopwatch.

← If the activity's resumed, start the stopwatch again if it was running previously.

The activity code continues over the page.

The activity code (continued)

Save the state of the stopwatch if it's about to be destroyed.

```java
@Override
public void onSaveInstanceState(Bundle savedInstanceState) {
    savedInstanceState.putInt("seconds", seconds);
    savedInstanceState.putBoolean("running", running);
    savedInstanceState.putBoolean("wasRunning", wasRunning);
}

//Start the stopwatch running when the Start button is clicked.
public void onClickStart(View view) {
    running = true;
}
```

This gets called when the Start button is clicked.

```java
//Stop the stopwatch running when the Stop button is clicked.
public void onClickStop(View view) {
    running = false;
}
```

This gets called when the Stop button is clicked.

```java
//Reset the stopwatch when the Reset button is clicked.
public void onClickReset(View view) {
    running = false;
    seconds = 0;
}
```

This gets called when the Reset button is clicked.

The runTimer() method uses a Handler to increment the seconds and update the text view.

```java
//Sets the number of seconds on the timer.
private void runTimer() {
    final TextView timeView = (TextView)findViewById(R.id.time_view);
    final Handler handler = new Handler();
    handler.post(new Runnable() {
        @Override
        public void run() {
            int hours = seconds/3600;
            int minutes = (seconds%3600)/60;
            int secs = seconds%60;
            String time = String.format("%d:%02d:%02d",
                    hours, minutes, secs);
            timeView.setText(time);
            if (running) {
                seconds++;
            }
            handler.postDelayed(this, 1000);
        }
    });
}
```

Stopwatch

app/src/main

java

com.hfad.stopwatch

Stopwatch
Activity.java

BE the Activity

On the right, you'll see some activity code. Your job is to play like you're the activity and say which code will run in each of the situations below. We've labeled the code we want you to consider. We've done the first one to start you off.

User starts the activity and starts using it.

Code segments A, G, D. The activity is created, then it's made visible, then it receives the focus.

User starts the activity, starts using it, then switches to another app.

↙ This one's tough.

User starts the activity, starts using it, rotates the device, switches to another app, then goes back to the activity.

```
...
class MyActivity extends Activity{

    protected void onCreate(
            Bundle savedInstanceState) {
    (A) //Run code A
        ...
    }

    protected void onPause() {
    (B) //Run code B
        ...
    }

    protected void onRestart() {
    (C) //Run code C
        ...
    }

    protected void onResume() {
    (D) //Run code D
        ...
    }

    protected void onStop() {
    (E) //Run code E
        ...
    }

    protected void onRecreate() {
    (F) //Run code F
        ...
    }

    protected void onStart() {
    (G) //Run code G
        ...
    }

    protected void onDestroy() {
    (H) //Run code H
        ...
    }
}
```

BE the Activity Solution

On the right, you'll see some activity code. Your job is to play like you're the activity and say which code will run in each of the situations below. We've labeled the code we want you to consider. We've done the first one to start you off.

User starts the activity and starts using it.

Code segments A, G, D. The activity is created, then it's made visible, then it receives the focus.

User starts the activity, starts using it, then switches to another app.

Code segments A, G, D, B, E. The activity is created, then it's made visible and receives the focus. When the user switches to another app, it loses the focus and is no longer visible to the user

User starts the activity, starts using it, rotates the device, switches to another app, then goes back to the activity.

Code segments A, G, D, B, E, H, A, G, D, B, E, C, G, D. First, the activity is created, made visible, and receives the focus. When the device is rotated, the activity loses the focus, stops being visible, and is destroyed. It's then created again, made visible, and receives the focus. When the user switches to another app and back again, the activity loses the focus, loses visibility, becomes visible again, and regains the focus.

```java
...
class MyActivity extends Activity{

    protected void onCreate(
            Bundle savedInstanceState) {
      A  //Run code A
         ...
    }

    protected void onPause() {
      B  //Run code B
         ...
    }

    protected void onRestart() {
      C  //Run code C
         ...
    }

    protected void onResume() {
      D  //Run code D
         ...
    }

    protected void onStop() {
      E  //Run code E
         ...
    }

    protected void onRecreate() {
      F  //Run code F
         ...
    }

    protected void onStart() {
      G  //Run code G
         ...
    }

    protected void onDestroy() {
      H  //Run code H
         ...
    }
}
```

There's no lifecycle method called onRecreate().

Your handy guide to the lifecycle methods

Method	When it's called	Next method
onCreate()	When the activity is first created. Use it for normal static setup, such as creating views. It also gives you a `Bundle` giving the previously saved state of the activity.	`onStart()`
onRestart()	When your activity has been stopped just before it gets started again.	`onStart()`
onStart()	When your activity is becoming visible. It's followed by `onResume()` if the activity comes into the foreground, or `onStop()` if the activity is made invisible.	`onResume()` or `onStop()`
onResume()	When your activity is in the foreground.	`onPause()`
onPause()	When your activity is no longer in the foreground because another activity is resuming. The next activity isn't resumed until this method finishes, so any code in this method needs to be quick. It's followed by `onResume()` if the activity returns to the foreground, or `onStop()` if it becomes invisible.	`onResume()` or `onStop()`
onStop()	When the activity is no longer visible. This can be because another activity is covering it, or because the activity's being destroyed. It's followed by `onRestart()` if the activity becomes visible again, or `onDestroy()` if the activity is going to be destroyed.	`onRestart()` or `onDestroy()`
onDestroy()	When your activity is about to be destroyed or because the activity is finishing.	None

Your Android Toolbox

You've got Chapter 4 under your belt and now you've added the activity lifecycle to your toolbox.

You can download the full code for the chapter from https://tinyurl.com/HeadFirstAndroid.

BULLET POINTS

- Each app runs in its own process by default.

- Only the main thread can update the user interface.

- Use a `Handler` to schedule code, or post code to a different thread.

- A device configuration change results in the activity being destroyed and re-created.

- Your activity inherits the lifecycle methods from the Android `Activity` class. If you override any of these methods, you need to call up to the method in the superclass.

- `onSaveInstanceState(Bundle)` enables your activity to save its state before the activity gets destroyed. You can use the `Bundle` to restore state in `onCreate()`.

- You add values to a `Bundle` using `bundle.put*("name", value)`. You retrieve values from the bundle using `bundle.get*("name")`.

- `onCreate()` and `onDestroy()`, deal with the birth and death of the activity.

- `onRestart()`, `onStart()` and `onStop()` deal with the visibility of the activity.

- `onResume()` and `onPause()` deal with when the activity gains and loses the focus.

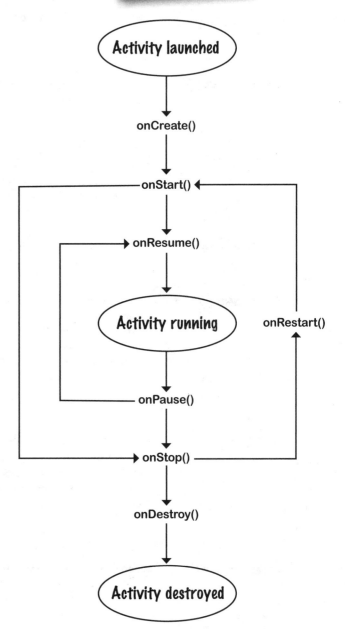

5 the user interface

Enjoy the View *

Now remember, it's layout_row="18", layout_column="56". Not "behind the white one".

Let's face it, you need to know how to create great layouts.

If you're building apps you want people to *use*, you need to make sure they **look just the way you want**. So far we've only scratched the surface when it comes to creating layouts, so it's time to **look a little deeper**. We'll introduce you to more **types of layout** you can use, and we'll also take you on a tour of the **main GUI components** and **how you use them**. By the end of the chapter, you'll see that even though they all look a little different, all layouts and GUI components have *more in common than you might think*.

Your user interface is made up of layouts and GUI components

As you already know, a layout defines what a screen looks like, and you define it using XML. Layouts usually contain GUI components such as buttons and text fields. Your user interacts with these to make your app do something.

All the apps you've seen in the book so far have used relative layouts, but there are other types of layout you can use as well to get your app to look exactly how you want.

In this chapter, we're going to introduce some of the other layouts you'll want to use in your apps, and also more of the GUI components you can use to make your app more interactive. Let's start with the layouts.

Three key layouts: relative, linear, and grid

Layouts come in several flavors, and each one has their own policy to follow when deciding where to position the views it contains. Here are three of the key ones. Don't worry about the details for now, over the next few pages we're going to take you through each one.

RelativeLayout

A **relative layout** displays its views in relative positions. You define the position of each view relative to other views in the layout, or relative to its parent layout. As an example, you can choose to position a text view relative to the top of the parent layout, a spinner underneath the text view, and a button relative to the bottom of the parent layout.

LinearLayout

A **linear layout** displays views next to each other either vertically or horizontally. If it's vertically, the views are displayed in a single column. If it's horizontally, the views are displayed in a single row.

GridLayout

A **grid layout** divides the screen into a grid of rows, columns, and cells. You specify how many columns your layout should have, where you want your views to appear, and how many rows or columns they should span.

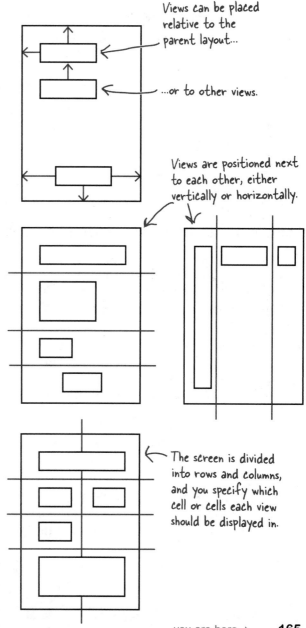

Views can be placed relative to the parent layout...

...or to other views.

Views are positioned next to each other, either vertically or horizontally.

The screen is divided into rows and columns, and you specify which cell or cells each view should be displayed in.

RelativeLayout
LinearLayout
GridLayout

RelativeLayout displays views in relative positions

As you already know, a relative layout allows you to position views relative to the parent layout, or relative to other views in the layout.

You define a relative layout using the `<RelativeLayout>` element like this:

This tells Android you're using a relative layout. →

```
<RelativeLayout xmlns:android="http://schemas.android.com/apk/res/android"
        android:layout_width="match_parent"
        android:layout_height="match_parent"
```

The layout_width and layout_height specify what size you want the layout to be.

```
   ...>   ← There may be other attributes too.
   ...
</RelativeLayout>
```

The `xmlns:android` attribute is used to specify the Android namespace, and you must always set it to `"http://schemas.android.com/apk/res/android"`.

You MUST set the layout width and height

The `android:layout_width` and `android:layout_height` attributes specify how wide and high you want the layout to be. **These attributes are mandatory for all types of layout and view**.

You can set `android:layout_width` and `android:layout_height` to `"match_parent"`, `"wrap_content"` or a specific size such as 10dp - 10 density-independent pixels. `"wrap_content"` means that you want the layout to be just big enough to hold all of the views inside it, and `"match_parent"` means that you want the layout to be as big as its parent—in this case, as big as the device screen minus any padding. You will usually set the layout width and height to `"match_parent"`.

You may sometimes see `android:layout_width` and `android:layout_height` set to `"fill_parent"`. `"fill_parent"` was used in older versions of Android, and it's now replaced by `"match_parent"`. `"fill_parent"` is deprecated.

Geek Bits

What are density-independent pixels?

Some devices create very sharp images by using very tiny pixels. Other devices are cheaper to produce because they have fewer, larger pixels. You use density-independent pixels (dp) to avoid creating interfaces that are overly small on some devices, and overly large on others. A measurement in density-independent pixels is roughly the same size across all devices.

Adding padding

If you want there to be a bit of space around the edge of the layout, you can set `padding` attributes. These attributes tell Android how much padding you want between each of the layout's sides and its parent. Here's how you would tell Android you want to add padding of 16dp around all edges of the layout:

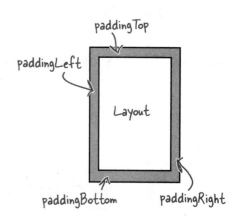

padding Top

paddingLeft

Layout

paddingBottom

paddingRight

```
<RelativeLayout ...
    android:paddingBottom="16dp"
    android:paddingLeft="16dp"
    android:paddingRight="16dp"
    android:paddingTop="16dp">
    ...
</RelativeLayout>
```

Add padding of 16dp.

The `android:padding*` attributes are optional, and you can use them with **any layout or view**.

In the above example, we've hardcoded the padding and set it to 16dp. An alternative approach is to specify the padding in a dimension resource file instead. Using a dimension resource file makes it easier to maintain the padding of all the layouts in your app.

You use a dimension resource file by setting the padding attributes in your layout file to the name of a dimension resource like this:

```
<RelativeLayout ...
    android:paddingLeft="@dimen/activity_horizontal_margin"
    android:paddingRight="@dimen/activity_horizontal_margin"
    android:paddingTop="@dimen/activity_vertical_margin"
    android:paddingBottom="@dimen/activity_vertical_margin">
```

The paddingLeft and paddingRight attributes are set to @dimen/activity_ horizontal_margin.

The paddingTop and paddingBottom attributes are set to @dimen/activity_ vertical_margin.

Android then looks up the values of the attributes at runtime in the dimension resource file. This file is located in the *app/src/main/res/ values* folder, and it's usually called *dimens.xml*:

```
<resources>
    <dimen name="activity_horizontal_margin">16dp</dimen>
    <dimen name="activity_vertical_margin">16dp</dimen>
</resources>
```

The layout looks up the padding values from these dimen resources.

When you create a new Android Studio project and add an activity to it, the IDE will usually create this for you.

Positioning views relative to the parent layout

RelativeLayout
LinearLayout
GridLayout

When you use a relative layout, you need to tell Android where you want its views to appear relative to other views in the layout, or to its parent. A view's parent is the layout that contains the view.

If you want a view to always appear in a particular position on the screen, irrespective of the screen size or orientation, you need to position the view relative to its *parent*. As an example, here's how you'd make sure a button always appears in the top-right corner of the layout:

```
<RelativeLayout ... >
    <Button
        android:layout_width="wrap_content"
        android:layout_height="wrap_content"
        android:text="@string/click_me"
        android:layout_alignParentTop="true"
        android:layout_alignParentRight="true" />
</RelativeLayout>
```

The layout contains the button, so the layout is the button's parent.

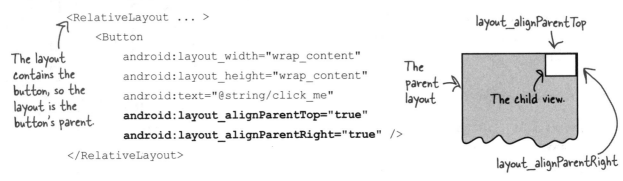

layout_alignParentTop

The parent layout

The child view.

layout_alignParentRight

The lines of code

```
android:layout_alignParentTop="true"
android:layout_alignParentRight="true"
```

mean that the top edge of the button is aligned to the top edge of the layout, and the right edge of the button is aligned to the right edge of the layout. This will be the case no matter what the screen size or orientation of your device:

The button appears in the top-right corner if the screen orientation is portrait or landscape, irrespective of screen size.

If your layout includes padding, there'll be a gap between the edges of the view and the edges of the screen.

Attributes for positioning views relative to the parent layout

Here are some of the most common attributes for positioning views relative to their parent layout. Add the attribute you want to the view you're positioning, then set its value to `"true"`:

```
android:attribute="true"
```

Attribute	What it does
android:layout_alignParentBottom	Aligns the bottom edge of the view to the bottom edge of the parent.
android:layout_alignParentLeft	Aligns the left edge of the view to the left edge of the parent.
android:layout_alignParentRight	Aligns the right edge of the view to the right edge of the parent.
android:layout_alignParentTop	Aligns the top edge of the view to the top edge of the parent.
android:layout_centerInParent	Centers the view horizontally and vertically in the parent.
android:layout_centerHorizontal	Centers the view horizontally in the parent.
android:layout_centerVertical	Centers the view vertically in the parent.

The view is aligned to the parent's left and bottom edges.

The view is aligned to the parent's right and top edges.

Positioning views relative to other views

RelativeLayout
LinearLayout
GridLayout

In addition to positioning views relative to the parent layout, you can also position views *relative to other views*. You do this when you want views to stay aligned in some way, irrespective of the screen size or orientation.

In order to position a view relative to another view, the view you're using as an anchor must be given an ID using the `android:id` attribute:

android:id="@+id/button_click_me"

The syntax `"@+id"` tells Android to include the ID as a resource in its resource file *R.java*. If you miss out the `"+"`, Android won't add the ID as a resource and you'll get errors in your code.

Here's how you create a layout with two buttons, with one button centered in the middle of the layout, and the second button positioned underneath the first:

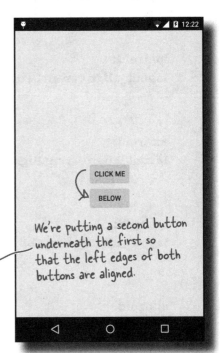

```
<RelativeLayout ... >
    <Button
        android:id="@+id/button_click_me"
        android:layout_width="wrap_content"
        android:layout_height="wrap_content"
        android:layout_centerInParent="true"
        android:text="@string/click_me" />

    <Button
        android:layout_width="wrap_content"
        android:layout_height="wrap_content"
        android:layout_alignLeft="@+id/button_click_me"
        android:layout_below="@+id/button_click_me"
        android:text="@string/new_button_text" />
</RelativeLayout>
```

We're using this button as an anchor for the second one, so it needs an ID.

We're putting a second button underneath the first so that the left edges of both buttons are aligned.

The lines

```
android:layout_alignLeft="@+id/button_click_me"
android:layout_below="@+id/button_click_me"
```

ensure that the second button has its left edge aligned to the left edge of the first button, and is always positioned beneath it.

Attributes for positioning views relative to other views

Here are some more of the attributes you can use when positioning views relative to another view. Add the attribute to the view you're positioning, and sets its value to the view you're positioning relative to:

```
android:attribute="@+id/view_id"
```

Attribute	What it does
android:layout_above	Put the view above the view you're anchoring it to.
android:layout_below	Puts the view below the view you're anchoring it to.
android:layout_alignTop	Aligns the top edge of the view to the top edge of the view you're anchoring it to.
android:layout_alignBottom	Aligns the bottom edge of the view to the bottom edge of the view you're anchoring it to.
android:layout_alignLeft	Aligns the left edge of the view to the left edge of the view you're anchoring it to.
android:layout_alignRight	Aligns the right edge of the view to the right edge of the view you're anchoring it to.
android:layout_toLeftOf	Puts the right edge of the view to the left of the view you're anchoring it to.
android:layout_toRightOf	Puts the left edge of the view to the right of the view you're anchoring it to.

Your view goes above

CLICK ME

The view you're anchoring it to

Your view goes below

CLICK ME

CLICK ME

Align the view's top edges

Align the view's bottom edges

CLICK ME

Align the view's left edges

CLICK ME

Align the view's right edges

CLICK ME

CLICK ME

Your view goes to the left

CLICK ME

Your view goes to the right

Use margins to add distance between views

When you use any of the layout attributes to position a view, the layout doesn't leave much of a gap. You can increase the size of the gap between views by adding one or more **margins** to the view.

As an example, suppose you wanted to put one view below another, but add 50dp of extra space between the two. To do that, you'd add a margin of 50dp to the top of the bottom view:

```
<RelativeLayout ... >
    <Button
        android:id="@+id/button_click_me"
        ... />

    <Button
        android:layout_width="wrap_content"
        android:layout_height="wrap_content"
        android:layout_alignLeft="@+id/button_click_me"
        android:layout_below="@+id/button_click_me"
        android:layout_marginTop="50dp"
        android:text="@string/button_below" />
</RelativeLayout>
```

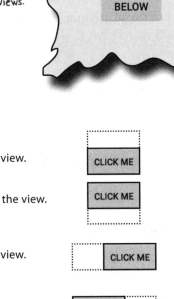

Adding a margin to the top of the bottom button adds extra space between the two views.

Here's a list of the margins you can use to give your views extra space. Add the attribute to the view, and set its value to the size of margin you want:

```
android:attribute="10dp"
```

Attribute	What it does	
android:layout_marginTop	Adds extra space to the top of the view.	CLICK ME
android:layout_marginBottom	Adds extra space to the bottom of the view.	CLICK ME
android:layout_marginLeft	Adds extra space to the left of the view.	CLICK ME
android:layout_marginRight	Adds extra space to the right of the view.	CLICK ME

RelativeLayout: a summary

Before we move on to our next type of layout, here's a summary of
how you create relative layouts.

How you specify a relative layout

You specify a relative layout using `<RelativeLayout>`. You must
specify the layout width and height, but padding is optional:

```
<RelativeLayout xmlns:android="http://schemas.android.com/apk/res/android"
    android:layout_width="match_parent"
    android:layout_height="match_parent"
    android:paddingBottom="16dp"
    android:paddingLeft="16dp"
    android:paddingRight="16dp"
    android:paddingTop="16dp"...>
    ...
</RelativeLayout>
```

You can position views relative to the layout of another view

You specify where each view should be positioned by adding layout
attributes to it. These attributes can position the view relative to the
parent layout—for example, in the bottom right corner, or centered.
You can also use attributes to position views relative to another view.
You anchor one view to another using the view's ID.

You can add margins to views to increase the space around them

When you use any of the layout attributes to position a view, the layout
doesn't leave much of a gap. You can increase the size of the gap
between views by adding one or more margins to the view:

```
android:layout_marginTop="5dp"
android:layout_marginBottom="5dp"
android:layout_marginLeft="5dp"
android:layout_marginRight="5dp"
```

So far we've just been working with the relative layout, but there's
another layout that's commonly used too: the **linear layout**. Let's
take a closer look.

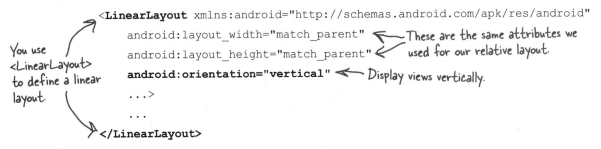

RelativeLayout
LinearLayout
GridLayout

LinearLayout displays views in a single row or column

A linear layout displays its views next to each other, either vertically or horizontally. If it's vertically, the views are displayed in a single column. If it's horizontally, the views are displayed in a single row.

How you define a linear layout

You define a linear layout using the `<LinearLayout>` element like this:

```
<LinearLayout xmlns:android="http://schemas.android.com/apk/res/android"
    android:layout_width="match_parent"
    android:layout_height="match_parent"
    android:orientation="vertical"
    ...>
    ...
</LinearLayout>
```

You use `<LinearLayout>` to define a linear layout.

These are the same attributes we used for our relative layout.

Display views vertically.

The `android:layout_width`, `android:layout_height` and `android:orientation` attributes are mandatory. `android:layout_width` and `android:layout_height` specify the layout width and height, just as it does with the relative layout. You use the `android:orientation` attribute to specify which direction you want to arrange views in.

You arrange views vertically using:

android:orientation="vertical"

You arrange views horizontally using:

android:orientation="horizontal"

A linear layout with a vertical orientation.

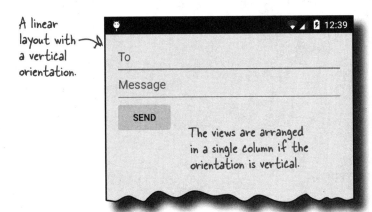

The views are arranged in a single column if the orientation is vertical.

A linear layout with a horizontal orientation.

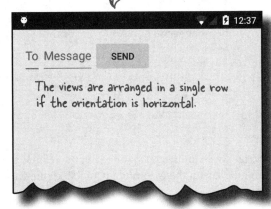

The views are arranged in a single row if the orientation is horizontal.

A linear layout displays views in the order they appear in the layout XML

When you define a linear layout, you add views to the layout in the order in which you want them to appear. So if you want a text view to appear above a button, you *must* define the text view first:

```
<LinearLayout ... >
    <TextView
        android:layout_width="wrap_content"
        android:layout_height="wrap_content"
        android:text="@string/textView1" />

    <Button
        android:layout_width="wrap_content"
        android:layout_height="wrap_content"
        android:text="@string/click_me" />
</LinearLayout>
```

If you define the text view above the button in the XML, the text view will appear above the button when displayed.

With a linear layout, you only need to give your views IDs if you're explicitly going to refer to them in your activity code. This is because the linear layout figures out where each view should be positioned based on the order in which they appear in the XML. Views don't need to refer to other views in order to specify where they should be positioned.

Just as with the relative layout, you can specify the width and height of any views using android:layout_width and android:layout_height. The code:

```
android:layout_width="wrap_content"
```

means that you want the view to be just wide enough for its content to fit inside it—for example, the text displayed on a button or in a text view. The code:

```
android:layout_width="match_parent"
```

means that you want the view to be as wide as the parent layout.

android:layout_width and android:layout_height are mandatory attributes for all views, no matter which layout you use.

They can take the values wrap_content, match_parent, or a specific dimension value such as 16dp.

Let's change up a basic linear layout

RelativeLayout
LinearLayout
GridLayout

At first glance, a linear layout can seem basic and inflexible. After all, all it does is arrange views in a particular order. To give you more flexibility, you can tweak your layouts appearance using some more of its attributes. To show you how this works, we're going to transform a basic linear layout.

The layout is composed of two editable text fields and a button. To start with, these text fields are simply displayed vertically on the screen like this:

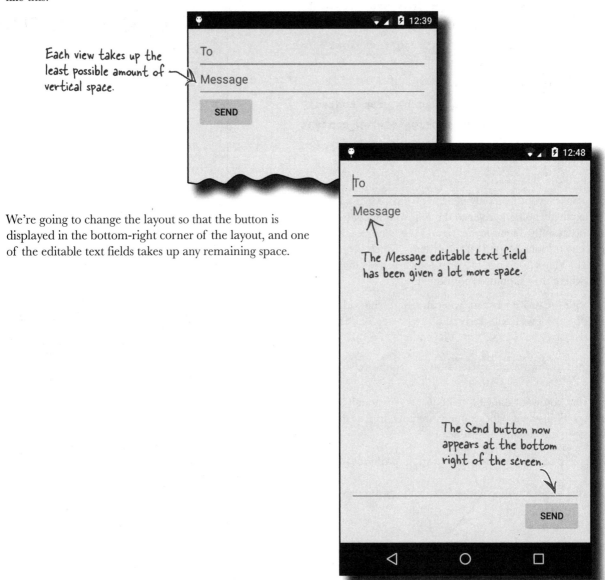

Each view takes up the least possible amount of vertical space.

The Message editable text field has been given a lot more space.

The Send button now appears at the bottom right of the screen.

We're going to change the layout so that the button is displayed in the bottom-right corner of the layout, and one of the editable text fields takes up any remaining space.

Here's the starting point for the linear layout

The linear layout contains two editable text fields and a button. The button is labeled "Send", and the editable text fields contain hint text values of "To" and "Message".

Hint text in an editable text field is text that's displayed when the text field is empty. It's used to give users a hint as to what sort of text they should enter. You define hint text using the `android:hint` attribute:

```
<LinearLayout xmlns:android="http://schemas.android.com/apk/res/android"
    xmlns:tools="http://schemas.android.com/tools"
    android:layout_width="match_parent"
    android:layout_height="match_parent"
    android:paddingBottom="16dp"
    android:paddingLeft="16dp"
    android:paddingRight="16dp"
    android:paddingTop="16dp"
    android:orientation="vertical"
    tools:context=".MainActivity" >

    <EditText
        android:layout_width="match_parent"
        android:layout_height="wrap_content"
        android:hint="@string/to" />

    <EditText
        android:layout_width="match_parent"
        android:layout_height="wrap_content"
        android:hint="@string/message" />

    <Button
        android:layout_width="wrap_content"
        android:layout_height="wrap_content"
        android:text="@string/send" />
</LinearLayout>
```

The editable text fields are as wide as the parent layout.

android:hint displays a hint to the user as to what they should type in the editable text field.

The values of these strings are defined in Strings.xml as usual.

All of these views take up just as much vertical space in the layout as they need for their contents. So how do we make the Message text field taller?

Make a view streeeeetch by adding weight

RelativeLayout
LinearLayout
GridLayout

All of the views in our basic layout take up just as much vertical space as they need for their content. What we actually want is to make the Message text field stretch to take up any vertical space in the layout that's not being used by the other views.

We want to make the Message text field stretch vertically so that it fills any spare space in the layout.

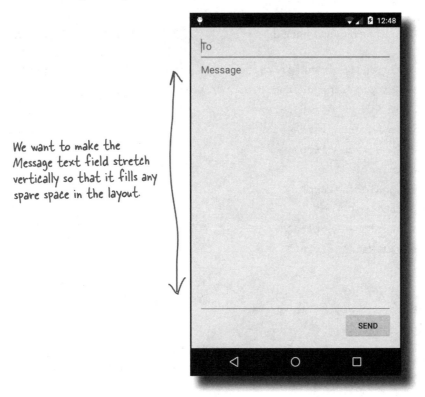

In order to do this, we need to allocate some **weight** to the Message text field. Allocating weight to a view is a way of telling it to stretch to take up extra space in the layout.

You assign weight to a view using

```
android:layout_weight="number"
```

where `number` is some number greater than 0.

When you allocate weight to a view, the layout first of all makes sure that each view has enough space for its content. It makes sure that each button has space for its text, each editable text field has space for its hint, and so on. Once it's done that, the layout takes any extra space, and divides it proportionally between the views with a weight of 1 or greater.

Adding weight to one view

We need the Message editable text field to take up any extra space in the layout. To do this, we'll set its `layout_weight` attribute to 1. As this is the only view in the layout with a weight value, this will make the text field stretch vertically to fill the remainder of the screen. Here's the code:

```
<LinearLayout ... >
    <EditText
        android:layout_width="match_parent"
        android:layout_height="wrap_content"
        android:hint="@string/to" />

    <EditText
        android:layout_width="match_parent"
        android:layout_height="0dp"
        android:layout_weight="1"
        android:hint="@string/message" />

    <Button
        android:layout_width="wrap_content"
        android:layout_height="wrap_content"
        android:text="@string/send" />
</LinearLayout>
```

This <EditText> and the <Button> have no layout_weight attribute set. They'll take up as much room as their content needs, but no more.

This view is the only one with any weight. It will expand to fill the space that's not needed by any of the other views.

The height of the view will be determined by the linear layout based on the layout_weight. Setting the layout_height to 0dp is more efficient than setting it to "wrap_content".

Giving the message editable text field a weight of 1 means that it takes up all of the extra space that's not used by the other views in the layout. This is because neither of the other two views have been allocated any weight in the layout XML.

The Message view has a weight of 1. As it's the only view with its weight attribute set, it expands to take up any extra vertical space in the layout.

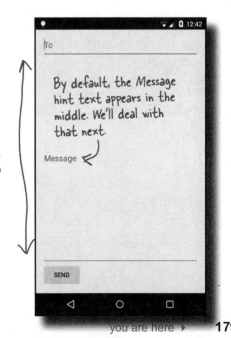

By default, the Message hint text appears in the middle. We'll deal with that next.

RelativeLayout
LinearLayout
GridLayout

Adding weight to multiple views

In this example, we only had one view with a weight attribute set. But what if we had *more* than one?

Suppose we gave the To text field a weight of 1, and the Message text field a weight of 2 like this:

```
<LinearLayout ... >
    ...
    <EditText
        android:layout_width="match_parent"
        android:layout_height="0dp"
        android:layout_weight="1"
        android:hint="@string/to" />

    <EditText
        android:layout_width="match_parent"
        android:layout_height="0dp"
        android:layout_weight="2"
        android:hint="@string/message" />
    ...
</LinearLayout>
```

To figure out how much extra space each view takes up, start by adding together the `layout_weight` attributes for each view. In our case, this is 1+2=3. The amount of extra space taken up by each view will be the view's weight divided by the total weight. The To view has a weight of 1, so this means it will take up 1/3 of the remaining space in the layout. The Message view has a weight of 2, so it will take up 2/3 of the remaining space.

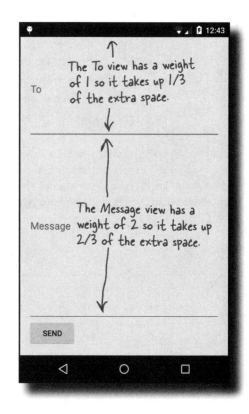

The To view has a weight of 1 so it takes up 1/3 of the extra space.

The Message view has a weight of 2 so it takes up 2/3 of the extra space.

Use gravity to specify where text appears in a view

The next thing we need to do is move the hint text inside the Message text field. At the moment, it's centered vertically inside the view. We need to change it so that the text appears at the top of the text field. We can achieve this using the `android:gravity` attribute.

The `android:gravity` attribute lets you specify how you want to position the contents of a view inside the view—for example, how you want to position text inside a text field. If you want the text inside a view to appear at the top, the following code will do the trick:

android:gravity="top"

We'll add an `android:gravity` attribute to the Message text field so that the hint text moves to the top of the view:

```
<LinearLayout ... >
    ...
    <EditText
        android:layout_width="match_parent"
        android:layout_height="0dp"
        android:layout_weight="1"
        android:gravity="top"        ← Display the text inside the text field
        android:hint="@string/message" />        at the top of the text field.
    ...
</LinearLayout>
```

Test drive

Adding the `android:gravity` attribute to the Message text field moves the hint text to the top of the view, just like we want.

You'll find a list of the other values you can use with the `android:gravity` attribute on the next page.

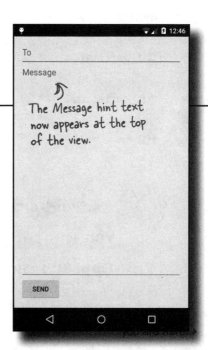

We need to move the Message hint text from the center of the view to the top.

The Message hint text now appears at the top of the view.

RelativeLayout
LinearLayout
GridLayout

Using the android:gravity attribute: a list of values

Here are some more of the values you can use with the `android:gravity` attribute. Add the attribute to your view, and set its value to one of the values below:

```
android:gravity="value"
```

Value	What it does
top	Puts the view's contents at the top of the view.
bottom	Puts the view's contents at the bottom of the view.
left	Puts the view's contents at the left of the view.
right	Puts the view's contents at the right of the view.
center_vertical	Centers the view's contents vertically.
center_horizontal	Centers the view's contents horizontally.
center	Centers the view's contents vertically and horizontally.
fill_vertical	Make the view's contents fill the view vertically.
fill_horizontal	Make the view's contents fill the view horizontally.
fill	Make the view's contents fill the view.

android:gravity lets you say where you want the view's contents to appear inside the view.

Move the button to the right with layout_gravity

There's one final change we need to make to our layout. The Send button currently appears in the bottom-left corner. We need to move it over to the right so that it's in the bottom-right corner instead. To do this, we'll use the `android:layout_gravity` attribute.

The `android:layout_gravity` attribute lets you specify where you want a view in a linear layout to appear in its enclosing space. You can use it to push a view to the right, for instance, or center the view horizontally. To move our button to the right, we'd need to add the following to the button:

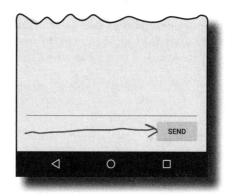

android:layout_gravity="right"

> But why do we need to use layout_gravity to move the button? Earlier on we saw the layout_alignRight attribute—surely that would do it?

The android:layout_alignRight attribute only applies to relative layouts.

Layouts have some attributes in common, such as `android:layout_width` and `android:layout_height`. Many attributes, however, are specific to one particular type of attribute.

Most of the attributes we saw for the relative layout don't apply to linear layouts. Linear layouts use the concept of gravity instead, so we have to use

```
android:layout_gravity="right"
```

if we want to move a view to the right.

You'll see a list of some of the other values you can use with the `android:layout_gravity` attribute on the next page.

RelativeLayout
LinearLayout
GridLayout

More values you can use with the android:layout_gravity attribute

Here are some of the values you can use with the
`android:layout_gravity` attribute. Add the attribute to
your view, and set its value to one of the values below:

```
android:layout_gravity="value"
```

Value	What it does
top, bottom, left, right	Puts the view at the top, bottom, left, or right of its container.
start, end	Puts the view at the start or end of its container.
center_vertical, center_horizontal	Centers the view vertically or horizontally in its container.
center	Centers the view vertically and horizontally in its container.
fill_vertical, fill_horizontal	Grow the view so that it fills its container in a vertical or horizontal direction.
fill	Grow the view so that it fills its container in a vertical and horizontal direction.

android:layout_gravity lets you say where you
want views to appear in their available space.

android:layout_gravity deals with the placement
of the view itself, whereas android:gravity deals
with how to display the view contents.

The full linear layout code

Here's the full code for the linear layout:

```
<LinearLayout xmlns:android="http://schemas.android.com/apk/res/android"
    xmlns:tools="http://schemas.android.com/tools"
    android:layout_width="match_parent"
    android:layout_height="match_parent"
    android:paddingBottom="16dp"
    android:paddingLeft="16dp"
    android:paddingRight="16dp"
    android:paddingTop="16dp"
    android:orientation="vertical"
    tools:context=".MainActivity" >

    <EditText
        android:layout_width="match_parent"
        android:layout_height="wrap_content"
        android:hint="@string/to" />

    <EditText
        android:layout_width="match_parent"
        android:layout_height="0dp"
        android:layout_weight="1"
        android:gravity="top"
        android:hint="@string/message" />

    <Button
        android:layout_width="wrap_content"
        android:layout_height="wrap_content"
        android:layout_gravity="right"
        android:text="@string/send" />

</LinearLayout>
```

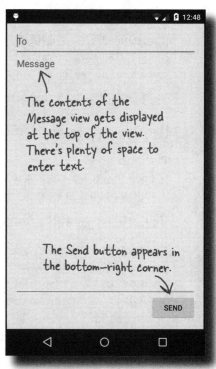

The contents of the Message view gets displayed at the top of the view. There's plenty of space to enter text.

The Send button appears in the bottom-right corner.

android:gravity is different to android:layout_gravity. android:gravity relates to the contents of the view, android:layout_gravity relates to the view itself.

RelativeLayout
LinearLayout
GridLayout

LinearLayout: a summary

Here's a summary of how you create linear layouts.

How you specify a linear layout

You specify a linear layout using `<LinearLayout>`. You must specify the layout width, height, and orientation, but padding is optional:

```
<LinearLayout xmlns:android="http://schemas.android.com/apk/res/android"
    android:layout_width="match_parent"
    android:layout_height="match_parent"
    android:orientation="vertical"
    ...>
    ...
</LinearLayout>
```

Views get displayed in the order they appear

When you define a linear layout, you add views to the layout in the order in which you want them to appear.

Stretch views using weight

By default, all views take up just as much space as necessary for their content. If you want to make one or more of your views take up more space, you can use the `weight` attribute to make it stretch:

```
android:layout_weight="1"
```

Use gravity to specify where a view's contents appear in a view

The `android:gravity` attribute lets you specify how you want to position the contents of a view inside the view—for example, how you want to position text inside a text field.

Use layout_gravity to specify where a view appears in its enclosing space

The `android:layout_gravity` attribute lets you specify where you want a view in a linear layout to appear in its enclosing space. You can use it to push a view to the right, for instance, or center the view horizontally.

That's everything we've covered on linear layouts. There's one more view group we're going to look at: the **grid layout**.

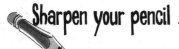

Sharpen your pencil

Here's the layout XML for the Beer Adviser app we created in Chapter 2. Change it to a linear layout that produces the output below.

```xml
<RelativeLayout xmlns:android="http://schemas.android.com/apk/res/android"
    xmlns:tools="http://schemas.android.com/tools"
    android:layout_width="match_parent"
    android:layout_height="match_parent"
    android:paddingBottom="16dp"
    android:paddingLeft="16dp"
    android:paddingRight="16dp"
    android:paddingTop="16dp"
    tools:context=".FindBeerActivity" >

    <Spinner
        android:id="@+id/color"
        android:layout_width="wrap_content"
        android:layout_height="wrap_content"
        android:layout_alignParentTop="true"
        android:layout_centerHorizontal="true"
        android:layout_marginTop="37dp"
        android:entries="@array/beer_colors" />

    <Button
        android:id="@+id/find_beer"
        android:layout_width="wrap_content"
        android:layout_height="wrap_content"
        android:layout_alignLeft="@+id/color"
        android:layout_below="@+id/color"
        android:text="@string/find_beer"
        android:onClick="onClickFindBeer" />

    <TextView
        android:id="@+id/brands"
        android:layout_width="wrap_content"
        android:layout_height="wrap_content"
        android:layout_alignLeft="@+id/find_beer"
        android:layout_below="@+id/find_beer"
        android:layout_marginTop="18dp"
        android:text="@string/brands" />
</RelativeLayout>
```

It won't win any "most stylish layout" awards, but see if you can change the XML to produce this.

⬇ 🤖	▼◢ 🔋 10:42

light ▼ **FIND BEER!** Jail Pale Ale
Gout Stout

Sharpen your pencil
Solution

Here's the layout XML for the Beer Adviser app we created in Chapter 2. Change it to a linear layout that produces the output below.

Change it to a linear layout.

```
<RelativeLinearLayout xmlns:android="http://schemas.android.com/apk/res/android"
    xmlns:tools="http://schemas.android.com/tools"
    android:layout_width="match_parent"
    android:layout_height="match_parent"
    android:paddingBottom="16dp"
    android:paddingLeft=" 16dp"
    android:paddingRight="16dp"
    android:paddingTop="16dp"
    android:orientation="horizontal"
    tools:context=".FindBeerActivity" >
```

Linear layouts use an android:orientation attribute. Use "horizontal" to display views next to each other horizontally.

```
    <Spinner
        android:id="@+id/color"
        android:layout_width="wrap_content"
        android:layout_height="wrap_content"
        android:layout_alignParentTop="true"
        android:layout_centerHorizontal="true"
        android:layout_marginTop="37dp"
        android:entries="@array/beer_colors" />
```

We don't need these lines.

```
    <Button
        android:id="@+id/find_beer"
        android:layout_width="wrap_content"
        android:layout_height="wrap_content"
        android:layout_alignLeft="@+id/color"
        android:layout_below="@+id/color"
        android:text="@string/find_beer"
        android:onClick="onClickFindBeer" />
```

We don't need these lines.

```
    <TextView
        android:id="@+id/brands"
        android:layout_width="wrap_content"
        android:layout_height="wrap_content"
        android:layout_alignLeft="@+id/find_beer"
        android:layout_below="@+id/find_beer"
        android:layout_marginTop="18dp"
        android:text="@string/brands" />
```

We don't need these lines.

Change it to a linear layout.

```
</RelativeLinearLayout>
```

light ▼   **FIND BEER!**   Jail Pale Ale
Gout Stout

🔻◢ 🔋 10:42

GridLayout displays views in a grid

A grid layout splits the screen up into a grid of rows and columns, and allocates views to cells:

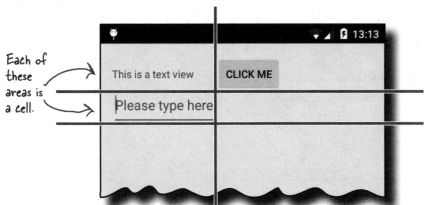

Each of these areas is a cell.

Watch it!

GridLayout requires API level 14 or above.

If you plan on using a grid layout, make sure your app uses a minimum SDK of API 14.

How you define a grid layout

You define a grid layout in a similar way to how you define the other types of layout, this time using the **<GridLayout>** element:

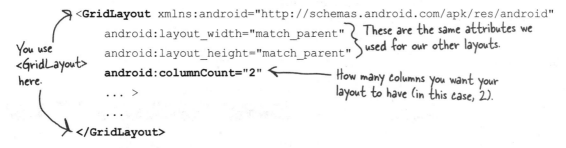

```
<GridLayout xmlns:android="http://schemas.android.com/apk/res/android"
        android:layout_width="match_parent"
        android:layout_height="match_parent"
        android:columnCount="2"
        ... >
        ...
</GridLayout>
```

You use <GridLayout> here.

These are the same attributes we used for our other layouts.

How many columns you want your layout to have (in this case, 2).

You specify how many columns you want the grid layout to have using:

android:columnCount="number"

where `number` is the number of columns. You can also specify a maximum number of rows using:

android:rowCount="number"

but in practice you can usually let Android figure this out based on the number of views in the layout. Android will include as many rows as is necessary to display the views.

RelativeLayout
LinearLayout
GridLayout

Adding views to the grid layout

You can add views to a grid layout in a similar way to how you add views to a linear layout:

```
<GridLayout ... >

    <TextView
        android:layout_width="wrap_content"
        android:layout_height="wrap_content"
        android:text="@string/textview" />

    <Button
        android:layout_width="wrap_content"
        android:layout_height="wrap_content"
        android:text="@string/click_me" />

    <EditText
        android:layout_width="wrap_content"
        android:layout_height="wrap_content"
        android:hint="@string/edit" />

</GridLayout>
```

Just like a linear layout, there's no need to give your views IDs unless you're explicitly going to refer to them in your activity code. The views don't need to refer to each other within the layout, so they don't need to have IDs for this purpose.

By default, the grid layout positions your views in the order in which they appear in the XML. So if you have a grid layout with two columns, the grid layout will put the first view in the first position, the second view in the second position, and so on.

The downside of this approach is that if you remove one of your views from the layout, it can drastically change the appearance of the layout. To get around this, you specify where you want each view to appear, and how many columns you want it to span.

Let's create a new grid layout

To see this in action, we'll create a grid layout that specifies which cells we want views to appear in, and how many columns they should span. The layout is composed of a text view containing the text "To", an editable text field that contains hint text of "Enter email address", an editable text field that contains hint text of "Message", and a button labeled "Send":

This is similar to the example we used with the linear layout, except that there's now a To text field at the top, and the Send button is centered horizontally at the bottom.

Here's what we're going to do

1 **Sketch the user interface, and split it into rows and columns.**
This will make it easier for us to see how we should construct our layout.

2 **Build up the layout row by row.**

RelativeLayout
LinearLayout
GridLayout

We'll start with a sketch

The first thing we'll do to create our new layout is sketch it out. That way
we can see how many rows and columns we need, where each view should
be positioned, and how many columns each view should span.

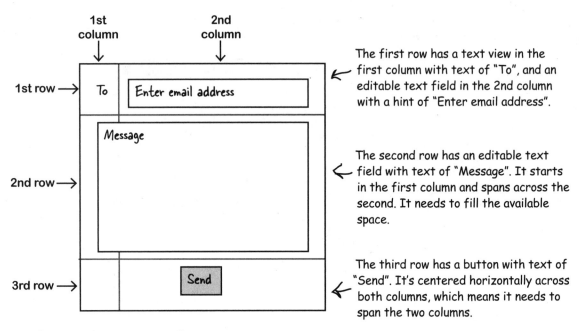

The first row has a text view in the
first column with text of "To", and an
editable text field in the 2nd column
with a hint of "Enter email address".

The second row has an editable text
field with text of "Message". It starts
in the first column and spans across the
second. It needs to fill the available
space.

The third row has a button with text of
"Send". It's centered horizontally across
both columns, which means it needs to
span the two columns.

The grid layout needs two columns

We can position our views how we want if we use a grid layout with two columns:

```
<GridLayout xmlns:android="http://schemas.android.com/apk/res/android"
    xmlns:tools="http://schemas.android.com/tools"
    android:layout_width="match_parent"
    android:layout_height="match_parent"
    android:paddingBottom="16dp"
    android:paddingLeft="16dp"
    android:paddingRight="16dp"
    android:paddingTop="16dp"
    android:columnCount="2"
    tools:context=".MainActivity" >
</GridLayout>
```

Now that we have the basic grid layout defined, we can start adding views.

Row 0: add views to specific rows and columns

The first row of the grid layout is composed of a text view in the first column, and an editable text field in the second column. You start by adding the views to the layout:

| To | Enter email address |

```
<GridLayout...>
    <TextView
        android:layout_width="wrap_content"
        android:layout_height="wrap_content"
        android:text="@string/to" />

    <EditText
        android:layout_width="wrap_content"
        android:layout_height="wrap_content"
        android:layout_gravity="fill_horizontal"
        android:hint="@string/to_hint" />
</GridLayout>
```

You can use android:gravity and android:layout_gravity attributes with grid layouts.

← *You can use layout_gravity in grid layouts too. We're using fill_horizontal because we want the editable text field to fill the remaining horizontal space.*

Then you use the `android:layout_row` and `android:layout_column` attributes to say which row and column you want each view to appear in. The row and column indices start from 0, so if you want a view to appear in the first column and first row, you use:

```
android:layout_row="0"
android:layout_column="0"
```

Columns and rows start at 0, so this refers to the first row and first column.

Row and column indices start at 0. layout_column="n" refers to column n+1 in the display.

Let's apply this to our layout code by putting the text view in column 0, and the editable text field in column 1.

```
<GridLayout...>
    <TextView
        ...
        android:layout_row="0"
        android:layout_column="0"
        android:text="@string/to" />

    <EditText
        ...
        android:layout_row="0"
        android:layout_column="1"
        android:hint="@string/to_hint" />
</GridLayout>
```

Column 0 ↓   Column 1 ↓

Row 0 →

| To | Enter email address |

RelativeLayout
LinearLayout
GridLayout

Row 1: make a view span multiple columns

The second row of the grid layout is composed of an editable text field that starts in the first column and spans across the second. The view takes up all the available space.

To get a view to span multiple columns, you start by specifying which row and column you want the view to start in. We want the view to start in the first column of the second row, so we need to use:

```
android:layout_row="1"
android:layout_column="0"
```

We want our view to go across two columns, and we can do this using the `android:layout_columnSpan` attribute like this:

```
android:layout_columnSpan="number"
```

where `number` is the number of columns we want the view to span across. In our case, this is:

```
android:layout_columnSpan="2"
```

Putting it all together, here's the code for the Message view:

```
<GridLayout...>
    <TextView... />
    <EditText.../>          These are the views we added on the last page for row 0.
    <EditText
        android:layout_width="wrap_content"
        android:layout_height="wrap_content"
        android:layout_gravity="fill"      We want the view to fill the available space,
        android:gravity="top"              and for the text to appear at the top.
        android:layout_row="1"
        android:layout_column="0"          The view starts in column 0, and spans 2
        android:layout_columnSpan="2"      columns.
        android:hint="@string/message" />
</GridLayout>
```

Now that we've added the views for the first two rows, all we need to do is add the button.

Column 0   Column 1

Row 1 → | Message

Column span = 2

Row 2: make a view span multiple columns

We need the button to be centered horizontally across the two columns like this:

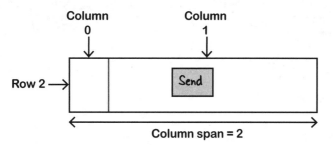

Column 0   Column 1

Row 2 →   Send

Column span = 2

Layout Magnets

We wrote some code to center the Send button in the third row of the grid layout, but a sudden breeze blew some of it away. See if you can reconstruct the code using the magnets below.

```
<GridLayout...>
    <TextView... />
    <EditText.../>
    <EditText.../>


    <Button
        android:layout_width="wrap_content"
        android:layout_height="wrap_content"

        android:layout_row=
                    ..............

        android:layout_column=
                    ..............

        android:layout_gravity=
                    ...................................

        android:layout_columnSpan=
                    ..............

        android:text="@string/send" />


</GridLayout>
```

These are the views we've already added.

fill_horizontal

"0"

"2"

"0"

"1"

"1"

"2"

center_horizontal

Answers on page 224

RelativeLayout
LinearLayout
GridLayout

The full code for the grid layout

```xml
<GridLayout xmlns:android="http://schemas.android.com/apk/res/android"
    xmlns:tools="http://schemas.android.com/tools"
    android:layout_width="match_parent"
    android:layout_height="match_parent"
    android:paddingBottom="16dp"
    android:paddingLeft="16dp"
    android:paddingRight="16dp"
    android:paddingTop="16dp"
    android:columnCount="2"
    tools:context=".MainActivity" >

    <TextView
        android:layout_width="wrap_content"
        android:layout_height="wrap_content"
        android:layout_row="0"
        android:layout_column="0"
        android:text="@string/to" />

    <EditText
        android:layout_width="wrap_content"
        android:layout_height="wrap_content"
        android:layout_gravity="fill_horizontal"
        android:layout_row="0"
        android:layout_column="1"
        android:hint="@string/to_hint" />

    <EditText
        android:layout_width="wrap_content"
        android:layout_height="wrap_content"
        android:layout_gravity="fill"
        android:gravity="top"
        android:layout_row="1"
        android:layout_column="0"
        android:layout_columnSpan="2"
        android:hint="@string/message" />

    <Button
        android:layout_width="wrap_content"
        android:layout_height="wrap_content"
        android:layout_row="2"
        android:layout_column="0"
        android:layout_gravity="center_horizontal"
        android:layout_columnSpan="2"
        android:text="@string/send" />
</GridLayout>
```

The button spans two columns, starting from row 2 column 1. It's centered horizontally.

GridLayout: a summary

Here's a summary of how you create grid layouts.

How you specify a grid layout

You specify a grid layout using `<GridLayout>`. You specify how many columns you need using the `android:columnCount` attribute. You say how many rows you need using the `android:rowCount` attribute:

```
<GridLayout xmlns:android="http://schemas.android.com/apk/res/android"
    android:layout_width="match_parent"
    android:layout_height="match_parent"
    android:columnCount="2"
    ... >
    ...
</GridLayout>
```

Specify which row and column each view should start in

You use the `android:layout_row` and `android:layout_column` attributes to say which row and column you want each view to appear in. The row and column indices start from 0, so if you want a view to appear in the first column and first row, you use:

```
android:layout_row="0"
android:layout_column="0"
```

Specify how many columns each view should span

You use the `android:layout_columnSpan` attribute to specify how many columns each view should span. If you want a view to span across two columns, for instance, you use:

```
android:layout_columnSpan="2"
```

BE the Layout

Three of the five screens below were
made from layouts on the opposite
page. Your job is to match each of
the three layouts to the
screen that the layout
would produce.

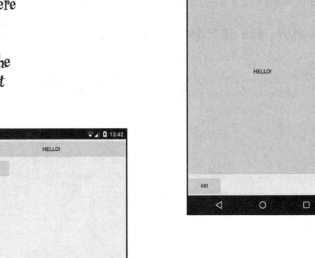

2
HELLO!
HI!

1
HELLO!

4
HELLO!
HI!

5
HELLO!
HI!

A

```xml
<GridLayout xmlns:android="http://schemas.android.com/apk/res/android"
    xmlns:tools="http://schemas.android.com/tools"
    android:layout_width="match_parent"
    android:layout_height="match_parent"
    android:columnCount="3"
    tools:context=".MainActivity" >
    <Button
        android:layout_width="wrap_content"
        android:layout_height="wrap_content"
        android:layout_gravity="fill"
        android:layout_columnSpan="3"
        android:text="@string/hello" />
</GridLayout>
```

B

```xml
<GridLayout xmlns:android="http://schemas.android.com/apk/res/android"
    xmlns:tools="http://schemas.android.com/tools"
    android:layout_width="match_parent"
    android:layout_height="match_parent"
    android:columnCount="2"
    tools:context=".MainActivity" >
    <Button
        android:layout_width="wrap_content"
        android:layout_height="wrap_content"
        android:layout_gravity="fill"
        android:layout_columnSpan="2"
        android:text="@string/hello" />
    <Button
        android:layout_width="wrap_content"
        android:layout_height="wrap_content"
        android:text="@string/hi" />
</GridLayout>
```

C

```xml
<GridLayout xmlns:android="http://schemas.android.com/apk/res/android"
    xmlns:tools="http://schemas.android.com/tools"
    android:layout_width="match_parent"
    android:layout_height="match_parent"
    android:columnCount="2"
    tools:context=".MainActivity" >
    <Button
        android:layout_width="wrap_content"
        android:layout_height="wrap_content"
        android:layout_row="0"
        android:layout_column="0"
        android:layout_columnSpan="2"
        android:text="@string/hello" />
    <Button
        android:layout_width="wrap_content"
        android:layout_height="wrap_content"
        android:layout_row="1"
        android:layout_column="0"
        android:text="@string/hi" />
</GridLayout>
```

BE the Layout Solution

Three of the five screens below were made from layouts on the opposite page. Your job is to match each of the three layouts to the screen that the layout would produce.

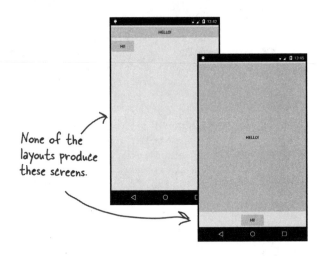

None of the layouts produce these screens.

1

A

```
<GridLayout xmlns:android=
        "http://schemas.android.com/apk/res/android"
    xmlns:tools="http://schemas.android.com/tools"
    android:layout_width="match_parent"
    android:layout_height="match_parent"
    android:columnCount="3"
    tools:context=".MainActivity" >
<Button
    android:layout_width="wrap_content"
    android:layout_height="wrap_content"
    android:layout_gravity="fill"
    android:layout_columnSpan="3"
    android:text="@string/hello" />
</GridLayout>
```

This has one button that fills the screen.

3

B

```
<GridLayout xmlns:android=
        "http://schemas.android.com/apk/res/android"
    xmlns:tools="http://schemas.android.com/tools"
    android:layout_width="match_parent"
    android:layout_height="match_parent"
    android:columnCount="2"
    tools:context=".MainActivity" >
<Button
    android:layout_width="wrap_content"
    android:layout_height="wrap_content"
    android:layout_gravity="fill"
    android:layout_columnSpan="2"
    android:text="@string/hello" />
<Button
    android:layout_width="wrap_content"
    android:layout_height="wrap_content"
    android:text="@string/hi" />
</GridLayout>
```

This button fills the screen, leaving space for another one underneath it.

```
<GridLayout xmlns:android=
        "http://schemas.android.com/apk/res/android"
    xmlns:tools="http://schemas.android.com/tools"
    android:layout_width="match_parent"
    android:layout_height="match_parent"
    android:columnCount="2"
    tools:context=".MainActivity" >
    <Button
        android:layout_width="wrap_content"
        android:layout_height="wrap_content"
        android:layout_row="0"
        android:layout_column="0"
        android:layout_columnSpan="2"
        android:text="@string/hello" />
    <Button
        android:layout_width="wrap_content"
        android:layout_height="wrap_content"
        android:layout_row="1"
        android:layout_column="0"
        android:text="@string/hi" />
</GridLayout>
```

Even though the button spans two columns, we didn't tell it to fill the screen horizontally.

Layouts and GUI components have a lot in common

You may have noticed that all layout types have attributes in common. Whichever type of layout you use, you must specify the layout width and height using the `android:layout_width` and `android:layout_height` attributes. This isn't just limited to layouts—the `android:layout_width` and `android:layout_height` are mandatory for all GUI components too.

This is because **all layouts and GUI components are subclasses of the Android `View` class**. Let's look at this in more detail.

GUI components are a type of View

You've already seen that GUI components are all types of views—behind the scenes, they are all subclasses of the `android.view.View` class. This means that all of the GUI components you use in your user interface have attributes and behavior in common. They can all be displayed on the screen, for instance, and they can say how tall or wide they should be. Each of the GUI components you use in your user interface take this basic functionality, and extend it.

android.view.View is the base class of all the GUI components you use to develop your apps.

android.widget. TextView is a direct subclass of the View class.

Spinners are a more complex type of View.

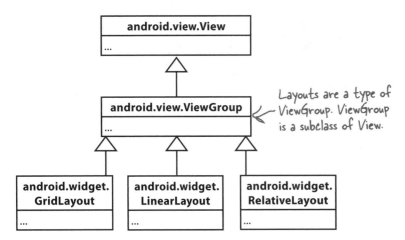

Layouts are a type of View called a ViewGroup

It's not just the GUI components that are a type of view. Under the hood, a layout is a special type of view called a **view group**. All layouts are subclasses of the `android.view.ViewGroup` class. A view group is a type of view that can contain other views.

Layouts are a type of ViewGroup. ViewGroup is a subclass of View.

A GUI component is a type of view, an object which takes up space on the screen.

A layout is a type of view group, which is a special type of view that can contain other views.

What being a view buys you

A `View` object occupies rectangular space on the screen. It includes the functionality all views need in order to lead a happy helpful life in Androidville. Here are some of the areas we think are the most important:

Getting and setting properties

Each view is a Java object behind the scenes, and that means you can get and set its properties in your activity code. As an example, you can retrieve the value selected in a spinner or change the text in a text view. The exact properties and methods you can access depend on the type of view.

To help you with this, each view can have an ID associated with it so that you can refer to it in your code.

Size and position

You can specify the width and height of views so that Android knows how big they need to be. You can also say whether any padding is needed around the view.

Once your view has been displayed, you can retrieve the position of the view, and its actual size on the screen.

Focus handling

Android handles how the focus moves depending on what the user does. This includes responding to any views that are hidden, removed, or made visible.

Event handling and listeners

Each of your views can respond to events. You can also create listeners so that you can react to things happening in the view. As an example, all views can react to getting or losing the focus, and a button (and all of its subclasses) can react to being clicked.

As a view group is also a type of view, this means that all layouts and GUI components share this common functionality.

Here are some of the View methods you can use in your activity code. As these are in the base View class, they're common to all views and view groups.

android.view.View
getId()
getHeight()
getWidth()
setVisibility(int)
findViewById(int)
isClickable()
isFocused()
requestFocus()
...

A layout is really a hierarchy of Views

The layout you define using XML gives you a *hierachical tree of views and view groups*. As an example, here's a relative layout containing a button and an editable text field. The relative layout is a view group, and the button and text field are both views. The view group is the view's parent, and the views are the view group's children:

`<RelativeLayout xmlns:android="http://schemas.android.com/apk/res/android"`

`... >`

> We've left out a lot of the XML. The key thing is the views the view group contains.

`<Button`

`android:id="@+id/send"`

`... />`

`<EditText`

`android:id="@+id/message"`

`... />`

`</RelativeLayout>`

The relative layout

ViewGroup

The button

View   **View**

The editable text field

Behind the scenes, when you build your app, the layout XML is converted to a `ViewGroup` object containing a tree of `Views`. In the example above, the button gets translated to a `Button` object, and the text view gets translated to a `TextView` object. `Button` and `TextView` are both subclasses of `View`.

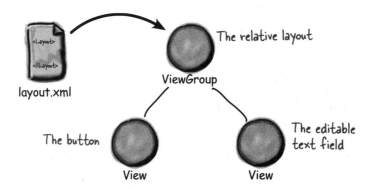

layout.xml

ViewGroup — The relative layout

The button — View

The editable text field — View

This is the reason why you can manipulate the views in your layout using Java code. Behind the scenes, all of the views are rendered to Java `View` objects.

Playing with views

Let's look at the most common GUI components. You've already seen some of these, but we'll review them anyway. We won't show you the whole API for each of these—just selected highlights to get you started.

Text view

Used for displaying text.

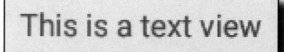

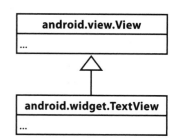

Defining it in XML

You define a text view in your layout using the `<TextView>` element. You use `android:text` to say what text you want it to display, usually by using a string resource:

```
<TextView
    android:id="@+id/text_view"
    android:layout_width="wrap_content"
    android:layout_height="wrap_content"
    android:text="@string/text" />
```

The `TextView` API includes many attributes to control the text view's appearance, such as the text size. To change the text size, you use the `android:textSize` attribute like this:

```
android:textSize="14sp"
```

You specify the text size using scale-independent pixels (sp). Scale-independent pixels take into account whether users want to use large fonts on their devices. A text size of 14sp will be physically larger on a device configured to use large fonts than on a device configured to use small fonts.

Using it in your activity code

You can change the text displayed in your text view using code like this:

```
TextView textView = (TextView) findViewById(R.id.text_view);
textView.setText("Some other string");
```

Edit Text

Like a text view, but editable.

Enter email address

Defining it in XML

You define an editable text view in XML using the `<EditText>` element. You use the `android:hint` attribute to give a hint to the user as to how to fill it in.

```
<EditText
    android:id="@+id/edit_text"
    android:layout_width="wrap_content"
    android:layout_height="wrap_content"
    android:hint="@string/edit_text" />
```

You can use the `android:inputType` attribute to define what type of data you're expecting the user to enter so that Android can help them. As an example, if you're expecting the user to enter numbers, you can use

```
android:inputType="number"
```

to provide them with a number keypad. Here are some more of our favorites:

You can find the entire list in the online Android developer documentation.

Value	What it does
phone	Provides a phone number keypad.
textPassword	Displays a text entry keypad, and your input is concealed.
textCapSentences	Capitalizes the first word of a sentence.
textAutoCorrect	Automatically corrects the text being input.

You can specify multiple input types using the | character. As an example, to capitalize the first word of a sentence and automatically correct any misspellings, you'd use:

```
android:inputType="textCapSentences|textAutoCorrect"
```

Using it in your activity code

You can retrieve the text entered in an editable text view like this:

```
EditText editText = (EditText) findViewById(R.id.edit_text);
String text = editText.getText().toString();
```

android.view.View

...

android.widget.TextView

...

android.widget.EditText

...

Button

Usually used to make your app do something when the button's clicked.

Defining it in XML

You define a button in XML using the <Button> element. You use the android:text attribute to say what text you want the button to display:

```
<Button
    android:id="@+id/button"
    android:layout_width="wrap_content"
    android:layout_height="wrap_content"
    android:text="@string/button_text" />
```

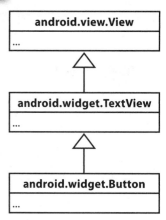

Using it in your activity code

You get the button to respond to the user clicking it by using the android:onClick attribute in the layout XML, and setting it to the name of the method you want to call in your activity code:

```
android:onClick="onButtonClicked"
```

You then define the method in your activity like this:

```
/** Called when the button is clicked */
public void onButtonClicked(View view) {
    // Do something in response to button click
}
```

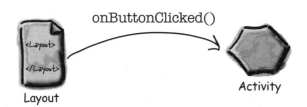

onButtonClicked()

Layout   Activity

Toggle button

A toggle button allows you to choose between two states by clicking a button.

This is what the toggle button looks like when it's off.

When you click the toggle button, it changes to being on.

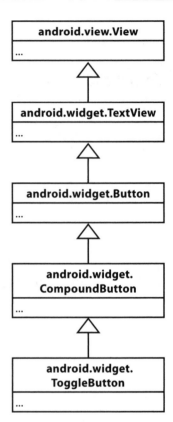

android.view.View

...

android.widget.TextView

...

android.widget.Button

...

android.widget.
CompoundButton

...

android.widget.
ToggleButton

...

Defining it in XML

You define a toggle button in XML using the `<ToggleButton>` element. You use the `android:textOn` and `android:textOff` attributes to say what text you want the button to display depending on the state of the button:

```
<ToggleButton
    android:id="@+id/toggle_button"
    android:layout_width="wrap_content"
    android:layout_height="wrap_content"
    android:textOn="@string/on"
    android:textOff="@string/off" />
```

Using it in your activity code

You get the toggle button to respond to the user clicking it by using the `android:onClick` attribute in the layout XML. You give it the name of the method you want to call in your activity code:

```
android:onClick="onToggleButtonClicked"
```

This is exactly the same as calling a method when a normal button gets clicked.

You then define the method in your activity like this:

```
/** Called when the toggle button is clicked */
public void onToggleClicked(View view) {
    // Get the state of the toggle button.
    boolean on = ((ToggleButton) view).isChecked();
    if (on) {
        // On
    } else {
        // Off
    }
}
```

This returns true if the toggle button is on, and false if the toggle button is off.

Switch

A switch is a slider control that acts in the same way as a toggle button.

This is the switch →  ┌ This is the
when it's off.   switch when
                                            it's on.

Watch it!

A Switch requires API level 14 or above.

If you want to use a switch in your app, make sure it uses a minimum SDK of API level 14.

Defining it in XML

You define a toggle button in XML using the `<Switch>` element. You use the `android:textOn` and `android:textOff` attributes to say what text you want the switch to display depending on the state of the switch:

```
<Switch
    android:id="@+id/switch_view"
    android:layout_width="wrap_content"
    android:layout_height="wrap_content"
    android:textOn="@string/on"
    android:textOff="@string/off" />
```

Using it in your activity code

You get the switch to respond to the user clicking it by using the `android:onClick` attribute in the layout XML, and setting it to the name of the method you want to call in your activity code:

```
android:onClick="onSwitchClicked"
```

You then define the method in your activity like this:

```
/** Called when the switch is clicked */
public void onSwitchClicked(View view) {
    // Is the switch on?
    boolean on = ((Switch) view).isChecked();

    if (on) {
        // On
    } else {
        // Off
    }
}
```

This is very similar code to that used with the toggle button.

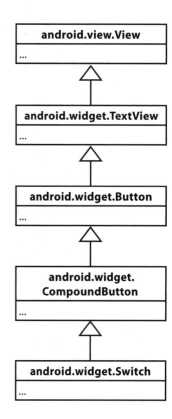

```
android.view.View
...
```
△
```
android.widget.TextView
...
```
△
```
android.widget.Button
...
```
△
```
android.widget.
CompoundButton
...
```
△
```
android.widget.Switch
...
```

Check boxes

Check boxes let you display multiple options to users. They can then select whichever options they want. Each of the checkboxes can be checked or unchecked independently of any others.

Here we have two checkboxes. Users can choose milk, sugar, both milk and sugar, or neither.

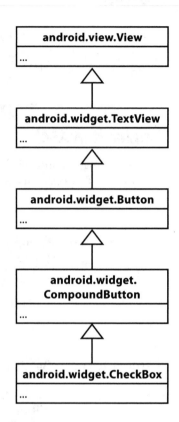

Defining them in XML

You define each checkbox in XML using the <CheckBox> element. You use the android:text attribute to display text for each option:

```xml
<CheckBox android:id="@+id/checkbox_milk"
    android:layout_width="wrap_content"
    android:layout_height="wrap_content"
    android:text="@string/milk" />


<CheckBox android:id="@+id/checkbox_sugar"
    android:layout_width="wrap_content"
    android:layout_height="wrap_content"
    android:text="@string/sugar" />
```

Using them in your activity code

You can find whether a particular checkbox is checked using the isChecked() method. It returns true if the checkbox is checked:

```java
CheckBox checkbox = (CheckBox) findViewById(R.id.checkbox_milk);
boolean checked = checkbox.isChecked();
if (checked) {
    //do something
}
```

Checkboxes (continued)

Just like buttons, you can respond to the user clicking a checkbox by using the android:onClick attribute in the layout XML, and setting it to the name of the method you want to call in your activity code:

```
<CheckBox android:id="@+id/checkbox_milk"
    android:layout_width="wrap_content"
    android:layout_height="wrap_content"
    android:text="@string/milk"
    android:onClick="onCheckboxClicked"/>

<CheckBox android:id="@+id/checkbox_sugar"
    android:layout_width="wrap_content"
    android:layout_height="wrap_content"
    android:text="@string/sugar"
    android:onClick="onCheckboxClicked"/>
```

In this case, the onCheckboxClicked() method will get called no matter which checkbox gets clicked. We could have specified a different method for each checkbox if we'd wanted to.

You then define the method in your activity like this:

```
public void onCheckboxClicked(View view) {
    // Has the checkbox that was clicked been checked?
    boolean checked = ((CheckBox) view).isChecked();

    // Retrieve which checkbox was clicked
    switch(view.getId()) {
        case R.id.checkbox_milk:
            if (checked)
                // Milky coffee
            else
                // Black as the midnight sky on a moonless night
            break;
        case R.id.checkbox_sugar:
            if (checked)
                // Sweet
            else
                // Keep it bitter
            break;
    }
}
```

Radio buttons

These let you display multiple options to the user. The user can select a single
option.

Use radio buttons to restrict the users choice to just one option.

Defining them in XML

You start by defining a radio group, a special type of view group, using the
<RadioGroup> tag. Within this, you then define individual radio buttons
using the <RadioButton> tag:

```
<RadioGroup android:id="@+id/radio_group"
    android:layout_width="match_parent"
    android:layout_height="wrap_content"
    android:orientation="vertical">

    <RadioButton android:id="@+id/radio_cavemen"
        android:layout_width="wrap_content"
        android:layout_height="wrap_content"
        android:text="@string/cavemen" />

    <RadioButton android:id="@+id/radio_astronauts"
        android:layout_width="wrap_content"
        android:layout_height="wrap_content"
        android:text="@string/astronauts" />

</RadioGroup>
```

You can choose to display the radio buttons in a horizontal or vertical list.

Using them in your activity code

You can find which radio button is selected using the
getCheckedRadioButtonId() method:

```
RadioGroup radioGroup = findViewById(R.id.radioGroup);
int id = radioGroup.getCheckedRadioButtonId();
if (id == -1){
    //no item selected
}
else{
    RadioButton radioButton = findViewById(id);
}
```

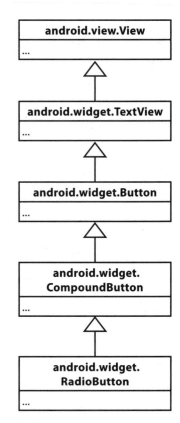

The radio group
containing the radio
buttons is a subclass
of LinearLayout.
You can use the
same attributes with
a radio group as you
can with a linear
layout.

Radio buttons (continued)

You can respond to the user clicking a radio button by using the `android:onClick` attribute in the layout XML, and setting it to the name of the method you want to call in your activity code:

```
<RadioGroup android:id="@+id/radio_group"
    android:layout_width="match_parent"
    android:layout_height="wrap_content"
    android:orientation="vertical">

    <RadioButton android:id="@+id/radio_cavemen"
        android:layout_width="wrap_content"
        android:layout_height="wrap_content"
        android:text="@string/cavemen"
        android:onClick="onRadioButtonClicked" />

    <RadioButton android:id="@+id/radio_astronauts"
        android:layout_width="wrap_content"
        android:layout_height="wrap_content"
        android:text="@string/astronauts"
        android:onClick="onRadioButtonClicked" />
</RadioGroup>
```

You then define the method in your activity like this:

```
public void onRadioButtonClicked(View view) {
    RadioGroup radioGroup = findViewById(R.id.radioGroup);
    int id = radioGroup.getCheckedRadioButtonId();
    switch(id) {
        case R.id.radio_cavemen:
            // Cavemen win
            break;
        case R.id.radio_astronauts:
            // Astronauts win
            break;
    }
}
```

Spinner

As you've already seen, a spinner gives you a drop-down list of values from which only one can be selected.

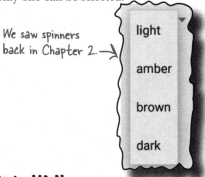

We saw spinners back in Chapter 2.

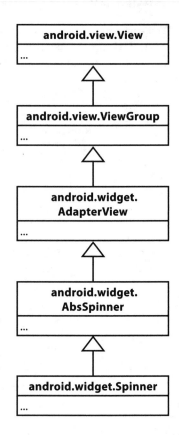

Defining it in XML

You define a spinner in XML using the `<Spinner>` element. You add a static array of entries to the spinner by using the `android:entries` attribute and setting it to an array of strings.

```
<Spinner
    android:id="@+id/spinner"
    android:layout_width="wrap_content"
    android:layout_height="wrap_content"
    android:entries="@array/spinner_values" />
```

There are other ways of populating the spinner, which you'll see later in the book.

You can add an array of strings to *strings.xml* like this:

```
<string-array name="spinner_values">
    <item>light</item>
    <item>amber</item>
    <item>brown</item>
    <item>dark</item>
</string-array>
```

Using it in your activity code

You can get the value of the currently selected item by using the `getSelectedItem()` method and converting it to a `String`:

```
Spinner spinner = (Spinner) findViewById(R.id.spinner);
String string = String.valueOf(spinner.getSelectedItem());
```

Image views

You use an image view to display an image:

An image view contains an image. →

```
android.view.View
...
```

△

```
android.widget.ImageView
...
```

↑

The ImageView class is a direct subclass of View.

Adding an image to your project

You first need to add an image file to your project as a drawable resource. If you expand the *app/src/main/res* folder in your project, you should see that there's a folder called *drawable*. This is the default location for image resources. To add an image file to this folder, you simply drag the image file to it.

If you want, you can use different image files depending on the screen density of the device. This means you can display higher-resolution images on higher-density screens, and lower-resolution images on lower-density screens. To do this, you create different *drawable* folders in *app/src/main/res* for the different screen densities. The name of the folder relates to the screen density of the device:

You create a new folder by switching to the Project view of your folder structure, highlighting the res folder, and choosing File, New..., Android resource directory.

`android-ldpi`	Low-density screens, around 120 dpi.
`android-mdpi`	Medium-density screens, around 160 dpi.
`android-hdpi`	High-density screens, around 240 dpi.
`android-xhdpi`	Extra-high-density screens, around 320 dpi.
`android-xxhdpi`	Extra-extra-high-density screens, around 480 dpi.
`android-xxxhdpi`	Extra-extra-extra high-density screens, around 640 dpi.

Depending on what version of Android Studio you're running, the IDE may create some of these folders for you automatically.

You then put different resolution images in each of the *drawable** folders, making sure that each of the image files has the same name. Android decides which image to use at runtime, depending on the screen density of the device it's running on. As an example, if the device has an extra high density screen, it will use the image located in the *drawable-xhdpi* folder.

If an image is added to just one of the folders, Android will use the same image file for all devices. It's common to use the *drawable* folder for this purpose.

Images: the layout XML

You define an image view in XML using the <ImageView> element. You use the android:src attribute to specify what image you want to display. You use the android:contentDescription attribute to add a string description of the image so that your app is more accessible:

```
<ImageView
    android:layout_width="200dp"
    android:layout_height="100dp"
    android:src="@drawable/starbuzz_logo"
    android:contentDescription="@string/starbuzz_logo" />
```

The android:src attribute takes a value of the form "@drawable/image_name", where image_name is the name of the image (without its extension). Image resources are prefixed with @drawable. @drawable tells Android that it's an image resource located in one or more of the *drawable* folders.

Using it in your activity code

You can set the image source and description in your activity code using the setImageResource() and setContentDescription() methods:

```
ImageView photo = (ImageView)findViewById(R.id.photo);
int image = R.drawable.starbuzz_logo;
String description = "This is the logo";
photo.setImageResource(image);
photo.setContentDescription(description);
```

This code looks for the image resource called starbuzz_logo in the *drawable** folders, and sets it as the source of an image view with an ID of photo. When you need to refer to an image resource in your activity code, you use R.drawable.image_name where image_name is the name of the image (without its extension)

Adding images to buttons

In addition to displaying images in image views, you can also display images on buttons.

Displaying text and an image on a button

To display text on a button with an image to the right of it, use the android:drawableRight attribute and specify the image to be used:

```
<Button
    android:layout_width="wrap_content"
    android:layout_height="wrap_content"
    android:drawableRight="@drawable/android"
    android:text="@string/click_me" />
```

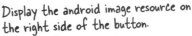

Display the android image resource on the right side of the button.

If you want to display the image on the left, use the android:drawableLeft attribute:

```
<Button
    android:layout_width="wrap_content"
    android:layout_height="wrap_content"
    android:drawableLeft="@drawable/android"
    android:text="@string/click_me" />
```

Use the android:drawableBottom attribute to display the image underneath the text:

```
<Button
    android:layout_width="wrap_content"
    android:layout_height="wrap_content"
    android:drawableBottom="@drawable/android"
    android:text="@string/click_me" />
```

The android:drawableBottom attribute displays the image above the text:

```
<Button
    android:layout_width="wrap_content"
    android:layout_height="wrap_content"
    android:drawableTop="@drawable/android"
    android:text="@string/click_me" />
```

Image Button

An image button is just like a button, except it contains an image and no text.

Defining it in XML

You define an image button in XML using the <ImageButton> element. You use the android:src attribute to say what image you want the image button to display:

```
<ImageButton
    android:id="@+id/button"
    android:layout_width="wrap_content"
    android:layout_height="wrap_content"
    android:src="@drawable/button_icon />
```

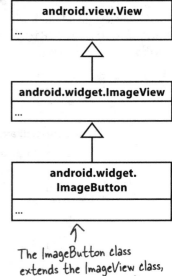

The ImageButton class extends the ImageView class, not the Button class. Does that surprise you?

Using it in your activity code

You get the image button to respond to the user clicking it by using the android:onClick attribute in the layout XML, and setting it to the name of the method you want to call in your activity code:

```
android:onClick="onButtonClicked"
```

You then define the method in your activity like this:

```
/** Called when the image button is clicked */
public void onButtonClicked(View view) {
    // Do something in response to button click
}
```

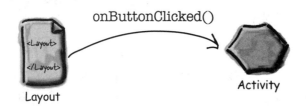

onButtonClicked()

Layout

Activity

Scroll views

If you add lots of views to your layouts, you may have problems on devices with smaller screens—most layouts don't come with scrollbars to allow you to scroll down the page. As an example, when we added seven large buttons to a linear layout, we couldn't see all of them.

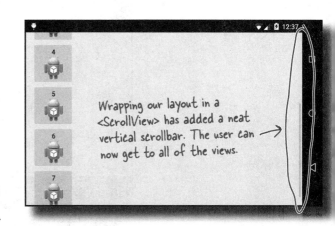

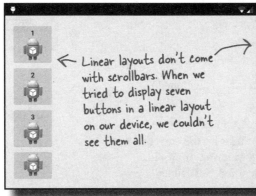

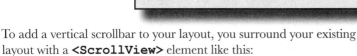
← Linear layouts don't come with scrollbars. When we tried to display seven buttons in a linear layout on our device, we couldn't see them all.

To add a vertical scrollbar to your layout, you surround your existing layout with a **<ScrollView>** element like this:

```
<ScrollView xmlns:android="http://schemas.android.com/apk/res/android"
    xmlns:tools="http://schemas.android.com/tools"
    android:layout_width="match_parent"
    android:layout_height="match_parent"
    tools:context=".MainActivity" >
```

Move these attributes from the original layout to the <ScrollView> as the <ScrollView> is now the root element.

```
    <LinearLayout
        android:layout_width="match_parent"
        android:layout_height="match_parent"
        android:paddingBottom="16dp"
        android:paddingLeft="16dp"
        android:paddingRight="16dp"
        android:paddingTop="16dp"
        android:orientation="vertical" >
    ...
    </LinearLayout>
</ScrollView>
```

Wrapping our layout in a <ScrollView> has added a neat vertical scrollbar. The user can now get to all of the views. →

To add a horizontal scrollbar to your layout, wrap your existing layout inside a **<HorizontalScrollView>** element instead.

Toasts

There's one final widget we want to show you in this chapter: a toast. A toast is a simple pop-up message you can display on the screen.

Toasts are purely informative, as the user can't interact with them. While a toast is displayed, the activity stays visible and interactive. The toast automatically disappears when it times out.

Using it in your activity code

You create a toast using activity code only. You can't define one in your layout.

To create a toast, you call the `Toast.makeText()` method, and pass it three parameters: a `Context` (usually `this` for the current activity), a `CharSequence` that's the message you want to display, and an `int` duration. Once you've created the toast, you call its `show()` method to display it.

Here's the code you would use to create a toast that appears on screen for a short duration:

```java
CharSequence text = "Hello, I'm a Toast!";
int duration = Toast.LENGTH_SHORT;

Toast toast = Toast.makeText(this, text, duration);
toast.show();
```

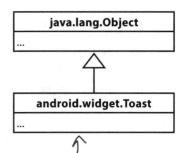

A Toast isn't actually a type of View. They're a useful way of giving the user a short message, though, so we're sneaking it into this chapter.

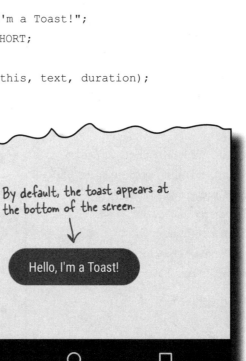

By default, the toast appears at the bottom of the screen.

Hello, I'm a Toast!

It's time for you to try out some of the views we've introduced you to this chapter. Create a layout that will create this screen:

You probably won't want to write the code here, but why not experiment in the IDE?

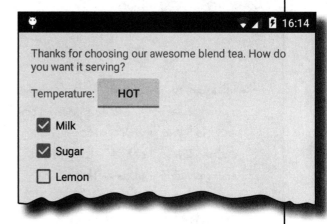

Here's one of the many ways in which you can create the layout. Don't worry if your code looks different, as there are many different solutions.

```
<GridLayout xmlns:android="http://schemas.android.com/apk/res/android"
    xmlns:tools="http://schemas.android.com/tools"
    android:layout_width="match_parent"
    android:layout_height="match_parent"
    android:paddingBottom="16dp"
    android:paddingLeft="16dp"
    android:paddingRight="16dp"
    android:paddingTop="16dp"
    android:columnCount="2"
    tools:context=".MainActivity" >

    <TextView
        android:layout_width="wrap_content"
        android:layout_height="wrap_content"
        android:layout_row="0"
        android:layout_column="0"
        android:layout_columnSpan="2"
        android:text="@string/message" />

    <TextView
        android:layout_width="wrap_content"
        android:layout_height="wrap_content"
        android:layout_row="1"
        android:layout_column="0"
        android:text="@string/temp" />
```

We used a grid layout, but you could have used a relative layout instead.

← We'll use two columns.

Display a text view at the top that spans both columns.

← All of the views need strings to be added to strings.xml.

Add a temperature label to the next row in the first column.

We used a toggle button to display whether the drink should be served hot or cold, and put it in row 1, column 1.

```
<ToggleButton
    android:layout_width="wrap_content"
    android:layout_height="wrap_content"
    android:layout_row="1"
    android:layout_column="1"
    android:textOn="@string/hot"
    android:textOff="@string/cold" />

<CheckBox android:id="@+id/checkbox_milk"
    android:layout_width="wrap_content"
    android:layout_height="wrap_content"
    android:layout_row="2"
    android:layout_column="0"
    android:text="@string/milk" />

<CheckBox android:id="@+id/checkbox_sugar"
    android:layout_width="wrap_content"
    android:layout_height="wrap_content"
    android:layout_row="3"
    android:layout_column="0"
    android:text="@string/sugar" />

<CheckBox android:id="@+id/checkbox_lemon"
    android:layout_width="wrap_content"
    android:layout_height="wrap_content"
    android:layout_row="4"
    android:layout_column="0"
    android:text="@string/lemon" />

</GridLayout>
```

We used a checkbox for each of the values (Milk, Sugar, and Lemon). We put each one on a separate row.

Layout Magnets Solution

We wrote some code to center the Send button in the third row of the grid layout, but a sudden breeze blew some of it away. See if you can reconstruct the code using the magnets below.

```
<GridLayout...>
    <TextView... />
    <EditText.../>
    <EditText.../>
```
These are the views we've already added.

```
<Button
        android:layout_width="wrap_content"
        android:layout_height="wrap_content"

        android:layout_row=    "2"
```
The button starts at row 2, column 0.

```
        android:layout_column=    "0"
```
We want to center it horizontally.

```
        android:layout_gravity=    center_horizontal
```

```
        android:layout_columnSpan=    "2"
```
It spans two columns.

```
        android:text="@string/send" />

</GridLayout>
```

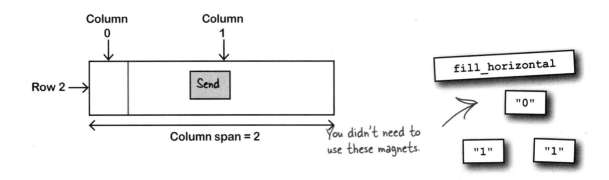

Your Android Toolbox

You've got Chapter 5 under your belt and now you've added views and view groups to your toolbox.

BULLET POINTS

- GUI components are all types of view. They are all subclasses of the `android.view.View` class.

- All layouts are subclasses of the `android.view.ViewGroup` class. A view group is a type of view that can contain multiple views.

- The layout XML file gets converted to a ViewGroup containing a hierarchical tree of views.

- A relative layout displays child views relative to other views, or relative to the parent layout.

- A linear layout lists views either horizontally or vertically. You specify the direction using the `android:orientation` attribute.

- A grid layout divides the screen into a grid of cells so that you can specify which cell (or cells) each view should occupy. Use `android:columnCount` to say how many columns there should be. Use `android:layout_row` and `android:layout_column` to say which cell you want each view to appear in. Use `android:layout_columnSpan` to say how many columns the view should spread across.

- Use `android:padding*` attributes to specify how much padding you want there to be around a view.

- Use `android:layout_weight` in a linear layout if you want a view to use up extra space in the layout.

- `android:layout_gravity` lets you say where you want views to appear in their available space.

- `android:gravity` lets you say where you want the contents to appear inside the view.

- `<ToggleButton>` defines a toggle button which allows you to choose between two states by clicking a button.

- `<Switch>` defines a switch control that behaves in the same way as a toggle button. It requires API level 14 or above.

- `<CheckBox>` defines a checkbox.

- To define a group of radio buttons, first use `<RadioGroup>` to define the radio group. Then put individual radio buttons in the radio group using `<RadioButton>`.

- Use `<ImageView>` to display an image.

- `<ImageButton>` defines a button with no text, just an image.

- Add scrollbars using `<ScrollView>` or `<HorizontalScrollView>`.

- A `Toast` is a pop-up message.

6 list views and adapters

Getting Organized

Sheesh! So many ideas... However will I turn all of these into the most downloaded app of the year?

Want to know how best to structure your Android app?

You've learned about some of the basic building blocks that are used to build apps, and now **it's time to get organized**. In this chapter, we'll show you how you can take a bunch of ideas and **structure them into an awesome app**. We'll show you how **lists of data** can form the core part of your app design, and how **linking them together** can create a **powerful and easy-to-use app**. Along the way, you'll get your first glimpse of using **event listeners** and **adapters** to make your app more dynamic.

Every app starts with ideas

When you first come up with an idea for an app, you'll have lots of thoughts about what the app should contain.

As an example, the guys at Starbuzz want a new app to entice more customers to their stores. These are some of the ideas they came up with for what the app should include:

These are all ideas that users of the app will find useful. But how do you take all of these ideas and organize them into an intuitive, well-organized app?

Categorize your ideas:
top-level, category, and detail/edit activities

A useful way to bring order to these ideas is to categorize them into three different types of activity: **top-level** activities, **category** activities, and **detail/edit** activities.

Top-level activities

A top-level activity contains the things that are most important to the user, and gives them an easy way of navigating to them. In most apps, the first activity the user sees will be a top-level activity.

Category activities

Category activities show the data that belongs to a particular category, often in a list. These type of activities are often used to help the user navigate to detail/edit activities. An example of a category activity is a list of all the drinks available at Starbuzz.

Detail/edit activities

Detail/edit activities display details for a particular record, let the user edit the record, or allow the user to enter new records. An example of a detail/edit activity would be an activity that shows the user the details of a particular drink.

Once you've categorized your activities, you can use them to construct a hierarchy showing how the user will navigate between activities.

Exercise

Think of an app you'd like to create. What activities should it include? Organize these activities into top-level activities, category activities, and detail/edit activities.

Navigating through the activities

When you categorize the ideas you have into top-level, category, and detail/edit activities, you can use these categorizations to figure out how to navigate through your app. In general, you want your users to navigate from top-level activities to detail/edit activities via category activities.

Top-level activities go at the top

These are the activities your user will encounter first, so they go at the top.

Category activities go between top-level and detail/edit activities

Your users will navigate from the top-level activity to the category activities. In complex apps, you might have several layers of categories and subcategories.

Detail/edit activities

These form the bottom layer of the activity hierarchy. Users will navigate to these from the category activities.

As an example, suppose a user wanted to look at details of one of the drinks that Starbuzz serves. To do this, she would launch the app, and be presented with the top-level activity start screen showing her a list of options. The user would click on the option to display a list of drinks. To see details of a particular drink, she would then click on her drink of choice from the list.

Use ListViews to navigate to data

When you structure your app in this way, you need a way of navigating between your activities. A common approach used in this situation is to use **list views**. A list view allows you to display a list of data that you can then use to navigate through the app.

As an example, on the previous page, we said we'd have a category activity that displays a list of the drinks sold by Starbuzz. Here's what the activity might look like:

This is a ListView containing a list of drinks. →

The activity uses a list view to display all the drinks that are sold by Starbuzz. To navigate to a particular drink, the user clicks on one of the drinks, and the details of that drink are displayed.

If you click on the Latte option in the ListView, you get shown the details for the Latte.

We're going to spend the rest of this chapter showing you how to use list views to implement this approach using the Starbuzz app as an example.

We're going to build the Starbuzz app

part of

Rather than build all the category and detail/edit activities required for the entire Starbuzz app, **we're going to focus on just the drinks.** We're going to build a top-level activity that the user will see when they launch the app, a category activity that will display a list of drinks, and a detail/edit activity that will display details of a single drink.

The top-level activity

When the user launches the app, she will be presented with the top-level activity, the main entry point of the app. This activity includes an image of the Starbuzz logo, and a navigational list containing entries for Drinks, Food, and Stores.

When the user clicks on an item in the list, the app uses her selection to navigate to a separate activity. As an example, if the user clicks on Drinks, the app starts a category activity relating to drinks.

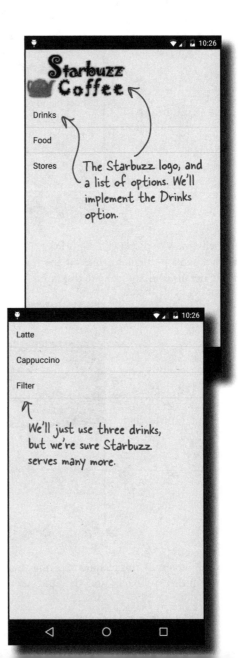

The Starbuzz logo, and a list of options. We'll implement the Drinks option.

The drinks category activity

This activity is launched when the user chooses Drinks from the navigational list in the top-level activity. The activity displays a list of all the drinks that are available at Starbuzz. The user can click on one of these drinks to see more details of it.

We'll just use three drinks, but we're sure Starbuzz serves many more.

The drink detail activity

The drink activity is launched when the user clicks on one of the drinks listed by the drink category activity.

This activity displays details of the drink the user has selected, such as its name, an image of what it looks like, and a desciption.

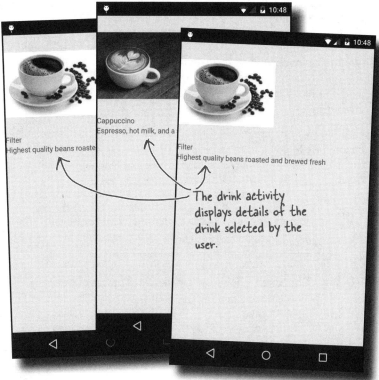

The drink activity displays details of the drink selected by the user.

How the user navigates through the app

The user navigates from the top-level activity to the drink category activity by clicking on the "Drinks" item in the top-level activity. She then navigates to the drink activity by clicking on a drink.

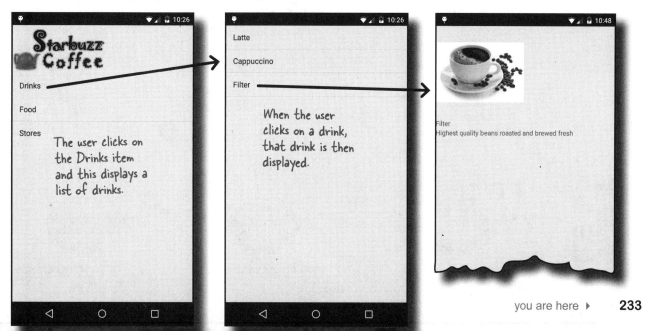

The user clicks on the Drinks item and this displays a list of drinks.

When the user clicks on a drink, that drink is then displayed.

The Starbuzz app structure

The app contains three activities. `TopLevelActivity` is the app's top-level activity and allows the user to navigate through the app. `DrinkCategoryActivity` is a category activity; it contains a list of all the drinks. The third activity, `DrinkActivity`, displays details of a given drink.

For now, we're going to hold the drink data in a Java class. In a later chapter, we're going to move it into a database, but for now we want to focus on building the rest of the app without teaching you about databases too.

① When the app gets launched, it starts activity TopLevelActivity.
The activity uses layout *activity_top_level.xml*. The activity displays a list of options for Drinks, Food, and Stores.

② The user clicks on Drinks in TopLevelActivity.
This launches activity `DrinkCategoryActivity`. This activity displays a list of drinks.

> DrinkCategoryActivity doesn't need you to create a layout for it. You'll see why later in the chapter.

③ Details of the drinks are held in the *Drink.java* class file.
`DrinkCategoryActivity` gets the values for its list of drinks from this class.

④ The user clicks on a drink in DrinkCategoryActivity.
This launches activity `DrinkActivity`. The activity uses layout *activity_drink.xml*.

⑤ DrinkActivity gets details of the drink from the *Drink.java* class file.

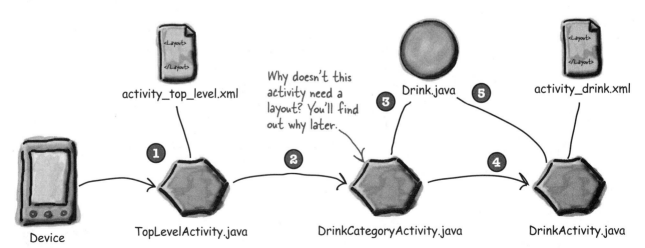

activity_top_level.xml

Why doesn't this activity need a layout? You'll find out why later.

Drink.java ⑤

activity_drink.xml

Device   ① TopLevelActivity.java   ② DrinkCategoryActivity.java ③   ④ DrinkActivity.java

Here are the steps

There are a number of steps we'll go through to build the app:

1 **Add the Drink class and image resources.**
The class contains details of the available drinks, and we'll use images of the drinks and Starbuzz logo in the app.

2 **Create TopLevelActivity and its layout.**
This is the entry point for the app. It needs to display the Starbuzz logo and include navigational list of options. `TopLevelActivity` needs to launch `DrinkCategoryActivity` when the Drink option is clicked.

3 **Create DrinkCategoryActivity.**
`DrinkCategoryActivity` contains a list of all the drinks that are available. When a drink is clicked, it needs to launch `DrinkCategory`.

4 **Create DrinkActivity and its layout.**
`DrinkActivity` displays details of the drink the user clicked on in `DrinkCategoryActivity`.

Create the project

You create the project for the app in exactly the same way you did for the previous chapters.

Create a new Android project for an application named "Starbuzz" with a package name of `com.hfad.starbuzz`. The minimum SDK should be API 15. You'll need an activity called "TopLevelActivity" and a layout called "activity_top_level".

→ **Add resources**
TopLevelActivity
DrinkCategoryActivity
DrinkActivity

The Drink class

Add resources
TopLevelActivity
DrinkCategoryActivity
DrinkActivity

We'll start by adding the `Drink` class to the app. *Drink.java* is a pure Java class file that activities will get their drink data from. The class defines an array of three drinks, where each drink is composed of a name, description, and image resource ID. Add the class to the *com.hfad.starbuzz* package in the *app/ src/main/java* folder in your project, giving it a class name of `Drink`. Then save your changes.

```java
package com.hfad.starbuzz;

public class Drink {
    private String name;
    private String description;
    private int imageResourceId;

    //drinks is an array of Drinks
    public static final Drink[] drinks = {
        new Drink("Latte", "A couple of espresso shots with steamed milk",
                R.drawable.latte),
        new Drink("Cappuccino", "Espresso, hot milk, and a steamed milk foam",
                R.drawable.cappuccino),
        new Drink("Filter", "Highest quality beans roasted and brewed fresh",
                R.drawable.filter)
    };

    //Each Drink has a name, description, and an image resource
    private Drink(String name, String description, int imageResourceId) {
        this.name = name;
        this.description = description;
        this.imageResourceId = imageResourceId;
    }

    public String getDescription() {
        return description;
    }

    public String getName() {
        return name;
    }

    public int getImageResourceId() {
        return imageResourceId;
    }

    public String toString() {
        return this.name;
    }
}
```

Each Drink has a name, description, and image resource ID. The image resource ID refers to drink images we'll add to the project on the next page.

drinks is an array of three Drinks.

These are images of the drinks. We'll add these next.

The Drink constructor

These are getters for the private variables.

The String representation of a Drink is its name.

Starbuzz
app/src/main
java
com.hfad.starbuzz
Drink.java

The image files

The `Drink` code includes three image resources for its drinks with ids of `R.drawable.latte`, `R.drawable.cappuccino` and `R.drawable.filter`. These are so we can show the user images of the drinks. `R.drawable.latte` refers to an image file called *latte*, `R.drawable.cappuccino` refers to an image file called *cappuccino*, and `R.drawable.filter` refers to a file called *filter*.

We need to add these image files to the project, along with an image of the Starbuzz logo so that we can use it in our top-level activity. To do this, download the files *starbuzz-logo.png*, *cappuccino.png*, *filter.png*, and *latte.png* from *https://tinyurl.com/HeadFirstAndroid*. Then drag the file to the *app/src/main/res/drawable* folder in your Starbuzz project.

When you add images to your apps, you need to decide whether to display different images for different density screens. In our case, we're going to use the same resolution image irrespective of screen density, so we've put a single copy of the images in one folder. If you decide to cater for different screen densities in your own apps, put images for the different screen densities in the appropriate *drawable** folders as described in Chapter 5.

Here are the four image files. You add them to Android Studio by dragging them to the drawable folder.

When you save images to your project, Android assigns each of them an ID in the form `R.drawable.image_name`. As an example, the file *latte.png* is given an ID of `R.drawable.latte`, which matches the value of the latte's image resource ID in the `Drink` class.

Drink

name: "Latte"

description: "A couple of expresso shots with steamed milk"

imageResourceId: R.drawable.latte

The image latte.png is given an ID of R.drawable.latte.

R.drawable.latte

Now that we've added the `Drink` class and image resources to the project, let's work on the activities. We'll start with the top-level activity.

Add resources
TopLevelActivity
DrinkCategoryActivity
DrinkActivity

The top-level layout contains an image and a list

When we created our project, we called our default activity *TopLevelActivity.java*, and its layout *activity_top_level.xml*. We need to change the layout so it displays an image and a list.

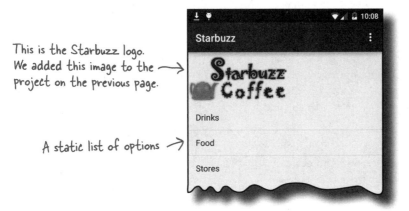

This is the Starbuzz logo. We added this image to the project on the previous page. →

A static list of options →

You saw how to display images in Chapter 5 using an image view. In this case, we need an image view that displays the Starbuzz logo, so we'll create one that uses *starbuzz_logo.png* as its source.

Here's the code to define the image view in the layout:

```
<ImageView
    android:layout_width="200dp"
    android:layout_height="100dp"
    android:src="@drawable/starbuzz_logo"
    android:contentDescription="@string/starbuzz_logo" />
```

These are the dimensions we want the image to have.

The source of the image is the starbuzz_logo.png file we added to the app.

Adding a content description makes your app more accessible.

When you use an image view in your app, you use the `android:contentDescription` attribute to add a description of the image; this makes your app more accessible. In our case, we're using a string value of `"@string/starbuzz_logo"`. Add this to *strings.xml*:

```
<resources>
    ...
    <string name="starbuzz_logo">Starbuzz logo</string>
</resources>
```

That's everything we need to add the image to the layout, so let's move on to the list.

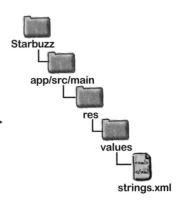

Starbuzz

app/src/main

res

values

strings.xml

Use a list view to display the list of options

As we said earlier, a list view allows you to display a vertical list of data that you can then use to navigate through the app. We're going to add a list view to the layout that displays the list of options, and later on we'll use it to navigate to a different activity.

How to define a list view in XML

You add a list view to your layout using the **<ListView>** element. You then add an array of entries to the list view by using the android:entries attribute and setting it to an array of strings. The array of strings then gets displayed in the list view as a list of text views.

Here's how you add a list view to your layout that gets its values from an array of strings called options:

```
<ListView    ←—This defines the list view.
    android:id="@+id/list_options"
    android:layout_width="match_parent"
    android:layout_height="wrap_content"
    android:entries="@array/options" />
```

The values in the list view are defined by the options array.

You define the array in exactly the same way that you did earlier in the book, by adding it to *strings.xml* like this:

```
<resources>
    ...
    <string-array name="options">
        <item>Drinks</item>
        <item>Food</item>
        <item>Stores</item>
    </string-array>
</resources>
```

Starbuzz
app/src/main
res
values
strings.xml

This populates the list view with three values: Drinks, Food, and Stores.

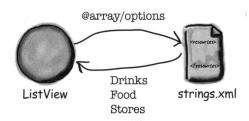

@array/options

ListView
Drinks
Food
Stores
strings.xml

The entries attribute populates the ListView with values from the options array. Each item in the ListView is a TextView.

Drinks

Food

Stores

android.view.View
...

android.view.ViewGroup
...

android.widget. AdapterView
...

android.widget.ListView
...

The full top-level layout code

Here's our layout code in full (make sure you change your code
to match ours):

```xml
<LinearLayout xmlns:android="http://schemas.android.com/apk/res/android"
    xmlns:tools="http://schemas.android.com/tools"
    android:layout_width="match_parent"
    android:layout_height="match_parent"
    android:orientation="vertical"
    tools:context=".TopLevelActivity" >
```

We're using a linear layout with a vertical orientation. This will display our list view directly underneath the Starbuzz logo.

```xml
    <ImageView
        android:layout_width="200dp"
        android:layout_height="100dp"
        android:src="@drawable/starbuzz_logo"
        android:contentDescription="@string/starbuzz_logo" />
```

Starbuzz
└ app/src/main
  └ res
    └ layout
      └ activity_top_level.xml

```xml
    <ListView
        android:id="@+id/list_options"
        android:layout_width="match_parent"
        android:layout_height="wrap_content"
        android:entries="@array/options" />
</LinearLayout>
```

Test drive

Make sure you've applied all the changes to *activity_top_level.xml*,
and also updated *strings.xml*. When you run the app, you should
see the Starbuzz logo displayed on the device screen with the
list view underneath it. The list view displays the three values
from the options array.

If you click on any of the options in the list, nothing happens,
as we haven't told the list view to respond to clicks yet. The
next thing we'll do is see how you get list views to respond to
clicks and launch a second activity.

These are the values in the options array.

Get ListViews to respond to clicks with a Listener

You make the items in a list view respond to clicks by implementing an **event listener.**

An event listener allows you to listen for events that take place in your app, such as when views get clicked, when they receive or lose the focus, or when the user presses a hardware key on their device. By implementing an event listener, you can tell when your user performs a particular action—such as clicking on an item in a list view—and respond to it.

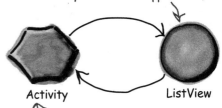

The ListView needs to know the Activity cares what happens to it.

Activity   **ListView**

The ListView tells the Activity when an item gets clicked so the Activity can react.

OnItemClickListener listens for item clicks

When you want to get items in a list view to respond to clicks, you need to create an `OnItemClickListener` and implement its `onItemClick()` method. The `OnItemClickListener` listens for when items are clicked, and the `onItemClick()` method lets you say how your activity should respond to the click. The `onItemClick()` method includes several parameters that you can use to find out which item was clicked, such as a reference to the view item that was clicked, its position in the list view (starting at 0), and the row ID of the underlying data.

We want to start `DrinkCategoryActivity` when the first item in the list view is clicked—the item at position 0. If the item at position 0 is clicked, we need to create an intent to start `DrinkCategoryActivity`. Here's the code to create the listener:

OnItemClickListener is a nested class with the AdapterView class. A ListView is a subclass of AdapterView.

```
AdapterView.OnItemClickListener itemClickListener = new AdapterView.OnItemClickListener(){
    public void onItemClick(AdapterView<?> listView,     ← The view that was clicked (in this case,
                            View itemView,                   the list view).
                            int position,     These give you more about which item was clicked in the
                            long id) {        list view such as the item view and its position.
        if (position == 0) {
            Intent intent = new Intent(TopLevelActivity.this, DrinkCategoryActivity.class);
            startActivity(intent);
        }
    }
};
```

Drinks is the first item in the list view, so it's at position 0.

The intent's coming from TopLevelActivity.

It needs to launch DrinkCategoryActivity.

Once you've created the listener, you need to add it to the `ListView`.

Set the listener to the list view

Add resources
TopLevelActivity
DrinkCategoryActivity
DrinkActivity

Once you've created the OnClickItemListener, you need
to attach it to the list view. You do this using the ListView
setOnItemClickListener() method. The method takes one
argument, the listener itself:

```
AdapterView.OnItemClickListener itemClickListener = new AdapterView.OnItemClickListener(){
    public void onItemClick(AdapterView<?> listView,

        ...

    }
};
ListView listView = (ListView) findViewById(R.id.list_options);
listView.setOnItemClickListener(itemClickListener);
```

This is the listener we just created.

Adding the listener to the list view is crucial, as it's this step that makes the
listener get notified when the user clicks on items in the list view. If you
don't do this, the items in your list view won't be able to respond to clicks.

You've now seen everything you need in order to get the
TopLevelActivity list view to respond to clicks.

What happens when you run the code

1 The onCreate() method in TopLevelActivity creates an
onItemClickListener and links it to the activity's ListView.

TopLevelActivity   ListView   onItemClickListener

2 When the user clicks on an item in the list view, the
onItemClickListener's onItemClick() method gets called.
If the Drinks item is clicked, the onItemClickListener creates an intent to start
DrinkCategoryActivity.

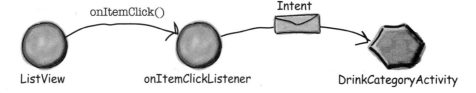

onItemClick()   Intent

ListView   onItemClickListener   DrinkCategoryActivity

The full TopLevelActivity code

Here's the complete code for `TopLevelActivity.java`.
Replace the code the wizard created for you with the code below,
then save your changes:

```java
package com.hfad.starbuzz;

import android.app.Activity;
import android.content.Intent;
import android.os.Bundle;
import android.widget.AdapterView;
import android.widget.ListView;
import android.view.View;
```

We're using these extra classes.

Starbuzz
app/src/main
java
com.hfad.starbuzz
TopLevel Activity.java

```java
public class TopLevelActivity extends Activity {

    @Override
    protected void onCreate(Bundle savedInstanceState) {
        super.onCreate(savedInstanceState);
        setContentView(R.layout.activity_top_level);
        //Create an OnItemClickListener
        AdapterView.OnItemClickListener itemClickListener =
                            new AdapterView.OnItemClickListener(){
            public void onItemClick(AdapterView<?> listView,
                                    View v,
                                    int position,
                                    long id) {
                if (position == 0) {
                    Intent intent = new Intent(TopLevelActivity.this,
                                        DrinkCategoryActivity.class);
                    startActivity(intent);
                }
            }
        };
        //Add the listener to the list view
        ListView listView = (ListView) findViewById(R.id.list_options);
        listView.setOnItemClickListener(itemClickListener);
    }
}
```

Create the listener.

Implement its onItemClick() method.

Launch DrinkCategoryActivity if the user clicks on the Drinks item. We'll create this activity next, so don't worry if Android Studio says it doesn't exist.

Add the listener to the list view.

Where we've got to

Add resources
TopLevelActivity
DrinkCategoryActivity
DrinkActivity

So far we've added *Drink.java* to our app and created
`TopLevelActivity` and its layout.

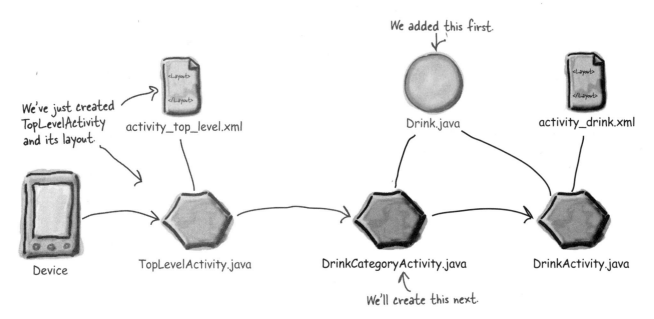

We added this first.

Drink.java   activity_drink.xml

We've just created
TopLevelActivity
and its layout.

activity_top_level.xml

Device   TopLevelActivity.java   DrinkCategoryActivity.java   DrinkActivity.java

We'll create this next.

The next thing we need to do is create
`DrinkCategoryActivity` so that it gets
launched when the user clicks on the Drinks option in
`TopLevelActivity`.

there are no Dumb Questions

Q: Why did we have to create an event listener to get items
in the `ListView` to respond to clicks? Couldn't we have
just used its `android:onClick` attribute in the layout
code?

A: You can only use the `android:onClick` attribute
in activity layouts for buttons, or any views that are subclasses of
`Button` such as `CheckBoxes` and `RadioButtons`.

The `ListView` class isn't a subclass of `Button`, so using
the `android:onClick` attribute won't work. That's why you
have to implement your own listener.

Exercise

Here's some activity code from a separate project. When the user clicks on an item in a list view, the code is meant to display the text of that item in a text view. Does the code do what it's meant to? If not, why not? The text view has an ID of `text_view` and the list view has an ID of `list_view`.

```java
package com.hfad.ch06_ex;

import android.app.Activity;
import android.os.Bundle;
import android.widget.AdapterView;
import android.widget.ListView;
import android.widget.TextView;
import android.view.View;

public class MainActivity extends Activity {

    @Override
    protected void onCreate(Bundle savedInstanceState) {
        super.onCreate(savedInstanceState);
        setContentView(R.layout.activity_main);
        final TextView textView = (TextView) findViewById(R.id.text_view);
        AdapterView.OnItemClickListener itemClickListener =
                new AdapterView.OnItemClickListener(){
                    public void onItemClick(AdapterView<?> listView,
                                            View v,
                                            int position,
                                            long id) {
                        TextView item = (TextView) v;
                        textView.setText(item.getText());
                    }
                };
        ListView listView = (ListView) findViewById(R.id.list_view);
    }
}
```

Exercise Solution

Here's some activity code from a separate project. When the user clicks on an item in a list view, the code is meant to display the text of that item in a text view. Does the code do what it's meant to? If not, why not? The text view has an ID of `text_view` and the list view has an ID of `list_view`.

```java
package com.hfad.ch06_ex;

import android.app.Activity;
import android.os.Bundle;
import android.widget.AdapterView;
import android.widget.ListView;
import android.widget.TextView;
import android.view.View;

public class MainActivity extends Activity {

    @Override
    protected void onCreate(Bundle savedInstanceState) {
        super.onCreate(savedInstanceState);
        setContentView(R.layout.activity_main);
        final TextView textView = (TextView) findViewById(R.id.text_view);
        AdapterView.OnItemClickListener itemClickListener =
                new AdapterView.OnItemClickListener(){
                    public void onItemClick(AdapterView<?> listView,
                                            View v,
                                            int position,
                                            long id) {
                        TextView item = (TextView) v;
                        textView.setText(item.getText());
                    }
                };
        ListView listView = (ListView) findViewById(R.id.list_view);
    }
}
```

This is the item in the ListView that was clicked. → (points to `TextView item = (TextView) v;`)

It's a TextView, so we can get its text using getText(). → (points to `textView.setText(item.getText());`)

The code doesn't work as intended as the line of code

listView.setOnItemClickListener(itemClickListener);

is missing from the end of the code. Apart from that, the code's fine.

A category activity displays the data for a single category

As we said earlier, DrinkCategoryActivity is an example of a category activity. A category activity is one that shows the data that belongs to a particular category, often in a list. You then use the category activity to navigate to details of the data.

We're going to use DrinkCategoryActivity to display a list of drinks. When the user clicks on one of the drinks, we'll show them the details of that drink.

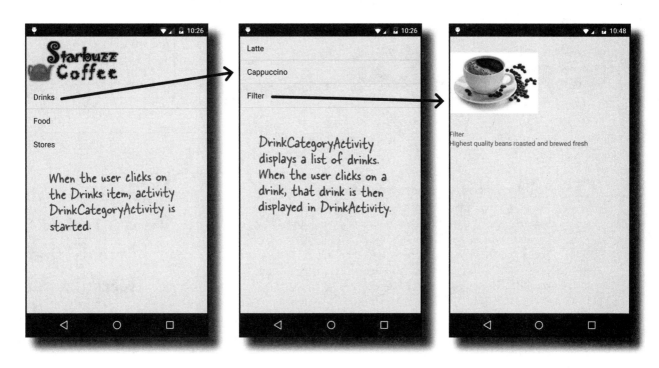

When the user clicks on the Drinks item, activity DrinkCategoryActivity is started.

DrinkCategoryActivity displays a list of drinks. When the user clicks on a drink, that drink is then displayed in DrinkActivity.

To do this, we'll create an activity containing a single list view that displays a list of all the drinks. As our activity only needs to contain a single list view with no other GUI components, we can use a special kind of activity called a **list activity**. So what's a list activity?

A ListActivity is an activity that contains only a list

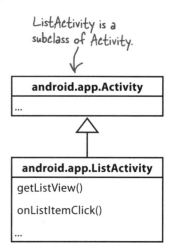

A list activity is type of activity that specializes in working with a list. It's automatically bound to a list view, so you don't need to create one yourself. Here's what one looks like:

A list activity comes complete with its own list view so you don't need to add it yourself. You still need to provide it with data, and you'll see how to do that soon.

ListActivity is a subclass of Activity.

android.app.Activity
...

android.app.ListActivity
getListView()
onListItemClick()
...

There are a couple of major advantages in using a list activity to display categories of data:

⭐ **You don't need to create your own layout.**
List activities define their own layout programmatically, so there's no XML layout for you to create or maintain. The layout the list activity generates includes a single list view. You access this list view in your activity code using the list activity's `getListView()` method. You need this to specify what data should be displayed in the list view.

⭐ **You don't have to implement your own event listener.**
The `ListActivity` class already implements an event listener that listens for when items in the list view are clicked. Instead of creating your own event listener and binding it to the list view, you just need to implement the list activity's `onListItemClick()` method. This makes it easier to get your activity to respond when the user clicks on items in the list view. You'll see this in action later on when we use the `onListItemClick()` method to start another activity.

Category activities generally need to display a single list view you can use to navigate to detail records, so list activities are good for this situation.

So what does the list activity code look like?

A ListActivity is a type of Activity that specializes in working with a ListView. It has a default layout that contains the ListView.

How to create a list activity

Here's what the basic code looks like to create a list activity. As you can see, it's very similar to creating an activity. Use the New Activity wizard to create a new activity in your project called `DrinkCategoryActivity`, then replace the contents of *DrinkCategoryActivity.java* with the code below:

Android Studio may automatically generate a layout file for you. We won't use it because list activities define their own layout.

```
package com.hfad.starbuzz;

import android.app.ListActivity;
import android.os.Bundle;

public class DrinkCategoryActivity extends ListActivity {

    @Override
    protected void onCreate(Bundle savedInstanceState) {
        super.onCreate(savedInstanceState);
    }
}
```

The activity needs to extend ListActivity, not Activity.

ListActivity inherits the onCreate() method from the Activity class. We'll add code to this method soon.

Starbuzz
app/src/main
java
com.hfad.starbuzz
DrinkCategory Activity.java

The above code creates a basic list activity called `DrinkCategoryActivity`. Because it's a list activity, it needs to extend the `ListActivity` class rather than `Activity`.

The other difference is that you don't need to use the `setContentView()` method to say what layout the list activity should use. This is because list activities define their own layouts so you don't need to create one yourself. The list activity handles this for you.

Just as with normal activities, list activities need to be registered in the *AndroidManifest.xml* file. This is so they can be used within your app. When you create your activity, Android Studio does this for you.

```
<application
    ... >
    <activity
        android:name=".TopLevelActivity"
        android:label="@string/app_name"
        ...
    </activity>
    <activity
        android:name=".DrinkCategoryActivity"
        android:label="@string/title_activity_drink_category" >
    </activity>
</application>
```

Here's the first activity we created.

Here's the new activity. Every activity needs an entry in AndroidManifest.xml.

Starbuzz
app/src/main
AndroidManifest.xml

Once you've created a list activity, you need to populate the list with data. Let's see how.

android:entries works for static array data held in strings.xml

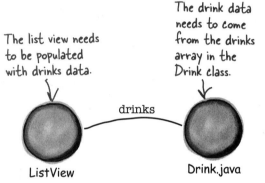

Add resources
TopLevelActivity
DrinkCategoryActivity
DrinkActivity

When we created our first activity `TopLevelActivity`, we could bind data to the list view using the `android:entries` attribute in our layout XML. This worked because the data was held as a static string array resource. The array was described in *strings.xml*, so we could easily refer to it using

```
android:entries="@array/options"
```

where `options` is the name of the string array.

Using `android:entries` only works if the data is a static array in *strings.xml*. But what if it isn't? What if the data is held in an array you've programmatically created in Java code, or held in a database? In this case, the `android:entries` attribute won't work.

If you need to bind your list view to data held in something other than a string array resource, you need to take a different approach; you need to write activity code to bind the data. In our case, we need to bind our list view to the `drinks` array in the `Drink` class.

The list view needs to be populated with drinks data.

The drink data needs to come from the drinks array in the Drink class.

drinks

ListView   Drink.java

For nonstatic data, use an adapter

If you need to display data in a list view that comes from a nonstatic source such as a Java array or database, you need to use an **adapter**. An adapter acts as a bridge between the data source and the list view:

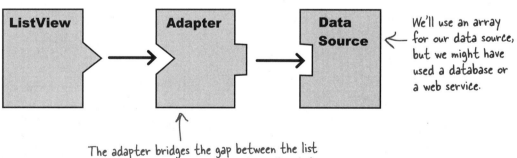

ListView → Adapter → Data Source

We'll use an array for our data source, but we might have used a database or a web service.

The adapter bridges the gap between the list view and the data source. Adapters allow list views to display data from a variety of sources.

There are several different types of adapter. For now, we're going to focus on **array adapters**.

Connect list views to arrays with an array adapter

An array adapter is a type of adapter that's used to bind arrays to views. You can use it with any subclass of the `AdapterView` class, which means you can use it with both list views and spinners.

In our case, we're going to use an array adapter to display data from the `Drink.drinks` array in the list view.

An adapter acts as a bridge between a View and a data source. An ArrayAdapter is a type of adapter that specializes in working with arrays.

This is our list view.

We'll create an array adapter to bind our list view to our array.

This is our array.

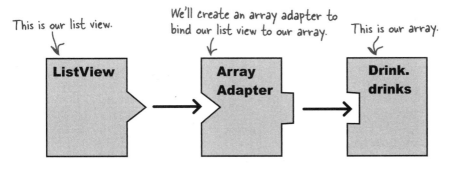

You use an array adapter by initializing the array adapter and attaching it to the list view.

To initialize the array adapter, you first specify what type of data is contained in the array you want to bind to the list view. You then pass it three parameters: a `Context` (usually the current activity), a layout resource that specifies how to display each item in the array, and the array itself.

Here's the code to create an array adapter that displays `Drink` data from the `Drink.drinks` array:

The array contains Drink objects.

```
ArrayAdapter<Drink> listAdapter = new ArrayAdapter<Drink>(
        this,
        android.R.layout.simple_list_item_1,
        Drink.drinks);
```

this is the current activity. The Activity class is a subclass of Context.

→this,

←The array

This is a built-in layout resource. It tells the array adapter to display each item in the array in a single text view.

You then attach the array adapter to the list view using the `ListView` `setAdapter()` method:

```
ListView listView = getListView();
listView.setAdapter(listAdapter);
```

Behind the scenes, the array adapter takes each item in the array, converts it to a `String` using its `toString()` method and puts each result into a text view. It then displays each text view as a single row in the list view.

Add the array adapter to DrinkCategoryActivity

Add resources
TopLevelActivity
DrinkCategoryActivity
DrinkActivity

We'll change the *DrinkCategoryActivity.java* code so that the list view uses an array adapter to get drinks data from the Drink class. We'll put the code in the onCreate() method so that the list view gets populated when the activity gets created.

Here's the full code for the activity (update your code to reflect ours, then save your changes):

```java
package com.hfad.starbuzz;

import android.app.ListActivity;
import android.os.Bundle;
import android.widget.ArrayAdapter;
import android.widget.ListView;

public class DrinkCategoryActivity extends ListActivity {

    @Override
    protected void onCreate(Bundle savedInstanceState) {
        super.onCreate(savedInstanceState);
        ListView listDrinks = getListView();
        ArrayAdapter<Drink> listAdapter = new ArrayAdapter<Drink>(
                this,
                android.R.layout.simple_list_item_1,
                Drink.drinks);
        listDrinks.setAdapter(listAdapter);
    }

}
```

We're using these extra classes.

Starbuzz
app/src/main
java
com.hfad.starbuzz
DrinkCategory
Activity.java

This populates the list view with data from the drinks array.

These are all the changes that you need to get your list view to display a list of the drinks from the Drink class.

These are the drinks from the Drink.drinks array.

What happens when you run the code

1 **When the user clicks on the Drinks option, DrinkCategoryActivity is launched.**
As DrinkCategoryActivity is a list activity, it has a default layout containing a single
ListView object. This layout is created behind the scenes in Java code, so it's not defined by
XML.

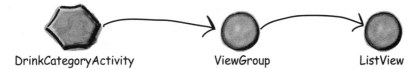

DrinkCategoryActivity   ViewGroup   ListView

2 **DrinkCategoryActivity creates an ArrayAdapter<Drink>, an array adapter
that deals with arrays of Drink objects.**

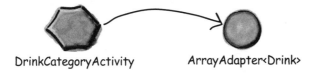

DrinkCategoryActivity   ArrayAdapter<Drink>

3 **The array adapter's source is the drinks array in the Drink class.**
It uses the Drink.toString() method to return the name of each drink.

Drink.toString()

DrinkCategoryActivity   ArrayAdapter<Drink>   Drink.drinks

4 **DrinkCategoryActivity makes the ListView use the array adapter using the
setAdapter() method.**
The list view uses it to display a list of the drink names.

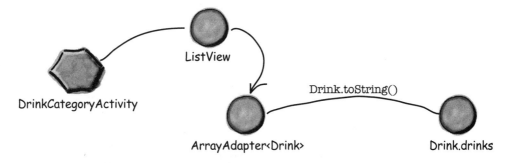

ListView

DrinkCategoryActivity

Drink.toString()

ArrayAdapter<Drink>   Drink.drinks

Test drive the app

When you run the app, `TopLevelActivity` gets displayed as before. When you click on the Drinks item, `DrinkCategoryActivity` is launched. It displays the names of all the drinks from the `Drink` Java class.

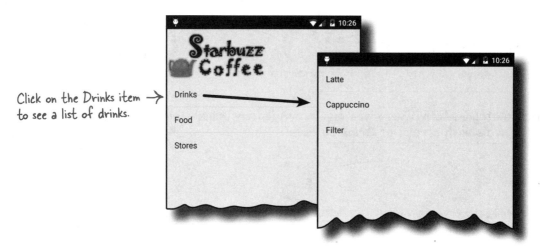

Click on the Drinks item to see a list of drinks.

App review: where we've got to

So far we've added *Drink.java* to our app, and created activities `TopLevelActivity` and `DrinkCategoryActivity`.

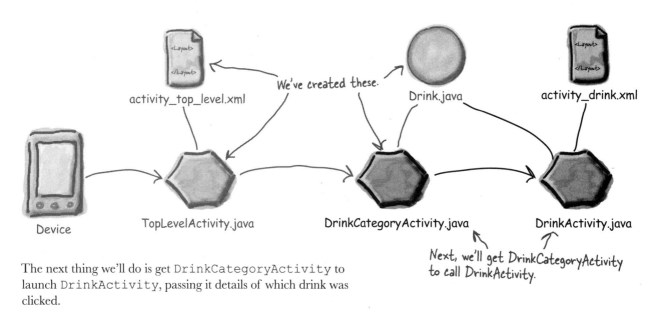

We've created these.

activity_top_level.xml

Drink.java

activity_drink.xml

Device   TopLevelActivity.java   DrinkCategoryActivity.java   DrinkActivity.java

Next, we'll get DrinkCategoryActivity to call DrinkActivity.

The next thing we'll do is get `DrinkCategoryActivity` to launch `DrinkActivity`, passing it details of which drink was clicked.

Pool Puzzle

Your **goal** is to create an activity that binds a Java array of colors to a spinner. Take code snippets from the pool and place them into the blank lines in the activity. You may **not** use the same snippet more than once, and you won't need to use all the snippets.

```
...
public class MainActivity extends Activity {

    String[] colors = new String[] {"Red", "Orange", "Yellow", "Green", "Blue"};

    @Override
    protected void onCreate(Bundle savedInstanceState) {
        super.onCreate(savedInstanceState);
        setContentView(R.layout.activity_main);
        Spinner spinner = (..............) findViewById(R.id.spinner);
        ArrayAdapter<..........> adapter = new ArrayAdapter<..............>(
                .........,
                android.R.layout.simple_spinner_item,
                colors);
        spinner...................(adapter);
    }
}
```

This displays each value in the array as a single row in the spinner.

Note: each thing from the pool can only be used once!

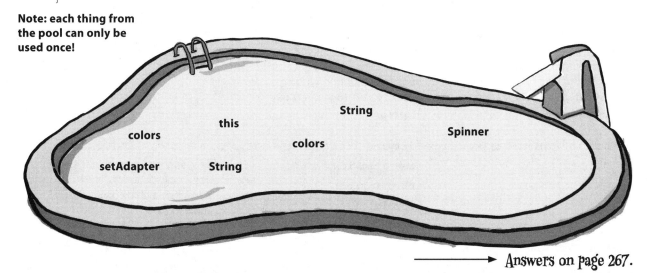

String

colors

this

Spinner

colors

setAdapter

String

Answers on page 267.

How we handled clicks in TopLevelActivity

Add resources
TopLevelActivity
DrinkCategoryActivity
DrinkActivity

Earlier on in the chapter, we needed to get `TopLevelActivity` to react to the user clicking items in the list view. To do that, we had to create an `OnItemClickListener`, implement its `onItemClick()` method, and assign it to the list view:

```
AdapterView.OnItemClickListener itemClickListener = new AdapterView.OnItemClickListener(){
    public void onItemClick(AdapterView<?> listView,        ← The list view
                            View itemView,
                            int position,        The item view that was clicked, its position in
                            long id) {           the list and the row ID of the underlying data.
        //Do something when an item is clicked
    }
};
ListView listView = (ListView) findViewById(R.id.list_options);
listView.setOnItemClickListener(itemClickListener);    ← Add the listener to the list view.
```

We had to set up an event listener in this way because list views aren't hardwired to respond to clicks in the way that buttons are.

So how should we get `DrinkCategoryActivity` to handle user clicks?

ListActivity implements an item click listener by default

There's a significant difference between `TopLevelActivity` and `DrinkCategoryActivity`. Whereas `TopLevelActivity` is a normal `Activity` object, `DrinkCategoryActivity` is a `ListActivity`, a special type of activity that's designed to work with list views.

This is significant when it comes to handling user clicks. A key difference between `Activity` and `ListActivity` is that the `ListActivity` class *already implements an on item click event listener*. Instead of creating your own event listener, **when you use a list activity you just need to implement the `onListItemClick()` method**.

```
public void onListItemClick(ListView listView,        ← These are the same arguments that the
                            View itemView,               onItemClick() method above has: the list
                            int position,                view, the item view that was clicked, its
                            long id) {                   position in the list, and the row ID of
        //Do something                                   the underlying data.
    }
```

Pass data to an activity using the ListActivity onListItemClick() method

When you use a list activity to display categories, you'll usually use the onListItemClick() method to start another activity that displays details of the item the user clicked. To do this, you create an intent that starts the second activity. You then add the ID of the item that was clicked as extra information so that the second activity can use it when the activity starts.

In our case, we want to start DrinkActivity and pass it the ID of the drink that was selected. DrinkActivity will then be able to use this information to display details of the right drink. Here's the code:

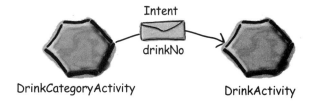

Intent

drinkNo

DrinkCategoryActivity

DrinkActivity

```
public void onListItemClick(ListView listView,        ←This gets called when an item's clicked.
                            View itemView,
                            int position,        DrinkCategoryActivity needs to start
                            long id) {           DrinkActivity.
    Intent intent = new Intent(DrinkCategoryActivity.this, DrinkActivity.class);
    intent.putExtra(DrinkActivity.EXTRA_DRINKNO, (int) id);    ←Add the ID of the item that
    startActivity(intent);                                        was clicked to the intent.
}                                                                 This is the index of the drink
                                                                  in the drinks array.
```

We're using a constant for the name of the extra information in the intent so that we know DrinkCategoryActivity and DrinkActivity are using the same String. We'll add the constant to DrinkActivity when we create the activity.

It's common practice to pass the ID of the item that was clicked as it's the ID of the underlying data. If the underlying data is an array, the ID is the index of the item in the array. If the underlying data comes from a database, the ID is the ID of the record in the table. Passing the ID of the item in this way means that it's easier for the second activity to get details of the data, and then display it.

That's everything we need to make DrinkCategoryActivity start DrinkActivity and tell it which drink was selected. The full activity code is on the next page.

The full DrinkCategoryActivity code

Add resources

TopLevelActivity

DrinkCategoryActivity

DrinkActivity

Here's the full code for *DrinkCategoryActivity.java* (add the new method to your code, then save your changes):

```java
package com.hfad.starbuzz;

import android.app.ListActivity;
import android.os.Bundle;
import android.widget.ArrayAdapter;
import android.widget.ListView;
import android.view.View;
import android.content.Intent;
```

We're using these extra classes.

Starbuzz

app/src/main

java

com.hfad.starbuzz

DrinkCategory
Activity.java

```java
public class DrinkCategoryActivity extends ListActivity {

    @Override
    protected void onCreate(Bundle savedInstanceState) {
        super.onCreate(savedInstanceState);
        ListView listDrinks = getListView();
        ArrayAdapter<Drink> listAdapter = new ArrayAdapter<Drink>(
                this,
                android.R.layout.simple_list_item_1,
                Drink.drinks);
        listDrinks.setAdapter(listAdapter);
    }

    @Override
    public void onListItemClick(ListView listView,
                                View itemView,
                                int position,
                                long id) {
        Intent intent = new Intent(DrinkCategoryActivity.this, DrinkActivity.class);
        intent.putExtra(DrinkActivity.EXTRA_DRINKNO, (int) id);
        startActivity(intent);
    }
}
```

Implement the onListItemClick() method so that DrinkActivity is launched when the user clicks on an item in the list view.

We're adding DrinkActivity next, so don't worry if Android Studio says it doesn't exist.

A detail activity displays data for a single record

As we said earlier, `DrinkActivity` is an example of a detail activity. A detail activity displays details for a particular record, and you generally navigate to it from a category activity.

We're going to use `DrinkActivity` to display details of the drink the user selects. The `Drink` class includes the drink name, description, and image resource ID, so we'll display this data in our layout. We'll include an image view for the drink image resource, and text views for the drink name and description.

Here's our layout code. Add a new activity to your project called `DrinkActivity` with a layout called `activity_drink`, then replace the contents of *activity_drink.xml* with this:

← *Make sure you create the new activity.*

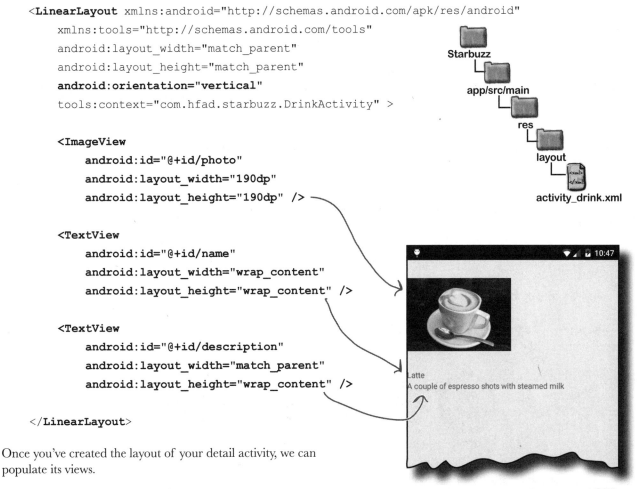

```xml
<LinearLayout xmlns:android="http://schemas.android.com/apk/res/android"
    xmlns:tools="http://schemas.android.com/tools"
    android:layout_width="match_parent"
    android:layout_height="match_parent"
    android:orientation="vertical"
    tools:context="com.hfad.starbuzz.DrinkActivity" >

    <ImageView
        android:id="@+id/photo"
        android:layout_width="190dp"
        android:layout_height="190dp" />

    <TextView
        android:id="@+id/name"
        android:layout_width="wrap_content"
        android:layout_height="wrap_content" />

    <TextView
        android:id="@+id/description"
        android:layout_width="match_parent"
        android:layout_height="wrap_content" />

</LinearLayout>
```

Once you've created the layout of your detail activity, we can populate its views.

Retrieve data from the intent

☑ Add resources
☑ TopLevelActivity
☑ DrinkCategoryActivity
→ **DrinkActivity**

As you've seen, when you get a category activity to start a detail activity, you get items in the category activity list view to respond to clicks. When an item is clicked, you create an intent to start the detail activity. You pass the ID of the item the user clicked as extra information in the intent.

When the detail activity is started, the detail activity can retrieve the extra information from the intent and use it to populate its views. In our case, we can use the information in the intent that started `DrinkActivity` to retrieve details of the drink the user clicked.

When we created `DrinkCategoryActivity`, we added the ID of the drink the user clicked as extra information in the intent. We gave it a label of `DrinkActivity.EXTRA_DRINKNO`, which we need to define as a constant in `DrinkActivity`:

```
public static final String EXTRA_DRINKNO = "drinkNo";
```

As you saw in Chapter 3, you can retrieve the intent that started an activity using the `getIntent()` method. If this intent has extra information, you can use the intent's `get*()` methods to retrieve it. Here's the code to retrieve the value of `EXTRA_DRINKNO` from the intent that started `DrinkActivity`:

```
int drinkNo = (Integer)getIntent().getExtras().get(EXTRA_DRINKNO);
```

Once you've retrieved the information from the intent, you can use it to get the data you need to display in your detail record.

In our case, we can use `drinkNo` to get details of the drink the user selected. `drinkNo` is the ID of the drink, the index of the drink in the `drinks` array. This means that you can get the drink the user clicked on using:

```
Drink drink = Drink.drinks[drinkNo];
```

This gives us a `Drink` object containing all the information we need to update the views attributes in the activity:

drink

name="Latte"
description="A couple of espresso shots with steamed milk"
imageResourceId=R.drawable.latte

Update the views with the data

When you update the views in your detail activity, you need to make sure that the values they display reflect the data you've derived from the intent.

Our detail activity contains two text views and an image view. We need to make sure that each of these is updated to reflect the details of the drink.

name
description
imageResourceId

drink

Drink Magnets

See if you can use the magnets below to populate the `DrinkActivity` views with the correct data.

```
...
//Get the drink from the intent
int drinkNo = (Integer)getIntent().getExtras().get(EXTRA_DRINKNO);
Drink drink = Drink.drinks[drinkNo];



//Populate the drink image
ImageView photo = (ImageView)findViewById(R.id.photo);

photo.......................................(drink.getImageResourceId());

photo..........................................(drink.getName());



//Populate the drink name
TextView name = (TextView)findViewById(R.id.name);

name..................(drink.getName());



//Populate the drink description
TextView description = (TextView)findViewById(R.id.description);

description................(drink.getDescription());
...
```

| setText |

| setContentDescription |

| setContent |

| setImageResourceId |

| setImageResource |

| setText |

Drink Magnets Solution

See if you can use the magnets below to populate the
DrinkActivity views with the correct data.

```
...
//Get the drink from the intent
int drinkNo = (Integer)getIntent().getExtras().get(EXTRA_DRINKNO);
Drink drink = Drink.drinks[drinkNo];


//Populate the drink image
ImageView photo = (ImageView)findViewById(R.id.photo);
```

You set the source of the image using setImageResource().

```
photo. setImageResource (drink.getImageResourceId());
```

This is needed to make the app more accessible.

```
photo. setContentDescription (drink.getName());
```

```
//Populate the drink name
TextView name = (TextView)findViewById(R.id.name);

name. setText (drink.getName());
```

Use setText() to set the text in a text view.

```
//Populate the drink description
TextView description = (TextView)findViewById(R.id.description);

description. setText (drink.getDescription());
...
```

You didn't need to use these.

setContent

setImageResourceId

The DrinkActivity code

Here's the code for *DrinkActivity.java* (replace the code the wizard gave you with the code below, then save your changes):

```java
package com.hfad.starbuzz;

import android.app.Activity;
import android.os.Bundle;
import android.widget.ImageView;
import android.widget.TextView;

public class DrinkActivity extends Activity {

    public static final String EXTRA_DRINKNO = "drinkNo";
```

Add EXTRA_DRINKNO as a constant.

```java
    @Override
    protected void onCreate(Bundle savedInstanceState) {
        super.onCreate(savedInstanceState);
        setContentView(R.layout.activity_drink);

        //Get the drink from the intent
        int drinkNo = (Integer)getIntent().getExtras().get(EXTRA_DRINKNO);
        Drink drink = Drink.drinks[drinkNo];
```

Use the drinkNo to get details of the drink the user chose.

```java
        //Populate the drink image
        ImageView photo = (ImageView)findViewById(R.id.photo);
        photo.setImageResource(drink.getImageResourceId());
        photo.setContentDescription(drink.getName());

        //Populate the drink name
        TextView name = (TextView)findViewById(R.id.name);
        name.setText(drink.getName());
```

Populate the views with the drink data.

```java
        //Populate the drink description
        TextView description = (TextView)findViewById(R.id.description);
        description.setText(drink.getDescription());
    }
}
```

Starbuzz
app/src/main
java
com.hfad.starbuzz
DrinkActivity.java

What happens when you run the app

① When the user starts the app, it launches TopLevelActivity.

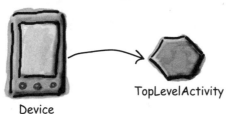

Device   TopLevelActivity

② The onCreate() method in TopLevelActivity creates an
onItemClickListener and links it to the activity's ListView.

TopLevelActivity   ListView   onItemClickListener

③ When the user clicks on an item in the list view, the
onItemClickListener's onItemClick() method gets called.

If the Drinks item was clicked, the `onItemClickListener` creates an intent to start
`DrinkCategoryActivity`.

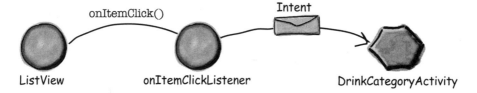

onItemClick()   Intent

ListView   onItemClickListener   DrinkCategoryActivity

④ **DrinkCategoryActivity is a ListActivity.**

The `DrinkCategoryActivity` list view uses an `ArrayAdapter<Drink>` to display a
list of drink names.

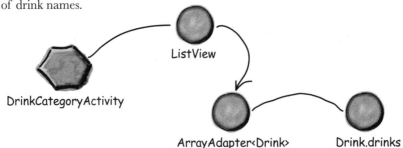

ListView

DrinkCategoryActivity

ArrayAdapter<Drink>   Drink.drinks

The story continues

5 When the user chooses a drink from the ListView, the onListItemClick() method gets called.

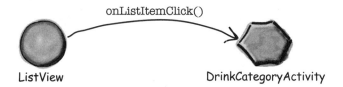

6 The DrinkCategoryActivity's onListItemClick() method creates an intent to start DrinkActivity, passing along the drink number as extra information.

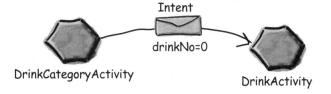

7 **DrinkActivity is launched.**
It retrieves the drink number from the intent, and gets details for the correct drink from the Drink class. It uses this information to update its views.

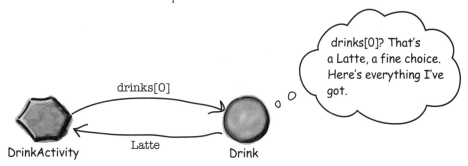

Test drive the app

When you run the app, `TopLevelActivity` gets displayed as before.

We implemented the Drinks part of the app. The other items won't do anything if you click on them.

When you click on the Drinks item, `DrinkCategoryActivity` is launched. It displays all the drinks from the `Drink` java class.

When you click on one of the drinks, `DrinkActivity` is launched and details of the drink the user selected are displayed.

We clicked on the Latte option...

...and here are details of the Latte.

Using these three activities, you can see how to structure your app into top-level activities, category activities, and detail/edit activities. Later on, we'll revisit the Starbuzz app so that you can see how you can retrieve the drinks from a database.

Pool Puzzle Solution

Your **goal** is to create an activity that binds a Java array of colors to a spinner. Take code snippets from the pool and place them into the blank lines in the activity. You may **not** use the same snippet more than once, and you won't need to use all the snippets.

```
...
public class MainActivity extends Activity {

    String[] colors = new String[] {"Red", "Orange", "Yellow", "Green", "Blue"};

    @Override
    protected void onCreate(Bundle savedInstanceState) {
        super.onCreate(savedInstanceState);
        setContentView(R.layout.activity_main);
        Spinner spinner = ( Spinner ) findViewById(R.id.spinner);
        ArrayAdapter< String > adapter = new ArrayAdapter< String >(
                this ,
                android.R.layout.simple_spinner_item,
                colors);
        spinner. setAdapter (adapter);
    }
}
```

We're using an array of type String.

Use setAdapter() to get the spinner to use the array adapter.

These code snippets were not needed here.

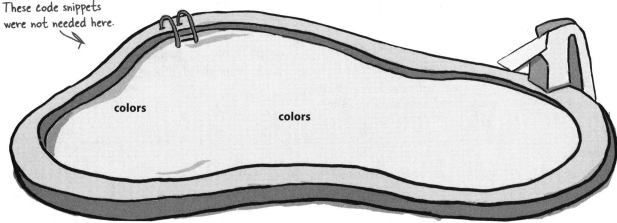

colors   colors

Your Android Toolbox

You've got Chapter 6 under your belt and now you've added list views and app design to your toolbox.

You can download the full code for the chapter from https://tinyurl.com/HeadFirstAndroid.

BULLET POINTS

- Sort your ideas for activities into top-level activities, category activities, and detail/edit activities. Use the category activities to navigate from the top-level activities to the detail/edit activities.

- Image resources go in one or more of the *drawable** folders. You reference them in your layout using `@drawable/image_name`. You access them in your activity code using `R.drawable.image_name`.

- An `ImageView` holds an image. Add it to your layout using `<ImageView>`. Use `android:src` to set its source, and `android:contentDescription` to give it an accessible label. The equivalent methods in Java are `setImageResource()` and `setContentDescription()`.

- A `ListView` displays items in a list. Add it to your layout using `<ListView>`.

- Use `android:entries` in your layout to populate the items in your list views from an array defined in *strings.xml*.

- A `ListActivity` is an `Activity` that comes with a `ListView`. You get a reference to the `ListView` using `getListView()`.

- A `ListActivity` has its own default layout, but you can replace it with your own.

- An adapter acts as a bridge between an `AdapterView` and a data source. `ListView`s and `Spinner`s are both types of `AdapterView`.

- An `ArrayAdapter` is an adapter that works with arrays.

- Handle click events on `Button`s using `android:onClick` in the layout code.

- Handle click events on a `ListView` in a `ListActivity` by implementing the `onListItemClick()` method.

- Handle click events elsewhere by creating a listener and implementing its click event.

7 fragments

Make it Modular

Doing the same job in different places... I guess that makes me a fragment.

You've seen how to create apps that work in the same way irrespective of the device they're running on.

But what if you want your app to **look and behave differently** depending on whether it's running on a **phone** or a **tablet**? In this chapter, we'll show you how to make your app choose the **most appropriate layout for the device screen size**. We'll also introduce you to **fragments**, a way of creating **modular code components** that can be **reused by different activities**.

Your app needs to look great on all devices

One of the great things about Android development is that you
can put the exact same app on devices with completely different
screen sizes and processors, and have them run in exactly the
same way. But that doesn't mean that they always have to *look*
exactly the same.

On a phone:

Take a look at this image of an app on
a phone. It displays a list of workouts,
and when you click on one, you are
shown the details of that workout.

Click on an item in a list, and
it launches a second activity.

On a tablet:

On a larger device,
like a tablet, you have
a lot more screen
space available. It
would be good if
all the information
appeared on the
same screen. On
the tablet, the list of
workouts only goes
part-way across the
screen, and when
you click on an item,
the details appear on
the right.

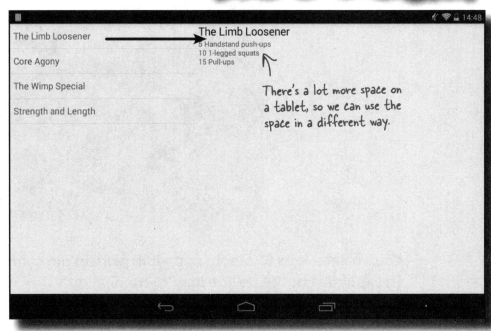

There's a lot more space on
a tablet, so we can use the
space in a different way.

To make the phone and tablet user interfaces look different from
each other, we can use separate layouts for large devices and
small devices.

Your app may need to behave differently too

It's not enough to simply have different layouts for different devices. You also need *different Java code* to run alongside the layouts so that the app can behave differently depending on the device. In our Workout app, for instance, we need to provide **one activity for tablets**, and **two activities for phones**.

On a phone:

Here we have two activities: one for the list and one for the details.

On a tablet:

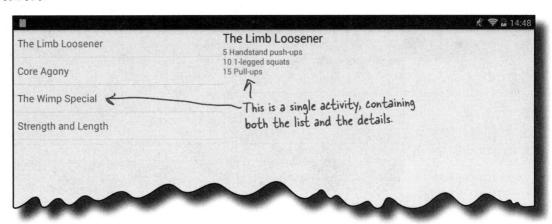

This is a single activity, containing both the list and the details.

But that means you might duplicate code

The second activity that runs only on phones will need to insert the details of a workout into the layout. But that code will also need to be available in the main activity for when the app is running on a tablet. *The same code needs to be run by multiple activities.*

Rather than duplicate the code in the two activities, we can use **fragments**. So what's a fragment?

Fragments allow you to reuse code

Fragments are like reusable components or subactivities. A
fragment is used to control part of a screen, and can be reused
between screens. This means we can create a fragment for the
list of workouts, and a fragment to display the details of a single
workout. These fragments can then be shared between layouts.

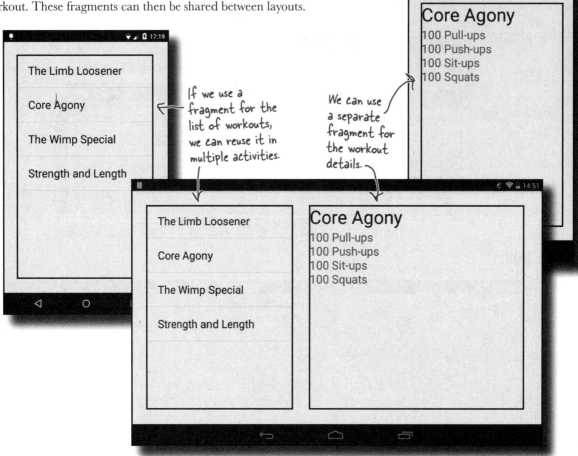

If we use a fragment for the list of workouts, we can reuse it in multiple activities.

We can use a separate fragment for the workout details.

A fragment has a layout

Just like an activity, a fragment has an associated layout. If
you design it carefully, the Java code can be used to control
everything within the interface. If the fragment code contains
all that you need to control its layout, it greatly increases the
chances that you'll be able to reuse it elsewhere in the app.

We're going to show you how to create and use fragments by
building the Workout app.

The Workout app structure

For most of this chapter, we're going to focus on building the version
of the app that displays two fragments alongside each other in a
single activity. Here's a breakdown of how the app is structured, and
what it does.

1 **When the app gets launched, it starts activity MainActivity.**
The activity uses layout *activity_main.xml*.

2 **The activity uses two fragments, WorkoutListFragment, and
WorkoutDetailFragment.**

3 **WorkoutListFragment displays a list of workouts.**
It uses *fragment_workout_list.xml* as its layout.

4 **WorkoutDetailFragment displays details of a workout.**
It uses *fragment_workout_detail.xml* as its layout.

5 **Both fragments get their workout data from *Workout.java*.**
Workout.java contains an array of Workouts.

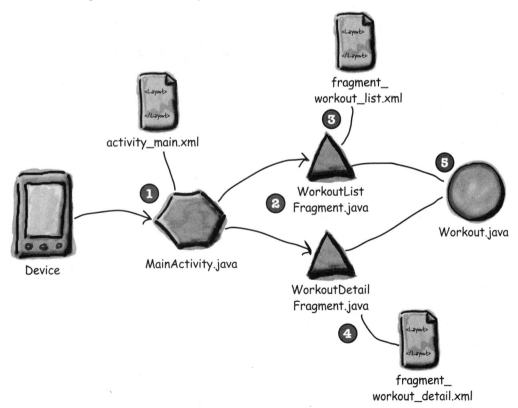

Here are the steps

There are a number of steps we'll go through to build the app:

1 **Create the fragments.**
We'll create two fragments. `WorkoutListFragment` will be used to display a list of workouts, and `WorkoutDetailFragment` will be used to display details of a specific workout. We'll display these fragments in a single activity. We'll also add a plain old Java `Workout` class that the fragments will use to get their data from.

2 **Link the two fragments.**
When we click on a workout in `WorkoutListFragment`, we want to display details of the workout in `WorkoutDetailFragment`.

3 **Create device-specific layouts.**
Finally, we're going to change our app so that it looks and behaves differently depending on what sort of device it's run on. If it's run on a device with a large screen, the fragments will be displayed alongside each other. If not, they'll be displayed in separate activities.

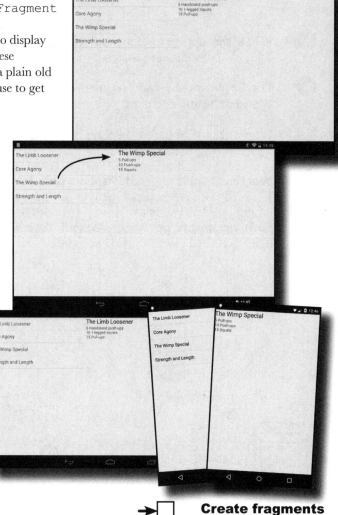

Create fragments
Link fragments
Device layouts

Create the project

You create the project for the app in exactly the same way you did for the previous chapters.

Create a new Android project with a blank activity for an application named "Workout" with a package name of `com.hfad.workout`. The minimum SDK should be *at least* API 17, as we'll use this app in the next chapter to cover areas that require API 17 or above. You'll need to specify an activity called "MainActivity" and a layout called "activity_main" so your code matches ours.

The Workout class

We'll start by adding the `Workout` class to the app.
Workout.java is a pure Java class file that the app will get workout data
from. The class defines an array of four workouts, where each workout
is composed of a name and description. Add the class to the *com.hfad.*
workout package in the *app/src/main/java* folder in your project, giving
it a class name of `Workout`. Then save your changes.

```java
package com.hfad.workout;
```
                                            Each Workout has a name and description.
```java
public class Workout {
    private String name;
    private String description;
```
                                    workouts is an array of four Workouts.
```java
    public static final Workout[] workouts = {
            new Workout("The Limb Loosener",
                    "5 Handstand push-ups\n10 1-legged squats\n15 Pull-ups"),
            new Workout("Core Agony",
                    "100 Pull-ups\n100 Push-ups\n100 Sit-ups\n100 Squats"),
            new Workout("The Wimp Special",
                    "5 Pull-ups\n10 Push-ups\n15 Squats"),
            new Workout("Strength and Length",
                    "500 meter run\n21 x 1.5 pood kettleball swing\n21 x pull-ups")
    };

    //Each Workout has a name and description
    private Workout(String name, String description) {
        this.name = name;
        this.description = description;
    }

    public String getDescription() {
        return description;
    }

    public String getName() {
        return name;
    }
```
                            These are getters for the private variables.
```java
    public String toString() {
        return this.name;
    }
}
```
                            The String representation of a Workout is its name.

Workout
  └─ *app/src/main*
        └─ *java*
              └─ *com.hfad.workout*
                    └─ *Workout.java*

The data will be used by the fragment `WorkoutDetailFragment`.
We'll create this fragment next.

How to add a fragment to your project

We're going to add a new fragment called `WorkoutDetailFragment` to the project to display details of a single workout. You add a new fragment in a similar way to how you add a new activity. In Android Studio, go to File→New...→Fragment→Fragment (Blank).

You will be asked to choose options for your new fragment. Give the fragment a name of "WorkoutDetailFragment", tick the option to create layout XML for it, and give the fragment layout a name of "fragment_workout_detail". Untick the options to include fragment factory methods and interface callbacks; these options generate extra code which you don't need to use. When you're done, click on the Finish button.

We suggest looking at the extra code Android generates for you after you've finished this book. You might find some of it useful depending on what you want to do.

Choose options for your new file

Creates a blank fragment that is compatible back to API level 4.

This is the name of the fragment.

Fragment Name: `WorkoutDetailFragment`

☑ Create layout XML?

Fragment Layout Name: `fragment_workout_detail`

This is the name of the fragment layout.

☐ Include fragment factory methods?   ☐ Include interface callbacks?

We don't want Android Studio creating a load of extra code for us, so we're unticking these options.

Fragment (Blank)

We're creating a blank fragment.

Generate event callbacks for communication with an Activity or other fragments

[Cancel] [Previous] [Next] [**Finish**]

When you click on the Finish button, Android Studio creates a new fragment file called *WorkoutDetailFragment.java* in the *app/src/main/java* folder, and a new layout file called *fragment_workout_detail.xml* in the *app/src/res/layout* folder.

Fragment layout code looks just like activity layout code

We'll start by updating the layout code for the fragment. Open the file *fragment_workout_detail.xml* in the *app/src/res/layout* folder, and replace its contents with the code below:

```xml
<?xml version="1.0" encoding="utf-8"?>
<LinearLayout xmlns:android="http://schemas.android.com/apk/res/android"
    android:layout_height="match_parent"
    android:layout_width="match_parent"
    android:orientation="vertical">
```

We're displaying the workout name and description in two separate TextViews.

```xml
    <TextView
        android:layout_width="wrap_content"
        android:layout_height="wrap_content"
        android:textAppearance="?android:attr/textAppearanceLarge"
        android:text=""
        android:id="@+id/textTitle" />
```

This is the workout name.

```xml
    <TextView
        android:layout_width="wrap_content"
        android:layout_height="wrap_content"
        android:text=""
        android:id="@+id/textDescription" />
```

This is the workout description.

```xml
</LinearLayout>
```

Core Agony
100 Pull-ups
100 Push-ups
100 Sit-ups
100 Squats

This is a fragment that we can use inside our activities.

As you can see, fragment layout code looks just like activity layout code. This is a very simple layout made up of two text views: a text view with large text to display the name of the workout, and a text view with smaller text to display the workout description. When you write your own fragment layout code, you can use any of the views and layouts you've already been using to write activity layout code.

Now that we've created a layout for our fragment to use, we'll look at the fragment code itself.

What fragment code looks like

The code for the fragment is held in *WorkoutDetailFragment.java* in the *app/ src/main/java* folder. Open this file now.

As you'd expect, Android Studio has generated Java code for you. Replace the code that Android Studio has generated with the code below:

```
package com.hfad.workout;

import android.app.Fragment;
import android.os.Bundle;
import android.view.LayoutInflater;
import android.view.View;
import android.view.ViewGroup;

public class WorkoutDetailFragment extends Fragment {

    @Override
    public View onCreateView(LayoutInflater inflater, ViewGroup container,
                             Bundle savedInstanceState) {
        return inflater.inflate(R.layout.fragment_workout_detail, container, false);
    }
}
```

The class extends the Android Fragment class.

This is the onCreateView() method. It's called when Android needs the fragment's layout.

↖ This tells Android which layout the fragment uses (in this case, it's fragment_workout_detail).

Workout
app/src/main
java
com.hfad.workout
WorkoutDetail
Fragment.java

The above code creates a basic fragment. As you can see, it's a class that extends the `android.app.Fragment` class. All fragments must subclass the `Fragment` class.

Our fragment also implements the `onCreateView()` method. The `onCreateView()` method gets called each time Android needs the fragment's layout, and it's where you say which layout the fragment uses. This method is optional, but as you need to implement it whenever you're creating a fragment with a layout, you'll need to implement it almost every time you create a fragment.

You specify the fragment's layout using the code

```
inflater.inflate(R.layout.fragment_workout_detail,
        container, false);
```

This is the fragment equivalent of an activity's `setContentView()` method. Just like `setContentView()`, you use it to say what layout the fragment should use. The container argument is passed by the activity that uses the fragment. It's the `ViewGroup` in the activity that the fragment layout needs to be inserted into.

Watch it!

All fragments must have a public no-argument constructor.

This is because Android uses it to reinstantiate the fragment when needed, and if it's not there, you'll get a runtime exception.

In practice, you only need to add one to your fragment code if you include another constructor with one or more arguments. This is because if a Java class contains no constructors, the Java compiler automatically adds a public no-argument constructor for you.

Adding a fragment to an activity's layout

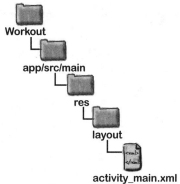

Workout

app/src/main

res

layout

activity_main.xml

When we created our project, Android Studio created an activity for us called *MainActivity.java*, and a layout called *activity_main.xml*. We're going to change the layout so that it contains the fragment we just created.

To do this, open the *activity_main.xml* file in the *app/src/main/res/layout* folder, and replace the code Android Studio has given you with the code below:

```xml
<?xml version="1.0" encoding="utf-8"?>
<LinearLayout xmlns:android="http://schemas.android.com/apk/res/android"
    android:orientation="horizontal"
    android:layout_width="match_parent"
    android:layout_height="match_parent">

    <fragment
        class="com.hfad.workout.WorkoutDetailFragment"
        android:id="@+id/detail_frag"
        android:layout_width="match_parent"
        android:layout_height="match_parent" />
</LinearLayout>
```

This adds the fragment WorkoutDetailFragment to the activity's layout.

As you can see, the layout contains one element, `<fragment>`. You use the `<fragment>` element to add a fragment to an activity's layout. You specify which fragment using the `class` attribute and setting it to the fully qualified name of the fragment. In our case, we're going to create a fragment called `WorkoutDetailFragment` in the `com.hfad.workout` package, so we use

class="com.hfad.workout.WorkoutDetailFragment"

We've created a fragment and got the activity to display it in its layout. So far, though, the fragment doesn't actually do anything. What we need to do next is get the activity to say which workout to display, and get the fragment to populate its views with details of the workout.

17:19

Core Agony
100 Pull-ups
100 Push-ups
100 Sit-ups
100 Squats

Passing the workout ID to the fragment

When you have an activity that uses a fragment, the activity will usually need to talk to it in some way. As an example, if you have a fragment that displays detail records, you need the activity to tell the fragment which record to display details of.

In our case, we need WorkoutDetailFragment to display details of a particular workout. To do this, we'll add a simple setter method to the fragment that sets the value of the workout ID. The activity will then be able to use this method to set the workout ID. Later on, we'll use the workout ID to update the fragment's views.

Here's the revised code for WorkoutDetailFragment (update your code with our changes):

```
package com.hfad.workout;

import android.app.Fragment;
import android.os.Bundle;
import android.view.LayoutInflater;
import android.view.View;
import android.view.ViewGroup;

public class WorkoutDetailFragment extends Fragment {
    private long workoutId;
    @Override
    public View onCreateView(LayoutInflater inflater, ViewGroup container,
                        Bundle savedInstanceState) {
        return inflater.inflate(R.layout.fragment_workout_detail, container, false);
    }

    public void setWorkout(long id) {
        this.workoutId = id;
    }
}
```

← This is the ID of the workout the user chooses. Later, we'll use it to set the values of fragment's views with the workout details.

← This is a setter method for the workout ID. The activity will use this method to set the value of the workout ID.

Workout

app/src/main

java

com.hfad.workout

WorkoutDetail Fragment.java

The activity needs to call the fragment's setWorkout() method and pass it the ID of a particular workout. Let's see how.

Get the activity to set the workout ID

Before an activity can talk to its fragment, the activity first needs to get a reference to it. To get a reference to the fragment, you first get a reference to the activity's **fragment manager** using the activity's getFragmentManager() method. You then use its findFragmentById() method to get a reference to the fragment:

This is the ID of the fragment in the activity's layout.

```
getFragmentManager().findFragmentById(R.id.fragment_id)
```

findFragmentById() is a bit like findViewById() except you use it to get a reference to a fragment.

The fragment manager is used to manage any fragments used by the activity. You use it to get references to fragments, and perform fragment transactions. You'll see more about this later in the chapter.

Here's our full activity code (replace the existing code in *MainActivity.java* with the code shown here):

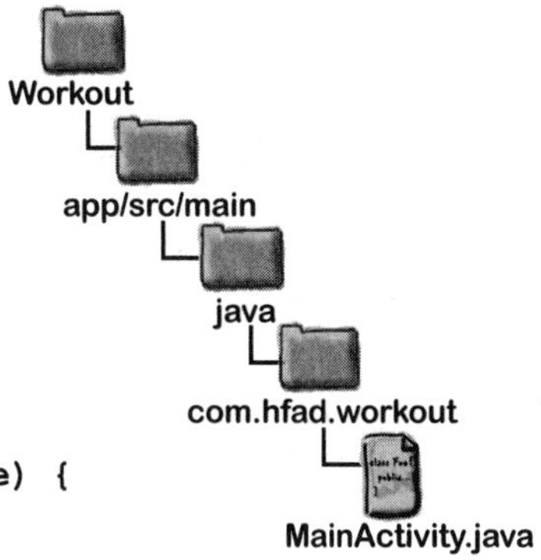

```java
package com.hfad.workout;

import android.app.Activity;
import android.os.Bundle;

public class MainActivity extends Activity {

    @Override
    protected void onCreate(Bundle savedInstanceState) {
        super.onCreate(savedInstanceState);
        setContentView(R.layout.activity_main);
        WorkoutDetailFragment frag = (WorkoutDetailFragment)
                        getFragmentManager().findFragmentById(R.id.detail_frag);
        frag.setWorkout(1);
    }
}
```

We're going to get WorkoutDetailFragment to display details of a workout here to check it's working.

Workout

app/src/main

java

com.hfad.workout

MainActivity.java

This gets us a reference to WorkoutDetailFragment. Its id in the activity's layout is detail_frag.

As you can see, we've got a reference to the fragment after calling setContentView(). This is really important, because before this, the fragment won't have been created.

We're using the code frag.setWorkout(1) to tell fragment which workout we want it to display details of. This is the custom method that we created in our fragment. For now, we're just setting the ID of the workout in the activity's onCreate() method so that we can see some data. Later on, we'll change it so that the user can select which workout they want to see.

The next thing we need to do is get the fragment to update its views when the fragment is displayed to the user. But before we can do this, we need to understand the fragment's lifecycle.

Activity states revisited

Just like an activity, a fragment has a number of key lifecycle methods that get called at particular times. It's important to know what these are and when they get called so your fragment works in just the way you want.

Fragments are contained within and controlled by activities, so the fragment lifecycle is closely linked to the activity lifecycle. Here's a reminder of the different states an activity goes through, and on the next page we'll show you how these relate to the fragment.

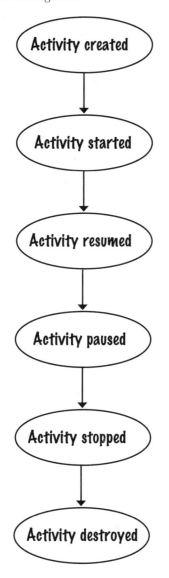

The activity is created when its onCreate() method runs.
At this point, the activity is initialized, but isn't visible.

The activity is started when its onStart() method runs.
The activity is visible, but doesn't have the focus.

The activity is resumed when its onResume() method runs.
The activity is visible, and has the focus.

The activity is paused when its onPause() method runs.
The activity is still visible, but no longer has the focus.

The activity is stopped when its onStop() method runs.
The activity is no longer visible, but still exists.

The activity is destroyed when its onDestroy() method runs.
The activity no longer exists.

The fragment lifecycle

A fragment's lifecycle is very similar to an activity's, but it has a few extra steps. This is because it needs to interact with the lifecycle of the activity that contains it. Here are the fragment lifecycle methods, along with where they fit in with the different activity states.

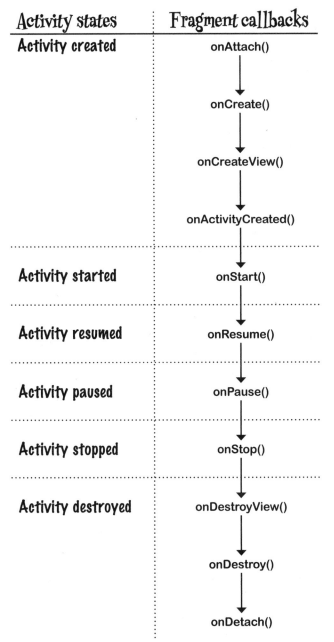

Activity states	Fragment callbacks
Activity created	onAttach()
	onCreate()
	onCreateView()
	onActivityCreated()
Activity started	onStart()
Activity resumed	onResume()
Activity paused	onPause()
Activity stopped	onStop()
Activity destroyed	onDestroyView()
	onDestroy()
	onDetach()

onAttach(Activity)
This happens when the fragment is associated with an activity.

onCreate(Bundle)
This is very similar to the activity's onCreate() method. It can be used to do the initial setup of the fragment.

onCreateView(LayoutInflater, ViewGroup, Bundle)
Fragments use a layout inflater to create their view at this stage.

onActivityCreated(Bundle)
This method is called when the onCreate() method of the activity has completed.

onStart()
The onStart() method is called when the fragment is about to become visible.

onResume()
Called when the fragment is visible and actively running.

onPause()
Called when the fragment is no longer interacting with the user.

onStop()
Called when the fragment is no longer visible to the user.

onDestroyView()
Gives the fragment the chance to clear away any resources that were associated with its view.

onDestroy()
In this method, the fragment can clear away any other resources it created.

onDetach()
When the fragment finally loses contact with the activity.

Your fragment inherits the lifecycle methods

Create fragments
Link fragments
Device layouts

As you saw earlier, your fragment extends the Android `fragment` class. This class gives your fragment access to the fragment lifecycle methods.

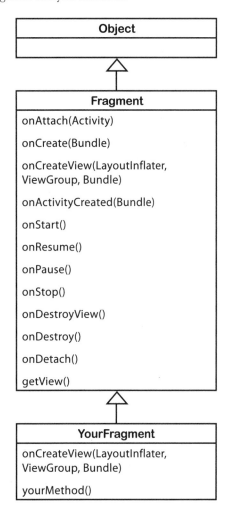

Object class
(java.lang.Object)

Fragment class
(android.app.Fragment)

The Fragment class implements default versions of the lifecycle methods. It also defines other methods that fragments need, such as getView().

YourFragment class
(com.hfad.foo)

Most of the behavior of your fragment is handled by superclass methods. All you do is override the methods you need.

Even though fragments have a lot in common with activities, the `Fragment` class doesn't extend the `Activity` class. This means that some methods that are available to activities aren't available to fragments.

Note that the `Fragment` class doesn't implement the `Context` class. Unlike an activity, a fragment isn't a type of context and therefore doesn't have direct access to global information about the application environment. Instead, fragments must access this information using the context of other objects such as its parent activity.

Set the view's values in the fragment's onStart() method

We need to get `WorkoutDetailFragment` to update its views with details of the workout. We need to do this when the activity is started, so we'll use the fragment's `onStart()` method. Here's the code:

```java
package com.hfad.workout;

import android.app.Fragment;
import android.os.Bundle;
import android.view.LayoutInflater;
import android.view.View;
import android.view.ViewGroup;
import android.widget.TextView;
```

We're using this class in the onStart() method.

```java
public class WorkoutDetailFragment extends Fragment {
    private long workoutId;

    @Override
    public View onCreateView(LayoutInflater inflater, ViewGroup container,
                             Bundle savedInstanceState) {
        return inflater.inflate(R.layout.fragment_workout_detail, container, false);
    }

    @Override
    public void onStart() {
        super.onStart();
        View view = getView();
        if (view != null) {
            TextView title = (TextView) view.findViewById(R.id.textTitle);
            Workout workout = Workout.workouts[(int) workoutId];
            title.setText(workout.getName());
            TextView description = (TextView) view.findViewById(R.id.textDescription);
            description.setText(workout.getDescription());
        }
    }
    public void setWorkout(long id) {
        this.workoutId = id;
    }
}
```

The getView() method gets the fragment's root View. We can then use this to get references to the workout title and description text views.

Workout
app/src/main
java
com.hfad.workout
WorkoutDetail Fragment.java

As we said on the previous page, fragments are distinct from activities, and therefore don't have all the methods that an activity does. Fragments don't include a `findViewById()` method, for instance. To get a reference to a fragment's views, we first have to get a reference to the fragment's root view using the `getView()` method, and use that to find its child views.

Now that we've got the fragment to update its views, let's take the app for a test drive.

> **You should always call up to the superclass when you implement any fragment lifecycle methods.**

Test drive the app

When we run the app, details of a workout appear on the device screen.

The app looks the same as if the workout details were displayed within an activity. Because the activity is using a *fragment* to display details of the workout, we can reuse the fragment in another activity if we want to.

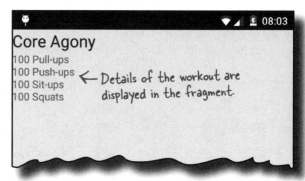

Details of the workout are displayed in the fragment.

What happens when you run the app

① When the app is launched, activity MainActivity gets created.

Device   MainActivity

② MainActivity passes the workout ID to WorkoutDetailFragment in its onCreate() method by calling the fragment's setWorkout() method.

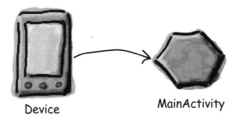

setWorkout(1)

MainActivity   WorkoutList Fragment

③ The fragment uses the value of the workout ID in its onStart() method to set the values of its views.

textTitle: CoreAgony

textDescription: 100 Pull ups
100 Push-ups
100 Sit ups
100 Squats

MainActivity   WorkoutList Fragment

Where we've got to

So far, we've created *MainActivity.java*, its layout *activity_main.xml*, the fragment *WorkoutDetailFragment.java*, its layout *fragment_workout_detail.xml*, and the plain old Java class file *Workout.java*. `MainActivity` uses `WorkoutListFragment` to display details of the workout, and it gets the workout data from the `Workout` class.

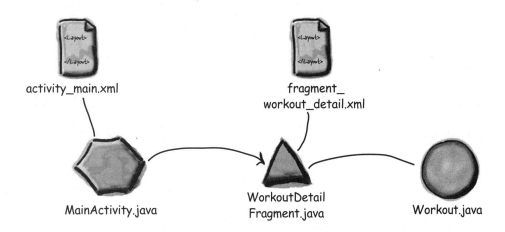

activity_main.xml   fragment_workout_detail.xml

MainActivity.java   WorkoutDetail Fragment.java   Workout.java

The next thing we need to do is create the fragment `WorkoutListFragment` to display a list of the workouts.

there are no Dumb Questions

Q: Why can't an activity get a fragment by calling the `findViewById()` method?

A: Because `findViewById()` always returns a `View` object and, surprisingly, fragments aren't views.

Q: Why isn't `findFragmentById()` an activity method like `findViewById()` is?

A: That's a good question. Fragments weren't available in early versions of Android. It uses the fragment manager as a way to add a whole bunch of useful code for managing fragments, without having to pack lots of extra code into the activity base class.

Q: Why don't fragments have a `findViewById()` method?

A: Because fragments aren't views or activities. Instead, you need to use the fragment's `getView()` method to get a reference to the fragment's root view, and then call the view's `findViewById()` method to get its child views.

Q: Activities need to be registered in *AndroidManifest.xml* so that the app can use them. Do fragments?

A: No. Activities need to be registered in *AndroidManifest.xml*, but fragments don't.

We need to create a fragment with a list

Now that we've got `WorkoutDetailFragment` working, we need to create a second fragment that contains a list of the different workouts. We'll then be able to use the fragments to create different user interfaces for phones and tablets.

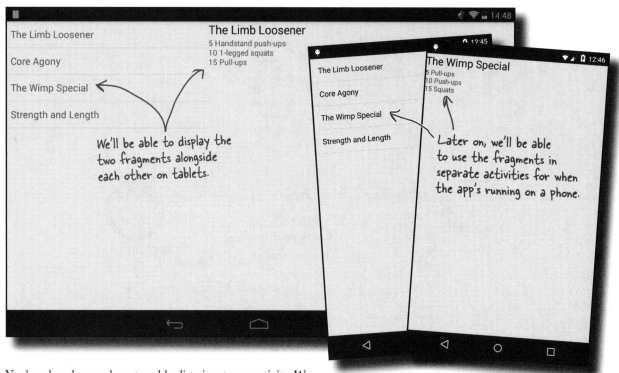

We'll be able to display the two fragments alongside each other on tablets.

Later on, we'll be able to use the fragments in separate activities for when the app's running on a phone.

You've already seen how to add a list view to an activity. We can create a fragment that contains a single list view, and then update it with the names of the workouts.

> So the fragment will contain just a single list. I wonder... When we wanted to use an activity that contained a single list, we used a ListActivity. Is there something similar for fragments?

He's right. We can use a type of fragment called a ListFragment.

We'll look at this on the next page.

A ListFragment is a fragment that contains only a list

A list fragment is type of fragment that specializes in working with a list. Just like a list activity, it's automatically bound to a list view, so you don't need to create one yourself. Here's what one looks like:

A list fragment comes complete with its own list view so you don't need to add it yourself. You just need to provide it with data.

| The Limb Loosener |
| Core Agony |
| The Wimp Special |
| Strength and Length |

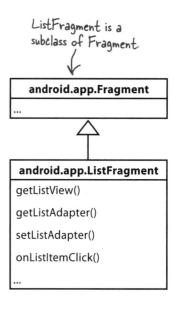

ListFragment is a subclass of Fragment.

android.app.Fragment
...

android.app.ListFragment
getListView()
getListAdapter()
setListAdapter()
onListItemClick()
...

Just as with a list activity, there are are a couple of major advantages in using a list fragment to display categories of data:

⭐ **You don't need to create your own layout.**
List fragments define their own layout programmatically, so there's no XML layout for you to create or maintain. The layout the list fragment generates includes a single list view. You access this list view in your activity code using the list fragment's `getListView()` method. You need this in order to specify what data should be displayed in the list view.

⭐ **You don't have to implement your own event listener.**
The `ListFragment` class is registered as a listener on the list view, and listens for when items in the list view are clicked. You use the list fragment's `onListItemClick()` method to get fragment to respond to clicks. You'll see this in action later on.

· So what does the list fragment code look like?

A ListFragment is a type of Fragment that's specializes in working with a ListView. It has a default layout that contains the ListView.

How to create a list fragment

You add a list fragment to your project in the same way you add a normal fragment. Go to File→New...→Fragment→Fragment (Blank). Give the fragment a name of "WorkoutListFragment", and then untick the options to create layout XML, and also the options to include fragment factory methods and interface callbacks. List fragments define their own layouts programmatically, so you don't need Android Studio to create one for you. When you click on the Finish button, Android Studio creates a new list fragment for you in a file called *WorkoutListFragment.java* in the *app/src/main/java* folder.

Here's what the basic code looks like to create a list fragment. As you can see, it's very similar to that of a normal fragment. Replace the code in `WorkoutListFragment` with the code below:

```
package com.hfad.workout;

import android.os.Bundle;
import android.app.ListFragment;
import android.view.LayoutInflater;
import android.view.View;
import android.view.ViewGroup;

public class WorkoutListFragment extends ListFragment {

    @Override
    public View onCreateView(LayoutInflater inflater, ViewGroup container,
                             Bundle savedInstanceState) {
        return super.onCreateView(inflater, container, savedInstanceState);
    }
}
```

The activity needs to extend ListFragment, not Fragment.

Workout
└ app/src/main
   └ java
      └ com.hfad.workout
         WorkoutList
         Fragment.java

Calling the superclass onCreateView() method gives you the default layout for the ListFragment.

The above code creates a basic list fragment called `WorkoutListFragment`. As it's a list fragment, it needs to extend the `ListFragment` class rather than `Fragment`.

The `onCreateView()` method is optional. The `onCreateView()` method gets called when the fragment's view gets created. We're including it in our code as we want to populate the fragment's list view with data as soon as it gets created. If you don't need your code to do anything at this point, you don't need to include the method.

Let's see how to add data to the list view.

We'll use an ArrayAdapter to set the values in the ListView

As mentioned in Chapter 6, you can connect data to a list view using an adapter. This is still the case when your list view is in a fragment; `ListView` is a subclass of the `AdapterView` class, and it's this class that allows a view to work with adapters.

We want to supply the list view in `WorkoutListFragment` with an array of workout names, so we'll use an array adapter to bind the array to the list view.

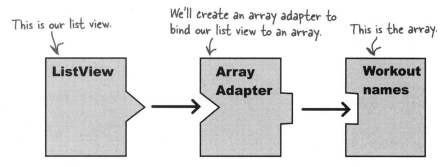

This is our list view.

We'll create an array adapter to bind our list view to an array.

This is the array.

ListView → **Array Adapter** → **Workout names**

A Fragment isn't a type of Context

As you've already seen, to create an array adapter that works with a list view, you use:

```
ArrayAdapter<DataType> listAdapter = new ArrayAdapter<DataType>(
                context, android.R.layout.simple_list_item_1, array);
```

where `DataType` is the type of data, `array` is the array and `context` is the current context.

When we used this in an activity, we could use `this` to get the current context. We could do this because an activity is a type of context—the `Activity` class is a subclass of the `Context` class.

As you saw earlier, the `Fragment` class *isn't* a subclass of the `Context` class, so using `this` won't work. Instead, you need to get the current context in some other way. If you're using the adapter in the fragment's `onCreateView()` method as we are here, you can use the `LayoutInflator` object's `getContext()` method to get the context instead:

```
ArrayAdapter<DataType> listAdapter = new ArrayAdapter<DataType>(
        inflator.getContext(), android.R.layout.simple_list_item_1, array);
```

This gets you the current context.

Once you've created the adapter, you bind it to the `ListView` using the fragment's `setListAdapter()` method:

```
setListAdapter(listAdapter);
```

Let's use an array adapter to populate the list view in our fragment with a list of workouts.

The updated WorkoutListFragment code

We've updated our *WorkoutListFragment.java* code so that it
populates the list view with the names of the workouts. Apply
the changes to your code, then save your changes:

```java
package com.hfad.workout;

import android.os.Bundle;
import android.app.ListFragment;
import android.view.LayoutInflater;
import android.view.View;
import android.view.ViewGroup;
import android.widget.ArrayAdapter;
```

We're using this class in the
← onCreateView() method.

Workout

app/src/main

java

com.hfad.workout

**WorkoutList
Fragment.java**

```java
public class WorkoutListFragment extends ListFragment {

    @Override
    public View onCreateView(LayoutInflater inflater, ViewGroup container,
                             Bundle savedInstanceState) {
        String[] names = new String[Workout.workouts.length];
        for (int i = 0; i < names.length; i++) {
            names[i] = Workout.workouts[i].getName();
        }
```

Create a String array of the workout names.

Create an array adapter.

```java
        ArrayAdapter<String> adapter = new ArrayAdapter<String>(
```

Get the context from →
the layout inflater.
```java
                inflater.getContext(), android.R.layout.simple_list_item_1,
                names);
        setListAdapter(adapter);
```
← Bind the array adapter to the list view.

```java
        return super.onCreateView(inflater, container, savedInstanceState);
    }
}
```

Now that the `WorkoutListFragment` contains a list of
workouts, let's see what it looks like by using it in our activity.

Display WorkoutListFragment in the MainActivity layout

We're going to add our new WorkoutListFragment to our MainActivity layout so that it appears to the left of WorkoutDetailFragment. Displaying fragments side by side in this manner is a common way of designing apps to work on tablets.

To do this, we'll use a linear layout with a horizontal orientation. We'll use layout weights to control how much horizontal space each fragment should take up.

Here's the code below (update your version of *activity_main.xml* to reflect our changes):

```xml
<?xml version="1.0" encoding="utf-8"?>
<LinearLayout xmlns:android="http://schemas.android.com/apk/res/android"
    android:orientation="horizontal"
    android:layout_width="match_parent"
    android:layout_height="match_parent">

    <fragment
        class="com.hfad.workout.WorkoutListFragment"
        android:id="@+id/list_frag"
        android:layout_width="0dp"
        android:layout_weight="2"
        android:layout_height="match_parent"/>

    <fragment
        class="com.hfad.workout.WorkoutDetailFragment"
        android:id="@+id/detail_frag"
        android:layout_width="0dp"
        android:layout_weight="3"
        android:layout_height="match_parent" />
</LinearLayout>
```

Display the list of workouts first.

Then display the workout details.

We're using layout_weight to control how much space each fragment should take up.

Workout
app/src/main
res
layout
activity_main.xml

Let's see what the app now looks like.

Test drive the app

When we run the app, a list of the workouts appears in a list on the left of the screen, and details of a single workout appears on the right. We hardcoded which workout should appear in our *MainActivity.java* code, so no matter which workout the user clicks on, details of the Core Agony workout will be displayed.

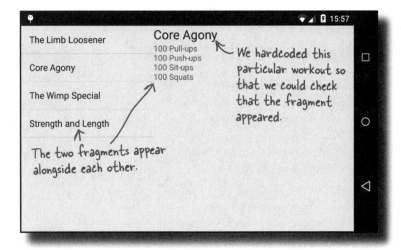

We hardcoded this particular workout so that we could check that the fragment appeared.

The two fragments appear alongside each other.

We need to get WorkoutDetailFragment to respond to clicks in WorkoutListFragment

Here's a reminder of where we've got to with our app. As you can see, we've now created all the components our app needs:

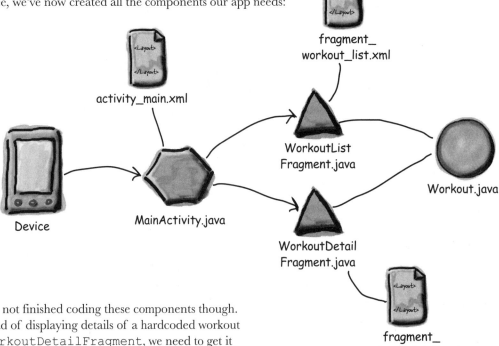

We're not finished coding these components though. Instead of displaying details of a hardcoded workout in WorkoutDetailFragment, we need to get it to display details of the workout the user clicks on in WorkoutListFragment.

Wiring up the list to the detail

There are a few ways that we can make the detail change when
an item is clicked on the list. We'll do something like this:

1 Add code to `WorkoutListFragment` that waits for a workout to be
clicked.

2 When that code runs, we'll call some code in *MainActivity.java* that...

3 ...will change the details in the detail fragment.

We don't want to write code in `WorkoutListFragment`
that talks *directly* to `WorkoutDetailFragment`. Can you
think why?

The answer is *reuse*. We want our fragments to know as little
as possible about the environment that contains it. The more
a fragment needs to know about the activity using it, the less
reusable it is.

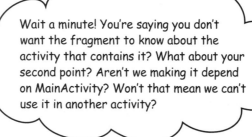

Wait a minute! You're saying you don't
want the fragment to know about the
activity that contains it? What about your
second point? Aren't we making it depend
on MainActivity? Won't that mean we can't
use it in another activity?

**We need to use an interface to decouple
the fragment from the activity.**

We need to decouple the fragment with an interface

We have two objects that need to talk to each other—the fragment and the activity—and we want them to talk without one side knowing too much about the other. The way we do that in Java is with an *interface*. When we define an interface, we're saying *what the minimum requirements are for one object to talk usefully to another*. It means that we'll be able to get the fragment to talk to any kind of activity, so long as that activity implements the interface.

We're going to create an interface called **WorkoutListListener**, that looks like this:

```
interface WorkoutListListener {
    void itemClicked(long id);
};
```

So long as an activity implements this interface, we'll be able to tell it that an item on the list fragment has been clicked. This is what will happen at runtime:

1   The WorkoutListListener will tell the fragment that it wants to listen.

2   A user will click on a workout in the list.

3   The onListItemClicked() method in the list-fragment will be called.

4   That method will then call the WorkoutListListener's itemClicked() method with the ID of the workout that was clicked

But when will the activity say that it's listening?

When will the activity tell the fragment that it's ready to receive updates about what item's been clicked? If you look back at the fragment lifecycle, you'll see that when the fragment is attached to the activity, the fragment's onAttach() method is called with the value of the activity:

```
@Override
public void onAttach(Activity activity) {
    ...
}
```

We can use this method to register the activity with the fragment. Let's take a look at the code.

First, add the interface to the list fragment

We've updated our *WorkoutListFragment.java* code to add a listener
(apply the changes to your code, then save your work):

```java
package com.hfad.workout;

import android.os.Bundle;
import android.app.ListFragment;
import android.view.LayoutInflater;
import android.view.View;
import android.view.ViewGroup;
import android.widget.ArrayAdapter;
import android.app.Activity;          Import these classes.
import android.widget.ListView;

public class WorkoutListFragment extends ListFragment {

    static interface WorkoutListListener {
        void itemClicked(long id);
    };
                                      Add the listener to the fragment.
    private WorkoutListListener listener;

    @Override
    public View onCreateView(LayoutInflater inflater, ViewGroup container,
                             Bundle savedInstanceState) {
        String[] names = new String[Workout.workouts.length];
        for (int i = 0; i < names.length; i++) {
            names[i] = Workout.workouts[i].getName();
        }
        ArrayAdapter<String> adapter = new ArrayAdapter<String>(
                inflater.getContext(), android.R.layout.simple_list_item_1,
                names);
        setListAdapter(adapter);
        return super.onCreateView(inflater, container, savedInstanceState);
    }

    @Override
    public void onAttach(Activity activity) {      This is called when the
        super.onAttach(activity);                   fragment gets attached
        this.listener = (WorkoutListListener)activity;   to the activity.
    }

    @Override
    public void onListItemClick(ListView l, View v, int position, long id) {
        if (listener != null) {
            listener.itemClicked(id);      Tell the listener when an item
        }                                   in the ListView is clicked.
    }
}
```

Folder path: Workout → app/src/main → java → com.hfad.workout → WorkoutList Fragment.java

Then make the activity implement the interface

Now we need to make *MainActivity.java* implement the
WorkoutListListener interface we just created. Update your
code with our changes below:

```
package com.hfad.workout;

import android.app.Activity;
import android.os.Bundle;

public class MainActivity extends Activity
                implements WorkoutListFragment.WorkoutListListener {

    @Override
    protected void onCreate(Bundle savedInstanceState) {
        super.onCreate(savedInstanceState);
        setContentView(R.layout.activity_main);
        WorkoutDetailFragment frag = (WorkoutDetailFragment)
                    getFragmentManager().findFragmentById(R.id.detail_frag);
        frag.setWorkout(1);
    }

    @Override
    public void itemClicked(long id) {
        //The code to set the detail will go here
    }
}
```

Implement the listener defined in WorkoutListFragment.

We'll remove these lines as we're no longer hardcoding which workout to display.

This method is defined in the listener.

Workout
app/src/main
java
com.hfad.workout
MainActivity.java

When an item is clicked in the fragment, the itemClicked()
method in the activity will be called. We can put code in this
method to show the details of the workout that's just been selected.

But how do we update the workout details?

The WorkoutDetailFragment updates its views when the
fragment is started. But once the fragment is displayed on screen,
how do we get the fragment to update the details?

You might be thinking that we could play with the fragment's
lifecycle so that we get it to update. Instead, **we'll replace the
detail fragment with a *brand-new* detail fragment, each
time we want its text to change**.

There's a really good reason why...

You want fragments to work with the back button

Suppose a user clicks on one workout, then a second workout. When they click on the back button, they're going to expect to be returned back to the first workout they chose.

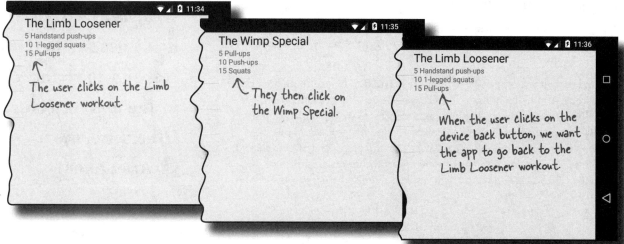

The Limb Loosener
5 Handstand push-ups
10 1-legged squats
15 Pull-ups

The user clicks on the Limb Loosener workout.

The Wimp Special
5 Pull-ups
10 Push-ups
15 Squats

They then click on the Wimp Special.

The Limb Loosener
5 Handstand push-ups
10 1-legged squats
15 Pull-ups

When the user clicks on the device back button, we want the app to go back to the Limb Loosener workout.

In every app we've built so far, the back-button has returned the user to the previous activity. Now that we're using fragments, we need to understand what happens when you click the back button.

Welcome to the back stack

The back stack is the list of places that you've visited on the device. Each place is a **transaction** on the back stack.

A lot of transactions move you from one activity to another:

> Transaction: Go to inbox activity
> Transaction: Go to 'compose new mail' activity
> Transaction: Go to sent mail activity

These are all separate transactions.

So when you go to a new activity, a transaction to do that is recorded on the back stack. If ever you press the back button, that transaction is reversed, and you're returned to the activity you were at before.

But back stack transactions don't *have* to be activities. They can just be changes to the fragments on the screen:

> Transaction: Replace the 'Strength and length' detail fragment with a 'Core agony' fragment
> Transaction: Replace the 'Core agony' fragment with 'The wimp special'

That means that *fragment* changes can be undone with the back button, just like *activity* changes can.

Don't update—instead, replace

Instead of updating the views in `WorkoutDetailFragment`, we will replace it with a new instance of `WorkoutDetailFragment` set up to display details of the next workout that's been selected. That way, we can store the fragment replacement inside a back stack transaction, and the user will be unable to undo the change by hitting the back button. But how do we replace one fragment with another?

We'll need to begin by making a change in the *activity_main.xml* layout file. Instead of inserting `WorkoutDetailFragment` directly, we'll use a **frame layout**.

A frame layout is a type of view group that's used to block out an area on the screen. You define it using the `<FrameLayout>` element. You use it to display single items—in our case, a fragment. We'll put our fragment in a frame layout so that we can control its contents programmatically. Whenever an item in the `WorkoutListFragment` list view gets clicked, we'll replace the contents of the frame layout with a new instance of `WorkoutDetailFragment` that displays details of the correct workout:

Add a fragment to an activity using \<fragment\> if you don't need it to respond to changes in the user interface. Otherwise, use a \<FrameLayout\>.

```xml
<?xml version="1.0" encoding="utf-8"?>
<LinearLayout xmlns:android="http://schemas.android.com/apk/res/android"
    android:orientation="horizontal"
    android:layout_width="match_parent"
    android:layout_height="match_parent">

    <fragment
        class="com.hfad.workout.WorkoutListFragment"
        android:id="@+id/list_frag"
        android:layout_width="0dp"
        android:layout_weight="2"
        android:layout_height="match_parent"/>

    <del>\<fragment\></del>
    <FrameLayout
        <del>class="com.hfad.workout.WorkoutDetailFragment"</del>
        <del>android:id="@+id/detail_frag"</del>
        android:id="@+id/fragment_container"
        android:layout_width="0dp"
        android:layout_weight="3"
        android:layout_height="match_parent" />

</LinearLayout>
```

We're going to display the fragment inside a FrameLayout.

We'll add the fragment to the frame layout programmatically.

Workout

app/src/main

res

layout

activity_main.xml

Next, we'll write the code to add the fragment to the frame layout.

Using fragment transactions

You replace the fragment at runtime inside a **fragment transaction**. A fragment transaction is a set of changes you want to apply relating to the fragment, all at the same time.

To create a fragment transaction, you start by getting a `FragmentTransaction` from the fragment manager:

```
WorkoutDetailFragment fragment = new WorkoutDetailFragment();

FragmentTransaction transaction = getFragmentManager().beginTransaction();
```

↖ The start of the fragment transaction

You then specify all the actions you want to group together in the transaction. In our case, we want to replace the fragment in the frame layout, and we do this using the fragment's `replace()` method:

```
transaction.replace(R.id.fragment_container, fragment);
```

↖ This replaces the fragment held in the fragment container.

where `R.id.fragment_container` is the ID of the container containing the fragment. You may also add a fragment to a container using the `add()` method, or remove a fragment using the `remove()` method:

```
transaction.add(R.id.fragment_container, fragment);
transaction.remove(fragment);
```

← You can add or remove fragments if you want. In our example, we don't need to.

You can use the `setTransition()` method to say what sort of transition animation you want for this transaction.

```
transaction.setTransition(transition);
```

← You don't have to set a transition.

where `transition` is the type of animation. Options for this are `TRANSIT_FRAGMENT_CLOSE` (a fragment is being removed from the stack), `TRANSIT_FRAGMENT_OPEN` (a fragment is being added), `TRANSIT_FRAGMENT_FADE` (the fragment should fade in and out) and `TRANSIT_NONE` (no animation).

Once you've specified all the actions you want to take as part of the transaction, you can use the `addToBackStack()` method to add the transaction to the back stack of transactions. This allows the user to go back to a previous state of the fragment when they press the Back button. The `addToBackStack()` method takes one parameter, a `String` name you can use to label the transaction:

```
transaction.addToBackStack(null);
```

← Most of the time you won't need to retrieve the transaction, so it can be set to null.

To commit the changes to the activity, you call the `commit()` method:

```
transaction.commit();
```

The `commit()` method applies the changes.

The updated MainActivity code

We want to get a new instance of `WorkoutDetailFragment` that displays the correct workout, display the fragment in the activity using a fragment transaction, and then add the transaction to the back button back stack. Here's the full code:

```
package com.hfad.workout;

import android.app.Activity;
import android.os.Bundle;
import android.app.FragmentTransaction;

public class MainActivity extends Activity
                  implements WorkoutListFragment.WorkoutListListener {

    @Override
    protected void onCreate(Bundle savedInstanceState) {
        super.onCreate(savedInstanceState);
        setContentView(R.layout.activity_main);
    }

    @Override
    public void itemClicked(long id) {
        WorkoutDetailFragment details = new WorkoutDetailFragment();
        FragmentTransaction ft = getFragmentManager().beginTransaction();
        details.setWorkout(id);
        ft.replace(R.id.fragment_container, details);
        ft.addToBackStack(null);
        ft.setTransition(FragmentTransaction.TRANSIT_FRAGMENT_FADE);
        ft.commit();
    }
}
```

We're using a fragment transaction, so we need to import the FragmentTransaction class.

Start the fragment transaction.

Replace the fragment and add it to the back stack.

Get the new and old fragments to fade in and out

Commit the transaction.

Let's see what happens when we run the code.

Workout

app/src/main

java

com.hfad.workout

MainActivity.java

Test drive the app

When we run the app, a list of the workouts appears in a list on the left of the screen. When we click on one of the workouts, details of that workout appear on the right. If we click on another workout and then click on the back button, details of the workout we chose previously appear on the screen.

The right side of the screen is empty when you start the app, as the user hasn't chosen a workout yet.

When the user clicks on the Limb Loosener workout, its details get displayed.

The user clicks on the Wimp Special workout and its details get displayed.

When the user clicks on the back button, the app goes back to the Limb Loosener workout.

The app seems to be working fine as long as you don't rotate the screen. If you change the screen orientation, there's a problem. Let's see what happens.

Rotating the device breaks the app

☑ **Create fragments**
→ □ **Link fragments**
□ **Device layouts**

When you rotate the app, there's a problem. Regardless of which workout you've chosen, when you rotate the device, the app displays details of the first workout.

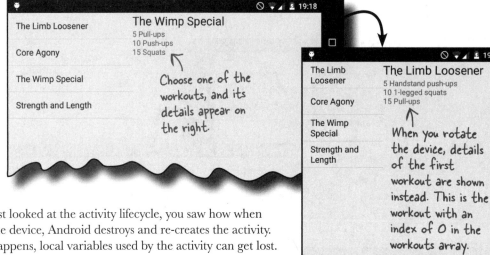

Choose one of the workouts, and its details appear on the right.

When you rotate the device, details of the first workout are shown instead. This is the workout with an index of 0 in the workouts array.

When we first looked at the activity lifecycle, you saw how when you rotate the device, Android destroys and re-creates the activity. When this happens, local variables used by the activity can get lost. If the activity uses a fragment, **the fragment gets destroyed and re-created along with the activity**. This means that any local variables used by the fragment can also lose their state.

In our `WorkoutDetailFragment`, we use a local variable called `workoutId` to store the ID of the workout the user clicks on in the `WorkoutListFragment` list view. When the user rotates the device, `workoutId` loses its current value and it's set to 0 by default. The fragment then displays details of the workout with an ID of 0—the first workout in the list.

You deal with this problem in a fragment in a similar way to how you deal with it in an activity. You first override the fragment's `onSaveInstanceState()` method, and put the local variable whose state you want to save in the method's `Bundle` parameter:

```java
public void onSaveInstanceState(Bundle savedInstanceState) {
    savedInstanceState.putLong("workoutId", workoutId);
}
```

The `onSaveInstanceState()` method gets called before the fragment is destroyed.

You then retrieve the value from the `Bundle` in the fragment's `onCreateView()` method:

```java
if (savedInstanceState != null) {
    workoutId = savedInstanceState.getLong("workoutId");
}
```

We can use it to get the previous state of the workoutId variable.

We'll show you the revised code on the next page.

The WorkoutDetailFragment code

```java
package com.hfad.workout;

...  ← No new imports are required so we've skipped them.

public class WorkoutDetailFragment extends Fragment {
    private long workoutId;

    @Override
    public View onCreateView(LayoutInflater inflater, ViewGroup container,
                             Bundle savedInstanceState) {
        if (savedInstanceState != null) {
            workoutId = savedInstanceState.getLong("workoutId");  ← Set the value of the workoutId.
        }
        return inflater.inflate(R.layout.fragment_workout_detail, container, false);
    }

    @Override
    public void onStart() {
        super.onStart();
        View view = getView();
        if (view != null) {
            TextView title = (TextView) view.findViewById(R.id.textTitle);
            Workout workout = Workout.workouts[(int) workoutId];
            title.setText(workout.getName());
            TextView description = (TextView) view.findViewById(R.id.textDescription);
            description.setText(workout.getDescription());
        }
    }

    @Override
    public void onSaveInstanceState(Bundle savedInstanceState) {
        savedInstanceState.putLong("workoutId", workoutId);
    }

    public void setWorkout(long id) {
        this.workoutId = id;
    }
}
```

Save the value of the workoutId in the savedInstanceState Bundle before the fragment gets destroyed. We're retrieving it in the onCreateView() method.

Workout

app/src/main

java

com.hfad.workout

WorkoutDetail
Fragment.java

When you click on one of the workouts, its details continue to be displayed when you rotate the device.

The Wimp Special
5 Pull-ups
10 Push-ups
15 Squats

The Limb Loosener
Core Agony
The Wimp Special
Strength and Length

19:18

The Limb Loosener
Core Agony
The Wimp Special
Strength and

The Wimp Special
5 Pull-ups
10 Push-ups
15 Squats

19:27

Phone versus tablet

There's one more thing we want to do with our Workout app. We want to make the app behave differently depending on whether we're running it on a phone or a tablet.

On a tablet

If we're running the app on a tablet, we want it to look and behave how it does now. We want the list of workouts and the workout details to appear side by side in the same activity. When you click on a workout, its details appear alongside it.

On a phone

If we're running the app on a phone, we want the app to behave differently. We want the list of workouts to appear in one activity and take up the full screen of the device. When you click on a workout, this will launch a second activity that displays details of the workout.

These are two → different activities, each one displaying a different fragment.

The phone and tablet app structures

Here's how the tablet and phone versions of the app need to work:

On a tablet

The tablet version of the app will work in the same way the app does currently:

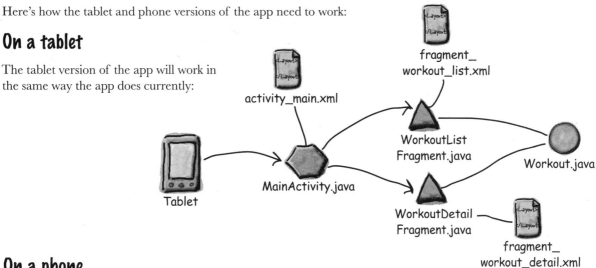

On a phone

Instead of using both fragments inside `MainActivity`, `MainActivity` will use `WorkoutListFragment` and `DetailActivity` will use `WorkoutDetailFragment`. `MainActivity` will start `DetailActivity` when the user clicks on a workout.

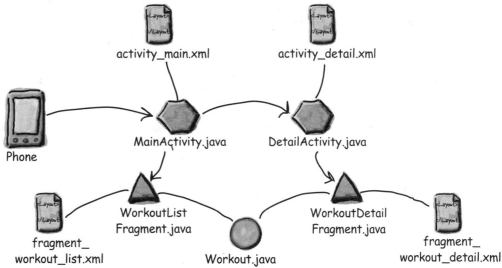

We need to get the app to look and behave differently depending on whether the app is run on a phone or a tablet. To help us do this, let's see how we can get our app to choose a different layout depending on the type of device it's running on.

Put screen-specific resources in screen-specific folders

Earlier in the book, you saw how you could get different devices to use image resources appropriate to their screen size by putting different sized images in the different *drawable* folders. As an example, you put images you want devices with high density screens to use in the *drawable-hdpi* folder.

You can do something similar with other resources such as layouts, menus, and values. If you want to create multiple versions of the same resources for different screen specs, you just need to create multiple resource folders with an appropriate name. The device will then load the resources at runtime from the folder that's the closest match to its screen spec.

As an example, if you want to have one layout for large screen devices, and a couple of other layouts for other devices, you put the layout for the large device in the *app/src/main/res/layout-large* folder, and the layouts for the other devices in the *app/src/main/res/layout* folder. When the app gets run on a device with a large screen, the device will use the layout in the *layout-large* folder:

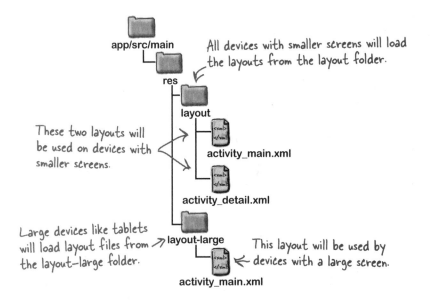

app/src/main

All devices with smaller screens will load the layouts from the layout folder.

res

layout

These two layouts will be used on devices with smaller screens.

activity_main.xml

activity_detail.xml

Large devices like tablets will load layout files from the layout-large folder.

layout-large

This layout will be used by devices with a large screen.

activity_main.xml

On the next page, we'll show you all the different options you can use for your resource folder names.

The different folder options

You can put all kinds of resources (drawables or images, layouts, menus, and values) in different folders to specify which types of device they should be used with. The screen-specific folder name can include screen size, density, orientation and aspect ratio, each part separated by hyphens. As an example, if you want to create a layout that will only be used by very large tablets in landscape mode, you would create a folder called *layout-xlarge-land* and put the layout file in that folder. Here are the different options you can use for the folder names:

You **must** specify a resource type.

Screen density is based on dots per inch.

Resource type	Screen size	Screen density	Orientation	Aspect ratio
drawable	-small	-ldpi	-land	-long
layout	-normal	-mdpi	-port	-notlong
menu	-large	-hdpi		
mipmap	-xlarge	-xhdpi		
values		-xxhdpi		
		-xxxhdpi		
		-nodpi		
		-tvdpi		

A mipmap resource is used for application icons. Older versions of Android Studio use drawables instead.

long is for screens that have a very high value for height.

This is for density-independent resources. Use -nodpi for any image resources you don't want to scale (e.g., a folder called drawable-nodpi).

Android decides at runtime which resources to use by looking for the best match. If there's no exact match, it will use resources designed for a smaller screen than the current one. If resources are only available for screens larger than the current one, Android won't use them and the app will crash.

If you only want your app to work on devices with particular screen sizes, you can specify this in `AndroidManifest.xml` using the `<supports-screens>` attribute. As an example, if you don't want your app to run on devices with small screens, you'd use

```
<supports-screens android:smallScreens="false"/>
```

Using the different folder names, you can create layouts that are specific for phones and tablets. Let's start with the tablet version of our app.

For more information on the settings on this page, see
https://developer.android.com/guide/practices/screens_support.html

BE the Folder Structure

Below you'll see the code for an activity. You want to display one layout when it runs on devices with large sized screens, and another layout when it runs on devices with normal sized screens. Which of these folder structures will allow you to do that?

← Here's the activity.

```java
import android.app.Activity;
import android.os.Bundle;

public class MainActivity extends Activity {

    @Override
    protected void onCreate(Bundle savedInstanceState) {
        super.onCreate(savedInstanceState);
        setContentView(R.layout.activity_main);
        ...
    }
}
```

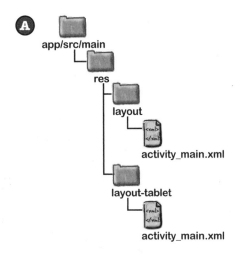

A

app/src/main

res

layout

activity_main.xml

layout-tablet

activity_main.xml

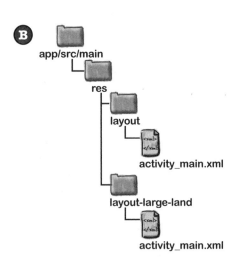

B

app/src/main

res

layout

activity_main.xml

layout-large-land

activity_main.xml

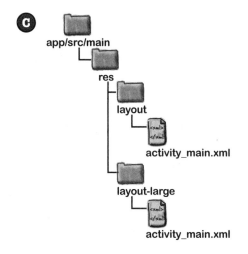

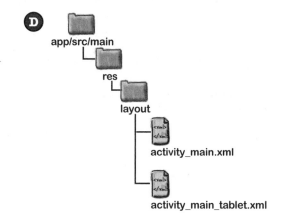

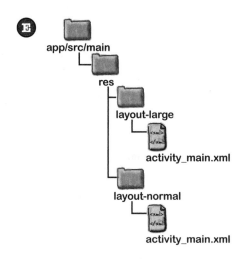

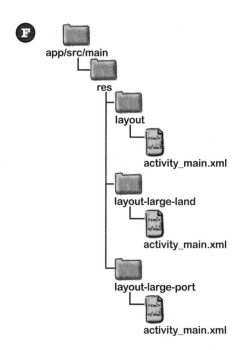

BE the Folder Structure Solution

Below you'll see the code for an activity. You want to display one layout when it runs on devices with large sized screens, and another layout when it runs on devices with smaller sized screens. Which of these folder structures will allow you to do that?

```java
import android.app.Activity;
import android.os.Bundle;

public class MainActivity extends Activity {

    @Override
    protected void onCreate(Bundle savedInstanceState) {
        super.onCreate(savedInstanceState);
        setContentView(R.layout.activity_main);
        ...
    }
}
```

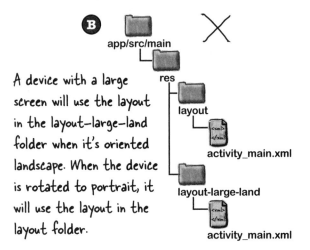

A

Android doesn't recognize the folder name layout-tablet. activity_main.xml in the layout folder will be displayed on all devices.

B

A device with a large screen will use the layout in the layout-large-land folder when it's oriented landscape. When the device is rotated to portrait, it will use the layout in the layout folder.

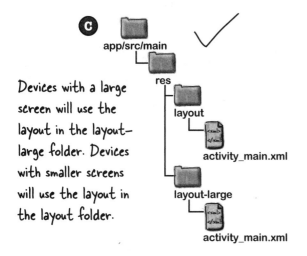

C Devices with a large screen will use the layout in the layout-large folder. Devices with smaller screens will use the layout in the layout folder.

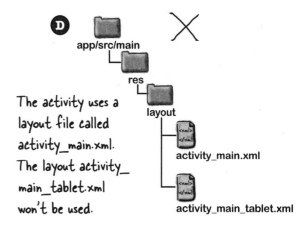

D The activity uses a layout file called activity_main.xml. The layout activity_main_tablet.xml won't be used.

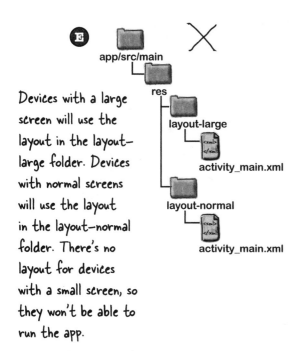

E Devices with a large screen will use the layout in the layout-large folder. Devices with normal screens will use the layout in the layout-normal folder. There's no layout for devices with a small screen, so they won't be able to run the app.

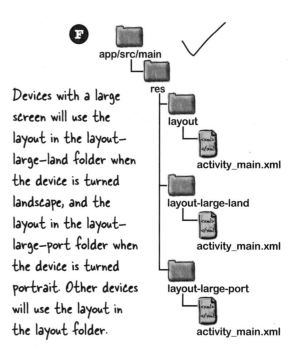

F Devices with a large screen will use the layout in the layout-large-land folder when the device is turned landscape, and the layout in the layout-large-port folder when the device is turned portrait. Other devices will use the layout in the layout folder.

Tablets use layouts in the layout-large folder

Getting the tablet version of our app up and running is easy—all we need to do is put our existing activity layout file *activity_main.xml* into the *app/src/main/res/layout-large* folder. The layout in this folder will then only be used by devices with a large screen.

If the *app/src/main/res/layout-large* folder doesn't exist in your Android Studio project, you'll need to create it. To do this, switch to the Project view of your folder structure, highlight the *app/src/main/res* folder in the folder explorer, and choose File→New...→Directory. When prompted, give the folder a name of "layout-large". When you click on the OK button, Android Studio will create the new *app/src/main/res/layout-large* folder for you.

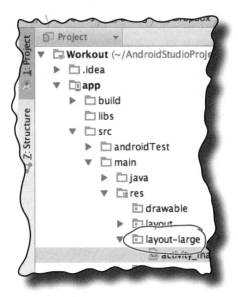

To copy the *activity_main.xml* layout file, highlight the file in the explorer, and choose the Copy command from the Edit menu. Then highlight the new `layout-large` folder, and choose the Paste command from the Edit menu. Android Studio will copy the *activity_main.xml* file into the *app/src/main/res/layout-large* folder.

If you open the file, it should look like this:

```xml
<?xml version="1.0" encoding="utf-8"?>
<LinearLayout xmlns:android="http://schemas.android.com/apk/res/android"
    android:orientation="horizontal"
    android:layout_width="match_parent"
    android:layout_height="match_parent">

    <fragment
        class="com.hfad.workout.WorkoutListFragment"
        android:id="@+id/list_frag"
        android:layout_width="0dp"
        android:layout_weight="2"
        android:layout_height="match_parent"/>

    <FrameLayout
        android:id="@+id/fragment_container"
        android:layout_width="0dp"
        android:layout_weight="3"
        android:layout_height="match_parent" />
</LinearLayout>
```

We've not changed the layout, just copied it to the layout-large folder.

Workout
app/src/main
res
layout-large
activity_main.xml

This layout will be used by devices with a large screen, so when the app is run on a tablet, the two fragments will be displayed side by side. Next, let's deal with the phone layouts.

The MainActivity phone layout

When the app runs on a phone, we want `MainActivity` to just display `WorkoutListFragment`, and not `WorkoutDetailFragment`. To do this, we'll update the code in *activity_main.xml* in the *app/src/main/res/layout* folder so that it just contains `WorkoutListFragment`. Any phones that run the app will use the layout in the *layout* folder, whereas any tablets will use the layout in the *layout-large* folder.

To do this, open the *activity_main.xml* file in the *app/src/main/res/layout* folder, then replace the XML with the code below:

We just want MainActivity to display WorkoutListFragment on a phone.

```xml
<?xml version="1.0" encoding="utf-8"?>
<fragment xmlns:android="http://schemas.android.com/apk/res/android"
    class="com.hfad.workout.WorkoutListFragment"
    android:id="@+id/list_frag"
    android:layout_width="match_parent"
    android:layout_height="match_parent"/>
```

Make sure you edit activity_main.xml in the layout folder.

```
Workout
  └ app/src/main
        └ res
            └ layout
                └ activity_main.xml
```

As `MainActivity` only needs to display `WorkoutListFragment` when it's running on a phone, there's no need for us to create a separate layout that contains the `<fragment>` element. This is only necessary when you need to display multiple fragments.

Note that the version of *activity_main.xml* in the *layout* folder doesn't contain the `fragment_container` frame layout, whereas the version of *activity_main.xml* in the *layout-large* folder does. This is because only the version of *activity_main.xml* in the *layout-large* folder needs to display `WorkoutDetailFragment`. Later on, we'll be able to use this fact to figure out which layout the app's using on the user's device.

The next thing we need to do is create a second activity that uses `WorkoutDetailFragment`.

To get our app to look different on a phone and a tablet, we're juggling two different layouts with the same name.

Take the next few pages slowly, and double-check you're updating the correct version of the layout.

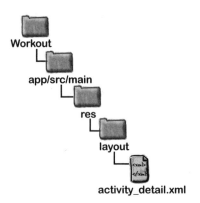

☑ **Create fragments**
☑ **Link fragments**
→☐ **Device layouts**

Phones will use DetailActivity to display details of the workout

We're going to create a second activity called `DetailActivity`. This activity will contain `WorkoutDetailFragment`, and will be used by phones to display details of the workout the user selects.

Use the Android Studio New Activity wizard to create a new blank activity called *DetailActivity.java* with a layout called *activity_detail.xml*. This layout needs to be in the *app/src/main/res/layout* folder so that any device can use it.

The layout just needs to contain the fragment `WorkoutDetailFragment`. Update the code in *activity_detail.xml* as follows:

Workout
app/src/main
res
layout
activity_detail.xml

```xml
<?xml version="1.0" encoding="utf-8"?>
<fragment xmlns:android="http://schemas.android.com/apk/res/android"
    class="com.hfad.workout.WorkoutDetailFragment"
    android:id="@+id/detail_frag"
    android:layout_width="match_parent"
    android:layout_height="match_parent"/>
```

← *DetailActivity will just display WorkoutDetailFragment.*

As well as updating the *activity_detail* layout, we need to update `DetailActivity` itself. If the app is running on a phone, `MainActivity` will need to start `DetailActivity` using an intent. This intent will need to include the ID of the workout the user has selected as extra information. The `DetailActivity` will then need to pass this to the `WorkoutDetailFragment` using its `setWorkout()` method.

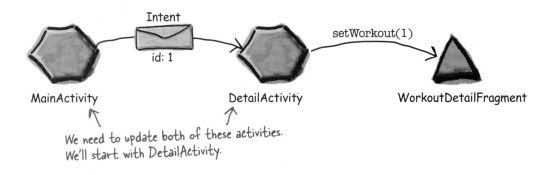

Intent
id: 1

setWorkout(1)

MainActivity   DetailActivity   WorkoutDetailFragment

We need to update both of these activities. We'll start with DetailActivity.

Pool Puzzle

Your **job** is to take code segments from the pool and place them into the blank lines in *DetailActivity.java*. You may **not** use the same code segment more than once, and you won't need to use all the code segments. Your **goal** is to get the workout ID from the intent, and pass it to WorkoutDetailFragment.

```java
package com.hfad.workout;

import android.app.Activity;
import android.os.Bundle;

public class DetailActivity extends Activity {
    public static final String EXTRA_WORKOUT_ID = "id";

    @Override
    protected void onCreate(Bundle savedInstanceState) {
        super.onCreate(savedInstanceState);
        setContentView(R.layout.activity_detail);
        .......................................... workoutDetailFragment = ( .......................................... )
            .......................................... (R.id.detail_frag);
        int workoutId = (int) getIntent().getExtras().get(EXTRA_WORKOUT_ID);
        workoutDetailFragment.setWorkout(workoutId);
    }
}
```

We're using a constant for the name of the extra information in the intent so that we know MainActivity and DetailActivity are using the same String.

These code snippets were not needed here.

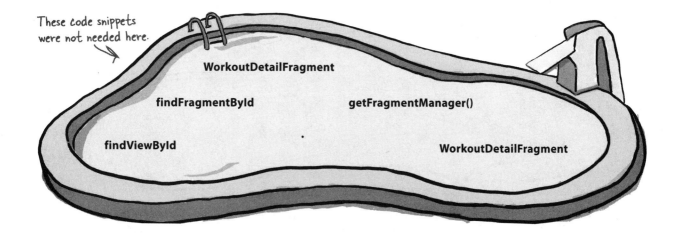

WorkoutDetailFragment

findFragmentById

getFragmentManager()

findViewById

WorkoutDetailFragment

Pool Puzzle Solution

Your **job** is to take code segments from the pool and place them into the blank lines in *DetailActivity.java*. You may **not** use the same code segment more than once, and you won't need to use all the code segments. Your **goal** is to get the workout ID from the intent, and pass it to WorkoutDetailFragment.

```java
package com.hfad.workout;

import android.app.Activity;
import android.os.Bundle;

public class DetailActivity extends Activity {
    public static final String EXTRA_WORKOUT_ID = "id";

    @Override
    protected void onCreate(Bundle savedInstanceState) {
        super.onCreate(savedInstanceState);
        setContentView(R.layout.activity_detail);
        WorkoutDetailFragment workoutDetailFragment = ( WorkoutDetailFragment )
                getFragmentManager() . findFragmentById (R.id.detail_frag);
        int workoutId = (int) getIntent().getExtras().get(EXTRA_WORKOUT_ID);
        workoutDetailFragment.setWorkout(workoutId);
    }
}
```

We get a reference to a fragment by calling the fragment manager's findFragmentById() method.

These code snippets were not needed here.

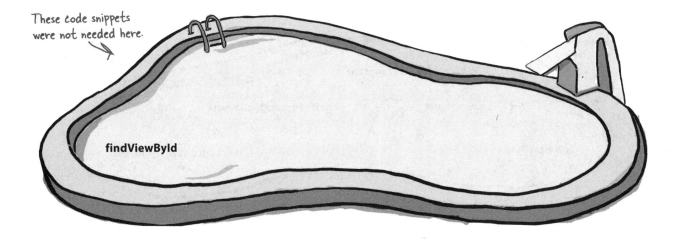

findViewById

The full DetailActivity code

Here's the full code for `DetailActivity` (replace the code
Android Studio has generated for you with the code below):

```
package com.hfad.workout;

import android.app.Activity;
import android.os.Bundle;

public class DetailActivity extends Activity {
    public static final String EXTRA_WORKOUT_ID = "id";

    @Override
    protected void onCreate(Bundle savedInstanceState) {
        super.onCreate(savedInstanceState);
        setContentView(R.layout.activity_detail);
        WorkoutDetailFragment workoutDetailFragment = (WorkoutDetailFragment)
                getFragmentManager().findFragmentById(R.id.detail_frag);
        int workoutId = (int) getIntent().getExtras().get(EXTRA_WORKOUT_ID);
        workoutDetailFragment.setWorkout(workoutId);
    }
}
```

Workout
app/src/main
java
com.hfad.workout
DetailActivity.java

Get a reference to the fragment.

Get the ID of the workout the user clicked on from the intent.

Pass the workout ID to the fragment.

The `DetailActivity` code gets the ID of the workout from
the intent that started the activity. The next thing we need to do
is get `MainActivity` to start `DetailActivity`—but only if
the app's being run on a phone.

But how can we tell?

Use layout differences to tell which layout the device is using

We want `MainActivity` to perform different actions when the user clicks on a workout depending on whether the device is using *activity_main.xml* in the *layout* or *layout-large* folder.

If the app is running on a phone, the device will be using *activity_main.xml* in the *layout* folder. This layout doesn't include `WorkoutDetailFragment`, so if the user clicks on a workout, we want `MainActivity` to start `DetailActivity`.

If the app is running on a tablet, the device will be using *activity_main.xml* in the *layout-large* folder. This layout includes a frame layout with an ID of `fragment_container` that's used to display `WorkoutDetailFragment`. If the user clicks on a workout in this case, we need to display a new instance of `WorkoutDetailFragment` in the `fragment_container` frame layout.

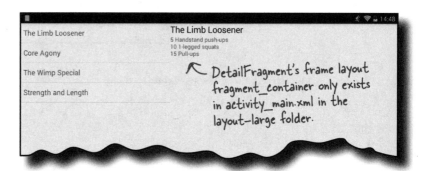

DetailFragment's frame layout fragment_container only exists in activity_main.xml in the layout-large folder.

We can deal with both these situations in `MainActivity` by checking which layout the device is using. We can tell this by looking for a view with an ID of `fragment_container`.

If `fragment_container` exists, the device must be using *activity_main.xml* in the *layout-large* folder, so we know we have to display a new instance of `WorkoutDetailFragment` when the user clicks on a workout. If `fragment_container` doesn't exist, the device must be using the version of *activity_main.xml* in the *layout* folder, so we need to start `DetailActivity` instead.

The revised MainActivity code

Here's the full code for *MainActivity.java* (update your code with our changes):

```
package com.hfad.workout;

import android.app.Activity;
import android.app.FragmentTransaction;
import android.content.Intent;
import android.os.Bundle;
import android.view.View;
```
> We're using these extra classes in the itemClicked() method.

```
public class MainActivity extends Activity
                implements WorkoutListFragment.WorkoutListListener {

    @Override
    protected void onCreate(Bundle savedInstanceState) {
        super.onCreate(savedInstanceState);
        setContentView(R.layout.activity_main);
    }
```
> Get a reference to the frame layout that contains WorkoutDetailFragment. This will exist if the app is being run on a device with a large screen.

```
    @Override
    public void itemClicked(long id) {
        View fragmentContainer = findViewById(R.id.fragment_container);
        if (fragmentContainer != null) {
            WorkoutDetailFragment details = new WorkoutDetailFragment();
            FragmentTransaction ft = getFragmentManager().beginTransaction();
            details.setWorkout(id);
            ft.replace(R.id.fragment_container, details);
            ft.addToBackStack(null);
            ft.setTransition(FragmentTransaction.TRANSIT_FRAGMENT_FADE);
            ft.commit();
        } else {
            Intent intent = new Intent(this, DetailActivity.class);
            intent.putExtra(DetailActivity.EXTRA_WORKOUT_ID, (int)id);
            startActivity(intent);
        }
    }
}
```
> We only need to run this code if the frame layout is there.

> If the frame layout isn't there, the app must be running on a device with a smaller screen. Start DetailActivity, passing it the ID of the workout.

Let's see what happens when we run the app.

Test drive the app

When you run the app on a tablet, it appears just as before. A list of the workout names appears on the left of the screen, and when you click on one of the workouts, its details appear on the right.

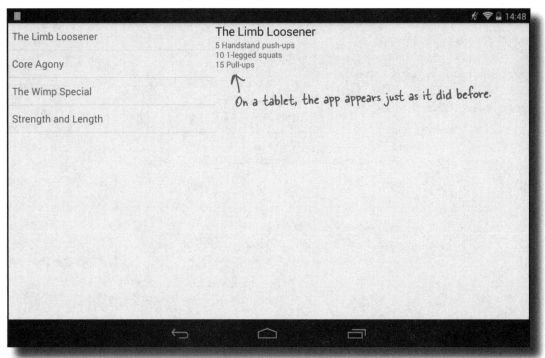

On a tablet, the app appears just as it did before.

When you run the app on a phone, the list of workout names appears on the screen. When you click on one of the workouts, its details are displayed in a separate activity.

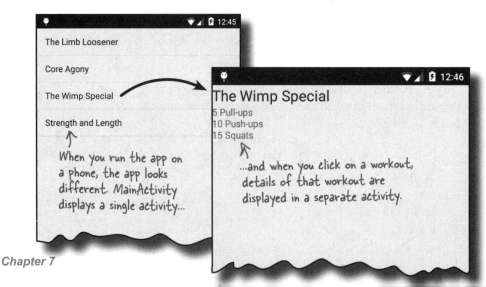

When you run the app on a phone, the app looks different. MainActivity displays a single activity...

...and when you click on a workout, details of that workout are displayed in a separate activity.

Your Android Toolbox

You've got Chapter 7 under your belt and now you've added fragments to your toolbox.

Fragment Lifecycle Methods

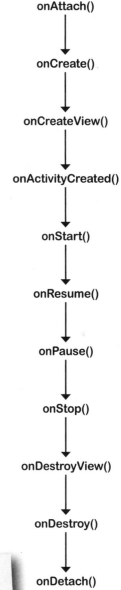

onAttach()

↓

onCreate()

↓

onCreateView()

↓

onActivityCreated()

↓

onStart()

↓

onResume()

↓

onPause()

↓

onStop()

↓

onDestroyView()

↓

onDestroy()

↓

onDetach()

BULLET POINTS

- A fragment is used to control part of a screen. It can be reused across multiple activities.

- A fragment has an associated layout.

- A fragment is a subclass of the `android.app.Fragment` class.

- The `onCreateView()` method gets called each time Android needs the fragment's layout.

- Add a fragment to an activity's layout using the `<fragment>` element and adding a `class` attribute.

- The fragment lifecycle methods tie in with the states of the activity that contains the fragment.

- The `Fragment` class doesn't extend the `Activity` class or implement the `Context` class.

- Fragments don't have a `findViewById()` method. Instead, use the `getView()` method to get a reference to the root view, then call the view's `findViewById()` method.

- A list fragment is a fragment that comes complete with a `ListView`. You create one by subclassing `ListFragment`.

- If you need to get a fragment to respond to changes in the user interface, use the `<FrameLayout>` element.

- Use fragment transactions to make a set of changes to an existing fragment and add to the back stack.

- Make apps look different on different devices by putting separate layouts in device-appropriate folders.

> You can download the full code for the chapter from https://tinyurl.com/HeadFirstAndroid.

8 nested fragments

Dealing with Children

> The Back button was going crazy, transactions everywhere. So I hit them with the getChildFragmentManager() method and BAM! Everything went back to normal.

You've seen how using fragments in activities allow you to reuse code and make your apps more flexible.

In this chapter, we're going to show you **how to nest one fragment inside another**.

You'll see how to use the **child fragment manager** to tame unruly fragment transactions.

Along the way you'll see why **knowing the differences between activities and fragments** is so important.

Creating nested fragments

In Chapter 7, you saw how to create fragments, how to include them in activities, and how to connect them together. To do this, we created a list fragment displaying a list of workouts, and a fragment displaying details of a single workout.

It's not just activities that can contain fragments—fragments can be nested inside other fragments. So that you can see this in action, we're going to add a stopwatch fragment to our workout detail fragment.

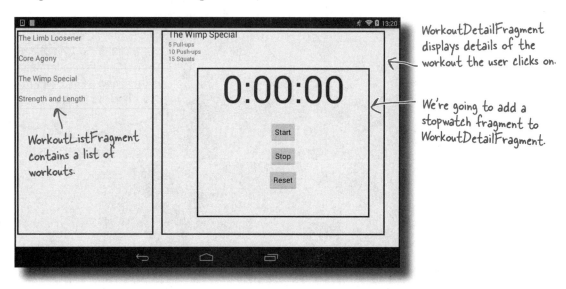

WorkoutDetailFragment displays details of the workout the user clicks on.

We're going to add a stopwatch fragment to WorkoutDetailFragment.

WorkoutListFragment contains a list of workouts.

We'll add a new stopwatch fragment

We're going to add a new stopwatch fragment called *StopwatchFragment.java* that uses a layout called *fragment_stopwatch.xml*. We're going to base the fragment on the stopwatch activity we created back in Chapter 4.

We already know that activities and fragments behave in similar ways, but we also know that a fragment is a distinct type of object—a fragment is not a subclass of activity. **Is there some way we could rewrite that activity code so that it works like a fragment?**

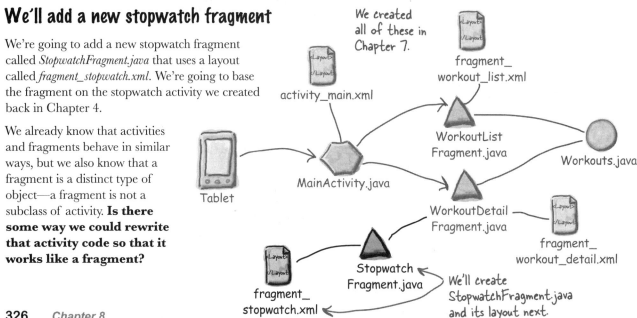

We created all of these in Chapter 7.

fragment_workout_list.xml

activity_main.xml

WorkoutList Fragment.java

Workouts.java

Tablet

MainActivity.java

WorkoutDetail Fragment.java

fragment_workout_detail.xml

Stopwatch Fragment.java

We'll create StopwatchFragment.java and its layout next.

fragment_stopwatch.xml

Fragments and activities have similar lifecycles...

To understand how to rewrite an activity as a fragment, we
need to think a little about the similarities and differences
between them. If we looks at the lifecycles of fragments and
activities, we'll see that they're very similar:

Lifecycle Method	Activity?	Fragment?
onAttach()		✓
onCreate()	✓	✓
onCreateView()		✓
onActivityCreated()		✓
onStart()	✓	✓
onPause()	✓	✓
onResume()	✓	✓
onStop()	✓	✓
onDestroyView()		✓
onRestart()	✓	
onDestroy()	✓	✓
onDetach()		✓

...but the methods are slightly different

Fragment lifecycle methods are almost the same as activity lifecycle
methods, but there's one major difference: activity lifecycle
methods are **protected** and fragment lifecycle methods are
public. And we've already seen that the way fragments create a
layout from a layout resource file is different.

Also, in a fragment, we can't call methods like findViewById()
directly. Instead, we need to find a reference to a View object, and
then call view.findViewById().

With these similarities and differences in mind, it's time you started
to write some code...

Sharpen your pencil

This is the code for `StopwatchActivity` we wrote earlier. You're going to convert this code into a fragment called `StopwatchFragment`. With a pencil, make the changes you need. Keep the following things in mind:

- Instead of a layout file called *activity_stopwatch.xml*, it will use a layout called *fragment_stopwatch.xml*.

- Make sure the access restrictions on the methods are correct.

- How will you specify the layout?

- The `runTimer()` method won't be able to call `findViewById()`, so you might want to pass a view object into `runTimer()`.

```java
public class StopwatchActivity extends Activity {
    //Number of seconds displayed on the stopwatch.
    private int seconds = 0;  // ← The number of seconds that have passed.
    //Is the stopwatch running?
    private boolean running;  // ← running says whether the stopwatch is running.
    private boolean wasRunning;  // ← wasRunning says whether the stopwatch was running
                                 //   before the stopwatch was paused.

    @Override
    protected void onCreate(Bundle savedInstanceState) {
        super.onCreate(savedInstanceState);
        setContentView(R.layout.activity_stopwatch);
        if (savedInstanceState != null) {
            seconds = savedInstanceState.getInt("seconds");
            running = savedInstanceState.getBoolean("running");
            wasRunning = savedInstanceState.getBoolean("wasRunning");
            if (wasRunning) {
                running = true;
            }
        }
        runTimer();  // ← Start the runTimer() method.
    }

    @Override
    protected void onPause() {  // ← Stop the stopwatch if the activity is paused.
        super.onPause();
        wasRunning = running;
        running = false;
    }
```

> If the activity was destroyed and re-created, restore the state of the variables from the savedInstanceState Bundle.

```
    @Override
    protected void onResume() {          ←— Start the stopwatch if the activity is resumed.
        super.onResume();
        if (wasRunning) {
            running = true;
        }
    }
                                 Save the activity's state before
                                 the activity is destroyed.
    @Override                   ↙
    protected void onSaveInstanceState(Bundle savedInstanceState) {
        savedInstanceState.putInt("seconds", seconds);
        savedInstanceState.putBoolean("running", running);
        savedInstanceState.putBoolean("wasRunning", wasRunning);
    }

    public void onClickStart(View view) {
        running = true;                    ↖
    }

    public void onClickStop(View view) {  ←— Start, stop or reset the stopwatch
        running = false;                       depending on which button is clicked.
    }
                                          ↖
    public void onClickReset(View view) {
        running = false;
        seconds = 0;               Use a Handler to post code to
    }                              increment the number of seconds and
                                   update the text view every second.
    private void runTimer() {    ↙
        final TextView timeView = (TextView) findViewById(R.id.time_view);
        final Handler handler = new Handler();
        handler.post(new Runnable() {
            @Override
            public void run() {
                int hours = seconds / 3600;
                int minutes = (seconds % 3600) / 60;
                int secs = seconds % 60;
                String time = String.format("%d:%02d:%02d",
                        hours, minutes, secs);
                timeView.setText(time);
                if (running) {
                    seconds++;
                }
                handler.postDelayed(this, 1000);
            }
        });
    }
}
```

Sharpen your pencil
Solution

This is the code for StopwatchActivity we wrote earlier. You're going to convert this code into a fragment called StopwatchFragment. With a pencil, make the changes you need. Keep the following things in mind:

- Instead of a layout file called *activity_stopwatch.xml*, it will use a layout called *fragment_stopwatch.xml*.

- Make sure the access restrictions on the methods are correct.

- How will you specify the layout?

- The runTimer() method won't be able to call findViewById(), so you might want to pass a view object into runTimer().

This is the new name.

```java
public class ~~StopwatchActivity~~ StopwatchFragment extends ~~Activity~~ Fragment {
    //Number of seconds displayed on the stopwatch.
    private int seconds = 0;
    //Is the stopwatch running?
    private boolean running;
    private boolean wasRunning;
```

We're extending Fragment, not Activity.

← This method needs to be public.

```java
    @Override
    ~~protected~~ public void onCreate(Bundle savedInstanceState) {
        super.onCreate(savedInstanceState);
        ~~setContentView(R.layout.activity_stopwatch);~~
        if (savedInstanceState != null) {
            seconds = savedInstanceState.getInt("seconds");
            running = savedInstanceState.getBoolean("running");
            wasRunning = savedInstanceState.getBoolean("wasRunning");
            if (wasRunning) {
                running = true;
            }
        }
        ~~runTimer();~~
    }
```

← You don't set a fragment's layout in its onCreate() method.

We can leave this code in the onCreate() method.

← We're not calling runTimer() yet because we've not set the layout—we don't have any views yet.

We set the fragment's layout in the onCreateView() method.

```java
    @Override
    public View onCreateView(LayoutInflater inflater, ViewGroup container,
                             Bundle savedInstanceState) {
        View layout = inflater.inflate(R.layout.fragment_stopwatch, container, false);
        runTimer(layout);
        return layout;
    }
```

← Pass the layout view to the runTimer() method.

← This method needs to be public.

```java
    @Override
    ~~protected~~ public void onPause() {
        super.onPause();
        wasRunning = running;
        running = false;
    }
```

```
@Override            ← This method needs to be public.
protected public   void onResume() {
    super.onResume();
    if (wasRunning) {
        running = true;
    }
}

@Override            ← This method needs to be public.
protected public   void onSaveInstanceState(Bundle savedInstanceState) {
    savedInstanceState.putInt("seconds", seconds);
    savedInstanceState.putBoolean("running", running);
    savedInstanceState.putBoolean("wasRunning", wasRunning);
}

public void onClickStart(View view) {
    running = true;
}

public void onClickStop(View view) {
    running = false;
}

public void onClickReset(View view) {
    running = false;
    seconds = 0;
}
                                    ← The runTimer() method now takes a View.
private void runTimer( View view ) {
    final TextView timeView = (TextView) view.findViewById(R.id.time_view);
    final Handler handler = new Handler();   ← Use the view parameter to call findViewById().
    handler.post(new Runnable() {
        @Override
        public void run() {
            int hours = seconds / 3600;
            int minutes = (seconds % 3600) / 60;
            int secs = seconds % 60;
            String time = String.format("%d:%02d:%02d",
                    hours, minutes, secs);
            timeView.setText(time);
            if (running) {
                seconds++;
            }
            handler.postDelayed(this, 1000);
        }
    });
}
}
```

The StopwatchFragment code

We'll add `StopwatchFragment` to our Workout project so that we can use it in our app. You do this in the same way you did in Chapter 7. Go to File→New...→Fragment→Fragment (Blank). Give the fragment a name of "StopwatchFragment", a layout name of "fragment_stopwatch", and untick the options for including fragment factory methods and interface callbacks.

When you click on the Finish button, Android Studio creates a new fragment for you in a file called *StopwatchFragment.java* in the *app/src/main/java* folder. Replace the fragment code Android Studio gives you with the following code (this is the code you updated in the exercise on the previous page):

```
package com.hfad.workout;

import android.os.Bundle;
import android.os.Handler;
import android.app.Fragment;
import android.view.LayoutInflater;
import android.view.View;
import android.view.ViewGroup;
import android.widget.TextView;

public class StopwatchFragment extends Fragment {
    //Number of seconds displayed on the stopwatch.
    private int seconds = 0;      // The number of seconds that have passed.
    //Is the stopwatch running?
    private boolean running;      // running says whether the stopwatch is running.
    private boolean wasRunning;   // wasRunning says whether the stopwatch was running
                                  // before the stopwatch was paused.

    @Override
    public void onCreate(Bundle savedInstanceState) {
        super.onCreate(savedInstanceState);
        if (savedInstanceState != null) {    // Restore the state of the variables
                                             // from the savedInstanceState Bundle.
            seconds = savedInstanceState.getInt("seconds");
            running = savedInstanceState.getBoolean("running");
            wasRunning = savedInstanceState.getBoolean("wasRunning");
            if (wasRunning) {
                running = true;
            }
        }
    }
}
```

Workout

app/src/main

java

com.hfad.workout

Stopwatch
Fragment.java

The StopwatchFragment code (continued)

```
@Override
public View onCreateView(LayoutInflater inflater, ViewGroup container,
                         Bundle savedInstanceState) {
    View layout = inflater.inflate(R.layout.fragment_stopwatch, container, false);
    runTimer(layout);
    return layout;
}
```

Set the fragment's layout, and start the runTimer() method passing in the layout.

```
@Override
public void onPause() {
    super.onPause();
    wasRunning = running;
    running = false;
}
```

If the fragment's paused, record whether the stopwatch was running and stop it.

Workout

app/src/main

java

com.hfad.workout

Stopwatch Fragment.java

```
@Override
public void onResume() {
    super.onResume();
    if (wasRunning) {
        running = true;
    }
}
```

If the stopwatch was running before it was paused, set it running again.

```
@Override
public void onSaveInstanceState(Bundle savedInstanceState) {
    savedInstanceState.putInt("seconds", seconds);
    savedInstanceState.putBoolean("running", running);
    savedInstanceState.putBoolean("wasRunning", wasRunning);
}
```

Put the values of the variables in the Bundle before the activity is destroyed. These are used when the user turns the device.

```
public void onClickStart(View view) {
    running = true;
}
```

This code needs to run when the user clicks on the Start button.

The code continues on the next page.

The StopwatchFragment code (continued)

```java
public void onClickStop(View view) {
    running = false;
}
```

This code needs to run when the user clicks on the Stop button.

```java
public void onClickReset(View view) {
    running = false;
    seconds = 0;
}
```

This code needs to run when the user clicks on the Reset button.

```java
private void runTimer(View view) {
    final TextView timeView = (TextView) view.findViewById(R.id.time_view);
    final Handler handler = new Handler();
    handler.post(new Runnable() {
        @Override
        public void run() {
            int hours = seconds / 3600;
            int minutes = (seconds % 3600) / 60;
            int secs = seconds % 60;
            String time = String.format("%d:%02d:%02d",
                    hours, minutes, secs);
            timeView.setText(time);
            if (running) {
                seconds++;
            }
            handler.postDelayed(this, 1000);
        }
    });
}
```

Putting the code in a Handler means it can run in the background thread.

Display the number of seconds that have passed in the stopwatch.

If the stopwatch is running, increment the number of seconds.

Run the Handler code every second.

Workout

app/src/main

java

com.hfad.workout

Stopwatch
Fragment.java

That's all the Java code we need for our
StopwatchFragment. The next thing we need to do is say
what the fragment should look like by updating the layout code
Android Studio gave us.

The StopwatchFragment layout

We'll use the same layout for StopwatchFragment as we used in our original Stopwatch app. Replace the contents of *fragment_stopwatch.xml* with the code below:

```xml
<?xml version="1.0" encoding="utf-8"?>
<RelativeLayout xmlns:android="http://schemas.android.com/apk/res/android"
    xmlns:tools="http://schemas.android.com/tools"
    android:layout_width="match_parent"
    android:layout_height="match_parent">

    <TextView
        android:id="@+id/time_view"
        android:layout_width="wrap_content"
        android:layout_height="wrap_content"
        android:layout_alignParentTop="true"
        android:layout_centerHorizontal="true"
        android:layout_marginTop="0dp"
        android:text=""
        android:textAppearance="?android:attr/textAppearanceLarge"
        android:textSize="92sp" />

    <Button
        android:id="@+id/start_button"
        android:layout_width="wrap_content"
        android:layout_height="wrap_content"
        android:layout_below="@+id/time_view"
        android:layout_centerHorizontal="true"
        android:layout_marginTop="20dp"
        android:onClick="onClickStart"
        android:text="@string/start" />

    <Button
        android:id="@+id/stop_button"
        android:layout_width="wrap_content"
        android:layout_height="wrap_content"
        android:layout_below="@+id/start_button"
        android:layout_centerHorizontal="true"
        android:layout_marginTop="10dp"
        android:onClick="onClickStop"
        android:text="@string/stop" />
```

Workout
app/src/main
res
layout
fragment_
stopwatch.xml

The number of hours, minutes, and seconds that have passed.

The Start button

The Stop button

0:00:00

Start

Stop

Reset ← The Reset button code is on the next page.

The StopwatchFragment layout (continued)

```
<Button
    android:id="@+id/reset_button"
    android:layout_width="wrap_content"
    android:layout_height="wrap_content"
    android:layout_below="@+id/stop_button"
    android:layout_centerHorizontal="true"
    android:layout_marginTop="10dp"
    android:onClick="onClickReset"
    android:text="@string/reset" />
</RelativeLayout>
```

The Reset button

The StopwatchFragment layout uses String values

The XML code in *fragment_stopwatch.xml* uses string values for the text on the Start, Stop, and Reset buttons. We need to add these to *strings.xml*:

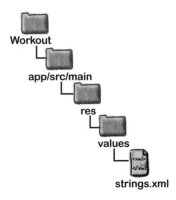

```
...
    <string name="start">Start</string>
    <string name="stop">Stop</string>
    <string name="reset">Reset</string>
...
```

These are the button labels.

The Stopwatch fragment looks just like it did when it was an activity. The difference is that we can now use it in other activities and fragments.

The stopwatch looks the same as it did when it was an activity. Because it's now a fragment, we can reuse it in different activities and fragments.

The next thing we need to do is display it when we show the user details of the workout they choose.

Adding the stopwatch fragment to WorkoutDetailFragment

We're going to add the `StopwatchFragment` inside the `WorkoutDetailFragment`. The user interface of `MainActivity` on a tablet will link together like this:

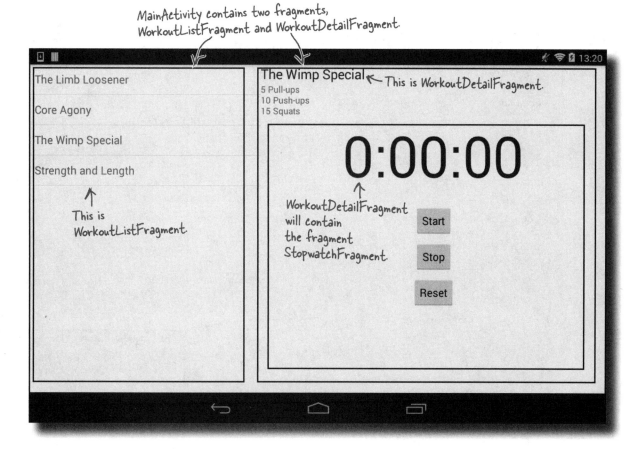

MainActivity contains two fragments, WorkoutListFragment and WorkoutDetailFragment.

This is WorkoutDetailFragment.

This is WorkoutListFragment.

WorkoutDetailFragment will contain the fragment StopwatchFragment.

We need to add it programmatically

You've seen that there are two ways of adding a fragment, using a *layout* file and writing *Java code*. If you add a fragment to another fragment's layout the result can be flaky, so we're going to add the `StopwatchFragment` to the `WorkoutDetailFragment` using Java code. That means we're going to do it in *almost* the same way that we added the `WorkoutDetailFragment` to the activity. There's just one difference which we'll come to.

If you nest fragments inside fragments, you need to add the nested fragment programmatically.

Add a FrameLayout where the fragment should appear

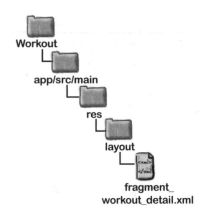

As you saw in Chapter 7, to add a fragment programmatically using Java code, you add a frame layout to your layout where you want the fragment to go.

We want to put our `StopwatchFragment` in `WorkoutDetailFragment` underneath the workout name and description. We'll add a frame layout underneath the name and description text views that will be used to contain `StopwatchFragment`:

```xml
<?xml version="1.0" encoding="utf-8"?>
<LinearLayout xmlns:android="http://schemas.android.com/apk/res/android"
    android:layout_height="match_parent"
    android:layout_width="match_parent"
    android:orientation="vertical">

    <TextView
        android:layout_width="wrap_content"
        android:layout_height="wrap_content"
        android:textAppearance="?android:attr/textAppearanceLarge"
        android:text=""
        android:id="@+id/textTitle" />

    <TextView
        android:layout_width="wrap_content"
        android:layout_height="wrap_content"
        android:text=""
        android:id="@+id/textDescription" />

    <FrameLayout
        android:id="@+id/stopwatch_container"
        android:layout_width="match_parent"
        android:layout_height="match_parent" />
</LinearLayout>
```

Now that we've added the frame layout to the layout, we need to add the fragment to it in our Java code.

The Limb Loosener
5 Handstand push-ups
10 1-legged squats
15 Pull-ups

This is the FrameLayout we'll put the fragment in.

Then display the fragment in Java code

We want to add `StopwatchFragment` to the frame layout when `WorkoutDetailFragment`'s view gets created. We'll do this in a similar way to how we did in Chapter 7, by replacing the fragment that's displayed in the frame layout using a fragment transaction. Here's a reminder of the code we used in Chapter 7:

Create a new instance of the fragment you wish to display.

```
WorkoutDetailFragment details = new WorkoutDetailFragment();
FragmentTransaction ft = getFragmentManager().beginTransaction();
ft.replace(R.id.fragment_container, details);
ft.addToBackStack(null);
ft.setTransition(FragmentTransaction.TRANSIT_FRAGMENT_FADE);
ft.commit();
```

Start the fragment transaction.

Replace the fragment and add it to the back stack.

Commit the transaction.

Get the new and old fragments to fade in and out

We used the above code to replace the fragment that's displayed in an activity, but this time there's a key difference. Instead of replacing the fragment that's displayed in an *activity*, we want to replace the fragment that's displayed in a *fragment*. This means that we need to make a small change to how we create the fragment transaction.

When we wanted to display a fragment in an activity, we created the fragment transaction using the activity's fragment manager like this:

This gets a reference to the activity's fragment manager.

```
FragmentTransaction ft = getFragmentManager().beginTransaction();
```

The `getFragmentManager()` method gets the fragment manager associated with the *fragment's parent activity*. This means that the fragment transaction is linked to the activity.

When you want to display fragments inside another fragment, you need to use a slightly different fragment manager. You need to use the fragment manager associated with the *parent fragment* instead. This means that any fragment transactions will be linked to the parent fragment rather than the activity.

To get the fragment manager that's associated with the parent fragment, you use the `getChildFragmentManager()` method. This means that the code to begin the transaction looks like this:

This gets a reference to the fragment's fragment manager.

```
FragmentTransaction ft = getChildFragmentManager().beginTransaction();
```

So what difference does using `getChildFragmentManager()` make in practice?

getFragmentManager() creates transactions at the activity lavel

Let's first look at what would happen if our
`WorkoutDetailFragment` used `getFragmentManager()` to
create the fragment transaction to display `StopwatchFragment`.

When someone clicks on a workout, we want the app to display the
details of the workout and the stopwatch. `MainActivity` creates
a transaction to display `WorkoutDetailFragment`. If we use
`getFragmentManager()` to display the `StopwatchFragment` as
well, we'll have two transactions on the back stack.

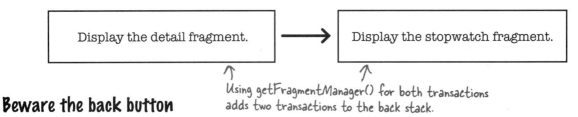

Using getFragmentManager() for both transactions
adds two transactions to the back stack.

Beware the back button

The problem with using two transactions to display the workout is that
weird things happen if the user presses the back button.

When a user clicks on a workout, and then clicks the back button, they
will expect the screen to go back to how it looked before. But **the back
button simply undoes the last transaction on the back stack**.
That means if we create two transactions to the workout detail and the
stopwatch, if the user clicks the back button then all that will happen is
the stopwatch will be removed. They have to click it again to remove the
workout detail section.

Nested fragments need nested transactions

The problem of having multiple transactions for nested fragments was why the child fragment manager was created. The transactions created by the child fragment manager fit *inside* the main transactions. So when we add the `StopwatchFragment` to the `WorkoutDetailFragment` using a transaction created by `getChildFragmentManager().beginTransaction()`, the transactions are nested like this:

Display the detail fragment.

Display the stopwatch fragment.

Using getChildFragmentManager() to display the stopwatch means that the transaction to display the stopwatch is nested inside the transaction to display the detail fragment.

The back stack has one transaction that contains the second transaction. When someone presses the back button, the *display-the-detail-fragment* transaction is undone, and that will mean that the *display-the-stopwatch-fragment* transaction is undone at the same time. When the user presses the back button, the app behaves correctly:

This time the user has to press the Back button just once to undo both the workout detail and stopwatch transactions.

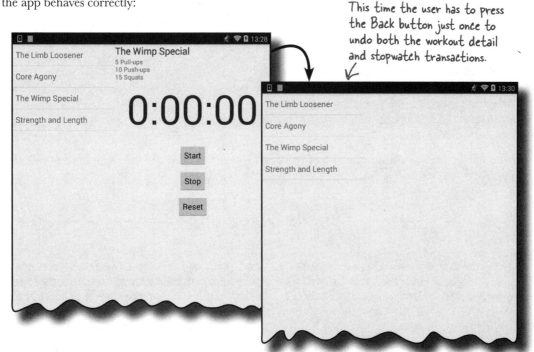

Display the fragment in its parent's onCreateView() method

We want to add `StopwatchFragment` to the frame layout when `WorkoutDetailFragment`'s view gets created. When `WorkoutDetailFragment`'s view gets created, its `onCreateView()` method gets called, so we'll add a fragment transaction to the `onCreateView()` method to display `StopwatchFragment`. Here's the code:

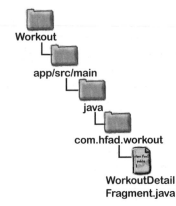

Workout

app/src/main

java

com.hfad.workout

WorkoutDetail Fragment.java

```java
@Override
public View onCreateView(LayoutInflater inflater, ViewGroup container,
                         Bundle savedInstanceState) {
    if (savedInstanceState != null) {
        workoutId = savedInstanceState.getLong("workoutId");
    }
    FragmentTransaction ft = getChildFragmentManager().beginTransaction();
    StopwatchFragment stopwatchFragment = new StopwatchFragment();
    ft.replace(R.id.stopwatch_container, stopwatchFragment);
    ft.addToBackStack(null);
    ft.setTransition(FragmentTransaction.TRANSIT_FRAGMENT_FADE);
    ft.commit();
    return inflater.inflate(R.layout.detail, container, false);
}
```

Start the transaction.

Add the transaction to the back stack.

Commit the transaction.

Replace the fragment in the frame layout.

Set the transition animation style.

As you can see, the code looks almost identical to the code used to display a fragment inside an activity. The key difference is that we're displaying a fragment inside another fragment, so we need to use `getChildFragmentManager()` instead of `getFragmentManager()`.

We'll show you the full code for `WorkoutDetailFragment` on the next page, and then see how it runs.

there are no Dumb Questions

Q: I can see that the child fragment manager handles the case where I put one fragment inside another. But what if I put one fragment inside another, inside another, inside another...?

A: The transactions will all be nested within each other, leaving just a single transaction at the activity level. So the nested set of child transactions will be undone by a single Back button click.

The full WorkoutDetailFragment code

Here's the full code for *WorkoutDetailFragment.java*:

```
package com.hfad.workout;

import android.app.Fragment;
import android.os.Bundle;
import android.view.LayoutInflater;
import android.view.View;
import android.view.ViewGroup;
import android.widget.TextView;
import android.app.FragmentTransaction;

public class WorkoutDetailFragment extends Fragment {
    private long workoutId;

    @Override
    public View onCreateView(LayoutInflater inflater, ViewGroup container,
                             Bundle savedInstanceState) {
        if (savedInstanceState != null) {
            workoutId = savedInstanceState.getLong("workoutId");
        }
        FragmentTransaction ft = getChildFragmentManager().beginTransaction();
        StopwatchFragment stopwatchFragment = new StopwatchFragment();
        ft.replace(R.id.stopwatch_container, stopwatchFragment);
        ft.addToBackStack(null);
        ft.setTransition(FragmentTransaction.TRANSIT_FRAGMENT_FADE);
        ft.commit();
        return inflater.inflate(R.layout.fragment_workout_detail, container, false);
    }

    @Override
    public void onStart() {
        super.onStart();
        View view = getView();
        if (view != null) {
            TextView title = (TextView) view.findViewById(R.id.textTitle);
            Workout workout = Workout.workouts[(int) workoutId];
            title.setText(workout.getName());
            TextView description = (TextView) view.findViewById(R.id.textDescription);
            description.setText(workout.getDescription());
        }
    }

    @Override
    public void onSaveInstanceState(Bundle savedInstanceState) {
        savedInstanceState.putLong("workoutId", workoutId);
    }

    public void setWorkout(long id) {
        this.workoutId = id;
    }
}
```

We're using the FragmentTransaction class, so we're importing it.

Use a fragment transaction to add the stopwatch fragment to the frame layout.

These methods don't need to change.

Workout

app/src/main

java

com.hfad.workout

WorkoutDetail Fragment.java

Test drive the app

Now that you've added the code to display the stopwatch, let's run the app and check that it works.

If you select one of the workouts, the workout detail appears along with the stopwatch. If you click on the Back button, the whole screen goes back to how it looked before:

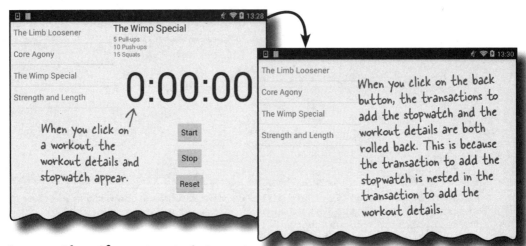

When you click on a workout, the workout details and stopwatch appear.

When you click on the back button, the transactions to add the stopwatch and the workout details are both rolled back. This is because the transaction to add the stopwatch is nested in the transaction to add the workout details.

But there's a problem if you try to interact with the stopwatch

If you try to press one of the buttons on the stopwatch, a weird thing happens. The app crashes:

Click on one of the buttons in the stopwatch...

...and the app crashes.

Let's look at what went wrong.

Why does the app crash if you press a button?

When we converted the stopwatch activity into a fragment, we
didn't change any of the code relating to the buttons. We know
this code worked great when it was in an activity, so why should it
cause the app to crash in a fragment?

Here's the error output from Android Studio. Can you see what
may have caused the problem?

Yikes.

```
01-24 17:37:00.326    2400-2400/com.hfad.fraghack E/AndroidRuntime: FATAL EXCEPTION: main
    Process: com.hfad.fraghack, PID: 2400
    java.lang.IllegalStateException: Could not find a method onClickStart(View) in the activity
    class com.hfad.fraghack.MainActivity for onClick handler on view class android.widget.
    Button with id 'start_button'
            at android.view.View$1.onClick(View.java:3994)
            at android.view.View.performClick(View.java:4756)
            at android.view.View$PerformClick.run(View.java:19749)
            at android.os.Handler.handleCallback(Handler.java:739)
            at android.os.Handler.dispatchMessage(Handler.java:95)
            at android.os.Looper.loop(Looper.java:135)
            at android.app.ActivityThread.main(ActivityThread.java:5221)
            at java.lang.reflect.Method.invoke(Native Method)
            at java.lang.reflect.Method.invoke(Method.java:372)
            at com.android.internal.os.ZygoteInit$MethodAndArgsCaller.run(ZygoteInit.java:899)
            at com.android.internal.os.ZygoteInit.main(ZygoteInit.java:694)
     Caused by: java.lang.NoSuchMethodException: onClickStart [class android.view.View]
            at java.lang.Class.getMethod(Class.java:664)
            at java.lang.Class.getMethod(Class.java:643)
            at android.view.View$1.onClick(View.java:3987)
            at android.view.View.performClick(View.java:4756)
            at android.view.View$PerformClick.run(View.java:19749)
            at android.os.Handler.handleCallback(Handler.java:739)
            at android.os.Handler.dispatchMessage(Handler.java:95)
            at android.os.Looper.loop(Looper.java:135)
            at android.app.ActivityThread.main(ActivityThread.java:5221)
            at java.lang.reflect.Method.invoke(Native Method)
            at java.lang.reflect.Method.invoke(Method.java:372)
            at com.android.internal.os.ZygoteInit$MethodAndArgsCaller.run(ZygoteInit.java:899)
            at com.android.internal.os.ZygoteInit.main(ZygoteInit.java:694)
```

Let's look at the StopwatchFragment layout code

In the layout code for the StopwatchFragment, we're binding
the buttons to methods in the same way that we did for an activity, by
using the android:onClick attribute to say which method should
be called when each button is clicked:

We're using the same layout for the stopwatch now that it's a fragment as we did when it was an activity.

```xml
<?xml version="1.0" encoding="utf-8"?>
<RelativeLayout xmlns:android="http://schemas.android.com/apk/res/android"
    ...
    <Button
        android:id="@+id/start_button"
        android:layout_width="wrap_content"
        android:layout_height="wrap_content"
        android:layout_below="@+id/time_view"
        android:layout_centerHorizontal="true"
        android:layout_marginTop="20dp"
        android:onClick="onClickStart"
        android:text="@string/start" />

    <Button
        android:id="@+id/stop_button"
        android:layout_width="wrap_content"
        android:layout_height="wrap_content"
        android:layout_below="@+id/start_button"
        android:layout_centerHorizontal="true"
        android:layout_marginTop="10dp"
        android:onClick="onClickStop"
        android:text="@string/stop" />

    <Button
        android:id="@+id/reset_button"
        android:layout_width="wrap_content"
        android:layout_height="wrap_content"
        android:layout_below="@+id/stop_button"
        android:layout_centerHorizontal="true"
        android:layout_marginTop="10dp"
        android:onClick="onClickReset"
        android:text="@string/reset" />
</RelativeLayout>
```

Workout
app/src/main
res
layout
fragment_
stopwatch.xml

We're using the android:onClick attributes in the layout to say which methods should be called when each button is clicked.

So why should we have a problem now that we're using a fragment?

The onClick attribute calls methods in the activity, not the fragment

There's a big problem with using the `android:onClick` attribute to say which method should be called when a view is clicked. The attribute specifies which method should be called in the **current activity**. This is fine when the views are in an *activity*'s layout. When the views are in a *fragment* this leads to problems. Instead of calling methods in the fragment, Android calls methods in the parent activity. If it can't find the methods in this activity, the app crashes.

The problem occurs regardless of whether the fragment is included in an activity, or nested inside another fragment. It applies to *all* fragments.

It's not just buttons that have this problem. The `android:onClick` attribute can be used with any views that are subclasses of the `Button` class. This includes checkboxes, radio buttons, switches, and toggle buttons.

Now we *could* move the methods out of the fragment into the activity, but that approach has a major disadvantage. It would mean that the fragment is no longer self-contained—if we wanted to reuse the fragment in another activity, we'd need to include the code in *that* activity too. Instead, we'll deal with it in the fragment.

Whenever I see android:onClick, I assume it's all about **me**. **My** methods run, not the fragment's.

Activity

How to make button clicks call methods in the fragment

There are two things you need to do in order to get buttons in a fragment to call methods in the fragment instead of the activity:

1 **Remove references to android:onClick in the fragment layout.**
Buttons attempt to call methods in the activity when the `android:onClick` attribute is used, so these need to be removed from the fragment layout.

2 **Bind the buttons to methods in the fragment by implementing an onClickListener.**
This will ensure that the right methods are called when the buttons are clicked.

Let's do this now in our `StopwatchFragment`.

First, remove the onClick attributes from the fragment's layout

The first thing we'll do is remove the `android:onClick` lines of code from the fragment's layout. This will stop Android trying to call methods in the activity when the buttons are clicked:

```xml
<?xml version="1.0" encoding="utf-8"?>
<RelativeLayout xmlns:android="http://schemas.android.com/apk/res/android"
    ...
    <Button
        android:id="@+id/start_button"
        android:layout_width="wrap_content"
        android:layout_height="wrap_content"
        android:layout_below="@+id/time_view"
        android:layout_centerHorizontal="true"
        android:layout_marginTop="20dp"
        android:onClick="onClickStart"
        android:text="@string/start" />

    <Button
        android:id="@+id/stop_button"
        android:layout_width="wrap_content"
        android:layout_height="wrap_content"
        android:layout_below="@+id/start_button"
        android:layout_centerHorizontal="true"
        android:layout_marginTop="10dp"
        android:onClick="onClickStop"
        android:text="@string/stop" />

    <Button
        android:id="@+id/reset_button"
        android:layout_width="wrap_content"
        android:layout_height="wrap_content"
        android:layout_below="@+id/stop_button"
        android:layout_centerHorizontal="true"
        android:layout_marginTop="10dp"
        android:onClick="onClickReset"
        android:text="@string/reset" />
</RelativeLayout>
```

Workout

app/src/main

res

layout

fragment_
stopwatch.xml

Remove the onClick attributes for each of the buttons in the stopwatch.

The next thing is to get the fragment to respond to button clicks.

Make the fragment implement OnClickListener

To make the buttons call methods in `StopwatchFragment` when they are clicked, we'll make the fragment implement the `View.OnClickListener` interface like this:

This turns the fragment into an OnClickListener.

```
public class StopwatchFragment extends Fragment implements View.OnClickListener {

    ...

}
```

This turns `StopwatchFragment` into a type of `View.OnClickListener` so that it can respond to when views are clicked.

You tell the fragment how to respond to clicks by implementing the `View.OnClickListener` `onClick()` method. This method gets called whenever a view in the fragment is clicked.

```
@Override
public void onClick(View v) {     ← You must override the onClick()
                                    method in your fragment code.
    ...

}
```

The `onClick()` method has a single `View` parameter. This is the view that the user clicks on. You can use the `View` `getId()` method to find out which view the user clicked on, and then decide how to react.

Code Magnets

See if you can complete the `StopwatchFragment` `onClick()` method. You need to call the `onClickStart()` method when the Start button is clicked, the `onClickStop()` method when the Stop button is clicked, and the `onClickReset()` method when the Reset button is clicked.

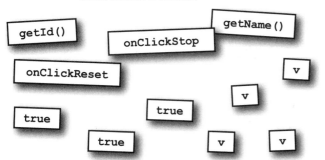

```
@Override
public void onClick(View v) {

    switch (........ . ..............) {
        case R.id.start_button:

            onClickStart(...........);
            break;
        case R.id.stop_button:

            ......................(..........);
            break;
        case R.id.reset_button:

            ......................(..........);
    }

}
```

Code Magnets Solution

See if you can complete the `StopwatchFragment onClick()` method. You need to call the `onClickStart()` method when the Start button is clicked, the `onClickStop()` method when the Stop button is clicked, and the `onClickReset()` method when the Reset button is clicked.

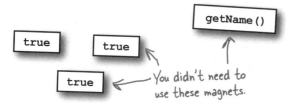

	`true`	
`true`		
	`true`	

You didn't need to use these magnets.

```
@Override
public void onClick(View v) {
    switch ( v . getId() ) {
        case R.id.start_button:

            onClickStart( v );
            break;
        case R.id.stop_button:

            onClickStop ( v );
            break;
        case R.id.reset_button:

            onClickReset ( v );
    }

}
```

The StopwatchFragment onClick() method

Here's the code to implement the `StopwatchFragment` `onClick()` method so that the correct method gets called when each button is clicked:

```
@Override
public void onClick(View v) {          This is the View the user clicked on.
    switch (v.getId()) {          Check which View was clicked.
        case R.id.start_button:
            onClickStart(v);          If the Start button was clicked,
            break;                    call the onClickStart() method.
        case R.id.stop_button:        If the Stop button was clicked,
            onClickStop(v);           call the onClickStop() method.
            break;
        case R.id.reset_button:       If the Reset button was clicked,
            onClickReset(v);          call the onClickReset() method.
            break;
    }
}
```

There's just one more thing we need to do: we need to attach the listener to the buttons in the fragment.

Attach the OnClickListener to the buttons

To make the views respond to clicks, you need to call
each view's setOnClickListener() method.
The setOnClickListener() method takes
an OnClickListener object as a parameter. As
StopwatchFragment implements the OnClickListener
interface, we can use this to pass the fragment as the
OnClickListener.

As an example, here's how you attach the OnClickListener to
the Start button:

Get a reference to the button.
↓

```
Button startButton = (Button) layout.findViewById(R.id.start_button);
startButton.setOnClickListener(this);  ←  Attach the listener to the button.
```

The call to each view's setOnClickListener() method
needs to be made after the fragment's views have been created.
This means they need to go in the StopwatchFragment
onCreateView() method like this:

```
@Override
public View onCreateView(LayoutInflater inflater, ViewGroup container,
                         Bundle savedInstanceState) {
    View layout = inflater.inflate(R.layout.stopwatch, container, false);
    runTimer(layout);
    Button startButton = (Button) layout.findViewById(R.id.start_button);
    startButton.setOnClickListener(this);
    Button stopButton = (Button) layout.findViewById(R.id.stop_button);
    stopButton.setOnClickListener(this);
    Button resetButton = (Button) layout.findViewById(R.id.reset_button);
    resetButton.setOnClickListener(this);
    return layout;
}
```
↑
This attaches the listener to each of the buttons.

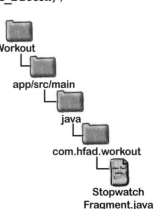

Workout

app/src/main

java

com.hfad.workout

Stopwatch
Fragment.java

We'll show you the full StopwatchFragment code on the next
page.

The StopwatchFragment code

Here's the revised code for *StopwatchFragment.java*:

```
package com.hfad.workout;
...
import android.widget.Button;

public class StopwatchFragment extends Fragment implements View.OnClickListener {
    //Number of seconds displayed on the stopwatch.
    private int seconds = 0;
    //Is the stopwatch running?
    private boolean running;
    private boolean wasRunning;

    @Override
    public void onCreate(Bundle savedInstanceState) {
        super.onCreate(savedInstanceState);
        if (savedInstanceState != null) {
            seconds = savedInstanceState.getInt("seconds");
            running = savedInstanceState.getBoolean("running");
            wasRunning = savedInstanceState.getBoolean("wasRunning");
            if (wasRunning) {
                running = true;
            }
        }
    }

    @Override
    public View onCreateView(LayoutInflater inflater, ViewGroup container,
                             Bundle savedInstanceState) {
        View layout = inflater.inflate(R.layout.stopwatch, container, false);
        runTimer(layout);
        Button startButton = (Button) layout.findViewById(R.id.start_button);
        startButton.setOnClickListener(this);
        Button stopButton = (Button) layout.findViewById(R.id.stop_button);
        stopButton.setOnClickListener(this);
        Button resetButton = (Button) layout.findViewById(R.id.reset_button);
        resetButton.setOnClickListener(this);
        return layout;
    }
```

We're using the Button class, so we'll import it.

The fragment needs to implement the View.OnClickListener interface.

We're not changing the onCreate() method.

Update the onCreateView() method to attach the listener to the buttons.

Workout

app/src/main

java

com.hfad.workout

Stopwatch
Fragment.java

The StopwatchFragment code (continued)

```
@Override
public void onClick(View v) {
    switch (v.getId()) {
        case R.id.start_button:
            onClickStart(v);
            break;
        case R.id.stop_button:
            onClickStop(v);
            break;
        case R.id.reset_button:
            onClickReset(v);
            break;
    }
}

...

public void onClickStart(View view) {
    running = true;
}

public void onClickStop(View view) {
    running = false;
}

public void onClickReset(View view) {
    running = false;
    seconds = 0;
}
...
}
```

As we're implementing the OnClickListener interface, we need to override the onClick() method.

Call the appropriate method in the fragment for the button that was clicked.

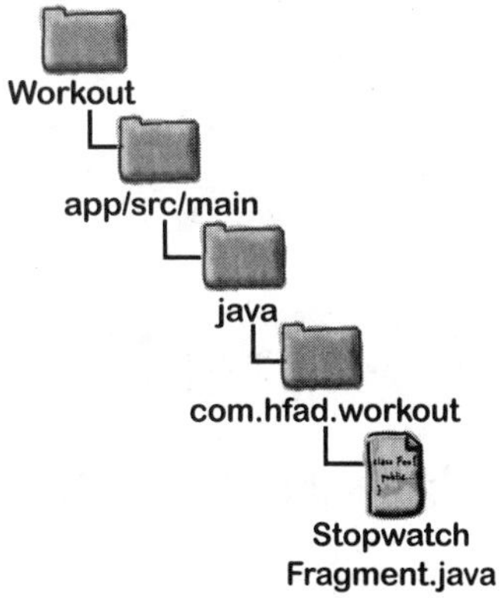

Workout

app/src/main

java

com.hfad.workout

Stopwatch Fragment.java

These are the same methods that we had before. They'll get called when the buttons are clicked.

Let's see what happens when we run the app.

Test drive the app

Now when you run the app, the buttons on the stopwatch work correctly.

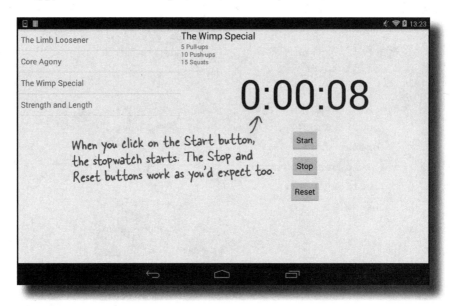

When you click on the Start button, the stopwatch starts. The Stop and Reset buttons work as you'd expect too.

But there's a problem when you rotate the device

If you start the stopwatch and then rotate the device, something strange happens. The stopwatch is reset to 0:

Start the stopwatch and then rotate the device.

When you rotate the device, the stopwatch gets reset back to 0. What's going on?

We've seen before that changing the screen orientation can reset the views. So what happens to fragments when you change the orientation?

Rotating the device re-creates the activity

As you already know, when you're running an app and rotate the device, the activity that's running gets destroyed and re-created. All variables in the activity code are set back to their default values; if you want to save these values before the activity's destroyed, you need to use the activity's `onSaveInstanceState()` method.

But what if the activity contains a fragment? You've already seen that the activity and fragment lifecycles are closely related, but what happens to the fragment when you rotate the device?

What happens to the fragment when you rotate the device

1 **An activity contains a fragment.**

Activity   Fragment

2 **When the user rotates the device, the activity is destroyed along with the fragment.**

The story continues...

③ The activity is re-created and its onCreate() method is called.

The onCreate() method includes a call to setContentView().

onCreate()

Activity

④ When the activity's setContentView() method runs, it reads the activity's layout and replays its fragment transactions.

The fragment is re-created in line with its latest transaction.

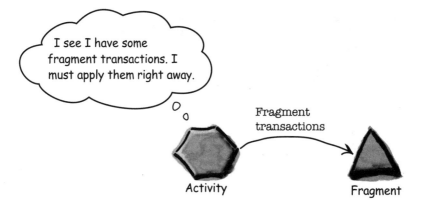

I see I have some fragment transactions. I must apply them right away.

Fragment transactions

Activity

Fragment

When you rotate the device, the fragment *should* go back to the same state it was in before the device was rotated. So why, in our case, has the stopwatch been reset? To get some clues, let's look at the WorkoutDetailFragment onCreateView() method.

onCreateView() runs **AFTER** the transactions have been replayed

The onCreateView() method runs after the activity has replayed all of the activity's fragment transactions. Here's the method. Can you see why the stopwatch gets reset to 0 seconds when the device is rotated?

onCreateView() method in the fragment runs after the activity has replayed all of its fragment transactions.

```
    @Override
    public View onCreateView(LayoutInflater inflater, ViewGroup container,
                            Bundle savedInstanceState) {
        if (savedInstanceState != null) {
            workoutId = savedInstanceState.getLong("workoutId");
        }
        FragmentTransaction ft = getChildFragmentManager().beginTransaction();
        StopwatchFragment stopwatchFragment = new StopwatchFragment();
        ft.replace(R.id.stopwatch_container, stopwatchFragment);
        ft.addToBackStack(null);
        ft.setTransition(FragmentTransaction.TRANSIT_FRAGMENT_FADE);
        ft.commit();
        return inflater.inflate(R.layout.fragment_workout_detail, container, false);
    }
```

This runs if WorkoutDetailFragment has saved its state prior to being destroyed.

This replaces the stopwatch fragment with a brand-new one.

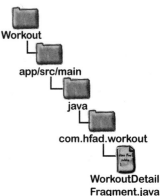

Workout

app/src/main

java

com.hfad.workout

WorkoutDetail
Fragment.java

The onCreateView() method includes a fragment transaction that replaces the stopwatch fragment with a brand-new one. This means that two things happen:

1 The activity replays its fragments transactions, putting the stopwatch fragment in the state it was in before the device was rotated.

2 The onCreateView() method gets rid of the stopwatch fragment the activity reinstated, and replaces it with a brand-new one. As it's a new version of the fragment, the stopwatch is reset to 0.

To stop this from happening, we need to make sure we only replace the fragment if the savedInstanceState Bundle is null. This will mean that a brand-new StopwatchFragment is only displayed when the activity is first created.

The WorkoutDetailFragment code

Here's the full code for *WorkoutDetailFragment.java*:

```
package com.hfad.workout;

...

public class WorkoutDetailFragment extends Fragment {
    private long workoutId;

    @Override
    public View onCreateView(LayoutInflater inflater, ViewGroup container,
                             Bundle savedInstanceState) {
        if (savedInstanceState != null) {
            workoutId = savedInstanceState.getLong("workoutId");
        } else {
            FragmentTransaction ft = getChildFragmentManager().beginTransaction();
            StopwatchFragment stopwatchFragment = new StopwatchFragment();
            ft.replace(R.id.stopwatch_container, stopwatchFragment);
            ft.addToBackStack(null);
            ft.setTransition(FragmentTransaction.TRANSIT_FRAGMENT_FADE);
            ft.commit();
        }
        return inflater.inflate(R.layout.fragment_workout_detail, container, false);
    }

    @Override
    public void onStart() {
        super.onStart();
        View view = getView();
        if (view != null) {
            TextView title = (TextView) view.findViewById(R.id.textTitle);
            Workout workout = Workout.workouts[(int) workoutId];
            title.setText(workout.getName());
            TextView description = (TextView) view.findViewById(R.id.textDescription);
            description.setText(workout.getDescription());
        }
    }

    @Override
    public void onSaveInstanceState(Bundle savedInstanceState) {
        savedInstanceState.putLong("workoutId", workoutId);
    }

    public void setWorkout(long id) {
        this.workoutId = id;
    }
}
```

The only change we need to make is to put the transaction in an else statement. The transaction will only run if savedInstanceState is null.

Let's see what happens when we run the code.

Test drive the app

Run the app, start the stopwatch, then rotate the device. Let's
see what happens to the stopwatch.

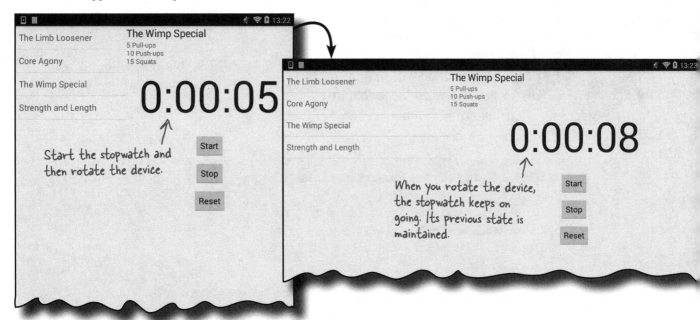

Start the stopwatch and
then rotate the device.

When you rotate the device,
the stopwatch keeps on
going. Its previous state is
maintained.

The stopwatch keeps going. Even though rotating the
device means that the activity is destroyed, the fragment
transactions replay successfully. We're no longer replacing
StopwatchFragment with a brand-new fragment.

there are no Dumb Questions

**Q: If I use the `android:onClick` attribute in my
fragment layout code, will Android really try to call a method in
my activity?**

A: Yes, it will. Rather than use the `android:onClick`
attribute to get views to respond to clicks, implement an
`OnClickListener` instead.

**Q: Does this apply to nested fragments, or fragments in
general?**

A: It's common behavior with all fragments, irrespective of
whether they're nested inside another fragment.

Q: Should I use fragments in my own apps?

A: That depends on your app and what you want to achieve.
One of the major benefits of using fragments is that you can use
them to support a wide range of different screen sizes. You can, say,
choose to display fragments side by side on tablets and on separate
screens on smaller devices. You'll also see some more ways in
which using fragments can be useful in the next couple of chapters...

BE the Fragment

Below are two pieces of fragment layout code, and on the next page there are two pieces of fragment Java code. Your job is to play like you're the fragment and say which combination will display a message when the switch in the layout is on.

A
```xml
<LinearLayout xmlns:android="http://schemas.android.com/apk/res/android"
    xmlns:tools="http://schemas.android.com/tools"
    android:layout_width="match_parent"
    android:layout_height="match_parent"
    android:orientation="vertical"
    tools:context="com.hfad.ch10ex.SwitchFragment">

    <Switch
        android:id="@+id/switch_view"
        android:layout_width="wrap_content"
        android:layout_height="wrap_content" />
</LinearLayout>
```

These are the two pieces of fragment layout code.

B
```xml
<LinearLayout xmlns:android="http://schemas.android.com/apk/res/android"
    xmlns:tools="http://schemas.android.com/tools"
    android:layout_width="match_parent"
    android:layout_height="match_parent"
    android:orientation="vertical"
    tools:context="com.hfad.ch10ex.SwitchFragment">

    <Switch
        android:id="@+id/switch_view"
        android:layout_width="wrap_content"
        android:layout_height="wrap_content"
        android:onClick="onClick" />
</LinearLayout>
```

C
```java
public class SwitchFragment extends Fragment implements View.OnClickListener{

    @Override
    public View onCreateView(LayoutInflater inflater, ViewGroup container,
                            Bundle savedInstanceState) {
        return inflater.inflate(R.layout.fragment_switch, container, false);
    }

    @Override
    public void onClick(View v) {
        if (v.getId() == R.id.switch_view) {
            if (((Switch) v).isChecked()) {
                Toast.makeText(v.getContext(), "On", Toast.LENGTH_SHORT).show();
            }
        }
    }
}
```

These are the two pieces of
fragment Java code.

D
```java
public class SwitchFragment extends Fragment implements View.OnClickListener{

    @Override
    public View onCreateView(LayoutInflater inflater, ViewGroup container,
                            Bundle savedInstanceState) {
        View layout = inflater.inflate(R.layout.fragment_switch, container, false);
        Switch switchView = (Switch) layout.findViewById(R.id.switch_view);
        switchView.setOnClickListener(this);
        return layout;
    }

    @Override
    public void onClick(View v) {
        if (v.getId() == R.id.switch_view) {
            if (((Switch) v).isChecked()) {
                Toast.makeText(v.getContext(), "On", Toast.LENGTH_SHORT).show();
            }
        }
    }
}
```

BE the Fragment Solution
Below are two pieces of fragment layout
code, and on the next page there are two
pieces of fragment Java code. Your job
is to play like you're the
fragment and say which
combination will display a
message when the switch in
the layout is on.

A
```
<LinearLayout xmlns:android="http://schemas.android.com/apk/res/android"
    xmlns:tools="http://schemas.android.com/tools"
    android:layout_width="match_parent"
    android:layout_height="match_parent"
    android:orientation="vertical"
    tools:context="com.hfad.ch10ex.SwitchFragment">

    <Switch
        android:id="@+id/switch_view"
        android:layout_width="wrap_content"
        android:layout_height="wrap_content" />
</LinearLayout>
```

This is the correct layout code.

B
```
<LinearLayout xmlns:android="http://schemas.android.com/apk/res/android"
    xmlns:tools="http://schemas.android.com/tools"
    android:layout_width="match_parent"
    android:layout_height="match_parent"
    android:orientation="vertical"
    tools:context="com.hfad.ch10ex.SwitchFragment">

    <Switch
        android:id="@+id/switch_view"
        android:layout_width="wrap_content"
        android:layout_height="wrap_content"
        android:onClick="onClick" />
</LinearLayout>
```

The Switch in this layout code uses the
android:onClick attribute. This will call
code in the activity, not the fragment.

C

```java
public class SwitchFragment extends Fragment implements View.OnClickListener{

    @Override
    public View onCreateView(LayoutInflater inflater, ViewGroup container,
                             Bundle savedInstanceState) {
        return inflater.inflate(R.layout.fragment_switch, container, false);
    }

    @Override
    public void onClick(View v) {
        if (v.getId() == R.id.switch_view) {
            if (((Switch) v).isChecked()) {
                Toast.makeText(v.getContext(), "On", Toast.LENGTH_SHORT).show();
            }
        }
    }
}
```

✗   *This code implements View.OnClickListener, but doesn't set the listener to the Switch. The onClick() method never gets called.*

D

```java
public class SwitchFragment extends Fragment implements View.OnClickListener{

    @Override
    public View onCreateView(LayoutInflater inflater, ViewGroup container,
                             Bundle savedInstanceState) {
        View layout = inflater.inflate(R.layout.fragment_switch, container, false);
        Switch switchView = (Switch) layout.findViewById(R.id.switch_view);
        switchView.setOnClickListener(this);
        return layout;
    }

    @Override
    public void onClick(View v) {
        if (v.getId() == R.id.switch_view) {
            if (((Switch) v).isChecked()) {
                Toast.makeText(v.getContext(), "On", Toast.LENGTH_SHORT).show();
            }
        }
    }
}
```

✓   *This is the correct Java code. When the Switch is clicked, the onClick() method runs.*

Your Android Toolbox

You've got Chapter 8 under your belt and now you've added nested fragments to your toolbox.

You can download the full code for the chapter from https://tinyurl.com/HeadFirstAndroid.

BULLET POINTS

- Fragments can contain other fragments.

- If you're nesting a fragment in another fragment, you need to add the nested fragment programmatically in Java code.

- When you perform transactions on a nested fragment, use `getChildFragmentManager()` to create the transaction.

- If you use the `android:onClick` attribute in a fragment, Android will look for a method of that name in the fragment's parent activity.

- Instead of using the `android:onClick` attribute in a fragment, make the fragment implement the `View.OnClickListener` interface and implement its `onClick()` method.

- When the device configuration changes, the activity and its fragments get destroyed. When the activity is re-created, it replays its fragment transactions in the `onCreate()` method's call to `setContentView()`.

- The fragment's `onCreateView()` method runs after the activity has replayed its fragment transactions.

9 action bars

Taking Shortcuts

Everybody likes a shortcut.

And in this chapter you'll see how to add shortcuts to your apps using **action bars**. We'll show you how to start other activities by *adding action items* to your action bar, how to share content with other apps using the *share action provider*, and how to navigate up your app's hierarchy by implementing *the action bar's Up button*. Along the way, you'll see how to give your app a consistent look and feel using **themes**, and introduce you to the *Android support library package*.

Great apps have a clear structure

Back in Chapter 6, we looked at ways of structuring an app to create the best user experience. Remember that when you create an app, you will have three different types of screen:

Top-level screens

This is usually the first activity in your app that your user sees.

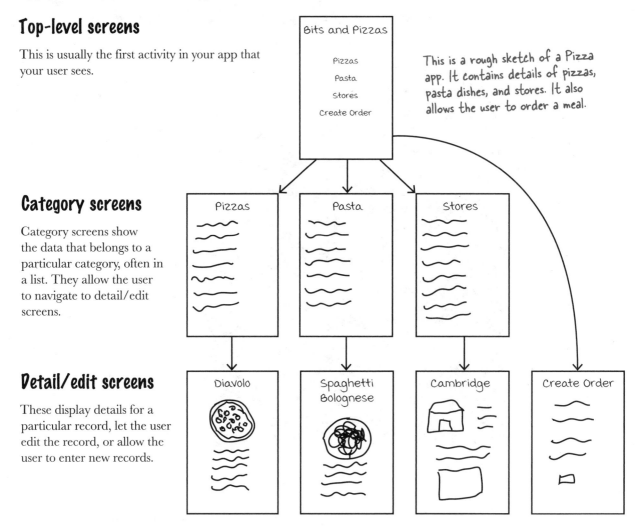

This is a rough sketch of a Pizza app. It contains details of pizzas, pasta dishes, and stores. It also allows the user to order a meal.

Category screens

Category screens show the data that belongs to a particular category, often in a list. They allow the user to navigate to detail/edit screens.

Detail/edit screens

These display details for a particular record, let the user edit the record, or allow the user to enter new records.

They also have great shortcuts

If a user's going to use your app a lot, they'll want quick ways to get around. We're going to look at navigational views that will give your user shortcuts around your app, providing more space in your app for actual content. Let's begin by taking a closer look at the top-level screen in the above Pizza app.

Different types of navigation

In the top-level screen of the Pizza app, there's a list of options for places in the app the user can go to.

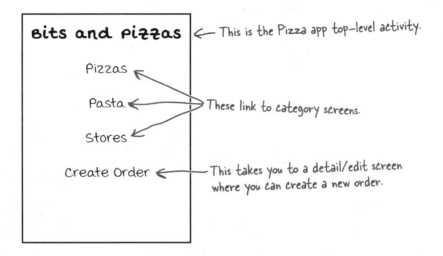

Bits and Pizzas ← This is the Pizza app top-level activity.

Pizzas

Pasta ← These link to category screens.

Stores

Create Order ← This takes you to a detail/edit screen where you can create a new order.

The first three options link to category activities; the first presents the user with a list of pizzas, the second a list of pasta, and the third displays a list of stores. You can think of the category activities as being **passive**. They display information and help you get around.

The fourth option links to a detail/edit activity that allows the user to create an order. This option is **active**. It allows the user to create something.

You generally deal with active and passive navigation options in different ways. In this chapter, we're going to look at how you deal with active navigation options.

Using actions for navigation

In Android apps, active navigational options are usually added to the action bar. The action bar is the bar you often see at the top of activities. It's the place where common actions are displayed, so it normally includes buttons that are best described using verbs such as Create, Search, or Edit.

In the Pizza app, we can make it easy for the user to place an order wherever they are in the app by adding an action bar to the top of every activity. The action bar will include a Create Order button so the user has access to it wherever they are.

Let's take a closer look at how you add action bars to your apps.

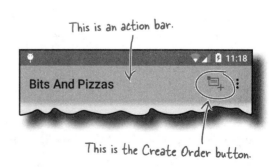

This is an action bar.

This is the Create Order button.

Let's start with the action bar

The action bar has a number of uses:

- ★ For displaying the app or activity name so that the user knows where in the app they are. As an example, an email app might use it to indicate whether the user is in her inbox or junk folder.

- ★ For making key actions prominent in a way that's predictable—for example, sharing content or performing searches.

- ★ For navigating to other activities to perform an action.

To add an action bar, you need to use a **theme** that includes an action bar. A theme is a style that's applied to an entire activity or application so that your app has a consistent look and feel. It controls such things as the color of the activity background and action bar, and the style of the text. Android has a number of built-in themes you can use.

Themes

Android comes with a bunch of built-in themes. You can find a whole list in the Android R.style reference documentation:

http://developer.android.com/reference/android/R.style.html

API level 11 and above

If you want your apps to run on API level 11 or above, you add an action bar by applying `Theme.Holo` or one of its subclasses. This is what you'll need to do most of the time. For API level 21 or above, you have the added option of using one of the newer `Theme.Material` themes. There are several different themes to choose from depending on what appearance you want your app to have. As an example, applying a theme of `Theme.Material.Light.DarkActionBar` will give you activities with a light background and a dark action bar.

Theme.
Material.
Light.

Theme.
Holo.
Light.

These are examples of two different themes.

API level 7 or above

If you need to support older devices running API level 7 or above, you can still add an action bar but you need to do it slightly differently. You first need to change your activities so that they extend the class `android.support.v7.app.ActionBarActivity` instead of the `android.app.Activity` class. You must then apply one of the `Theme.AppCompat` themes.

You only need to take this approach if you intend to support older devices running API levels 7, 8, 9, or 10. Most devices run a higher API level than this.

The `ActionBarActivity` class and the `Theme.AppCompat` themes are included in the **Android support libraries**. Let's look at these in more detail.

The Android support libraries

As time passes, Android continued to add new features. But what if you want to use the latest Android widgets on a device that's two or three years old? The Android support libraries are a set of code libraries that you can include in your project. They're primarily there for backward compatibility, as they allow you to use newer features of Android in older devices.

Some features of Android are only available in the support libraries, so if you need to use these features in your app, you need to use the support library. As an example, the `DrawerLayout` APIs allow you to create a navigation drawer you can pull out from the side of the screen, and these APIs are currently only available in the v4 support library.

The Android support library package includes several support libraries. Each one targets a base API level and includes a specific set of features. The name of the support library reflects the lowest version number of Android the library is compatible with. The v4 support library, for instance, can be used with API level 4 and higher. Similarly, the v7 support libraries can be used with API level 7 and higher. Each of these libraries undergo revisions to include new features and bug fixes.

The classes in a support library are stored within packages named `android.support.v*`. As an example, the v4 library has classes in the `android.support.v4` package.

Here are some of the libraries in the Android support library package:

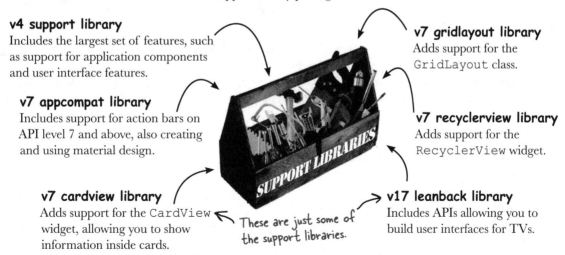

v4 support library
Includes the largest set of features, such as support for application components and user interface features.

v7 appcompat library
Includes support for action bars on API level 7 and above, also creating and using material design.

v7 cardview library
Adds support for the `CardView` widget, allowing you to show information inside cards.

v7 gridlayout library
Adds support for the `GridLayout` class.

v7 recyclerview library
Adds support for the `RecyclerView` widget.

v17 leanback library
Includes APIs allowing you to build user interfaces for TVs.

These are just some of the support libraries.

Android Studio will often add support libraries to your project by default. To see this, let's create a new project to prototype the Pizza app and see if there are any references to them.

Your project may include support libraries

We're going to build a prototype of the Pizza app that supports API level 17 and above. Create a new Android project with a blank activity for an application named "Bits and Pizzas" with a package name of *com.hfad.bitsandpizzas*. The minimum SDK should be API level 17. Specify an activity called "MainActivity", a layout called "activity_main" and a menu resource called "menu_main".

We're going to look at how your new project may be using support libraries by default. First, let's look at *MainActivity.java*. Here's the code that Android Studio created for us. By default, MainActivity extends the android. support.v7.app.ActionBarActivity class. In other words, it's using a v7 support library:

```
package com.hfad.bitsandpizzas;

import android.support.v7.app.ActionBarActivity;
...
public class MainActivity extends ActionBarActivity {
    ...
}
```

The android.support.v7 in the ActionBarActivity import tells you it's from v7 appcompat library.

Your MainActivity.java code may look different. It depends on the behavior of the IDE you're using.

The ActionBarActivity class is used in conjunction with the Theme. AppCompat themes to add action bars to apps that support API levels between 7 and 10. If you use the ActionBarActivity class as the superclass for your activities, you *have* to use one of these themes or your app won't run. You *can't* use more recent themes, such as Material.

Even if you remove references to ActionBarActivity from your app, the v7 support library may still be a dependency in your project. You can see this by going to File→Project Structure. When you click on the app module and choose Dependencies, you may find there's a reference to the v7 appcompat library:

Android Studio automatically added the v7 appcompat library as a dependency. Depending on which version of Android Studio you're using, you may or may not have this.

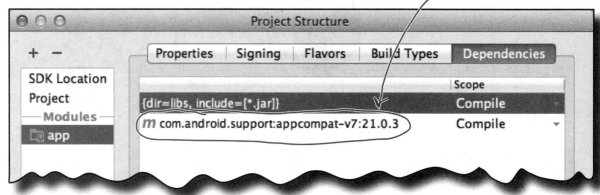

We'll get the app to use up to date themes

We want our prototype app to include action bars. The app supports devices running a minimum of API level 17, so we don't need to provide backward compatibility by using `ActionBarActivity` and `Theme.AppCompat`. Instead, we'll bring the look more up to date by using a Holo theme by default, and get it to switch to a Material theme if it's running on API level 21.

To do this, we need to do two things:

1 **Make sure the activity code doesn't reference ActionBarActivity.**
If it does, we'll only be able to use a `Theme.AppCompat` theme.

2 **Apply the themes.**
We'll get the app to pick up the right theme for the API level it's running on.

We're going to keep the dependency on the v7 appcompat library as this has an impact on the code you'll write later on.

Change MainActivity to use an Activity

We'll start by making sure that *MainActivity.java* uses the `Activity` class and not `ActionBarActivity`. Update your code so that it looks like the code below:

```java
package com.hfad.bitsandpizzas;

import android.app.Activity;
import android.os.Bundle;

public class MainActivity extends Activity {

    @Override
    protected void onCreate(Bundle savedInstanceState) {
        super.onCreate(savedInstanceState);
        setContentView(R.layout.activity_main);
    }
}
```

Make sure your activity extends Activity, not ActionBarActivity. If you use ActionBarActivity, you can't use the Holo or Material themes, Android forces you to use an AppCompat theme.

BitsAndPizzas
  app/src/main
    java
      com.hfad.bitsandpizzas
        MainActivity.java

Now that we know `MainActivity` doesn't use `ActionBarActivity`, we'll look at how you apply a theme.

Apply a theme in AndroidManifest.xml

As you've already seen, the app's *AndroidManifest.xml* file provides essential information about the app such as what activities it contains. It also includes a number of attributes that have an impact on your action bars.

BitsAndPizzas

app/src/main

AndroidManifest.xml

Here's the *AndroidManifest.xml* code Android Studio created for us (we've highlighted the key areas):

```
<manifest xmlns:android="http://schemas.android.com/apk/res/android"
    package="com.hfad.bitsandpizzas" >
    <application
        android:allowBackup="true"
        android:icon="@mipmap/ic_launcher"
        android:label="@string/app_name"
        android:theme="@style/AppTheme" >
        <activity
            android:name=".MainActivity"
            android:label="@string/app_name" >
            ...
        </activity>
    </application>
</manifest>
```

The app's icon. Android Studio provides one by default.

User-friendly name of the app

The theme

User-friendly name of the activity

The label

The icon

▼ ⬛ 🔋 16:08

Bits And Pizzas

The **android:icon** attribute is used to assign an icon to the app. The icon is used as the launcher icon for the app, and if the theme you're using displays an icon in the action bar, it will use this icon.

The icon can be a drawable or mipmap resource. A mipmap is an image that can be used for application icons, and they're held in *mipmap** folders in *app/src/main/res*. Just as with drawables, you can add different images for different screen densities by adding them to an appropriately named *mipmap* folder. As an example, an icon in the *mipmap-hdpi* folder will be used by devices with high-density screens. You refer to mipmap resources in your layout using @mipmap.

Android Studio creates default application icons for you for different screen densities. Older versions of Android Studio put the icons in the drawable folders, and newer versions put them in the mipmap folders.

The **android:label** attribute assigns a user-friendly label to the app or activity, depending on whether it's used in the <application> or <activity> attribute. The action bar displays the current activity's label. If the current activity has no label, it uses the app's label instead.

The **android:theme** attribute specifies the theme. Using this attribute in the <application> element applies it to the entire app. Using it in the <activity> element applies it to a single activity.

Our android:theme attribute has the value "@style/AppTheme". The @style prefix means that the theme is defined in a **style resource file**. So what's a style resource file?

Define styles in style resource files

A style resource file holds details of any themes you want to use.

When you create a project in Android Studio, the IDE creates a default style resource file for you called *styles.xml* located in the *app/src/main/res/values* folder. It will look something like this:

Don't worry if Android Studio has used a different theme—we'll change it on the next page.

```
<resources>
    <!-- Base application theme. -->
    <style name="AppTheme" parent="Theme.AppCompat.Light.DarkActionBar">
        <!-- Customize your theme here. -->
    </style>
</resources>
```

The style resource file contains one or more styles. Each style is defined using the `<style>` element.

Each style must have a name, which you define with the `name` attribute. The style must have a name so that the `android:theme` attribute in *AndroidManifest.xml* can refer to it. In our case, the style has a name of `"AppTheme"`, so *AndroidManifest.xml* can refer to is using `"@style/AppTheme"`.

The `parent` attribute specifies where the style should inherit its properties from. In the case above, this is `"Theme.AppCompat.Light.DarkActionBar"`.

You can also use the style resource file to customize the look of your app by modifying the properties of an existing theme. To do this, you add an `<item>` element to the `<style>` that describes the modification you want to make. As an example, here's how you'd modify the theme so that all the activities have a red background:

BitsAndPizzas
└ **app/src/main**
  └ **res**
    └ **values**
      └ **styles.xml**

```
<resources>
    <style name="AppTheme" parent="Theme.AppCompat.Light.DarkActionBar">
        <item name="android:background">#FF0000</item>
    </style>
</resources>
```

This line turns the backgrounds of your activities red.

We're not going to go into detail about customizing themes here. If you want to learn more we suggest you look at the online reference documentation: *http://developer.android.com/guide/topics/ui/themes.html*.

On the next page, we're going to change the theme used by the app.

Set the default theme in styles.xml

We're going to change the app so that it uses `Theme.Holo.Light` by default, and switches to using `Theme.Material.Light` if the app's running on API level 21.

We'll start by changing the default theme. To do this, open the style resource file *styles.xml* located in the *app/src/main/res/values* folder. This is the default style resource file. By default, we want to use a theme of `Theme.Holo.Light`, so this needs to be reflected in the `<style>` attribute like this:

```
<resources>
    <style name="AppTheme" parent="android:Theme.Holo.Light">
        <!-- Customize your theme here. -->
    </style>
</resources>
```

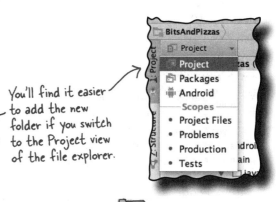

Use a Material theme on newer devices

As you saw in Chapter 8, you can use different folder structures to get your app to use different resources at runtime. As an example, you saw how to get your app to use different layout files depending on the size of the device screen.

Here, we need the app to use a different style resource depending on the API level the app's running on. To get the app to use a particular resource if the app's running on API level 21, we can create a new values-v21 resource file and add the resource to this folder.

To do this, create a new folder in the *app/src/main/res* folder called *values-v21*. Then copy the file *styles.xml* from the *values* folder, and paste it in the *values-v21* folder.

> You'll find it easier to add the new folder if you switch to the Project view of the file explorer.

We want the app to use a Material theme if it's running on API level 21, so edit *styles.xml* in the *values-v21* folder so that it uses a theme of `Theme.Material.Light`:

```
<resources>
    <style name="AppTheme" parent="android:Theme.Material.Light">
        <!-- Customize your theme here. -->
    </style>
</resources>
```

> We'll use this theme if the device is running API level 21.

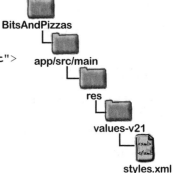

The style name we're using in each style resource file should be the same, because this enables an appropriate theme to be used at runtime. Let's see how.

What happens when you run the app

① When you run the app, Android sees that it needs to apply the theme described by @style/AppTheme.

Android

I must use the style called AppTheme that's the best fit for this device.

② If the app's running on API level 21, it uses the style called AppTheme in the values-21 folder.

The style specifies a theme of Theme.Material.Light, so it applies this theme.

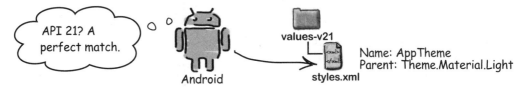

API 21? A perfect match.

Android

values-v21

styles.xml

Name: AppTheme
Parent: Theme.Material.Light

③ If the app's running on an API level below 21, it uses the style called AppTheme in the values folder.

The style specifies a theme of Theme.Holo.Light, so this theme is applied instead.

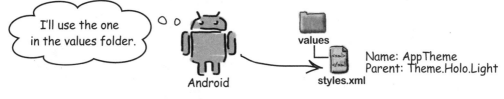

I'll use the one in the values folder.

Android

values

styles.xml

Name: AppTheme
Parent: Theme.Holo.Light

Test drive the app

When you run the app, MainActivity has an action bar. If you run the app on a device that has API level 21, the app uses a theme of Theme.Material.Light. If you run the app on a device with a lower API level, it uses a theme of Theme.Holo.Light.

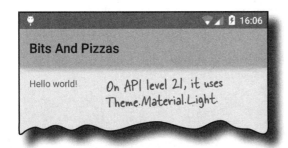

Bits And Pizzas

Hello world!

On API level 21, it uses Theme.Material.Light.

Bits And Pizzas

Hello world!

On a lower API level, it uses Theme.Holo.Light.

Adding action items to the action bar

Most of the time, you'll want to add action items to the action bar. These are buttons or text in the action bar you can click on to make something happen. As an example, we're going to add a "Create Order" button to our action bar.

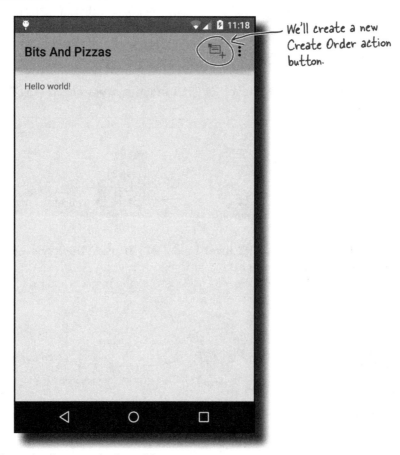

We'll create a new Create Order action button.

To add action items to the action bar, you do three things:

1 **Define the action items in a menu resource file.**

2 **Get the activity to inflate the menu resource.**
You do this by implementing the onCreateOptionsMenu() method.

3 **Add code to say what each item should do when clicked.**
You do this by implementing the onOptionsItemSelected() method.

We'll start with the menu resource file.

The menu resource file

When you create a project containing an activity, Android Studio creates a default menu resource file for you. We told Android Studio to call this file *menu_main.xml*, and it created it in the *app/src/main/res/menu* folder. All menu resource files go in this folder.

Our default action bar.

Here's the menu resource file Android Studio created for us. It describes a single Settings action item that appears in the action bar overflow:

```
<menu xmlns:android="http://schemas.android.com/apk/res/android"
      xmlns:tools="http://schemas.android.com/tools"
      xmlns:app="http://schemas.android.com/apk/res-auto"
      tools:context=".MainActivity">

    <item android:id="@+id/action_settings"
          android:title="@string/action_settings"
          android:orderInCategory="100"
          app:showAsAction="never" />
</menu>
```

This is the Settings action item.

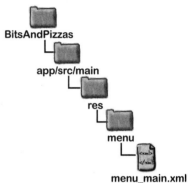

Each menu resource file has a `<menu>` element at its root. A menu resource file defines a single menu, or set of items to be added to the action bar. Your app can contain multiple resource files, and this is useful if you want different activities to have different items on their action bars.

Items are added to the menu using the `<item>` element. Each action item is described using a separate `<item>`. The `<item>` element has a number of attributes you can use, here are some of the most common ones:

android:id	Gives the item a unique ID. You need this in order to refer to the item in your activity code.
android:icon	The item's icon. This is a drawable or mipmap resource.
android:title	The item's text. This may not get displayed if your item has an icon if there's not space in the action bar for both. If the item appears in the action bar's overflow, only the text will be displayed.
android:orderInCategory	An integer value that helps Android decide the order in which items should appear in the action bar.

The code above uses another attribute, `showAsAction`. We'll look at this on the next page.

The menu showAsAction attribute

The showAsAction attribute is used to say how you want the item to appear in the action bar. As an example, you can use it to get an item to appear in the overflow rather than the main action bar, or to place an item on the main action bar only if there's room. The attribute can take the following values:

"ifRoom"	Place the item in the action bar if there's space. If there's not space, put it in the overflow.
"withText"	Include the item's title text.
"never"	Put the item in the overflow area, and never in the main action bar.
"always"	Always place the item in the main area of the action bar. This value should be used sparingly; if you apply this to many items, they may overlap each other.

Let's look again at the showAsAction attribute in the menu resource code. Notice how the showAsAction attribute is prefixed with app: not android:

```
<menu xmlns:android="http://schemas.android.com/apk/res/android"
    xmlns:app="http://schemas.android.com/apk/res-auto"    ← This adds the app namespace.
    ...>

    <item android:id="@+id/action_settings"    ⎫
        android:title="@string/action_settings" ⎬  The ID, title, and orderInCategory
                                                     attributes use the android namespace.
        android:orderInCategory="100"
        app:showAsAction="never" />    ← showAsAction uses the app namespace.
</menu>
```

Earlier in the chapter, you saw how our project had a dependency on the v7 appcompat library. The v7 appcompat library doesn't include showAsAction in the android namespace.

If your project has a dependency on the v7 appcompat library, showAsAction must be prefixed with app:, and the <menu> attribute must include an attribute of

```
xmlns:app="http://schemas.android.com/apk/res-auto"
```

*If your project has **no** dependency on the v7 appcompat library,* showAsAction must be prefixed with android:, not app:. You can also omit the attribute

```
xmlns:app="http://schemas.android.com/apk/res-auto"
```

from the <menu> element.

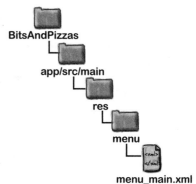

BitsAndPizzas

app/src/main

res

menu

menu_main.xml

Add a new action item

We're going to add a new item to the action bar for creating orders. The item will have a title of "Create Order" and an icon.

When you use icons in your action bar, you can create your own or use icons from the Android action bar icon pack. The icon pack contains many standard icons you can use in your apps.

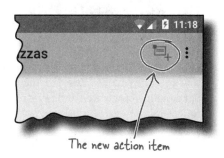

The new action item

We're going to use the `ic_action_new_event` icon from the icon pack. First, download the icon pack from *https://developer.android.com/design/downloads/index.html*. If you expand it, you'll see there are many different icons for different themes and screen sizes.

The `ic_action_new_event` icons are located in the *Action Bar Icons/holo_light/05_content_new_event* folder. There are different icons for different screen sizes, indicated by their folder name. You need to copy the icons to appropriate folders in your project. Copy the icon in the *drawable-hdpi* folder to the *drawable_hdpi* folder in your project, and so on.

If Android Studio hasn't created the folders for you, you'll need to create them yourself.

Once you've added the icons, add a new `action_create_order` string resource to *strings.xml*:

```
<string name="action_create_order">Create Order</string>
```
We'll use this for the action item's title.

Then add the menu item to *menu_main.xml*:

```
<menu xmlns:android="http://schemas.android.com/apk/res/android"
    xmlns:tools="http://schemas.android.com/tools"
    xmlns:app="http://schemas.android.com/apk/res-auto"
    tools:context=".MainActivity">

    <item android:id="@+id/action_create_order"
        android:title="@string/action_create_order"
        android:icon="@drawable/ic_action_new_event"
        android:orderInCategory="1"
        app:showAsAction="ifRoom" />

    <item android:id="@+id/action_settings"
        android:title="@string/action_settings"
        android:orderInCategory="100"
        app:showAsAction="never" />
</menu>
```

The new item is displayed as an icon on the action bar if there's room for it.

BitsAndPizzas
app/src/main
res
menu
menu_main.xml

Now that you've added action items to the menu resource file, you need to add the items to your action bar in your activity code. Let's see how.

Inflate the menu in the activity with the onCreateOptionsMenu() method

Once you've created a menu resource file, you add the items it contains to the action bar by implementing the activity's `onCreateOptionsMenu()` method. It runs when the action bar's menu gets created and takes one parameter, a `Menu` object representing the action bar.

Here's our `onCreateOptionsMenu()` method:

```
package com.hfad.bitsandpizzas;

import android.view.Menu;   ← The onCreateOptionsMenu()
...                           method uses the Menu class.


public class MainActivity extends Activity {

    ...
                              Implementing this method adds any items in
                              the menu resource file to the action bar.
    @Override                        ↓
    public boolean onCreateOptionsMenu(Menu menu) {
        // Inflate the menu; this adds items to the action bar if it is present.
        getMenuInflater().inflate(R.menu.menu_main, menu);
        return super.onCreateOptionsMenu(menu);
    }
}
```

BitsAndPizzas

app/src/main

java

com.hfad.bitsandpizzas

MainActivity.java

You add items to the action bar using

```
getMenuInflater().inflate(R.menu.menu_main, menu);
```

↙ This is a Menu object that represents the action bar.

↑ This is the menu resource file.

This takes the menu items in the *menu_main.xml* menu resource file, and adds them to the action bar `Menu` object.

React to action item clicks with the onOptionsItemSelected() method

You get your activity to react to when an action item in the action bar is clicked by implementing the onOptionsItemSelected() method. This method runs whenever an item in the action bar is clicked.

The onOptionsItemSelected() method takes one attribute, a MenuItem object that represents the item on the action bar that was clicked. You can use the MenuItem's getItemId() method to get the ID of the item on the action bar that was clicked so that you can perform an appropriate action, such as starting a new activity.

Here's the code for our onOptionsItemSelected() method:

```
package com.hfad.bitsandpizzas;

import android.view.MenuItem;
...


public class MainActivity extends Activity {

    ...

    @Override
    public boolean onOptionsItemSelected(MenuItem item) {
        switch (item.getItemId()) {
            case R.id.action_create_order:
                //Code to run when the Create Order item is clicked
                return true;
            case R.id.action_settings:
                //Code to run when the settings item is clicked
                return true;
            default:
                return super.onOptionsItemSelected(item);
        }
    }

}
```

← The onOptionsItemSelected() method uses this class.

The MenuItem object is the item on the action bar that was clicked.

Check which item was clicked.

We need to get the Create Order item to do something.

Android Studio created a Settings item for us. You'd put code to get it to do something here.

Returning true tells Android you've dealt with the item being clicked.

BitsAndPizzas

app/src/main

java

com.hfad.bitsandpizzas

MainActivity.java

We're going to get the Create Order action item to start a new activity called OrderActivity when it's clicked.

Create OrderActivity

We need to create a new activity called `OrderActivity` so our
Create Order action item can launch it.

Start by creating a new blank activity. Give it a name of
"OrderActivity", a layout name of "activity_order", a title of
"Create Order", and a menu resource name of "menu_order".

Here's the code for *OrderActivity.java*. Make sure that your code
reflects ours. In particular, make sure that `OrderActivity`
extends the `Activity` class and not `ActionBarActivity`.
This is because you can only use one of the `Theme.AppCompat`
themes with `ActionBarActivity`, and we want to use the
Holo and Material themes .

```
package com.hfad.bitsandpizzas;

import android.app.Activity;    ← Make sure that OrderActivity
                                   extends Activity, not
import android.os.Bundle;         ActionBarActivity.
                                        ↓
public class OrderActivity extends Activity {

    @Override
    protected void onCreate(Bundle savedInstanceState) {
        super.onCreate(savedInstanceState);
        setContentView(R.layout.activity_order);
    }

}
```

BitsAndPizzas

app/src/main

java

com.hfad.bitsandpizzas

OrderActivity.java

We've not included the `onCreateOptionsMenu()`
and `onOptionsItemSelected()` methods in our
`OrderActivity` code, as we don't need `OrderActivity` to
display menu items from the menu resource file in its action bar.
These methods would need to be added if we ever did want to
display menu items.

Now that we've created `OrderActivity`, let's get the Create
Order action item in `MainActivity` to start it.

Start OrderActivity with the Create Order action item

We want to get the Create Order action item in the `MainActivity` action bar to start `OrderActivity` when it's clicked. To do this, we need to update `MainActivity`'s `onOptionsItemSelected()` method. We'll start `OrderActivity` using an intent.

Here's the code we need to change:

```java
package com.hfad.bitsandpizzas;

import android.content.Intent;    ⟵ We need to use the Intent class.
...

public class MainActivity extends Activity {
...

    @Override
    public boolean onOptionsItemSelected(MenuItem item) {
        switch (item.getItemId()) {
            case R.id.action_create_order:
                //Code to run when the Create Order item is clicked
                Intent intent = new Intent(this, OrderActivity.class);
                startActivity(intent);
                return true;
            case R.id.action_settings:
                //Code to run when the settings item is clicked
                return true;
            default:
                return super.onOptionsItemSelected(item);
        }
    }
}
```

This intent is used to start OrderActivity when the Create Order action item is clicked.

BitsAndPizzas

app/src/main

java

com.hfad.bitsandpizzas

MainActivity.java

When the Create Order action item is clicked, it will create an intent that starts `OrderActivity`.

We'll show you the full *MainActivity.java* code on the next page.

The full MainActivity.java code

```java
package com.hfad.bitsandpizzas;

import android.app.Activity;
import android.content.Intent;
import android.os.Bundle;
import android.view.Menu;
import android.view.MenuItem;

public class MainActivity extends Activity {

    @Override
    protected void onCreate(Bundle savedInstanceState) {
        super.onCreate(savedInstanceState);
        setContentView(R.layout.activity_main);
    }

    @Override
    public boolean onCreateOptionsMenu(Menu menu) {
        // Inflate the menu; this adds items to the action bar if it is present.
        getMenuInflater().inflate(R.menu.menu_main, menu);
        return super.onCreateOptionsMenu(menu);
    }

    @Override
    public boolean onOptionsItemSelected(MenuItem item) {
        switch (item.getItemId()) {
            case R.id.action_create_order:
                //Code to run when the Create Order item is clicked
                Intent intent = new Intent(this, OrderActivity.class);
                startActivity(intent);
                return true;
            case R.id.action_settings:
                //Code to run when the settings item is clicked
                return true;
            default:
                return super.onOptionsItemSelected(item);
        }
    }
}
```

BitsAndPizzas

app/src/main

java

com.hfad.bitsandpizzas

MainActivity.java

Add items to the action bar.

Start OrderActivity when the Create Order item is clicked.

Test drive the app

When you run the app, a new Create Order action item is displayed in the `MainActivity` action bar. When you click on the action item, it starts `OrderActivity`.

Here's the Create Order action item.

Clicking on the Create Order action item starts OrderActivity.

Don't worry if your action item doesn't appear in the main action bar.

The action item may appear in the overflow instead. This is due to a bug in some revisions of the v7 appcompat library. If this is a problem in your app, report it to Google.

---

there are no Dumb Questions

Q: My app already includes a label and icon. Where did they come from?

A: When you create an Android project using an IDE like Android Studio, the IDE creates a bunch of code for you. This includes things such as the app label and icon.

Q: Can you use action bars if you want to support an API below level 7?

A: No, you can't. This isn't that big a deal, though, because very few devices run API level 7 or below.

Q: Why do I have to use `ActionBarActivity` if I want to support an API below level 11?

A: You have to use the Android support library to add an action bar in this case.

Q: Would I ever want to use different themes for different API levels?

A: You might. Material was introduced with API level 21, so you might want apps to use this theme if it's available.

Q: You say you can apply themes to activities individually. Would I ever want to do that?

A: Yes, you might. The Holo and Material themes have several subclasses of themes that give activities a slightly different appearance. If you want to give one of your activities a different look, you might want it to use a different theme.

Sharing content on the action bar

The next thing we'll look at is how to use an action provider with your action bar. An action provider is an item you add to your action bar that handles its own appearance and behavior.

We're going to concentrate on using the share action provider. The share action provider allows users to share content in your app with other apps such as Gmail. As an example, you could use it to let users send details of a particular pizza to one of their contacts.

The share action provider defines its own icon, so you don't have to add it yourself. When you click on it, it provides you with a list of apps you can use to share content.

You share the content with an intent

To get the share action provider to share content, you pass it an intent. The intent you pass it defines the content you want to share, and its type. As an example, if you define an intent that passes text with an ACTION_SEND action, the share action will offer you a list of apps on your device that are capable of sharing this type of data.

This is what the share action looks like on the action bar. When you click on it, it gives you a list of apps that you can use to share content.

1 **Your activity creates an intent and passes it to the share action provider.**
The intent describes the content that needs to be shared, its type, and an action.

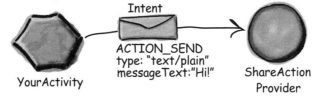

YourActivity

Intent
ACTION_SEND
type: "text/plain"
messageText:"Hi!"

ShareAction
Provider

2 **When the user clicks on the share action, the share action uses the intent to present the user with a list of apps that can deal with it.**
The user chooses an app, and the share action provider passes the intent to the app's activity that can handle it.

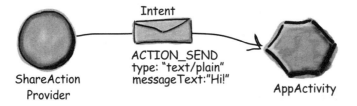

ShareAction
Provider

Intent
ACTION_SEND
type: "text/plain"
messageText:"Hi!"

AppActivity

Add a share action provider to menu_main.xml

You add a share action to the action bar by including it in the menu resource file.

To start, add a new `action_share` string to *strings.xml*. We'll use it to add a title to the share action in case it appears in the overflow:

```xml
<string name="action_share">Share</string>
```

You add the share action to the menu resource file using the `<item>` element as before. This time, however, you need to specify that you're using a share action provider. You do this by adding an attribute of `android:actionProviderClass` and setting it to `android.widget.ShareActionProvider`.

Here's the code to add the share action:

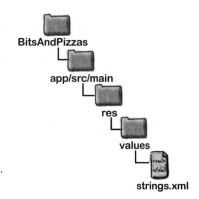

```xml
<menu xmlns:android="http://schemas.android.com/apk/res/android"
    xmlns:app="http://schemas.android.com/apk/res-auto"
    xmlns:tools="http://schemas.android.com/tools"
    tools:context=".MainActivity">

    <item android:id="@+id/action_create_order"
        ... />

    <item android:id="@+id/action_share"
        android:title="@string/action_share"
        android:orderInCategory="2"
        app:showAsAction="ifRoom"
        android:actionProviderClass="android.widget.ShareActionProvider" />

    <item android:id="@+id/action_settings"
        ... />

</menu>
```

Display the share action provider in the action bar if there's room.

This is the share action provider class.

When you add a share action to your menu resource file, there's no need to include an icon. The share action provider already defines one.

Now that we've added the share action to the action bar, let's specify what content to share.

Specify the content with an intent

To get the share action to share content when it's clicked, you need to tell it what to share in your activity code. You do this by passing the share action provider an intent using its `setShareIntent()` method. Here's how you'd get the share action to share some default text when it's clicked:

```
package com.hfad.bitsandpizzas;

...

import android.widget.ShareActionProvider;

public class MainActivity extends Activity {

    private ShareActionProvider shareActionProvider;

    ...                             Add a ShareActionProvider private
    @Override                       variable.
    public boolean onCreateOptionsMenu(Menu menu) {
        getMenuInflater().inflate(R.menu.menu_main, menu);
        MenuItem menuItem = menu.findItem(R.id.action_share);
        shareActionProvider = (ShareActionProvider) menuItem.getActionProvider();
        setIntent("This is example text");
        return super.onCreateOptionsMenu(menu);
    }

    private void setIntent(String text) {
        Intent intent = new Intent(Intent.ACTION_SEND);
        intent.setType("text/plain");
        intent.putExtra(Intent.EXTRA_TEXT, text);
        shareActionProvider.setShareIntent(intent);
    }
}
```

Get a reference to the share action provider and assign it to the private variable. Then call the setIntent() method.

We created the setIntent() method. It creates an intent, and passes it to the share action provider using its setShareIntent() method.

BitsAndPizzas

app/src/main

java

com.hfad.bitsandpizzas

MainActivity.java

You need to call the share action provider's `setShareIntent()` method whenever the content you wish to share has changed. As an example, if you're flicking through images in a photo app, you need to make sure you share the current photo.

We'll show you our full activity code on the next page, and then we'll see what happens when the app runs.

The full MainActivity.java code

Here's the full activity code for *MainActivity.java*:

```java
package com.hfad.bitsandpizzas;

import android.app.Activity;
import android.content.Intent;
import android.os.Bundle;
import android.view.Menu;
import android.view.MenuItem;
import android.widget.ShareActionProvider;

public class MainActivity extends Activity {

    private ShareActionProvider shareActionProvider;

    @Override
    protected void onCreate(Bundle savedInstanceState) {
        super.onCreate(savedInstanceState);
        setContentView(R.layout.activity_main);
    }

    @Override
    public boolean onCreateOptionsMenu(Menu menu) {
        // Inflate the menu; this adds items to the action bar if it is present.
        getMenuInflater().inflate(R.menu.menu_main, menu);
        MenuItem menuItem = menu.findItem(R.id.action_share);
        shareActionProvider = (ShareActionProvider) menuItem.getActionProvider();
        setIntent("This is example text");
        return super.onCreateOptionsMenu(menu);
    }

    private void setIntent(String text) {
        Intent intent = new Intent(Intent.ACTION_SEND);
        intent.setType("text/plain");
        intent.putExtra(Intent.EXTRA_TEXT, text);
        shareActionProvider.setShareIntent(intent);
    }
```

We're using the ShareActionProvider class, so we need to import it.

This sets the default text that the share action provider should share.

The code continues over the page.

The MainActivity.java code (continued)

```java
@Override
public boolean onOptionsItemSelected(MenuItem item) {
    switch (item.getItemId()) {
        case R.id.action_create_order:
            //Code to run when the Create Order item is clicked
            Intent intent = new Intent(this, OrderActivity.class);
            startActivity(intent);
            return true;
        case R.id.action_settings:
            //Code to run when the settings item is clicked
            return true;
        default:
            return super.onOptionsItemSelected(item);
    }
}
```

BitsAndPizzas
app/src/main
java
com.hfad.bitsandpizzas
MainActivity.java

This method hasn't changed.

Test drive the app

When you run the app, the share action is displayed in the action bar. When you click on it, it gives you a list of apps to choose from that can accept the intent we want to share. When you choose an app, it shares the default text.

Remember, the share action may appear in the action bar overflow instead of on the main area of the action bar.

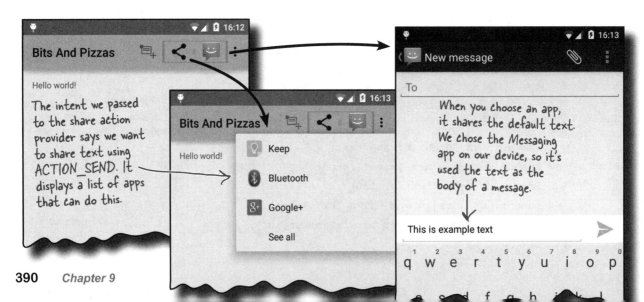

The intent we passed to the share action provider says we want to share text using ACTION_SEND. It displays a list of apps that can do this.

When you choose an app, it shares the default text. We chose the Messaging app on our device, so it's used the text as the body of a message.

Enabling Up navigation

If you have an app that contains a hierarchy of activities, you can enable the Up button on the action bar to navigate through the app using hierarchical relationships. As an example, `MainActivity` in our app includes an action item on its action bar that starts a second activity, `OrderActivity`. If we enable the Up button on `OrderActivity`'s action bar, the user will be able to return to `MainActivity` by clicking on it.

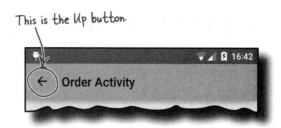
This is the Up button.

Click on the Create Order action to go to OrderActivity.

Click on the Up button...

...to go to MainActivity.

Up navigation may sound the same as using the Back button, but it's different. The Back button allows users to work their way back through the history of activities they've been to. The Up button, on the other hand, is purely based on the app's hierarchical structure.

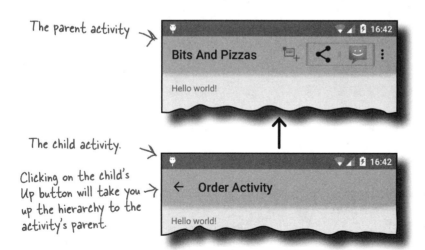

The parent activity

The child activity.

Clicking on the child's Up button will take you up the hierarchy to the activity's parent.

Use the Back button to navigate back to the previous activity.

Use the Up button to navigate up the app's hierarchy.

So that you can see this in action, we're going to enable the Up button on `OrderActivity`'s action bar. When you click on it, it will display `MainActivity`.

Setting an activity's parent

The Up button enables the user to navigate up a hierarchy of activities in the app. You declare this hierarchy in *AndroidManifest.xml* by specifying the parent of each activity. As an example, we want the user to be able to navigate from `OrderActivity` to `MainActivity` when they press the Up button, so this means that `MainActivity` is the parent of `OrderActivity`

From API level 16, you specify the parent activity using the `android:parentActivityName` attribute. For older versions of Android, you need to include a `<meta-data>` element that includes the name of the parent activity. Here are both approaches in our *AndroidManifest.xml*:

```xml
<?xml version="1.0" encoding="utf-8"?>
<manifest xmlns:android="http://schemas.android.com/apk/res/android"
    package="com.hfad.bitsandpizzas" >
    <application
        android:allowBackup="true"
        android:icon="@mipmap/ic_launcher"
        android:label="@string/app_name"
        android:theme="@style/AppTheme" >

        <activity
            android:name=".MainActivity"
            android:label="@string/app_name" >
            <intent-filter>
                <action android:name="android.intent.action.MAIN" />
                <category android:name="android.intent.category.LAUNCHER" />
            </intent-filter>
        </activity>

        <activity
            android:name=".OrderActivity"
            android:label="@string/title_activity_order"
            android:parentActivityName=".MainActivity">
            <meta-data
                android:name="android.support.PARENT_ACTIVITY"
                android:value=".MainActivity" />
        </activity>

    </application>
</manifest>
```

BitsAndPizzas

app/src/main

AndroidManifest.xml

Apps at API level 16 or above use this line. It says that OrderActivity's parent is MainActivity.

You only need to add the <meta-data> element if you're supporting apps below API level 16. We've only included it so you can see what it looks like, and including it doesn't do any harm.

Finally, we need to enable the Up button in `OrderActivity`.

Adding the Up button

You enable the Up button from within your activity code. You first get a reference to the action bar using the activity's `getActionBar()` method. You then call the action bar's `setDisplayHomeAsUpEnabled()` method, passing it a value of `true`.

Watch it!

If you enable the Up button for an activity, you must specify its parent.

If you don't, you'll get a null pointer exception when you call the setDisplayHomeAsUpEnabled() method.

```
ActionBar actionBar = getActionBar();
actionBar.setDisplayHomeAsUpEnabled(true);
```

We want to enable the Up button in `OrderActivity`, so we'll add the code to the `onCreate()` method in *OrderActivity.java*. Here's our full activity code:

```
package com.hfad.bitsandpizzas;

import android.app.ActionBar;          We're using the ActionBar
import android.app.Activity;           class, so we need to import it.
import android.os.Bundle;


public class OrderActivity extends Activity {

    @Override
    protected void onCreate(Bundle savedInstanceState) {
        super.onCreate(savedInstanceState);
        setContentView(R.layout.activity_order);
        ActionBar actionBar = getActionBar();
        actionBar.setDisplayHomeAsUpEnabled(true);
    }
}
                    This enables the Up button
                    in the action bar.
```

BitsAndPizzas
app/src/main
java
com.hfad.bitsandpizzas
OrderActivity.java

Let's see what happens when we run the app.

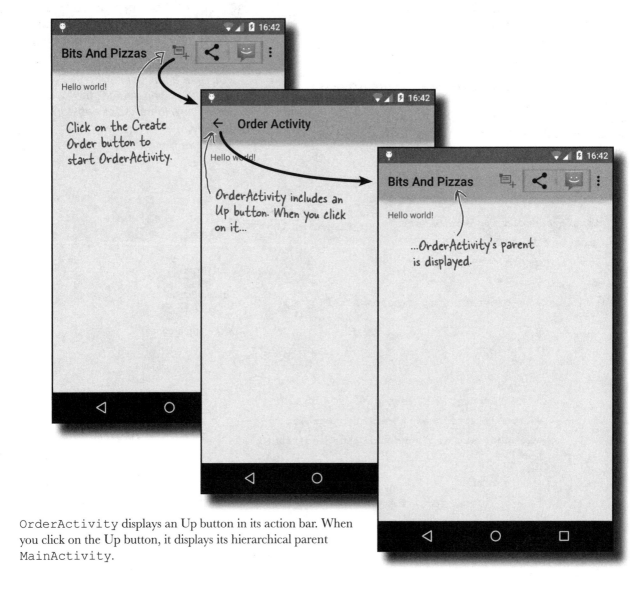

Test drive the app

When you run your app and click on the Create Order action item, OrderActivity is displayed as before.

Click on the Create Order button to start OrderActivity.

OrderActivity includes an Up button. When you click on it...

...OrderActivity's parent is displayed.

OrderActivity displays an Up button in its action bar. When you click on the Up button, it displays its hierarchical parent MainActivity.

Your Android Toolbox

You've got Chapter 9 under your belt and now you've added action bars to your toolbox.

You can download the full code for the chapter from https://tinyurl.com/HeadFirstAndroid.

BULLET POINTS

- To add an action bar to apps supporting API level 11 or above apply one of the Holo or Material themes.

- Add an action bar to apps supporting API level 7 or above by applying an AppCompat theme and using the `ActionBarActivity` class. If you use `ActionBarActivity`, you must use an AppCompat theme.

- `ActionBarActivity` and the AppCompat themes are in the v7 appcompat support library.

- The `android:theme` attribute in *AndroidManifest.xml* specifies which theme to apply.

- You define styles in a style resource file using the `<style>` element. The `name` attribute gives the style a name. The `parent` attribute specifies where the style should inherit its properties from.

- The default folder for style resource files is *app/src/main/res/values*. Put a style resource file in the *app/src/main/res/values-v21* folder if you want it to be used on API level 21.

- Add action items to your action bar by adding items to a menu resource file.

- Add the items in the menu resource file to the action bar by implementing the activity's `onCreateOptionsMenu()` method.

- Say what items should do when clicked by implementing the activity's `onOptionsItemSelected()` method.

- You can share content by adding the share action provider to your action bar. Add it by including it in your menu resource file. Call its `setShareIntent()` method to pass it an intent describing the content you wish to share.

- Add an Up button to your action bar to navigate up the app's hierarchy. Specify the hierarchy in *AndroidManifest.xml*. Use the `ActionBar setDisplayHomeAsUpEnabled()` method to enable the Up button.

10 navigation drawers

Going Places

> I know I'll never get lost so long as I have my lucky navigation drawers.

Apps are so much better when they're easy to navigate.

In this chapter, we're going to introduce you to the **navigation drawer**, a slide-out panel that appears when you swipe the screen with your finger or click an icon on the action bar. We'll show you how to use it to display a **list of links** that take you to **all the major hubs of your app**. You'll also see how **switching fragments** makes those hubs **easy to get to** and **fast to display**.

The Pizza app revisited

In Chapter 9, we showed you a sketch of the top-level screen of the Pizza app. It contained a list of options to places in the app the user could go to. The first three options linked to category screens for pizzas, pasta, and stores, and the final option links to a detail/edit screen where the user could create an order.

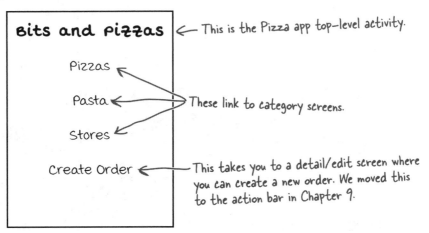

Bits and Pizzas ← This is the Pizza app top-level activity.

Pizzas
Pasta → These link to category screens.
Stores

Create Order ← This takes you to a detail/edit screen where you can create a new order. We moved this to the action bar in Chapter 9.

So far you've seen how you can add action items to the action bar. This approach is best used for active options such as creating an order, but what about the category screens? As these are more passive and used for navigating through the app, we'll take a different approach.

We're going to add the Pizzas, Pasta, and Stores options to a **navigation drawer**. A navigation drawer is a slide-out panel that contains links to the main parts of the app. These main parts are called the **major hubs** of the app, and they are typically the main navigation points within the app—the top-level screens and the categories:

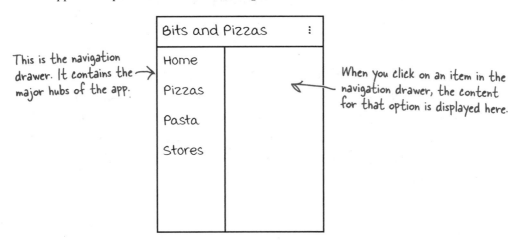

This is the navigation drawer. It contains the major hubs of the app.

Bits and Pizzas ⋮

Home

Pizzas

Pasta

Stores

When you click on an item in the navigation drawer, the content for that option is displayed here.

Navigation drawers deconstructed

You implement a navigation drawer using a special type of layout called a **DrawerLayout**. The DrawerLayout manages two views:

⭐ A view for the main content. This is usually a FrameLayout so that you can display and switch fragments.

⭐ A view for the navigation drawer, usually a ListView.

By default, the DrawerLayout displays the view containing the main content. It looks just like a normal activity:

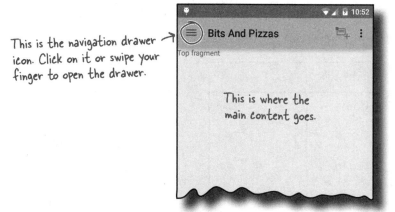

This is the navigation drawer icon. Click on it or swipe your finger to open the drawer.

This is where the main content goes.

When you click on the navigation drawer icon or swipe your finger from the edge of the screen, the view for the navigation drawer slides over the main content:

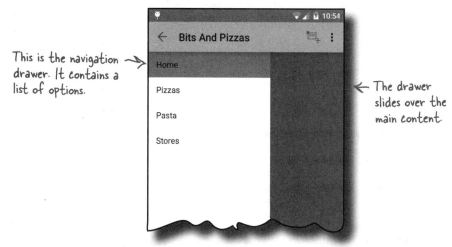

This is the navigation drawer. It contains a list of options.

The drawer slides over the main content.

This content can then be used to navigate through the app.

So how does this affect the structure of the Pizza app?

The Pizza app structure

We're going to change `MainActivity` so that it uses a drawer layout. It will contain a frame layout for displaying fragments, and a list view to display a list of options.

The list view will contain options for Home, Pizzas, Pasta, and Stores so that the user can easily navigate to the major hubs of the app. We'll create fragments for these different options. This means that we'll be able to switch the fragments at runtime, and the user will be able to access the navigation drawer from each of the different screens.

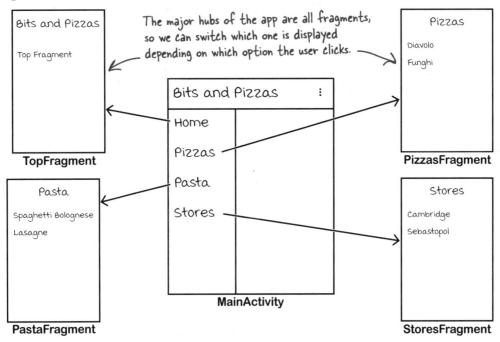

Here are the steps we'll go through to do this:

1 **Create fragments for the major hubs.**

2 **Create and initialize the navigation drawer.**
The navigation drawer will contain a `ListView` displaying the list of options.

3 **Get the ListView to respond to item clicks.**
This will allow the user to navigate to the major hubs of the app.

4 **Add an ActionBarDrawerToggle.**
This lets the user control the drawer through the action bar and allows the activity to respond to drawer open and close events.

We'll start by creating the fragments.

Adding a navigation drawer takes a *lot* of code.

We're going to spend the rest of the chapter showing you how to add one, and we'll show you the entire *MainActivity.java* code at the end.

Create TopFragment

We'll use `TopFragment` to display the top-level content. For now, we'll use it to display the text "Top fragment" so that we know which fragment we're displaying. Create a new blank fragment with a fragment name of TopFragment and a layout name of fragment_top.

We're using a blank fragment for all of our fragments as we're going to replace all the code Android Studio generates for us.

Here's the code for *TopFragment.java*:

```java
package com.hfad.bitsandpizzas;

import android.os.Bundle;
import android.app.Fragment;
import android.view.LayoutInflater;
import android.view.View;
import android.view.ViewGroup;

public class TopFragment extends Fragment {

    @Override
    public View onCreateView(LayoutInflater inflater, ViewGroup container,
                             Bundle savedInstanceState) {
        return inflater.inflate(R.layout.fragment_top, container, false);
    }
}
```

TopFragment.java is a plain fragment.

BitsAndPizzas
└─ app/src/main
   └─ java
      └─ com.hfad.bitsandpizzas
         └─ TopFragment.java

Add the following string resource to *strings.xml*; we'll use this in our fragment layout:

```xml
<string name="title_top">Top fragment</string>
```

Add this to strings.xml. We'll use it in the layout so we know when TopFragment is being displayed.

Here's the code for *fragment_top.xml*:

```xml
<RelativeLayout xmlns:android="http://schemas.android.com/apk/res/android"
    xmlns:tools="http://schemas.android.com/tools"
    android:layout_width="match_parent"
    android:layout_height="match_parent"
    tools:context=".MainActivity">
    <TextView
        android:text="@string/title_top"
        android:layout_width="wrap_content"
        android:layout_height="wrap_content" />
</RelativeLayout>
```

BitsAndPizzas
└─ app/src/main
   └─ res
      └─ layout
         └─ fragment_top.xml

Create PizzaFragment

We'll use a ListFragment called PizzaFragment to display the list of pizzas. Create a new blank fragment with a fragment name of PizzaFragment, and untick the option to create a layout. This is because list fragments don't need a layout—they use their own.

Next, add a new string array resource called "pizzas" to *strings.xml* (this contains the names of the pizzas):

```
<string-array name="pizzas">
    <item>Diavolo</item>      ← Add the array of pizzas to strings.xml.
    <item>Funghi</item>
</string-array>
```

Then change the code for *PizzaFragment.java* so that it's a ListFragment. Its list view should be populated with the pizza names. Here's the code:

```
package com.hfad.bitsandpizzas;

import android.app.ListFragment;
import android.os.Bundle;
import android.view.LayoutInflater;
import android.view.View;
import android.view.ViewGroup;
import android.widget.ArrayAdapter;

public class PizzaFragment extends ListFragment {

    @Override
    public View onCreateView(LayoutInflater inflater, ViewGroup container,
                             Bundle savedInstanceState) {
        ArrayAdapter<String> adapter = new ArrayAdapter<String>(
                inflater.getContext(),
                android.R.layout.simple_list_item_1,
                getResources().getStringArray(R.array.pizzas));
        setListAdapter(adapter);
        return super.onCreateView(inflater, container, savedInstanceState);
    }
}
```

We'll use a ListFragment to display the list of pizzas.

BitsAndPizzas

app/src/main

java

com.hfad.bitsandpizzas

PizzaFragment.java

Create PastaFragment

We'll use a `ListFragment` called `PastaFragment` to display the list of pasta. Create a new blank fragment with a fragment name of PastaFragment. You can untick the option to create a layout as list fragments use their own layouts.

Next, add a new string array resource called "pasta" to *strings.xml* (this contains the names of the pasta):

```
<string-array name="pasta">
    <item>Spaghetti Bolognese</item>    ← Add the array of pasta to strings.xml.
    <item>Lasagne</item>
</string-array>
```

Then change the code for *PastaFragment.java* so that it's a `ListFragment`. Its list view should be populated with the pasta names. Here's the code:

```java
package com.hfad.bitsandpizzas;

import android.app.ListFragment;
import android.os.Bundle;
import android.view.LayoutInflater;
import android.view.View;
import android.view.ViewGroup;
import android.widget.ArrayAdapter;

public class PastaFragment extends ListFragment {

    @Override
    public View onCreateView(LayoutInflater inflater, ViewGroup container,
                             Bundle savedInstanceState) {
        ArrayAdapter<String> adapter = new ArrayAdapter<String>(
                inflater.getContext(),
                android.R.layout.simple_list_item_1,
                getResources().getStringArray(R.array.pasta));
        setListAdapter(adapter);
        return super.onCreateView(inflater, container, savedInstanceState);
    }
}
```

We'll use a ListFragment to display the list of pasta.

BitsAndPizzas

app/src/main

java

com.hfad.bitsandpizzas

PastaFragment.java

Create StoresFragment

→ ☐ **Add fragments**
 ☐ **Create drawer**
 ☐ **ListView clicks**
 ☐ **ActionBarDrawerToggle**

We'll use a ListFragment called StoresFragment to display the list of pasta. Create a new blank fragment with a fragment name of "StoresFragment." Untick the option to create a layout as list fragments define their own layouts.

Next, add a new string array resource called "stores" to *strings.xml* (this contains the names of the stores):

```
<string-array name="stores">
    <item>Cambridge</item>
    <item>Sebastopol</item>
</string-array>
```

← Add the array of stores to strings.xml.

Then change the code for *StoresFragment.java* so that it's a ListFragment. Its list view should be populated with the store names. Here's the code:

```
package com.hfad.bitsandpizzas;

import android.app.ListFragment;
import android.os.Bundle;
import android.view.LayoutInflater;
import android.view.View;
import android.view.ViewGroup;
import android.widget.ArrayAdapter;

public class StoresFragment extends ListFragment {

    @Override
    public View onCreateView(LayoutInflater inflater, ViewGroup container,
                             Bundle savedInstanceState) {
        ArrayAdapter<String> adapter = new ArrayAdapter<String>(
                inflater.getContext(),
                android.R.layout.simple_list_item_1,
                getResources().getStringArray(R.array.stores));
        setListAdapter(adapter);
        return super.onCreateView(inflater, container, savedInstanceState);
    }
}
```

BitsAndPizzas
app/src/main
java
com.hfad.bitsandpizzas
StoresFragment.java

We'll use a ListFragment to display the list of stores.
↓

Add the DrawerLayout

Next, we'll change the layout of *MainActivity.java* so that it uses a
DrawerLayout. As we said earlier, this will contain a FrameLayout
that will display fragments, and a ListView for the navigation drawer.

You create the DrawerLayout using code like this:

The layout uses the DrawerLayout from the v4 support library. The v7 appcompat library includes the v4 support library.

```
<android.support.v4.widget.DrawerLayout
    xmlns:android="http://schemas.android.com/apk/res/android"
    android:id="@+id/drawer_layout"
    android:layout_width="match_parent"
    android:layout_height="match_parent">
```

The FrameLayout will be used to display fragments.

```
    <FrameLayout
        android:layout_width="match_parent"
        android:layout_height="match_parent"
        ... />
```

The ListView describes the drawer.

```
    <ListView
        android:layout_width="240dp"
        android:layout_height="match_parent"
        ... />
</android.support.v4.widget.DrawerLayout>
```

The DrawerLayout is the root component of the new layout. That's
because it needs to control everything that appears on the screen.
The DrawerLayout class comes from the v4 support library, so
we use its full class path of android.support.v4.widget.
DrawerLayout.

The first element in the DrawerLayout is used to display the content.
In our case, this is a FrameLayout that we'll use to display fragments.
You want this to be as large as possible, so you set its layout_width
and layout_height attributes to "match_parent".

The second element in the DrawerLayout defines the drawer itself.
If you use a ListView, this will display a drawer that contains a list
of options. You usually want this to partially fill the screen horizontally
when it slides out, so you set its layout_height attribute to
"match_parent" and its layout_width attribute to a fixed width.

We'll show you the full code for *activity_main.xml* on the next page.

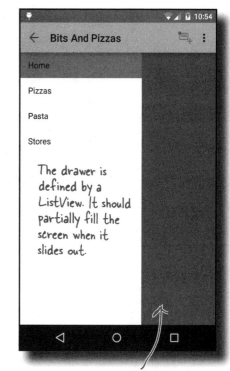

The drawer is defined by a ListView. It should partially fill the screen when it slides out.

The content goes in a FrameLayout. You want the content to fill the screen. At the moment, it's partially hidden by the drawer.

The full code for activity_main.xml

Here's the full code for *activity_main.xml*:

```
<android.support.v4.widget.DrawerLayout
    xmlns:android="http://schemas.android.com/apk/res/android"
    android:id="@+id/drawer_layout"
    android:layout_width="match_parent"
    android:layout_height="match_parent">

    <FrameLayout
        android:id="@+id/content_frame"
        android:layout_width="match_parent"
        android:layout_height="match_parent" />

    <ListView android:id="@+id/drawer"
        android:layout_width="240dp"
        android:layout_height="match_parent"
        android:layout_gravity="start"
        android:choiceMode="singleChoice"
        android:divider="@android:color/transparent"
        android:dividerHeight="0dp"
        android:background="#ffffff"/>

</android.support.v4.widget.DrawerLayout>
```

Fragments will be displayed in the FrameLayout.

BitsAndPizzas
app/src/main
res
layout
activity_main.xml

The ListView describes the drawer.

← *The drawer width.*

← *Where to place the drawer.*

← *Select one item at a time.*

↖ *Switch off the divider lines between items and set the background color of the drawer.*

Take a careful note of the settings we're using with the <ListView> element, as any navigation drawer you create is likely styled in a similar way.

To set the size of the drawer, you use the layout_width and layout_height attributes. We've set layout_width to "240dp" so that the drawer is 240dp wide when it's open.

Setting the layout_gravity attribute to "start" places the drawer on the left in languages where text runs from left to right, and places it on the right in countries where text runs from right to left.

The divider, dividerHeight, and background attributes are used to switch off divider lines between the options and set the background color.

Finally, setting the choiceMode attribute to "singleChoice" means only one item can be selected at a time.

Watch it!

If your project doesn't include a dependency on the v7 appcompat support library, the navigation drawer code in this chapter won't work.

You manage dependencies by navigating to File→Project Structure→App→Dependencies.

Initialize the drawer's list

Now that we've added a drawer layout to *activity_main.xml*, we need to specify its behavior in *MainActivity.java*. The first thing we'll do is populate the list view. To do this, we'll add an array of options to *strings.xml*. We'll then use an array adapter to populate the list.

Here's the array of strings you need to add to *strings.xml* (each item in the array refers to which fragment you want to display when it's clicked):

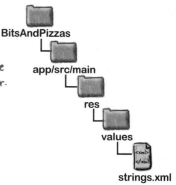

BitsAndPizzas

app/src/main

res

values

strings.xml

```xml
<string-array name="titles">
    <item>Home</item>
    <item>Pizzas</item>
    <item>Pasta</item>
    <item>Stores</item>
</string-array>
```

These are the options that will be displayed in the navigation drawer. Add the array to strings.xml.

We'll populate the list view in *MainActivity.java*'s onCreate() method. We'll use private variables for the array and list view as we'll need these later on. Here's the code:

```java
...
import android.widget.ArrayAdapter;
import android.widget.ListView;

public class MainActivity extends Activity {
    ...
    private String[] titles;
    private ListView drawerList;

    @Override
    protected void onCreate(Bundle savedInstanceState) {
        ...
        titles = getResources().getStringArray(R.array.titles);
        drawerList = (ListView)findViewById(R.id.drawer);
        drawerList.setAdapter(new ArrayAdapter<String>(this,
            android.R.layout.simple_list_item_activated_1, titles));
    }
    ...
}
```

We're using these classes, so we need to import them.

BitsAndPizzas

app/src/main

java

com.hfad.bitsandpizzas

MainActivity.java

We'll use these in other methods later on, so add them as private class variables.

Use an ArrayAdapter to populate the ListView.

Using simple_list_item_activated_1 means that the item the user clicks on is highlighted.

Now that we've populated the list view with a list of options, we'll get the list to respond to item clicks.

Use an OnItemClickListener to respond to clicks in the list view

You get the list view to respond to clicks in the same way that we did in Chapter 6, by using an `onItemClickListener`. We're going to create the listener, implement its `onItemClick()` method, and assign the listener to the list view. Here's the code:

BitsAndPizzas
└ app/src/main
   └ java
      └ com.hfad.bitsandpizzas
         └ MainActivity.java

```
...
import android.view.View;          ← We're using these
import android.widget.AdapterView;    classes, so we need to
                                      import them.

public class MainActivity extends Activity {
    ...
                        This describes the OnItemClickListener.
                                    ↓
    private class DrawerItemClickListener implements ListView.OnItemClickListener {
        @Override
        public void onItemClick(AdapterView<?> parent, View view, int position, long id) {
            //Code to run when the item gets clicked
        }                          ↑
    };            When the user clicks on an item in the navigation
                  drawer, the onItemClick() method gets called.


    @Override
    protected void onCreate(Bundle savedInstanceState) {
        ...
        drawerList.setOnItemClickListener(new DrawerItemClickListener());
    }            ↖
};      Add a new instance of our OnItemClickListener to the drawer's ListView.
```

The `onItemClick()` method needs to include the code you want to run when the user clicks on an item in the list view. We'll get it to call a new `selectItem()` method, passing in the position of the selected item. We'll write this method next.

The method should do three things:

⭐ Switch the fragment in the frame layout.

⭐ Change the title in the action bar to reflect the layout.

⭐ Close the navigation drawer.

You already know everything you need in order to do the first of these tasks, so have a go at the exercise on the next page.

Code Magnets

When the user clicks on an item in the navigation drawer list view, we need to display the correct fragment in the `content_frame` frame layout. See if you can finish the code below.

> Home
>
> Pizzas
>
> Pasta
>
> Stores

These are the items in the ListView.

```java
private void selectItem(int position) {
    Fragment fragment;

    switch(.....................) {
        case 1:

            fragment = ...............................................;
            break;
        case 2:

            fragment = ...............................................;
            break;
        case 3:

            fragment = ...............................................;
            break;
        default:

            fragment = ...............................................;
    }

    FragmentTransaction ft = getFragmentManager()...........................................;

    ft.replace(R.id.content_frame, .......................);

    ft.addToBackStack(null);
    ft.setTransition(FragmentTransaction.TRANSIT_FRAGMENT_FADE);

    ft........................;
}
```

beginTransaction()

new   position

PizzaFragment()

TopFragment()

new   fragment

StoresFragment()

PastaFragment()

new   commit()

new

Code Magnets Solution

When the user clicks on an item in the navigation drawer list view, we need to display the correct fragment in the `content_frame` frame layout. See if you can finish the code below.

| Home |
| Pizzas |
| Pasta |
| Stores |

These are the items in the ListView.

```
private void selectItem(int position) {
    Fragment fragment;
    switch( position ) {
        case 1:

            fragment = new PizzaFragment() ;
            break;
        case 2:

            fragment = new PastaFragment() ;
            break;
        case 3:

            fragment = new StoresFragment() ;
            break;
        default:

            fragment = new TopFragment() ;
    }

    FragmentTransaction ft = getFragmentManager(). beginTransaction() ;

    ft.replace(R.id.content_frame, fragment );
    ft.addToBackStack(null);
    ft.setTransition(FragmentTransaction.TRANSIT_FRAGMENT_FADE);

    ft. commit() ;
}
```

Check the position in the drawer's ListView of the item that was clicked.

Create a type of fragment that's appropriate for the position. If the user clicks on "Pizzas", for example, create a PizzaFragment.

By default, create a TopFragment.

Begin a fragment transaction to replace the fragment that's displayed.

Commit the transaction.

The selectItem() method so far

Here's our revised *MainActivity.java* code (when an item in the navigation drawer gets clicked, it calls the `selectItem()`, which method displays a fragment):

```
...
import android.app.Fragment;
import android.app.FragmentTransaction;

public class MainActivity extends Activity {
    ...
    private class DrawerItemClickListener implements ListView.OnItemClickListener {
        @Override
        public void onItemClick(AdapterView<?> parent, View view, int position, long id) {
            selectItem(position);
        }
    };

    private void selectItem(int position) {
        Fragment fragment;
        switch(position) {
            case 1:
                fragment = new PizzaFragment();
                break;
            case 2:
                fragment = new PastaFragment();
                break;
            case 3:
                fragment = new StoresFragment();
                break;
            default:
                fragment = new TopFragment();
        }
        FragmentTransaction ft = getFragmentManager().beginTransaction();
        ft.replace(R.id.content_frame, fragment);
        ft.addToBackStack(null);
        ft.setTransition(FragmentTransaction.TRANSIT_FRAGMENT_FADE);
        ft.commit();
    }
}
```

BitsAndPizzas

app/src/main

java

com.hfad.bitsandpizzas

MainActivity.java

← Call the selectItem() method when an item gets clicked.

← Check the position of the item that was clicked.

← Use the position to create the right type of fragment. The "Pizzas" option is at position 1, for instance, so in this case create a PizzaFragment.

← Create a TopFragment by default

↑ Use fragment transaction to replace the fragment that's displayed.

Now that the `selectItem()` method displays the correct fragment, we'll get it to change the action bar title.

Changing the action bar title

Add fragments ✓
Create drawer ✓
ListView clicks
ActionBarDrawerToggle

In addition to switching the fragment that's displayed, we need to change the title of the action bar so that it reflects which fragment is displayed. By default, we want the action bar to display the name of the app, but if the user clicks on the Pizzas option, for example, we want to change the action bar title to "Pizzas". This will help the user know where they are in the app.

To do this, we'll use the position of the chosen item to get the title that should be displayed from the titles array. We'll then update the action bar title using the **ActionBar setTitle()** method. We'll put this in a separate method as we'll need it later on. Here's the code:

```
private void selectItem(int position) {
    ...
    //Set the action bar title
    setActionBarTitle(position);    ← Call the setActionTitle()
}                                      method, passing it the position
                                       of the item that was clicked on.

private void setActionBarTitle(int position) {
    String title;                   If the user clicks on the "Home" option, use
    if (position == 0){            ↙ the app name for the title.
        title = getResources().getString(R.string.app_name);
    } else {
        title = titles[position];  ← Otherwise, get the String from the titles array for
    }                                 the position that was clicked and use that
    getActionBar().setTitle(title);  ← Display the title in the action bar.
}
```

BitsAndPizzas
app/src/main
java
com.hfad.bitsandpizzas
MainActivity.java

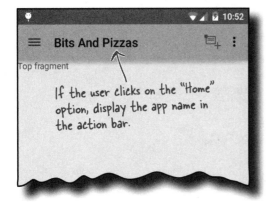

If the user clicks on the "Home" option, display the app name in the action bar.

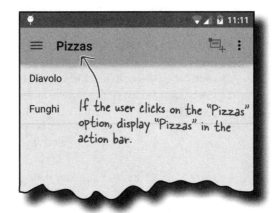

If the user clicks on the "Pizzas" option, display "Pizzas" in the action bar.

Closing the navigation drawer

The final thing we'll get the selectItem() code to do is
close the navigation drawer. This saves the user from closing it
themselves.

You close the drawer by getting a reference to the
DrawerLayout and calling its **closeDrawer()** method.
The closeDrawer() method takes one parameter, the View
that you're using for the navigation drawer. In our case, it's the
ListView that displays the list of options:

```
private void selectItem(int position) {
    ...
    //Close the drawer
    DrawerLayout drawerLayout = (DrawerLayout) findViewById(R.id.drawer_layout);
    drawerLayout.closeDrawer(drawerList);
}
```

Get a reference to the DrawerLayout.

drawerList is the DrawerLayout's drawer. This tells
the DrawerLayout to close the drawerList drawer.

The entire screen is
the DrawerLayout. It
contains a FrameLayout
where the content goes,
and a ListView which is
used for the drawer.

You need to tell the
DrawerLayout to close
its ListView drawer.

Now that you've seen all the components needed for the
selectItem() code, let's look at the full code and how it's
used in MainActivity.

The updated MainActivity.java code

☑ **Add fragments**
☑ **Create drawer**
→ ☑ **ListView clicks**
ActionBarDrawerToggle

Here's the updated code for *MainActivity.java*:

```
package com.hfad.bitsandpizzas;

...

import android.support.v4.widget.DrawerLayout;
```
← DrawerLayout is in the v4 support library.

BitsAndPizzas → app/src/main → java → com.hfad.bitsandpizzas → MainActivity.java

```
public class MainActivity extends Activity {
    ...
    private DrawerLayout drawerLayout;
```
← Add the DrawerLayout as a private variable, as we'll use it in multiple methods.

```
    private class DrawerItemClickListener implements ListView.OnItemClickListener {
        @Override
        public void onItemClick(AdapterView<?> parent, View view, int position, long id) {
            //Code to run when an item in the navigation drawer gets clicked
            selectItem(position);
```
← Call the selectItem() method.
```
        }
    };


    @Override
    protected void onCreate(Bundle savedInstanceState) {
        super.onCreate(savedInstanceState);
        setContentView(R.layout.activity_main);
        titles = getResources().getStringArray(R.array.titles);
        drawerList = (ListView)findViewById(R.id.drawer);
        drawerLayout = (DrawerLayout) findViewById(R.id.drawer_layout);
```
Get a reference to the DrawerLayout.
```
        //Populate the ListView
        drawerList.setAdapter(new ArrayAdapter<String>(this,
                android.R.layout.simple_list_item_activated_1, titles));
        drawerList.setOnItemClickListener(new DrawerItemClickListener());
        if (savedInstanceState == null) {
            selectItem(0);
```
← If the MainActivity is newly created, use the selectItem() method to display TopFragment.
```
        }
    }
```

The code continues →
on the next page.

The MainActivity.java code (continued)

```java
private void selectItem(int position) {
    // update the main content by replacing fragments
    Fragment fragment;
    switch(position) {
        case 1:
            fragment = new PizzaFragment();
            break;
        case 2:
            fragment = new PastaFragment();
            break;
        case 3:
            fragment = new StoresFragment();
            break;
        default:
            fragment = new TopFragment();
    }
    FragmentTransaction ft = getFragmentManager().beginTransaction();
    ft.replace(R.id.content_frame, fragment);
    ft.addToBackStack(null);
    ft.setTransition(FragmentTransaction.TRANSIT_FRAGMENT_FADE);
    ft.commit();
    //Set the action bar title
    setActionBarTitle(position);
    //Close drawer
    drawerLayout.closeDrawer(drawerList);
}


private void setActionBarTitle(int position) {
    String title;
    if (position == 0){
        title = getResources().getString(R.string.app_name);
    } else {
        title = titles[position];
    }
    getActionBar().setTitle(title);
}
...
}
```

Get the right fragment to display.

Display the fragment using a fragment transaction.

← *Set the action bar title.*

← *Close the drawer.*

If the user clicks on the "Home" option, use the app name for the title.

← *Otherwise, get the String from the titles array for the position that was clicked and use that*

← *Display the title in the action bar.*

... ← *We've omitted the onCreateOptionsMenu() and onOptionsItemSelected() methods from our original ManActivity code, as these haven't changed.*

BitsAndPizzas

app/src/main

java

com.hfad.bitsandpizzas

MainActivity.java

Get the drawer to open and close

So far we've added a navigation drawer to `MainActivity`, populated it with a list of the major hubs in the app, and got the activity to respond when an item is clicked. The next thing we'll look at is how to open and close the drawer, and how to respond to its state.

There are a couple of reasons why you might want to respond to the state of the navigation drawer. First, you might want to change the title of the action bar when the navigation drawer opens and closes. You might, say, want to display the app name when the drawer is open, and display the selected fragment when the drawer is closed.

Another reason relates to the action items on the action bar. When the drawer is open, you may want to hide some or all of these action items so that the user can only click on them when the drawer is closed.

Over the next few pages, we're going to show you how to set up a `DrawerListener` so that you can listen for `DrawerLayout` events. We'll use it to hide the share action on the action bar when the navigation drawer is open, and make it visible again when the drawer closes.

Add fragments
Create drawer
ListView clicks
ActionBarDrawerToggle

We know it seems like you have to take care of a lot of things when you create a navigation drawer.

Even though the code might seem complex, stick with it and you'll be fine.

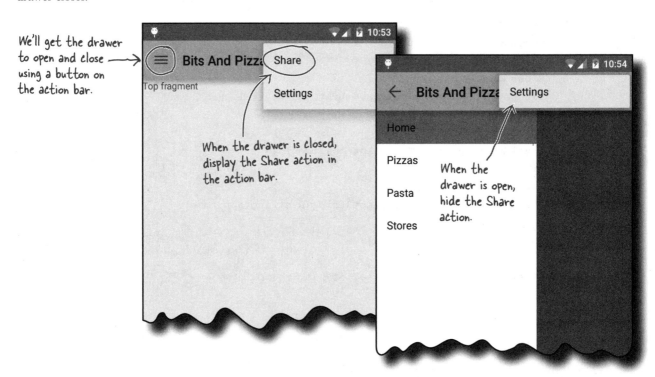

We'll get the drawer to open and close using a button on the action bar.

When the drawer is closed, display the Share action in the action bar.

When the drawer is open, hide the Share action.

Using an ActionBarDrawerToggle

The best way of setting up a DrawerListener is to use an **ActionBarDrawerToggle**. An ActionBarDrawerToggle is a special type of DrawerListener that works with an action bar. It allows you to listen for DrawerLayout events like a normal DrawerListener, and it also lets you open and close the drawer by clicking on an icon on the action bar.

You start by creating two String resources in *strings.xml* that describe the "open drawer" and "close drawer" actions. These are needed for accessibility:

```
<string name="open_drawer">Open drawer</string>
<string name="close_drawer">Close drawer</string>
```

Add these to strings.xml. They're needed for the ActionBarDrawerToggle.

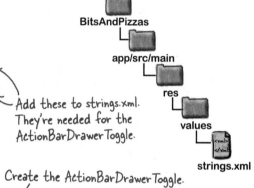

Then create a new ActionBarDrawerToggle by calling its constructor and passing it four parameters: a Context (usually this for the current Context), the DrawerLayout, and the two String resources. You then override the ActionBarDrawerToggle's **onDrawerClosed()** and **onDrawerOpened()** methods:

Create the ActionBarDrawerToggle.

```
ActionBarDrawerToggle drawerToggle = new ActionBarDrawerToggle(this, drawerLayout,
                R.string.open_drawer, R.string.close_drawer) {

    //Called when a drawer has settled in a completely closed state
    @Override
    public void onDrawerClosed(View view) {
        super.onDrawerClosed(view);
        //Code to run when the drawer is closed
    }

    //Called when a drawer has settled in a completely open state.
    @Override
    public void onDrawerOpened(View drawerView) {
        super.onDrawerOpened(drawerView);
        //Code to run when the drawer is open
    }
};
```

This method gets called when the drawer is closed.

This method gets called when the drawer is open.

Once you've created the ActionBarDrawerToggle, you set it to the DrawerLayout using the DrawerLayout's setDrawerListener() method:

Set the ActionBarDrawerToggle as the DrawerLayout's drawer listener.

```
drawerLayout.setDrawerListener(drawerToggle);
```

BitsAndPizzas
app/src/main
java
com.hfad.bitsandpizzas
MainActivity.java

Modifying action bar items at runtime

☑ Add fragments
☑ Create drawer
☑ ListView clicks
→ **ActionBarDrawerToggle**

If you have items on your action bar that are specific to the contents of a particular fragment, you may want to hide them when the drawer is open, and display them again when the drawer is open. When you need to modify the contents of the action bar in this way, you have to do two things.

First, you need to call the activity's **invalidateOptionsMenu()** method. This tells Android that the menu items that need to be on the action bar have changed and should be re-created.

When you call the invalidateOptionsMenu() method, the activity's onPrepareOptionsMenu() method gets called. You can override this method to specify how the menu items need to change.

We're going to change the visibility of the share action on our action bar depending on whether the drawer is open or closed. We therefore need to call the invalidateOptionsMenu() method in the onDrawerClosed() and onDrawerOpened() methods of the ActionBarDrawerToggle:

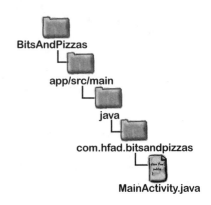

```java
public void onDrawerClosed(View view) {
    super.onDrawerClosed(view);
    invalidateOptionsMenu();
}


public void onDrawerOpened(View drawerView) {
    super.onDrawerOpened(drawerView);
    invalidateOptionsMenu();
}
```

The invalidateOptionsMenu() method tells Android to re-create the menu items. We want to change the visibility of the Share action if the drawer is opened or closed, so we call it in the onDrawerOpened() and onDrawerClosed() methods.

We then use the activity's onPrepareOptionsMenu() method to set the visibility of the share action:

```java
//Called whenever we call invalidateOptionsMenu()
@Override
public boolean onPrepareOptionsMenu(Menu menu) {
    // If the drawer is open, hide action items related to the content view
    boolean drawerOpen = drawerLayout.isDrawerOpen(drawerList);
    menu.findItem(R.id.action_share).setVisible(!drawerOpen);
    return super.onPrepareOptionsMenu(menu);
}
```

The onPrepareOptionsMenu() method gets called whenever invalidateOptionsMenu() gets called.

Set the Share action's visibility to false if the drawer is open, set it to true if it isn't.

On the next page, we'll take you through the full code.

The file path diagram shows:
BitsAndPizzas → app/src/main → java → com.hfad.bitsandpizzas → MainActivity.java

The updated MainActivity.java code

Here's the revised code for *MainActivity.java*:

```
...
import android.support.v7.app.ActionBarDrawerToggle;

public class MainActivity extends Activity {
    ...
    private ActionBarDrawerToggle drawerToggle;

    @Override
    protected void onCreate(Bundle savedInstanceState) {
        ...

        //Create the ActionBarDrawerToggle
        drawerToggle = new ActionBarDrawerToggle(this, drawerLayout,
                R.string.open_drawer, R.string.close_drawer) {
            //Called when a drawer has settled in a completely closed state
            public void onDrawerClosed(View view) {
                super.onDrawerClosed(view);
                invalidateOptionsMenu();
            }
            //Called when a drawer has settled in a completely open state.
            public void onDrawerOpened(View drawerView) {
                super.onDrawerOpened(drawerView);
                invalidateOptionsMenu();
            }
        };
        drawerLayout.setDrawerListener(drawerToggle);
    }


    //Called whenever we call invalidateOptionsMenu()
    @Override
    public boolean onPrepareOptionsMenu(Menu menu) {
        // If the drawer is open, hide action items related to the content view
        boolean drawerOpen = drawerLayout.isDrawerOpen(drawerList);
        menu.findItem(R.id.action_share).setVisible(!drawerOpen);
        return super.onPrepareOptionsMenu(menu);
    }
    ...
}
```

ActionBarDrawerToggle is in the v7 appcompat library.

Set this as a private variable, as we'll use it in multiple methods.

BitsAndPizzas

app/src/main

java

com.hfad.bitsandpizzas

MainActivity.java

Call invalidateOptionsMenu() when the drawer is opened or closed.

Set the DrawerLayout's drawer listener as the ActionBarDrawerToggle.

Set the visibility of the Share action when the drawer is opened and closed.

☑ Add fragments
☑ Create drawer
☑ ListView clicks
→ ☐ **ActionBarDrawerToggle**

Enable the drawer to open and close

We've added a navigation drawer to `MainActivity`, populated it with a list of options, got the activity to respond when an option is clicked, and seen how to hide action items when the drawer is open. The final thing we'll do is let the user open and close the drawer by clicking on an icon in the action bar.

As we said earlier, this functionality is one of the advantages of using an `ActionBarDrawerToggle`. To switch it on, we need to add some extra code. We'll take you through the code changes individually, then show you the full *MainActivity.java* code right at the end.

The ActionBarDrawerToggle lets you use the action bar's Up button to open and close the drawer.

First, you enable the icon in the action bar. You do that using these two method calls in the activity's `onCreate()` method:

```java
getActionBar().setDisplayHomeAsUpEnabled(true);
getActionBar().setHomeButtonEnabled(true);
```

Enable the Up button so you can use it for the drawer.

These lines of code enable the activity's Up button. As we're using an `ActionBarDrawerToggle`, the Up button will be used to activate the drawer instead of navigating up the app's hierarchy.

Next, you need to get the `ActionBarDrawerToggle` to handle being clicked. To do this, you call its `onOptionsItemSelected()` method from within the activity's `onOptionsItemSelected()` method like this:

```java
@Override
public boolean onOptionsItemSelected(MenuItem item) {
    if (drawerToggle.onOptionsItemSelected(item)) {
        return true;
    }
    //Code to handle the rest of the action items
    ...
    }
}
```

You need to add these lines of code to the onOptionsItemSelected() method so that the ActionBarDrawerToggle can handle being clicked.

The code

```java
drawerToggle.onOptionsItemSelected(item)
```

returns `true` if the `ActionBarDrawerToggle` has handled being clicked. If it returns `false`, this means that another action item in the action bar has been clicked, and the rest of the code in the activity's `onOptionsItemSelected()` method will run.

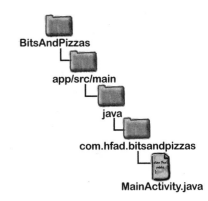

BitsAndPizzas

app/src/main

java

com.hfad.bitsandpizzas

MainActivity.java

Syncing the ActionBarDrawerToggle state

There are just two more things we need to do in order to get our
`ActionBarDrawerToggle` working properly.

First, we need to call the `ActionBarDrawerToggle`'s
`syncState()` method from within the activity's `postCreate()`
method. The `syncState()` method synchronizes the state of the
drawer icon with the state of the `DrawerLayout`.

We'd love it if the navigation drawer handled this for you automatically, but it doesn't. You have to handle it yourself.

Syncing the state means that the drawer icon appears one way when the drawer is closed, and another way when the drawer is open.

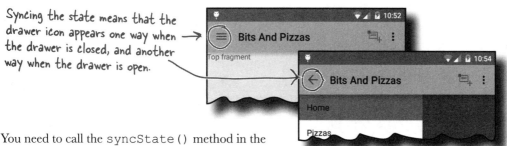

You need to call the `syncState()` method in the
activity's `onPostCreate()` method so that the
`ActionBarDrawerToggle` is in the right state after the
activity is created:

You need to add this method to your activity so that the state of the ActionBarDrawerToggle is in sync with the state of the drawer.

```
@Override
protected void onPostCreate(Bundle savedInstanceState) {
    super.onPostCreate(savedInstanceState);
    // Sync the toggle state after onRestoreInstanceState has occurred.
    drawerToggle.syncState();
}
```

Finally, if the device configuration changes, we need to pass details
of the configuration change to the `ActionBarDrawerToggle`.
We do this by calling the `ActionBarDrawerToggle`'s
`onConfigurationChanged()` method from within the
activity's `onConfigurationChanged()` method:

```
@Override
public void onConfigurationChanged(Configuration newConfig) {
    super.onConfigurationChanged(newConfig);
    drawerToggle.onConfigurationChanged(newConfig);
}
```

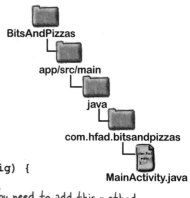

BitsAndPizzas

app/src/main

java

com.hfad.bitsandpizzas

MainActivity.java

You need to add this method to your activity so that any configuration changes get passed to the ActionBarDrawerToggle.

We'll show you where the latest code changes fit into *MainActivity.
java* on the next page, and then we'll see what happens when we
run the app.

The updated MainActivity.java code

☑ Add fragments
☑ Create drawer
☑ ListView clicks
→ ☑ **ActionBarDrawerToggle**

Here's the revised code for *MainActivity.java*:

```
...
import android.content.res.Configuration;
```
Import this class as it's used by the onConfigurationChanged() method.

```
public class MainActivity extends Activity {

    ...
    private ActionBarDrawerToggle drawerToggle;

    @Override
    protected void onCreate(Bundle savedInstanceState) {

        ...
        getActionBar().setDisplayHomeAsUpEnabled(true);
        getActionBar().setHomeButtonEnabled(true);
    }
```
Enable the Up icon so it can be used by the ActionBarDrawerToggle.

```
    @Override
    protected void onPostCreate(Bundle savedInstanceState) {
        super.onPostCreate(savedInstanceState);
        drawerToggle.syncState();
    }
```
Sync the state of the ActionBarDrawerToggle with the state of the drawer.

```
    @Override
    public void onConfigurationChanged(Configuration newConfig) {
        super.onConfigurationChanged(newConfig);
        drawerToggle.onConfigurationChanged(newConfig);
    }
```
Pass any configuration changes to the ActionBarDrawerToggle.

```
    @Override
    public boolean onOptionsItemSelected(MenuItem item) {
        if (drawerToggle.onOptionsItemSelected(item)) {
            return true;
        }
        //Code to handle the rest of the action items
        switch (item.getItemId()) {
            ...
        }
    }
    ...
}
```
Let the ActionBarDrawerToggle handle being clicked.

BitsAndPizzas

app/src/main

java

com.hfad.bitsandpizzas

MainActivity.java

Test drive the app

When we run the app, `MainActivity` is displayed. It features a working navigation drawer:

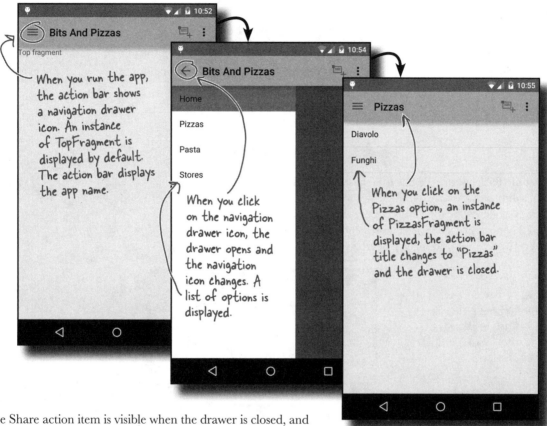

When you run the app, the action bar shows a navigation drawer icon. An instance of TopFragment is displayed by default. The action bar displays the app name.

When you click on the navigation drawer icon, the drawer opens and the navigation icon changes. A list of options is displayed.

When you click on the Pizzas option, an instance of PizzasFragment is displayed, the action bar title changes to "Pizzas" and the drawer is closed.

The Share action item is visible when the drawer is closed, and hidden when the drawer is open:

The Share action is visible if the drawer is closed.

The Share action is hidden if the drawer is open.

There's just one thing we need to sort out: we need to make sure the correct title in the action bar is displayed when the device is rotated or the user presses the back button. So what currently happens?

The title and fragment are getting out of sync

When we click on one of the options in the navigation drawer, the title in the action bar reflects the fragment that's displayed. As an example, if you click on the Pizzas option, the action bar title gets set to "Pizzas":

When you click on items in the navigation drawer, the title gets updated correctly. ⟶

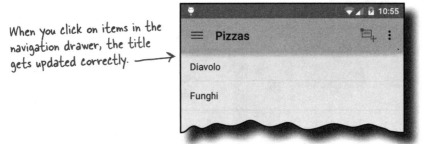

If you click on the Back button, the title isn't updated to reflect the fragment that's displayed. As an example, suppose you click on the Stores option, followed by the Pizzas option. A list of pizzas is displayed and the title reflects this. If you then click on the Back button, `StoresFragment` is displayed but the title is "Pizzas":

The action bar title stays the same when we click on the Back button. In this case, it says "Pizzas" when a list of stores is displayed ⟶

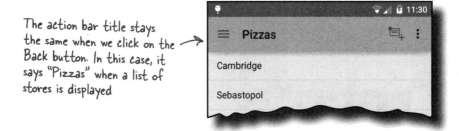

If you rotate the device, the title reverts to "Bits and Pizzas" irrespective of what fragment is displayed:

The action bar title is reset when you rotate the device. ⟶

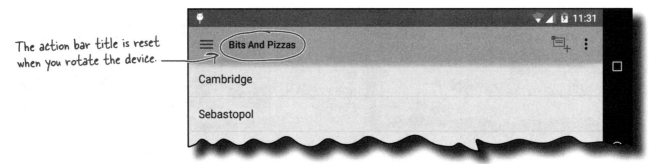

Let's fix these problems, starting with keeping the action bar title in sync when the device is rotated.

Dealing with configuration changes

As you already know, when you rotate your device, the current activity gets destroyed and re-created. This means that any user interface changes you have made are lost, including changes to the action bar title.

Just as we did in earlier chapters, we'll use the activity's `onSaveInstanceState()` method to save the position of the currently selected item in the navigation drawer. We can then use this in the `onCreate()` method to update the title in the action bar.

Here are the code changes:

```
...
public class MainActivity extends Activity {
    ...
    private int currentPosition = 0;
                                      ↖
                        Set currentPosition to 0 by default.
    @Override
    protected void onCreate(Bundle savedInstanceState) {
        ...
        //Display the correct fragment.
        if (savedInstanceState != null) {
            currentPosition = savedInstanceState.getInt("position");
            setActionBarTitle(currentPosition);
        } else {
            selectItem(0);
        }
        ...              ↖
    }          If the activity's newly created,
               display TopFragment.

    private void selectItem(int position) {
        currentPosition = position;  ←── Update currentPosition when an item is selected.
        ...
    }

    @Override
    public void onSaveInstanceState(Bundle outState) {
        super.onSaveInstanceState(outState);
        outState.putInt("position", currentPosition);
    }              ↖
    ...          Save the state of currentPosition if
}                the activity's going to be destroyed.
```

If the activity has been destroyed and re-created, set the value of currentPosition from the activity's previous state and use it to set the action bar title.

BitsAndPizzas

app/src/main

java

com.hfad.bitsandpizzas

MainActivity.java

Reacting to changes on the back stack

The final thing we need to address is how to make the action bar
title reflect the fragment that's displayed when the user clicks on
the back button. We can do this by adding a **FragmentManager.
OnBackStackChangedListener** to the activity's fragment
manager.

The FragmentManager.OnBackStackChangedListener
interface listens for changes to the back stack. This includes when a
fragment transaction is added to the back stack, and when the user
clicks on the back button to navigate to a previous back stack entry.

You add an OnBackStackChangedListener to the activity's
fragment manager like this:

```
getFragmentManager().addOnBackStackChangedListener(
    new FragmentManager.OnBackStackChangedListener() {
        public void onBackStackChanged() {
            //Code to run when the back stack changes
        }
    }
);
```

*You add a new FragmentManager.
OnBackStackChangedListener,
implementing its onBackStackChanged()
method. This method is called whenever
the back stack changes.*

When the back stack changes, the
OnBackStackChangedListener's onBackStackChanged()
method gets called. Any code you want to run when the user clicks
on the back button should be added to this method.

When the onBackStackChanged() method gets called, we want
to do three things.

★ Update the currentPosition variable so that it reflects the position
in the list view of the currently displayed fragment.

★ Call the setActionBarTitle() method, passing it the value of
currentPosition.

★ Make sure that the right option in the navigation drawer's list view is
highlighted by calling its setItemChecked() method.

Each of these depends on us knowing the position in the list view of
the currently displayed fragment. So how do we work this out?

Adding tags to fragments

To work out what the value of `currentPosition` should be, we'll check what type of fragment is currently attached to the activity. As an example, if the attached fragment is an instance of `PizzaFragment`, we'll set `currentPosition` to 1.

We'll get a reference to the currently attached fragment by adding a `String` tag to each fragment. We'll then use the fragment manager's `findFragmentByTag()` method to retrieve the fragment.

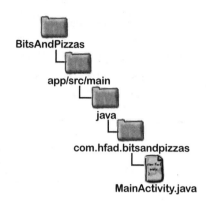

You add a tag to a fragment as part of a fragment transaction. Here's the current fragment transaction we're using in our `selectItem()` method to replace the fragment that's currently displayed:

```
FragmentTransaction ft = getFragmentManager().beginTransaction();

ft.replace(R.id.content_frame, fragment);

ft.addToBackStack(null);

ft.setTransition(FragmentTransaction.TRANSIT_FRAGMENT_FADE);

ft.commit();
```

To add a tag to the fragment, you add an extra `String` parameter to the `replace()` method in the transaction:

```
FragmentTransaction ft = getFragmentManager().beginTransaction();

ft.replace(R.id.content_frame, fragment, "visible_fragment");

ft.addToBackStack(null);

ft.setTransition(FragmentTransaction.TRANSIT_FRAGMENT_FADE);

ft.commit();
```

This adds a tag of "visible_fragment" to the fragment as it's added to the back stack.

In the above code, we're adding a tag of `"visible_fragment"` to the `replace()` method. Every fragment that's displayed in `MainActivity` will be tagged with this value.

Next, we'll use the fragment manager's `findFragmentByTag()` method to get a reference to the currently attached fragment.

Find the fragment using its tag

To retrieve the fragment that's currently attached to the activity, we'll pass the tag we set as part of the fragment transaction to the findFragmentByTag() method:

Find a fragment with a tag of "visible_fragment".

```
FragmentManager fragMan = getFragmentManager();
Fragment fragment = fragMan.findFragmentByTag("visible_fragment");
```

The findFragmentByTag() method starts by searching all fragments that are currently attached to the activity. If it can find no fragment with the correct tag, it then searches through all fragments on the back stack. By giving all fragments the same tag of "visible_fragment", the above code will get a reference to the fragment that's currently attached to the activity.

Here's the full code for the OnBackStackListener. We're using the findFragmentByTag() method to get a reference to the currently attached fragment. We're then checking which type of fragment it's an instance of so we can work out the value of currentPosition:

This gets the fragment currently attached to the activity.

```
getFragmentManager().addOnBackStackChangedListener(
    new FragmentManager.OnBackStackChangedListener() {
        public void onBackStackChanged() {
            FragmentManager fragMan = getFragmentManager();
            Fragment fragment = fragMan.findFragmentByTag("visible_fragment");
            if (fragment instanceof TopFragment) {
                currentPosition = 0;
            }
            if (fragment instanceof PizzaFragment) {
                currentPosition = 1;
            }
            if (fragment instanceof PastaFragment) {
                currentPosition = 2;
            }
            if (fragment instanceof StoresFragment) {
                currentPosition = 3;
            }
            setActionBarTitle(currentPosition);
            drawerList.setItemChecked(currentPosition, true);
        }
    }
);
```

Check what type of fragment it is, and set currentPosition accordingly.

Set the action bar title and highlight the correct item in the drawer ListView.

BitsAndPizzas → **app/src/main** → **java** → **com.hfad.bitsandpizzas** → **MainActivity.java**

That's all the code we need to get our action bar titles to sync with the displayed fragment when the user clicks on the Back button. Before we see it running, let's look at the full code for *MainActivity.java*.

The full MainActivity.java code

Here's the entire code for *MainActivity.java*:

```
package com.hfad.bitsandpizzas;

import android.app.Activity;
import android.app.Fragment;
import android.app.FragmentManager;
import android.app.FragmentTransaction;
import android.content.Intent;
import android.content.res.Configuration;
import android.os.Bundle;
import android.support.v7.app.ActionBarDrawerToggle;
import android.view.Menu;
import android.view.MenuItem;
import android.view.View;
import android.widget.AdapterView;
import android.widget.ArrayAdapter;
import android.widget.ListView;
import android.widget.ShareActionProvider;
import android.support.v4.widget.DrawerLayout;


public class MainActivity extends Activity {

    private ShareActionProvider shareActionProvider;
    private String[] titles;
    private ListView drawerList;
    private DrawerLayout drawerLayout;
    private ActionBarDrawerToggle drawerToggle;
    private int currentPosition = 0;

    private class DrawerItemClickListener implements ListView.OnItemClickListener {
        @Override
        public void onItemClick(AdapterView<?> parent, View view, int position, long id) {
            //Code to run when an item in the navigation drawer gets clicked
            selectItem(position);
        }
    };
```

We're using the FragmentManager class, so we need to import it.

These are all the classes used in the code.

BitsAndPizzas
app/src/main
java
com.hfad.bitsandpizzas
MainActivity.java

We're using all these private variables.

The OnItemClickListener's onItemClick() method gets called when the user clicks on an item in the drawer's ListView.

Call the selectItem() method when an item in the drawer ListView is clicked.

The code continues on the next page.

MainActivity.java (continued)

```
@Override
protected void onCreate(Bundle savedInstanceState) {
    super.onCreate(savedInstanceState);
    setContentView(R.layout.activity_main);
    titles = getResources().getStringArray(R.array.titles);
    drawerList = (ListView)findViewById(R.id.drawer);
    drawerLayout = (DrawerLayout) findViewById(R.id.drawer_layout);
    //Initialize the ListView
    drawerList.setAdapter(new ArrayAdapter<String>(this,
            android.R.layout.simple_list_item_activated_1, titles));
    drawerList.setOnItemClickListener(new DrawerItemClickListener());
    //Display the correct fragment.
    if (savedInstanceState != null) {
        currentPosition = savedInstanceState.getInt("position");
        setActionBarTitle(currentPosition);
    } else {
        selectItem(0);
    }
    //Create the ActionBarDrawerToggle
    drawerToggle = new ActionBarDrawerToggle(this, drawerLayout,
            R.string.open_drawer, R.string.close_drawer) {


        //Called when a drawer has settled in a completely closed state
        @Override
        public void onDrawerClosed(View view) {
            super.onDrawerClosed(view);
            invalidateOptionsMenu();
        }


        //Called when a drawer has settled in a completely open state.
        @Override
        public void onDrawerOpened(View drawerView) {
            super.onDrawerOpened(drawerView);
            invalidateOptionsMenu();
        }
    };
```

Populate the drawer's ListView and get it to respond to clicks.

If the activity's been destroyed and re-created, set the correct action bar title.

Display TopFragment by default.

Call invalidateOptionsMenu when the drawer is open or closed because we want to change the action items displayed in the action bar.

BitsAndPizzas

app/src/main

java

com.hfad.bitsandpizzas

MainActivity.java

The code continues on the next page.

MainActivity.java (continued)

This code is still part of the onCreate() method.
↓

```
drawerLayout.setDrawerListener(drawerToggle);
getActionBar().setDisplayHomeAsUpEnabled(true);
getActionBar().setHomeButtonEnabled(true);
```
← Enable the Up icon on the action bar so we can use it to open the drawer.

```
getFragmentManager().addOnBackStackChangedListener(
    new FragmentManager.OnBackStackChangedListener() {
        public void onBackStackChanged() {
            FragmentManager fragMan = getFragmentManager();
            Fragment fragment = fragMan.findFragmentByTag("visible_fragment");
            if (fragment instanceof TopFragment) {
                currentPosition = 0;
            }
            if (fragment instanceof PizzaFragment) {
                currentPosition = 1;
            }
            if (fragment instanceof PastaFragment) {
                currentPosition = 2;
            }
            if (fragment instanceof StoresFragment) {
                currentPosition = 3;
            }
            setActionBarTitle(currentPosition);
            drawerList.setItemChecked(currentPosition, true);
        }
    }
);
}
```

This gets called when the back stack changes.

Check which class the fragment currently attached to the activity is an instance of, and set currentPosition accordingly.

Set the action bar title and highlight the correct item in the drawer ListView.

BitsAndPizzas

app/src/main

java

com.hfad.bitsandpizzas

MainActivity.java

The code continues on the next page.

MainActivity.java (continued)

We call the selectItem() method when the user
clicks on an item in the drawer's ListView.

BitsAndPizzas

app/src/main

java

com.hfad.bitsandpizzas

MainActivity.java

```java
private void selectItem(int position) {
    // update the main content by replacing fragments
    currentPosition = position;
    Fragment fragment;
    switch(position) {
        case 1:
            fragment = new PizzaFragment();
            break;
        case 2:
            fragment = new PastaFragment();
            break;
        case 3:
            fragment = new StoresFragment();
            break;
        default:
            fragment = new TopFragment();
    }
    FragmentTransaction ft = getFragmentManager().beginTransaction();
    ft.replace(R.id.content_frame, fragment, "visible_fragment");
    ft.addToBackStack(null);
    ft.setTransition(FragmentTransaction.TRANSIT_FRAGMENT_FADE);
    ft.commit();
    //Set the action bar title
    setActionBarTitle(position);
    //Close the drawer
    drawerLayout.closeDrawer(drawerList);
}
```

Decide which fragment to display
based on the position of the item the
user selects in the drawer's ListView.

Display the fragment.

Display the right title in the action bar.

Close the drawer.

The code continues
on the next page.

MainActivity.java (continued)

```java
@Override
public boolean onPrepareOptionsMenu(Menu menu) {
    // If the drawer is open, hide action items related to the content view
    boolean drawerOpen = drawerLayout.isDrawerOpen(drawerList);
    menu.findItem(R.id.action_share).setVisible(!drawerOpen);
    return super.onPrepareOptionsMenu(menu);
}
```

↖ Display the Share action if the drawer is closed, hide it if the drawer is open.

```java
@Override
protected void onPostCreate(Bundle savedInstanceState) {
    super.onPostCreate(savedInstanceState);
    // Sync the toggle state after onRestoreInstanceState has occurred.
    drawerToggle.syncState();
}
```

← Sync the state of the ActionBarDrawerToggle with the state of the drawer.

```java
@Override
public void onConfigurationChanged(Configuration newConfig) {
    super.onConfigurationChanged(newConfig);
    drawerToggle.onConfigurationChanged(newConfig);
}
```

↖ Pass details of any configuration changes to the ActionBarDrawerToggle.

```java
@Override
public void onSaveInstanceState(Bundle outState) {
    super.onSaveInstanceState(outState);
    outState.putInt("position", currentPosition);
}
```

↖ Save the state of currentPosition if the activity's destroyed.

BitsAndPizzas

app/src/main

java

com.hfad.bitsandpizzas

MainActivity.java

```java
private void setActionBarTitle(int position) {
    String title;
    if (position == 0){
        title = getResources().getString(R.string.app_name);
    } else {
        title = titles[position];
    }
    getActionBar().setTitle(title);
}
```

← Set the action bar title so it reflects the fragment that's displayed.

The code continues ⤵ on the next page.

MainActivity.java (continued)

Add items in the menu resource file to the action bar.

```java
@Override
public boolean onCreateOptionsMenu(Menu menu) {
    // Inflate the menu; this adds items to the action bar if it is present.
    getMenuInflater().inflate(R.menu.menu_main, menu);
    MenuItem menuItem = menu.findItem(R.id.action_share);
    shareActionProvider = (ShareActionProvider) menuItem.getActionProvider();
    setIntent("This is example text");
    return super.onCreateOptionsMenu(menu);
}

private void setIntent(String text) {
    Intent intent = new Intent(Intent.ACTION_SEND);
    intent.setType("text/plain");
    intent.putExtra(Intent.EXTRA_TEXT, text);
    shareActionProvider.setShareIntent(intent);
}
```

Pass the Share action an intent for it to share.

BitsAndPizzas
└ app/src/main
  └ java
    └ com.hfad.bitsandpizzas
      └ MainActivity.java

This method is called when the user clicks on an item in the action bar.

```java
@Override
public boolean onOptionsItemSelected(MenuItem item) {
    if (drawerToggle.onOptionsItemSelected(item)) {
        return true;
    }
```

If the ActionBarDrawerToggle is clicked, let it handle what happens.

```java
    switch (item.getItemId()) {
        case R.id.action_create_order:
            //Code to run when the Create Order item is clicked
            Intent intent = new Intent(this, OrderActivity.class);
            startActivity(intent);
            return true;
        case R.id.action_settings:
            //Code to run when the settings item is clicked
            return true;
        default:
            return super.onOptionsItemSelected(item);
    }
}
```

If the Create Order action is clicked, start OrderActivity.

Test drive the app

Let's see what happens when we run the app.

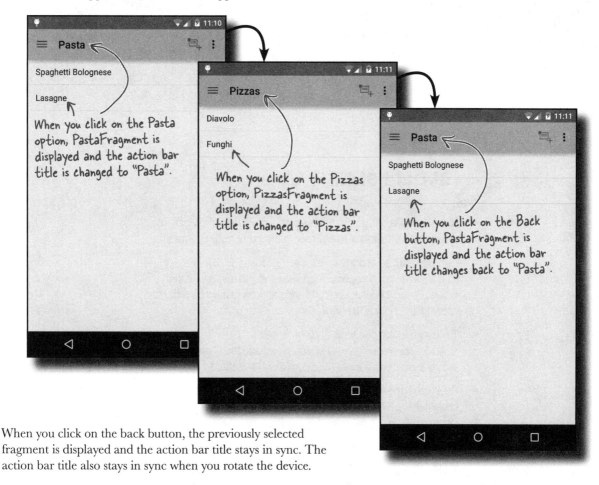

When you click on the Pasta option, PastaFragment is displayed and the action bar title is changed to "Pasta".

When you click on the Pizzas option, PizzasFragment is displayed and the action bar title is changed to "Pizzas".

When you click on the Back button, PastaFragment is displayed and the action bar title changes back to "Pasta".

When you click on the back button, the previously selected fragment is displayed and the action bar title stays in sync. The action bar title also stays in sync when you rotate the device.

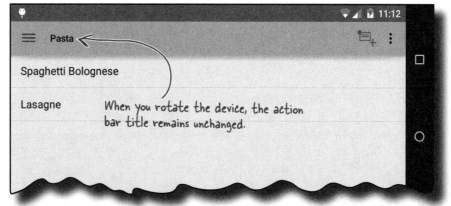

When you rotate the device, the action bar title remains unchanged.

Your Android Toolbox

You've got Chapter 10 under your belt and now you've added drawer layouts to your toolbox.

You can download the full code for the chapter from https://tinyurl.com/HeadFirstAndroid.

BULLET POINTS

- Use a `DrawerLayout` to create an activity with a navigation drawer. Use the drawer to navigate to the major hubs of your app.

- If you're using an action bar, use `ActionBarDrawerToggle` as a `DrawerListener`. This allows you to respond to the drawer opening and closing, and adds an icon to the action bar for opening and closing the drawer.

- To change action bar items at runtime, call `invalidateOptionsMenu()` and add the changes in the activity's `onPrepareOptionsMenu()` method.

- React to changes on the back stack by implementing the `FragmentManager.OnBackStackChangedListener()`.

- The fragment manager's `findFragmentByTag()` method searches for fragments with a given tag.

11 SQLite databases

Fire Up the Database

When I said I wanted persistence, I was talking about the database.

If you're recording high scores or saving tweets, your app will need to store data. And on Android you usually keep your data safe inside a **SQLite database**. In this chapter, we'll show you how to **create a database, add tables to it, and prepopulate it with data**, all with the help of the friendly **SQLite helper**. You'll then see how you can cleanly roll out **upgrades** to your database structure, and how to **downgrade** it if you need to pull any changes.

Back to Starbuzz

Back in Chapter 6, we created an app for Starbuzz. The app allows users to navigate through a series of screens so that they can see the drinks available at Starbuzz.

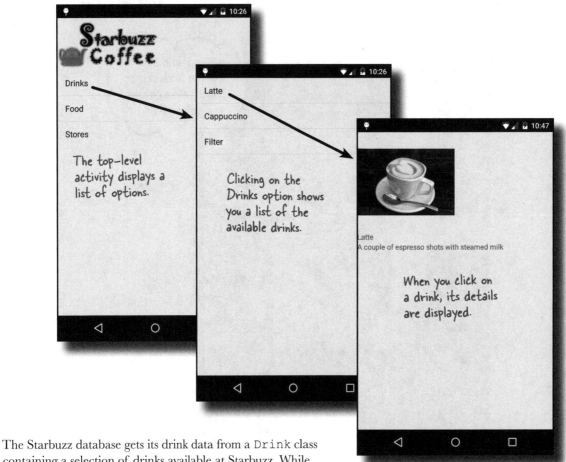

The top-level activity displays a list of options.

Clicking on the Drinks option shows you a list of the available drinks.

When you click on a drink, its details are displayed.

The Starbuzz database gets its drink data from a `Drink` class containing a selection of drinks available at Starbuzz. While this made building the first version of the app easier, there's a better way of storing and persisting data.

Over the next two chapters, we're going to change the Starbuzz database so that it gets its data from a SQLite database. In this chapter, we'll see how to create the database, and in the next chapter, we'll show you how to connect activities to it.

Android uses SQLite databases to persist data

All apps need to store data, and the main way you do that in Androidville
is with a **SQLite database**. Why SQLite?

⭐ **It's lightweight.**
Most database systems need a special database server process
in order to work. SQLite doesn't, a SQLite database is just a
file. When you're not using the database, it doesn't use up any
processor time. That's important on a mobile device, because
we don't want to drain the battery.

⭐ **It's optimized for a single user.**
Our app is the only thing that will talk to the database, so
we shouldn't have to identify ourselves with a username and
password.

⭐ **It's stable and fast.**
SQLite databases are amazingly stable. They can handle
database transactions, which means if you're updating several
pieces of data and screw up, SQLite can roll the data back.
Also, the code that reads and writes the data is written in
optimized C code. Not only is it fast, but it also reduces the
amount of processor power it needs.

> We're going to go through the <u>basics</u> of SQLite in this chapter.
>
> If you plan on doing a lot of database heavy lifting in your apps, we suggest you do more background reading on SQLite and SQL.

Where's the database stored?

Android automatically creates a folder for each app where the app's
database can be stored. When we create a database for the Starbuzz app,
it will be stored in the following folder:

com.hfad.starbuzz is the app's unique identifier.

/data/data/com.hfad.starbuzz/databases

An app can store several databases in this folder. Each database
consists of two files.

The first file is the **database file** and has the same name
as your database—for example, "starbuzz". This is the main
SQLite database file. All of your data is stored in this file.

The second file is the **journal file**. It has the same name
as your database, with a suffix of "-journal"—for example,
"starbuzz-journal". The journal file contains all of the changes
made to your database. If there's a problem, Android will use
the journal to undo (or rollback) your latest changes.

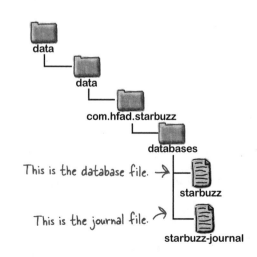

data

data

com.hfad.starbuzz

databases

This is the database file. →
starbuzz

This is the journal file. ↗
starbuzz-journal

Android comes with SQLite classes

Android uses a set of classes that allows you to manage a SQLite database. There are three types of object that do the bulk of this work.

The SQLite Helper

You create a SQLite helper by extending the `SQLiteOpenHelper` class. This enables you to create and manage databases.

The SQLite Database

The `SQLiteDatabase` class gives you access to the database. It's like a `SQLConnection` in JDBC.

Cursors

A `Cursor` lets you read from and write to the database. It's like a `ResultSet` in JDBC.

We're going to use these objects to show you how to create a SQLite database your app can use to persist data by replacing the `Drink` class with a SQLite database.

---
there are no
Dumb Questions

Q: If there's no username and password on the database, how is it kept secure?

A: The directory where an app's databases are stored is only readable by the app itself. The database is secured down at the operating system level.

Q: Can I write an Android app that talks to some other kind of external database, such as Oracle?

A: There's no reason why you can't access other databases over a network connection, but be careful to conserve the resources used by Android. For example, you might use less battery power if you access your database via a web service. That way, if you're not talking to the database, you're not using up any resources.

Q: Why doesn't Android use JDBC to access SQLite databases?

A: We know we're going to be using a SQLite database, so using JDBC would be overkill. Those layers of database drivers that make JDBC so flexible would just drain the battery on an Android device.

Q: Is the database directory inside the app's directory?

A: No. It's kept in a separate directory from the app's code. That way, the app can be overwritten with a newer version, but the data in the database will be kept safe.

The current Starbuzz app structure

Here's a reminder of the current structure of the Starbuzz app:

1 **TopLevelActivity contains a list of options for Drinks, Food, and Stores.**

2 **When the user clicks on the Drinks option, it launches DrinkCategoryActivity.**
This activity displays a list of drinks that it gets from the Java `Drink` class.

3 **When the user clicks on a drink, its details get displayed in DrinkActivity.**
`DrinkActivity` gets details of the drink from the Java `Drink` class.

The app currently gets its data from the Drink class.

activity_top_level.xml   Drink.java   activity_drink.xml

Device   **1** TopLevelActivity.java   **2** DrinkCategoryActivity.java   **3** DrinkActivity.java

How does the app structure need to change if we're to use a SQLite database?

— Do this!

We're going to update the Starbuzz app in this chapter, so open your original Starbuzz project in Android Studio.

We'll change the app to use a database

We'll use a SQLite helper to create a SQLite database we can use with our Starbuzz app. We're going to replace our Drink Java class with a database, so we need our SQLite helper to do the following:

1 **Create the database.**
Before we can do anything else, we need to get the SQLite helper to create version 1 (the first version) of our Starbuzz database.

2 **Create the Drink table and populate it with drinks.**
Once we have a database, we can create a table in it. The table structure needs to reflect the attributes in the current Drink class, so it needs to be able to store the name, description, and image resource ID of each drink. We'll then add three drinks to it.

The app has the same structure as before except that we're replacing the file *Drink.java* with a SQLite helper and a SQLite Starbuzz database. The SQLite helper will maintain the Starbuzz database, and provide access to it for the other activities. We'll change the activities to use the database in the next chapter.

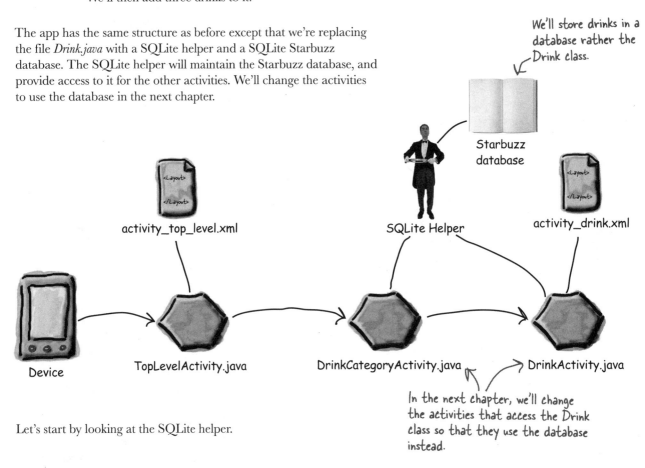

We'll store drinks in a database rather the Drink class.

Starbuzz database

SQLite Helper

activity_top_level.xml

activity_drink.xml

Device

TopLevelActivity.java

DrinkCategoryActivity.java

DrinkActivity.java

In the next chapter, we'll change the activities that access the Drink class so that they use the database instead.

Let's start by looking at the SQLite helper.

The SQLite helper manages your database

The **SQLiteOpenHelper** class is there to help you create and maintain your SQLite databases. Think of it as a personal assistant who's there to take care of the general database housekeeping.

Let's look at some typical tasks that the SQLite helper can assist you with:

Creating the database

When you first install an app, the database file won't exist. The SQLite helper will make sure the database file is created with the correct name and with the correct table structures installed.

Getting access to the database

Our app shouldn't need to know all of the details about where the database file is, so the SQLite helper can serve us with an easy-to-use database object whenever we need it. At all hours, day or night.

The SQLite helper

Keeping the database shipshape

The structure of the database will probably change over time, and the SQLite helper can be relied upon to convert an old version of a database into a shiny, spiffy new version, with all the latest database structures it needs.

Create the SQLite helper

You create a SQLite helper by writing a class that extends the
SQLiteOpenHelper class. When you do this, you ***must*** override
the onCreate() and onUpgrade() methods. These methods are
mandatory.

The onCreate() method gets called when the database first gets
created on the device. The method should include all the code
needed to create the tables you need for your app.

The onUpgrade() method gets called when the database needs to
be upgraded. As an example, if you need to make table changes to
your database after it's been released, this is the method to do it in.

In our app, we're going to use a SQLite helper called
StarbuzzDatabaseHelper. Create this class in your Starbuzz
project by highlighting the *app/src/main/java/com.hfad.starbuzz* folder
in your project folder explorer, and navigating to File→New...→Java
Class. Give the class a name of "StarbuzzDatabaseHelper", then
replace its contents with the code below:

```
package com.hfad.starbuzz;

import android.database.sqlite.SQLiteOpenHelper;
import android.content.Context;
import android.database.sqlite.SQLiteDatabase;

class StarbuzzDatabaseHelper extends SQLiteOpenHelper {

    StarbuzzDatabaseHelper(Context context) {
    }

    @Override
    public void onCreate(SQLiteDatabase db) {
    }

    @Override
    public void onUpgrade(SQLiteDatabase db, int oldVersion, int newVersion) {
    }
}
```

SQLite helpers must extend the SQLiteOpenHelper class.

The onCreate() and onUpgrade() methods are mandatory. We've left them empty for now, and we'll look at them in more detail throughout the chapter.

Create database
Create table

java.lang.Object
...

android.database.sqlite. SQLiteOpenHelper

| onCreate(SQLiteDatabase) |
| onUpgrade(SQLiteDatabase, int, int) |
| onDowngrade(SQLiteDatabase, int, int) |
| onOpen(SQLiteDatabase) |
| getReadableDatabase() |
| getWritableDatabase() |
| ... |

The SQLiteOpenHelper class is a subclass of Object.

Starbuzz
app/src/main
java
com.hfad.starbuzz
StarbuzzDatabase Helper.java

To get the SQLite helper to do something, we need to add code to its
methods. The first thing to do is tell the SQLite helper what database
it needs to create.

1. Specify the database

There are two pieces of information the SQLite helper needs in order to create the database.

First, we need to give the database a name. By giving the database a name, we make sure that the database remains on the device when it's closed. If we don't, the database will only be created in memory, so once the database is closed, it will disappear.

Creating databases that are only held in memory can be useful when you're testing your app.

The second piece of information we need to provide is the version of the database. The database version needs to be an integer value, starting at 1. The SQLite helper uses this version number to determine whether the database needs to be upgraded.

Name: "starbuzz"
Version: 1

You specify the database name and version by passing them to the constructor of the SQLiteOpenHelper superclass. We're going to give our database a name of "starbuzz", and as it's the first version of the database, we'll give it a version number of 1. Here's the code we need (update your version of *StarbuzzDatabaseHelper. java* with the code below):

SQLite database

```
...
class StarbuzzDatabaseHelper extends SQLiteOpenHelper {

    private static final String DB_NAME = "starbuzz"; // the name of our database
    private static final int DB_VERSION = 1; // the version of the database

    StarbuzzDatabaseHelper(Context context) {
        super(context, DB_NAME, null, DB_VERSION);
    }
...
}
```

We're calling the constructor of the SQLiteOpenHelper superclass, and passing it the database name and version.

This parameter is an advanced feature relating to cursors. We're covering cursors in the next chapter.

The constructor specifies details of the database, but the database doesn't get created at that point. The SQLite helper waits until the app needs to access the database, and the database gets created at that point.

Once you've told the SQLite helper what database to create, you can specify its tables.

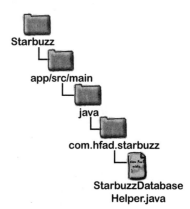

Starbuzz

app/src/main

java

com.hfad.starbuzz

StarbuzzDatabase
Helper.java

We've done everything we need to get the database created when we need it.

Create database
Create table

Inside a SQLite database

The data inside a SQLite database is stored in tables. A table contains several rows, and each row is split into columns. A column contains a single piece of data, like a number of a piece of text.

You need to create a table for each distinct piece of data that you want to record. In the Starbuzz app, for example, we'll need to create a table for the drink data. It will look something like this:

The columns in the table are _id, NAME, DESCRIPTION, and IMAGE_RESOURCE_ID. The Drink class contained similarly named attributes.

_id	NAME	DESCRIPTION	IMAGE_RESOURCE_ID
1	"Latte"	"Espresso and steamed milk"	54543543
2	"Cappuccino"	"Espresso, hot milk and steamed-milk foam"	654334453
3	"Filter"	"Our best drip coffee"	44324234

Some columns can be specified as primary keys. A primary key uniquely identifies a single row. If you say that a column is a primary key, then the database won't allow you to store rows with duplicate keys.

We recommend that your tables have a single integer primary key column called _id. This is because Android code is hardwired to expect a numeric _id column, so not having one can cause you problems later on.

Storage classes and data-types

Each column in a table is designed to store a particular type of data. For example, in our DRINK table, the DESCRIPTION column will only ever store text data. Here are the main data types you can use in SQLite, and what they can store:

INTEGER	Any integer type
TEXT	Any character type
REAL	Any floating-point number
NUMERIC	Booleans, dates, and date-times
BLOB	Binary Large Object

Unlike most database systems, you don't need to specify the column size in SQLite. Under the hood, the data type is translated into a much broader storage class. This means you can say very generally what kind of data you're going to store, but you're not forced to be specific about the size of data.

It's an Android convention to call your primary key columns _id. Android code expects there to be an _id column on your data. Ignoring this convention will make it harder to get the data out of your database and into your user interface.

You create tables using Structured Query Language (SQL)

Every application that talks to SQLite needs to use a standard database language called Structured Query Language. SQL is used by almost every type of database. If you want to create the DRINK table, you will need to do it in SQL.

This is the SQL command to create the table: *The _id column is the primary key.*

```
CREATE TABLE DRINK (_id INTEGER PRIMARY KEY AUTOINCREMENT,
                    NAME TEXT,
                    DESCRIPTION TEXT,
                    IMAGE_RESOURCE_ID INTEGER)
```

The table name   *These are the table columns.*

The CREATE TABLE command says what columns you want in the table, and what the data type is of each column. The _id column is the primary key of the table, and the special keyword AUTOINCREMENT means that when we store a new row in the table, SQLite will automatically generate a unique integer for it.

The onCreate() method is called when the database is created

The SQLite helper is in charge of creating the SQLite database the first time it needs to be used. First, an empty database is created on the device, and then the SQLite helper onCreate() method is called.

The onCreate() method is passed a SQLiteDatabase object as a parameter. We can use this to run our SQL command with the method:

```
SQLiteDatabase.execSQL(String sql);
```
Execute the SQL in the String on the database.

This method has one parameter, the SQL you want to execute.

Here's the full code for the onCreate() method:

```java
@Override
public void onCreate(SQLiteDatabase db){
    db.execSQL("CREATE TABLE DRINK ("
            + "_id INTEGER PRIMARY KEY AUTOINCREMENT, "
            + "NAME TEXT, "
            + "DESCRIPTION TEXT, "
            + "IMAGE_RESOURCE_ID INTEGER);");
}
```

This gives us an empty DRINK table, but what if we want to prepopulate it with data?

The SQLiteDatabase class gives you access to the database.

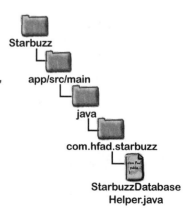

Starbuzz
app/src/main
java
com.hfad.starbuzz
StarbuzzDatabase
Helper.java

Insert data using the insert() method

The SQLiteDatabase class contains several methods that enable you to insert, update, and delete data. We'll look at these methods over the next few pages, starting with inserting data.

If you need to prepopulate a SQLite table with data, you can use the **SQLiteDatabase insert()** method. This method allows you to insert data into the database, and returns the ID of the record once it's been inserted. If the method is unable to insert the record, it returns a value of -1.

To use the `insert()` method, you need to specify the table you want to insert into, and the values you're inserting. You say what values you want to insert by creating a **ContentValues** object. A `ContentValues` object is used to hold name/value pairs of data:

```
ContentValues drinkValues = new ContentValues();
```

You add name/value pairs of data to the `ContentValues` object using its **put()** method. We want to use it to insert a row of data into the DRINK table, so we'll populate it with the name of each column in the DRINK table, and the value we want to go in each field:

```
ContentValues drinkValues = new ContentValues();
drinkValues.put("NAME", "Latte");
drinkValues.put("DESCRIPTION", "Espresso and steamed milk");
drinkValues.put("IMAGE_RESOURCE_ID", R.drawable.latte);
```

```
┌──────────────────────────┐
│    java.lang.Object      │
│    ...                   │
└──────────────────────────┘
            △
┌──────────────────────────┐
│  android.database.sqlite.│
│      SQLiteDatabase      │
├──────────────────────────┤
│ execSQL(String)          │
├──────────────────────────┤
│ insert(String, String, ContentValues) │
├──────────────────────────┤
│ update(String, ContentValues, String, String[]) │
├──────────────────────────┤
│ delete(String, String, String[]) │
├──────────────────────────┤
│ ...                      │
└──────────────────────────┘
```

The SQLiteDatabase class is a subclass of Object.

This will put the value "Espresso and steamed milk" in the DESCRIPTION column.

You need a separate call to the put() method for each value you want to enter.

Finally, we'll use the `SQLiteDatabase insert()` method to insert the values into the DRINK table:

```
db.insert("DRINK", null, drinkValues);
```

Running these lines of code will insert the Latte record into the DRINK table:

_id	NAME	DESCRIPTION	IMAGE_RESOURCE_ID
1	"Latte"	"Espresso and steamed milk"	54543543

A shiny new record gets inserted into the table.

The `insert()` method takes the following general form:

```
db.insert(String table, String nullColumnHack, ContentValues values);
```

This inserts a single row into the table. To insert multiple rows, you need to make repeated calls to the insert() method.

The `nullColumnHack String` value is optional and most of the time you'll want to set it to null like we did in the code above. It's there in case the `ContentValues` object is empty and you want to insert an empty row into your table. SQLite won't let you insert an empty row without you specifying the name of at least one column; the `nullColumnHack` parameter allows you to specify one of the columns.

Update records with the update() method

You update existing records in SQLite using the SQLiteDatabase update() method. This method allows you to update records in the database, and returns the number of records it's updated. To use the update() method, you need to specify the table you want to update records in, the values you want to update, and the conditions for updating them. Here's what it looks like:

```
public int update (String table,
                   ContentValues values,
                   String whereClause,
                   String[] whereArgs)
```

As an example, here's how you'd change the value of the DESCRIPTION column to "Tasty" where the name of the drink is "Latte":

```
ContentValues drinkValues = new ContentValues();
drinkValues.put("DESCRIPTION", "Tasty");   ← This will put the value "Tasty" in the DESCRIPTION column.
db.update("DRINK",
        drinkValues,              ── Update the DESCRIPTION column to "Tasty"
        "NAME = ?",         ←      in the DRINK table where NAME = "Latte".
        new String[] {"Latte"});
```

_id	NAME	DESCRIPTION	IMAGE_RESOURCE_ID
1	"Latte"	~~"Espresso and steamed milk"~~ "Tasty"	54543543

The first parameter of the update() method is the name of the table you want to update (in this case, the DRINK table).

The second parameter specifies what values you want to update. Just as you did with the insert() method, you say what values you want to update by creating a ContentValues object to hold name/value pairs of data:

```
ContentValues drinkValues = new ContentValues();
drinkValues.put("DESCRIPTION", "Tasty");
```

The third parameter gives conditions for which records you want to update. In the above example, "NAME = ?" means that the NAME column should be equal to some value. The ? symbol is a placeholder symbol for this value. The query uses the contents of the last parameter to say what the value should be (in this case, "Latte").

You can also specify multiple criteria, and we'll show you this on the next page.

Watch it!

If you set the last two parameters of the update() method to null, ALL records in the table will be updated.

As an example, the code

```
db.update("DRINK",
        drinkValues,
        null, null);
```

will update all records in the DRINK table.

Create database
Create table

Multiple conditions

If you want to apply multiple conditions to your query, you need to make
sure you specify the conditions in the same order you specify the values. As an
example, here's how you'd update records from the DRINK table where the
name of the drink is "Latte", or the drink description is "Our best drip coffee".

```
db.update("DRINK",
          drinkValues,
          "NAME = ? OR DESCRIPTION = ?",
          new String[] {"Latte", "Our best drip coffee"});
```

*This means: Where NAME = "Latte" or
DESCRIPTION = "Our best drip coffee".*

The condition values must be Strings, even if the column you're applying the
condition to doesn't contain Strings. If this is the case, you need to convert
your values to Strings. As an example, here's how you'd return DRINK
records where the _id is 1:

```
db.update("DRINK",
          drinkValues,
          "_id = ?",
          new String[] {Integer.toString(1)});
```

*Convert the int 1
to a String value.*

Delete records with the delete() method

The SQLiteDatabase delete() method works in a similar way to the
update() method you've just seen. It takes the following form:

```
public int delete (String table,
                   String whereClause,
                   String[] whereArgs)
```

As an example, here's how you'd delete all records from the database where
the name of the drink is "Latte":

```
db.delete("DRINK",
          "NAME = ?",
          new String[] {"Latte"});
```

Can you see how similar this is to the update() method?

The entire row is deleted

_id	NAME	DESCRIPTION	IMAGE_RESOURCE_ID
1	"Latte"	"Espresso and steamed milk"	54543543

The first parameter is the name of the table you want to delete records from
(in this case, DRINK). The second and third arguments allow you to describe
conditions to specify exactly which records you wish to delete (in this case,
where NAME = "Latte").

Now that you've seen the kinds of operations you can do to manipulate data
in a SQLite table, you have everything that you need to create a SQLite
database and create tables and prepoplute them with data. On the next page,
we'll put this into practice in our SQLite helper code.

The StarbuzzDatabaseHelper code

Here's the complete code for *StarbuzzDatabaseHelper.java* (update your code to reflect our changes):

Starbuzz

app/src/main

java

com.hfad.starbuzz

StarbuzzDatabase Helper.java

```java
package com.hfad.starbuzz;

import android.content.ContentValues;
import android.content.Context;
import android.database.sqlite.SQLiteDatabase;
import android.database.sqlite.SQLiteOpenHelper;

class StarbuzzDatabaseHelper extends SQLiteOpenHelper{

    private static final String DB_NAME = "starbuzz"; // the name of our database
    private static final int DB_VERSION = 1; // the version of the database

    StarbuzzDatabaseHelper(Context context){
        super(context, DB_NAME, null, DB_VERSION);
    }

    @Override
    public void onCreate(SQLiteDatabase db){
        db.execSQL("CREATE TABLE DRINK (_id INTEGER PRIMARY KEY AUTOINCREMENT, "
                + "NAME TEXT, "
                + "DESCRIPTION TEXT, "
                + "IMAGE_RESOURCE_ID INTEGER);");
        insertDrink(db, "Latte", "Espresso and steamed milk", R.drawable.latte);
        insertDrink(db, "Cappuccino", "Espresso, hot milk and steamed-milk foam",
                        R.drawable.cappuccino);
        insertDrink(db, "Filter", "Our best drip coffee", R.drawable.filter);
    }

    @Override
    public void onUpgrade(SQLiteDatabase db, int oldVersion, int newVersion) {
    }

    private static void insertDrink(SQLiteDatabase db, String name,
                                    String description, int resourceId) {
        ContentValues drinkValues = new ContentValues();
        drinkValues.put("NAME", name);
        drinkValues.put("DESCRIPTION", description);
        drinkValues.put("IMAGE_RESOURCE_ID", resourceId);
        db.insert("DRINK", null, drinkValues);
    }
}
```

Say what the database name and version is. It's the first version of the database, so the version should be 1.

onCreate() gets called when the database first gets created, so we're using it to create the table and insert data.

Create the DRINK table.

Insert each drink in a separate row.

onUpgrade() gets called when the database needs to be upgraded. We'll look at this next.

We need to insert several drinks, so we created a separate method to do this.

Create database
Create table

What the SQLite helper code does

① **The user installs the app and launches it.**
When the app needs to access the database, the SQLite helper checks to see if the database already exists.

You need a database, sir? Let me see if it's already there for you.

SQLite helper

② **If the database doesn't exist, it gets created.**
It's given the name and version number specified in the SQLite helper.

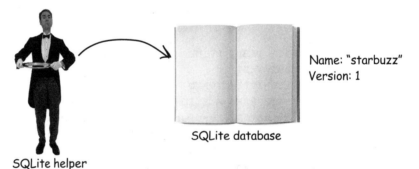

SQLite database

Name: "starbuzz"
Version: 1

SQLite helper

③ **When the database is created, the onCreate() method in the SQLite helper is called.**
It adds a DRINK table to the database, and populates it with records.

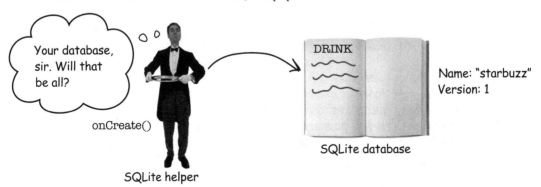

Your database, sir. Will that be all?

onCreate()

DRINK

SQLite database

Name: "starbuzz"
Version: 1

SQLite helper

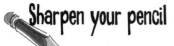

Sharpen your pencil

Here's the `onCreate()` method of a `SQLiteOpenHelper` class. Your job is to say what values have been inserted into the NAME and DESCRIPTION columns of the DRINK table when the `onCreate()` method has finished running.

```java
@Override
public void onCreate(SQLiteDatabase db) {
    ContentValues espresso = new ContentValues();
    espresso.put("NAME", "Espresso");
    ContentValues americano = new ContentValues();
    americano.put("NAME", "Americano");
    ContentValues latte = new ContentValues();
    latte.put("NAME", "Latte");
    ContentValues filter = new ContentValues();
    filter.put("DESCRIPTION", "Filter");
    ContentValues mochachino = new ContentValues();
    mochachino.put("NAME", "Mochachino");

    db.execSQL("CREATE TABLE DRINK ("
            + "_id INTEGER PRIMARY KEY AUTOINCREMENT, "
            + "NAME TEXT, "
            + "DESCRIPTION TEXT);");
    db.insert("DRINK", null, espresso);
    db.insert("DRINK", null, americano);
    db.delete("DRINK", null, null);
    db.insert("DRINK", null, latte);
    db.update("DRINK", mochachino, "NAME = ?", new String[] {"Espresso"});
    db.insert("DRINK", null, filter);
}
```

You don't → need to enter the value of the _id column.

_id	NAME	DESCRIPTION

Sharpen your pencil Solution

Here's the `onCreate()` method of a `SQLiteOpenHelper` class. Your job is to say what values have been inserted into the NAME and DESCRIPTION columns of the DRINK table when the `onCreate()` method has finished running.

```java
@Override
public void onCreate(SQLiteDatabase db) {
    ContentValues espresso = new ContentValues();
    espresso.put("NAME", "Espresso");
    ContentValues americano = new ContentValues();
    americano.put("NAME", "Americano");
    ContentValues latte = new ContentValues();
    latte.put("NAME", "Latte");
    ContentValues filter = new ContentValues();
    filter.put("DESCRIPTION", "Filter");
    ContentValues mochachino = new ContentValues();
    mochachino.put("NAME", "Mochachino");

    db.execSQL("CREATE TABLE DRINK ("
            + "_id INTEGER PRIMARY KEY AUTOINCREMENT, "
            + "NAME TEXT, "
            + "DESCRIPTION TEXT);");
    db.insert("DRINK", null, espresso);
    db.insert("DRINK", null, americano);
    db.delete("DRINK", null, null);
    db.insert("DRINK", null, latte);
    db.update("DRINK", mochachino, "NAME = ?", new String[] {"Espresso"});
    db.insert("DRINK", null, filter);
}
```

← Create the table, adding _id, NAME, DESCRIPTION columns.

← Insert Espresso in the NAME column.

← Insert Americano in the NAME column.

← Delete all the drinks.

← Insert Latte in the NAME column.

↖ Set NAME to Mochachino where NAME is Espresso. No records get updated.

↑ Insert Filter in the DESCRIPTION column.

_id	NAME	DESCRIPTION
	Latte	
		Filter

What if you need to change the database?

So far, you've seen how to create a SQLite database that your app will be able to use to persist data. But what if you need to make changes to the database at some future stage?

As an example, suppose lots of users have already installed your Starbuzz app on their devices, and you want to a add a new FAVORITE column to the DRINK table. How would you distribute this change to new and existing users?

> Well, we could change the CREATE TABLE statement in the onCreate() method, but that doesn't feel entirely right to me. I mean, what if a device already has the old version of the database installed?

When you need to change an app's database, there are two key scenarios you have to deal with.

The first scenario is that the user has never installed your app before, and doesn't have the database installed on her device. In this case, the SQLite helper creates the database the first time the database needs to be accessed, and runs its `onCreate()` method.

The second scenario is where the user installs a new version of your app which includes a different version of the database. If the SQLite helper spots that the database that's installed is out of date, it will call either the `onUpgrade()` or `onDowngrade()` method.

So how can the SQLite helper tell if the database is out of date?

Upgrade database

SQLite databases have a version number

The SQLite helper can tell whether the SQLite database needs updating by looking at its version number. You specify the version of the database in the SQLite helper by passing it to the `SQLiteOpenHelper` superclass in its constructor.

Earlier on, we specified the version number of the database like this:

```
. . .
    private static final String DB_NAME = "starbuzz";
    private static final int DB_VERSION = 1;


    StarbuzzDatabaseHelper(Context context) {
        super(context, DB_NAME, null, DB_VERSION);
    }
. . .
```

When the database gets created, its version number gets set to the version number in the SQLite helper, and the SQLite helper `onCreate()` method gets called.

When you want to update the database, you change the version number in the SQLite helper code. To *upgrade* the database, specify a number that's larger than you had before, and to *downgrade* your database, specify a number that's lower:

```
. . .
    private static final int DB_VERSION = 2;
. . .
```
← Here we're increasing the version number, so the database will get upgraded.

Most of the time, you'll want to upgrade the database, so specify a number that's larger. This is because you usually only downgrade your database when you want to pull changes you made in a previous upgrade.

When the user installs the latest version of the app on her device, the first time the app needs to use the database, the SQLite helper checks its version number against that of the database on the device.

If the version number in the SQLite helper code is **higher** than that of the database, it calls the SQLite helper **onUpgrade()** method. If the version number in the SQLite helper code is **lower** than that of the database, it calls the **onDowngrade()** method instead.

Once it's called either of these methods, it changes the version number of the database to match the version number in the SQLite helper.

Geek Bits

SQLite databases support a version number that's used by the SQLite helper, and an internal schema version. Whenever a change is made to the database schema, such as the table structure, the database increments the schema version by 1. You have no control over this value, it's just used internally by SQLite.

Upgrading the database: an overview

Here's what happens when you release a new version of the app
where you've changed the SQLite helper version number from 1 to 2:

① **The user installs the new release of the app and runs it.**

User   Device

② **If this is the first time the user has installed the app, the database
doesn't exist, so the SQLite helper creates it.**
The SQLite helper gives the database the name and version number specified in the
SQLite helper code.

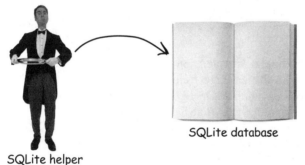

Name: "starbuzz"
Version: 2

*The SQLite helper gives the
database a version number
of 2 if this is the version
number specified in the
SQLite helper code.*

SQLite database

SQLite helper

③ **When the database is created, the onCreate() method in the SQLite
helper is called.**
The onCreate() method includes code to populate the database.

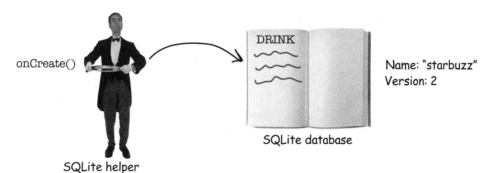

onCreate()

DRINK

Name: "starbuzz"
Version: 2

SQLite database

SQLite helper

The story continues...

4 **If the user installed a previous version of the app and accessed the database, the database already exists.**
    If the database already exists, the SQLite helper doesn't re-create it.

> Very good, sir, I see you already have version 1 of the database.

SQLite helper

Name: "starbuzz"
Version: 1

SQLite database

5 **The SQLite helper checks the version number of the database against the version number in the SQLite helper code.**
    If the SQLite helper version number is higher than the database version, it calls the onUpgrade() method. If the SQLite helper version number is lower than the database version, it calls the onDowngrade() method. It then changes the database version number to reflect the version number in the SQLite helper code.

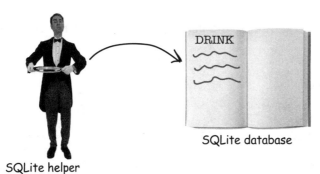

SQLite helper

SQLite database

Name: "starbuzz"
Version: ✗ 2

The SQLite helper runs the onUpgrade() method (if the new version number is higher) and updates the database version number.

How the SQLite helper makes decisions

Here's a summary of what the SQLite helper does depending on whether the database already exists and the version number of the database.

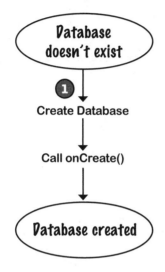

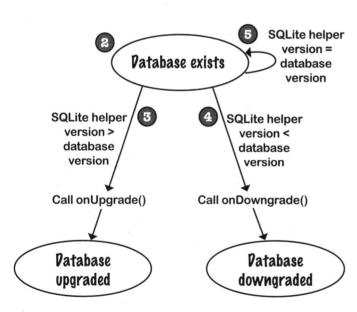

① **If the database doesn't already exist, the SQLite helper creates the database, and the helper onCreate() method runs.**

② **If the database already exists, the SQlite helper checks the version number held on the database with the version number in the helper.**

③ **If the version number in the SQLite helper is larger than the version number held on the database, the onUpgrade() method is called.**
The SQlite helper then updates the database version number.

④ **If the version number in the SQLite helper is smaller than the version number held on the database, the onDowngrade() method is called.**
The SQlite helper then updates the database version number.

⑤ **If the version number in the SQLite helper is the same as the version number held on the database, neither method is called.**
The database is already up to date.

Now that you've seen under what circumstances the onUpgrade() and onDowngrade() methods get called, let's find out more about how you use them.

→ □ **Upgrade database**

Upgrade your database with onUpgrade()

The `onUpgrade()` method has three parameters—the SQLite database, the version number of the database itself, and the new version of the database that's passed to the `SQLiteOpenHelper` superclass:

The current version of the database

The new version described in the SQLite helper code

```
@Override
public void onUpgrade(SQLiteDatabase db, int oldVersion, int newVersion) {
    //Your code goes here
}
```

Remember, to upgrade the database, the new version must be higher than the old version.

The version numbers are important, as you can use them to say what database changes should be made depending on which version of the database the user already has. As an example, suppose you needed to run code when the database is currently at version 1. Your code would look like this:

```
@Override
public void onUpgrade(SQLiteDatabase db, int oldVersion, int newVersion) {
    if (oldVersion == 1) {
        //Code to run if the database version is 1
    }
}
```

This code will only run if the user's database is at version 1.

You can also use the version numbers to apply successive updates like this:

```
@Override
public void onUpgrade(SQLiteDatabase db, int oldVersion, int newVersion) {
    if (oldVersion == 1) {
        //Code to run if the database version is 1
    }
    if (oldVersion < 3) {
        //Code to run if the database version is 1 or 2
    }
}
```

This code will only run if the user's database is at version 1.

This code will run if the user's database is at version 1 or 2. If the user has version 1 of the database, it will run both sets of code.

Using this approach means that you can make sure that the user gets all the database changes applied that they need, irrespective of which version they have installed.

The `onDowngrade()` method works in a similar way to the `onUpgrade()` method. Let's take a look on the next page.

Downgrade your database with onDowngrade()

The onDowngrade() method isn't used as often as the onUpgrade() method, as it's used to revert your database to a previous version. This can be useful if you release a version of your app that includes database changes, but you then discover that there are bugs. The onDowngrade() method allows you to pull the changes and set the database back to its previous version.

Just like the onUpgrade() method, the onDowngrade() method has three parameters—the SQLite database you want to downgrade, the version number of the database itself, and the new version of the database that's passed to the SQLiteOpenHelper superclass:

```
@Override
public void onDowngrade(SQLiteDatabase db, int oldVersion, int newVersion) {
    //Your code goes here
}
```

To downgrade the database, the new version must be lower than the old version.

Just as with the onUpgrade() method, you can use the version numbers to revert changes specific to a particular version. As an example, if you needed to make changes to the database when the database version number is 3, you'd use code like following:

```
@Override
public void onDowngrade(SQLiteDatabase db, int oldVersion, int newVersion) {
    if (oldVersion == 3) {
        //Code to run if the database version is 3
    }
}
```

This code will run if the user has version 3 of the database, but you want to downgrade it to a lower version.

Let's put this into practice by upgrading the database.

Let's upgrade the database

Suppose we need to upgrade our database to add a new column to the DRINK table. As we want all new and existing users to get this change, we need to make sure that it's included in both the onCreate() and onUpgrade() methods. The onCreate() method will make sure that all new users get the new column, and the onUpgrade() method will make sure that all existing users get it too.

Rather than put similar code in both the onCreate() and onUpgrade() methods, we're going to create a separate updateMyDatabase() method, called by both the onCreate() and onUpgrade() methods. We'll move the code that's currently in the onCreate() method to this new updateMyDatabase() method, and we'll add extra code to create the extra column. Using this approach means that you can put all of your database code in one place, and more easily keep track of what changes you've made each time you've updated the database:

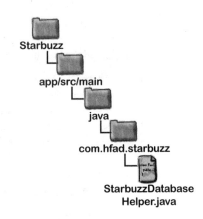

Starbuzz
app/src/main
java
com.hfad.starbuzz
StarbuzzDatabase
Helper.java

```java
...
@Override
public void onCreate(SQLiteDatabase db) {
    updateMyDatabase(db, 0, DB_VERSION);
}
```
← Rather than create the DRINK table here, we'll get our updateMyDatabase() method to do it.

```java
@Override
public void onUpgrade(SQLiteDatabase db, int oldVersion, int newVersion) {
    updateMyDatabase(db, oldVersion, newVersion);
}
```
← Call the updateMyDatabase() method from onUpgrade(), passing along the parameters.

```java
private void updateMyDatabase(SQLiteDatabase db, int oldVersion, int newVersion) {
    if (oldVersion < 1) {
        db.execSQL("CREATE TABLE DRINK (_id INTEGER PRIMARY KEY AUTOINCREMENT, "
                + "NAME TEXT, "
                + "DESCRIPTION TEXT, "
                + "IMAGE_RESOURCE_ID INTEGER);");
        insertDrink(db, "Latte", "Espresso and steamed milk", R.drawable.latte);
        insertDrink(db, "Cappuccino", "Espresso, hot milk and steamed-milk foam",
                R.drawable.cappuccino);
        insertDrink(db, "Filter", "Our best drip coffee", R.drawable.filter);
    }
    if (oldVersion < 2) {
        //Code to add the extra column
    }
}
...
```

This is the code we had in our onCreate() method.

← This code will run if the user already has version 1 of the database.

BE the SQLite Helper

On the right, you'll see some SQLite helper code. Your job is to play like you're the SQLite helper and say which code will run for each of the users below. We've labeled the code we want you to consider. We've done the first one to start you off.

User 1 runs the app for the first time.

Code segment A. The user doesn't have the database, so the onCreate() method runs.

User 2 has database version 1.

User 3 has database version 2.

User 4 has database version 3.

User 5 has database version 4.

User 6 has database version 5.

```
...

class MyHelper extends SQLiteOpenHelper{

    StarbuzzDatabaseHelper(Context context){
        super(context, "fred", null, 4);
    }

    @Override
    public void onCreate(SQLiteDatabase db){
    A   //Run code A
        ...
    }

    @Override
    public void onUpgrade(SQLiteDatabase db,
                          int oldVersion,
                          int newVersion){
        if (oldVersion < 2) {
        B   //Run code B
            ...
        }
        if (oldVersion == 3) {
        C   //Run code C
            ...
        }
        D   //Run code D
        ...
    }

    @Override
    public void onDowngrade(SQLiteDatabase db,
                            int oldVersion,
                            int newVersion){
        if (oldVersion == 3) {
        E   //Run code E
            ...
        }
        if (oldVersion < 6) {
        F   //Run code F
            ...
        }
    }
}
```

BE the SQLite Helper Solution

On the right you'll see some SQLite helper code. Your job is to play like you're the SQLite helper and say which code will run for each of the users below. We've labeled the code we want you to consider. We've done the first one to start you off.

User 1 runs the app for the first time.

Code segment A. The user doesn't have the database, so the onCreate() method runs.

User 2 has database version 1.

Code segment B then D. The database needs to be upgraded with oldVersion == 1.

User 3 has database version 2.

Code segment D. The database needs to be upgraded with oldVersion == 2.

User 4 has database version 3.

Code segment C then D. The database needs to be upgraded with oldVersion == 3.

User 5 has database version 4.

None. The user has the correct version of the database.

User 6 has database version 5.

Code segment F. The database needs to be downgraded with oldVersion == 5.

```
...

class MyHelper extends SQLiteOpenHelper{

    StarbuzzDatabaseHelper(Context context){
        super(context, "fred", null, 4);
    }
```
The new version of the database is 4.
```
    @Override
    public void onCreate(SQLiteDatabase db){
    A   //Run code A
        ...
    }
```
The onCreate() method will only run if the user doesn't have the database.
```
    @Override
    public void onUpgrade(SQLiteDatabase db,
                    int oldVersion,
                    int newVersion){
        if (oldVersion < 2) {
        B   //Run code B
            ...
        }
        if (oldVersion == 3) {
        C   //Run code C
            ...
        }
    D   //Run code D
        ...
    }
```
This will run if the user has version 1.

This will run if the user has version 3.

This will run if the user has version 1, 2, or 3.
```
    @Override
    public void onDowngrade(SQLiteDatabase db,
                    int oldVersion,
                    int newVersion){
        if (oldVersion == 3) {
        E   //Run code E
            ...
        }
        if (oldVersion < 6) {
        F   //Run code F
            ...
        }
    }
}
```
This will never run. If the user has version 3, her database needs to be upgraded, not downgraded.

This will run if the user has version 5. For onDowngrade() to run, the user must have a version greater than 4, as that's the current version number of the helper.

Upgrading an existing database

When you need to upgrade your database, there are two types of actions
you might want to perform:

⚙ **Change the database records.**
Earlier on in the chapter, you saw how to insert, update, or delete records in
your database using the `SQLiteDatabase insert()`, `update()`, and
`delete()` methods. You may add more records when you upgrade the
database, or change or remove the records that are already there.

⚙ **Change the database structure.**
You've already seen how you can create tables in the database. You may
also want to add columns to existing tables, rename tables, or remove tables
completely.

We'll look at how to perform these actions over the next few pages,
starting with changing the database structure to add columns to existing
tables.

Add new columns to tables using SQL

Earlier on in the chapter, you saw how you could create tables using the
SQL CREATE TABLE command like this:

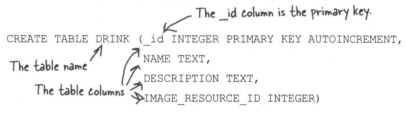

```
CREATE TABLE DRINK (_id INTEGER PRIMARY KEY AUTOINCREMENT,
                    NAME TEXT,
                    DESCRIPTION TEXT,
                    IMAGE_RESOURCE_ID INTEGER)
```

The _id column is the primary key.
The table name
The table columns

You can also use SQL to change an existing table using the ALTER
TABLE command. As an example, here's what the command looks like
to add a column to a table:

```
ALTER TABLE DRINK
ADD COLUMN FAVORITE NUMERIC
```

← *The table name*
← *The column you want to add*

In the example above, we're adding a column called FAVORITE that
holds numeric values to the DRINK table.

On the next page, we'll show you how to rename a table, or remove it
from the database.

→ ☐ **Upgrade database**

Renaming tables

You can also use the ALTER TABLE command to rename a table. As
an example, here's how you'd rename the DRINK table to FOO:

```
ALTER TABLE DRINK
```
← The current table name
```
RENAME TO FOO
```
← The new name of the table

Delete tables by dropping them

In addition to creating and altering tables, you can delete them using
the DROP TABLE command:

```
DROP TABLE DRINK
```
← The name of the table you want to remove

This command is useful if you have a table in your database schema
that you know you don't need any more, and want to remove it in
order to save space.

Execute the SQL using execSQL()

As you saw earlier in the chapter, you can execute SQL commands
using the SQLiteDatabase execSQL() method:

```
SQLiteDatabase.execSQL(String sql);
```

As an example, here's how you'd execute SQL to add a new
FAVORITE column to the DRINK table:

```
db.execSQL("ALTER TABLE DRINK ADD COLUMN FAVORITE NUMERIC;");
```

You can use the execSQL() method any time you need to execute
SQL on the database.

Now that you've seen the sorts of actions you might want to
perform when upgrading your database, let's apply this to
StarbuzzDatabaseHelper.java.

The full SQLite helper code

Here's the full code for *StarbuzzDatabaseHelper.java* that will add a
new FAVORITE column to the DRINK table. Update your code to
match ours (the changes are in bold):

```
package com.hfad.starbuzz;

import android.content.ContentValues;
import android.content.Context;
import android.database.sqlite.SQLiteDatabase;
import android.database.sqlite.SQLiteOpenHelper;

class StarbuzzDatabaseHelper extends SQLiteOpenHelper{

    private static final String DB_NAME = "starbuzz"; // the name of our database
    private static final int DB_VERSION = 2; // the version of the database

    StarbuzzDatabaseHelper(Context context){
        super(context, DB_NAME, null, DB_VERSION);
    }

    @Override
    public void onCreate(SQLiteDatabase db){
        updateMyDatabase(db, 0, DB_VERSION);
    }

    @Override
    public void onUpgrade(SQLiteDatabase db, int oldVersion, int newVersion) {
        updateMyDatabase(db, oldVersion, newVersion);
    }
```

Starbuzz
└ app/src/main
  └ java
    └ com.hfad.starbuzz
      └ StarbuzzDatabase
        Helper.java

Changing the version number to a larger
integer enables the SQLite helper to
spot that you want to upgrade the
database.

We'll put the code from the onCreate()
method in the updateMyDatabase() method.

The code to upgrade the database is
in our updateMyDatabase() method.

The code continues over the page.

Upgrade database

The SQLite helper code (continued)

```java
private void updateMyDatabase(SQLiteDatabase db, int oldVersion, int newVersion) {
    if (oldVersion < 1) {
        db.execSQL("CREATE TABLE DRINK (_id INTEGER PRIMARY KEY AUTOINCREMENT, "
                    + "NAME TEXT, "
                    + "DESCRIPTION TEXT, "
                    + "IMAGE_RESOURCE_ID INTEGER);");
        insertDrink(db, "Latte", "Espresso and steamed milk", R.drawable.latte);
        insertDrink(db, "Cappuccino", "Espresso, hot milk and steamed-milk foam",
                    R.drawable.cappuccino);
        insertDrink(db, "Filter", "Our best drip coffee", R.drawable.filter);
    }
    if (oldVersion < 2) {
        db.execSQL("ALTER TABLE DRINK ADD COLUMN FAVORITE NUMERIC;");
    }
}
```

Add a numeric FAVORITE column to the DRINK table.

```java
private static void insertDrink(SQLiteDatabase db, String name,
                                String description, int resourceId) {
    ContentValues drinkValues = new ContentValues();
    drinkValues.put("NAME", name);
    drinkValues.put("DESCRIPTION", description);
    drinkValues.put("IMAGE_RESOURCE_ID", resourceId);
    db.insert("DRINK", null, drinkValues);
}
}
```

The new code in the SQLite helper means that existing users will get the new FAVORITE column added to the DRINK table the next time they access the database. It also means that any new users will get the complete database created for them, including the new column.

We'll go through what happens when the code runs on the next page.

What happens when the code runs

1 When the database first needs to be accessed, the SQLite helper checks whether the database already exists.

You need a database, sir? Let me see if it's already there for you.

SQLite helper

2 If the database doesn't exist, the SQLite helper creates it and runs its onCreate() method.

Our onCreate() method code calls the updateMyDatabase() method. This creates the DRINK table (including the extra column) and populates the table with records.

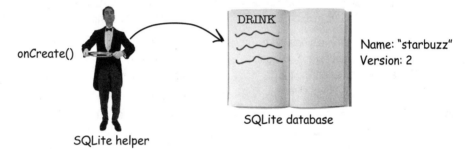

onCreate()

SQLite helper

DRINK

SQLite database

Name: "starbuzz"
Version: 2

3 If the database already exists, the SQLite helper checks the version number of the database against the version number in the SQLite helper code.

If the SQLite helper version number is higher than the database version, it calls the onUpgrade() method. If the SQLite helper version number is lower than the database version, it calls the onDowngrade() method. Our SQLite helper version number is higher than that of the database, so the onUpgrade() method is called. It calls the updateMyDatabase() method, and this adds an extra column called FAVORITE to the DRINK table.

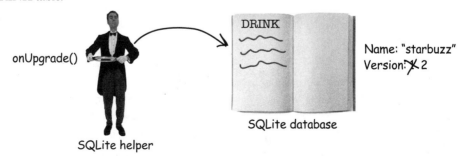

onUpgrade()

SQLite helper

DRINK

SQLite database

Name: "starbuzz"
Version: ~~1~~ 2

Your Android Toolbox

You've got Chapter 11 under your belt and now you've added creating, updating, and upgrading databases to your toolbox.

You can download the full code for the chapter from https://tinyurl.com/HeadFirstAndroid.

BULLET POINTS

- Android uses SQLite as its backend database to persist data.

- The `SQLiteDatabase` class gives you access to the SQLite database.

- A SQLite helper lets you create and manage SQLite databases. You create a SQLite helper by extending the `SQLiteOpenHelper` class.

- You must implement the `SQLiteOpenHelper onCreate()` and `onUpgrade()` methods.

- The database gets created the first time it needs to be accessed. You need to give the database a name and version number, starting at 1. If you don't give the database a name, it will just get created in memory.

- The `onCreate()` method gets called when the database first gets created.

- The `onUpgrade()` method gets called when the database needs to be upgraded.

- Execute SQL using the `SQLiteDatabase execSQL(String)` method.

- Add records to tables using the `insert()` method.

- Update records using the `update()` method.

- Remove records from tables using the `delete()` method.

12 cursors and asynctasks

Connecting to Databases

My doInBackground() method's awesome. If I left it all to Mr. Main Event can you imagine how slow he'd be?

So how do you connect your app to a SQLite database?

So far you've seen how to create a SQLite database using a SQLite helper. The next step is to get your activities to access it. In this chapter, you'll find out **how to use cursors to get data from the database**, **how to navigate cursors,** and **how to get data from them**. You'll then find out how to use **cursor adapters** to connect them to list views. Finally, you'll see how writing efficient **multithreaded code** with **AsyncTask**s will keep your app speedy.

The story so far...

In Chapter 11, you saw how to write a SQLite helper to create a database, and how to add tables and prepopulate them with data. You also saw how to make the SQLite helper deal with database upgrades so that you can change the structure of the database and manipulate the data it contains by upgrading it.

In this chapter, we're going to show you how to get your activities to interact with the database so that your user can read from and write to the database using your app.

Here's the current state of our Starbuzz app:

We've created the SQLite helper and added code so it can create the Starbuzz database. It's not being used by any activities yet.

Starbuzz database

SQLite Helper

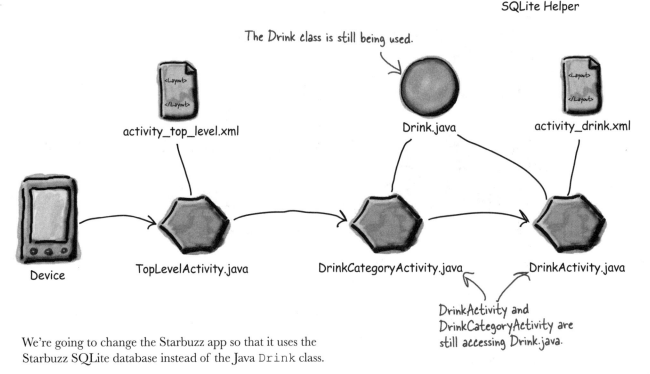

The Drink class is still being used.

activity_top_level.xml

Drink.java

activity_drink.xml

Device

TopLevelActivity.java

DrinkCategoryActivity.java

DrinkActivity.java

DrinkActivity and DrinkCategoryActivity are still accessing Drink.java.

We're going to change the Starbuzz app so that it uses the Starbuzz SQLite database instead of the Java `Drink` class.

We'll change the app to use the database

There are two activities that use the Drink class. We need to get them to read data from the SQLite database with assistance from the SQLite helper. Here's what we'll do:

1 **Update the Drink code in DrinkActivity.**
DrinkActivity uses the Drink class to display the details it has for a given drink. We'll change the activity so that it retrieves the record for that drink from the Starbuzz database.

2 **Update the Drink code in DrinkCategoryActivity.**
DrinkCategoryActivity uses the Drink class to display a list of all the drinks. We'll change this so that the activity displays a list of all the records in the DRINK table.

3 **Let users choose their favorite drinks.**
In Chapter 11, we upgraded the database so that the DRINK table includes a FAVORITE column. We'll change the app so that users can flag which drinks are their favorites, and display a list of these favorites in TopLevelActivity.

Here's what the structure of the app will look like:

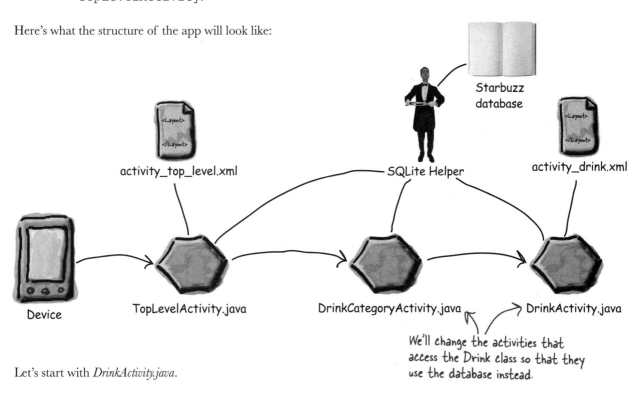

Starbuzz database

activity_top_level.xml

SQLite Helper

activity_drink.xml

Device

TopLevelActivity.java

DrinkCategoryActivity.java

DrinkActivity.java

We'll change the activities that access the Drink class so that they use the database instead.

Let's start with *DrinkActivity.java*.

The current DrinkActivity code

DrinkActivity
DrinkCategoryActivity
Favorites

Here's a reminder of what the current *DrinkActivity.java* code looks like. The onCreate() method gets the drink number selected by the user, gets the drink details from the Drink class, and then populates the activity's views using the drink attributes:

> DrinkActivity displays details of the drink the user selected.

> Cappuccino
> Espresso, hot milk, and a steamed milk foam

```java
package com.hfad.starbuzz;

import android.app.Activity;
import android.os.Bundle;
import android.widget.ImageView;
import android.widget.TextView;

public class DrinkActivity extends Activity {

    public static final String EXTRA_DRINKNO = "drinkNo";

    @Override
    protected void onCreate(Bundle savedInstanceState) {
        super.onCreate(savedInstanceState);
        setContentView(R.layout.activity_drink);

        //Get the drink from the intent
        int drinkNo = (Integer)getIntent().getExtras().get(EXTRA_DRINKNO);
        Drink drink = Drink.drinks[drinkNo];

        //Populate the drink image
        ImageView photo = (ImageView)findViewById(R.id.photo);
        photo.setImageResource(drink.getImageResourceId());
        photo.setContentDescription(drink.getName());

        //Populate the drink name
        TextView name = (TextView)findViewById(R.id.name);
        name.setText(drink.getName());

        //Populate the drink description
        TextView description = (TextView)findViewById(R.id.description);
        description.setText(drink.getDescription());
    }
}
```

> Starbuzz
> app/src/main
> java
> com.hfad.starbuzz
> DrinkActivity.java

This is the drink the user selected.

Use the drink number from the intent to get the drink from the Drink class. We'll need to change this so the drink comes from the database.

We need to populate the views in the layout with values from the database, not from the Drink class.

Get data from the database with a cursor

Our current `DrinkActivity` code depends on being able to get details of a particular drink from the `Drink` class. How do we change this so that we can retrieve drink details from the Starbuzz database instead? *How do you change an activity so that it reads data from a database?*

The solution is to use a **cursor**.

Cursors give you access to database data

A cursor gives you access to database recordsets. You specify what data you want access to, and the cursor brings back the records from the database. You then navigate through the records supplied by the cursor.

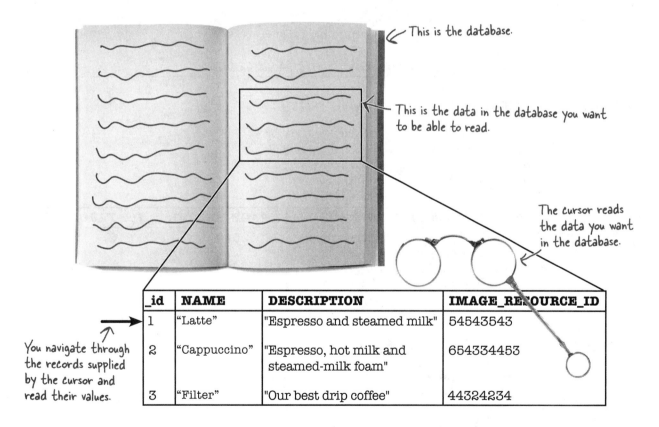

This is the database.

This is the data in the database you want to be able to read.

The cursor reads the data you want in the database.

You navigate through the records supplied by the cursor and read their values.

_id	NAME	DESCRIPTION	IMAGE_RESOURCE_ID
1	"Latte"	"Espresso and steamed milk"	54543543
2	"Cappuccino"	"Espresso, hot milk and steamed-milk foam"	654334453
3	"Filter"	"Our best drip coffee"	44324234

You create a cursor by specifying what data you want access to using a database query. So what's a query?

DrinkActivity
DrinkCategoryActivity
Favorites

A query lets you say what records you want from the database

A database query gives you a way of saying exactly which records you want access to from the database. As an example, you can say you want to access all the data from the DRINK table, or just those drinks whose name begins with "L". The more you can restrict the data you return, the more efficient your query will be.

Specify the table and columns

The first thing to specify in your query is which table you want to get records from, and which columns you need.

Return the data from the NAME and DESCRIPTION columns in the DRINK table.

_id	NAME	DESCRIPTION	IMAGE_RESOURCE_ID	FAVORITE
1	"Latte"	"Espresso and steamed milk"	54543543	0
2	"Cappuccino"	"Espresso, hot milk and steamed-milk foam"	654334453	0
3	"Filter"	"Our best drip coffee"	44324234	0

Declare any conditions that restrict your selection

Once you've said what columns you want, you can filter your data by declaring any conditions the data must meet. In our app, for example, we want to retrieve the drink the user selected, and we can do this by only returning records where the drink _id has a particular value.

Return data where _id is 1.

_id	NAME	DESCRIPTION	IMAGE_RESOURCE_ID	FAVORITE
1	"Latte"	"Espresso and steamed milk"	54543543	0
2	"Cappuccino"	"Espresso, hot milk and steamed-milk foam"	654334453	0
3	"Filter"	"Our best drip coffee"	44324234	0

Other stuff you can use queries for

If you expect your query to return several rows of data, you might find it useful to say what order you want the records to be in. As an example, you might want to order the drink records in drink name order. You can also use queries to group the data in some way, and apply aggregate functions to it. As an example, you might want to return a count of how many drinks there are and display it in your app.

So how do you create a query?

The SQLiteDatabase query() method lets you build SQL using a query builder

You can build a query using the SQLiteDatabase query() method. The query() method returns an object of type Cursor, which your activities can use to access the database.

Here is the basic form of the query() method:

```
public Cursor query(String table,
                    String[] columns,
                    String selection,
                    String[] selectionArgs,
                    String groupBy,
                    String having,
                    String orderBy)
```

↑
The query() method returns a Cursor.

The table and columns you want to access.

Use these if you want to apply conditions.

Use these if you want to aggregate the data.

Do you want the data in a particular order?

You can use this version of the query() method to specify which table you want to return data from, which columns you want, what conditions you want to apply to the data, what data aggregations you need, and how you want the data ordered.

There are several other overloaded versions of the query() method which allow you to add extra details to your query, such as whether you want each row to be unique, and the maximum number of rows you want to be returned. We're not going to go into all these variations, but if you're interested, you can find a full list of the overloaded methods in the online Android documentation:

http://developer.android.com/reference/android/database/ sqlite/SQLiteDatabase.html

Over the next few pages, we'll go through some of the most common ways in which you might want to use the query() method.

Behind the scenes, Android uses the query() method to construct an SQL SELECT statement.

DrinkActivity
DrinkCategoryActivity
Favorites

Specifying table and columns

The simplest type of database query you can create is to return all
the records for particular columns without specifying criteria. To do
this, put the name of the table as the first parameter, and a `String`
array of the column names as the second. As an example, here's
how you'd use the `query()` method to return the contents of the
name and description columns from the DRINK table:

*Put each column you want back as a
separate value in a String array.*

```
Cursor cursor = db.query("DRINK",
                         new String[] {"NAME", "DESCRIPTION"},
                         null, null, null, null, null);
```

*This query only uses the first two
parameters, hence the null values.*

*The query returns all the data from
the NAME and DESCRIPTION
columns in the DRINK table.*

NAME	DESCRIPTION
"Latte"	"Espresso and steamed milk"
"Cappuccino"	"Espresso, hot milk and steamed-milk foam"
"Filter"	"Our best drip coffee"

Restrict your query by applying conditions

You can apply conditions to your database query by specifying what
values particular columns should have using the third and fourth
query parameters. As an example, here's how you'd say you only
want to return records from the DRINK table where the name of
the drink is "Latte":

```
Cursor cursor = db.query("DRINK",
                 new String[] {"NAME", "DESCRIPTION"},
                 "NAME = ?",
                 new String[] {"Latte"},
                 null, null, null);
```

*This means "where the contents
of the NAME column is 'Latte'".*

The third parameter `"NAME = ?"` means that the NAME column
should equal some value. The `?` symbol is a placeholder symbol for
this value. The query uses the contents of the fourth parameter to
say what the value should be (in this case, "Latte").

*The query returns all the data from the NAME
and DESCRIPTION columns in the DRINK table
where the value of the NAME column is "Latte".*

NAME	DESCRIPTION
"Latte"	"Espresso and steamed milk"

Applying multiple conditions to your query

If you want to apply multiple conditions to your query, you need to make sure you specify the conditions in the same order you specify the values. As an example, here's how you'd return records from the DRINK table where the name of the drink is "Latte", or the drink description is "Our best drip coffee".

```
Cursor cursor = db.query("DRINK",
                new String[] {"NAME", "DESCRIPTION"},
                "NAME = ? OR DESCRIPTION = ?",
                new String[] {"Latte", "Our best drip coffee"},
                null, null, null);
```

This means "where NAME is 'Latte' or DESCRIPTION is "Our best drip coffee"".

The query returns all the data from the NAME and DESCRIPTION columns in the DRINK table where the value of the NAME column is "Latte" or the value of the DESCRIPTION column is "Our best drip coffee".

NAME	DESCRIPTION
"Latte"	"Espresso and steamed milk"
"Filter"	"Our best drip coffee"

If you specify the conditions in a different order to the values, your cursor will return the wrong data. As an example, it might pair the value "Latte" with the DESCRIPTION column rather than the NAME column. This wouldn't return any records.

You specify conditions as String values

The condition values must be `Strings`. If the column you're applying the condition to doesn't contain text, you still need to convert your values to `Strings`. As an example, here's how you'd return DRINK records where the _id is 1:

```
Cursor cursor = db.query("Drink",
                    new String[] {"NAME", "DESCRIPTION"},
                    "_id = ?",
                    new String[] {Integer.toString(1)},
                    null, null, null);
```

Convert the int 1 to a String value.

The query returns all the data from the NAME and DESCRIPTION columns in the DRINK table where the value of the _id column is 1.

_id	NAME	DESCRIPTION
1	"Latte"	"Espresso and steamed milk"

Order data in your query

If you want to display data in your app in a particular order, you can use the query to sort the data by a particular column. This can be useful if, for example, you want to display drink names in alphabetical order.

By default, the data in the table appears in _id order as this was the order in which data was entered:

_id	NAME	DESCRIPTION	IMAGE_RESOURCE_ID	FAVORITE
1	"Latte"	"Espresso and steamed milk"	54543543	1
2	"Cappuccino"	"Espresso, hot milk and steamed-milk foam"	654334453	0
3	"Filter"	"Our best drip coffee"	44324234	0

If you wanted to retrieve data from the NAME and FAVORITE column in ascending NAME order, you could use the following:

```
Cursor cursor = db.query("DRINK",
        new String[] {"_id", "NAME", "FAVORITE"},
        null, null, null, null,
        "NAME ASC");  ← Order by NAME in ascending order.
```

NAME	FAVORITE
"Cappuccino"	0
"Filter"	0
"Latte"	1

The ASC keyword means that you want to order that column in ascending order. Columns are ordered in ascending order by default, so if you want you can omit the ASC. To order the data in descending order instead, you'd use DESC.

You can sort by multiple columns too. As an example, here's how you'd order by FAVORITE in descending order, followed by NAME in ascending order:

```
Cursor cursor = db.query("DRINK",
        new String[] {"_id", "NAME", "FAVORITE"},
        null, null, null, null,
        "FAVORITE DESC, NAME");  ← Order by FAVORITE in
                                    descending order, then
                                    NAME in ascending order.
```

NAME	FAVORITE
"Latte"	1
"Cappuccino"	0
"Filter"	0

You've now seen the most common ways of using the query() method, but there are still more things you can do.

Using SQL functions in queries

If you're familiar with SQL functions, the great news is you can use them in queries. They allow you to retrieve things like the number of rows in a table, the average value of a column, or the highest value.

Here are some of the most useful SQL functions you can use in your queries:

AVG()	The average value
COUNT()	The number of rows
SUM()	The sum
MAX()	The largest value
MIN()	The smallest value

As an example, if you wanted to count how many drinks there are in the DRINK table, you could use the SQL COUNT () function to count the number of values in the _id column:

```
Cursor cursor = db.query("DRINK",
                    new String[] {"COUNT(_id) AS count"},
                    null, null, null, null, null);
```

This returns the number of drinks in a column labeled "count"

The query returns the number of rows in the DRINK table. ⟶

count
3

If the DRINK table contained an extra PRICE column that gave the price of each drink, you could find out the average drink price using the SQL AVG () function to find the average value of the PRICE column:

```
Cursor cursor = db.query("DRINK",
                    new String[] {"AVG(PRICE) AS price"},
                    null, null, null, null, null);
```

price
4.17

⟵ *Our DRINK table doesn't contain a PRICE column, but if it did, we could use it to get the average drink price.*

SQL GROUP BY and HAVING clauses

DrinkActivity
DrinkCategoryActivity
Favorites

If you're familiar with the GROUP BY and HAVING clauses of SQL, you can use these in the fifth and sixth parameters of the query() method.

As an example, suppose you wanted to find out how many drinks there are for each value of FAVORITE. To do this, you'd create a query to return the FAVORITE column and a count of drinks. You'd then group by the FAVORITE column to return the number of drinks there are for each value of FAVORITE:

We're not teaching you SQL in this book, just giving you a glimpse of what you can do.

If you think this is something you'll find useful, we suggest picking up a copy of *Head First SQL*.

```
Cursor cursor = db.query("DRINK",
                    new String[] {"FAVORITE", "COUNT(_id) AS count"},
                    null, null,
                    "FAVORITE",
                    null, null);
```

Group by the FAVORITE column.

Return the FAVORITE column and the number of drinks.

If the data in the DRINKS table looks like this:

_id	NAME	DESCRIPTION	IMAGE_RESOURCE_ID	FAVORITE
1	"Latte"	"Espresso and steamed milk"	54543543	1
2	"Cappuccino"	"Espresso, hot milk and steamed-milk foam"	654334453	0
3	"Filter"	"Our best drip coffee"	44324234	0

the query will return data like this:

FAVORITE	count
1	1
0	2

There's 1 drink where FAVORITE has a value of 1, and 2 drinks where FAVORITE has a value of 0.

Now that you've seen how to create a cursor using the query() method, it's time for you to have a go at creating one for the Starbuzz app.

Code Magnets

In our code for `DrinkActivity`, we want to get the name, description, and image resource ID for the drink passed to it in an intent. Can you construct a `query()` method that will do that?

```
...

int drinkNo = (Integer)getIntent().getExtras().get(EXTRA_DRINKNO);

Cursor cursor = db.query(................,

        new String[] {.........................,...................,...............................},

        "..........................",

        new String[] {..............................................},

        null, null,null);

...
```

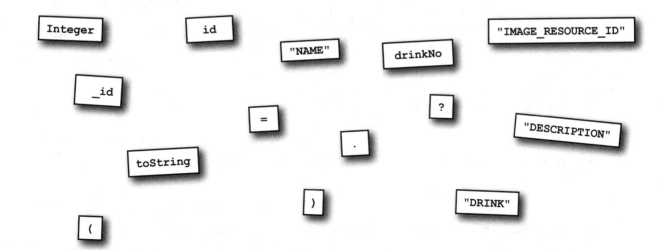

Code Magnets Solution

In our code for DrinkActivity we want to get the name, description and image resource ID for the drink passed to it in an intent. Can you construct a query() method that will do that?

```
...

int drinkNo = (Integer)getIntent().getExtras().get(EXTRA_DRINKNO);

Cursor cursor = db.query( "DRINK" ,
```
← We want to access the DRINK table.

Get the NAME, DESCRIPTION, and IMAGE_RESOURCE_ID columns.
```
    new String[] { "NAME" , "DESCRIPTION" , "IMAGE_RESOURCE_ID" },

    " _id = ? ",
```
← Where _id matches the drinkNo.
```
    new String[] { Integer . toString ( drinkNo ) },

    null, null,null);

...
```
drinkNo is an int, so needed to be converted to a String.

id

Get a reference to the database

Over the past few pages, you've seen how to build a query that returns a cursor. The query() method is defined in the SQLiteDatabase class, which means in order to call it we need to get a reference to our Starbuzz database. The SQLiteOpenHelper class implements a couple of methods that can help us with this: **getReadableDatabase()** and **getWritableDatabase()**. Each of these methods returns an object of type SQLiteDatabase, which gives us access to the database. You call the methods like this:

A cursor lets you read data from the database.

```
SQLiteOpenHelper starbuzzDatabaseHelper = new StarbuzzDatabaseHelper(this);

SQLiteDatabase db = starbuzzDatabaseHelper.getReadableDatabase();
```

and

```
SQLiteOpenHelper starbuzzDatabaseHelper = new StarbuzzDatabaseHelper(this);

SQLiteDatabase db = starbuzzDatabaseHelper.getWritableDatabase();
```

So what's the difference between these two methods?

getReadableDatabase() versus getWritableDatabase()

You're probably thinking that getReadableDatabase() returns a read-only database object, and getWritableDatabase() returns one that's writable. In fact, most of the time getReadableDatabase() and getWritableDatabase() ***both return a reference to the same database object***. This database object can be used to read and write data to the database. So why is there a getReadableDatabase() method if it returns the same object as the getWriteableDatabase() method?

The key difference between the getReadableDatabase() and getWritableDatabase() methods is what happens if it's not possible to write to the database. This can happen if the disk is full, for instance.

If you use the getWritableDatabase() method in this case, the method will fail, and throw a **SQLiteException**. But if you use the getReadableDatabase() method, the method will try to get a read-only reference to the database. It may still throw a SQLiteException if it can't get read-only access to the database.

If you only need read data from a database, you're best off using the getReadableDatabase() method. If you need to write to the database, ← use the getWritableDatabase() method instead.

*You'll **probably** be able to write to the database if you use getReadableDatabase(), but it's not guaranteed.*

getReadableDatabase()

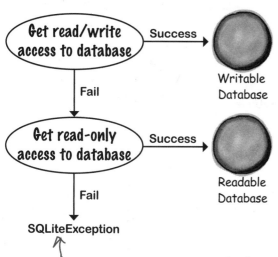

getReadableDatabase() tries to get read/write access to the database first. If it fails, it then tries to get read-only access to the database. If it still can't get access, it throws a SQLiteException.

getWritableDatabase()

getWritableDatabase() tries to get read/write access to the database. If it fails, it throws a SQLiteException.

DrinkActivity
DrinkCategoryActivity
Favorites

The code for getting a cursor

Putting all of this together, here's the code for getting a cursor. We'll
use this code later in the onCreate() method of our activity.

*We don't need to write to
the database so we're using
getReadableDatabase().*

```
try {
    SQLiteOpenHelper starbuzzDatabaseHelper = new StarbuzzDatabaseHelper(this);
    SQLiteDatabase db = starbuzzDatabaseHelper.getReadableDatabase();
    Cursor cursor = db.query("DRINK",
                        new String[] {"NAME", "DESCRIPTION", "IMAGE_RESOURCE_ID"},
                        "_id = ?",
                        new String[] {Integer.toString(drinkNo)},
                        null, null,null);

    //Code to do something with the cursor

} catch(SQLiteException e) {
    Toast toast = Toast.makeText(this, "Database unavailable", Toast.LENGTH_SHORT);
    toast.show();
}
```

*The cursor
contains a single
record as the _id
column contains
unique records.*

*We have the cursor,
but we still need to
do something with it.*

Display a message if the database is unavailable.

What the code does

1 **The starbuzzDatabaseHelper is created.**

starbuzzDatabaseHelper

2 **starbuzzDatabaseHelper creates a SQLiteDatabase object called db.**

starbuzzDatabaseHelper   db

2 **The cursor is created by calling the SQLiteDatabase query() method.**

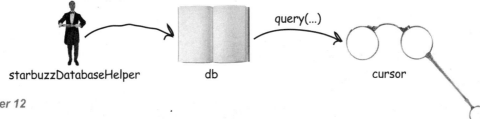

query(...)

starbuzzDatabaseHelper   db   cursor

To read a record from a cursor, you first need to navigate to it

You've now seen how to create a cursor; you use the `SQLiteDatabase query()` method to say what data you want the cursor to return. But that's not the end of the story— we need to read values from it.

Whenever you need to retrieve values from a particular record in a cursor, you first need to navigate to that record. You need to do this irrespective of how many records are returned by the cursor.

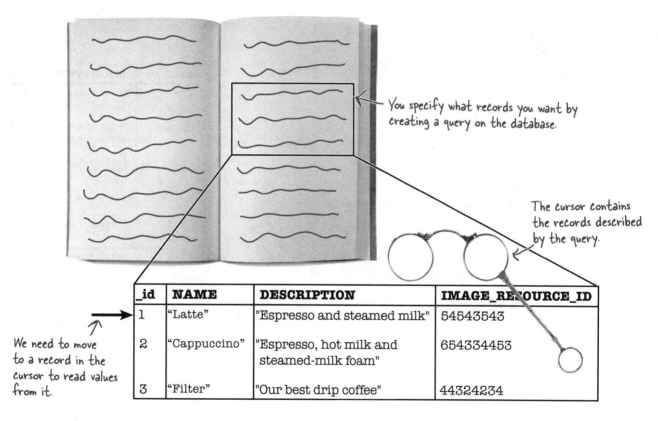

You specify what records you want by creating a query on the database.

The cursor contains the records described by the query.

We need to move to a record in the cursor to read values from it.

_id	NAME	DESCRIPTION	IMAGE_RESOURCE_ID
1	"Latte"	"Espresso and steamed milk"	54543543
2	"Cappuccino"	"Espresso, hot milk and steamed-milk foam"	654334453
3	"Filter"	"Our best drip coffee"	44324234

On the next page, we'll look at how you navigate cursors.

DrinkActivity
DrinkCategoryActivity
Favorites

Navigating cursors

There are four main methods you use to navigate through the records in a cursor. These methods are moveToFirst(), moveToLast(), moveToPrevious(), and moveToNext().

To get access to the first record returned by the cursor, you can use its moveToFirst() method (it returns a value of true if it finds a record, and false if the cursor hasn't returned any records):

```
if (cursor.moveToFirst()) {

    //Do something

};
```

Move to the first row.

NAME	DESCRIPTION
"Latte"	"Espresso and steamed milk"
Cappuccino	"Espresso, hot milk and steamed-milk foam"
Filter	"Our best drip coffee"

If you want to navigate to the last record returned by the cursor, you can use the moveToLast() method instead (just like the moveToFirst() method, it returns a value of true if it finds a record, and false if it doesn't):

```
if (cursor.moveToLast()) {

    //Do something

};
```

NAME	DESCRIPTION
"Latte"	"Espresso and steamed milk"
Cappuccino	"Espresso, hot milk and steamed-milk foam"
Filter	"Our best drip coffee"

Move to the last row.

To iterate through the records in the cursor, you use the moveToPrevious() and moveToNext() methods.

The moveToPrevious() method moves you to the previous record in the cursor (it returns true if it succeeds in moving to the previous record, and false if it fails—which could be because it's already at the first record, or because the cursor doesn't contain any records):

```
if (cursor.moveToPrevious()) {

    //Do something

};
```

NAME	DESCRIPTION
"Latte"	"Espresso and steamed milk"
Cappuccino	"Espresso, hot milk and steamed-milk foam"
Filter	"Our best drip coffee"

Move to the previous row.

The moveToNext() method works in the same way as the moveToPrevious() method, except that it moves you to the next record in the cursor (it returns true if it succeeds in moving to the next record, and false if it fails):

```
if (cursor.moveToNext()) {

    //Do something

};
```

NAME	DESCRIPTION
"Latte"	"Espresso and steamed milk"
Cappuccino	"Espresso, hot milk and steamed-milk foam"
Filter	"Our best drip coffee"

Move to the next row.

Once you've navigated to a record in your cursor, you can access its values. We'll look at that on the next page.

Getting cursor values

Once you've moved to a record in a cursor, you can retrieve values from it so that you can display them in your activity's views. You retrieve a value from the current record in a cursor using its `get*()` methods. The exact method you use for this depends on the type of value you want to retrieve. As an example, the `getString()` method returns the value of a column as a `String`, and the `getInt()` method returns the value of a column as an `int`. Each of the methods takes a single parameter, the column index.

As an example, here's the query we used to create our cursor:

```
Cursor cursor = db.query ("Drink",
                new String[] {"NAME", "DESCRIPTION", "IMAGE_RESOURCE_ID"},
                "_id = ?",
                new String[] {Integer.toString(1)},
                null, null,null);
```

The cursor has three columns: NAME, DESCRIPTION, and IMAGE_RESOURCE_ID. The first two columns, NAME and DESCRIPTION, contain data of type `String`. The third column, IMAGE_RESOURCE_ID, contains data of type `int`.

Column 0   Column 1   Column 2

NAME	DESCRIPTION	IMAGE_RESOURCE_ID
"Latte"	"Espresso and steamed milk"	54543543

Suppose you wanted to get the value of the NAME column for the current record. NAME is the first column in the cursor, and contains `String` values. You'd therefore get the contents of the NAME column using the `getString()` method like this:

String name = cursor.getString(0); ← This is the first column in the cursor.

Similarly, suppose you wanted to get the contents of the IMAGE_RESOURCE_ID column. This is the third column in the cursor, and contains `int` values, so you'd use the code:

int imageResource = cursor.getInt(2);

You can find details of all the cursor get methods in http://developer.android.com/reference/android/database/Cursor.html.

Finally, close the cursor and database

Once you've finished retrieving values from the cursor, you need to close the cursor and the database in order to release their resources. You do this by calling the cursor and database **close()** methods:

cursor.close();

db.close();

We've now covered all the code we need to replace the code in `DrinkActivity` so that it gets its data from the Starbuzz database. Let's look at the code.

The DrinkActivity code

Here's the full code for *DrinkActivity.java* (apply the changes in bold to your code, then save your work):

```java
package com.hfad.starbuzz;

import android.app.Activity;
import android.os.Bundle;
import android.widget.ImageView;
import android.widget.TextView;
import android.widget.Toast;
import android.database.Cursor;
import android.database.sqlite.SQLiteDatabase;
import android.database.sqlite.SQLiteException;
import android.database.sqlite.SQLiteOpenHelper;
```

We're using these extra classes in the code.

Starbuzz
app/src/main
java
com.hfad.starbuzz
DrinkActivity.java

```java
public class DrinkActivity extends Activity {

    public static final String EXTRA_DRINKNO = "drinkNo";

    @Override
    protected void onCreate(Bundle savedInstanceState) {
        super.onCreate(savedInstanceState);
        setContentView(R.layout.activity_drink);

        //Get the drink from the intent
        int drinkNo = (Integer)getIntent().getExtras().get(EXTRA_DRINKNO);

        //Create a cursor
        try {
            SQLiteOpenHelper starbuzzDatabaseHelper = new StarbuzzDatabaseHelper(this);
            SQLiteDatabase db = starbuzzDatabaseHelper.getReadableDatabase();
            Cursor cursor = db.query ("DRINK",
                    new String[] {"NAME", "DESCRIPTION", "IMAGE_RESOURCE_ID"},
                    "_id = ?",
                    new String[] {Integer.toString(drinkNo)},
                    null, null,null);
```

This is the ID of the drink the user chose.

Create a cursor that gets the NAME, DESCRIPTION, and IMAGE_RESOURCE_ID data from the DRINK table where _id matches drinkNo.

The code continues on the next page.

The DrinkActivity code (continued)

Starbuzz

app/src/main

java

com.hfad.starbuzz

DrinkActivity.java

```
//Move to the first record in the Cursor
if (cursor.moveToFirst()) {
```
← There's only one record in the cursor, but we still need to move to it.

The name of the drink is the first item in the cursor, the description is the second column, and the image resource ID is the third. That's because we told the cursor to use the NAME, DESCRIPTION, and IMAGE_RESOURCE_ID columns from the database in that order.

```
    //Get the drink details from the cursor
    String nameText = cursor.getString(0);
    String descriptionText = cursor.getString(1);
    int photoId = cursor.getInt(2);

    //Populate the drink name
    TextView name = (TextView)findViewById(R.id.name);
    name.setText(nameText);
```
← Use the data from the cursor to populate the views.

```
    //Populate the drink description
    TextView description = (TextView)findViewById(R.id.description);
    description.setText(descriptionText);

    //Populate the drink image
    ImageView photo = (ImageView)findViewById(R.id.photo);
    photo.setImageResource(photoId);
    photo.setContentDescription(nameText);
}
cursor.close();
db.close();
```
← Close the cursor and database.

```
} catch(SQLiteException e) {
    Toast toast = Toast.makeText(this, "Database unavailable", Toast.LENGTH_SHORT);
    toast.show();
}
```
↑ If a SQLiteException is thrown, this means there's a problem with the database. In this case, we'll use a Toast to display a message to the user.

```
    }
}
```

So that's the DrinkActivity code complete. Let's see what's next.

Relax

Connecting your activities to a database takes more code than using a Java class.

But if you take your time working through the code in this chapter, you'll be fine.

What we've done so far

Now that we've finished updating the *DrinkActivity.java* code, let's look at the app structure diagram to see what we've done, and what we need to do next.

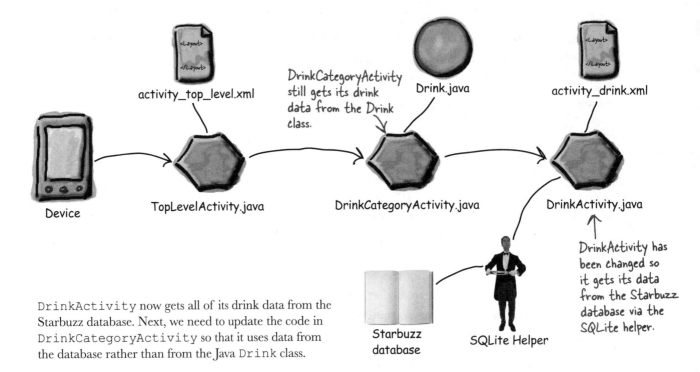

activity_top_level.xml

DrinkCategoryActivity still gets its drink data from the Drink class.

Drink.java

activity_drink.xml

Device

TopLevelActivity.java

DrinkCategoryActivity.java

DrinkActivity.java

DrinkActivity has been changed so it gets its data from the Starbuzz database via the SQLite helper.

Starbuzz database

SQLite Helper

`DrinkActivity` now gets all of its drink data from the Starbuzz database. Next, we need to update the code in `DrinkCategoryActivity` so that it uses data from the database rather than from the Java `Drink` class.

---

there are no Dumb Questions

Q: How much SQL do I need to know to create cursors?

A: It's useful to have an understanding of SQL SELECT statements, as behind the scenes the `query()` method translates to one. In general, your queries probably won't be too complex, but SQL knowledge is a useful skill.

Q: You said that if the database can't be accessed, a SQLiteException is thrown. How should I deal with it?

A: First, check the exception details. The exception might be caused by an error in SQL syntax which you can then rectify.

How you handle the exception depends on the impact it has on your app. As an example, if you can get read access to the database but can't write to it, you can still give the user read-only access to the database, but you might want to tell the user that you can't save their changes. Ultimately, it all depends on your app.

The current DrinkCategoryActivity code

Here's a reminder of what the current *DrinkCategoryActivity.java* code looks like. The onCreate() method populates a ListView with drinks using an ArrayAdapter. The onListItemClick() method adds the drink the user selects to an intent, and then starts DrinkActivity:

> ▼ ◢ ▣ 10:26
>
> | Latte | |
> | Cappuccino | *DrinkCategoryActivity* |
> | Filter | *displays a list of drinks.* |

Starbuzz

app/src/main

java

com.hfad.starbuzz

DrinkCategory Activity.java

```java
package com.hfad.starbuzz;

import android.app.ListActivity;
import android.os.Bundle;
import android.widget.ArrayAdapter;
import android.widget.ListView;
import android.view.View;
import android.content.Intent;

public class DrinkCategoryActivity extends ListActivity {

    @Override
    protected void onCreate(Bundle savedInstanceState) {
        super.onCreate(savedInstanceState);
        ListView listDrinks = getListView();
        ArrayAdapter<Drink> listAdapter = new ArrayAdapter<Drink>(
                this,
                android.R.layout.simple_list_item_1,
                Drink.drinks);
        listDrinks.setAdapter(listAdapter);
    }

    @Override
    public void onListItemClick(ListView listView,
                                View itemView,
                                int position,
                                long id) {
        Intent intent = new Intent(DrinkCategoryActivity.this, DrinkActivity.class);
        intent.putExtra(DrinkActivity.EXTRA_DRINKNO, (int)id);
        startActivity(intent);
    }

}
```

At the moment, we're using an ArrayAdapter to bind an array to the ListView. We need to replace this code so that the data comes from a database instead.

How do we replace the array data in the ListView?

The `listDrinks` list view gets its data from the `Drink.drinks` array. Now, what we *could* do is read the list of drinks from the database, and then store them in an array that we pass to the array adapter.

That would work, but can you think of a reason why that might be a bad idea?

We could just read the data from the database and store it in an array.

Then we could keep array adapter and the rest of the code would be the same. But is this a good idea?

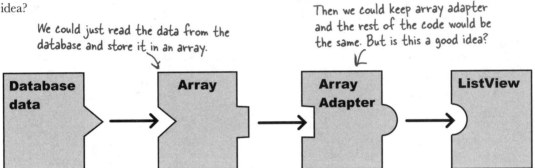

For our very small database, there's no real problem in reading all of the data from the database and storing it in an array in memory. But if you have an app that stores a very large amount of data, then it's going to take some time to read it all out of the database. It may also take a lot of memory to store it all in an array some place.

Instead, we're going to switch from using an `ArrayAdapter` to a **CursorAdapter**.

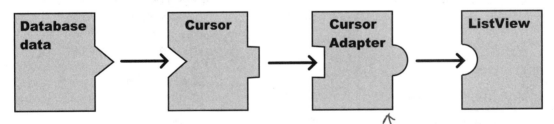

A `CursorAdapter` is just like an `ArrayAdapter`, except instead of getting its data from an array, it reads the data from a cursor.

Let's look at how it works.

Our data is in the form of a cursor, so we can use a CursorAdapter to plug it into the ListView.

A CursorAdapter reads just enough data

Let's pretend that our database is a lot larger. For example, let's say Starbuzz massively extended its range of artisan coffees for the hipster market. Instead of *three* types of coffee, the different combinations of extra shots, milk, and granola sprinkles might mean that we need to store *300* drinks in the database. But we can only see a few at a time in the list.

The `ListView` can only display a limited number of items at one time. On a small device, it might only initially show, say, the first 11 coffees. If we were using an array, we would have to read all 300 coffees from the database into the array before we could display any on the screen.

That's not how it works with a `CursorAdapter`.

 The ListView gets displayed on the screen.
When the list is first displayed, it will be sized to fit the screen. Let's say it has space to show five items.

These are the items the ListView has space to display. We're using five to keep things simple, but in practice it's likely to be more.

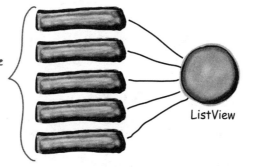

The ListView asks its adapter for the first five items.
The `ListView` doesn't know where the data is coming from—whether it's an array or a database—but it *does* know that it will be given the data by its adapter. So it makes a request to the adapter for the first five drinks.

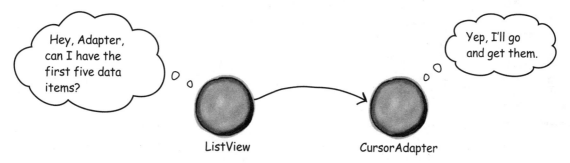

Hey, Adapter, can I have the first five data items?

Yep, I'll go and get them.

ListView   CursorAdapter

The story continues

DrinkActivity
DrinkCategoryActivity
Favorites

3 **The CursorAdapter asks its cursor to read five rows from the database.**
A `CursorAdapter` is given a cursor when it's constructed, and it will ask the cursor for data only when it needs it.

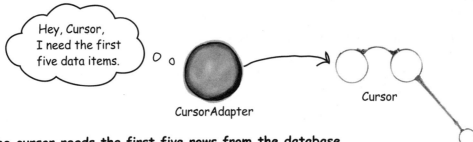

Hey, Cursor, I need the first five data items.

CursorAdapter

Cursor

4 **The cursor reads the first five rows from the database.**
Even though the database table contains 300 rows, the cursor only needs to read the first five. That's a lot more efficient, and it means that the screen can start displaying data much sooner.

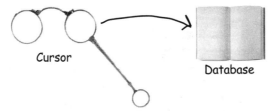

Cursor

Database

5 **The user scrolls the list.**
As the user scrolls the list, the `CursorAdapter` asks the cursor to read a few more rows from the database. If the user scrolls the list just a little, and uncovers one new item, the cursor will read one more row from the database.

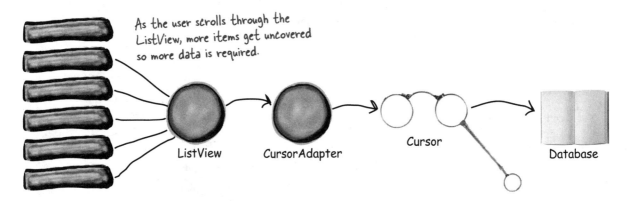

As the user scrolls through the ListView, more items get uncovered so more data is required.

ListView   CursorAdapter   Cursor   Database

So a `CursorAdapter` is a lot more efficient than the `ArrayAdapter`. It only reads the data it needs. That means it's faster and takes up less memory, and speed and memory are both important things to keep in mind.

A SimpleCursorAdapter maps data to views

We're going to create a simple cursor adapter to use with our app. A `SimpleCursorAdapter` is an implementation of `CursorAdapter` that can be used in most cases where you need to display cursor data in a list view. It takes columns from a cursor, and maps them to `TextViews` or `ImageViews`.

In our case, we want to display a list of drink names in our `DrinkCategoryActivity` list view, so we'll use a simple cursor adapter to map the name of each drink to a text view in the list view:

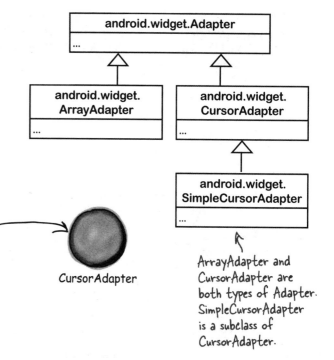

Our ListView displays each drink name in a separate TextView.

ArrayAdapter and CursorAdapter are both types of Adapter. SimpleCursorAdapter is a subclass of CursorAdapter.

First, create the cursor

The first thing to think about when creating a cursor to use with a cursor adapter is what columns the cursor needs to contain. The cursor should include all the columns that need to be displayed in the list view, along with a column called _id. The _id column must be included, or the cursor adapter won't work. So why's that?

In Chapter 11, we mentioned that it was an Android convention to give the primary key column in a table the name _id. This is so integral to Android that *the cursor adapter assumes that this column will be there*, and uses it to uniquely identify each row in the cursor. When you use a cursor adapter with a list view, the list view uses this column to identify which row the user has clicked.

As we're using a cursor adapter to display the names of the drinks, our cursor must contain the _id and NAME columns like this:

```
cursor = db.query("DRINK", new String[]{"_id", "NAME"},
            null, null, null, null, null);
```

We must include the _id column, even though we're not displaying its data.

On the next page, we'll use the cursor to create the cursor adapter.

Creating the SimpleCursorAdapter

To create a simple cursor adapter, you need to tell it how you want the data to be displayed, which cursor to use, and which columns should be mapped to which views. Here's how you'd create a simple cursor adapter to display a list of drink names:

This is the cursor from the previous page.

```
cursor = db.query("DRINK", new String[]{"_id", "NAME"},
                  null, null, null, null, null);

CursorAdapter listAdapter = new SimpleCursorAdapter(this,
                  android.R.layout.simple_list_item_1,
                  cursor,
                  new String[]{"NAME"},
                  new int[]{android.R.id.text1},
                  0);

listDrinks.setAdapter(listAdapter);
```

This is the same layout we used with the array adapter. It displays a single value for each row in the list view.

This is the cursor. →

Display the contents of the NAME column in the ListView text views.

Use setAdapter() to connect the adapter to the list view.

Just as we did with the array adapter, we're using `android.R.layout.simple_list_item_1` to tell Android that we want to display each row in the cursor as a single text view in the list view. This text view has an ID of `android.R.id.text1`.

The general form of the `SimpleCursorAdapter` constructor looks like this:

How to display the data. You can use the same layout you used with an array adapter.

```
SimpleCursorAdapter adapter = new SimpleCursorAdapter(Context context,
                                  int layout,
                                  Cursor cursor,
                                  String[] fromColumns,
                                  int[] toViews,
                                  int flags)
```

The cursor you create. The cursor should include the _id column, and the data you want to appear.

Which columns in the cursor to match to which views

Used to determine the behavior of the cursor.

The `context` and `layout` parameters are exactly the same ones you used when you created an array adapter. `context` is the current context, and `layout` says how you want to display the data. Instead of saying which array we need to get our data from, we need to specify which cursor contains the data using the cursor parameter. You then use `fromColumns` to specify which columns in the cursor you want to use, and `toViews` to say which views you want to display them in.

The `flags` parameter is generally set to 0, which is the default. The alternative is to set it to `FLAG_REGISTER_CONTENT_OBSERVER` to register a content observer that will be notified when the content changes. We're not covering this here, as it can lead to memory leaks. Later in the chapter, you'll see how to deal with the underlying data changing.

Closing the cursor and database

When we introduced you to cursors earlier in the chapter, we said that you needed to close the cursor and database after you'd finished with it in order to release their resources. In our `DrinkActivity` code, we used a cursor to retrieve drink details from the database, and once we'd used these values with our views, we immediately closed the cursor and database.

When you use a cursor adapter, it works slightly differently; the cursor adapter needs the cursor to stay open in case it needs to retrieve more data from it. This will happen if the user scrolls down the list of items in the list view, and needs to see more data.

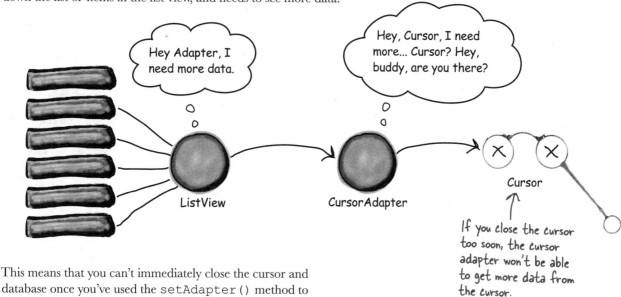

This means that you can't immediately close the cursor and database once you've used the `setAdapter()` method to connect it to your list view. Instead, you can use the activity's `onDestroy()` method to close them. As the activity's being destroyed, there's no further need for the cursor or database connection, so they can be closed:

```
public void onDestroy(){
    super.onDestroy();
    cursor.close();
    db.close();
}
```
Close the cursor and database when the activity is destroyed.

On the next page, see if you can update the code for `DrinkCategoryActivity`.

Pöōl Puzzle

Your **job** is to take code segments from the pool and place them into the blank lines in *DrinkCategoryActivity.java*. You may **not** use the same code segment more than once, and you won't need to use all the code segments. Your **goal** is to populate the ListView with a list of drinks from the database.

```
. . .
public class DrinkCategoryActivity extends ListActivity {

    private SQLiteDatabase db;
    private Cursor cursor;

    @Override
    protected void onCreate(Bundle savedInstanceState) {
        super.onCreate(savedInstanceState);
        ListView listDrinks = getListView();

        try {
            ................................. starbuzzDatabaseHelper = new StarbuzzDatabaseHelper(this);
            db = starbuzzDatabaseHelper. ................................. ;
```

Starbuzz
app/src/main
java
com.hfad.starbuzz
DrinkCategory
Activity.java

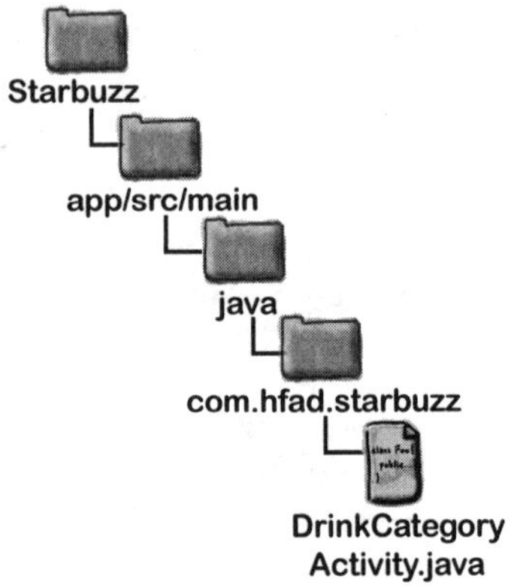

The code continues on the next page →

Note: each thing from the pool can only be used once!

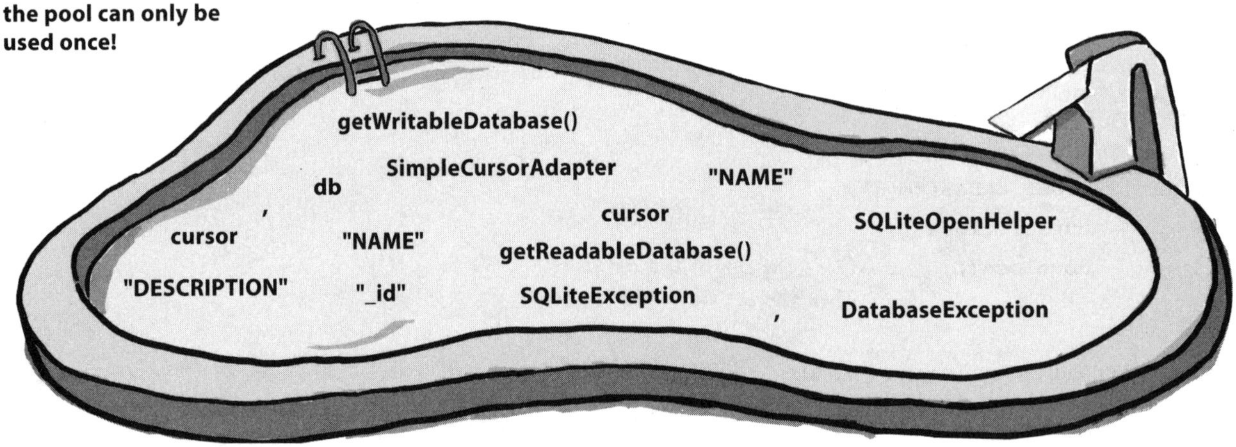

getWritableDatabase()
SimpleCursorAdapter
"NAME"
db
cursor
cursor
"NAME"
SQLiteOpenHelper
getReadableDatabase()
"DESCRIPTION"
"_id"
SQLiteException
DatabaseException
,
,

```
        cursor = db.query("DRINK",
                        new String[]{.................................................},
                        null, null, null, null, null);


        CursorAdapter listAdapter = new .........................(this,
                                    android.R.layout.simple_list_item_1,
                                    ................. ,
                                    new String[]{.................},
                                    new int[]{android.R.id.text1},
                                    0);
        listDrinks.setAdapter(listAdapter);


    } catch(.................................. e) {
        Toast toast = Toast.makeText(this, "Database unavailable", Toast.LENGTH_SHORT);
        toast.show();
    }
}


@Override
public void onDestroy(){
    super.onDestroy();
    .................close();
    .................close();
}


@Override
public void onListItemClick(ListView listView,
                            View itemView,
                            int position,
                            long id) {
    Intent intent = new Intent(DrinkCategoryActivity.this, DrinkActivity.class);
    intent.putExtra(DrinkActivity.EXTRA_DRINKNO, (int)id);
    startActivity(intent);
}
}
```

Starbuzz

app/src/main

java

com.hfad.starbuzz

DrinkCategory Activity.java

Pool Puzzle Solution

Your **job** is to take code segments from the pool and place them into the blank lines in *DrinkCategoryActivity.java*. You may **not** use the same code segment more than once, and you won't need to use all the code segments. Your **goal** is to populate the ListView with a list of drinks from the database.

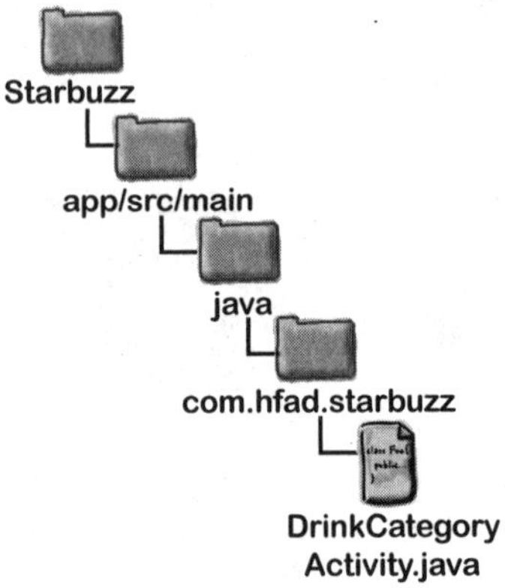

```
...
public class DrinkCategoryActivity extends ListActivity {

    private SQLiteDatabase db;
    private Cursor cursor;

    @Override
    protected void onCreate(Bundle savedInstanceState) {
        super.onCreate(savedInstanceState);
        ListView listDrinks = getListView();
```

You get a reference to the database using a SQLiteOpenHelper.

```
        try {
            SQLiteOpenHelper starbuzzDatabaseHelper = new StarbuzzDatabaseHelper(this);
            db = starbuzzDatabaseHelper. getReadableDatabase() ;
```

We're reading from the database, so we just need read-only access.

Starbuzz
app/src/main
java
com.hfad.starbuzz
DrinkCategory Activity.java

These code snippets were not needed here.

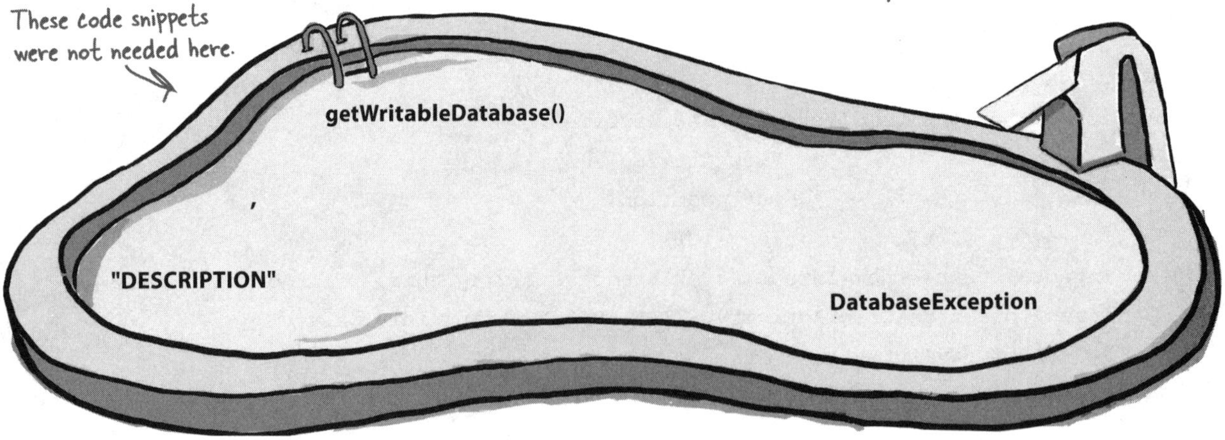

getWritableDatabase()

"DESCRIPTION"

DatabaseException

The cursor must include the _id column, or the adapter won't work. It must also include the NAME column so that we can display a list of drink names.

```java
cursor = db.query("DRINK",
                new String[]{"_id", "NAME"                    },
                null, null, null, null, null);
```

We're using a SimpleCursorAdapter.

```java
CursorAdapter listAdapter = new SimpleCursorAdapter(this,
                android.R.layout.simple_list_item_1,
```

Use the cursor we just created. →
```java
                cursor,
```
Display the contents of the NAME column.
```java
                new String[]{"NAME"},
                new int[]{android.R.id.text1},
                0);
listDrinks.setAdapter(listAdapter);
```

If the database is unavailable, we'll catch the SQLiteException.
```java
} catch( SQLiteException e) {
    Toast toast = Toast.makeText(this, "Database unavailable", Toast.LENGTH_SHORT);
    toast.show();
    }
}
```

```java
@Override
public void onDestroy(){
    super.onDestroy();
    cursor.close();    ←  Close the cursor before you
    db.close();    ←      close the database.
}
```

Starbuzz
app/src/main
java
com.hfad.starbuzz
DrinkCategory Activity.java

```java
@Override
public void onListItemClick(ListView listView,
                    View itemView,
                    int position,
                    long id) {
    Intent intent = new Intent(DrinkCategoryActivity.this, DrinkActivity.class);
    intent.putExtra(DrinkActivity.EXTRA_DRINKNO, (int)id);
    startActivity(intent);
}
}
```

The revised code for DrinkCategoryActivity

DrinkActivity
DrinkCategoryActivity
Favorites

Here's the full code for *DrinkCategoryActivity.java*, replacing the array adapter with a cursor adapter (the changes are in bold):

```
package com.hfad.starbuzz;

import android.app.ListActivity;
import android.content.Intent;
import android.os.Bundle;
import android.view.View;
import android.widget.ListView;
import android.database.Cursor;
import android.database.sqlite.SQLiteDatabase;
import android.database.sqlite.SQLiteException;
import android.database.sqlite.SQLiteOpenHelper;
import android.widget.CursorAdapter;
import android.widget.SimpleCursorAdapter;
import android.widget.Toast;
import android.widget.SimpleCursorAdapter;
```

Starbuzz

app/src/main

java

com.hfad.starbuzz

DrinkCategory
Activity.java

We're using these extra classes, so you need to import them.

```
public class DrinkCategoryActivity extends ListActivity {
    private SQLiteDatabase db;
    private Cursor cursor;
```

We're adding these as private variables so we can close the database and cursor in our onDestroy() method.

```
    @Override
    protected void onCreate(Bundle savedInstanceState) {
        super.onCreate(savedInstanceState);
        ListView listDrinks = getListView();

        try {
            SQLiteOpenHelper starbuzzDatabaseHelper = new StarbuzzDatabaseHelper(this);
            db = starbuzzDatabaseHelper.getReadableDatabase();
```

↖ Get a reference to the database.

```
            cursor = db.query("DRINK",
                        new String[]{"_id", "NAME"},
                        null, null, null, null, null);
```

Create the cursor.

The code continues on the next page.

The DrinkCategoryActivity code (continued)

Create the cursor adapter.

```
CursorAdapter listAdapter = new SimpleCursorAdapter(this,
                              android.R.layout.simple_list_item_1,
                              cursor,
                              new String[]{"NAME"},
                              new int[]{android.R.id.text1},
                              0);
    listDrinks.setAdapter(listAdapter);
} catch(SQLiteException e) {
    Toast toast = Toast.makeText(this, "Database unavailable", Toast.LENGTH_SHORT);
    toast.show();
    }
}
```

Map the contents of the NAME column to the text in the ListView. →

We're still using an adapter, but this time it's a cursor adapter.

Display a message to the user if a SQLiteException gets thrown.

```
@Override
public void onDestroy(){
    super.onDestroy();
    cursor.close();
    db.close();
}
```

← We're closing the database and cursor in the activity's onDestroy() method. The cursor will stay open until the cursor adapter no longer needs it.

Starbuzz

app/src/main

java

com.hfad.starbuzz

DrinkCategory
Activity.java

```
@Override
public void onListItemClick(ListView listView,
                            View itemView,
                            int position,
                            long id) {
    Intent intent = new Intent(DrinkCategoryActivity.this, DrinkActivity.class);
    intent.putExtra(DrinkActivity.EXTRA_DRINKNO, (int)id);
    startActivity(intent);
    }
}
```

← We didn't need to change this method.

Let's try running the app.

Test drive the app

Make the changes to the code, and then build and redeploy the app.
When you do that, you'll see that the app looks exactly the same as before.

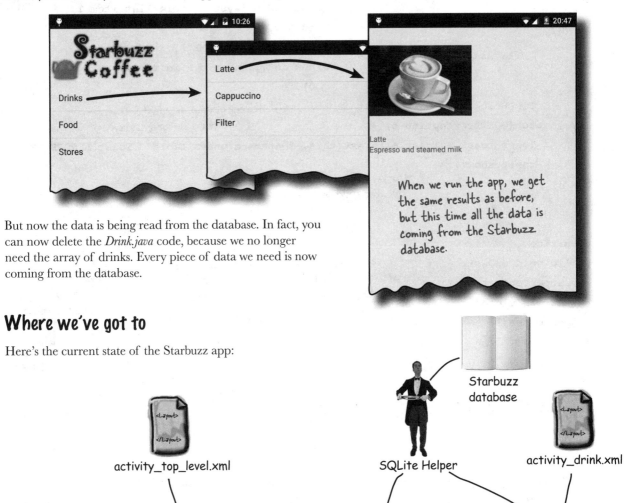

When we run the app, we get the same results as before, but this time all the data is coming from the Starbuzz database.

But now the data is being read from the database. In fact, you can now delete the *Drink.java* code, because we no longer need the array of drinks. Every piece of data we need is now coming from the database.

Where we've got to

Here's the current state of the Starbuzz app:

Starbuzz database

activity_top_level.xml

SQLite Helper

activity_drink.xml

Device

TopLevelActivity.java

DrinkCategoryActivity.java

DrinkActivity.java

We've changed the activities that access the Drink class so that they use the database instead.

There's one more change we're going to make to the app.
We're going to get the app to update data in the database.

Put important information in the top-level activity

When we first created our Starbuzz app, we designed the top-level activity to be very simple. The top-level activity is the first activity that the user sees when they launch your app, and all the Starbuzz one contains is an image and three navigation items which could be moved into a navigation drawer. It's a good idea to keep your user interface simple, but is this *too* simple?

The design of your top-level activity needs careful thought, as it's the first thing that your user sees. Ideally, it should contain content that's useful for new and existing users. One way of achieving this is to think about what your users will want to do in your app, and then give them a means of doing this from the front screen. As an example, if you were designing an app to play music, you might want to include the most recent albums the user has played in the top-level activity so that they're easy for the user to find.

We're going to change the Starbuzz top-level activity by adding the users favorite drinks to it, and allowing them to click straight through to the drink they select.

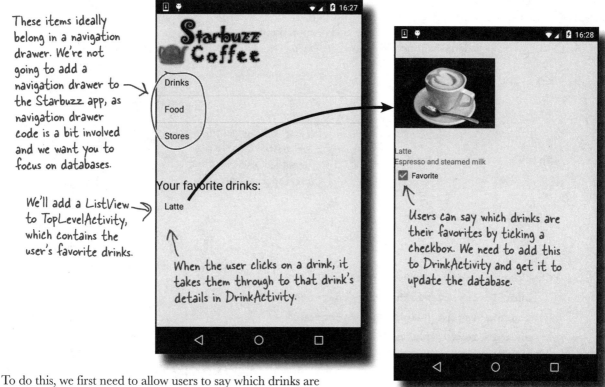

These items ideally belong in a navigation drawer. We're not going to add a navigation drawer to the Starbuzz app, as navigation drawer code is a bit involved and we want you to focus on databases.

We'll add a ListView to TopLevelActivity, which contains the user's favorite drinks.

When the user clicks on a drink, it takes them through to that drink's details in DrinkActivity.

Users can say which drinks are their favorites by ticking a checkbox. We need to add this to DrinkActivity and get it to update the database.

To do this, we first need to allow users to say which drinks are their favorites.

DrinkActivity
DrinkCategoryActivity
Favorites

Add favorites to DrinkActivity

In Chapter 11, we added a FAVORITE column to the DRINK table in the Starbuzz database. We'll use this column to let users indicate whether a particular drink is one of their favorites so that we know which drinks to display in `TopLevelActivity`. We'll let users edit drinks within `DrinkActivity`, as this activity displays details of the drink.

To do this, we need to add a new view to *activity_drink.xml* that will be used to edit and display the value of the FAVORITE column. The type of view you use in a layout depends on what type of data you need to use it for. We need a view that will allow the user to choose true/false values, so we're going to use a checkbox.

We'll add a checkbox so users can record their favorites.

First, add a String resource called `favorite` to *strings.xml* (we'll use this as a label for the checkbox):

```xml
<string name="favorite">Favorite</string>
```

Then add the checkbox to *activity_drink.xml*. We're giving it an ID of `favorite`, and using its `android:text` attribute to display its label. We're also setting its `android:onClick` attribute to "onFavoriteClicked" so that the `onFavoriteClicked()` method in `DrinkActivity` will be called when the user clicks on the checkbox.

```xml
<LinearLayout ...>
    <ImageView android:id="@+id/photo"
        ... />

    <TextView android:id="@+id/name"
        ... />

    <TextView android:id="@+id/description"
        ... />

    <CheckBox android:id="@+id/favorite"
        android:layout_width="wrap_content"
        android:layout_height="wrap_content"
        android:text="@string/favorite"
        android:onClick="onFavoriteClicked"/>
</LinearLayout>
```

These are the photo, name, and description views we added when we first created the activity.

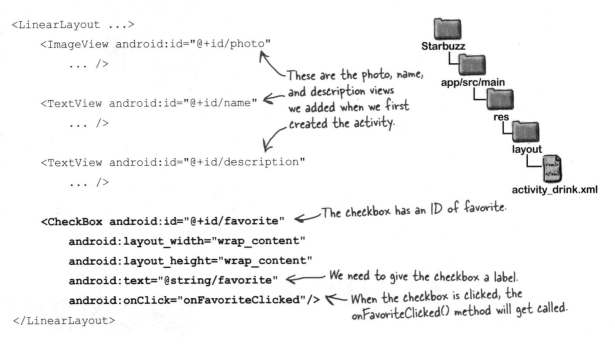

Starbuzz

app/src/main

res

layout

activity_drink.xml

The checkbox has an ID of favorite.

We need to give the checkbox a label.

When the checkbox is clicked, the onFavoriteClicked() method will get called.

Add a new column to the cursor

The next thing is to change the `DrinkActivity` code so that the favorite checkbox displays the value of the FAVORITE column that's in the database.

We can retrieve the value of the FAVORITE column in the same way that we did for the other views in the activity, by adding the FAVORITE column to our cursor. We can then retrieve the value of the FAVORITE column from the cursor, and set the value of the checkbox to that value. Here's the relevant part of the onCreate() method:

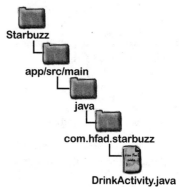

Starbuzz
app/src/main
java
com.hfad.starbuzz
DrinkActivity.java

```java
protected void onCreate(Bundle savedInstanceState) {
    ...
    SQLiteOpenHelper starbuzzDatabaseHelper = new StarbuzzDatabaseHelper(this);
    SQLiteDatabase db = starbuzzDatabaseHelper.getReadableDatabase();
    Cursor cursor = db.query ("DRINK",
                new String[] {"NAME", "DESCRIPTION", "IMAGE_RESOURCE_ID", "FAVORITE"},
                "_id = ?",
                new String[] {Integer.toString(drinkNo)},
                null, null,null);
```

Add the FAVORITE column to the cursor.

```java
    //Move to the first record in the Cursor
    if (cursor.moveToFirst()) {
        //Get the drink details from the cursor
        String nameText = cursor.getString(0);
        String descriptionText = cursor.getString(1);
        int photoId = cursor.getInt(2);
        boolean isFavorite = (cursor.getInt(3) == 1);
        ...
        //Populate the favorite checkbox
        CheckBox favorite = (CheckBox)findViewById(R.id.favorite);
        favorite.setChecked(isFavorite);
        ...
    }
}
```

Get the value of the FAVORITE column. It's stored in the database as 1 for true, 0 for false.

Set the value of the favorite checkbox.

That's enough to make sure the value of the FAVORITE column is displayed in the checkbox. Next, we need to get the checkbox to update the database when it's clicked.

DrinkActivity
DrinkCategoryActivity
Favorites

Respond to clicks to update the database

When we added the checkbox to *activity_drink.xml*, we set the android:onClick attribute to onFavoriteClicked(). This means that whenever the checkbox is clicked, the onFavoriteClicked() method in the activity will get called. We need to get this method to update the database with the current value of the checkbox. If the user checks or unchecks the checkbox, the onFavoriteClicked() method will get called and the user's change will be saved to the database.

In Chapter 11, you saw how to use SQLiteDatabase methods to change the data held in a SQLite database. You saw how to use the insert() method to insert data, the delete() method to delete data, and the update() method to update existing records.

You can use these methods to change data from within your activity. As an example, you could use the insert() method to add new drink records to the DRINK table, or the delete() method to delete them. In our case, we want to update the DRINK table's FAVORITE column with the value of the checkbox, and we can do this using the update() method.

As a reminder, the update() method takes the following form:

```
database.update(String table,
                ContentValues values,
                String whereClause,
                String[] whereArgs);
```

where table is the name of the table you want to update, and values is a ContentValues object containing name/value pairs of the columns you want to update and the values you want to set them to. The whereClause and whereArgs parameters specify which records you want to update

You already know everything you need to get DrinkActivity to update the FAVORITE column for the current drink when the checkbox is clicked, so have a go at the following exercise.

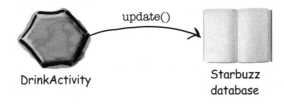

DrinkActivity   update()   Starbuzz database

Code Magnets

In our code for `DrinkActivity` we want to update the FAVORITE column in the database with the value of the favorite checkbox. Can you construct the `onFavoriteClicked()` method so that it will do that?

```java
public class DrinkActivity extends Activity {
...

    //Update the database when the checkbox is clicked

    public void onFavoriteClicked(......................){

        int drinkNo = (Integer)getIntent().getExtras().get(EXTRA_DRINKNO);
        CheckBox favorite = (CheckBox)findViewById(R.id.favorite);

        .............................. drinkValues = new ...........................;

        drinkValues.put(........................., favorite.isChecked());

        SQLiteOpenHelper starbuzzDatabaseHelper =
                              new StarbuzzDatabaseHelper(DrinkActivity.this);
        try {

            SQLiteDatabase db = starbuzzDatabaseHelper..............................;

            db.update(...................,...........................,

                                ........................., new String[] {Integer.toString(drinkNo)});
            db.close();
        } catch(SQLiteException e) {
            Toast toast = Toast.makeText(this, "Database unavailable", Toast.LENGTH_SHORT);
            toast.show();
        }
    }
}
```

`drinkValues`

`"FAVORITE"`

`View view`   `"_id = ?"`   `ContentValues`

`"DRINK"`

`ContentValues()`

`getReadableDatabase()`   `favorite`

`getWritableDatabase()`

Code Magnets Solution

DrinkActivity
DrinkCategoryActivity
Favorites

In our code for `DrinkActivity` we want to update the FAVORITE column in the database with the value of the favorite checkbox. Can you construct the `onFavoriteClicked()` method so that it will do that?

```
public class DrinkActivity extends Activity {

...

    //Update the database when the checkbox is clicked

    public void onFavoriteClicked( View view ) {

        int drinkNo = (Integer)getIntent().getExtras().get(EXTRA_DRINKNO);
        CheckBox favorite = (CheckBox)findViewById(R.id.favorite);

        ContentValues drinkValues = new ContentValues() ;

        drinkValues.put( "FAVORITE" , favorite.isChecked());

        SQLiteOpenHelper starbuzzDatabaseHelper =
                              new StarbuzzDatabaseHelper(DrinkActivity.this);
        try {

            SQLiteDatabase db = starbuzzDatabaseHelper. getWritableDatabase() ;

            db.update( "DRINK" , drinkValues ,

                      "_id = ?" , new String[] {Integer.toString(drinkNo)});
            db.close();
        } catch(SQLiteException e) {
            Toast toast = Toast.makeText(this, "Database unavailable", Toast.LENGTH_SHORT);
            toast.show();
        }
    }
}
```

We need read/write access to the database to update it.

You didn't need to use these magnets.

getReadableDatabase()

favorite

The DrinkActivity code

Here's the full code for *DrinkActivity.java* (changes are in bold):

```java
package com.hfad.starbuzz;

import android.app.Activity;
import android.os.Bundle;
import android.widget.ImageView;
import android.widget.TextView;
import android.widget.Toast;
import android.database.Cursor;
import android.database.sqlite.SQLiteDatabase;
import android.database.sqlite.SQLiteException;
import android.database.sqlite.SQLiteOpenHelper;
import android.view.View;
import android.widget.CheckBox;
import android.content.ContentValues;
```

We're using these extra classes.

```java
public class DrinkActivity extends Activity {

    public static final String EXTRA_DRINKNO = "drinkNo";

    @Override
    protected void onCreate(Bundle savedInstanceState) {
        super.onCreate(savedInstanceState);
        setContentView(R.layout.activity_drink);

        //Get the drink from the intent
        int drinkNo = (Integer)getIntent().getExtras().get(EXTRA_DRINKNO);

        //Create a cursor
        try {
            SQLiteOpenHelper starbuzzDatabaseHelper = new StarbuzzDatabaseHelper(this);
            SQLiteDatabase db = starbuzzDatabaseHelper.getWritableDatabase();
            Cursor cursor = db.query ("DRINK",
                    new String[] {"NAME", "DESCRIPTION", "IMAGE_RESOURCE_ID", "FAVORITE"},
                    "_id = ?",
                    new String[] {Integer.toString(drinkNo)},
                    null, null,null);

            //Move to the first record in the Cursor
            if (cursor.moveToFirst()) {

                //Get the drink details from the cursor
                String nameText = cursor.getString(0);
                String descriptionText = cursor.getString(1);
                int photoId = cursor.getInt(2);
                boolean isFavorite = (cursor.getInt(3) == 1);
```

You need read/write access to the database to update it.

Add the FAVORITE column to the cursor.

Get the value of the FAVORITE column.

The code continues on the next page.

The DrinkActivity code (continued)

```java
            //Populate the drink name
            TextView name = (TextView)findViewById(R.id.name);
            name.setText(nameText);

            //Populate the drink description
            TextView description = (TextView)findViewById(R.id.description);
            description.setText(descriptionText);

            //Populate the drink image
            ImageView photo = (ImageView)findViewById(R.id.photo);
            photo.setImageResource(photoId);
            photo.setContentDescription(nameText);

            //Populate the favorite checkbox
            CheckBox favorite = (CheckBox)findViewById(R.id.favorite);
            favorite.setChecked(isFavorite);
        };
        cursor.close();
        db.close();
    } catch(SQLiteException e) {
        Toast toast = Toast.makeText(this, "Database unavailable", Toast.LENGTH_SHORT);
        toast.show();
    }
}
```

Populate the checkbox.

```java
//Update the database when the checkbox is clicked
public void onFavoriteClicked(View view){
    int drinkNo = (Integer)getIntent().getExtras().get("drinkNo");
    CheckBox favorite = (CheckBox)findViewById(R.id.favorite);
    ContentValues drinkValues = new ContentValues();
    drinkValues.put("FAVORITE", favorite.isChecked());
    SQLiteOpenHelper starbuzzDatabaseHelper =
                        new StarbuzzDatabaseHelper(DrinkActivity.this);
    try {
        SQLiteDatabase db = starbuzzDatabaseHelper.getWritableDatabase();
        db.update("DRINK", drinkValues,
                        "_id = ?", new String[] {Integer.toString(drinkNo)});
        db.close();
    } catch(SQLiteException e) {
        Toast toast = Toast.makeText(this, "Database unavailable", Toast.LENGTH_SHORT);
        toast.show();
    }
}
}
```

Add the value of the favorite checkbox to the drinkValues ContentValues object.

Update the FAVORITE column to the value of the checkbox.

Display a message if there's a problem with the database.

Display favorites in TopLevelActivity

The final thing we need to do is display the user's favorite drinks in
`TopLevelActivity`.

★ **We need to add a new ListView to the layout.**
This will display a list of the user's favorite drinks.

★ **We need to populate the ListView.**
We'll populate the list with the user's favorite drinks from the database.

★ **We need to get the ListView to respond to clicks.**
If the user clicks on one of their favorite drinks, we'll display details of
the drink in `DrinkActivity`.

Applying all of these changes will enable us to display the user's
favorite drinks in `TopLevelActivity`.

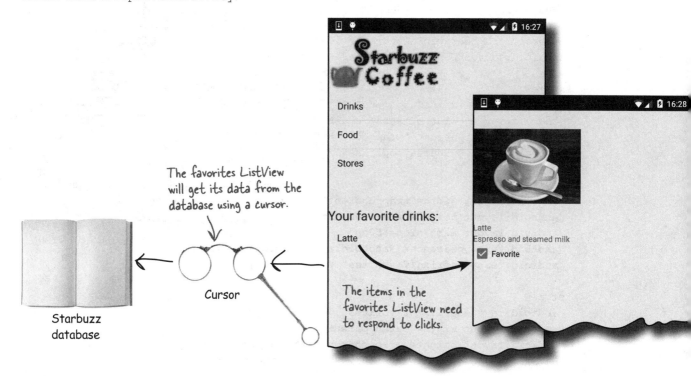

The favorites ListView
will get its data from the
database using a cursor.

Cursor

Starbuzz
database

The items in the
favorites ListView need
to respond to clicks.

Over the next few pages, we'll go through the code to do this.

Display the favorite drinks in activity_top_level.xml

DrinkActivity
DrinkCategoryActivity
Favorites

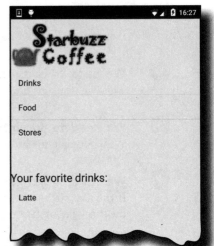

As we said on the previous page, we're going to add a list view to *activity_top_level.xml*, which we'll use to display a list of the user's favorite drinks. We'll also add a text view to display a heading for the list.

First, add the following String resource to *strings.xml* (we'll use this for the text view's text):

```xml
<string name="favorites">Your favorite drinks:</string>
```

Next, update *activity_top_level.xml* to add the text view and list view like this:

```xml
<LinearLayout ... >
    <ImageView
        android:layout_width="200dp"
        android:layout_height="100dp"
        android:src="@drawable/starbuzz_logo"
        android:contentDescription="@string/starbuzz_logo" />

    <ListView
        android:id="@+id/list_options"
        android:layout_width="match_parent"
        android:layout_height="wrap_content"
        android:entries="@array/options" />

    <TextView
        android:layout_width="wrap_content"
        android:layout_height="wrap_content"
        android:layout_marginTop="50dp"
        android:textAppearance="?android:attr/textAppearanceLarge"
        android:text="@string/favorites" />

    <ListView
        android:id="@+id/list_favorites"
        android:layout_width="match_parent"
        android:layout_height="wrap_content" />
</LinearLayout>
```

The layout already contains the Starbuzz logo and list view.

We'll add a text view to display the text "Your favorite drinks". We'll put this in a string called favorites.

The list_favorites ListView will display the user's favorite drinks.

Starbuzz
app/src/main
res
layout
activity_top_level.xml

Those are all the changes we need to make to *activity_top_level.xml*. Next, we need to update *TopLevelActivity.java*.

What changes are needed for TopLevelActivity.java

The next thing we need to do is display the users favorite drinks in the list view we just added, and get the list view to respond to clicks. To do this, we need to do the following:

 We need to create a cursor to populate the ListView.
The cursor will return all drinks where the FAVORITE column has been set to 1—all drinks that the user has flagged as being a favorite. Just as we did in our code for `DrinkCategoryActivity`, we can connect the cursor to the `ListView` using a `CursorAdapter`.

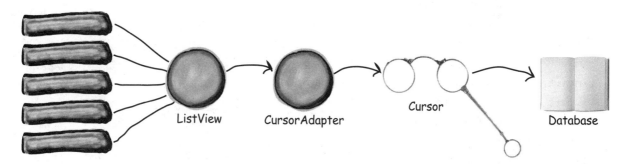

 We need to create an onItemClickListener so that the ListView can respond to clicks.
If the user clicks on one of her favorite drinks, we can create an intent that starts `DrinkActivity`, passing it the ID of the drink that was clicked. This will show the user details of the drink they've just chosen.

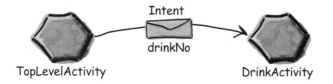

You've already seen the code you need to do this, so over the next few pages, we'll give you the full code for *TopLevelActivity. java*.

The new top-level activity code

DrinkActivity
DrinkCategoryActivity
Favorites

Here's the new code we need to add to *TopLevelActivity.java* (there's a lot of new code, so go through it carefully and take your time):

```java
package com.hfad.starbuzz;

import android.app.Activity;
import android.content.Intent;
import android.os.Bundle;
import android.widget.AdapterView;
import android.widget.ListView;
import android.view.View;
import android.database.Cursor;
import android.database.sqlite.SQLiteOpenHelper;
import android.database.sqlite.SQLiteException;
import android.database.sqlite.SQLiteDatabase;
import android.widget.SimpleCursorAdapter;
import android.widget.CursorAdapter;
import android.widget.Toast;
```

We're using all these extra classes.

Starbuzz
└ **app/src/main**
  └ **java**
    └ **com.hfad.starbuzz**
      └ **TopLevel Activity.java**

```java
public class TopLevelActivity extends Activity {

    private SQLiteDatabase db;
    private Cursor favoritesCursor;
```

We're adding these as private variables so that we have access to them in the onDestroy() method.

```java
    @Override
    protected void onCreate(Bundle savedInstanceState) {
        super.onCreate(savedInstanceState);
        setContentView(R.layout.activity_top_level);
```

The code continues on the next page.

The TopLevelActivity code (continued)

```
//Create an OnItemClickListener for the Options ListView
AdapterView.OnItemClickListener itemClickListener =
       new AdapterView.OnItemClickListener(){
           public void onItemClick(AdapterView<?> listView,
                                    View v,
                                    int position,
                                    long id) {
               if (position == 0) {
                   Intent intent = new Intent(TopLevelActivity.this,
                           DrinkCategoryActivity.class);
                   startActivity(intent);
               }
           }
       };
```

This is code we originally had in our onCreate() method. It populates the options list view and gets the list view to respond to clicks. We still need this code.

```
//Add the listener to the Options ListView
ListView listView = (ListView) findViewById(R.id.list_options);
listView.setOnItemClickListener(itemClickListener);
```

Get the favorites list view.

```
//Populate the list_favorites ListView from a cursor
ListView listFavorites = (ListView) findViewById(R.id.list_favorites);
try{
    SQLiteOpenHelper starbuzzDatabaseHelper = new StarbuzzDatabaseHelper(this);
    db = starbuzzDatabaseHelper.getReadableDatabase();
    favoritesCursor = db.query("DRINK",
        new String[] { "_id", "NAME"},
        "FAVORITE = 1",
        null, null, null, null);
```

Create a cursor that gets the values of the _id and NAME columns where FAVORITE=1.

Get the names of the user's favorite drinks.

The code continues → on the next page.

The TopLevelActivity code (continued)

```
            CursorAdapter favoriteAdapter =
                    new SimpleCursorAdapter(TopLevelActivity.this,
                            android.R.layout.simple_list_item_1,
                            favoritesCursor,
                            new String[]{"NAME"},
                            new int[]{android.R.id.text1}, 0);
            listFavorites.setAdapter(favoriteAdapter);
        } catch(SQLiteException e) {
            Toast toast = Toast.makeText(this, "Database unavailable", Toast.LENGTH_SHORT);
            toast.show();
        }

        //Navigate to DrinkActivity if a drink is clicked
        listFavorites.setOnItemClickListener(new AdapterView.OnItemClickListener() {
            @Override
            public void onItemClick(AdapterView<?> listView, View v, int position, long id)
{

                Intent intent = new Intent(TopLevelActivity.this, DrinkActivity.class);
                intent.putExtra(DrinkActivity.EXTRA_DRINKNO, (int)id);
                startActivity(intent);
            }
        });
    }

    //Close the cursor and database in the onDestroy() method
    @Override
    public void onDestroy(){
        super.onDestroy();
        favoritesCursor.close();
        db.close();
    }
}
```

Use the cursor in the cursor adapter.

Display the names of the → drinks in the ListView.

Display a message if there's a problem with the database

This will get called if an item ⤹ in the list view is clicked.

If the user clicks on one of the items in the favorites ListView, create an intent to start DrinkActivity passing along the ID of the drink.

Starbuzz
  └ app/src/main
      └ java
          └ com.hfad.starbuzz
              └ **TopLevel Activity.java**

Close the cursor and database when the activity is destroyed.

The above code populates a list view with the user's favorite drinks. When the user clicks on one of these drinks, an intent starts DrinkActivity and passes it the ID of the drink. Details of the drink are then displayed. We'll show you this running on the next page, along with a problem we need to sort out.

Test drive the app

When we open the app, the new text view
and new favorites list view are displayed in
`TopLevelActivity`, as you'd expect. No drinks
are displayed in the list view because no drinks
have been chosen as favorites yet.

The favorites ListView
is here. It isn't visible, as
there are no drinks in it

When we navigate to `DrinkActivity`, a new
checkbox is displayed. If we click on it, this flags
that the drink is a favorite.

Here's the checkbox we
added. Clicking on it
updates the Starbuzz
database.

When we go back to `TopLevelActivity`, the drink we selected as
a favorite isn't displayed in the favorites list view. It only appears if we
rotate the device.

 **BRAIN POWER**

Why do you think the drink we chose as a favorite
doesn't appear in the list view until we rotate the
screen? Think about this before turning the page.

Still no drinks. What
do you think happened?

DrinkActivity
DrinkCategoryActivity
Favorites

Cursors don't automatically refresh

If the user chooses a new favorite drink by navigating through the app to
`DrinkActivity`, the new favorite drink isn't automatically displayed in
the favorites list view in `TopLevelActivity`. This is because **cursors
retrieve data when the cursor gets created**. In our case, the cursor is
created in the activity `onCreate()` method, so it gets its data when the
activity is created. When the user navigates through the other activities,
`TopLevelActivity` is stopped, not destroyed and re-created.

When you start a second
activity, the second activity
is stacked on top of the
first. The first activity isn't
destroyed. Instead, it's paused
then stopped, as it loses the
focus and stops being visible to
the user.

Cursors don't automatically keep track of whether the underlying data in the
database has changed. If the underlying data changes after the cursor's been
created, the cursor doesn't get updated. It still contains the original records,
and none of the changes.

*If you update the data
in the database...*

*...the cursor won't
see it if the cursor's
already been created.*

_id	NAME	DESCRIPTION	IMAGE_RESOURCE_ID	FAVORITE
1	"Latte"	"Espresso and steamed milk"	54543543	1
2	"Cappuccino"	"Espresso, hot milk and	654334453	0
3	"Filter"			

_id	NAME	DESCRIPTION	IMAGE_RESOURCE_ID	FAVORITE
1	"Latte"	"Espresso and steamed milk"	54543543	0
2	"Cappuccino"	"Espresso, hot milk and steamed-milk foam"	654334453	0
3	"Filter"	"Our best drip coffee"	44324234	0

So how do we get around this?

Change the cursor with changeCursor()

The solution is to change the underlying cursor used by the favorites list view to a new version when the user returns to `TopLevelActivity`. If we do this in the activity's `onRestart()` method, the data in the ListView will get refreshed when the user returns to `TopLevelActivity`. Any new favorite drinks the user has chosen will be displayed, and any drinks that are no longer flagged as favorites will be removed from the list.

To do this, we can use the `CursorAdapter changeCursor()` method. The `changeCursor()` method replaces the cursor currently used by a cursor adapter to a new one, and closes the old cursor. Here's what the method looks like:

```java
public void changeCursor(Cursor newCursor)
```
← *This is the new cursor you want the cursor adapter to use.*

The `changeCursor()` method takes one parameter, the new cursor. Here's an example of the code in action:

```java
//Create the new cursor
StarbuzzDatabaseHelper starbuzzDatabaseHelper = new StarbuzzDatabaseHelper(this);
SQLiteDatabase db = starbuzzDatabaseHelper.getReadableDatabase();
Cursor cursor = db.query("DRINK",
                new String[] { "_id", "NAME"},
                "FAVORITE = 1",
                null, null, null, null);
```
← *You create a new cursor in exactly the same way you did before.*

```java
//Get the CursorAdapter used by the ListView
ListView listFavorites = (ListView)findViewById(R.id.list_favorites);
CursorAdapter adapter = (CursorAdapter) listFavorites.getAdapter();
```
You get the ListView's adapter using the getAdapter() method.

```java
//Change the cursor used by the CursorAdapter to the new one we just created
adapter.changeCursor(cursor);
```
← *Change the cursor used by the cursor adapter to the new one.*

We'll show you the revised code for *TopLevelActivity.java* on the next few pages.

DrinkActivity
DrinkCategoryActivity
Favorites

The revised TopLevelActivity.java code

Here's the full *TopLevelActivity.java* code (our changes are in bold):

```
package com.hfad.starbuzz;
...

public class TopLevelActivity extends Activity {
    ...
    @Override
    protected void onCreate(Bundle savedInstanceState) {
        ...
    }

    //Close the cursor and database in the onDestroy() method
    @Override
    public void onDestroy(){
        ...
    }

    public void onRestart() {
        super.onRestart();
        try{
            StarbuzzDatabaseHelper starbuzzDatabaseHelper = new StarbuzzDatabaseHelper(this);
            db = starbuzzDatabaseHelper.getReadableDatabase();
            Cursor newCursor = db.query("DRINK",
                    new String[] { "_id", "NAME"},
                    "FAVORITE = 1",
                    null, null, null, null);
            ListView listFavorites = (ListView)findViewById(R.id.list_favorites);
            CursorAdapter adapter = (CursorAdapter) listFavorites.getAdapter();
            adapter.changeCursor(newCursor);
            favoritesCursor = newCursor;
        } catch(SQLiteException e) {
            Toast toast = Toast.makeText(this, "Database unavailable", Toast.LENGTH_SHORT);
            toast.show();
        }
    }
}
```

These methods haven't changed.

This gets called when the user returns to TopLevelActivity.

You create a new cursor in exactly the same way you did before.

Change the cursor used by the cursor adapter to the new one.

Get the list view's adapter.

Display a message if there's a problem with the database.

Starbuzz

app/src/main

java

com.hfad.starbuzz

**TopLevel
Activity.java**

That's all the code we need for our top-level activity. Let's take it for a spin and see how it works.

Test drive the app

This time when we flag a drink as being a favorite, it appears in
`TopLevelActivity`. When we click on the drink, the app shows
us the details of that drink.

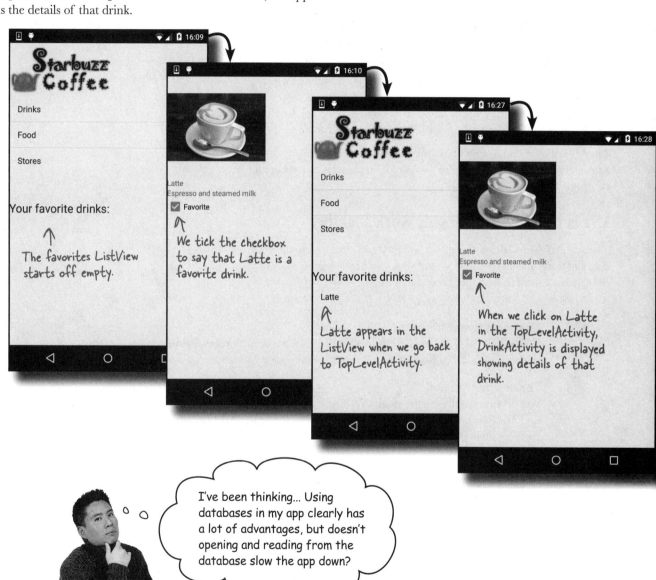

The favorites ListView starts off empty.

We tick the checkbox to say that Latte is a favorite drink.

Latte appears in the ListView when we go back to TopLevelActivity.

When we click on Latte in the TopLevelActivity, DrinkActivity is displayed showing details of that drink.

> I've been thinking... Using
> databases in my app clearly has
> a lot of advantages, but doesn't
> opening and reading from the
> database slow the app down?

Databases are powerful, but they can be slow.

That means that even though our app works, we need to keep
an eye on performance...

Databases can make your app go in sloooo-moooo....

Think about what your app has to do when it opens a database. It first needs to go searching through the flash to find the database file. If the database file isn't there, it needs to go create a blank database. Then it needs to run all of the SQL commands to create tables inside the database and any initial data it needs. Finally, it needs to fire off some queries to get the data out of there.

That takes time. For a tiny database like the one used in the Starbuzz app, it's not a lot of time. But as a database gets bigger and bigger, that time will increase and increase. Before you know it, your app will lose its mojo and will be slower than YouTube on Thanksgiving.

There's not a lot you can do about the speed of creating and reading from a database, but there *is* a lot you can do to prevent it slowing up your interface.

Life is better when threads work together

The big problem with accessing a slow database is that can make your app feel unresponsive. To understand why, you need to think about how threads work in Android. Since Lollipop, there are three kinds of threads you need to think about:

⭐ **The main event thread**
This is the real workhorse in Android. It listens for intents, it receives touch messages from the screen, and it calls all of the methods inside your activities.

⭐ **The render thread**
You don't normally interact with this thread, but it reads a list of requests for screen updates and then calls the low-level graphics hardware to repaint the screen and make your app look pretty.

⭐ **All of the other thread that you create**

If you're not careful, your app will do almost all of its work on the main event thread. Why? Because it's the main event thread that runs your event methods. If you just drop your database code into the `onCreate()` method (as we did in the Starbuzz app) then the main event thread will be busy talking to the database, instead of rushing off to look for any events from the screen or other apps. If your database code takes a long time, users will feel like they're being ignored.

So the trick is to **move your database code off the main event thread and run it in a custom thread in the background**.

 Sharpen your pencil

We're going to run the DrinkActivity database code in a background thread, but before we rush off and start hacking code, let's take a moment to think about what we need to do.

The code that we have at the moment does three different things. Which thread do you think each block of code should run on? Choose the type of thread you think each should run on.

A **Set up the interface.**

```
super.onCreate(savedInstanceState);
setContentView(R.layout.activity_drink);
int drinkNo = (Integer)getIntent().getExtras().get(EXTRA_DRINKNO);
```

Main event thread	A background thread

← Choose whether you think each block of code should be run on the main event thread or a background thread.

B **Talk to the database.**

```
SQLiteOpenHelper starbuzzDatabaseHelper = new StarbuzzDatabaseHelper(this);
SQLiteDatabase db = starbuzzDatabaseHelper.getReadableDatabase();
Cursor cursor = db.query ("Drink",...
```

Main event thread	A background thread

C **Update the views with the database data.**

```
name.setText(...);
description.setText(...);
photo.setImageResource(...);
```

Main event thread	A background thread

Sharpen your pencil
Solution

We're going to run the `DrinkActivity` database code in a background thread, but before we rush off and start hacking code, let's take a moment to think about what we need to do.

The code that we have at the moment does three different things. Which thread do you think each block of code should run on? Choose the type of thread you think each should run on.

A ## Set up the interface.

```
super.onCreate(savedInstanceState);
setContentView(R.layout.activity_drink);
int drinkNo = (Integer)getIntent().getExtras().get(EXTRA_DRINKNO);
```

Main event thread	A background thread
✓	

We always create the user interface on the main thread.

B ## Talk to the database.

```
SQLiteOpenHelper starbuzzDatabaseHelper = new StarbuzzDatabaseHelper(this);
SQLiteDatabase db = starbuzzDatabaseHelper.getReadableDatabase();
Cursor cursor = db.query ("Drink",...
```

Main event thread	A background thread
	✓

We want to run the database code in the background because it's slow.

C ## Update the views with the database data.

```
name.setText(...);
description.setText(...);
photo.setImageResource(...);
```

← We **must** to run the code to update the views on the main thread, otherwise we get an exception.

Main event thread	A background thread
✓	

What code goes on which thread?

When you use databases in your app, it's a good idea to run database code in a background thread, and update views with the database data in the main event thread. We're going to work through the `onFavoritesClicked()` method in the `DrinkActivity` code so that you can see how to approach this sort of problem.

Here's the code for the method (we've split it into sections, which we'll describe below):

```
//Update the database when the checkbox is clicked
public void onFavoriteClicked(View view){
```

1
```
    int drinkNo = (Integer)getIntent().getExtras().get(EXTRA_DRINKNO);
    CheckBox favorite = (CheckBox)findViewById(R.id.favorite);
    ContentValues drinkValues = new ContentValues();
    drinkValues.put("FAVORITE", favorite.isChecked());
```

2
```
    SQLiteOpenHelper starbuzzDatabaseHelper =
                        new StarbuzzDatabaseHelper(DrinkActivity.this);
    try {
        SQLiteDatabase db = starbuzzDatabaseHelper.getWritableDatabase();
        db.update("DRINK", drinkValues,
                        "_id = ?", new String[] {Integer.toString(drinkNo)});
        db.close();
    } catch(SQLiteException e) {
```

3
```
        Toast toast = Toast.makeText(this, "Database unavailable", Toast.LENGTH_SHORT);
        toast.show();
    }
}
```

1 **Code that needs to be run before the database code**
The first few lines of code gets the value of the favorite checkbox, and puts it in the `drinkValues ContentValues` object. This code must be run before the database code.

2 **Database code that needs to be run on a background thread**
This updates the DRINK table.

3 **Code that needs to be run after the database code**
If the database is unavailable, we want to display a message to the user. This must run on the main event thread.

We're going to implement the code using an **AsyncTask**. So what's that, anyway?

AsyncTask performs asynchronous tasks

The AsyncTask class lets you perform operations in the background. When they've finished running, it then allows you to update views in the main event thread. If the task is repetitive, you can even use it to publish the progress of the task while it's running.

You create an AsyncTask by extending the AsyncTask class, and implementing its doInBackground() method. The code in this method runs in a background thread, so it's the perfect place for you to put database code. The AsyncTask class also has an onPreExecute() method that runs before doInBackground(), and an onPostExecute() method that runs afterward. There's an onProgressUpdate() method if you need to publish task progress.

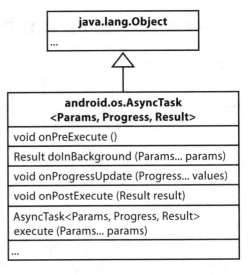

Here's what it looks like:

```java
private class MyAsyncTask extends AsyncTask<Params, Progress, Result>

    protected void onPreExecute() {
        //Code to run before executing the task
    }

    protected Result doInBackground(Params... params) {
        //Code that you want to run in a background thread
    }

    protected void onProgressUpdate(Progress... values) {
        //Code that you want to run to publish the progress of your task
    }

    protected void onPostExecute(Result result) {
        //Code that you want to run when the task is complete
    }
}
```

AsyncTask is defined by three generic parameters: Params, Progress, and Results. Params is the type of object used to pass any task parameters to the doInBackground() method, Progress is the type of object used to indicate task progress, and Result is the type of the task result. You can set any of these to Void if you're not going to use them.

We'll go through this over the next few pages by creating a new AsyncTask called UpdateDrinkTask we can use to update drinks in the background. Later on, we'll add this to our DrinkActivity code.

The onPreExecute() method

We'll start with the onPreExecute() method. This gets called
before the background task begins, and it's used to set up the
task. It's called on the main event thread, so it has access to views
in the user interface. The onPreExecute() method takes no
parameters, and has a void return type.

We're going to use the onPreExecute() method to get the
value of the favorite checkbox, and put it in the drinkValues
ContentValues object. This is because we need access to the
checkbox in order to do this, and it must be done before any of our
database code can be run. We're using a separate attribute outside
the method for the drinkValues ContentValues object so
that other methods in the class can access it.

Here's the code:

```
private class UpdateDrinkTask extends AsyncTask<Params, Progress, Result> {

    ContentValues drinkValues;

    protected void onPreExecute() {
        CheckBox favorite = (CheckBox)findViewById(R.id.favorite);
        drinkValues = new ContentValues();
        drinkValues.put("FAVORITE", favorite.isChecked());
    }

    ...

}
```

*Before we run the database code, we need
to get the value of the favorite checkbox.*

Next, we'll look at the doInBackground() method.

The doInBackground() method

The doInBackground() method runs in the background immediately after onPreExecute(). You define what type of parameters the task should receive, and what the return type should be.

We're going to use the doInBackground() method for our database code so that it runs in a background thread. We'll pass it the ID of the drink we need to update, and we'll use a Boolean return value, so we can tell whether the code ran successfully:

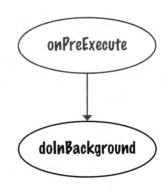

```
private class UpdateDrinkTask extends AsyncTask<Integer, Progress, Boolean> {

    ContentValues drinkValues;
```

You change this to Integer to match the parameter of the doInBackground() method.

You change this to Boolean to match the return type of the doInBackground() method.

```
    ...

    protected Boolean doInBackground(Integer... drinks) {
        int drinkNo = drinks[0];
        SQLiteOpenHelper starbuzzDatabaseHelper =
                            new StarbuzzDatabaseHelper(DrinkActivity.this);
        try {
            SQLiteDatabase db = starbuzzDatabaseHelper.getWritableDatabase();
            db.update("DRINK", drinkValues,
                        "_id = ?", new String[] {Integer.toString(drinkNo)});
            db.close();
            return true;
        } catch (SQLiteException e) {
            return false;
        }
    }

    ...

}
```

This code runs in a background thread.

This is an array of Integers, but we'll just include one item, the drink ID.

The update() method uses the drinkValues object that the onPreExecute() method created.

Next, we'll look at the onProgressUpdate() method.

The onProgressUpdate() method

The onProgressUpdate() method is called on the main event thread, so has access to views in the user interface. You can use this method to display progress to the user by updating views on the screen. You define what type of parameters the method should have.

The onProgressUpdate() method runs if a call to publishProgress() is made by the doInBackground() method like this:

```
protected Boolean doInBackground(Integer... count) {
    for (int i = 0; i < count; i++) {
        publishProgress(i);    This calls the onProgressUpdate()
    }                          method, passing in a value of i.
}

protected void onProgressUpdate(Integer... progress) {
    setProgress(progress[0]);
}
```

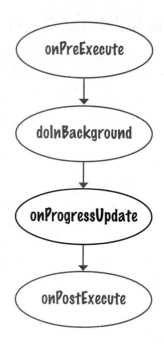

We're not publishing the progress of our task, so we don't need to implement this method. We'll indicate that we're not using any objects for task progress by changing the signature of UpdateDrinkTask:

We're not using the onProgressUpdate() method, so this is Void.

```
private class UpdateDrinkTask extends AsyncTask<Integer, Void, Boolean> {

    ...

}
```

Finally, we'll look at the onPostExecute() method.

The onPostExecute() method

The onPreExecute() method is called after the background task has finished. It's called on the main event thread, so has access to views in the user interface. You can use this method to present the results of the task to the user. The onPostExecute() method gets passed the results of the doInBackground() method, so must take parameters that match the doInBackground() return type.

We're going to use the onPostExecute() method to check whether the database code in the doInBackground() method ran successfully. If it didn't, we'll display a message to the user. We're doing this in the onPostExecute() method as this method can update the user interface; the doInBackground() method runs in a background thread, so can't update views.

Here's the code:

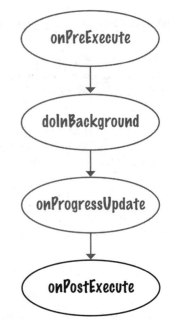

```java
private class UpdateDrinkTask extends AsyncTask<Integer, Void, Boolean> {
```

This is Boolean, as our doInBackground()
method returns a Boolean.

```java
    ...

    protected void onPostExecute(Boolean success) {
        if (!success) {
            Toast toast = Toast.makeText(DrinkActivity.this,
                          "Database unavailable", Toast.LENGTH_SHORT);
            toast.show();
        }
    }
}
```

Pass the Toast the
DrinkActivity context.

The AsyncTask class

When we first introduced the AsyncTask class, we said it was defined by three generic parameters: Params, Progress, and Results. You specify what these are by looking at the type of parameters used by your doInBackground(), onProgressUpdate(), and onPostExecute() methods. Params is the type of the doInBackground() parameters, Progress is the type of the onProgressUpdate() parameters, and Result is the type of the onPostExecute() method:

```
private class MyAsyncTask extends AsyncTask<Params, Progress, Result>

    protected void onPreExecute() {
        //Code to run before executing the task
    }

    protected Result doInBackground(Params... params) {
        //Code that you want to run in a background thread
    }

    protected void onProgressUpdate(Progress... values) {
        //Code that you want to run to publish the progress of your task
    }

    protected void onPostExecute(Result result) {
        //Code that you wan to run when the task is complete
    }
}
```

In our example, doInBackground() takes Integer parameters, and onPostExecute() takes a Boolean parameter. We're not using the onProgressUpdate() method. This means that in our example, Params is Integer, Progress is Void and Result is Boolean:

```
private class UpdateDrinkTask extends AsyncTask<Integer, Void, Boolean> {
    ...
    protected Boolean doInBackground(Integer... drinks) {
        ...
    }

    protected void onPostExecute(Boolean... success) {
        ...
    }
}
```

You now know everything you need to create a task—let's see how you run it.

Execute the AsyncTask

You run the task by calling your `AsyncTask`'s `execute()` method. If your `doInBackground()` method takes parameters, you add these to the `execute()` method. As an example, we want to pass the drink the user chose to the `AsyncTask`'s `doInBackground()` method, so we call it using:

```
int drinkNo = (Integer)getIntent().getExtras().get(EXTRA_DRINKNO);
new UpdateDrinkTask().execute(drinkNo);
```

The type of parameter you pass with the `execute()` method must match the type of parameter expected by the `AsyncTask doInBackground()` method. Our `doInBackground()` method takes `Integer` parameters, so we need to pass integers:

```
protected Boolean doInBackground(Integer... drinks) {
    ...
}
```

We're going to execute `UpdateDrinkTask` in `DrinkActivity`'s `onFavoritesClicked()` method. Here's what the method looks like:

```
//Update the database when the checkbox is clicked
public void onFavoriteClicked(View view){
    int drinkNo = (Integer)getIntent().getExtras().get(EXTRA_DRINKNO);
    CheckBox favorite = (CheckBox)findViewById(R.id.favorite);
    ContentValues drinkValues = new ContentValues();
    drinkValues.put("FAVORITE", favorite.isChecked());
    SQLiteOpenHelper starbuzzDatabaseHelper =
                        new StarbuzzDatabaseHelper(DrinkActivity.this);
    try {
        SQLiteDatabase db = starbuzzDatabaseHelper.getWritableDatabase();
        db.update("DRINK", drinkValues, "_id = ?", new String[] {Integer.toString(drinkNo)});
        db.close();
    } catch(SQLiteException e) {
        Toast toast = Toast.makeText(this, "Database unavailable", Toast.LENGTH_SHORT);
        toast.show();
    }

    new UpdateDrinkTask().execute(drinkNo);
}
```

All of this code is replaced by our AsyncTask.

Execute the AsyncTask and pass it the drink ID.

We'll show you the new *DrinkActivity.java* code on the next page.

The DrinkActivity.java code

When you create an `AsyncTask`, you add it as an inner class to the activity that needs to use it. We're going to add our `UpdateDrinkTask` class as an inner class to *DrinkActivity.java*. We'll execute the task in `DrinkActivity`'s `onFavoriteClicked()` method so that the task updates the database in the background when the user clicks on the favorite checkbox.

Here's the code:

```
package com.hfad.starbuzz;

...

import android.os.AsyncTask;  ← Import the AsyncTask class.

public class DrinkActivity extends Activity {

... ← We don't need to change the onCreate() method, so we've left it out.

    //Update the database when the checkbox is clicked
    public void onFavoriteClicked(View view){
        int drinkNo = (Integer)getIntent().getExtras().get(EXTRA_DRINKNO);
        new UpdateDrinkTask().execute(drinkNo);  ← Execute the task.
    }

    //Inner class to update the drink.        Add the AsyncTask to the activity as an inner class.
    private class UpdateDrinkTask extends AsyncTask<Integer, Void, Boolean> {
        ContentValues drinkValues;

                                              Before the database code runs, put the value of the
        protected void onPreExecute() {       checkbox in the drinkValues ContentValues object.
            CheckBox favorite = (CheckBox)findViewById(R.id.favorite);
            drinkValues = new ContentValues();
            drinkValues.put("FAVORITE", favorite.isChecked());
        }
```

The code continues →
on the next page.

The DrinkActivity.java code (continued)

Run the database code in a background thread.

```java
protected Boolean doInBackground(Integer... drinks) {
    int drinkNo = drinks[0];
    SQLiteOpenHelper starbuzzDatabaseHelper =
                        new StarbuzzDatabaseHelper(DrinkActivity.this);
    try {
        SQLiteDatabase db = starbuzzDatabaseHelper.getWritableDatabase();
        db.update("DRINK", drinkValues,
                        "_id = ?", new String[] {Integer.toString(drinkNo)});
        db.close();
        return true;
    } catch (SQLiteException e) {
        return false;
    }
}
```

Update the value of the FAVORITE column.

Starbuzz

app/src/main

java

com.hfad.starbuzz

DrinkActivity.java

```java
protected void onPostExecute(Boolean success) {
    if (!success) {
        Toast toast = Toast.makeText(DrinkActivity.this,
                        "Database unavailable", Toast.LENGTH_SHORT);
        toast.show();
    }
}
```

If the database code didn't run OK, display a message to the user.

That's everything you need in order to create an `AsyncTask`. When the user clicks on the favorite checkbox in `DrinkActivity`, the database gets updated in the background.

In an ideal world, all of your database code should run in the background. We're not going to change our other Starbuzz activities to do this, but why not have a go yourself?

A summary of the AsyncTask steps

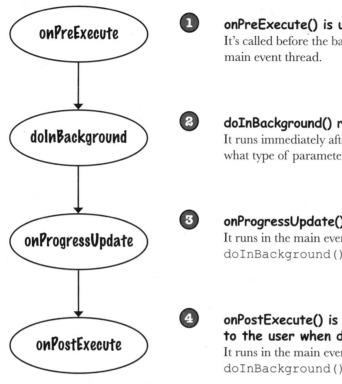

1 **onPreExecute() is used to set up the task.**
It's called before the background task begins, and runs on the main event thread.

2 **doInBackground() runs in the background thread.**
It runs immediately after onPreExecute(). You can specify what type of parameters it has, and what its return type is.

3 **onProgressUpdate() is used to display progress.**
It runs in the main event thread when the doInBackground() method calls publishProgress().

4 **onPostExecute() is used to display the task outcome to the user when doInBackground has finsihed.**
It runs in the main event thread. It takes the return value of doInBackground() as a parameter.

there are no Dumb Questions

Q: I've written code before that just ran the database code and it was fine. Do I really need to run it in the background?

A: For really small databases, like the one in the Starbuzz app, you probably won't notice the time it takes to access the database. But that's just because the database is small. If you use a larger database, or if you run an app on a slower device, the time it takes to access the database will be significant. So yes, you should *always* run database code in the background.

Q: Remind me - why is it bad to update a view from the background thread?

A: The short answer is that it will throw an exception if you try. The longer answer is that multi-threaded user interfaces are hugely buggy. Android avoided the problem by simply banning them.

Q: Which part of the database code is slowest? Opening the database, or reading data from it?

A: There's no general way of knowing. If your database has a complex data structure, then the first time you open the database will take a long time because it will need to create all the tables. If you're running a complex query, that might take a very long time. In general, play it safe and run everything in the background.

Q: If it take a few seconds to read data from the database, what will the user see?

A: The user will see blank views until the database code sets the values.

Q: Why have you put the database code for just one activity in an AsyncTask?

A: We wanted to show you how to use AsyncTasks in one activity as an example. In the real world, you should do this for the database code in all your activities.

Your Android Toolbox

You've got Chapter 12 under your belt and now you've added connecting your app to SQLite databases to your toolbox.

> You can download the full code for the chapter from https://tinyurl.com/HeadFirstAndroid.

BULLET POINTS

- A `Cursor` lets you read from and write to the database.

- You create a cursor by calling the `SQLiteDatabase query()` method. Behind the scenes, this builds a SQL SELECT statement.

- The `getWritableDatabase()` method returns a `SQLiteDatabase` object that allows you to read from and write to the database.

- The `getReadableDatabase()` returns a `SQLiteDatabase` object. This gives you read-only access to the database. It may also allow you to read from and write to the database, but this isn't guaranteed.

- Navigate through a cursor using the `moveTo*()` methods.

- Get values from a cursor using the `get*()` methods.

- Close cursors and database connections after you've finished with them.

- A `CursorAdapter` is an adapter that works with cursors. Use `SimpleCursorAdapter` to populate a `ListView` with the values returned by a cursor.

- Design your app so that you put useful content in your top-level activity.

- The `CursorAdapter changeCursor()` method replaces the cursor currently used by a cursor adapter to a new cursor that you provide. It then closes the old cursor.

- Run your database code in a background thread using `AsyncTask`.

13 services

At Your Service

Did I mention I run a ProtectionRacketService?

There are some operations you want to keep on running, irrespective of which app has the focus.

As an example, If you start playing a music file in a music app, you'd probably expect it to keep on playing when you switch to another app. In this chapter, you'll see how to use **services** to deal with situations just like this. Along the way, you'll see how to use some of **Android's built-in services**. You'll see how to to keep your users informed with the **notification service**, and how the **location service** can tell you where you're located.

Services work behind the scenes

An Android app is a collection of activities and other components. The bulk of your code is there to interact with the user, but sometimes you need to do things in the background. You might want to download a large file, stream a piece of music, or listen for a message from the server.

These kinds of tasks aren't what activities are designed to do. In simple cases, you can create a thread, but if you're not careful your activity code will start to get complex and unreadable.

That's why **services** were invented. A service is an application component like an activity but without a user interface. They have a simpler lifecycle than an activity, and they come with a bunch of features that make it easy to write code that will run in the background while the user is doing something else.

There are two types of service

Services come in two different flavors:

 **Started services**

A started service can run in the background indefinitely, even when the activity that started it is destroyed. If you wanted to download a large file from the Internet, you would probably create it as a started service. Once the operation is done, the service stops.

Bound services

A bound service is bound to another component such as an activity. The activity can interact with it, send requests, and get results. A bound service runs as long as components are bound to it. When components are no longer bound to it, the service is destroyed. If you wanted to create an odometer to measure the distance traveled by a vehicle, you'd probably use a bound service. This way, any activities bound to the service could keep asking the service for updates on the distance traveled.

In this chapter, we're going to create two services: a started service and a bound service. We'll start with the started service.

The started service app

We're going to create a new project that contains an
activity called `MainActivity`, and a service called
`DelayedMessageService`. Whenever `MainActivity` calls
`DelayedMessageService`, it will wait for 10 seconds and then
display a piece of text.

← MainActivity will use this layout.

activity_main.xml

The activity will pass → text to the service.

MainActivity.java

1...2..3...4...5...6...7 ...8...9...10... Here's the text.

The service will ← display the text after 10 seconds.

DelayedMessageService.java

We're going to do this in three stages:

1 **Display the message in the log.**
We'll start by displaying the message in the log so that we can check
the service works OK. We can look at the log in Android Studio.

2 **Display the message in a Toast.**
We'll get the message to appear in a pop-up toast so that you don't
have to keep your device connected to Android Studio in order to
see it working.

3 **Display the message in a Notification.**
We'll get `DelayedMessageService` to use Android's built-in
notification service to display the message in a notification. This will
mean that the user will be able to look at the message at a later time.

Create the project

We'll start by creating the project. Create a new Android project for
an application named "Joke" with a package name of `com.hfad.`
`joke`. The minimum SDK should be API 16 so that it will work
with most devices. You'll need a blank activity called "MainActivity"
and a layout called "activity_main" so that your code matches ours.

The next thing we need to do is create the service.

We're going to create an IntentService

You create a new service by extending either the `Service` class or the `IntentService` class.

The `Service` class is the base class for creating services. It provides you with basic service functionality, and you'll usually extend this class if you want to create a bound service.

The `IntentService` class is a subclass of `Service` that's designed to handle intents. You'll usually extend this class if you want to create a started service.

As we're creating a started service, we're going to add a new intent service to the project. To do this, go to File→New... and select the Service option. When prompted, choose the option to create a new `IntentService`. Give the service a name of `DelayedMessageService`, and untick the option to include helper start method. This is because we're going to replace the code that Android Studio generates for us.

You implement an intent service by extending the `IntentService` class and implementing its `onHandleIntent()` method. This method should contain the code you want to run when the service is called:

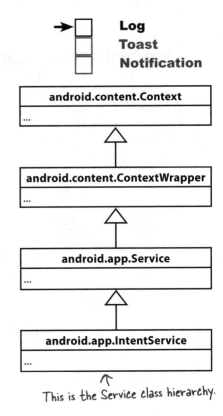

This is the Service class hierarchy.

```java
package com.hfad.joke;

import android.app.IntentService;
import android.content.Intent;
```

Extend the IntentService class.

```java
public class DelayedMessageService extends IntentService {

    public DelayedMessageService() {
        super("DelayedMessageService");
    }

    @Override
    protected void onHandleIntent(Intent intent) {
        //Code to do something
    }
}
```

Put the code you want the service to run in the onHandleIntent() method.

Joke
app/src/main
java
com.hfad.joke
DelayedMessage
Service.java

We'll show you an overview of this on the next page.

The IntentService from 50,000 feet

We're using an `IntentService` to create a started service, so lets's take a look at how they work.

1 **An activity says what service it needs to call by creating an explicit intent.**
The intent specifies the service it's intended for.

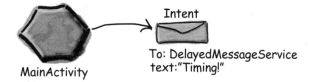

MainActivity → Intent — To: DelayedMessageService text:"Timing!"

2 **The intent is passed to the service.**

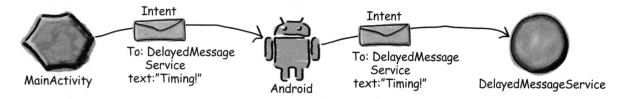

MainActivity → Intent — To: DelayedMessage Service text:"Timing!" → Android → Intent — To: DelayedMessage Service text:"Timing!" → DelayedMessageService

3 **The service starts and handles the intent.**
The `IntentService onHandleIntent()` method gets called and runs in a separate thread. If the service is passed multiple intents, it deals with them in sequence, one at a time. Once the service has finished running, it stops.

> Aha, some text. I know how to handle that. 1...2...3...4...

DelayedMessageService

As you can see, a service is started in the same way that you start an activity: by creating an intent. The difference is that when you start a service, what's on screen doesn't change because the service has no user interface.

We want `DelayedMessageService` to display a message in Android's log. Before we update the service, let's look at how you log messages.

Log
Toast
Notification

How to log messages

Adding messages to a log can be a useful way of checking your code is working the way you want. You tell Android what to log in your Java code, and when the app's running, you check the output in Android's log, or logcat.

You log messages using one of the following methods in the `Android.util.Log` class:

Log.v(String tag, String message)	Logs a verbose message.
Log.d(String tag, String message)	Logs a debug message.
Log.i(String tag, String message)	Logs an information message.
Log.w(String tag, String message)	Logs a warning message.
Log.e(String tag, String message)	Logs an error message.

Each message is composed of a `String` tag you use to identify the source of the message, and the message itself. As an example, to log a verbose message that's come from `DelayedMessageService`, you use the `Log.v()` method like this:

```
Log.v("DelayedMessageService", "This is a message");
```

You can view the logcat in Android Studio, and filter by the different types of message. To see the logcat, select the Android option at the bottom of your project screen in Android Studio and then select the Devices|logcat tab:

> There's also a Log.wtf() method you can use to report exceptions that should never happen. According to the Android documentation, wtf means "What a Terrible Failure". We know it means "Welcome to Fiskidagurinn", which refers to the Great Fish Day festival held annually in Dalvik, Iceland. Android Developers can often be heard to say "My AVD just took 8 minutes to boot up. WTF??" as a tribute to the small town that gave its name to the standard Android executable bytecode format.

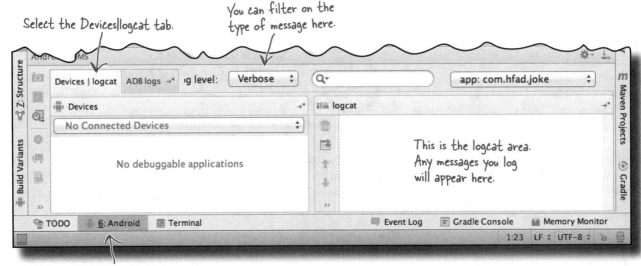

Select the Devices|logcat tab.

You can filter on the type of message here.

This is the logcat area. Any messages you log will appear here.

Select the Android option.

The full DelayedMessageService code

We want our service to get a piece of text from an intent, wait for 10 seconds, then display the piece of text in the log. To do this, we'll create a `showText()` method to log the text, and then call it from the `onHandleIntent()` method after a delay.

Here's the full code for *DelayedMessageService.java* (replace the code Android Studio has created for you with this code):

```java
package com.hfad.joke;

import android.app.IntentService;
import android.content.Intent;
import android.util.Log;
```

Extend the IntentService class.

```java
public class DelayedMessageService extends IntentService {

    public static final String EXTRA_MESSAGE = "message";
```

Use a constant to pass a message from the activity to the service.

```java
    public DelayedMessageService() {
        super("DelayedMessageService");
    }
```

Call the super constructor.

This method contains the code you want to run when the service receives an intent.

```java
    @Override
    protected void onHandleIntent(Intent intent) {
        synchronized (this) {
            try {
                wait(10000);
            } catch (InterruptedException e) {
                e.printStackTrace();
            }
        }
        String text = intent.getStringExtra(EXTRA_MESSAGE);
        showText(text);
    }
```

Wait 10 seconds.

Get the text from the intent

Call the showText() method.

```java
    private void showText(final String text) {
        Log.v("DelayedMessageService", "The message is: " + text);
    }
}
```

This logs a piece of text so we can see it in the logcat through Android Studio.

Joke

app/src/main

java

com.hfad.joke

DelayedMessage
Service.java

Log
Toast
Notification

You declare services in AndroidManifest.xml

Just like activities, services need to be declared in *AndroidManifest.xml* using the `<service>` element. This is so that Android can call the service; if a service isn't declared in *AndroidManifest.xml*, Android can't call it.

Android Studio declares the service in *AndroidManifest.xml* for you automatically when you create a new service. Here's what the code looks like:

```xml
<?xml version="1.0" encoding="utf-8"?>
<manifest xmlns:android="http://schemas.android.com/apk/res/android"
    package="com.hfad.joke" >
    <application
        ... >

        <activity
            ...
        </activity>

        <service
            android:name=".DelayedMessageService"
            android:exported="false" >
        </service>
    </application>
</manifest>
```

You declare a service in AndroidManifest.xml like this. Android Studio should do this for you automatically.

Joke

app/src/main

AndroidManifest.xml

The service name has a . in front of it so that Android can combine it with the package name to derive the fully qualified class name.

The `<service>` element contains two attributes.

The `android:name` attribute tells Android what the name of the service is—in our case, `DelayedMessageService`.

The `android:exported` attribute tells Android whether the service can be used by other apps. Setting it to `false` means that the service will only be used within the current app.

Now that we have a service, we need to run it by getting an activity to call it.

Add a button to activity_main.xml

We're going to get `MainActivity` to start
`DelayedMessageService` whenever a button is clicked.
We'll start by adding the button to `MainActivity`'s layout.

First, add the following values to *strings.xml* (we'll use them in
our activity and layout code):

```
<string name="button_response">Timing!</string>
<string name="button_text">What is the secret of comedy?</string>
```

← We're using both these strings in the app.

Next, update *activity_main.xml* so that `MainActivity`
displays a button:

```
<RelativeLayout xmlns:android="http://schemas.android.com/apk/res/android"
    xmlns:tools="http://schemas.android.com/tools"
    android:layout_width="match_parent"
    android:layout_height="match_parent"
    tools:context=".MainActivity">

    <Button
        android:layout_width="wrap_content"
        android:layout_height="wrap_content"
        android:text="@string/button_text"
        android:id="@+id/button"
        android:onClick="onClick"
        android:layout_alignParentTop="true"
        android:layout_centerHorizontal="true" />
</RelativeLayout>
```

This creates a button. When it's clicked, the onClick() method in the activity will get called.

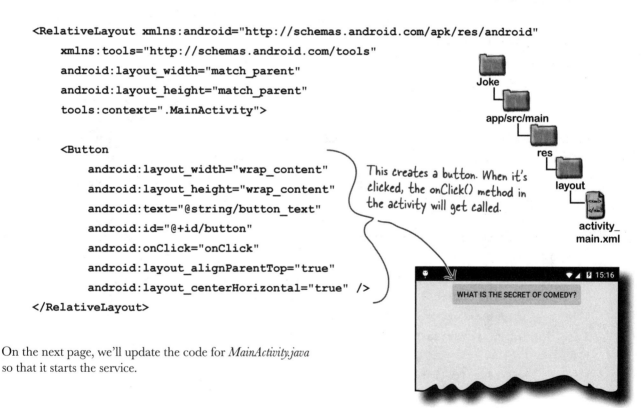

On the next page, we'll update the code for *MainActivity.java*
so that it starts the service.

Log
Toast
Notification

You start a service using startService()

You start a service from an activity in a similar way to how you start another activity. You create an explicit intent that's directed at the service you want to start. You then start the service using the startService() method:

```
Intent intent = new Intent(this, DelayedMessageService.class);
startService(intent);
```

Starting a service is just like starting an activity, except you use startService() instead of startActivity().

We'll use this in MainActivity's onClick() method so that the service gets started whenever its button gets clicked. Here's the code:

```
package com.hfad.joke;

import android.app.Activity;
import android.content.Intent;
import android.os.Bundle;
import android.view.View;


public class MainActivity extends Activity {

    @Override
    protected void onCreate(Bundle savedInstanceState) {
        super.onCreate(savedInstanceState);
        setContentView(R.layout.activity_main);
    }

    public void onClick(View view) {
        Intent intent = new Intent(this, DelayedMessageService.class);
        intent.putExtra(DelayedMessageService.EXTRA_MESSAGE,
                        getResources().getString(R.string.button_response));
        startService(intent);
    }
}
```

We're using these classes.

This will run when the button gets clicked.

Create the intent.

Add text to the intent.

Start the service.

Joke
app/src/main
java
com.hfad.joke
DelayedMessage
Service.java

That's all the code we need to get our activity to start the service. Let's see what happens when we run the app.

Test drive the app

When you run the app, `MainActivity` is displayed. It contains a single button:

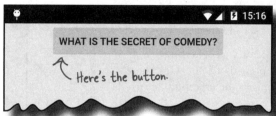

WHAT IS THE SECRET OF COMEDY?

Here's the button.

Press the button, switch back to Android Studio, and watch the logcat output in the lower-right corner of the IDE. After 10 seconds, the word "Timing!" appears in the logcat.

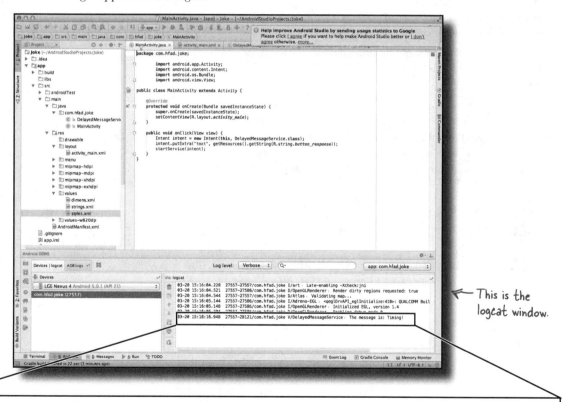

This is the logcat window.

```
03-20 15:18:16.948  27557-28121/com.hfad.joke V/DelayedMessageService: The message is: Timing!
```

Now that we know the service works, let's make it display a message on the screen so you don't have to keep your device plugged into your computer to see it running.

After a 10-second delay, the message is displayed in the log.

We want to send a message to the screen

Services don't have user interfaces like activities do, but that doesn't mean that they don't need to keep the user informed about stuff that's happening. The user might need to know when a file has been downloaded, for instance.

In our case, it would be a lot neater if we could display a message in a toast on the screen instead of in the log. There's just one thing—any code that updates the user interface needs to run in the main thread

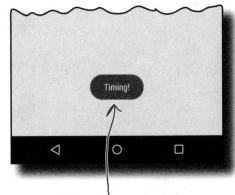

We'll get the service to display a message in a toast.

Screen updates require the main thread

As you've seen, when you use an intent service, you put the code you want to run in the onHandleIntent() method. This code then runs in the background in a separate thread. This is great for code that you want to run in the background, but not so great if you want to update the user interface. This is because you can only update the user interface in the main thread.

To get around this, we'll use a handler. As we said back in Chapter 4, a handler lets you post code that needs to be run to a separate thread. We can use the handler post() method to post the code to create a toast to the main thread. The code will then run on the main thread and the toast will get displayed correctly.

To get the code working, we need to do the following:

⭐ Create a handler in the main thread.

⭐ Use the Handler post() method in the service onHandleIntent() method to display a toast.

The first thing we need to look at is how to create a handler in the main thread.

onStartCommand() runs on the main thread

To create a handler on the main thread, we need to create a `Handler` object in a method that runs on the main thread. We can't use the `onHandleIntent()` method, as this runs in a background thread. Instead, we'll use the `onStartCommand()` method.

The `onStartCommand()` method gets called every time the intent service is started. The `onStartCommand()` method runs on the main thread, and runs before the `onHandleIntent()` method. If we create a handler in the `onStartCommand()` method, we'll be able to use it to post code to the main thread in the `onHandleIntent()` method:

```
...
public class DelayedMessageService extends IntentService {

    private Handler handler;    ← Add the handler as a private variable so
                                   different methods can access it.
    ...

                        This method runs on the main thread, so it
                        creates a new handler on the main thread.
    @Override          ↙
    public int onStartCommand(Intent intent, int flags, int startId) {
        handler = new Handler();
        return super.onStartCommand(intent, flags, startId);
    }
                        ↑
            Call the IntentService onStartCommand() method.
    @Override
    protected void onHandleIntent(Intent intent) {
        //Use the handler to post code to the main thread
    }
    ...

}
```

When you use the `onStartCommand()`, you must call its super implementation using:

```
super.onStartCommand(intent, flags, startId)
```

This is so that the intent service can properly handle the life of its background thread.

On the next page, we'll show you the full code for *DelayedMessageService.java* and then look at it running.

Joke
└ app/src/main
  └ java
    └ com.hfad.joke
      └ DelayedMessage
        Service.java

The full DelayedMessageService.java code

Log
Toast
Notification

```java
package com.hfad.joke;

import android.app.IntentService;
import android.content.Intent;
import android.os.Handler;
import android.widget.Toast;
```

← *We're using these extra classes.*

```java
public class DelayedMessageService extends IntentService {

    public static final String EXTRA_MESSAGE = "message";
    private Handler handler;
```

← *Add the handler as a new private variable.*

```java
    public DelayedMessageService() {
        super("DelayedMessageService");
    }
```

Create the handler on the main thread.
↓

```java
    @Override
    public int onStartCommand(Intent intent, int flags, int startId) {
        handler = new Handler();
        return super.onStartCommand(intent, flags, startId);
    }
```

We're not changing this method.
↙

```java
    @Override
    protected void onHandleIntent(Intent intent) {
        synchronized (this) {
            try {
                wait(10000);
            } catch (InterruptedException e) {
                e.printStackTrace();
            }
        }
        String text = intent.getStringExtra(EXTRA_MESSAGE);
        showText(text);
    }
```

```java
    private void showText(final String text) {
        handler.post(new Runnable() {
```

← *Post the Toast code to the main thread using the handler.*

```java
            @Override
            public void run() {
                Toast.makeText(getApplicationContext(), text, Toast.LENGTH_LONG).show();
            }
        });
    }
}
```

↑
This is the context you want to display the toast in.
There's more about this on the next page.

Joke
app/src/main
java
com.hfad.joke
DelayedMessage
Service.java

The application context

Let's take a closer look at the line of code that displays the toast:

```
Toast.makeText(getApplicationContext(), text, Toast.LENGTH_LONG).show();
```

The first parameter of the `Toast.makeText()` method is the context in which you want the toast to appear. When you create a toast in an activity, you use `this` to pass it the instance of the current activity.

This doesn't work in a service, because the service context doesn't have access to the screen. Whenever you need a context in a service in situations like this, you must use `getApplicationContext()` instead. This gives us the context for whatever app happens to be in the foreground when the code is run. It means that the service will be able to make a toast appear, even if we've switched to a different app.

Test drive the app

Let's try running our app again.

When you click on the button in `MainActivity`, a toast appears after 10 seconds. The toast appears irrespective of which app has the focus.

If you click on the button multiple times in quick succession, multiple toasts appear about 10 seconds apart. The service deals with each intent it receives, one at a time.

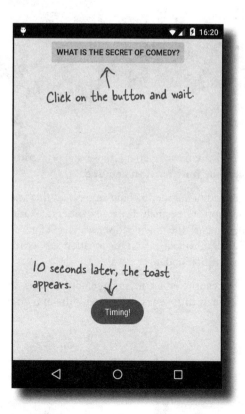

Can we improve on using Toasts?

We now know how to send a piece of text to the screen using a toast. That's useful if we want to tell the user that, say, the very long download of a file has completed. But the truth is toasts don't really stand out that much, and if you're not looking at the screen at exactly the right moment, you don't even see them. If we really want to keep the user informed about important stuff, we need to replace our toast with a **notification**.

Notifications are messages that appear in a list at the top of the screen. If the user doesn't happen to see the notification at the time it was created, it doesn't matter. She can still see them by dragging her finger down from the top of the screen to open the navigation drawer.

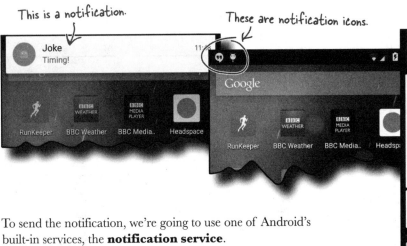

This is a notification.

These are notification icons.

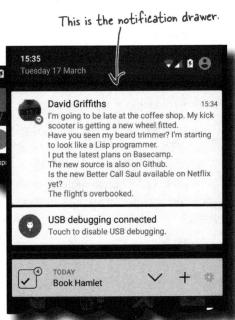

This is the notification drawer.

To send the notification, we're going to use one of Android's built-in services, the **notification service**.

Android comes with a number of built-in services that you can use in your app. These include the alarm service (used for controlling alarms), the download service (used for requesting HTTP downloads), and the location service (used for controlling location updates).

You use the notification service to manage notifications. We'll give you an overview of how it will fit in with the app on the next page.

How you use the notification service

Here's an overview of how our app will work with the Android notification service:

1 **MainActivity starts DelayedMessageService by passing it an intent.**

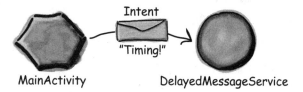

2 **DelayedMessageService creates a new Notification object.**
The Notification object contains details of how the notification should be configured, such as its text, title, and icon.

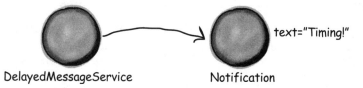

3 **DelayedMessageService creates a NotificationManager object to access Android's notification service.**
DelayedMessageService passes the Notification object to the NotificationManager, and the notification gets displayed.

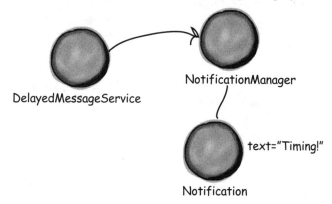

We'll start by creating the notification.

You create notifications using a notification builder

You create a notification using a notification builder to create a new `Notification` object. The notification builder allows you to create a notification with a specific set of features, without writing too much code. Each notification must include a small icon, a title, and some text.

Here's an example of the code you use to create a notification. It displays a high priority notification that vibrates when the notification appears and disappears once it's clicked:

```
Notification notification =  new Notification.Builder(this)
    .setSmallIcon(R.mipmap.ic_launcher)
    .setContentTitle(getString(R.string.app_name))
    .setContentText(text)
    .setAutoCancel(true)
    .setPriority(Notification.PRIORITY_MAX)
    .setDefaults(Notification.DEFAULT_VIBRATE)
    .build();
```

This displays a small notification icon—in this case, the mipmap called ic_launcher.

Set the title and text.

Make the notification disappear when clicked.

Give it a maximum priority and set it to vibrate to get a large "heads up" notification.

These are just some of the properties that you can set. You can also set things like visibility to control whether the notification will appear on the lock-screen, a number to display a count next to the notification in case you want to send many notifications from the same app, and a sound to make the notification make a noise. You can find out more about these properties here:

https://developer.android.com/reference/android/app/ Notification.Builder.html

It's also a good idea to say which activity should be displayed when the user clicks on the notification. In our case, for instance, we can get Android to display `MainActivity` when the notification is clicked. We'll show you how to do this on the next page.

Watch it!

Some of the notification properties require API level 16 or above.

If you need to support older devices, you won't be able to use all of the properties.

Getting your notification to start an activity

You get a notification to start an activity when it's clicked using a **pending intent**. A pending intent is an intent an app can pass to other applications so that they can submit the intent on your app's behalf at a later time.

Here are the steps you go through to create the pending intent:

1. Create an explicit intent

First, you create a simple explicit intent directed to the activity you want to start when the notification is clicked. In our case, we'll start `MainActivity`:

This is a normal intent that starts MainActivity.

```
Intent intent = new Intent(this, MainActivity.class);
```

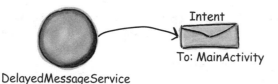

DelayedMessageService

Intent
To: MainActivity

2. Pass the intent to the TaskStackBuilder

Next, we use a `TaskStackBuilder` to make sure that the back button will play nicely when the activity gets started. The `TaskStackBuilder` allows you to access the history of activities used by the back button. We need to get the back stack related to the activity, and then add the intent we just created to it:

Create a TaskStackBuilder.

```
TaskStackBuilder stackBuilder = TaskStackBuilder.create(this);
stackBuilder.addParentStack(MainActivity.class);
stackBuilder.addNextIntent(intent);
```

These lines make the back button work properly when the activity is started.

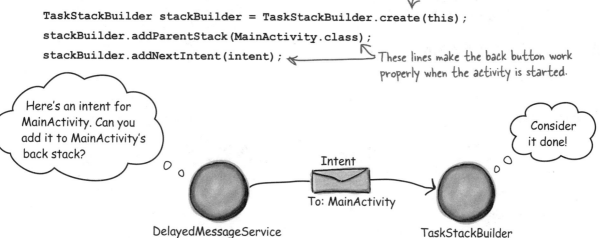

Here's an intent for MainActivity. Can you add it to MainActivity's back stack?

Consider it done!

DelayedMessageService

Intent
To: MainActivity

TaskStackBuilder

The story continues on the next page.

3. Get the pending intent from the TaskStackBuilder

Next, we get the pending intent from the `TaskStackBuilder` using its `getPendingIntent()` method. The `getPendingIntent()` method takes two `int` parameters, a request code that can be used to identify the intent, and a flag that specifies the pending intent's behavior.

Here are the different flag options:

`FLAG_CANCEL_CURRENT`	If a matching pending intent already exists, cancel it before generating a new one.
`FLAG_NO_CREATE`	If a matching pending intent doesn't already exist, don't create one and return null.
`FLAG_ONE_SHOT`	The pending intent can only be used once.
`FLAG_UPDATE_CURRENT`	If a matching pending intent already exists, keep it and replace its extra data with the contents of the new intent.

In our case, we'll use FLAG_UPDATE_CURRENT to modify any existing pending intent. Here's the code:

```
PendingIntent pendingIntent =
        stackBuilder.getPendingIntent(0, PendingIntent.FLAG_UPDATE_CURRENT);
```

This creates the pending intent.

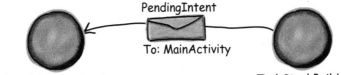

4. Add the intent to the notification

Finally, you add the pending intent to the notification using the `setContentIntent()` method:

```
notification.setContentIntent(pendingIntent);
```
Add the pending intent to the notification so that MainActivity starts when it's clicked.

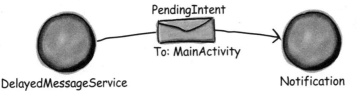

Once you've given the notification a pending intent telling it which activity to start when it's clicked, all that's left is to display it.

Send the notification using the notification service

So far we've looked at how to create and configure a notification. The next thing is to pass it to the Android notification service so that it appears on the device.

You access Android's built-in services using the `getSystemService()` method. It takes one argument, the name of the service you want to use.

In our case, we want to use the notification service, so we use code like this:

This is an ID we'll use for the notification.

```
public static final int NOTIFICATION_ID = 5453;
...

NotificationManager notificationManager =
            (NotificationManager) getSystemService(Context.NOTIFICATION_SERVICE);
notificationManager.notify(NOTIFICATION_ID, notification);
```

This is how you access Android's notification service.

Use the notification service to display the notification we created.

The `NOTIFICATION_ID` is used to identify the notification. If we send another notification with the same ID, it will replace the current notification. This is useful if you want to update an existing notification with new information.

The notification service deals will all of the issues involved in a background service sending updates to the screen. This means that you no longer need to use a handler in order to update the user interface; the notification service handles it for you.

On the next page, we'll show you the updated code for `DelayedMessageService`.

there are no Dumb Questions

Q: Why do I need to include an icon in a notification?

A: The notification system needs an icon to display the notification at the very top of the screen.

Q: What happens if I don't set the priority and switch vibrate on?

A: The notification will still be sent, but it won't pop up on your screen. You'll still see it listed in the navigation drawer.

The full code for DelayedMessageService.java

Log
Toast
Notification

Here's the full code for *DelayedMessageService.java*. It now uses a notification instead of a toast to display a message:

```java
package com.hfad.joke;

import android.app.IntentService;
import android.app.Notification;
import android.app.NotificationManager;
import android.app.PendingIntent;
import android.app.TaskStackBuilder;
import android.content.Context;
import android.content.Intent;
import android.os.Handler;
import android.widget.Toast;

public class DelayedMessageService extends IntentService {

    public static final String EXTRA_MESSAGE = "message";
    private Handler handler;
    public static final int NOTIFICATION_ID = 5453;

    public DelayedMessageService() {
        super("DelayedMessageService");
    }

    @Override
    protected void onHandleIntent(Intent intent) {
        synchronized (this) {
            try {
                wait(10000);
            } catch (InterruptedException e) {
                e.printStackTrace();
            }
        }
        String text = intent.getStringExtra(EXTRA_MESSAGE);
        showText(text);
    }
```

We're using these extra classes.

We're no longer displaying a Toast, so we don't need these imports.

We no longer need a Handler.

This is used to identify the notification. It could be any number, we just decided on 5453.

We're not changing this method.

The DelayedMessageService.java code (continued)

```
@Override
public int onStartCommand(Intent intent, int flags, int startId) {
    handler = new Handler();
    return super.onStartCommand(intent, flags, startId);
}
```

We're no longer using a Handler, so we don't need this method.

```
private void showText(final String text) {
    handler.post(new Runnable() {
        @Override
        public void run() {
            Toast.makeText(getApplicationContext(), text, Toast.LENGTH_LONG).show();
        }
    });
```

We're no longer displaying the message using a Toast.

```
        Intent intent = new Intent(this, MainActivity.class);
        TaskStackBuilder stackBuilder = TaskStackBuilder.create(this);
        stackBuilder.addParentStack(MainActivity.class);
        stackBuilder.addNextIntent(intent);
        PendingIntent pendingIntent =
                stackBuilder.getPendingIntent(0, PendingIntent.FLAG_UPDATE_CURRENT
                );
        Notification notification = new Notification.Builder(this)
                .setSmallIcon(R.mipmap.ic_launcher)
                .setContentTitle(getString(R.string.app_name))
                .setAutoCancel(true)
                .setPriority(Notification.PRIORITY_MAX)
                .setDefaults(Notification.DEFAULT_VIBRATE)
                .setContentIntent(pendingIntent)
                .setContentText(text)
                .build();
        NotificationManager notificationManager =
                (NotificationManager) getSystemService(Context.NOTIFICATION_SERVICE);
        notificationManager.notify(NOTIFICATION_ID, notification);
    }
}
```

Create an intent.

Use a TaskStackBuilder to make the back button play nicely and create the pending intent.

Build the notification.

Display the notification using the Android notification service.

That's all the code we need for our started service. Let's go through what happens when the code runs.

What happens when you run the code

Before you see the app up and running, let's go through what
happens when the code runs:

1 **MainActivity starts DelayedMessageService by passing it an intent.**
The intent contains the message `MainActivity` wants
`DelayedMessageService` to display.

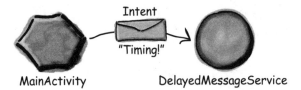

2 **DelayedMessageService waits for 10 seconds.**

3 **DelayedMessageService creates an intent for MainActivity.**

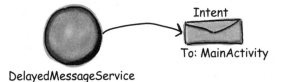

4 **DelayedMessageService creates a TaskStackBuilder and asks it to
add the intent to MainActivity's back stack.**

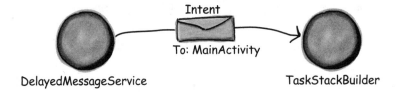

The story continues

5 The TaskStackBuilder use the intent to create a pending intent and passes it to DelayedMessageService.

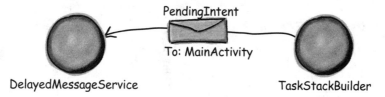

PendingIntent
To: MainActivity

DelayedMessageService   TaskStackBuilder

6 DelayedMessageService creates a Notification object, sets details of how it should be configured, and passes it the pending intent.

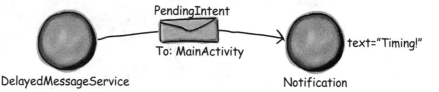

PendingIntent
To: MainActivity

text="Timing!"

DelayedMessageService   Notification

7 DelayedMessageService creates a NotificationManager object to access Android's notification service and passes it the Notification.
The notification service displays the notification.

PendingIntent
To: MainActivity
text="Timing!"

DelayedMessageService   NotificationManager   Notification

8 When the user clicks on the Notification, the Notification uses its pending intent to start MainActivity.

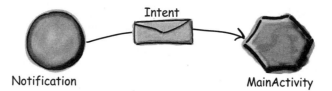

Intent

Notification   MainActivity

Let's take the app for a test drive.

Test drive the app

When you click on the button in `MainActivity`, a
notification is displayed after 10 seconds. You'll receive the
notification irrespective of which app you're in.

Click on the button.

After a delay, the notification appears. On older devices, you might need to open the notification drawer to see it.

When you click on the notification, Android returns you to
`MainActivity`.

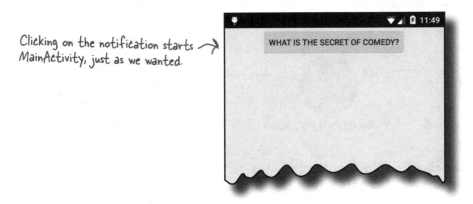

Clicking on the notification starts MainActivity, just as we wanted.

So far you've seen how to create a started service that displays
a notification using the Android notification service. After an
exercise, we'll look at how you create a bound service.

Service Magnets

Below you'll see most of the code needed to create a started service
called WombleService that plays a *.mp3* file in the background,
and an activity that uses it. See if you can finish off the code.
← This is the service.

```java
public class WombleService extends ................................ {

    public WombleService() {
        super("WombleService");
    }


    @Override
    protected void ..................................... (Intent intent) {
        MediaPlayer mediaPlayer =
                    MediaPlayer.create(getApplicationContext(), R.raw.wombling_song);
        mediaPlayer.start();
    }
}
```

*This uses the Android MediaPlayer class to play a file called
wombling_song.mp3. The file is located in the res/raw folder.*

```java
public class MainActivity extends Activity {
```
← This is the activity.

```java

    @Override
    protected void onCreate(Bundle savedInstanceState) {
        super.onCreate(savedInstanceState);
        setContentView(R.layout.activity_main);
    }


    public void onClick(View view) {
        Intent intent = new Intent(this, ...............................................);

        ............................... (intent);
    }
}
```

`onHandleIntent`

`startActivity`

`WombleService.class`   `IntentService`   `startService`   `WombleService`

Service Magnets Solution

Below you'll see most of the code needed to create a started service called `WombleService` that plays a *.mp3* file in the background, and an activity that uses it. See if you can finish off the code.

> ← This is the service. It extends the IntentService class.

```java
public class WombleService extends  IntentService  {

    public WombleService() {
        super("WombleService");
    }
```

> The code needs to run in the onHandleIntent() method.

```java
    @Override
    protected void  onHandleIntent  (Intent intent) {
        MediaPlayer mediaPlayer =
                MediaPlayer.create(getApplicationContext(), R.raw.wombling_song);
        mediaPlayer.start();
    }
}
```

> ← This is the activity.

```java
public class MainActivity extends Activity {

    @Override
    protected void onCreate(Bundle savedInstanceState) {
        super.onCreate(savedInstanceState);
        setContentView(R.layout.activity_main);
    }
```

> Create an explicit intent directed at WombleService.class.

```java
    public void onClick(View view) {
        Intent intent = new Intent(this, WombleService.class );

        startService (intent);
    }
}
```

> ↑ Start the service.

> You didn't need to use these magnets.

`startActivity`

`WombleService`

Bound services are more interactive

As we said earlier, a started service runs in the background indefinitely, even when the activity that started it is destroyed. Once the operation is done, the service stops itself.

A **bound service** is bound to another component such as an activity. The activity can interact with it, send requests, and get results. To see this in action, we're going to create a new app that uses a bound service that will work like an odometer to track the distance traveled by a vehicle.

How the odometer app will work

We're going to create a new project with an activity called MainActivity, and a service called OdometerService. MainActivity will use OdometerService to get the distance traveled.

1 **MainActivity binds to OdometerService.**
MainActivity uses the OdometerService getMiles() method to ask for the number of miles traveled.

2 **The OdometerService uses the Android location services to keep track of when the device moves.**
It uses these locations to calculate how far the device has traveled.

3 **The OdometerService returns the distance traveled to MainActivity.**
MainActivity displays the distance traveled to the user.

This is built-in to Android. Our OdometerService will use it to listen for changes in location.

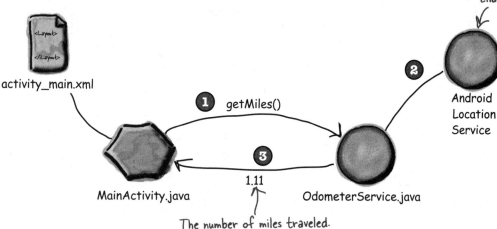

activity_main.xml

1 getMiles()

3

1.11

MainActivity.java   OdometerService.java

Android Location Service

The number of miles traveled.

We'll start by creating the service. Let's see what we need to do.

The steps needed to create the OdometerService

Binder
Location
getMiles()

There are a few steps we need to go through in order to
create the OdometerService:

1 **Define an OdometerBinder.**

A Binder object allows activities to bind to services. We'll define a
subclass of Binder called OdometerBinder that will enable our
activity to connect to the OdometerService.

OdometerBinder

2 **Create a LocationListener and register it with Android's
location service.**

This will allow the OdometerService to listen for changes in the
device location and work out the distance traveled in meters.

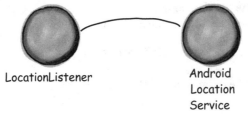

LocationListener

Android
Location
Service

2 **Create a public getMiles() method.**

The activity will be able to use this to get the number of miles traveled.

getMiles()

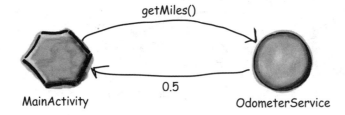

MainActivity

0.5

OdometerService

We'll start by creating a new project for our Odometer app.

Create a new Odometer project

Create a new Android project for an application named "Odometer" with a package name of `com.hfad.odometer`. The minimum SDK should be API 16 so that it will work with most devices. You'll need a blank activity called "MainActivity" and a layout called "activity_main" so that your code matches ours.

We're going to add a new service to the project. This time we're going to use a service that extends the `Service` class and not the `IntentService` class. This is because the `IntentService` class is intended for services that handle intents, as we did in the previous example. In this case, we're going to start the service by binding to it so there's no advantage in using the `IntentService` class.

You add a service that extends the `Service` class in a similar way to how we added a service earlier. Go to File→New... and select the Service option. When prompted, choose the option to create a new Service (not an IntentService), and give the service a name of "OdometerService". Untick the "exported" option as this only needs to be true if you want services outside this app to access the service. Make sure that the "enabled" option is ticked; if it isn't, the activity won't be able to run the app.

Here's what the code looks like to create a bound service based on the `Service` class:

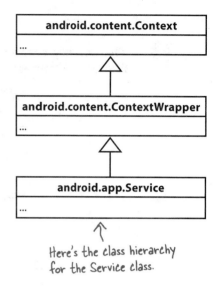

Here's the class hierarchy for the Service class.

```
package com.hfad.odometer;

import android.app.Service;
import android.content.Intent;
import android.os.IBinder;

public class OdometerService extends Service {

    @Override
    public IBinder onBind(Intent intent) {
        //Code to bind the service
    }
}
```

The class extends the Service class.

The onBind() method is used for binding components to the service.

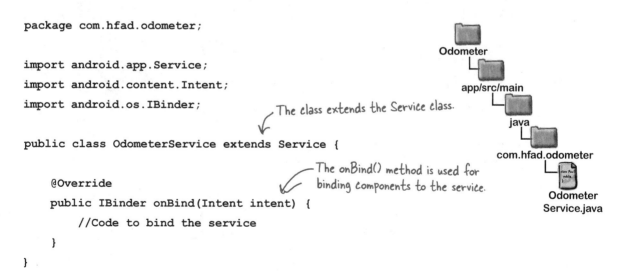

Odometer
app/src/main
java
com.hfad.odometer
Odometer
Service.java

The `onBind()` method is used to bind the service to an activity. We'll look at how binding works on the next page.

How binding works

This is how an activity binds to a bound service:

1 **The activity creates a ServiceConnection object.**

A ServiceConnection is used to form a connection with the service.

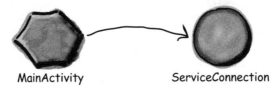

MainActivity   ServiceConnection

2 **The activity passes an Intent down the connection to the service.**

The intent contains any additional information the activity needs to pass to the service.

MainActivity   ServiceConnection   OdometerService

3 **The bound service creates a Binder object.**

The Binder contains a reference to the bound service. The service sends the Binder back along the connection.

MainActivity   ServiceConnection   OdometerService

4 **When the activity receives the Binder, it takes out the Service object and starts to use the service directly.**

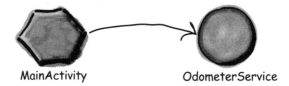

MainActivity   OdometerService

To allow the activity to bind to the service, we need to get the service to create the Binder object, and pass it to the activity using its onBind() method.

Define the Binder

When an activity asks to bind to a service using a service connection, the connection calls the onBind() method of the service. The onBind() method returns a Binder back to the connection. This is then passed back to the activity.

When you create a bound service, you need to define the Binder yourself. We're going to define a Binder called OdometerBinder by declaring it as an inner class like this:

— When you create a bound service, you need to provide a Binder implementation.

```
public class OdometerBinder extends Binder {
    OdometerService getOdometer() {
        return OdometerService.this;
    }
}
```

The activity will use this method to get a reference to the OdometerService.

We'll then return an instance of the OdometerBinder in the service onBind() method:

```
...
import android.os.Binder;
import android.os.IBinder;

public class OdometerService extends Service {
    private final IBinder binder = new OdometerBinder();

    public class OdometerBinder extends Binder {
        OdometerService getOdometer() {
            return OdometerService.this;
        }
    }
...
    @Override
    public IBinder onBind(Intent intent) {
        return binder;
    }
}
```

We're using these classes.

The Binder implementation.

The onBind() method returns an IBinder. This is an interface the Binder class implements.

Odometer

app/src/main

java

com.hfad.odometer

Odometer
Service.java

When the activity binds to the service with a service connection, the connection will call the onBind() method, which will return the OdometerBinder object. When the activity receives ← *You'll see this in action when we create an activity that uses the service.* the OdometerBinder from the connection, it will use the getOdometer() method to get the OdometerService object.

Get the service to do something

The next thing we need to is get our service to do something. We want our service to be able to tell the activity how far the device has traveled. There are two things we need to do to enable this:

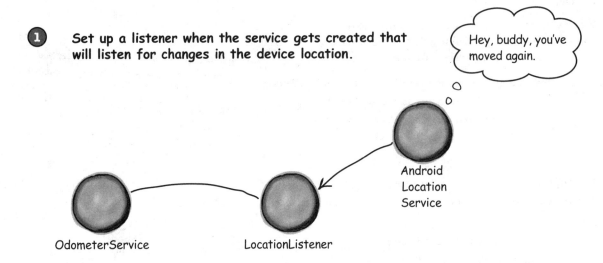

1 **Set up a listener when the service gets created that will listen for changes in the device location.**

Hey, buddy, you've moved again.

OdometerService   LocationListener   Android Location Service

2 **Return the number of miles traveled to the activity whenever the activity asks for it.**

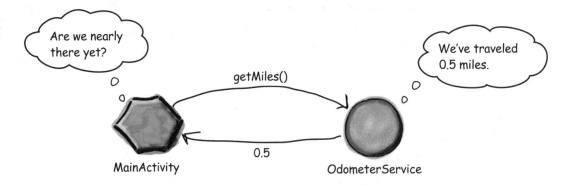

Are we nearly there yet?

We've traveled 0.5 miles.

getMiles()

0.5

MainActivity   OdometerService

Let's start by looking at what methods are available in the Service class that might be useful to us.

The Service class has four key methods

We're creating a bound service that extends the `Service` class. The `Service` class has four key methods that you might want to use:

Method.	When it's called	What you use it for
onCreate ()	When the service is first created	One-time setup procedures, such as instantiation
onStartCommand ()	When an activity starts the service using the `startService()` method	You don't need to implement this method if your service isn't a started service; it will only run if the service is started using `startService()`
onBind ()	When an activity wants to bind to the service	You must always implement this method by returning an `IBinder` object; if you don't want activities to bind to the service, return null instead
onDestroy ()	When the service is no longer being used and is about to be destroyed	Use this method to clean up any resources

In our case, we want to start getting location updates when the service is created. As this is a one-time setup, we'll do this in the `onCreate()` method:

```
@Override
public void onCreate() {    ← This is what the Service onCreate() method looks like.
    //Code to set up the listener
}
```

On the next page, we'll look at how we can get location updates.

Location, location, location...

If you want to find out the location of your device, you use the Android location service. The location service uses information from the GPS system and the names and strengths of nearby WiFi networks to find your location on the surface of the Earth.

You start by creating a **LocationListener**. A location listener is used for getting updates on when the device location has changed. You create the location listener like this:

This is the new LocationListener.

```
LocationListener listener = new LocationListener() {
    @Override
    public void onLocationChanged(Location location) {
        //Code to keep track of the distance
    }

    @Override
    public void onProviderDisabled(String arg0) {}

    @Override
    public void onProviderEnabled(String arg0) {}

    @Override
    public void onStatusChanged(String arg0, int arg1, Bundle bundle) {}
};
```

This method gets called whenever the LocationListener is told the device location has changed. The Location parameter describes the current location.

You need to override these methods too, but they can be left empty. They get called when the GPS is enabled or disabled, or if its status has changed. We don't need to react to any of these events.

To keep track of distances in location, you need to override the LocationListener onLocationChanged() method. This method has one parameter, a Location object that represents the device current location.

You can find the distance in meters between two locations using the Location distanceTo() method. As an example, if you use a Location object called lastLocation to record the device's last location, you can find the distance in meters between the locations using:

```
double distanceInMeters = location.distanceTo(lastLocation);
```

We'll show you the full code for the listener on the next page.

Add the LocationListener to the service

Here's the revised code for *OdometerService.java* (the onCreate()
method includes a location listener that keeps track of the distance the
device has traveled):

```
...
public class OdometerService extends Service {

    private static double distanceInMeters;
    private static Location lastLocation = null;
    ...
```

We're storing the distance traveled in meters and
the last location as static private variables.

```
    @Override
    public void onCreate() {
        LocationListener listener = new LocationListener() {
```

Create the listener.

```
            @Override
            public void onLocationChanged(Location location) {
                if (lastLocation == null) {
                    lastLocation = location;
                }
```

If it's our first location, set lastLocation to
the current Location.

```
                distanceInMeters += location.distanceTo(lastLocation);
                lastLocation = location;
            }
```

Add the distance between this location and the
last to the distanceInMeters variable, and set
lastLocation to the current Location.

```
            @Override
            public void onProviderDisabled(String arg0) {}

            @Override
            public void onProviderEnabled(String arg0) {}
```

We need to override these
methods, as they're part of
the LocationListener interface.

```
            @Override
            public void onStatusChanged(String arg0, int arg1, Bundle bundle) {}
        };
    }
}
```

Odometer

app/src/main

java

com.hfad.odometer

Odometer
Service.java

Now that we've created a listener, we need to register it with the location
service.

Binder
Location
getMiles()

Registering the LocationListener

You register the location listener with the Android location service using a `LocationManager` object. A location manager gives you access to the location service, and you create one like this:

```
LocationManager locManager = (LocationManager)getSystemService(Context.LOCATION_SERVICE);
```

This is how you access the Android location service.

We used the getSystemService() method earlier to get access to Android's notification service.

The `getSystemService()` method returns a reference to a system level service. In this case, we want to use Android's location service, so we use:

```
getSystemService(Context.LOCATION_SERVICE);
```

Once you have a location manager, you can use its `requestLocationUpdates()` method to register the location listener with the location service, and specify criteria for how often you want the listener to get updated. The `requestLocationUpdates()` method takes four parameters: a GPS provider, the minimum time interval between location updates in milliseconds, the minimum distance between location updates in meters, and a `LocationListener`.

Here's how you'd use the method to get updates every second when the device has moved more than a meter:

```
locManager.requestLocationUpdates(LocationManager.GPS_PROVIDER,
                            1000,
                            1,
                            listener);
```

This is the GPS provider.

The time in milliseconds.

The distance in meters. →

This is the LocationListener we created.

We can use this in the `Service` `onCreate()` method to register the listener we created with the location service and make sure it gets regular updates. Here's the code:

```
@Override
public void onCreate() {
    LocationListener listener = new LocationListener() {...};
    LocationManager locManager = (LocationManager)getSystemService(Context.LOCATION_SERVICE);
    locManager.requestLocationUpdates(LocationManager.GPS_PROVIDER, 1000, 1, listener);
}
```

We want to set up the listener and register it with the location service when the service is created.

That's everything we need to register the listener with the location service and get it to keep track of the distance traveled. Next, we need to get it to report back to the activity.

Tell the activity the distance traveled

If you remember, there were two things we needed our service to do.

The first thing we needed was to get it to keep track of the distance traveled by the device. We've now done this by creating a location listener and registering it with the location service.

The second thing we need is to get the service to tell the activity how far the device has traveled so that it can tell the user. To do this, we'll create a simple getMiles() method in the service that converts the current distance traveled into miles. The activity will call this method whenever it want to know the distance.

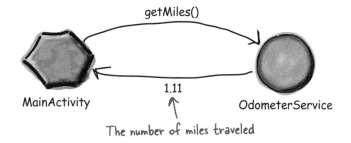

Here's what the getMiles() method looks like:

```java
public double getMiles() {
    return this.distanceInMeters / 1609.344;
}
```

This converts the distance traveled in meters into miles. We could make this calculation more precise if we wanted to, but it's accurate enough for our purposes.

The method takes the current distance traveled in meters, then divides it by 1609.344 to get the distance traveled in miles.

That's everything we need for our *OdometerService.java* code. We'll show you the full code on the next page.

The full OdometerService.java code

Here's the full code for our bound service *OdometerService.java*:

Binder
Location
getMiles()

```java
package com.hfad.odometer;

import android.app.Service;
import android.content.Context;
import android.content.Intent;
import android.location.Location;
import android.location.LocationListener;
import android.location.LocationManager;
import android.os.Binder;
import android.os.Bundle;
import android.os.IBinder;
```

These are all the classes we're using.

Odometer
app/src/main
java
com.hfad.odometer
Odometer
Service.java

```java
public class OdometerService extends Service {

    private final IBinder binder = new OdometerBinder();
    private static double distanceInMeters;
    private static Location lastLocation = null;
```

These are the private variables we're using.

```java
    public class OdometerBinder extends Binder {
        OdometerService getOdometer() {
            return OdometerService.this;
        }
    }
```

When you create a bound service, you have to define a Binder object. It enables the activity to bind to the service.

```java
    @Override
    public IBinder onBind(Intent intent) {
        return binder;
    }
```

This gets called when the activity binds to the service.

The OdometerService.java code (continued)

Set up the location listener when the service is created.

```java
@Override
public void onCreate() {
    LocationListener listener = new LocationListener() {
        @Override
        public void onLocationChanged(Location location) {
            if (lastLocation == null) {
                lastLocation = location;
            }
            distanceInMeters += location.distanceTo(lastLocation);
            lastLocation = location;
        }

        @Override
        public void onProviderDisabled(String arg0) {}

        @Override
        public void onProviderEnabled(String arg0) {}

        @Override
        public void onStatusChanged(String arg0, int arg1, Bundle bundle) {}
    };
    LocationManager locManager = (LocationManager) getSystemService(Context.LOCATION_SERVICE);
    locManager.requestLocationUpdates(LocationManager.GPS_PROVIDER, 1000, 1, listener);
}

public double getMiles() {
    return this.distanceInMeters / 1609.344;
}
}
```

This is our implementation of the location listener.

Convert the distance traveled to miles and return it.

Register the location listener with the location service.

```
Odometer
  └ app/src/main
      └ java
          └ com.hfad.odometer
              └ Odometer
                Service.java
```

The code allows an activity to bind to it, and when asked, it tells the activity how far the device has traveled. There's one more thing we need to do with our service; we need to give the app permission to use the GPS.

Binder
Location
getMiles()

Update AndroidManifest.xml

When you create an app, Android allows you to perform most actions by default. But there are some actions that Android needs the user to give permission for in order for them to work correctly. One of these actions is using the device GPS. If your app needs to use the device GPS, the user needs to give permission when the app is installed.

You tell Android that your app needs permission to use the GPS using the <uses-permission> element like this:

We're adding this because we're using the device GPS in our app.

```
<manifest ... '>
    <uses-permission android:name="android.permission.ACCESS_FINE_LOCATION" />
    ...
</manifest>
```

If you don't include this permission in *AndroidManifest.xml*, the app will crash.

You also need to check that Android Studio has added your service to *AndroidManifest.xml*:

```
<manifest ... >

    <uses-permission android:name="android.permission.ACCESS_FINE_LOCATION" />

    <application
        ... >
        <activity
            ...
        </activity>

        <service
            android:name=".OdometerService"
            android:exported="false"
            android:enabled="true" >
        </service>
    </application>
</manifest>
```

Odometer

app/src/main

AndroidManifest.xml

All services need to be declared in AndroidManifest.xml.

We're setting this to false, as only this app will use the service.

The android:enabled attribute must either be set to true or omitted completely. If you set it to false, your app won't be able to use the service.

Let's revisit where we've got to with our app after an exercise.

Service Magnets

See if you can complete the code below to create a bound service called `NumberService` that returns a random number when its `getNumber()` method is called:

```
...
    public class NumberService extends Service {

        private final IBinder binder = new NumberBinder();
        private final Random random = new Random();

        public class .................................extends Binder {

            ................................. getNumberService() {
                return NumberService.this;
            }
        }

        @Override

        public .........................................(Intent intent) {

            ..........................................;
        }

        public int getNumber() {
            return random.nextInt(100);
        }                        ↖
    }              This code generates a random number.
```

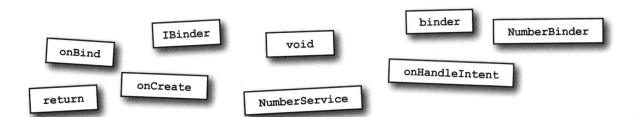

onBind

IBinder

void

binder

NumberBinder

return

onCreate

onHandleIntent

NumberService

Service Magnets Solution

See if you can complete the code below to create a bound service called `NumberService` that returns a random number when its `getNumber()` method is called.

```
...
public class NumberService extends Service {

    private final IBinder binder = new NumberBinder();
    private final Random random = new Random();

    public class  NumberBinder  extends Binder {        ← Define a NumberBinder class
                                                            that extends Binder.
         NumberService  getNumberService() {       ← The activity needs to
            return NumberService.this;                    get a reference to the
                                                          NumberService from the
        }                                                 Binder, so it needs to return
    }                                                     a NumberService object.

                        Override the onBind() method so the
                        activity can bind to the service.
    @Override

    public  IBinder    onBind  (Intent intent) {

        return    binder  ;     ← The onBind() method should return the Binder.

    }

    public int getNumber() {
        return random.nextInt(100);
    }

}
```

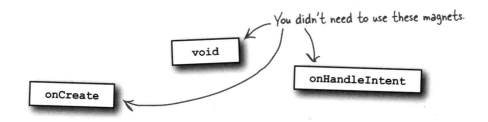

You didn't need to use these magnets.

void

onHandleIntent

onCreate

Where we've got to

Let's look again at what we want our app to do so we can see what's left:

1 **MainActivity binds to OdometerService.**
MainActivity uses the OdometerService getMiles() method to ask for the number of miles traveled.

2 **The OdometerService uses the Android location services to keep track of when the device moves.**
It uses these locations to calculate how far the device has traveled.

3 **The OdometerService returns the distance traveled to MainActivity.**
MainActivity displays the distance traveled to the user.

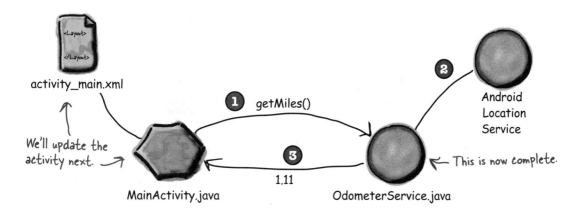

activity_main.xml

We'll update the activity next. →

MainActivity.java

1 getMiles()

3
1.11

OdometerService.java

2

Android Location Service

← This is now complete.

So far we've created the OdometerService. It uses the Android location services to track locations, and uses this to calculate the distance traveled.

The next thing we need to do is create MainActivity. We need to get it to bind to OdometerService, and then use the OdometerService getMiles() method to display the distance the device has traveled.

Update MainActivity's layout

Bind to Service
Display miles

These are the things we
need to do to MainActivity.

We need to get `MainActivity` to use the service to display
the number of miles traveled, so we'll start by updating the
layout file *activity_main.xml*. We'll add a text view to the layout
that we can use to display the mileage. We'll update the text
view every second in our Java code.

Here's the code for *activity_main.xml*:

```xml
<RelativeLayout xmlns:android="http://schemas.android.com/apk/res/android"
    xmlns:tools="http://schemas.android.com/tools"
    android:layout_width="match_parent"
    android:layout_height="match_parent"
    tools:context=".MainActivity">

    <TextView android:text=""
        android:id="@+id/distance"
        android:textAppearance="?android:attr/textAppearanceLarge"
        android:layout_width="match_parent"
        android:layout_height="match_parent"
        android:layout_centerHorizontal="true"
        android:singleLine="false"
        android:textSize="60dp"/>
</RelativeLayout>
```

We'll use the TextView
to display the distance.

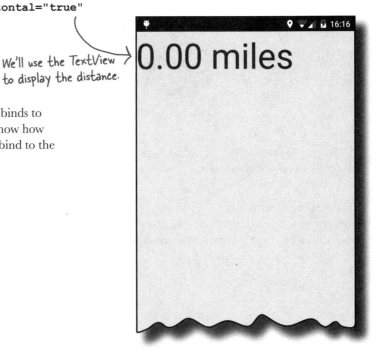

Next, we need to update the activity code so that it binds to
the service and updates the text view. We already know how
to update views, but what we don't know is how to bind to the
service. Let's see how it's done.

Create a ServiceConnection

Earlier on in the chapter, we said that an activity binds to a service using a `ServiceConnection` object. A `ServiceConnection` is an interface with two methods: `onServiceConnected()` and `onServiceDisconnected()`.

Main Activity → Service Connection → Odometer Service

The `onServiceConnected()` method is called when a connection to the service has been established and a `Binder` object is received from the service. You can use the binder to get a reference to the service.

The `onServiceDisconnected()` method is used when the connection to the service has been lost.

When you need an activity to bind to a service, you need to create your own implementation of the `ServiceConnection`. Here's ours:

```
...
public class MainActivity extends Activity {

    private OdometerService odometer;          ← We'll use this for the
                                                  OdometerService.
    private boolean bound = false;   ← Use this to store whether or not the
    ...                                 activity's bound to the service.

    private ServiceConnection connection = new ServiceConnection() {
        @Override
        public void onServiceConnected(ComponentName componentName, IBinder binder) {
            OdometerService.OdometerBinder odometerBinder =
                            (OdometerService.OdometerBinder) binder;
            odometer = odometerBinder.getOdometer();   ← Cast the Binder to an
            bound = true;                                 OdometerBinder, then use to get a
        }              ← When the service is connected,   reference to the OdometerService.
        @Override        set bound to true.
        public void onServiceDisconnected(ComponentName componentName) {
            bound = false;
        }         ↑
    };          When the service is disconnected,
}               set bound to false.
```

Folder diagram: Odometer → app/src/main → java → com.hfad.odometer → MainActivity.java

When the service is connected, the `onServiceConnected()` method uses the `Binder` object to get a reference to the service. We're also using the `onServiceConnected()` and `onServiceDisconnected()` methods to record whether the service is currently connected.

Bind to Service
Display miles

Bind to the service when the activity starts

We're going to use the connection to bind to the service when the activity becomes visible. As a reminder, when an activity becomes visible, its onStart() method gets called.

To bind to the service, you first create an explicit intent that's directed at the service you want to bind to. You then use the activity's bindService() method to bind to the service:

```
@Override
protected void onStart() {
    super.onStart();
    Intent intent = new Intent(this, OdometerService.class);
    bindService(intent, connection, Context.BIND_AUTO_CREATE);
}
```

MainActivity   *OdometerService*

This is an intent directed to the OdometerService.

This uses the intent and service connection to bind the activity to the service.

The code Context.BIND_AUTO_CREATE tells Android to create the service if it doesn't already exist.

Unbind from the service when the activity stops

When the activity loses visibility, we're going to unbind from the service. When an activity loses visibility, its onStop() method gets called.

You unbind from the service using the unbindService() connection. The method takes one parameter, our connection. We're going to check whether the service is bound when the activity loses visibility, and if it is, we'll unbind it:

```
@Override
protected void onStop() {
    super.onStop();
    if (bound) {
        unbindService(connection);
        bound = false;
    }
}
```

MainActivity   *OdometerService*

This uses the service connection to unbind from the service.

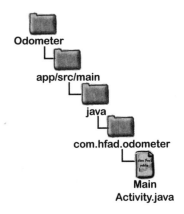

Odometer

app/src/main

java

com.hfad.odometer

Main
Activity.java

So far we have an activity that binds to the service when the activity starts, and unbinds from the service when the activity stops. The final thing we need to do is get the activity to ask the service for the distance traveled.

Display the distance traveled

Once you have a connection to the service, you can call its methods. We're going to call the `OdometerService getMiles()` method every second to get the distance traveled, and then use it to update the text view in the layout. We'll call the `getMiles()` method every second and update the text view each time it's called.

To do this, we're going to write a new method called `watchMileage()`. This works in exactly the same way as the `runTimer()` method we used in Chapter 4. The only difference is that it displays miles traveled instead of elapsed time.

Here's our `watchMileage()` method:

The activity will use the getMiles() method in the OdometerService to populate the TextView.

```java
private void watchMileage() {
    final TextView distanceView = (TextView) findViewById(R.id.distance);
    final Handler handler = new Handler();      // Create a new Handler.
    handler.post(new Runnable() {       // Call the post() method, passing in a new Runnable.
        @Override
        public void run() {
            double distance = 0.0;
            if (odometer != null) {
                distance = odometer.getMiles();
            }
            String distanceStr = String.format("%1$,.2f miles", distance);
            distanceView.setText(distanceStr);
            handler.postDelayed(this, 1000);
        }
    });
}
```

Get the text view.

If we've got a reference to the OdometerService, use its getMiles() method.

Format the miles.

Post the code in the Runnable to be run again after a delay of 1,000 milliseconds, or 1 second. As this line of code is included in the Runnable run() method, it will run every second (with a slight lag).

We'll then call this method in the activity's `onCreate()` method so that it starts running when the activity gets created:

```java
@Override
protected void onCreate(Bundle savedInstanceState) {
    ...
    watchMileage();
}
```

We'll show you the full code for `MainActivity` on the next page.

Odometer

app/src/main

java

com.hfad.odometer

Main
Activity.java

Bind to Service
Display miles

The full MainActivity.java code

Here's the complete code for *MainActivity.java*:

```java
package com.hfad.odometer;

import android.app.Activity;
import android.content.ComponentName;
import android.content.Context;
import android.content.Intent;
import android.content.ServiceConnection;
import android.os.Bundle;
import android.os.Handler;
import android.os.IBinder;
import android.widget.TextView;

public class MainActivity extends Activity {

    private OdometerService odometer;
    private boolean bound = false;
    private ServiceConnection connection = new ServiceConnection() {
        @Override
        public void onServiceConnected(ComponentName componentName, IBinder binder) {
            OdometerService.OdometerBinder odometerBinder =
                            (OdometerService.OdometerBinder) binder;
            odometer = odometerBinder.getOdometer();
            bound = true;
        }
        @Override
        public void onServiceDisconnected(ComponentName componentName) {
            bound = false;
        }
    };

    @Override
    protected void onCreate(Bundle savedInstanceState) {
        super.onCreate(savedInstanceState);
        setContentView(R.layout.activity_main);
        watchMileage();
    }
```

Odometer
app/src/main
java
com.hfad.odometer
Main
Activity.java

← We'll use this for the OdometerService.

← Use this to store whether or not the activity's bound to the service.

We need to define a ServiceConnection.

← Get a reference to the OdometerService when the service is connected.

← Call the watchMileage() function when the activity's created.

The MainActivity.java code (continued)

```java
@Override
protected void onStart() {
    super.onStart();
    Intent intent = new Intent(this, OdometerService.class);
    bindService(intent, connection, Context.BIND_AUTO_CREATE);
}
```

Bind the service when the activity starts.

```java
@Override
protected void onStop() {
    super.onStop();
    if (bound) {
        unbindService(connection);
        bound = false;
    }
}
```

Unbind the service when the activity stops.

Odometer

app/src/main

java

com.hfad.odometer

Main
Activity.java

This method updates the mileage that's displayed.

```java
private void watchMileage() {
    final TextView distanceView = (TextView) findViewById(R.id.distance);
    final Handler handler = new Handler();
    handler.post(new Runnable() {
        @Override
        public void run() {
            double distance = 0.0;
            if (odometer != null) {
                distance = odometer.getMiles();
            }
            String distanceStr = String.format("%1$,.2f miles", distance);
            distanceView.setText(distanceStr);
            handler.postDelayed(this, 1000);
        }
    });
}
```

If we've got a reference to the OdometerService, use its getMiles() method.

Update the distance every second.

That's all the code you need to get MainActivity to use the OdometerService. Let's see what happens when you run the code.

What happens when you run the code

Before you see the app up and running, let's go through what
happens when the code runs:

Bind to Service
Display miles

1 **When the MainActivity starts, the onStart() method creates a
ServiceConnection.**
It asks to bind to the `OdometerService`.

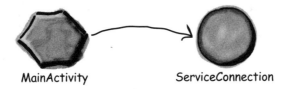

2 **The OdometerService starts and its onBind() method is called with a
copy of the intent from the MainActivity.**

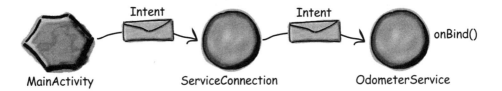

3 **The onBind() method returns a Binder object.**

The story continues

4 MainActivity gets a reference to OdometerService from the Binder and starts to use the service directly.

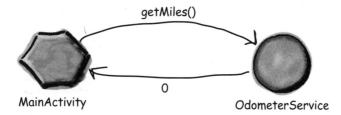

5 While MainActivity is running, the watchMileage() method calls the OdometerService getMiles() method every second and updates the screen.

6 When MainActivity stops, it disconnects from the OdometerService by calling unbindService().

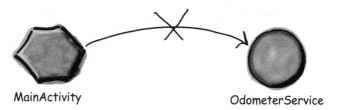

Let's run the app and see what it does.

Test drive the app

To see the app in action, you'll need to run it on a device that has a GPS. If you don't, the app won't work.

When you start the app, it says the distance traveled is 0 miles. An icon appears at the top of the device indicating that the location service has been activated:

The location service is up and running.

The app starts off displaying 0.00 miles.

0.00 miles

This number may go up slightly when you start the app. This is because it takes a few seconds for the GPS to home in on the device location, and it may initially misreport it.

1.11 miles

When you take your device for a walk, the distance displayed increases.

When you take your device on a road trip, the distance traveled increases.

We know you're full of great ideas for improving the Odometer app, so why not try them out? As an example, why not try adding Start, Stop, and Reset buttons?

Your Android Toolbox

You've got Chapter 13 under your belt and now you've added services to your toolbox.

You can download the full code for the chapter from https://tinyurl.com/HeadFirstAndroid.

BULLET POINTS

- A service is a component that can perform tasks in the background. It doesn't have a user interface.

- A started service can run in the background indefinitely, even when the activity that started it is destroyed. Once the operation is done, it stops itself.

- You declare services in *AndroidManifest.xml* using the `<service>` element.

- You can create a simple started service by extending the `IntentService` class and overriding its `onHandleIntent()` method. The `IntentService` class is designed for handling intents.

- You start a started service using the `startService()` method.

- If you override the `IntentService` `onStartCommand()` method, you must call its super implementation.

- You create a notification using a notification builder. You get your notification to start an activity using a pending intent. You then use Android's notification service to display the notification.

- A bound service is bound to another component such as an activity. The activity can interact with it and get results.

- You usually create a bound service by extending the `Service` class. You must define your own `Binder` object, and override the `onBind()` method. This is called when a component wants to bind to the service.

- The `Service` `onCreate()` method is called when the service is created. Use it for instantiation.

- The `Service` `onDestroy()` method is called when the service is about to be destroyed.

- You can use the Android location service to get the current location of the device. You create a `LocationListener`, and then register it with the location service. You can add criteria for how often the listener is notified of changes. When you use the device GPS, you need to add a permission for it in *AndroidManifest.xml*.

- To bind an activity to a service, you create a `ServiceConnection`. You override the `onServiceConnected()` method to get a reference to the service.

- You bind to the service using the `bindService()` method. You unbind from the service using the `unbindService()` method.

14 material design

Living in a Material World

One player comes off the pitch, another player moves straight in. Just like a recycler view.

With API level 21, Google introduced Material Design.

In this chapter, we'll look at **what Material Design is**, and how to make your apps fit in with it. We'll start by introducing you to **card views** you can reuse across your app for a **consistent look and feel**. Then we'll introduce you to the **recycler view**, the list view's flexible friend. Along the way, you'll see how to **create your own adapters**, and how to completely change the look of a recycler view with *just two lines of code*.

Welcome to Material Design

Material Design was launched with API level 21 and it's intended to give a consistent look and feel to all Android apps. The idea is that a user can switch from a Google app like the Play Store to an app designed by a third-party developer and instantly feel comfortable and know what to do. The *Material* part of the name comes from Material Design's visual style, which makes the parts of your interface look like overlapping pieces of material or paper:

Material Design uses animation and 3D effects likes drop-shadows to make it clear to the user how they can interact with the app. To do this, Material Design includes a set of support libraries that contains different widgets and themes for use in Material Design apps. In this chapter, we'll take a few of these widgets and use them to make the Pizza app we developed in Chapters 9 and 10 fit in with Material Design.

CardViews and RecyclerViews

Two of the most important Material Design widgets are recycler views and card views.

A **card view** is a container for other views. Card views have rounded corners, and a drop-shadow that makes them appear to be floating above the background. You can animate a card view so that it will appear to move when you push it.

A **recycler view** is like a new kind of list view A recycler view gets its name because it can efficiently reuse (or recycle) views to create the appearance of a list on the screen. A recycler view can be used to display card views.

We're going to change the Pizza app so that it uses card views and recycler views. We'll convert the app so that the list of pizzas goes

from this:

This is a normal ListView.

to this:

This is a recycler view containing two card views. Each card view contains the name and image of a pizza.

Geek Bits

Material Design uses a lot of 3D effects. But doesn't this slow your device? On most devices, the answer is *no*. If possible, the Material views will try to use the power of the graphics hardware to generate the drop-shadows in much the same way that a game would. That means that not only are generated shadows rendered beautifully, but they also take no extra time to draw. On older devices, the views will insert shadow images behind each view. That will take a little extra processing power and some extra memory. If you want to run your app on a very old device, it's best to check it against an actual device before release.

The Pizza app structure

We're going to change the app so that we use a card view and recycler view for the list of pizzas. Here's a breakdown of how the app will be structured and what it will do:

① **When the app gets launched, it starts MainActivity.**
The activity uses layout *activity_main.xml* and has a navigation drawer. When the user clicks on one of the options in the navigation drawer, it displays the appropriate fragment.

② **When the user clicks the Pizzas option, it displays PizzasMaterialFragment.**
`PizzasMaterialFragment` contains a recycler view.

③ **PizzaMaterialFragment uses an adapter, CaptionedImagesAdapter, to display card views showing an image and caption for each pizza.**
The card views are defined in *card_captioned_image.xml*. Pizza data is held in *Pizzas.java*.

④ **When the user clicks on a pizza, details of the pizza are displayed in PizzaDetailActivity.**

⑤ **When the user clicks on the Create Order action in the action bar of MainActivity or PizzaDetailActivity, OrderActivity is displayed.**

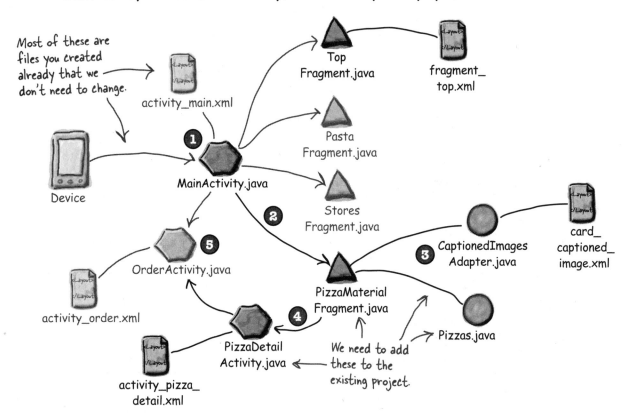

Most of these are files you created already that we don't need to change.

Device

activity_main.xml

① MainActivity.java

Top Fragment.java

fragment_ top.xml

Pasta Fragment.java

② Stores Fragment.java

CaptionedImages Adapter.java

③

card_ captioned_ image.xml

⑤ OrderActivity.java

PizzaMaterial Fragment.java

Pizzas.java

activity_order.xml

PizzaDetail Activity.java

④

We need to add these to the existing project.

activity_pizza_ detail.xml

Add the pizza data

We'll start by adding the pizza images to the Bits and Pizzas project. Download the files *diavolo.jpg* and *funghi.jpg* from *https://tinyurl.com/ HeadFirstAndroid*. Then drag them to the folder *app/src/main/res/drawable- nodpi*. If Android Studio hasn't created the folder for you, you'll need to create it.

We're putting the images in the *drawable-nodpi* folder because we want the device to use the same images, regardless of the dpi of the screen. If you wanted, you could create separate images for different device resolutions and put them in the appropriate *drawable** folder.

> **Do this!**
>
> **We're going to update the Pizza app in this chapter, so open your original Bits and Pizzas project in Android Studio.**

Add the Pizza class

We'll add a `Pizza` class to the app which the recycler view will get its pizza data from. The class defines an array of two pizzas, where each pizza is composed of a name and image resource ID. Add the class to the `com.hfad.bitsandpizzas` package in the *app/src/main/java* folder in your project, giving it a class name of `Pizza`. Then save your changes:

← In a real app, we might use a database for this. We're using a Java class here for simplicity.

```java
package com.hfad.bitsandpizzas;

public class Pizza {
    private String name;
    private int imageResourceId;

    public static final Pizza[] pizzas = {
            new Pizza("Diavolo", R.drawable.diavolo),
            new Pizza("Funghi", R.drawable.funghi)
    };

    private Pizza(String name, int imageResourceId) {
        this.name = name;
        this.imageResourceId = imageResourceId;
    }

    public String getName() {
        return name;
    }

    public int getImageResourceId() {
        return imageResourceId;
    }
}
```

Each Pizza has a name and image resource ID. The image resource ID refers to the drink images we added to the project above.

— The Pizza constructor

These are getters for the private variables.

BitsAndPizzas
└ app/src/main
  └ java
    └ com.hfad.bitsandpizzas
      └ Pizza.java

We're going to use a recycler view and card view in the app, and these require support libraries. We'll add these next.

Add the support libraries

Card views and recycler views come from the CardView and RecyclerView v7 libraries, so we need to add these libraries as dependencies. To do this, go to File→Project Structure. In the Project Structure window, select app and switch to the Dependencies tab. Then add library dependencies for recyclerview-v7 and cardview-v7.

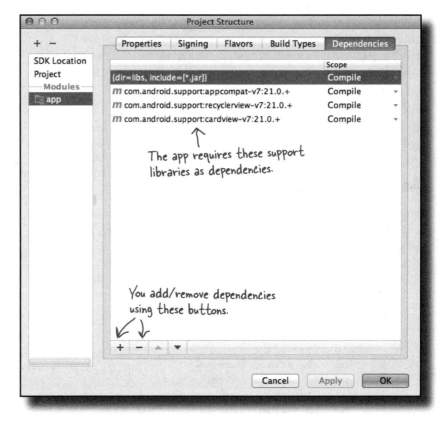

The app requires these support libraries as dependencies.

You add/remove dependencies using these buttons.

When you add dependencies, Android Studio records them in the *app/ build.gradle* file:

```
...
dependencies {
    compile fileTree(dir: 'libs', include: ['*.jar'])
    compile 'com.android.support:appcompat-v7:21.0.+'
    compile 'com.android.support:recyclerview-v7:21.0.+'
    compile 'com.android.support:cardview-v7:21.0.+'
}
```

Adding support libraries to the window above updates build.gradle behind the scenes.

BitsAndPizzas
app
build.gradle

If you wish, you can manage the library dependencies for your app by editing this file directly. It will have the same effect as adding dependencies in the Project Structure window.

Now that you've added the support libraries, we'll create the card view.

Create the CardView

You use card views to visually represent the basic data items in your app in a recognizable and coherent way. The basic data items in our Pizza Shop app are pizzas, pasta, and stores, so we're going to create a card view we can use to displays these items.

You create a card view by including it in a layout. You can either add it to an existing layout, or create a new layout file for it. Creating a new layout file for the card view means that you can use the card view inside a recycler view.

We want to use the card view inside a recycler view, so we're going to put it in its own layout file. To do this, add a new layout file to the *app/src/ main/res/layout* folder called *card_captioned_image.xml*.

You define a card view using code like this:

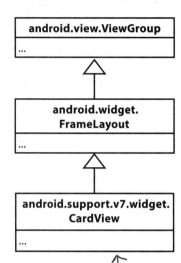

CardView is a subclass of FrameLayout.

─ This adds the CardView.

```
<android.support.v7.widget.CardView
    xmlns:android="http://schemas.android.com/apk/res/android"
    xmlns:card_view="http://schemas.android.com/apk/res-auto"
    android:id="@+id/card_view"
    android:layout_width="match_parent"
    android:layout_height="200dp"
    android:layout_margin="5dp"
    card_view:cardCornerRadius="4dp">
    ...
</android.support.v7.widget.CardView>
```

This gives the CardView rounded corners.

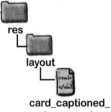

BitsAndPizzas

app/src/main

res

layout

card_captioned_
image.xml

The CardView class comes from the v7 CardView support library, so we have to use its full class path of android.support.v7.widget. CardView.

You give your card view rounded corners by adding a namespace of

> xmlns:card_view="http://schemas.android.com/apk/res-auto"

and using the card_view:cardCornerRadius attribute to set the corner radius. As an example, the code

> card_view:cardCornerRadius="4dp"

sets the card corner radius to 4dp.

You define the appearance of the card view by adding other views to it. In our case, we want to display an image and text in the card view. We'll show you the full code on the next page

The full card_captioned_image.xml code

Here's the full code for *card_captioned_image.xml* (we've added a linear
layout to the card view, and put an image view and text view inside the
linear layout; we've taken this approach because the `CardView` class
extends the `FrameLayout` class, and frame layouts are designed to hold
a single child view—in this case, the frame layout has a single child view of
a linear layout):

BitsAndPizzas

app/src/main

res

layout

**card_captioned_
image.xml**

```xml
<?xml version="1.0" encoding="utf-8"?>
<android.support.v7.widget.CardView
    xmlns:android="http://schemas.android.com/apk/res/android"
    xmlns:card_view="http://schemas.android.com/apk/res-auto"
    android:id="@+id/card_view"
    android:layout_width="match_parent"
    android:layout_height="200dp"
    android:layout_margin="5dp"
    card_view:cardCornerRadius="4dp">
```

The card view will be as wide as its
parent allows, and 200dp high.

```xml
    <LinearLayout
        android:layout_width="match_parent"
        android:layout_height="fill_parent"
        android:orientation="vertical">
```

The image will be as wide as
its parent allows. We're using
centerCrop to make sure the
image scales uniformly.

```xml
        <ImageView android:id="@+id/info_image"
            android:layout_height="0dp"
            android:layout_width="match_parent"
            android:layout_weight="1.0"
            android:scaleType="centerCrop"/>


        <TextView
            android:id="@+id/info_text"
            android:layout_marginLeft="5dp"
            android:layout_marginBottom="5dp"
            android:layout_height="wrap_content"
            android:layout_width="match_parent"/>
    </LinearLayout>
</android.support.v7.widget.CardView>
```

Diavolo

We'll be able to use this card view layout for any data items that consist of
a caption and an image, such as our pizza data.

The next thing we need to do is create a recycler view that will display a
list of our card views.

RecyclerViews use RecyclerView.Adapters

A recycler view is a more advanced version of a list view. Just like a list view, a recycler view is a scrollable container used for displaying sets of data. A recycler view, however, is more efficient at displaying large data sets. This is because a recycler view reuses (or recycles) views when they are no longer visible on screen, whereas a list view displays a new view for each item that appears on screen.

Just like a list view, you add data to a recycler view using an adapter. Unfortunately, recycler views don't work with any of the built-in adapters such as array adapters or cursor adapters. Instead, you have to create your own that's a subclass of the `RecyclerView.Adapter` class.

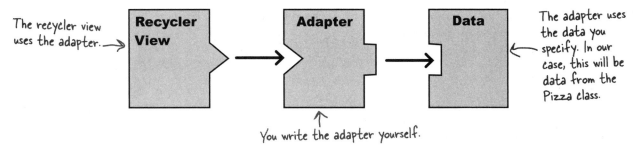

The recycler view uses the adapter. → **Recycler View** → **Adapter** → **Data** ← The adapter uses the data you specify. In our case, this will be data from the Pizza class.

You write the adapter yourself.

The adapter has two main jobs: to create each of the views that are visible within the recycler view, and to configure the view to match a piece of data.

In our case, the recycler view needs to display a list of cards, each containing an image view and a text view. This means that the adapter needs to create views for these items, and replace their contents when each item in the data set is no longer visible.

Over the next few pages, we're going to create a recycler view adapter. We need it to do three things:

1 **Specify what type of data the adapter should work with.**
We need to tell the adapter to use card views. Each card view needs to be populated with an image and its caption.

2 **Create the views.**
The adapter needs to create all of the views that will need to be displayed on screen.

3 **Bind the data to the views.**
The adapter needs to populate each of the views with data when it becomes visible.

We'll start by adding a `RecyclerView.Adapter` class to our project.

Create the basic adapter

We're going to create a recycler view adapter called
CaptionedImagesAdapter. Create a new class called
CaptionedImagesAdapter, then replace the code with the following:

```
package com.hfad.bitsandpizzas;

import android.support.v7.widget.RecyclerView;    ←—The RecyclerView class is in a support library.
import android.view.ViewGroup;

class CaptionedImagesAdapter extends RecyclerView.Adapter<CaptionedImagesAdapter.ViewHolder>{
    //Provide a reference to the views used in the recycler view
    public static class ViewHolder extends RecyclerView.ViewHolder {
        //Define the view holder ←— You need to define the ViewHolder.
    }                                    We'll do this on the next page.

    @Override
    public CaptionedImagesAdapter.ViewHolder onCreateViewHolder(
                    ViewGroup parent, int viewType){
        //Create a new view
    }
                            You need to implement these methods.
    @Override
    public void onBindViewHolder(ViewHolder holder, int position){
        //Set the values inside the given view
    }
                        You must implement this method too.
    @Override
    public int getItemCount(){
        //Return the number of items in the data set
    }
}
```

BitsAndPizzas

app/src/main

java

com.hfad.bitsandpizzas

CaptionedImages
Adapter.java

As you can see, the CaptionedImagesAdapter extends the
RecyclerView.Adapter class and implements its getItemCount(),
onCreateViewHolder(), and onBindViewHolder() methods.
The getItemCount() method is used to return the number of items
in the data set, the onCreateViewHolder() method is used to create
the views, and the onBindViewHolder() is used to set the values inside
the views. You must override these methods whenever you create your own
recycler view adapter

The class also defines a view holder, which you use to say what data the
adapter should work with. We'll look at this next.

Define the adapter's ViewHolder

A view holder provides a reference to the view or views for each data item in the recycler view. It's a holder for the views you want to display.

When you create a recycler view adapter, you need to create a view holder inside the adapter. You do this by extending the `RecyclerView.ViewHolder` class, and specifying what type of data it should hold.

Each data item in our recycler view is a card view, so we need to make our view holder store card views. Here's the code:

```
package com.hfad.bitsandpizzas;

...

import android.support.v7.widget.CardView;


class CaptionedImagesAdapter extends RecyclerView.Adapter<CaptionedImagesAdapter.ViewHolder>{
    //Provide a reference to the views used in the recycler view
    public static class ViewHolder extends RecyclerView.ViewHolder {
        private CardView cardView;
        public ViewHolder(CardView v) {
            super(v);
            cardView = v;
        }
    }

...

}
```

A ViewHolder holds one or more Views.

Each ViewHolder contains a CardView.

Our recycler view needs to display CardViews, so we specify that our ViewHolder contains CardViews. If you want to display another type of data in the recycler view, you define it here.

BitsAndPizzas
app/src/main
java
com.hfad.bitsandpizzas
CaptionedImages
Adapter.java

When you create a view holder, you must call the `ViewHolder` super constructor using:

```
super(v);
```

This is because the `ViewHolder` superclass includes metadata such as the item's position in the recycler view, and you need this for the adapter to work properly.

Now that we've created a view holder to store card views, we'll get the adapter to display the card views in the recycler view.

Create the ViewHolders

The recycler view maintains a fixed set of view holders that contain the views that appear in the list on the screen. The number of view holders depends on the size of the screen they need to appear on, and how much space each item takes up. To enable the recycler view to figure out how many view holders it needs to maintain, you need to tell it which layout to use for each view holder in the adapter's `onCreateViewHolder()` method.

When the recycler view is first constructed, it builds this set of view holders by repeatedly calling the adapter's `onCreateViewHolder()` method until all the view holders it needs have been created. The `onCreateViewHolder()` method takes two parameters: the `ViewGroup` parent object (the recycler view itself) and an `int` parameter called `viewType`. This is used if you want to display different kinds of views for different items in the list.

We want to create view holders that contains a card view based on our *card_captioned_image.xml* layout. Here's the code that will do that:

```
...

import android.view.LayoutInflater;


class CaptionedImagesAdapter extends RecyclerView.Adapter<CaptionedImagesAdapter.ViewHolder>{

    ...

    @Override
    public CaptionedImagesAdapter.ViewHolder onCreateViewHolder(
                ViewGroup parent, int viewType){
        CardView cv = (CardView) LayoutInflater.from(parent.getContext())
            .inflate(R.layout.card_captioned_image, parent, false);
        return new ViewHolder(cv);
    }
}
```

Specify what layout to use for the contents of the ViewHolder.

BitsAndPizzas

app/src/main

java

com.hfad.bitsandpizzas

CaptionedImages
Adapter.java

Now that the adapter can create the view holders in the recycler view, we need to get the adapter to populate the card views they contain with data.

Each card view displays an image and a caption

Each time the user scrolls the recycler view and a new item appears, the recycler view will take one of the view holders in its pool and call the onBindViewHolder() method to bind data to its contents. The code in the onBindViewHolder() method needs to set the contents of the views in the view holder so that they match the data.

In our case, the view holder contains card views that we need to populate with images and captions. To do this, we'll add a constructor to the adapter so that the recycler view can pass data to it. We'll then use the onBindViewHolder() method to bind the data to the card views.

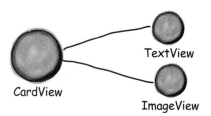

Each CardView contains a TextView and ImageView. We need to populate these with the caption and image of each pizza.

Create the constructor

The recycler view needs to pass arrays of captions and image IDs to the adapter, so we'll add a constructor that will take these as parameters. We'll store the arrays in instance variables. We'll also use the number of captions passed to the adapter to determine the number of items in the data set:

```
...
class CaptionedImagesAdapter extends RecyclerView.Adapter<CaptionedImagesAdapter.ViewHolder>{

    private String[] captions;
    private int[] imageIds;
```
We'll use these variables to hold the pizza data.

BitsAndPizzas
app/src/main
java
com.hfad.bitsandpizzas
CaptionedImages Adapter.java

```
...

    public CaptionedImagesAdapter(String[] captions, int[] imageIds){
        this.captions = captions;
        this.imageIds = imageIds;
    }
```
We'll pass the data to the adapter using its constructor.

```
    @Override
    public int getItemCount(){
        return captions.length;
    }
}
```
The length of the captions array equals the number of data items in the recycler view.

Now that the adapter can receive the data, we'll get the adapter to display it in the recycler view by writing the onBindViewHolder() method.

Add the data to the card views

The onBindViewHolder() method gets called whenever the recycler view needs to display data in a view holder. It takes two parameters: the view holder that data needs to be bound to, and the position in the data set of the data that needs to be bound.

We need to populate our card view with data. The card view contains two views, an image view with an ID of info_image, and a text view with an ID of info_text. We'll populate these with data from the captions and imageIds arrays.

Here's the code that will do that:

```
...
import android.widget.ImageView;          We're using these extra classes.
import android.widget.TextView;
import android.graphics.drawable.Drawable;


class CaptionedImagesAdapter extends RecyclerView.Adapter<CaptionedImagesAdapter.ViewHolder>{

    private String[] captions;
    private int[] imageIds;          These variables contain
                                     the captions and image
    ...                              resource IDs of the pizzas.


    public void onBindViewHolder(ViewHolder holder, int position){
        CardView cardView = holder.cardView;
        ImageView imageView = (ImageView)cardView.findViewById(R.id.info_image);
        Drawable drawable = cardView.getResources().getDrawable(imageIds[position]);
        imageView.setImageDrawable(drawable);
        imageView.setContentDescription(captions[position]);
        TextView textView = (TextView)cardView.findViewById(R.id.info_text);
        textView.setText(captions[position]);
    }
}
```

Display the image in the ImageView.

Display the caption in the TextView.

BitsAndPizzas

app/src/main

java

com.hfad.bitsandpizzas

CaptionedImages
Adapter.java

That's all the code we need for our adapter. We'll show you the full code on the next page.

The full code for CaptionedImagesAdapter.java

```java
package com.hfad.bitsandpizzas;

import android.support.v7.widget.RecyclerView;
import android.view.LayoutInflater;
import android.view.ViewGroup;
import android.support.v7.widget.CardView;
import android.widget.ImageView;
import android.widget.TextView;
import android.graphics.drawable.Drawable;
```

These are the classes we're using.

```java
class CaptionedImagesAdapter extends RecyclerView.Adapter<CaptionedImagesAdapter.ViewHolder>{

    private String[] captions;
    private int[] imageIds;

    public static class ViewHolder extends RecyclerView.ViewHolder{
        private CardView cardView;
        public ViewHolder(CardView v) {
            super(v);
            cardView = v;
        }
    }
```

Each ViewHolder will display a CardView.

```java
    public CaptionedImagesAdapter(String[] captions, int[] imageIds){
        this.captions = captions;
        this.imageIds = imageIds;
    }
```

Pass data to the adapter in its constructor.

```java
    @Override
    public CaptionedImagesAdapter.ViewHolder onCreateViewHolder(ViewGroup parent, int viewType){
        CardView cv = (CardView) LayoutInflater.from(parent.getContext())
                .inflate(R.layout.card_captioned_image, parent, false);
        return new ViewHolder(cv);
    }
```

Use our layout for the CardViews.

```java
    public void onBindViewHolder(ViewHolder holder, int position){
        CardView cardView = holder.cardView;
        ImageView imageView = (ImageView)cardView.findViewById(R.id.info_image);
        Drawable drawable = cardView.getResources().getDrawable(imageIds[position]);
        imageView.setImageDrawable(drawable);
        imageView.setContentDescription(captions[position]);
        TextView textView = (TextView)cardView.findViewById(R.id.info_text);
        textView.setText(captions[position]);
    }
```

Populate the CardView's ImageView and TextView with data.

```java
    @Override
    public int getItemCount(){
        return captions.length;
    }
}
```

The number of data items.

BitsAndPizzas

app/src/main

java

com.hfad.bitsandpizzas

CaptionedImages
Adapter.java

Create the recycler view

So far we've created a card view and an adapter. The next thing we need to do is create the recycler view. The recycler view will pass the adapter pizza data so that it can populate the card views with pizzas.

We're going to put the recycler view in a new fragment. This is because we're going to display it in `MainActivity` whenever the user clicks on the Pizzas option in the navigation drawer:

We'll start by creating the fragment. Add a new blank fragment to your project. Give the fragment a name of "PizzaMaterialFragment" and a layout name of "fragment_pizza_material".

On the next page, we'll add the recycler view to the layout.

Add the RecyclerView to the layout

You add a recycler view to the layout using the
`<android.support.v7.widget.RecyclerView>`
element.

Here's the code for *fragment_pizza_material.xml*; it contains a
recycler view with an ID of `pizza_recycler`:

```xml
<?xml version="1.0" encoding="utf-8"?>
<android.support.v7.widget.RecyclerView
    xmlns:android="http://schemas.android.com/apk/res/android"
    android:id="@+id/pizza_recycler"
    android:scrollbars="vertical"
    android:layout_width="match_parent"
    android:layout_height="match_parent"/>
```

This defines a RecyclerView with a vertical scrollbar.

BitsAndPizzas
└ **app/src/main**
  └ **res**
    └ **layout**
      └ fragment_pizza_
         material.xml

You add scrollbars to the recycler view using the
`android:scrollbars` attribute. We've set this to
`"vertical"` because we want our recycler view to display a
vertical list that will scroll vertically.

Now that we've added a recycler view to *fragment_pizza_material.
xml*, we need to add code to *PizzaMaterialFragment.java* to control
its behavior.

Using the adapter

In the code for *PizzaMaterialFragment.java*, we'll get the recycler
view to use the adapter. We need to tell the adapter what
data to use via the adapter's constructor, and then use the
`RecyclerView setAdapter()` method to assign the adapter
to the recycler view:

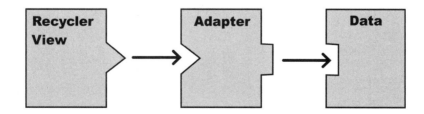

We'll show you the code for *PizzaMaterialFragment.java* on the next
page.

The PizzaMaterialFragment.java code

Here's the code for *PizzaMaterialFragment.java* (it creates an instance of
`CaptionedImagesAdapter`, tells it to use pizza names and images
for its data, and assigns the adapter to the recycler view):

```java
package com.hfad.bitsandpizzas;

import android.app.Fragment;
import android.os.Bundle;
import android.support.v7.widget.RecyclerView;
import android.view.LayoutInflater;
import android.view.View;
import android.view.ViewGroup;
```

← We're using these classes.

```java
public class PizzaMaterialFragment extends Fragment {

    @Override
    public View onCreateView(LayoutInflater inflater, ViewGroup container,
                             Bundle savedInstanceState) {
        RecyclerView pizzaRecycler = (RecyclerView)inflater.inflate(
                        R.layout.fragment_pizza_material, container, false);
```

↖ Use the layout we updated on the previous page.

```java
        String[] pizzaNames = new String[Pizza.pizzas.length];
        for (int i = 0; i < pizzaNames.length; i++) {
            pizzaNames[i] = Pizza.pizzas[i].getName();
        }
```

Add the pizza names to an array of Strings, and the pizza images to an array of ints.

```java
        int[] pizzaImages = new int[Pizza.pizzas.length];
        for (int i = 0; i < pizzaImages.length; i++) {
            pizzaImages[i] = Pizza.pizzas[i].getImageResourceId();
        }
```

Pass the arrays to the adapter.

```java
        CaptionedImagesAdapter adapter = new CaptionedImagesAdapter(pizzaNames, pizzaImages);
        pizzaRecycler.setAdapter(adapter);
        return pizzaRecycler;
    }
}
```

BitsAndPizzas

app/src/main

java

com.hfad.bitsandpizzas

PizzaMaterial
Fragment.java

There's just one more thing we need to do: we need to specify how
the views in the recycler view should be arranged.

A RecyclerView uses a layout manager to arrange its views

One of the ways in which a recycler view is more flexible than a list view is when it comes to arranging its views. A list view displays its views in a single vertical list, but a recycler view gives you more options. You can choose to display views in a linear list, a grid, or a staggered grid.

You specify how to arrange the views using a layout manager. The layout manager positions views inside a recycler view, and the type of layout manager you use determines how items are positioned:

LinearLayoutManager

This arranges items in a vertical or horizontal list.

GridLayoutManager

This arranges items in a grid.

StaggeredGrid LayoutManager

This arranges unevenly sized items in a staggered grid.

On the next page, we'll show you how to specify which layout manager to use.

Specifying the layout manager

You specify the layout manager, using the following lines of code:

```
LinearLayoutManager layoutManager = new LinearLayoutManager(getActivity());
pizzaRecycler.setLayoutManager(layoutManager);
```

This needs to be a Context. If you use this code in an activity, you use this instead of getActivity().

The above code tells the recycler view to use a
LinearLayoutManager, so all the views in the recycler view
will be displayed in a list:

When you use a LinearLayoutManager items are displayed in a linear list.

Using a layout manager means that it's easy to change the
appearance of your recycler view. If you want to display your views
in a grid instead, for instance, you just change the code to use a
GridLayoutManager instead:

```
GridLayoutManager layoutManager = new GridLayoutManager(getActivity(), 2);
pizzaRecycler.setLayoutManager(layoutManager);
```

This says that the GridLayoutManager should be two columns wide.

When you change it to a GridLayoutManager, items are displayed in a grid.

The full PizzaMaterialFragment.java code

Here's the full code for *PizzaMaterialFragment.java*:

```
package com.hfad.bitsandpizzas;

import android.app.Fragment;
import android.os.Bundle;
import android.support.v7.widget.LinearLayoutManager;
import android.support.v7.widget.RecyclerView;
import android.view.LayoutInflater;
import android.view.View;
import android.view.ViewGroup;

public class PizzaMaterialFragment extends Fragment {

    @Override
    public View onCreateView(LayoutInflater inflater, ViewGroup container,
                             Bundle savedInstanceState) {
        RecyclerView pizzaRecycler = (RecyclerView)inflater.inflate(
                        R.layout.fragment_pizza_material, container, false);

        String[] pizzaNames = new String[Pizza.pizzas.length];
        for (int i = 0; i < pizzaNames.length; i++) {
            pizzaNames[i] = Pizza.pizzas[i].getName();
        }

        int[] pizzaImages = new int[Pizza.pizzas.length];
        for (int i = 0; i < pizzaImages.length; i++) {
            pizzaImages[i] = Pizza.pizzas[i].getImageResourceId();
        }

        CaptionedImagesAdapter adapter = new CaptionedImagesAdapter(pizzaNames, pizzaImages);
        pizzaRecycler.setAdapter(adapter);
        LinearLayoutManager layoutManager = new LinearLayoutManager(getActivity());
        pizzaRecycler.setLayoutManager(layoutManager);
        return pizzaRecycler;
    }
}
```

We're using this class, so we need to import it.

BitsAndPizzas
app/src/main
java
com.hfad.bitsandpizzas
PizzaMaterial
Fragment.java

All this code stays the same.

We're going to display the CardViews in a linear list, so we're using a LinearLayoutManager.

Now that we've finished the recycler view code, let's change MainActivity so that it's displayed when the user clicks on the Pizzas option in the navigation drawer.

Get MainActivity to use the new PizzaMaterialFragment

When the user clicks on the Pizzas option, the `ListFragment` called `PizzaFragment` currently gets displayed. To display `PizzaMaterialFragment` instead, we need to replace all references to `PizzaFragment` in our `MainActivity` code with `PizzaMaterialFragment`.

`PizzaFragment` is used two times in *MainActivity.java*, in its `onCreate()` and `selectItem()` methods. Change these lines of code to use `PizzaMaterialFragment` instead:

```
package com.hfad.bitsandpizzas;
...
public class MainActivity extends Activity {
...
    @Override
    protected void onCreate(Bundle savedInstanceState) {
        ...
        getFragmentManager().addOnBackStackChangedListener(
            new FragmentManager.OnBackStackChangedListener() {
                public void onBackStackChanged() {
                    ...
                    if (fragment instanceof PizzaFragment) {
                    if (fragment instanceof PizzaMaterialFragment) {
                        currentPosition = 1;
                    }
                    ...
    }

    private void selectItem(int position) {
        ...
        switch(position) {
            case 1:
                fragment = new PizzaFragment();
                fragment = new PizzaMaterialFragment();
                break;
            ...
        }
    }
}
```

BitsAndPizzas

app/src/main

java

com.hfad.bitsandpizzas

MainActivity.java

We're using our new PizzaMaterialFragment instead of PizzaFragment. This means that when the user clicks on the Pizzas option in the navigation drawer, our shiny new recycler list will be displayed.

Before we run the app, let's go through what the code we've written so far will do.

What happens when the code runs

1 **The user clicks on the Pizzas option in the navigation drawer.**
Code in MainActivity runs to display PizzaMaterialFragment, and
PizzaMaterialFragment's onCreateView() method runs.

MainActivity   PizzaMaterialFragment   onCreateView()

2 **The PizzaMaterialFragment onCreateView() method creates a
LinearLayoutManager and assigns it to the recycler view.**
The LinearLayoutManager means that the views will be displayed in a list. As
the recycler view has a vertical scrollbar, the list will be displayed vertically.

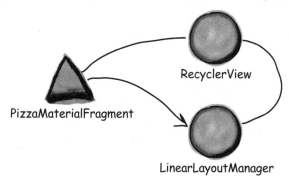

PizzaMaterialFragment   RecyclerView   LinearLayoutManager

3 **The PizzaMaterialFragment onCreateView() method creates a new
CaptionedImagesAdapter.**
It passes the names and images of the pizzas to the adapter using the adapter's
constructor, and sets the adapter to the recycler view.

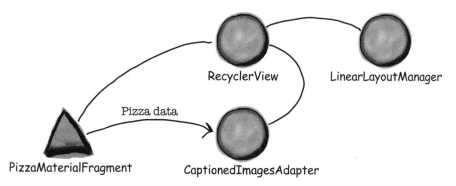

RecyclerView   LinearLayoutManager   Pizza data   PizzaMaterialFragment   CaptionedImagesAdapter

The story continues

④ The adapter creates a view holder for each of the CardViews the recycler view needs to display.

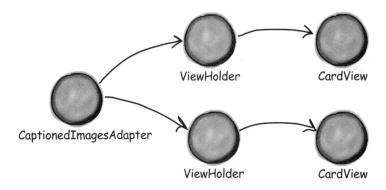

⑤ The adapter then binds the pizza names and images to the text view and image view in each card view.

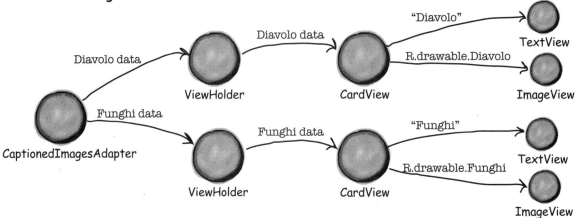

Next, let's run the app and see how it looks.

Test drive the app

Run the app, open the navigation drawer, and click on the
Pizzas option.

When you click on
the Pizzas option,
PizzaMaterialFragment
is displayed. It contains
a linear list of card
views populated with
pizza data.

The recycler view is displayed containing a linear list of
card views. Each card view contains pizza data.

RecyclerView Magnets

Use the magnets on this page and the next to create a new recycler view for the pasta dishes. The recycler view should contain a linear list of card views, each one displaying the name and image of a pasta dish.

↙ This is the code for the Pasta class.

```
package com.hfad.bitsandpizzas;

public class Pasta {
    private String name;
    private int imageResourceId;

    public static final................[] pastas = {
            new Pasta("Spaghetti Bolognese", R.drawable.spag_bol),
            new Pasta("Lasagne", R.drawable.lasagne)
    };

    private Pasta(String name, int imageResourceId) {
        this.name = name;
        this.imageResourceId = imageResourceId;
    }

    public String .....................{
        return name;
    }

    public int .........................{
        return imageResourceId;
    }
}
```

BitsAndPizzas
app/src/main
java
com.hfad.bitsandpizzas
Pasta.java

Magnets:

`getName()` `Pasta`

`android:scrollbars` `RecyclerView`

`android.support.v7.widget.RecyclerView`

`=`

`"vertical"` `getImageResourceId()`

This is the code for the layout. ↓

```
< ........................................................
    xmlns:android="http://schemas.android.com/apk/res/android"
    android:id="@+id/pasta_recycler"

    ........................................................

    android:layout_width="match_parent"
    android:layout_height="match_parent"/>
```

BitsAndPizzas
app/src/main
res
layout
fragment_pasta_material.xml

...

← This is the code for PastaMaterialFragment.java

```java
public class PastaMaterialFragment extends Fragment {

    @Override
    public View onCreateView(LayoutInflater inflater, ViewGroup container,
                             Bundle savedInstanceState) {
        RecyclerView pastaRecycler = (RecyclerView)inflater.inflate(

            ..................................................................., container, false);

        String[] pastaNames = new String[Pasta.pastas.length];
        for (int i = 0; i < pastaNames.length; i++) {
            pastaNames[i] = Pasta.pastas[i].getName();
        }

        int[] pastaImages = new int[Pasta.pastas.length];
        for (int i = 0; i < pastaImages.length; i++) {
            pastaImages[i] = Pasta.pastas[i].getImageResourceId();
        }

        ............................................... adapter =

                new ............................................ (pastaNames, ...........................);
        pastaRecycler.setAdapter(adapter);

        ...................................... layoutManager = new ........................................ (getActivity());
        pastaRecycler.setLayoutManager(layoutManager);
        return pastaRecycler;
    }
}
```

BitsAndPizzas
app/src/main
java
com.hfad.bitsandpizzas
Pasta Material Fragment.java

CaptionedImagesAdapter

ArrayAdapter

CaptionedImagesAdapter

LinearLayout

LinearLayoutManager

R.layout.fragment_pasta_material

pastaImages

LinearLayout

LinearLayoutManager

ArrayAdapter

RecyclerView Magnets Solution

Use the magnets on this page and the next to create a new recycler view for the pasta dishes. The recycler view should contain a linear list of card views, each one displaying the name and image of a pasta dish.

```java
package com.hfad.bitsandpizzas;

public class Pasta {
    private String name;
    private int imageResourceId;

    public static final Pasta[] pastas = {
            new Pasta("Spaghetti Bolognese", R.drawable.spag_bol),
            new Pasta("Lasagne", R.drawable.lasagne)
    };

    private Pasta(String name, int imageResourceId) {
        this.name = name;
        this.imageResourceId = imageResourceId;
    }

    public String getName() {
        return name;
    }

    public int getImageResourceId() {
        return imageResourceId;
    }
}
```

It's an array of Pasta objects.

These methods are used by PastaMaterialFragment.java.

BitsAndPizzas
  app/src/main
    java
      com.hfad.bitsandpizzas
        Pasta.java

RecyclerView

This is a spare magnet.

Add the recycler view to the layout.

```xml
<android.support.v7.widget.RecyclerView
    xmlns:android="http://schemas.android.com/apk/res/android"
    android:id="@+id/pasta_recycler"
    android:scrollbars="vertical"
    android:layout_width="match_parent"
    android:layout_height="match_parent"/>
```

Add vertical scrollbars.

BitsAndPizzas
  app/src/main
    res
      layout
        fragment_pasta_material.xml

```
...

public class PastaMaterialFragment extends Fragment {

    @Override
    public View onCreateView(LayoutInflater inflater, ViewGroup container,
                             Bundle savedInstanceState) {
        RecyclerView pastaRecycler = (RecyclerView)inflater.inflate(
```

Use this layout. → `R.layout.fragment_pasta_material` , container, false);

BitsAndPizzas
app/src/main
java
com.hfad.bitsandpizzas
Pasta Material Fragment.java

```
        String[] pastaNames = new String[Pasta.pastas.length];
        for (int i = 0; i < pastaNames.length; i++) {
            pastaNames[i] = Pasta.pastas[i].getName();
        }

        int[] pastaImages = new int[Pasta.pastas.length];
        for (int i = 0; i < pastaImages.length; i++) {
            pastaImages[i] = Pasta.pastas[i].getImageResourceId();
        }
```

We're using the CaptionedImagesAdapter we wrote earlier.

Pass the pasta names and images to the adapter.

`CaptionedImagesAdapter` adapter =

new `CaptionedImagesAdapter` (pastaNames, `pastaImages`);

```
        pastaRecycler.setAdapter(adapter);
```

`LinearLayoutManager` layoutManager = new `LinearLayoutManager` (getActivity());

```
        pastaRecycler.setLayoutManager(layoutManager);
        return pastaRecycler;
```

Use the LinearLayoutManager to display the card views in a linear list.

```
    }
}
```

You didn't need to use these magnets.

`LinearLayout`

`LinearLayout`   `ArrayAdapter`   `ArrayAdapter`

Where we've got to

Here's a reminder of where we've got to with our app:

1 **When the app gets launched, it starts MainActivity.**
The activity uses layout *activity_main.xml* and has a navigation drawer. When the user clicks on one of the options in the navigation drawer it displays the appropriate fragment.

2 **When the user clicks the Pizzas option, it displays PizzasMaterialFragment.**
`PizzasMaterialFragment` contains a recycler view.

3 **PizzaMaterialFragment uses an adapter, CaptionedImagesAdapter, to display card views showing an image and caption for each pizza.**
The card views are defined in *card_captioned_image.xml*.

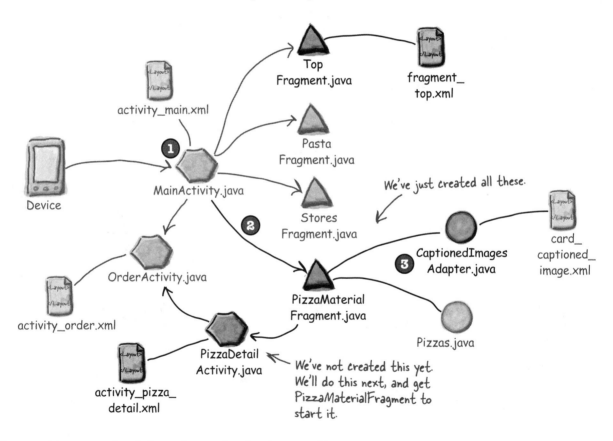

The next thing we need to do is get the recycler view to respond to clicks so it starts `PizzaDetailActivity` when the user clicks on one of the pizzas. `PizzaDetailActivity` will then display details of the pizza the user selected.

We'll create `PizzaDetailActivity` next.

Create PizzaDetailActivity

`PizzaDetailActivity` will display the name of the pizza the user selected, along with its image.

Create a new blank activity called "PizzaDetailActivity" with a layout name of "activity_pizza_detail" and a title of "Pizza Detail". Then update *activity_pizza_detail.xml* with the code below, which adds a text view and image view to the layout that we'll use to display details of the pizza:

```xml
<LinearLayout xmlns:android="http://schemas.android.com/apk/res/android"
    xmlns:tools="http://schemas.android.com/tools"
    android:layout_width="match_parent"
    android:layout_height="match_parent"
    android:orientation="vertical"
    tools:context="com.hfad.bitsandpizzas.PizzaDetailActivity">

    <TextView
        android:id="@+id/pizza_text"
        android:layout_width="wrap_content"
        android:layout_height="wrap_content"
        android:textAppearance="?android:attr/textAppearanceLarge" />

    <ImageView
        android:id="@+id/pizza_image"
        android:layout_height="wrap_content"
        android:layout_width="match_parent"
        android:adjustViewBounds="true"/>

</LinearLayout>
```

> BitsAndPizzas
> app/src/main
> res
> layout
> activity_pizza_detail.xml

PizzaDetailActivity contains a TextView and an ImageView. We'll put the name of the pizza in the TextView and the pizza's image in the ImageView.

We'll look at what we need the code for *PizzaDetailActivity.java* to do on the next page.

What PizzaDetailActivity.java needs to do

There are a few things that we need *PizzaDetailActivity.java* to do:

⭐ `PizzaDetailActivity`'s main purpose is to display the name and image of the pizza the user has selected. To do this, we'll get the ID of the pizza the user has selected from the intent that started the activity. We'll pass this to `PizzaDetailActivity` from `PizzaMaterialFragment` when the user clicks on one of the pizzas in the recycler view.

⭐ Back in Chapter 9, we created a menu resource file that describes items we wanted to add to the action bar. We'll use the `onCreateOptionsMenu()` to add these items to `PizzaDetailActivity`'s action bar.

⭐ The menu resource file describes a Share action that we can use to share information. We'll add an intent to the Share action that will share the name of the pizza the user has selected.

⭐ The menu resource file also describes a Create Order action. When the user clicks on this, we'll start `OrderActivity`.

⭐ We'll enable the `PizzaDetailActivity`'s Up button so that when the user clicks on it, they get returned to `MainActivity`.

Update AndroidManifest.xml

We'll start by updating *AndroidManifest.xml* to specify that `MainActivity` is the parent of `PizzaDetailActivity`. This means that when the user clicks on the Up button in `PizzaDetailActivity`'s action bar, `MainActivity` will be displayed:

```
<activity
    android:name=".PizzaDetailActivity"
    android:label="@string/title_activity_pizza_detail"
    android:parentActivityName=".MainActivity">
</activity>
```

MainActivity is PizzaDetailActivity's parent.

BitsAndPizzas
app/src/main
AndroidManifest.xml

Once you've done that, we'll look at how to get the recycler view to respond to clicks.

The code for PizzaDetailActivity.java

Here's the full code for *PizzaDetailActivity.java* (don't worry if it seems
like a lot, this is all code that you've seen before):

```java
package com.hfad.bitsandpizzas;

import android.app.Activity;
import android.content.Intent;
import android.os.Bundle;
import android.view.Menu;
import android.view.MenuItem;
import android.widget.ImageView;
import android.widget.ShareActionProvider;
import android.widget.TextView;
```

We're using these classes.

> BitsAndPizzas
> └ app/src/main
>   └ java
>   └ com.hfad.bitsandpizzas
>   └ PizzaDetailActivity.java

```java
public class PizzaDetailActivity extends Activity {

    private ShareActionProvider shareActionProvider;
    public static final String EXTRA_PIZZANO = "pizzaNo";
```

We'll use this constant to pass the ID of the pizza as extra information in the intent.

```java
    @Override
    protected void onCreate(Bundle savedInstanceState) {
        super.onCreate(savedInstanceState);
        setContentView(R.layout.activity_pizza_detail);

        //Enable the Up button
        getActionBar().setDisplayHomeAsUpEnabled(true);
```

← Enable the Up button.

```java
        //Display details of the pizza
        int pizzaNo = (Integer)getIntent().getExtras().get(EXTRA_PIZZANO);
        String pizzaName = Pizza.pizzas[pizzaNo].getName();
        TextView textView = (TextView)findViewById(R.id.pizza_text);
        textView.setText(pizzaName);
        int pizzaImage = Pizza.pizzas[pizzaNo].getImageResourceId();
        ImageView imageView = (ImageView)findViewById(R.id.pizza_image);
        imageView.setImageDrawable(getResources().getDrawable(pizzaImage));
        imageView.setContentDescription(pizzaName);
    }
```

Get the pizza the user chose from the intent.

Use the pizza ID to populate the TextView and ImageView.

The PizzaDetailActivity code (continued)

```
@Override
public boolean onCreateOptionsMenu(Menu menu) {
    getMenuInflater().inflate(R.menu.menu_main, menu);

    //Share the name of the pizza
    TextView textView = (TextView)findViewById(R.id.pizza_text);
    CharSequence pizzaName = textView.getText();
    MenuItem menuItem = menu.findItem(R.id.action_share);
    shareActionProvider = (ShareActionProvider) menuItem.getActionProvider();
    Intent intent = new Intent(Intent.ACTION_SEND);
    intent.setType("text/plain");
    intent.putExtra(Intent.EXTRA_TEXT, pizzaName);
    shareActionProvider.setShareIntent(intent);
    return true;
}

@Override
public boolean onOptionsItemSelected(MenuItem item) {
    switch (item.getItemId()) {
        case R.id.action_create_order:
            Intent intent = new Intent(this, OrderActivity.class);
            startActivity(intent);
            return true;
        default:
            return super.onOptionsItemSelected(item);
    }
}
```

Add items in the menu resource file to the action bar.

Set the default text to share in the Share action.

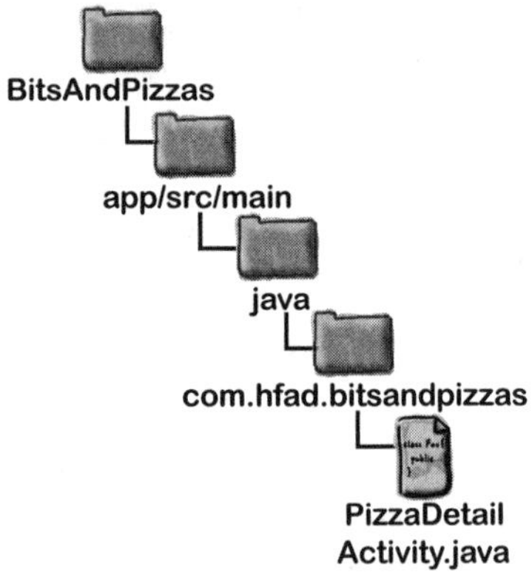

BitsAndPizzas

app/src/main

java

com.hfad.bitsandpizzas

PizzaDetail
Activity.java

Start OrderActivity when the user clicks on it in the action bar.

Once you've updated your *PizzaDetailActivity.java* code, we'll
look at how to get the recycler view to respond to clicks.

Getting a RecyclerView to respond to clicks

We need to get items in the recycler view to respond to clicks so that we can start `PizzaDetailActivity` when the user clicks on a particular pizza.

When you create a navigation list with a list view, you can respond to click events within the list by giving the list view an `OnItemClickListener`. The list view listens to each of the views that it contains, and if any of them are clicked, the list view calls its `OnItemClickListener`. That means that you can respond to list item clicks with very little code.

List views are able to do this because they inherit a bunch of functionality from a very deep hierarchy of superclasses. Recycler views, however, don't have such a rich set of built-in methods, as they don't inherit from the same superclasses:

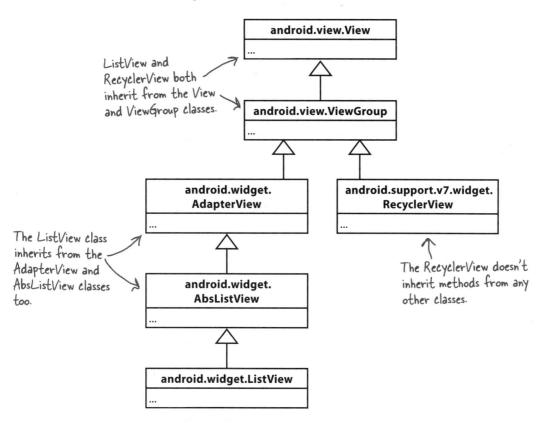

While this gives you more flexibility, it also means that with the recycler view you have to do a lot more of the work yourself. So how do we get the recycler view to respond to clicks?

You can listen to views from the adapter

If you want your recycler view to respond to clicks, you need to write the code yourself. In order to write event code, you need access to the views that appear inside the recycler view. So where do you do that?

The views are all created inside the `CaptionedImagesAdapter` class. When a view appears on screen, the recycler view calls the `onBindViewHolder()` code to make the card view match the details of the list item.

Let's say you want to send the user to an activity that displays a single pizza whenever a pizza card view is clicked. That means you *could* put some code inside the adapter to start an activity like this:

```java
class CaptionedImagesAdapter extends RecyclerView.Adapter<CaptionedImagesAdapter.ViewHolder>{
...
    public void onBindViewHolder(ViewHolder holder, int position){
        CardView cardView = holder.cardView;
        ImageView imageView = (ImageView)cardView.findViewById(R.id.info_image);
        Drawable drawable = cardView.getResources().getDrawable(imageIds[position]);
        imageView.setImageDrawable(drawable);
        TextView textView = (TextView)cardView.findViewById(R.id.info_text);
        textView.setText(captions[position]);
        cardView.setOnClickListener(new View.OnClickListener(){
            @Override
            public void onClick(View v) {
                Intent intent = new Intent(container.getContext(), PizzaDetailActivity.class);
                intent.putExtra(PizzaDetailActivity.EXTRA_PIZZANO, position);
                container.getContext().startActivity(intent);
            }
        });
    }
}
```

Adding this code to CaptionedImagesAdapter will start PizzaDetailActivity when a CardView is clicked.

But just because you *could* write this code, doesn't necessarily mean that you should.

BRAIN POWER

You *could* respond to a click event by adding code to your adapter class. Is there a reason why you *wouldn't* want to do that?

Keep your adapters reusable

If you deal with click events in the `CaptionedImagesAdapter` class, *you'll limit how that adapter can be used.* Think about the app we're building. We want to display lists of pizzas, pasta, and stores. In each case, we'll probably want to display a list of captioned images. If we modify the `CaptionedImagesAdapter` class so that clicks always send the user to an activity that displays details of a single pizza, we won't be able to use the `CaptionedImagesAdapter` for the pasta and stores lists. We'll have to create a separate adapter for each one.

Decouple your adapter with an interface

Instead, we'll keep the code that starts the activity outside of the adapter. When someone clicks on an item in the list, we want the adapter to call the fragment that contains the list and the fragment code can then fire off an intent to the next activity. That way we can reuse `CaptionedImagesAdapter` for the pizzas, pasta, and stores lists, and leave it to the fragments in each case to decide what happens in response to a click.

We're going to use a similar pattern to the one that allowed us to decouple a fragment from an activity. We'll create a `Listener` interface inside `CaptionedImagesAdapter` like this:

```java
public static interface Listener {
    public void onClick(int position);
}
```

We'll call the Listener's `onClick()` method whenever one of the card views in the recycler view is clicked. We'll then add code to `PizzaMaterialFragment` so that it implements the interface; this will allow the fragment to respond to clicks and start an activity.

This is what will happen at runtime:

1   A user will click on a card view in the recycler view.

2   The `Listener`'s `onClick()` method will be called.

3   The `onClick()` method is implemented in `PizzaMaterialFragment`. Code in the fragment starts `PizzaDetailActivity`.

Let's start by adding code to *CaptionedImagesAdapter.java*.

Add the interface to the adapter

We've updated our *CaptionedImagesAdapter.java* code to add the `Listener` interface and call its `onClick()` method whenever one of the card views is clicked (apply the changes to your code, then save your work):

```
package com.hfad.bitsandpizzas;

import android.graphics.drawable.Drawable;
import android.support.v7.widget.RecyclerView;
import android.view.LayoutInflater;
import android.view.View;          ← We're using this extra class, so import it.
import android.view.ViewGroup;
import android.support.v7.widget.CardView;
import android.widget.ImageView;
import android.widget.TextView;


class CaptionedImagesAdapter extends RecyclerView.Adapter<CaptionedImagesAdapter.ViewHolder>{

    private String[] captions;
    private int[] imageIds;
    private Listener listener;       ← Add the Listener as a private variable.

    public static interface Listener {      ← This is the interface.
        public void onClick(int position);
    }

    public static class ViewHolder extends RecyclerView.ViewHolder{
        private CardView cardView;
        public ViewHolder(CardView v) {
            super(v);
            cardView = v;              ↑
        }                          We're not changing these methods.
    }

    public CaptionedImagesAdapter(String[] captions, int[] imageIds){
        this.captions = captions;
        this.imageIds = imageIds;
    }
```

BitsAndPizzas
└ app/src/main
  └ java
    └ com.hfad.bitsandpizzas
      └ CaptionedImages
        Adapter.java

The CaptionedImagesAdapter.java code (continued)

```java
public void setListener(Listener listener){
    this.listener = listener;
}
```
← Activity's and fragments will use this method to register as a listener.

```java
@Override
public CaptionedImagesAdapter.ViewHolder onCreateViewHolder(ViewGroup parent, int viewType){
    CardView cv = (CardView) LayoutInflater.from(parent.getContext())
            .inflate(R.layout.card_captioned_image, parent, false);
    return new ViewHolder(cv);
}

public void onBindViewHolder(ViewHolder holder, final int position){
    CardView cardView = holder.cardView;
    ImageView imageView = (ImageView)cardView.findViewById(R.id.info_image);
    Drawable drawable = cardView.getResources().getDrawable(imageIds[position]);
    imageView.setImageDrawable(drawable);
    imageView.setContentDescription(captions[position]);
    TextView textView = (TextView)cardView.findViewById(R.id.info_text);
    textView.setText(captions[position]);
    cardView.setOnClickListener(new View.OnClickListener() {
        @Override
        public void onClick(View v) {
            if (listener != null) {
                listener.onClick(position);
            }
        }
    });
}
```

When the CardView is clicked, call the Listener onClick() method.

BitsAndPizzas
app/src/main
java
com.hfad.bitsandpizzas
CaptionedImages
Adapter.java

```java
@Override
public int getItemCount(){
    return captions.length;
}
```

Now that we've added a Listener to the adapter, we'll implement it in *PizzaMaterialFragment.java*.

Implement the listener in PizzaMaterialFragment.java

We'll implement CaptionedImagesAdapter's Listener interface in PizzaMaterialFragment so that when a card view in the recycler view is clicked, PizzaDetailActivity will be started. Here's the code:

```java
package com.hfad.bitsandpizzas;

import android.app.Fragment;
import android.content.Intent;
import android.os.Bundle;
import android.support.v7.widget.LinearLayoutManager;
import android.support.v7.widget.RecyclerView;
import android.view.LayoutInflater;
import android.view.View;
import android.view.ViewGroup;

public class PizzaMaterialFragment extends Fragment {

    @Override
    public View onCreateView(LayoutInflater inflater, ViewGroup container,
                             Bundle savedInstanceState) {
        RecyclerView pizzaRecycler = (RecyclerView)inflater.inflate(
                        R.layout.fragment_pizza_material, container, false);

        String[] pizzaNames = new String[Pizza.pizzas.length];
        for (int i = 0; i < pizzaNames.length; i++) {
            pizzaNames[i] = Pizza.pizzas[i].getName();
        }

        int[] pizzaImages = new int[Pizza.pizzas.length];
        for (int i = 0; i < pizzaImages.length; i++) {
            pizzaImages[i] = Pizza.pizzas[i].getImageResourceId();
        }
```

We're using an Intent to start the activity, so import the class.

BitsAndPizzas

app/src/main

java

com.hfad.bitsandpizzas

PizzaMaterial Fragment.java

This code stays the same.

The PizzaMaterialFragment.java code (continued)

```
        CaptionedImagesAdapter adapter = new CaptionedImagesAdapter(pizzaNames, pizzaImages);
        pizzaRecycler.setAdapter(adapter);
        LinearLayoutManager layoutManager = new LinearLayoutManager(getActivity());
        pizzaRecycler.setLayoutManager(layoutManager);

        adapter.setListener(new CaptionedImagesAdapter.Listener() {
            public void onClick(int position) {
                Intent intent = new Intent(getActivity(), PizzaDetailActivity.class);
                intent.putExtra(PizzaDetailActivity.EXTRA_PIZZANO, position);
                getActivity().startActivity(intent);
            }
        });
        return pizzaRecycler;
    }
}
```

This implements the Listener onClick() method. It starts PizzaDetailActivity, passing it the ID of the pizza the user chose.

BitsAndPizzas

app/src/main

java

com.hfad.bitsandpizzas

PizzaMaterial
Fragment.java

That's all the code we need to make views in the recycler view respond to clicks. By taking this approach, we can use the same adapter and card view for different types of data that is composed of an image view and text view.

PizzaMaterialFragment.java

PastaMaterialFragment.java

StoresMaterialFragment.java

CaptionedImages
Adapter.java

card_captioned_
image.xml

All of these fragments can use the same adapter and card view.

Let's see what happens when we run the code.

Test drive the app

Run the app, open the navigation drawer, and click on the Pizzas option. A list of card views is displayed, each one showing a different pizza, as before. Let's see what happens when you click on one of the pizzas:

When you click on the Pizzas option, PizzaMaterialFragment is displayed.

When you click on a pizza, its details are displayed in PizzaDetailActivity.

The card view responds to the click, and displays `PizzaDetailActivity`.

There's just one more thing we need to look at: the content we need to include in `TopFragment`.

Bring the content forward

When we first looked at the design of the Pizza app, `TopFragment` contained a list of navigation options. We moved these away from `TopFragment` using a combination of an action bar and navigation drawer, leaving `TopFragment` empty. So what should `TopFragment` contain?

`TopFragment` is our top-level screen, so it's the first screen that your users see when they start the app. Your top-level screen should be rewarding for both new and regular users, and one way you can do this is by bringing the content forward.

If you look at some of the Google apps on your device, there's one thing they have in common: they allow you to get to the main content of the app quickly by bringing some of it forward onto the top-level screen. The Calendar app displays upcoming events. Apps such as Play Books and Play Music display your recent actions and recommendations. They form the centerpiece of the top-level screen.

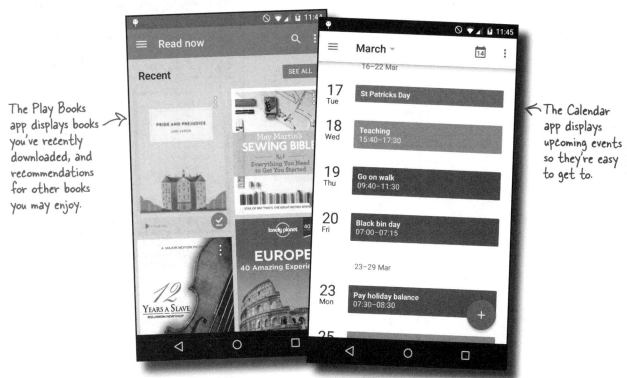

The Play Books app displays books you've recently downloaded, and recommendations for other books you may enjoy.

The Calendar app displays upcoming events so they're easy to get to.

We can bring the content forward in our Pizza app by displaying some of the food that's available in `TopFragment`. The good news is that you can do this with very little effort using the skills you've already learned in this chapter.

You're going to change `TopFragment` so that it displays introductory text and a recycler view that displays pizzas. First, write the layout code for *fragment_top.xml*. You need `TopFragment` to look like the image below.

This is what you want TopFragment to look like.

Sharpen your pencil

Next, add code to the box below to finish writing the code for *TopFragment.java* so that the recycler view is populated with two pizzas in a grid layout. If the user clicks on one of the pizzas, display its details in *PizzaDetailActivity.java*.

```java
...
public class TopFragment extends Fragment {

    @Override
    public View onCreateView(LayoutInflater inflater, ViewGroup container,
                             Bundle savedInstanceState) {
        RelativeLayout layout = (RelativeLayout)
                        inflater.inflate(R.layout.fragment_top, container, false);
```

Write →
your
code
here.

```java
        CaptionedImagesAdapter adapter =
                            new CaptionedImagesAdapter(pizzaNames, pizzaImages);
        pizzaRecycler.setAdapter(adapter);
        adapter.setListener(new CaptionedImagesAdapter.Listener() {
            public void onClick(int position) {
                Intent intent = new Intent(getActivity(), PizzaDetailActivity.class);
                intent.putExtra(PizzaDetailActivity.EXTRA_PIZZANO, position);
                getActivity().startActivity(intent);
            }
        });
        return layout;
    }
}
```

Most of the code is the same as for
PizzaMaterialFragment.java.

Exercise Solution

You're going to change `TopFragment` so that it displays introductory text and a recycler view that displays pizzas. First, write the layout code for *fragment_top.xml*. You need `TopFragment` to look like the image below.

Don't worry if your code looks different to ours. There are many different ways of creating a similar looking layout.

```xml
<RelativeLayout xmlns:android="http://schemas.android.com/apk/res/android"
    xmlns:tools="http://schemas.android.com/tools"
    android:layout_width="match_parent"
    android:layout_height="match_parent"
    android:paddingTop="16dp"
    android:paddingBottom="16dp"
    android:paddingRight="16dp"
    android:paddingLeft="16dp"
    tools:context=".MainActivity">
```

This is for the introductory text.

```xml
    <TextView
        android:layout_width="match_parent"
        android:layout_height="wrap_content"
        android:text="@string/welcome_text"
        android:id="@+id/welcome_text" />
```

This is for the recycler view.

```xml
    <android.support.v7.widget.RecyclerView
        android:id="@+id/pizza_recycler"
        android:scrollbars="vertical"
        android:layout_width="match_parent"
        android:layout_height="wrap_content"
        android:layout_below="@+id/welcome_text"
        android:layout_marginTop="10dp"/>
</RelativeLayout>
```

Sharpen your pencil
Solution

Next, add code to the box below to finish writing the code for *TopFragment.java* so that the recycler view is populated with two pizzas in a grid layout. If the user clicks on one of the pizzas, display its details in *PizzaDetailActivity.java*.

```
...
public class TopFragment extends Fragment {

    @Override
    public View onCreateView(LayoutInflater inflater, ViewGroup container,
                             Bundle savedInstanceState) {
        RelativeLayout layout = (RelativeLayout)
                        inflater.inflate(R.layout.fragment_top, container, false);
```

Your code may look different.

```
RecyclerView pizzaRecycler = (RecyclerView)layout.findViewById(R.id.pizza_recycler);
String[] pizzaNames = new String[2];
for (int i = 0; i < 2; i++) {
    pizzaNames[i] = Pizza.pizzas[i].getName();
}
int[] pizzaImages = new int[2];  ← We'll display two pizzas.
for (int i = 0; i < 2; i++) {
    pizzaImages[i] = Pizza.pizzas[i].getImageResourceId();
}                              ┌ Display the pizzas in a two-column grid.
GridLayoutManager layoutManager = new GridLayoutManager(getActivity(),2);
pizzaRecycler.setLayoutManager(layoutManager);
```

```
        CaptionedImagesAdapter adapter =
                                new CaptionedImagesAdapter(pizzaNames, pizzaImages);
        pizzaRecycler.setAdapter(adapter);
        adapter.setListener(new CaptionedImagesAdapter.Listener() {
            public void onClick(int position) {
                Intent intent = new Intent(getActivity(), PizzaDetailActivity.class);
                intent.putExtra(PizzaDetailActivity.EXTRA_PIZZANO, position);
                getActivity().startActivity(intent);
            }
        });
        return layout;
    }
}
```

Most of the code is the same as for
PizzaMaterialFragment.java.

The full code for fragment_top.xml

We've changed `TopFragment` so that it displays introductory text and two pizzas. We'll show you the full code over the next couple of pages.

First, add the following to *strings.xml*:

```xml
<string name="welcome_text">We offer a range of freshly baked pizza and pasta
dishes. Why not try some?</string>
```

Then update *fragment_top.xml* with the following code:

```xml
<RelativeLayout xmlns:android="http://schemas.android.com/apk/res/android"
    xmlns:tools="http://schemas.android.com/tools"
    android:layout_width="match_parent"
    android:layout_height="match_parent"
    android:paddingTop="16dp"
    android:paddingBottom="16dp"
    android:paddingRight="16dp"
    android:paddingLeft="16dp"
    tools:context=".MainActivity">

    <TextView
        android:layout_width="match_parent"
        android:layout_height="wrap_content"
        android:text="@string/welcome_text"
        android:id="@+id/welcome_text" />

    <android.support.v7.widget.RecyclerView
        android:id="@+id/pizza_recycler"
        android:scrollbars="vertical"
        android:layout_width="match_parent"
        android:layout_height="wrap_content"
        android:layout_below="@+id/welcome_text"
        android:layout_marginTop="10dp"/>
</RelativeLayout>
```

BitsAndPizzas
app/src/main
res
layout
fragment_top.xml

We're adding a TextView and RecyclerView to the layout.

On the next page, we'll show you the code for *TopFragment.java*.

The full code for TopFragment.java

```java
package com.hfad.bitsandpizzas;

import android.content.Intent;
import android.os.Bundle;
import android.app.Fragment;
import android.support.v7.widget.GridLayoutManager;
import android.support.v7.widget.RecyclerView;
import android.view.LayoutInflater;
import android.view.View;
import android.view.ViewGroup;
import android.widget.RelativeLayout;
```

We're using these classes.

BitsAndPizzas

app/src/main

java

com.hfad.bitsandpizzas

TopFragment.java

```java
public class TopFragment extends Fragment {

    @Override
    public View onCreateView(LayoutInflater inflater, ViewGroup container,
                             Bundle savedInstanceState) {
        RelativeLayout layout = (RelativeLayout)
                        inflater.inflate(R.layout.fragment_top, container, false);
        RecyclerView pizzaRecycler = (RecyclerView)layout.findViewById(R.id.pizza_recycler);
        String[] pizzaNames = new String[2];
        for (int i = 0; i < 2; i++) {
            pizzaNames[i] = Pizza.pizzas[i].getName();
        }
        int[] pizzaImages = new int[2];
        for (int i = 0; i < 2; i++) {
            pizzaImages[i] = Pizza.pizzas[i].getImageResourceId();
        }
        GridLayoutManager layoutManager = new GridLayoutManager(getActivity(),2);
        pizzaRecycler.setLayoutManager(layoutManager);
        CaptionedImagesAdapter adapter = new CaptionedImagesAdapter(pizzaNames, pizzaImages);
        pizzaRecycler.setAdapter(adapter);
        adapter.setListener(new CaptionedImagesAdapter.Listener() {
            public void onClick(int position) {
                Intent intent = new Intent(getActivity(), PizzaDetailActivity.class);
                intent.putExtra(PizzaDetailActivity.EXTRA_PIZZANO, position);
                getActivity().startActivity(intent);
            }
        });
        return layout;
    }
}
```

← Create arrays for the pizza names and images.

← Display the pizzas in a grid.

↖ Use the adapter to display the pizzas.

↑ Start PizzaDetailActivity when the user clicks on a pizza, passing it the position of the pizza.

Test drive the app

Let's see what happens when you run the app.

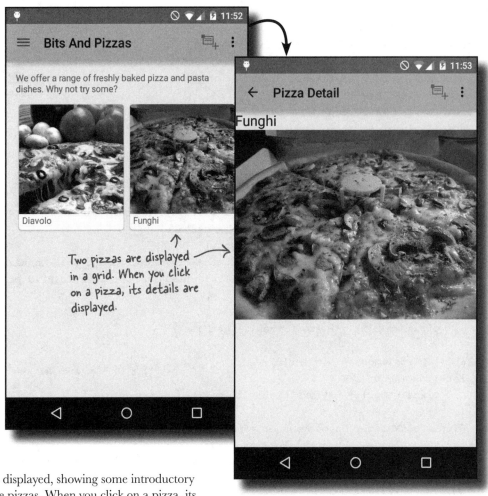

Two pizzas are displayed in a grid. When you click on a pizza, its details are displayed.

`TopFragment` is displayed, showing some introductory text and two of the pizzas. When you click on a pizza, its details are displayed in `PizzaDetailActivity`.

Your Android Toolbox

You've got Chapter 14 under your belt and now you've added Material Design to your tool box.

You can download the full code for the chapter from https://tinyurl.com/HeadFirstAndroid.

BULLET POINTS

- Card views and recycler views have their own support libraries.

- Add a card view to a layout using the `<android.support.v7.widget.CardView>` element.

- Give the card view rounded corners using the `cardCornerRadius` attribute. This requires a namespace of `"http://schemas.android.com/apk/res-auto"`.

- Recycler views work with adapters that are subclasses of `RecyclerView.Adapter`.

- When you create your own `RecyclerView.Adapter`, you must define the `ViewHolder` and implement the `onCreateViewHolder()`, `onBindViewHolder()`, and `getItemCount()` methods.

- You add a recycler view to a layout using the `<android.support.v7.widget.RecyclerView>` element. You give it a scrollbar using the `android:scrollbars` attribute.

- Use a layout manager to specify how items in a recycler view should be arranged. A `LinearLayoutManager` arranges items in a linear list, a `GridLayoutManager` arranges items in a grid, and a `StaggeredGridLayoutManager` arranges items in a staggered grid.

Leaving town...

It's been great having you here in Androidville

We're sad to see you leave, but there's nothing like taking what you've learned and putting it to use. There are still a few more gems for you in the back of the book and an index to read through, and then it's time to take all these new ideas and put them into practice. Bon voyage!

The Android Runtime

So **that's** what's going on under the hood...

Android apps need to run on devices with low-powered processors and very little memory.

Java apps can take up a lot of memory, and because they run inside their own Java Virtual Machine (JVM), Java apps can take a long time to start when they're running on low-powered machines. Android deals with this by not using the JVM for its apps. Instead, it uses a very different virtual machine called the **Android runtime (ART)**. In this appendix, we'll look at how ART gets your Java apps to run well on a small, low-powered device.

What is the Android runtime (ART)?

The Android runtime (ART) is thé system that runs your compiled code on an Android device. It first appeared on Android with the release of KitKat and became the standard way of running code in Lollipop.

ART is designed to run your compiled Android apps quickly and efficiently on small, low-powered devices.

ART is very different from the JVM

Java has been around for a very long time, and compiled Java programs have almost always run on Oracle's Java Virtual Machine (JVM). The JVM simulates a CPU chip, and it reads a compiled *.class* file that contains JVM machine code instructions called bytecodes. Traditionally you would compile *.java* source files into *.class* files. You would then run these using the JVM interpreter.

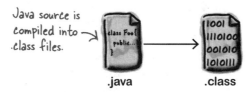

Java source is compiled into .class files.

.java → **.class**

ART is very different. When you compile an Android application, everything starts in the same way. You write *.java* source files and compile them into *.class* files, but then a tool called dx will convert the set of *.class* (or *.jar* archives) into a single file called *classes.dex*.

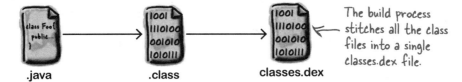

.java → **.class** → **classes.dex**

The build process stitches all the class files into a single classes.dex file.

This *classes.dex* file also contains bytecodes, but they are different from the bytecodes in a *.class* file. The *.dex* bytecodes are for a completely different virtual processor called **Dalvik**. In fact, dex stands for Dalvik Executable.

The Dalvik processor is kind of similar to the JVM. Both the JVM and Dalvik are virtual processors. They are both theoretical chips. But the Oracle JVM is a stack-based processor and Dalvik is a register-based processor. Some people believe that code for register-based processors can be tuned to be smaller and to run faster. By converting a whole set of different files into a single *classes.dex* file, the dx tool is able to make the compiled app a lot smaller because it can remove a lot of duplicated symbols that might appear in many *.class* files.

The *classes.dex* file is then compressed with a bunch of other resource and data files into a ZIP-compressed file called an application package or APK file. The *.apk* file is the final compiled application that can be installed on an Android device. This is the file that you'll eventually upload to the Google Play Store.

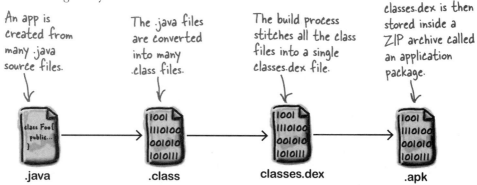

An app is created from many .java source files.

The .java files are converted into many .class files.

The build process stitches all the class files into a single classes.dex file.

classes.dex is then stored inside a ZIP archive called an application package.

.java → .class → classes.dex → .apk

How Android runs an APK file

The APK file is just a ZIP-compressed archive. When it's transferred to an Android device, it's stored in a directory called */data/ app/<package name>* and then the *classes.dex* file is extracted from it.

When the *classes.dex* file is extracted from the APK archive, it's converted into a native library. The Dalvik bytecodes become actual native machine code instructions that can be run directly by the device's CPU. This compiled library is then stored in the */data/dalvik-cache* directory. Android only needs to perform this native compilation step the first time that the app is run. From then on, the Android device can simply load and run the native library.

Android is just a version of the Linux operating system, and Linux doesn't normally have the ability to run Android apps. That's why each Android device runs a process called **Zygote**. Zygote is like an Android process that is already up and running. When you tell Android to start a new Android app, Zygote will create a forked version of itself. A forked process is just another copy of the process in memory. Linux can fork processes very quickly, so by forking the Zygote process and then loading the native library, an Android app can be loaded very quickly.

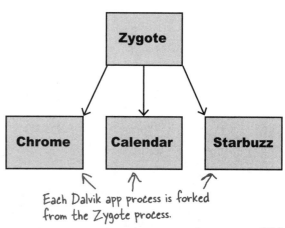

Each Dalvik app process is forked from the Zygote process.

Performance and size

Android devices usually have a lot less power and storage than machines that normally run Java code. ART uses *.dex* files that are normally smaller than their equivalent *.class* files. The Oracle JVM can compile some parts of the code it interprets using just-in-time compilation, which means that the JVM converts Java bytecode into machine code while it's running the code. This is fine for applications that run for a very long time, like application servers, but Android applications might be started and stopped regularly. By compiling all of the Dalvik bytecodes into a native library ahead of time, ART ensures that it only needs to compile the code once.

Finally, the Oracle Java runtime can take some time to start on low-powered devices. By using the Zygote process, Android is able to get apps up and running much more quickly. The Zygote process can also use shared memory to securely execute code that will be common to all Dalvik processes.

Security

An Android device might run code from many different developers, and it's important that each app is completely isolated from every other app. Without that separation, one app might breach the security of any other app on the device. To ensure that apps are isolated, Android will run each app in a separate process, with an automatically generated user account. This allows apps to be isolated using operating system security provided by Linux. If the Oracle Java runtime was used, each process would require its own Java process, which would greatly increase the memory required to run several apps.

The Android Debug Bridge

What better gift for the girl who has everything than a new command-line tool?

Why, darling, that's so thoughtful.

In this book, we've focused on using an IDE for all your Android needs.

But there are times when using a command-line tool can be plain useful, like those times when Android Studio can't see your Android device but you just *know* it's there. In this chapter, we'll introduce you to the **Android Debug Bridge (or adb)**, a command-line tool you can use to communicate with the emulator or Android devices.

adb: your command-line pal

Every time your development machine needs to talk to an Android device, whether it's a real device connected with a USB cable, or a virtual device running in an emulator, it does it by using the **Android Debug Bridge (adb)**. The adb is a process that's controlled by a command that's also called adb.

The `adb` command is stored in the `platform-tools` directory of the Android System Developer's Kit. On a Mac, you'll probably find it in */Users/<username>/Library/Android/sdk/platform-tools*. If you add the *platform-tools* directory to your `PATH`, you will be able to run adb from the command line.

In a terminal or at a command prompt, you can use it like this:

```
Interactive Session
$ adb devices
List of devices attached
emulator-5554      device
$
```

The `adb devices` command means "Tell me which Android devices you are connected to". The `adb` command works by talking to an adb server process, which runs in the background. The adb server is sometimes called the *adb dæmon* or *adbd*. When you enter an `adb` command in a terminal, a request is sent to network port 5037 on your machine. The adbd listens for commands to come in on this port. When Android Studio wants to run an app, or check the log output, or do anything else that involves talking to an Android device, it will do it via command port 5037.

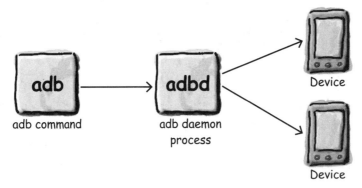

When the adbd receives a command, it will forward it to a separate adbd process that's running in the relevant Android device. This will then be able to make changes to the Android device or return the requested information.

Sometimes, if the adb server isn't running, the `adb` command will
need to start it:

```
Interactive Session
$ adb devices
* daemon not running. starting it now on port 5037 *
* daemon started successfully *
List of devices attached
emulator-5554       device
$
```

Likewise, if ever you plug in an Android device and Android
Studio can't see it, you can manually kill the adb server and restart
it:

```
Interactive Session
$ adb devices
List of devices attached
$ adb kill-server
$ adb start-server
* daemon not running. starting it now on port 5037 *
* daemon started successfully *
$ adb devices
List of devices attached
emulator-5554       device
$
```

By killing and restarting the server, you force adb to get back in
touch with any connected Android devices.

Running a shell

Most of the time you won't use adb directly; you'll let an IDE like Android Studio do the work for you. But there are times when it can be useful to go to the command line and interact with your devices directly.

One example is if you want to run a shell on your device:

```
Interactive Session
$ adb shell
root@generic_x86:/ #
```

The `adb shell` command will open up an interactive shell directly on the Android device. The `adb shell` command will only work when there is a single Android device connected, otherwise it won't know which Android device you want to talk to.

Once you open a shell to your device, you can run a lot of the standard Linux commands:

```
Interactive Session
$ adb shell
root@generic_x86:/ # ls
acct
cache
charger
config
d
data
default.prop
dev
etc
file_contexts
....
1|root@generic_x86:/ # df
Filesystem               Size     Used     Free    Blksize
/dev                    439.8M    60.0K   439.8M   4096
/mnt/asec               439.8M     0.0K   439.8M   4096
/mnt/obb                439.8M     0.0K   439.8M   4096
/system                 738.2M   533.0M   205.2M   4096
/data                   541.3M   237.8M   303.5M   4096
/cache                   65.0M     4.3M    60.6M   4096
/mnt/media_rw/sdcard    196.9M     4.5K   196.9M   512
/storage/sdcard         196.9M     4.5K   196.9M   512
root@generic_x86:/ #
```

Get the output from logcat

All of the apps running on your Android device sending their
output to a central stream called the logcat. You can see the live
output from the logcat by running the `adb logcat` command:

```
Interactive Session
$ adb logcat
--------- beginning of system
I/Vold    (  936): Vold 2.1 (the revenge) firing up
D/Vold    (  936): Volume sdcard state changing -1
(Initializing) -> 0 (No-Media)
W/DirectVolume(  936): Deprecated implied prefix pattern
detected, please use '/devices/platform/goldfish_mmc.0*'
instead
...
```

The logcat output will keep streaming until you stop it. It can be
useful to run `adb logcat` if you want to store the output in a
file. The `adb logcat` command is used by Android Studio to
produce the output you see in the Devices/logcat frame.

Copying files to/from your device

The `adb pull` and `adb push` commands can be used to
transfer files back and forth. For example, here we are copying the
/default.prop/ properties file into a local file called *1.txt*:

```
Interactive Session
$ adb pull /default.prop 1.txt
28 KB/s (281 bytes in 0.009s)
$ cat 1.txt
#
# ADDITIONAL_DEFAULT_PROPERTIES
#
ro.secure=0
ro.allow.mock.location=1
ro.debuggable=1
ro.zygote=zygote32
dalvik.vm.dex2oat-Xms=64m
dalvik.vm.dex2oat-Xmx=512m
dalvik.vm.image-dex2oat-Xms=64m
dalvik.vm.image-dex2oat-Xmx=64m
ro.dalvik.vm.native.bridge=0
persist.sys.usb.config=adb
$
```

And much, much more...

There are many, many commands that you can run using adb: you can back up and restore databases (very useful if you need to debug a problem with a database app), start the adb server on a different port, reboot machines, or just find out a lot of information about the running devices. To find out all the options available, just type adb on the command line:

```
Interactive Session
$ adb
Android Debug Bridge version 1.0.32
 -a                           - directs adb to listen on all
interfaces for a connection
 -d                           - directs command to the only
connected USB device
                                returns an error if more than
one USB device is present.
 -e                           - directs command to the only
running emulator.
returns an error if more than one emulator is ....
```

The Android Emulator

Ever felt like you were spending all your time waiting for the emulator?

There's no doubt that using the Android emulator is useful. It allows you to see how your app will run on devices other than the physical ones you have access to. But at times it can feel a little... sluggish. In this appendix, we're going to explain why the emulator can seem slow. Even better, we'll give you a few tips we've learned for **speeding it up**.

Why the emulator is so slow

When you're writing Android apps, you'll spend a lot of time waiting for the Android emulator to start up or deploy your code. Why is that? Why is the Android emulator so slooooooow? If you've ever written iPhone code, you will know how fast the iPhone simulator is. If it's possible for the iPhone, then why not for Android?

There's a clue in the name: the iPhone *Simulator* and the Android *Emulator*.

The iPhone Simulator simulates a device running the iOS operating system. All of the code for iOS is compiled to run natively on the Mac and the iPhone Simulator runs at Mac-native speed. That means it can simulate an iPhone boot-up in just a few seconds.

The Android Emulator works in a completely different way. An Android Emulator uses an open source application called QEMU (or Quick Emulator) to emulate the entire Android hardware device. It runs code that interprets machine code that's intended to be run by the device's processor. It has code that emulates the storage system, the screen, and pretty much every other piece of physical equipment on an Android device.

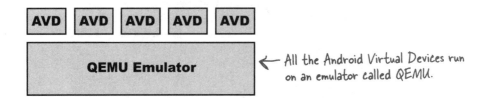

← All the Android Virtual Devices run on an emulator called QEMU.

An emulator like QEMU creates a much more realistic representation of a virtual device than something like the iPhone Simulator does, but the downside is that it has to do far more work for even simple operations like reading disk or displaying something on a screen. That's why the emulator takes so long to boot up a device. It has to pretend to be every little hardware component inside the device, and it has to interpret every single instruction.

How to speed up your Android development

1. Use a real device

The simplest way to speed up your development process is by using a real device. A real device will boot up much faster than an emulated one, and it will probably deploy and run apps a lot more quickly. If you want to develop on a real device, you may want to go into "Developer options" and check the Stay Awake option. This will prevent your device locking the screen, which is useful if you are repeatedly deploying to it.

2. Use an emulator snapshot

Booting up is one of the slowest things the emulator does. If you save a snapshot of the device while it's running, the emulator will be able to reset itself to this state without having to go through the boot-up process. To use a snapshot with your device, open the AVD manager from the Android Studio menu by selecting Tools→Android→AVD Manager, edit the AVD by clicking on the Edit symbol, then check the "Store a snapshot for faster startup" option.

This will save a snapshot of what the memory looks like when the device is running. The emulator will be able to restore the memory in this state without booting the device.

3. Use hardware acceleration

By default, the QEMU emulator will have to interpret each machine code instruction on the virtual device. That means it's very flexible because it can pretend to be lots of different CPUs, but it's one of the main reasons why the emulator is slow. Fortunately, there's a way to get your development machine to run the machine code instructions directly. There are two main types of Android Virtual Device: ARM machines and x86 machines. If you create an x86 Android device and your development machine is using a particular type of Intel x86 CPU, then you can configure your emulator to run the Android machine code instructions directly on your Intel CPU.

You will need to install Intel's Hardware Accelerated Execution Manager (HAXM). At the time of writing , you can find HAXM here:

← *If it's moved, a quick search should track it down.*

https://software.intel.com/en-us/android/articles/intel-hardware-accelerated-execution-manager

HAXM is a hypervisor. That means it can switch your CPU into a special mode to run virtual machine instructions directly. HAXM will only run on Intel processors that support Intel Virtualization Technology. If your development machine is compatible, then HAXM will make your AVD run much faster.

appendix iv: leftovers

The Top Ten Things (we didn't cover)

Oh my, look at the tasty treats we have left...

Even after all that, there's still a little more.

There are just a few more things we think you need to know. We wouldn't feel right about ignoring them, and we really wanted to give you a book you'd be able to lift without extensive training at the local gym. Before you put down the book, **read through these tidbits**.

1. Distributing your app

Once you've developed your app, you'll probably want to make it available to other users. You'll usually want to do this by releasing your app through an app marketplace such as Google Play.

There are two stages to this: preparing your app for release, and then releasing it.

Preparing your app for release

Before you can release your app, you need to configure, build, and test a release version of your app. This includes tasks such as deciding on an icon for your app and modifying *AndroidManifest.xml* so that only devices that are able to run your app are able to download it.

Before you release your app, make sure that you test it on at least one tablet and one phone to check that it looks the way you expect and its performance is acceptable.

You can find further details of how to prepare your app for release here:

http://developer.android.com/tools/publishing/preparing.html

Releasing your app

This stage includes publicizing your app, selling it, and distributing it.

To release your app on the Play Store, you need to register for a publisher account and use the Developer Console to publish your app. You can find further details here:

http://developer.android.com/distribute/googleplay/start.html

For ideas on how to best target your app to your users and build a buzz about it, we suggest you explore the documents here:

http://developer.android.com/distribute/index.html

2. Content providers

You've seen how to use intents to start activities in other apps. As an example, you can start the Messaging app to send the text you pass to it. But what if you want to use another app's data in your own app? What if you want to use Contacts data in your app to perform some task, or insert a new Calendar event?

You can't access another app's data by interrogating its database, Instead, you use a **content provider**. A content provider is an interface that allows apps to share data in a controlled way. It allows you to perform queries to read the data, insert new records, and update or delete existing records.

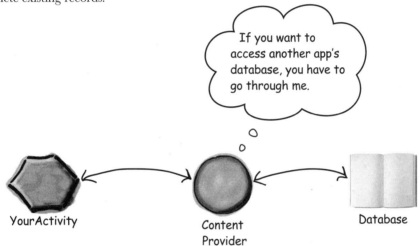

If you want other apps to use your data, you can create your own content provider.

You can find out more about the concept of content providers here:

http://developer.android.com/guide/topics/providers/content-providers.html

Here's a guide on using Contacts data in your app:

http://developer.android.com/guide/topics/providers/contacts-provider.html

Here's a guide on using Calendar data:

http://developer.android.com/guide/topics/providers/calendar-provider.html

3. The WebView class

If you want to provide your users with access to web content, you have two options. The first option is to develop a web app that users can access on their device using a browser. The second option is to use the `WebView` class.

The `WebView` class allows you to display the contents of a web page inside your activity's layout. You can use it to deliver an entire web app as a client application, or to deliver individual web pages. This approach is useful if there's content in your app you might need to update, such as an end-user agreement or user guide.

You add a `WebView` to your app by including it in your layout like this:

```
<WebView  xmlns:android="http://schemas.android.com/apk/res/android"
    android:id="@+id/webview"
    android:layout_width="match_parent"
    android:layout_height="match_parent" />
```

You tell it which web page to load using the `loadUrl()` method in your Java code like this:

```
WebView webView = (WebView) findViewById(R.id.webview);
webView.loadUrl("http://www.oreilly.com/");
```

You also need to specify that the app must have Internet access by adding the `INTERNET` permission to *AndroidManifest.xml*:

```
<manifest ... >
    <uses-permission android:name="android.permission.INTERNET" />
    ...
</manifest>
```

You can find out more about using web content in your apps here:

http://developer.android.com/guide/webapps/index.html

4. Animation

As Android devices use more of the power from their built-in graphics hardware, animation is being used more and more to improve the user's app experience.

There are several types of animation that you can perform in Android:

Property animation

Property animation relies on the fact that the visual components in an Android app use a lot of numeric properties to describe their appearance. If you change the value of a property like the height or the width of a view, you can make it animate. That's what property animation is: smoothly animating the properties of visual components over time.

View animations

A lot of animations can be created declaratively as XML resources. So you can have XML files that use a standard set of animations (like scaling, translation, and rotation) to create effects that you can call from your code. The wonderful thing about declarative view animations is that they are decoupled from your Java code, so they are very easy to port from one app project to another.

Activity transitions

Let's say you write an app that displays a list of items with names and images. You click on an item and you're taken to a detail view of it. The activity that shows you more detail will probably use the same image that appeared in the previous list activity.

Activity transitions allow you to animate view from one activity that will also appear in the next activity. So you can make an image from a list smoothly animate across the screen to the position it takes in the next activity. This will give your app a more seamless feel.

To learn more about Android animation see:

https://developer.android.com/guide/topics/graphics/index.html

To learn about activity transitions and Material Design, see:

https://developer.android.com/training/material/animations.html

5. Maps

An Android device can go everywhere with you, and so location and mapping are important features in many Google apps.

If you install the Google Play Services library, you can embed Google Maps directly into your app. It comes with the full power of the native app, plus you can do a huge amount of customization to make maps a fully integrated part of your app.

You insert a map into a layout as a fragment:

```
<fragment xmlns:android="http://schemas.android.com/apk/res/android"
    android:id="@+id/map"
    android:layout_width="match_parent"
    android:layout_height="match_parent"
    android:name="com.google.android.gms.maps.MapFragment"/>
```

Then you can programmatically access the map from your code as a GoogleMap object:

```
GoogleMap map = getMap();
```

And then you add your own features to the map. For example, you add polylines to it like this:

```
routeLine = map.addPolyline(new PolylineOptions()
                .width(ROUTE_THICKNESS_PIXELS)
                .color(Color.RED));
```

This is an app that has Google Maps embedded in it.

This is a polyline.

5. Maps (continued)

You can also listen to events on the app. With an
`OnCameraChangeListener` you can see when the
user moves the map to a different location, and with an
`OnMapClickListener` you can tell the latitude and
longitude of the point on the map where a user just clicked:

```
map.setOnCameraChangeListener(new OnCameraChangeListener() {
    @Override
    public void onCameraChange(CameraPosition cameraPosition) {
        // Dragged to a new place on the map
    }
});


map.setOnMapClickListener(new OnMapClickListener() {
    @Override
    public void onMapClick(LatLng latLng) {
        // Clicked at a latitude/longitude latLng
    }
});
```

To find out more about Google Maps and how you can
integrate them with your Android app, go to:

*https://developer.android.com/google/play-services/maps.
html*

6. Cursor loaders

If you do much work with databases or content providers,
sooner or later you'll encounter cursor loaders. A cursor loader
runs an asynchronous query in the background and returns
the results to the activity or fragment that called it. It manages
your cursor for you so that you don't have to. It also notifies
you if the data changes so that you can deal with it in your
views.

You can find out more about cursor loaders here:

*https://developer.android.com/training/load-data-
background/setup-loader.html*

7. Broadcast receivers

Suppose you want your app to react in some way when a system event occurs. You may, for example, have built a music app, and you want it to stop playing music if the headphones are removed. How can your app tell when these events occur?

System events include things like the device running low on power, a new incoming phone call, or the system getting booted. Android broadcasts these system events when they occur, and you can listen out for them by creating a broadcast receiver. Broadcast receivers allow you to subscribe to particular broadcast messages. This means that you can get your app to respond to system events.

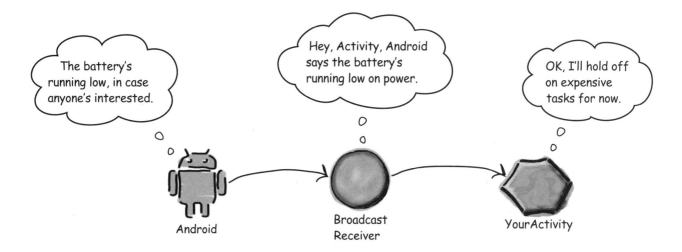

You can find out more about broadcast receivers here:

http://developer.android.com/reference/android/content/BroadcastReceiver.html

8. App widgets

An app widget is a small application view that you can add
to other apps or your home screen. It gives you direct access
to an app's core content or functionality from your home
screen without you having to launch the app.

Here's an example of an app widget:

This is an app widget. It gives you direct access to the app's core functionality.

To create an app widget, you need an `AppWidgetProviderInfo`
object, an `AppWidgetProvider` class implementation, and a
`View` layout. The `AppWidgetProviderInfo` object describes
metadata for the widget, such as its `AppWidgetProvider` class
and layout. It's defined in XML. The `AppWidgetProvider` class
implementation contains the methods that you need to interface with
the app widget. The `View` layout is an XML layout that describes
how the app widget should look.

To find out how you create your own app widgets, look here:

*http://developer.android.com/guide/topics/appwidgets/index.
html*

9. NinePatch graphics

A NinePatch graphic is a stretchable bitmap you can use as a view's background. The image is automatically resized depending on the contents of the view and the size of the screen. The clever bit is that you define which areas should stretch, and which areas shouldn't.

As an example, suppose you wanted to use the following image as the background of a button:

You need the image to be able to stretch so that it can accommodate different lengths of text, but you don't want the edges of the image to get distorted as it stretches:

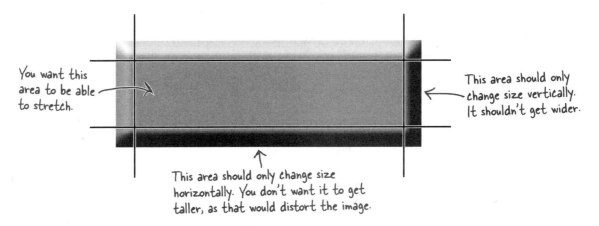

You want this area to be able to stretch.

This area should only change size vertically. It shouldn't get wider.

This area should only change size horizontally. You don't want it to get taller, as that would distort the image.

If you turn the image into a NinePatch graphic, you can get the image to stretch exactly how you want.

Android includes a tool called the Draw 9-patch tool that helps you create NinePatch images. You can find out more about the Draw 9-patch tool and NinePatch graphics in general by following this link:

http://developer.android.com/guide/topics/graphics/2d-graphics.html#nine-patch

10. Testing

All modern development relies heavily on testing, and Android comes with a lot of built-in support. As the main Android language is Java, you can use the standard Java testing frameworks, but Android takes things a whole step further by including a testing framework right in the SDK. In fact, Android Studio automatically creates a file hierarchy for tests every time you create a project.

Android testing is based on JUnit, with extensions specially built for Android. You can use `AndroidTestCases` for basic component testing. The framework includes mocks for objects like `Intents` and `Contexts` to make the testing of an individual component easier.

There's also a special `ApplicationTestCase` that's useful for testing that the basic configuration of files like *AndroidManifest.xml* is set up correctly.

The most impressive thing in the basic test framework is *Instrumentation Testing*. Android apps can be instrumented so that the interactions between a component and the operating system can be monitored and changed. This means that you can run tests directly on a device that can call the lifecycle methods of an activity and fire off intents to the operating system.

To find out more about the Android testing framework, go here:

http://d.android.com/tools/testing/testing_android.html

For more advanced scenario testing, you should look at the **Robotium** testing framework. Robotium builds on the instrumentation testing used in the basic Android framework, and takes it to a whole new level. With Robotium you can write test code that almost reads like the test scripts that manual testers perform.

For more information on Robotium go to:

https://code.google.com/p/robotium/

Index

M

X

Y

Have it your way.

O'Reilly eBooks

- Lifetime access to the book when you buy through oreilly.com
- Provided in up to four, DRM-free file formats, for use on the devices of your choice: PDF, .epub, Kindle-compatible .mobi, and Android .apk
- Fully searchable, with copy-and-paste, and print functionality
- We also alert you when we've updated the files with corrections and additions.

oreilly.com/ebooks/

Safari Books Online

- Access the contents and quickly search over 7000 books on technology, business, and certification guides
- Learn from expert video tutorials, and explore thousands of hours of video on technology and design topics
- Download whole books or chapters in PDF format, at no extra cost, to print or read on the go
- Early access to books as they're being written
- Interact directly with authors of upcoming books
- Save up to 35% on O'Reilly print books

See the complete Safari Library at safaribooksonline.com

©2014 O'Reilly Media, Inc. O'Reilly logo is a registered trademark of O'Reilly Media, Inc. 14373

Get even more for your money.

Join the O'Reilly Community, and register the O'Reilly books you own. It's free, and you'll get:

- $4.99 ebook upgrade offer
- 40% upgrade offer on O'Reilly print books
- Membership discounts on books and events
- Free lifetime updates to ebooks and videos
- Multiple ebook formats, DRM FREE
- Participation in the O'Reilly community
- Newsletters
- Account management
- 100% Satisfaction Guarantee

Signing up is easy:

1. Go to: oreilly.com/go/register
2. Create an O'Reilly login.
3. Provide your address.
4. Register your books.

Note: English-language books only

To order books online:
oreilly.com/store

For questions about products or an order:
orders@oreilly.com

To sign up to get topic-specific email announcements and/or news about upcoming books, conferences, special offers, and new technologies:
elists@oreilly.com

For technical questions about book content:
booktech@oreilly.com

To submit new book proposals to our editors:
proposals@oreilly.com

O'Reilly books are available in multiple DRM-free ebook formats. For more information:
oreilly.com/ebooks

O'REILLY®

©2014 O'Reilly Media, Inc. O'Reilly logo is a registered trademark of O'Reilly Media, Inc. 14373